Chinese Local Elites
and
Patterns of Dominance

This volume was sponsored by the Joint Committee on Chinese Studies of the American Council of Learned Societies and the Social Science Research Council, with funds provided by the National Endowment for the Humanities and the Andrew W. Mellon Foundation.

Chinese Local Elites
and
Patterns of Dominance

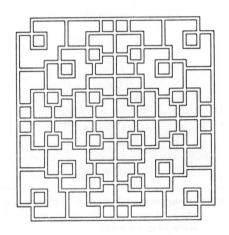

EDITED BY

Joseph W. Esherick
and
Mary Backus Rankin

UNIVERSITY OF CALIFORNIA PRESS

Berkeley   Los Angeles   London

University of California Press
Berkeley and Los Angeles, California

University of California Press, Ltd.
London, England

© 1990 by
The Regents of the University of California

First Paperback Printing 1993

Library of Congress Cataloging-in-Publication Data

Chinese local elites and patterns of dominance / edited by Joseph W.
Esherick and Mary Backus Rankin.

    p. cm.—(Studies on China; 11)

    Rev. versions of papers presented at the Conference on Chinese
Local Elites and Patterns of Dominance held in Aug. 1987 at Banff,
Canada; sponsored by the Joint Committee on Chinese Studies of
the American Council of Learned Societies and the Social Science
Research Council.

    Includes bibliographical references.

    ISBN 0-520-08434-9

    1. Elite (Social sciences)—China—Congresses. 2. China—Social
conditions—Congresses. I. Esherick, Joseph. II. Rankin, Mary
Backus. III. Joint Committee on Chinese Studies (U.S.)
IV. Conference on Chinese Local Elites and Patterns of Dominance
(1987: Banff, Alta.) V. Series.
HN740.Z9E426 1990
305.5'52'095109045—dc20   89-20258
                                                   CIP

Printed in the United States of America

1 2 3 4 5 6 7 8 9

The paper used in this publication meets the minimum requirements of
American National Standard for Information Sciences—Permanence of
Paper for Printed Library Materials, ANSI Z39.48-1984. ⊚ ™

STUDIES ON CHINA

A series of conference volumes sponsored by
the Joint Committee on Chinese Studies of the
American Council of Learned Studies and the
Social Science Research Council.

CONTENTS

vii

TABLES

ix

ILLUSTRATIONS

FIGURES

MAPS

PREFACE

In August 1987 the Joint Committee on Chinese Studies of the American Council of Learned Societies and the Social Science Research Council sponsored the Conference on Chinese Local Elites and Patterns of Dominance at Banff, Canada, with funds provided by the National Endowment for the Humanities. This topic grew out of the studies of Chinese local history and society during the 1970s and 1980s. The time had come to bring together the people working on different parts of China and to encourage the interaction of social historians with anthropologists and political scientists to build new generalizations and open new channels of debate about the nature of the Chinese elite. A further hope was that using theoretical concepts not specifically tied to the Chinese case might lead to future dialogues with scholars working on other cultures.

This intellectual background was reflected in perspectives and themes of the conference and this volume. Participants started by asking how elites in late imperial and republican China were defined by and operated in local contexts, and because these elites operated within inevitably unequal social structures the general themes of the conference revolved around patterns of dominance rather than, for instance, typologies or functions of elites. Focusing on elites as actors in local systems led to a theoretical awareness of the interaction of structure, process, and context in questions about how elites took initiatives to attain and maintain their local positions within larger structures not solely of their own making. Here the insights from anthropology were particularly useful, leading to definitions of elites based on their strategies and resources. Firm lines between functional elites like scholars, merchants, and militarists blurred as the conference looked at the often complex combinations of resources underlying elite dominance.

The conference papers underlined the regional as well as the functional diversity within the Chinese elite in contrast to the older image of a homogeneous degree-holding gentry. Emphasis on the practices of elites actively engaged in local arenas led to different perspectives on such issues as cultural unity and the role of the Chinese state. More emphasis was laid on how elites applied a general (and often state-fostered) cultural repertoire for their own purposes through such practices as patronage and the formation of networks and on how by doing so they defined themselves, shaped society, and created culture through interactions within their local communities as well as in relationship to the central state. Looking at how elites used symbols focused attention on the importance of cultural hegemony as well as more direct forms of economic, political, and military dominance in maintaining their positions in local society. Still another major topic was the interplay of continuity and change—a theme that highlighted both growing specialization in the modern period and the flexibility displayed by local elites in the face of the great economic, social, and political changes of the seventeenth through the twentieth century.

Formal planning for the conference began with a meeting in 1986. Keith Schoppa, William Rowe, and Stevan Harrell all deserve thanks for their role in defining the scope of the topic, and, as the one anthropologist at the meeting, Harrell was particularly helpful in explaining anthropological concepts to the historians. The eighteen papers presented at Banff covered a wide variety of topics pertaining to elites in local society. Historical background and some theoretical perspectives were provided at the opening session by Patricia B. Ebrey, "Some Dynamics of Elite Domination in Han through Song China," and Keith Schoppa, "Power, Legitimacy, and Symbol: Local Elites and the Jute Creek Embankment Case." Issues of continuity and change over time were then examined in William Rowe, "Success Stories: Lineage and Elite Status in Hanyang County, Hubei, c. 1368–1949," and Timothy Brook, "Elite Continuity in Yin County, Ningbo, 1371–1935." The kinds of dominance exercised by traders and industrial elites were the topics of Madeleine Zelin, "The Rise and Fall of the Furong (Sichuan) Elite: Merchant Dominance in Late Qing China," and Linda Grove, "Small-Town Merchants and Local Politics," set in localities of Shandong and Jiangsu. Changes occurring among gentry-merchant elites as China was pulled into the world economy were discussed by Lynda Bell, "From Compradore to County Magnate: Bourgeois Practice in the Wuxi County Silk Industry," and Hong-ming Yip, "Local Elites in a Dependent Economy: The Case of Twentieth-Century Weixian, Shandong Province." Relationships of elites to the state and the changing nature of local politics in the twentieth century were then examined by Helen Chauncey, "The Polity Below: Local Society and Republican Reform"; Lenore Barkan, "Patterns of Power: Thirty Years of Elite Politics in a Chinese County"; and David Strand, "Mediation, Representation, and Repression: Local Elites in 1920s Beijing."

Village elites and the contrasting village structures of authority in North and South China were discussed in Prasenjit Duara, "Elites and the Structure of Authority in the Villages of North China, 1900–1949," and Rubie S. Watson, "Corporate Property and Local Leadership in the Pearl River Delta, 1898–1941." Frontier elites and issues of ethnicity were the subjects of Jonathan Lipman, "Mosque, *Menhuan*, and Middleman: The Evolution of Hui Leadership in Northwest China," and Stevan Harrell, "From *Xiedou* to *Yijun*: The Decline of Ethnicity and the Transformation of the North Taiwan Local Elite, 1860–1895." On the last day three papers were presented about elites and the large processes of collective mobilization, social resistance, and revolution in the nineteenth and twentieth century: Bin Wong, "Tax Resistance: Patterns of Social Relations and Political Change"; Stephen Averill, "Local Elites and Communist Revolution in the Jiangxi Hill Country"; and Chen Yung-fa, "The Chinese Communists and the Huaibei Town-Elite."

The four discussants contributed strongly to the conference sessions. Robert Forster gave us his insights as an historian of European elites and, after the conference, wrote his comments on social continuity and change in a thought-provoking essay, "Comments: Some Perspectives of a European Historian of Elites." Joan Vincent commented as an anthropologist who had worked on Africa and Ireland and conducted a stimulating impromptu evening session on anthropological theory. Makota Ueda brought us the views of Japanese historians and provided an essay on "Japanese Scholarship on the Chinese Gentry" as well as an invaluable bibliography of recent publications in Japan. Philip Kuhn shared his knowledge derived from many years of studying the Chinese gentry and their relationship to the state. The demanding role of conference rapporteur was ably assumed by Blaine Gaustad, and Jason Parker of the American Council of Learned Societies gave advice and encouragement at all stages.

This volume is sponsored by the Joint Committee on Chinese Studies of the American Council of Learned Societies and the Social Science Research Council with funds provided by the Andrew W. Mellon Foundation. We thank Timothy Brook, Sherman Cochran, Paul Cohen, Prasenjit Duara, Lynda Grove, Richard Kraus, William Rowe, David Strand, and Ye Wa for their helpful comments on our introduction and conclusion, and we truly appreciate the help in the final production and editing from Amy Klatzkin and Lisa N. Jerry. Most particularly, however, we express our appreciation to all the scholars assembled at the Banff conference, whose excellent papers and enthusiastic discussions contributed so greatly to the views of Chinese elites put forth here.

CONTRIBUTORS

Stephen C. Averill is assistant professor of history at Michigan State University. He has published articles on Jiangxi society and the Communist movement in *Modern China* (1983) and the *Journal of Asian Studies* (1987). Currently he is completing a book manuscript on the origins of the Jiangxi Communist movement on the basis of the dissertation for his Ph.D. from Cornell University.

Lenore Barkan worked for the Social Security Administration and has been assistant professor of political science at Whitman College. She received her Ph.D. from the University of Washington and is currently revising her dissertation on the political interactions of Nationalists, Communists, and local leaders in Rugao County, Jiangsu, during the Chinese Republic.

Lynda S. Bell is assistant professor of history at the University of California, Riverside. She is co-author of *Chinese Communists and Rural Society, 1927–1934* (1978). Now she is working on a manuscript based on the dissertation for her Ph.D. from the University of California, Los Angeles, "Merchants, Peasants, and the State: The Organization and Politics of Chinese Silk Production, Wuxi County, 1870–1937."

Timothy Brook is assistant professor of history at the University of Toronto. He has published *Geographical Sources of Ming-Qing History* (1988) and *The Asiatic Mode of Production in China* (1989) and is currently working on a book manuscript on the Chinese gentry's patronage of Buddhist monasteries from the sixteenth to eighteenth centuries.

Prasenjit Duara is associate professor of history at University of Chicago. He is the author of *Culture, Power and the State: Rural North China, 1900–1942*. Currently he is engaged in a comparative study of nationalism and ethnicity in China and South Asia.

Joseph W. Esherick is professor of history at the University of California, San Diego. He is the author of *Reform and Revolution in China: The 1911 Revolution in Hunan and Hubei* (1976) and *The Origins of the Boxer Uprising* (1987). He is currently beginning a study of the Communist movement in the villages of northern Shaanxi province in northwestern China.

Edward A. McCord is assistant professor of history at the University of Florida. He received his Ph.D. from the University of Michigan. He has published an article on local militarization in *Modern China* and is currently working on a manuscript on the emergence of warlordism in republican China.

Mary Backus Rankin is an independent scholar of late imperial Chinese history. She is the author of *Early Chinese Revolutionaries: Radical Intellectuals in Shanghai and Chekiang, 1902–1911* (1971) and *Elite Activism and Political Transformation in China: Zhejiang Province, 1865–1911* (1986). Currently she is beginning a manuscript on the public sphere in late imperial China.

William T. Rowe is professor of history at the Johns Hopkins University. He is the author of *Hankow: Commerce and Society in a Chinese City, 1796–1889* (1984) and *Hankow: Conflict and Community in a Chinese City, 1796–1895* (1989). At present he is engaged in research on the eighteenth-century statecraft official, Chen Hongmou.

R. Keith Schoppa is professor of history at Valparaiso University. He is the author of *Chinese Elites and Political Change: Zhejiang Province in the Early Twentieth Century* (1982) and *Xiang Lake: Nine Centuries of Chinese Life* (1989). His current project is a manuscript, "Arenas of Revolution: Shen Dingyi and Chinese Society."

David Strand is associate professor of political science at Dickinson College. He is the author of *Rickshaw Beijing: City People and Politics in the 1920s* (1989) and is currently engaged in research for a book on the Chinese Communist Party in the 1930s and 1940s.

Rubie S. Watson is associate curator, Peabody Museum, and senior lecturer in anthropology, Harvard University. She is the author of *Inequality Among Brothers: Class and Kinship in South China* (1985). Currently she is working on gender in South China village societies.

Madeleine Zelin is professor of history at Columbia University. She has published *The Magistrate's Tael: Rationalizing Fiscal Reform in Eighteenth-Century Ch'ing China* (1984). At present she is preparing a manuscript on the late imperial socioeconomic history of the salt-producing industrial city of Zigong in Sichuan province.

INTRODUCTION

Joseph W. Esherick and Mary Backus Rankin

The revered Chinese philosopher Mencius wrote: "There are pursuits proper to great men and pursuits proper to lesser men. . . . Therefore it is said, 'Some labor with their hands, and some labor with their minds. Those who labor with their minds govern others. Those who labor with their hands are governed by others. Those who are governed provide food for others. Those who govern are provided with food by others.' This is universally regarded as just."[1] Few people would now openly subscribe to such explicitly elitist views. Until the nineteenth century, however, all complex civilizations accepted the notion that society was hierarchically ordered, that wealth and status would be unequally distributed, that certain people were properly qualified to rule, and that men and women owed deference to their social "betters." It was taken for granted that a society should have an elite. The only questions involved what type of elite it should be. What determined membership in the elite? How open was the elite? How unified was the elite? Did a single elite monopolize wealth, status, and power? Or did merchants, for example, have more wealth, aristocrats more status, and state functionaries more power?

When Western scholars interested in comparative sociology began to ask such questions about China, they readily associated elite status with office holding and the central bureaucratic state. From a European perspective the autocratic power of China's imperial bureaucracy was overwhelming: here was an enormous land of some four hundred million people ruled over by a bureaucracy of imperially appointed officials who qualified for office through state-sponsored examinations open to all, without regard for wealth or family pedigree.[2] This view of an all-powerful state readily associated elite status with state service. Thus Max Weber began his essay on the Chinese elite with the judgment that "for twelve centuries social rank in China has been determined more by qualification for office than by wealth."[3] In a similar

vein, the eminent sinologist Etiènne Balazs wrote of "the uninterrupted continuity of a ruling class of scholar-officials."[4]

The analytical purposes of the sociologist Weber and the sinologist Balazs
were virtually identical. Both sought to compare China to Western Europe
and to understand why China—with its enormous achievements in imperial
governance, in Confucian philosophy, in the high culture of painting and
poetry, and in such crafts as silk weaving and porcelain—had failed to break
through into capitalist production and industrial modernization. This was a
central concern of Weber's life work. He asked the same question of India,
and like so many others he came up with the answer of caste. In China he
focused instead on what he considered a unique, unified Chinese elite, the
literati, and the Confucian culture they embodied. Both Weber and Balazs
stressed the weakness of competing elites in China. The absence of a hereditary landed aristocracy or clerical hierarchy was one obvious contrast to
Europe, but Weber and Balazs were particularly concerned with explaining
the weakness of the bourgeoisie. Chinese cities, they both argued, were
administrative centers dominated by imperial bureaucrats and Confucian
scholar-officials, not self-governing communities of self-confident, world-
transforming capitalist entrepreneurs.[5] As a result, the Chinese scholar-
official elite ruled uncontested and essentially unchanged for centuries on
end.

Although such scholars as Weber and Balazs assumed that there was an
essentially homogeneous Chinese elite, this was not simply a political elite of
bureaucrats. It also included a vast number of former officials and potential
officials—all those who had passed the examinations and in the process
assimilated the ethics and assumptions, the manners and mores of Confucian
culture. Out of office, in their native counties, these men would be treated
with all the deference due their learning, their potential influence with the
bureaucracy, and their (or their families') usually substantial wealth in land.
They were *the* local elite. During the nineteenth century, English diplomatic
and missionary writers on China had introduced the term, "the Chinese
gentry," to describe this social group, which they considered similar to the
nonaristocratic/noncommoner rural landowning class in England. Despite
this analogy, Europeans in general found the gentry of China stubbornly
conservative, ignorant of the wider world, and fiercely proud. Most of the
West's difficulties in opening China to commerce and Christianity were
ascribed to the resistance of the gentry class.

When the first Western-trained Chinese social scientists looked at China's
traditional elite, they used the same term and shared many of the negative
views. To these Chinese nationalists, the gentry, with their commitment to
the humanistic education of Confucianism and their disdain for technical
knowledge or professional training, were responsible for China's backward-
ness. In the words of the London-trained anthropologist Fei Hsiao-tung, the
gentry

monopolized authority based on the wisdom of the past, spent time on literature, and tried to express themselves through art. . . . [T]he vested interests had
no wish to improve production but thought only of consolidating privilege.
Their main task was the perpetuation of established norms in order to set up a
guide for conventional behavior. A man who sees the world only through human relations is inclined to be conservative, because in human relations the
end is always mutual adjustment.[6]

Thus, before systematic study of Chinese society began in the mid-
twentieth century, there was already a substantial consensus on the nature of
the Chinese elite. The conclusions of sociologists and sinologists, of Western
China hands and Chinese nationalists were remarkably similar: China had a
single, culturally homogeneous elite called literati, scholar-officials or gentry.
This elite was closely tied to the imperial state, which conferred elite status
through the examination system (status which, by the late imperial period,
could be passed on to heirs only in limited ways and only by the highest
officials) and specified the Confucian curriculum that socialized the aspirants for examination degrees. This elite was remarkably enduring, so that
one scholar even described the entire period from 206 B.C. (the founding of
the Han dynasty) to 1948 (the year before the founding of the People's Republic) as one of "gentry society."[7] The gentry's divorce from manual labor
and technical knowledge, their humanistic resistance to professional training, their conservative commitment to Confucian values, and their stubbornly successful defense of their privileged position in society made them a
significant barrier to technical modernization and economic development in
China.

STUDIES OF THE LOCAL ELITE

As Western states grew stronger in the twentieth century and the weakness
of the Chinese imperial state was brutally demonstrated by the assaults of
Western imperialism, scholars began to doubt the power of "Oriental despotism." The lowest level of bureaucratic administration in China was the
county, numbering about 1,436 at the end of the eighteenth century.[8] This
meant that on average, each county magistrate was responsible for governing
almost three hundred thousand people. By contrast, there were about three
thousand persons per administrator under the ancien régime in France.[9] In
addition, because the "law of avoidance" prevented Chinese officials from
serving in their own province, the county magistrate was always an outsider, typically serving three years or less. Clearly, China's thinly spread
and weakly rooted state apparatus had a limited ability to penetrate local
society, and much of the governance fell to local elites operating outside the
formal bureaucracy.[10] Considerable scholarly attention was devoted to dis-
secting the anatomy of these local elites.

Gentry Studies. The earliest systematic studies of Chinese local elites were done by a generation of Chinese scholars working in American universities who defined Chinese elites as gentry and continued the Weberian mission of distinguishing them from Western elites. Their concern was the late imperial period—the Ming (1368–1644) and the Qing (1644–1911) dynasties—and they focused on the gentry's relationship to the bureaucratic state: their recruitment through the civil service examinations and their service to the state in local governance. Ch'ü T'ung-tsu stressed the gentry's role as intermediaries between the bureaucracy and the people, a role guaranteed by their legally protected access to local officials whose Confucian culture and training they shared. Ch'ü explicitly treated the gentry as "the local elite."[11] Chang Chung-li described the social position of the gentry: their fiscal and legal privileges (favorable land tax rates and immunity from corporal punishment) and their functions in education, public works, local defense, tax collection, and cultural leadership. He also addressed the question of stratification within the gentry and provided an extremely useful estimate of the size of the gentry class in the mid-Qing period.

Chang divided the gentry into upper and lower strata. At the top were about eighty thousand active and retired civil and military officials, including all who had passed the highest, metropolitan, level of the examination system and earned the *jinshi* degree (about two thousand five hundred in number for the more prestigious civil degree). About eighteen thousand men (combining civil and military) held the provincial *juren* degree, but failed to pass the *jinshi* or go on to official roles. The lowest level of the upper gentry were the *gongsheng* degree holders, about twenty-seven thousand in number. The total size of the upper gentry, which included all those qualified for regular appointment to office, was thus about 125,000 people at any given time. The lower gentry had qualified to take the examinations that would allow access to higher gentry status and official position but were not yet eligible for regular appointment. There were two main groups of lower gentry: 555,000 *shengyuan* who had passed exams at the county and prefectural level (of whom 460,000 were civil *shengyuan* and the rest military), and 310,000 *jiansheng*, virtually all of whom had purchased the degree. The total size of the degree-holding gentry class was thus about one million individuals, who, with their immediate families, represented about 1.3 percent of the Chinese population.[12]

Ho Ping-ti noted the strongly hierarchical organization of Chinese society and focused on the question of social mobility into the elite. He hypothesized that substantial mobility into the elite mitigated the inherent injustice of the hierarchical order and thus helped explain the persistent dominance of the gentry class. By analyzing the backgrounds of *jinshi* degree holders, he concluded that the gentry were quite open to new blood, and he stressed "the overwhelming power of the bureaucracy and the ability of the state

. . .to regulate the major channels of social mobility."[13] Robert Marsh similarly concluded in his detailed study of 572 Qing officials that there was significant circulation in and out of the bureaucracy, although this movement involved only a tiny fraction of the Chinese populace.[14]

In all these works, the Chinese elite was perceived as equivalent to the gentry class, defined by the single criterion of their examination degrees. Chang's second book, *The Income of the Chinese Gentry*, revealed significant occupational diversity within the gentry and underlined the importance of commercial wealth. Nonetheless, by defining elites as holders of state-conferred degrees, all these works stressed elite-state relations more than the role of elites in local society. More important, the uniformity of state-conferred degrees suggested a uniformity of local elites all across China. Little attention was paid to possible variations in elite types—and especially to the possibility that degree-holding gentry might be quite unimportant in some areas. Finally, the fundamentally sociological approach of these works lent a disturbingly static cast to their analysis. Defining eliteness by un-changing imperial degrees, titles, and offices suggested that however much quantitative rates of mobility might change, the basic nature of the Chinese elite remained the same. We remained trapped in Balazs's "uninterrupted continuity of a ruling class of scholar-officials."

The State and Local Society. The contribution of these early gentry studies was enormous, especially in distinguishing certain features of the Chinese elite. But by stressing the close ties between gentry and the bureaucratic state, they overlooked the obvious tensions. Japanese scholars have also iden-tified local elites with the gentry but have been much less concerned with links to the central state and more intent on elucidating local socioeconomic foundations of elite power; the implications of this perspective are evident in their discussions of "gentry landholding." In the Ming dynasty, the gentry were exempt from onerous corvée labor requirements. As a result, many peasants commended their land to gentry families to escape the corvée, not only substantially increasing gentry landholding but also significantly de-creasing imperial tax revenues. The widespread use of bond servants by elite families also gave them a coterie of personal dependents to bolster their domination of local society. According to an official report included in a Ming statute of 1479, "When moving about ["powerful magnates" who are honorary officials] ride in sedan chairs or on horses and take along a group of three to five bondservant companions (*puban*) who follow them on their rounds. Relying on their power and wealth they conspire to occupy the landed property of small peasants (*xiaomin*), forcefully drag away cows and horses and make the children of free people into bondservants (*nu*)."[15] Clearly such behavior conflicted with the interests of the bureaucratic state.

To some extent, excessive self-aggrandizement by the Ming gentry was responsible for both the fall of the dynasty to peasant rebellions and the Manchu invasion which led to founding the Qing dynasty in 1644. Under the Qing, the commutation of corvée labor duties to tax payments in silver and the elimination of most gentry tax privileges significantly reduced the structural conflict between state and gentry interests. In a widely influential formulation, Shigeta Atsushi saw this new Qing arrangement, not as "gentry landlordism" built on privileged status and personal dependency relations between master and bond servant, but as "gentry rule." Although Shigeta noted that the Qing state supported landlords' rent collection to guarantee state revenues from the land tax, he did not focus on the landlord-tenant dyad. All scholars agreed that the disappearance of most forms of personal dependence in the seventeenth and the eighteenth century made this dyad much less important. His notion of gentry rule was designed to encompass a much broader sociopolitical domination of local society, including influence over small peasants who owned their own land. Such peasant freeholders might still rely on local gentry for access to the local magistrate or for paternalistic relief in times of emergency. However, they no longer personally depended on an individual gentry "master" but instead socially depended on a preeminent gentry elite.[16]

Japanese scholarship has also been particularly important in elucidating local sources of gentry power as opposed to state-conferred status. Landholding, control of irrigation networks, local relief efforts, and other community activities all tended to serve gentry domination of local society. Several scholars pointed to the appearance of the term *xiangshen* (country gentry) in the sixteenth century and a growing gentry concern for their position in local society.[17] This scholarship suggested a secular trend toward the localization of elite power parallel to the "localist strategy" of lineage formation, militia organizing, and localized marriage alliances that Robert Hymes sees elites pursuing as early as the Southern Song (1127–1279).[18]

It is also clear that most of these phenomena could be understood as a cyclical process of elite-state competition for control of local society. As the Southern Song state weakened under nomadic pressure from the north, members of the local elite gained more opportunity to maneuver for local power and had less incentive to orient themselves toward a failing central state. The early Ming government severely restricted the prerogatives of the local gentry and strengthened the power of the bureaucratic state, but gradually the gentry expanded their landholdings and their privileges until the state was so weakened that it fell to peasant rebellion and Manchu invasion. With the early Qing state, the pendulum again swung in the direction of strong central governmental power.

Much literature on modern China—from the mid-nineteenth-century rebellions against the Qing through the Republican period (1911–1949)—also highlights declining central bureaucratic control over local society, with rural elites filling the power vacuum created when the imperial state weakened. This elite ascendancy is particularly evident in Philip Kuhn's study of gentry militia formation against the Taiping and other rebellions of the mid-nineteenth century. Local militarization led to "the supremacy of 'gentry managers'" as they assumed ever greater responsibility for local security, tax collection, and public works. The abolition of the examination system in 1905 and the collapse of the imperial system in 1911 did not end gentry rule in China: "China's rural elite survived into the twentieth century and indeed in some respects solidified its position in rural society."[19]

There is a strong tendency for this literature to view state-elite competition as a zero-sum game. The autocratic state seeks full fiscal and coercive power over rural society, while local elites—sometimes representing community interests, sometimes pursuing their own gain—seek to check the state's intrusion. Frederic Wakeman suggested a "dynamic oscillation" between integration into the imperial system and autonomy from it, a dialectic in which local elites and state functionaries checked each other's corruption to favor overall order.[20] Studies of merchant brokerage and taxfarming have also suggested more complex interaction of state and elite power: the state assigned powers over local taxes and markets to merchants in order to increase its own revenues, but these powers expanded in the nineteenth and the twentieth centuries with the advance of commercialization and the devolution of state power.[21] Nonetheless, most of this literature sees order as the product of state control. When elites organize it is a symptom of crisis, conflict, or the disintegration of established order.[22] In one volume of studies in this vein, a Middle Eastern specialist dared to ask:

> Would China look different if it were studied as the outcome of individual choices and actions rather than from the perspective of a total system? What would China look like from an approach which emphasized the differences between localities and provinces . . . ? Could informal or illegal phenomena, which seem to "deviate" from the Confucian conception of society and from the systematic ordering of Chinese society, be considered substantial realities in their own right rather than variant aspects of the Chinese system? Instead of seeing Chinese institutions as given forms for the organization of Chinese society, could they be interpreted as the outcomes of the informal dynamics of Chinese social life?[23]

In many respects, the present volume attempts to consider these questions, but its studies also build on several earlier analyses of the extrabureaucratic dynamics of local society.

Approaches from Local History. By shifting focus from state control or state certification of elite status to the activities of elites in local society, we develop more diverse pictures of local elites rather different from the scholar-gentry norm. Early twentieth-century field studies showed clear consensus among local residents about whom they considered the local gentry. However, many of these "gentry" possessed none of the normal academic qualifications for that status. One study in a Yunnanese county in Southwest China found several so-called gentry who had risen through corrupt dealings as military officers and one family whose members had killed an opium dealer for his cash, fled for a time, and later returned to establish themselves as respectable merchants and landlords.[24] A similar diversity of late imperial elite types emerged from local history research of the 1960s and 1970s.

Three studies stand out in this literature. Hilary Beattie's study of Tongcheng county, Anhui, directly challenged Chang Chung-li and Ho Ping-ti's focus on degree holders and suggested instead the importance of land and lineage. She explicitly sought to uncover the "long-term strategy" whereby certain families maintained elite status over long periods—a conclusion that clearly conflicted with Ho Ping-ti's stress on elite mobility. The strategy she identified was "a joint programme of systematic land investment coupled with education,"[25] in which lineage charitable estates were key, in both preserving the integrity of accumulated land and providing education in lineage schools.

Because education for the examinations was still central to Beattie's elite strategy, her local elite remained relatively close to the conventional mold. Johanna Meskill's *Chinese Pioneer Family* expanded the Chinese elite to include the very different figure of the local strongman. In the frontier society of eighteenth- and early nineteenth-century Taiwan, the local-elite family Meskill studied perpetuated its local dominance for more than a century through its military power and control of irrigation works. Only toward the end of the nineteenth century did the family show signs of gentrification, with the assumption of a cultured literati life-style.[26]

If Meskill's study, and the earlier Yunnan field work, taught us that frontier areas of China might differ significantly from the "gentry society" norm and that elite society might change significantly over time, Keith Schoppa's study of twentieth-century elites in Zhejiang showed that elites could vary significantly within a single province. Schoppa builds his model on a modified version of the core-periphery analysis used by G. William Skinner and demonstrates systematic variation in elite activities across space. Schoppa finds a more diverse, functionally specialized, commercialized, and politically organized elite in the prosperous lowland provincial core; a greater role of new military elites in the intermediate zones; and considerable continuity of entrenched oligarchies with generalized functions in the more isolated, hilly periphery.[27]

Schoppa's work is particularly important for us in treating the modern transformation of the local elite. Together with Mary Rankin's study of Zhejiang in the late Qing,[28] his book provides a comprehensive picture of elite organizing from the Taiping Rebellion of the mid-nineteenth century to the accession of the Nationalist government in 1927. By viewing the process from a local perspective, Rankin and Schoppa see not a disintegration of state power but elite activism, social mobilization, and political development at the local level. In their work, it is clear that this local elite activity is much broader, less defensive, and more enduring than the militia organizing stressed by Kuhn. Rankin and Schoppa stress the diversity of the local elite and the fusion of merchant and gentry groups, especially in the commercialized provincial core. Contrary to many twentieth-century images of a conservative gentry elite, both scholars demonstrate the elite's readiness to adopt new associational forms—chambers of commerce, educational associations, and a host of other professional associations and special interest organizations—following the removal of the long-standing Qing prohibitions on private association during the first decade of the twentieth century.

Recent research by historians in China reinforces this picture of a changing elite defined by wealth and local activity as well as degrees. Scholars in China have rarely focused on elites as such, although materials they have collected inform the studies in this volume, but their work on "capitalist sprouts" in Ming and Qing China has greatly illuminated the process of socioeconomic change since the sixteenth century. They document a striking expansion of commerce, development of interregional and foreign trade, and the rise of both household and factory handicraft production that changed social relations from the Ming onward.[29] The merchants leading this commercial expansion joined the gentry by buying land and cultivating literati life-styles, rather than remaining a distinct class. In doing so, they added commercial wealth to the resources available to elites, changed elite strategies for mobility and status maintenance, and opened arenas of activity outside the state-sanctioned paths of degree acquisition, office holding, and Confucian scholarship. The great merchant patrons of art and scholarship in the eighteenth century were only the most visible symbols of pervasive changes in the character of elites within the framework of gentry society and the late imperial polity.[30]

QUESTIONS AND CONCEPTS

The growing body of local history work has revealed that Chinese local elites were much more diverse, flexible, and changeable than earlier notions of gentry society suggested. Nonetheless, Chinese society remained profoundly hierarchical, and elite families (and the state) paid minute attention to rank, the marks of status, and culturally embedded relations of superior and inferior. People clearly knew who was higher and lower on the social scale.[31] The question of how then to identify, describe, and analyze the dominant

individuals and families in local arenas was pursued at the Conference on
Local Elites and Patterns of Dominance held in 1987 at Banff, Canada, and is
further examined in this volume of articles from the conference.

This central question suggests several corollaries. What strategies and
resources did local elites rely upon in their rise to local prominence, and by
what strategies and resources did they maintain their status? How important, in particular, was the state as either a source of wealth and status in
office and examination degrees or a potentially decisive actor in local political
processes? What were the critical arenas of local elite activity, and how were
these arenas related to each other? How long could elite families maintain
their prominence; that is, how much continuity was there in the local elite?
How different were local elites in different areas of China? What aspects of
the local environment help to explain regional variations in elite types? How
did the nature of local elites, and the strategies and resources on which they
relied, change over time? What process effected these changes, and what
were the crucial watersheds? In particular, how did twentieth-century elites
differ from late imperial elites? The last question is of central importance for
understanding the relationship of elites to processes of political and economic
development.

To answer these questions, we have supplemented the familiar Weberian
and Marxian analytical categories with the concepts used by anthropologists studying the practices of individuals within specific social structures. We
define local elites as any individuals or families that exercised dominance
within a local arena, thus deliberately avoiding a definition in terms of one
or more of the Weberian categories of wealth, status, and power.[32] Useful
as the Weberian categories are—and we will use them repeatedly in this
volume—they often suggest an association of merchants or industrialists
with wealth, aristocrats or gentry with status, and governmental officials with
power. If used to *define* an elite, not just to characterize elite types, these
categories tend to ossify social reality. One easily loses sight of changing
determinants of elite status and the complex interaction of wealth, status,
and power. Similarly, without denying the existence of classes in Chinese
society, we avoid defining an elite in terms of class. If "class" means simply
a shared relationship to the means of production, it becomes too narrow
and static a category to encompass the economic diversity of Chinese elites;
if it means the conscious articulation of that shared relationship, it refers to a
historical stage that had not yet arrived in China.[33] Patterns of dominance
not only call attention to an underlying coerciveness upholding the social
position of elites, but they also allow us to focus on the dynamic and pro-
cessual aspects of elite power and on the dialectical relationship of elites to
subordinate actors in local society.

Local elites act within local arenas; and in this volume we take "local" to
mean county (*xian*) level or lower. As we shall see, to maintain their position,

local elites often seek influence at higher levels of the administrative hierarchy or rely on external social connections and economic resources, but they focus their activity and purpose on the local arena. An arena is the environment, the stage, the surrounding social space, often the locale in which elites and other societal actors are involved. Arenas may be either geographical (village, county, nation) or functional (military, educational, political); and the concept of an arena includes the repertory of values, meanings, and resources of its constituent actors.[34]

Because the available resources and social environments of local arenas differ markedly across China, we would expect corresponding differences among local elites. Thus analyzing the characteristics of arenas both helps explain the observed diversity of Chinese local elites and calls attention to different social environments in China, rather than to the bureaucratically imposed uniformity through administrative divisions or examination degrees. When we recognize the higher level of commercialization in some arenas or the disturbed conditions producing local militarization in other places or times, we can better understand the different environments and resources available to elites in different areas of China and different periods of Chinese history, which naturally produce different types of elite. Therefore, we should neither anticipate that all county elites will be basically similar just because they operate in the same administrative subdivision nor expect that all holders of the lower *shengyuan* degree will act in the same way because they have the same formal rank. Only by careful attention to the social environment within which elites operate can we fully appreciate and understand the diversity of Chinese local elites.

To maintain their dominance, elites must control certain resources: material (land, commercial wealth, military power); social (networks of influence, kin groups, associations); personal (technical expertise, leadership abilities, religious or magical powers); or symbolic (status, honor, particular lifestyles, and all the cultural exchanges that inform Pierre Bourdieu's fruitful concept of "symbolic capital").[35] Elites, or would-be elites, use their resources in strategies designed to enhance or maintain their positions. The focus on strategies calls attention to the dynamic processes of creating and maintaining elite power. Human agents, active creators of their own history, pursue practices and strategies that, through repetition and over time, produce, maintain, and amend cultural structures. These structures in turn shape and constrain the social environment for subsequent activity in an arena.[36]

This dialectical interaction of strategy and structure provides a more dynamic picture of elite action than can be derived from structural analysis alone. Thus we can see how elites pursue strategies of lineage formation to protect family resources from division through partible inheritance; and how these lineages in turn become structures shaping the arenas in which elites contend. In a more modern context, elites advance their political objectives by forming associations, which then become resources in a new structure of political contention. The intersection of resource, strategy, and structure provides a convenient conceptual map for charting the rise, persistence, transformation, or decline of local elites.

The choice of terms to describe the actors in this volume is also influenced by the complexity of resources and strategies. We use "elite" because it can encompass all people—gentry, merchants, militarists, community leaders—at the top of local social structures and because the diverse resources of elite families often place them in more than one functional category. Gentry are thus only one, although a particularly important, type of elite in late imperial Chinese society. Going a step further, we have broadened the criteria defining gentry to include culture, life-styles, networks, and local reputation as well as degree holding. Gentry were the keepers of a particular set of cultural symbols that denoted refinement. These sociocultural attributes, associated with the literati image, conferred more distinctive status than the resources of land and wealth possessed by a still wider variety of elites.

This broader definition is intended neither to divorce the gentry from examination degrees nor to expand the term to be synonymous with "influential persons"—as it was indeed often used during the Republic. It would be hard to describe a family that failed to produce degree holders over long periods as gentry. Cultural expertise, symbolic display, patronage, and social alliances could, however, keep a family within the ranks of the *local* gentry during generations when it did not succeed in the examinations. Degrees might also function as cultural symbols buttressing claims to prominence within local social arenas as well as certificates of success in state-controlled examinations. Cultural mastery thus overlapped, but did not duplicate, the skills required for examination success. In both local and wider arenas the ability to write poetry was, for instance, a mark of elite refinement that was not directly oriented toward acquiring an official degree. Cultural display and symbols also helped set lower limits to the gentry category by distinguishing gentry, with or without degrees, from others, such as village community leaders, who lacked the same cultural credentials. Although a cultural definition of gentry is necessarily less precise than characterizations solely in terms of degree holding, it seems to reflect social dynamics more accurately by suggesting that gentry, like other elites, were defined not only by the state but also by themselves in relation to others in both their local arenas and the larger polity.

We have used "merchant" to include premodern industrialists and bankers as well as traders—and the merchants who appear in these pages are part of the local elite because of their wealth, often buttressed by resources commonly associated with the gentry, such as degrees (purchased or regular), landholding, cultural symbols, and community involvements. Given the frequent overlap between merchant and gentry resources and strategies, late imperial merchants do not generally fit the model of the European bourgeoisie, which originated as a legally, occupationally and socially distinct estate. Chinese bourgeoisie, in a loose sense more akin to "modern businessmen and professionals," enter our picture in the twentieth century after the introduction of Western-style industry, business, and specialized professions, but even then they also relied on some resources and strategies akin to those of the late imperial gentry. The changing circumstances behind such theoretical considerations are recorded in this volume's articles.

LOCAL ELITES IN HISTORICAL CONTEXT

The articles in this volume span the period from the fourteenth to the twentieth century, from the founding of the Ming dynasty to the onset of the Communist revolution. Arranged in roughly chronological order, the articles provide perspectives on the evolution of the Chinese elite in late imperial and modern times. Most of the detailed research focuses on the nineteenth and twentieth centuries: a period of continuous and sometimes wrenching social, economic, and political change.

We begin with three chapters on late imperial elites. This long period, from the fourteenth century to the early twentieth, includes the last two Chinese dynasties, the Ming and the Qing. At this time the techniques of centralized bureaucratic governance and the Confucian examination system that qualified men for office reached their highest level of sophistication. Degree-holding gentry were also the prototypical elites, especially in such stable and prosperous core areas as the Lower Yangzi. Timothy Brook opens the volume with a chapter on the Ming-Qing upper gentry of Ningbo. In a striking analysis of cultural hegemony at work, he argues that not only the examination degrees but also the cultural repertoires and associational networks of elite families allowed them to perpetuate their status over many generations, allowing one to speak of an "aristogenic elite."

William Rowe similarly argues for the very long continuity of elite families in Hanyang. Located along the middle reaches of the Yangzi River in the heart of China, the Hanyang region was sparsely populated at the beginning of the Ming. Rowe finds the Yuan-Ming transition a crucial period of elite formation, but in striking contrast to the Ningbo elite studied by Brook, these Hanyang families included remarkably few degree holders; instead, they perpetuated their position through occupational diversification, including substantial reliance on commerce, and an astute use of corporate lineages to marshal aggregate kinship resources and preserve elite status.

Continuing up the Yangzi, Madeleine Zelin's paper describes the operations of salt merchant families in Sichuan in the late Qing. The western province of Sichuan had been turned once again into a frontier region by the devastating rebellions during the seventeenth-century transition from Ming to Qing. Far from the political center, the elites of the town she studied owed their position to profits from salt wells, not governmental degrees. They adapted the lineage hall, most often associated with gentry strategies, to create commercial corporations to manage and preserve their family business interests. The elites in both Zelin's and Rowe's articles indicate the growing importance of mercantile activity, as national and regional trading networks expanded amid the general commercialization of late imperial Chinese society.

Late imperial China was far from stagnant before the mid-nineteenth century. Commercialization and indigenous industrialization were slowly changing the local elites. The series of late-eighteenth- and nineteenth-century rebellions, especially the monumental Taiping Rebellion of the 1850s and 1860s, destroyed some families, opened opportunities for others, and weakened state control over elite society. Following the forceful opening of China by the Opium War of 1839–1842, commercialization accelerated, industry and transport began to be mechanized, and powerful weapons and revolutionary ideas arrived from the West. The Qing state endorsed a full-fledged program of reform only after the disastrous failure of the antiforeign Boxer Uprising in 1900. The examination system was abolished in 1905, and diplomas from Western-style schools replaced the degrees that had formally certified gentry status. Chambers of commerce, industrial promotion bureaus, educational associations, and new voluntary associations provided the elite with opportunities to institutionalize local political power. After 1909, local and national assemblies were elected from limited constituencies. Thus local elites began to acquire formal political positions, and when the "law of avoidance" disappeared with the dynasty, men could hold administrative posts in their own localities. In the end, the late Qing reforms only accelerated demands for political change. When revolution broke out in 1911, it quickly gained the support of local and provincial elites. New republican forms replaced the imperial system in 1912, but central state power was not effectively reestablished. The ensuing "warlord period" was marked by political competition and warfare, and social changes accelerated without central direction.

Elite continuity and change across the watershed of the 1911 Revolution have long been critical issues in modern Chinese history. The next three chapters treat this transition from late imperial to Republican elites. Lynda Bell introduces the elite economic interests represented by the silk industrialists of Wuxi county, in the heart of the Lower Yangzi's Jiangnan core. These "hybrid types" emerged from the late imperial Lower Yangzi society in which elites were at once highly successful in examinations, much engaged in commerce, and increasingly involved in managing local affairs. However, when introducing new technology and managing a modern business dependent on foreign markets, the American-educated leader of Wuxi industry engaged in "bourgeois practice" similar to that of his Western counterparts. Industrial modernization also produced more powerful patterns of economic dominance over peasant households, dominance that differed from both the weaker controls exercised by earlier Jiangnan landlords and the European pattern of peasant migration to the cities during the early stages of industrialization.

Keith Schoppa's inquiry into local-elite politics in the Lower Yangzi carries issues of intra-elite conflcit and domination over peasants across the divide of the 1911 Revolution. His study of a water control dispute illustrates the elites' use of patronage, their manipulation of old cultural symbols, and their appropriation of the new discourse and institutions of representation. The article also underlines the effects of geographical location and overlapping arenas on local societies and the relative power of elites within them.

One unmistakable change in republican China was the prominence of military elites throughout the country. The first general steps in this direction occurred when local militia were formed to combat the Taiping and other rebellions from 1850 to the early 1870s—a process Philip Kuhn discusses in terms of the militarization of Chinese elites.[37] The late Qing promotion of military modernization to resist imperialism and the collapse of central state authority accelerated militarization in the early Republic. Edward McCord studies militia-warlord elites in the peripheral southwest where military power was more important than it ever became in the Lower Yangzi. Even there, McCord finds that military resources were paramount in maintaining dominance only in times of disorder; when the sociopolitical context was more stable, the family he studied developed its cultural and civil resources through education and examination degrees. Members also cultivated contacts in higher political arenas, a strategy that served them well when local elites moved into administrative posts in the confused years of the early Republic.

Each of these chapters shows us local elites aggressively responding to opportunities for association and reform in economic, political or military arenas. From the late Qing through the 1920s local elites were actively pressing for and profiting from the process of change. The founding of the Nanjing government by Chiang Kai-shek and the Nationalist (Guomindang) Party in 1927 ushered in a decade of centralized state-building that often left local elites, who lacked the legitimacy of previous county leaders, on the defensive. Lenore Barkan examines the changing character of elite-state relations in Rugao County on the northern edge of the Lower Yangzi core. There she finds a shift from prestigious, classically educated, community-oriented reformist leaders in the early twentieth century to more specialized, less prestigious men, who in the late 1920s were squeezed between the forces of the assertive Nationalist government in Nanjing (1928–1937) and dissenting

activists challenging the local establishment in the name of the masses. The
fragmentation of elite leadership and the stalemate between state and local
power partially explain the demise, in the 1930s, of the earlier, expansive
elite initiatives.

David Strand carries us further into the problem of elites caught between
state power and lower levels of society in his study of local leaders in the
national capital of Beijing during the warlord years. Strand contrasts long-
established elite strategies to protect their local authority through vertical
networks, patronage, and mediation with their simultaneous use of the associations of an emergent civil society. These associations not only provided
new resources to challenge state administrative authority, but, as Strand
further shows, the "counterelite" students, party activists, and labor organizers also used associations against the local establishment. New arenas of social conflict emerged, and elites were pushed into repressive acts when they
could no longer mediate ideologically charged disputes. Central state power
and mass politics constrained elites from above and below, but the two remained separate until later joined by the Communist revolution.

The communists, of course, rose to victory from village bases, and village
elites would become targets of land reform struggles. The articles by Rubie
Watson and Prasenjit Duara underline the striking differences between these
elites in the contrasting social environments of South and North China.
Watson studies a village in the New Territories of Hong Kong that illustrates
common characteristics of the southeast coast: commercialization, high
tenancy and landless rates among the peasantry, strong lineages, and the
ownership of half or more of the land by corporate ancestral estates. The
privileged position of village elites, resting on resources such as land, was
solidified by their interlocking roles as merchants, patrons, brokers, and
managers of lineage estates. Here we see corporate lineage used in another
way as a political resource for local domination.

Duara asks how elites of villages on the North China plain established
authority in a more fluid and less stratified society with few tenants and no
elaborate corporate lineages. He finds that cultural prestige, or "face," was
acquired by those middlemen who successfully brokered and guaranteed the
many contracts required for loans, leases, and land sales under customary
law. As community patrons, they dominated villagers who needed their outside connections and protection. When economic decline, warfare, and state
intrusion undermined the community-oriented brokers in the 1930s, they
were replaced, if at all, by more professional and often more predatory
brokers who hastened the impoverishment and disintegration of village
communities.

These issues of dominance and political change converge in Stephen Averill's chapter on the peripheral hill country of Jiangxi province where Mao
Zedong established the Central Soviet in the 1920s. Averill builds on a de-

tailed survey by Mao to provide a picture of economic stratification within the local elite, from the county's great families to the pettiest rural land-lords. He finds a fluid society in which the elite exercised "commanding collective dominance" but individual families were "remarkably insecure." The first Communists, children of insecure downwardly mobile elites, were exposed to new ideologies in schools at higher urban levels—an example of how overlapping arenas now both produced counterelites and reinforced ex-isting elite dominance. Hill-country schools became an arena through which these disaffected youths could enter the power structure. Communists reached out toward the peasantry through gangs and secret societies, but the early revolutionary movement tended to "expand and fracture in accordance with patterns of political interaction typical of hill-country elites."

REGIONAL VARIATIONS IN CHINESE LOCAL ELITES

In addition to describing historical changes in local elites, the chapters in this volume illustrate regional variations in the course of treating elites in six of G. William Skinner's original eight macroregions (maps 1.1 and 1.2).[38] Con-trasts have often been drawn between the ecologies and social organization of the Lower Yangzi, the southeastern coastal provinces, and the North China plain. However, geographical context is so important to understand-ing local elites in China that it is worth both summarizing characteristics of elites in these three major regions here and commenting briefly on the less studied elites of the Middle and Upper Yangzi regions and peripheral and frontier zones.[39]

The Lower Yangzi Elite. In late imperial times, the Lower Yangzi and its Jiangnan core was not only the wealthiest and most commercially developed region of China but also the most successful in producing degree-holding gentry.[40] Since the Ming the Jiangnan elite had also amassed substantial landholdings, with one seventeenth-century estimate asserting (probably with some exaggeration) that nine-tenths of the people were landless tenants.[41] By Qing times, the substantially urbanized gentry were living the leisured life of absentee landlords in administrative centers or the many small towns that lined the canals. Their scholarly and cultural activities set the standard for much of the nation, and our images of gentry society and literati culture are based on the Lower Yangzi region.[42] Jiangnan was also the most secure and least militarized area of China, and its cultural prominence reflected that fact.

The wealth and official status of the Lower Yangzi, especially the Jiang-nan, gentry gave them exceptional power, which the imperial state seemed to struggle endlessly to control. This gentry influence was enhanced by con-siderable social and cultural cohesiveness. Complex networks based upon

Map I.1. Provinces of China, Showing Locations of Studies in this Volume
SOURCE: G. William Skinner, *The City in Late Imperial China* (Stanford, 1977).

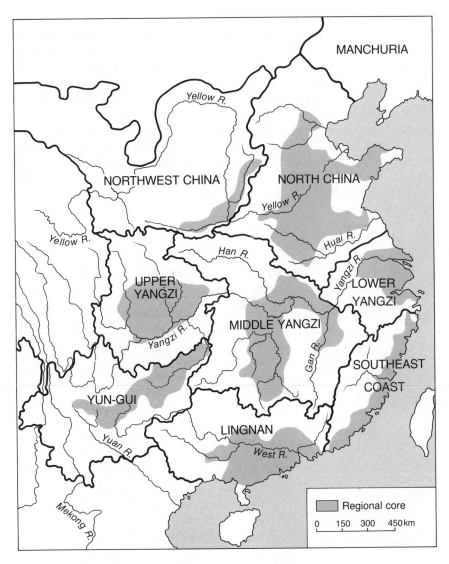

Map I.2. Physiographic Macroregions of China
SOURCE: G. William Skinner, *The City in Late Imperial China* (Stanford, 1977).

such practices and institutions as marriage alliances, philanthropic activities, academies, and poetry clubs, tied the Jiangnan gentry together and set them off in ways that promoted their cultural hegemony. Lower Yangzi elite families organized lineages and established charitable estates; but lineage lands were usually limited, and lineages less defensive and boundary-conscious than in the southeast. Networks linking the gentry generally outweighed kinship units dividing them.[43]

Although Lower Yangzi elites epitomized the gentry as degree holders and cultural leaders, they also exemplified the gentry's involvement in trade. As the most commercialized region of China, the Lower Yangzi provided more mercantile resources for elites to draw upon. Because there were too many degree holders to be employed in government service, some supported themselves as teachers, scholars, and managers, but others turned to trade. As foreign trade and the rise of Shanghai as China's leading commercial city expanded opportunities in the nineteenth and twentieth century, merchants and gentry were virtually fused.[44]

With such various resources to draw upon, Lower Yangzi elites were among those least dependent on the central state even though they had the closest connections with high officials. Their autonomy grew after the Taiping Rebellion when the numerous bureaus and agencies through which elites took charge of repairing the destruction permitted a qualitative new expansion of civil power, and the concentration of *lijin* (likin) taxes in the Yangzi valley (as in the southeast) provided more funds for local elite projects and greater tax-farming opportunities than in most of northern and western China.[45] When treaty ports like Shanghai provided partial havens for political organizing, elites were well prepared to translate their autonomy into political activity, culminating in elite participation in the 1911 Revolution and continued autonomy during the Republic.[46]

On the other hand, village elites with considerable land, managerial authority, and coercive power in their localities were relatively rare in Jiangnan, although they might be found elsewhere in the Lower Yangzi. After the Jiangnan landlords moved to towns and cities, there was less of a truly rural, community-oriented elite and few rural militia. Instead, absentee landlords acted in the villages through their agents and rent-collection bursaries supported by county governments.[47] In the southeast, rural landlords more closely tied to their local communities were more of a counterweight to county-level elites.[48]

Local Elites in the Southeast. Strong lineage organization was the most distinctive characteristic of rural society in the southeastern provinces of Guangdong, Fujian, and Taiwan, largely related to the frontier quality of these societies in the Ming and early Qing. Land had to be developed, and communities had to be defended; however, the scale of predation was small enough for an armed community to defend itself. Massive nomadic attacks and rebellions destroyed villages and scattered families in northern and western China, but the more manageable threats to rural society in the southeast reinforced the effect of hilly topography in producing cohesive and exclusive rural settlements. Complex lineage organization came later, influenced by Confucian norms and the officially sanctioned form of the ancestral estate, but it took its unique strength from the defensive need for community solidarity.[49]

Through lineage corporate property a foundation for the power of a characteristic local managerial elite was tied to kin-group constituencies. In many other ways, southeastern elites behaved much like those of the Lower Yangzi: turning to commercial ventures, following degree-holding strategies if they could move beyond the village level, and forming associations with other elites in the county seat or market towns. Foreign trade, developing from the sixteenth century onward, had more impact before the mid-nineteenth century than on any other region except Northwest China; in Fujian, it gave rise to absentee landlordism very similar to that produced by commercialization in Jiangnan.[50]

If such patterns were similar to the Lower Yangzi, the ways in which rural elites in the southeast exploited commercial resources reflected important differences as well. One of the most common methods was to exercise monopoly control and collect fees over local markets, ferries, or docks.[51] Clearly such exclusive arrangements would produce more territorial competition among elites than the commercial investments common in Jiangnan. Gentry associations frequently became "alliances" of kinship groups, rather than expressions of shared cuture and social interests.[52] Thus in the southeast, the vertical, kin-based structure of lineages seems stronger than horizontal gentry networks.

North China Elites. The unirrigated regions of North China—growing wheat, soy, corn, sorghum, and millet—were much poorer and more vulnerable to natural disasters than the rice-growing areas of the Yangzi and the southeast. Landlordism was generally undeveloped in North China, where landlords owned only about 10 percent of the land in Shandong and Hebei. When local elites did develop substantial landholdings, they tended to be in more commercially developed areas, along the southern Shandong portion of the Grand Canal or the northern littoral of the Shandong hills. There, by the nineteenth century, we see a fusion of landed and commercial wealth similar to the Lower Yangzi and southeastern patterns,[53] but in the vast regions without convenient water transport, and hence little commerce, local elites seem to have preserved more of the traditional Confucian disdain for mercantile activity.[54]

Scholars working on the North China plain have been impressed by the weakness of the degree-holding gentry elite in predominantly rural counties. In the last half of the nineteenth century, the fifty-three counties of western Shandong produced only 413 holders of the provincial *juren* degree. Thus the average county, with a population of about 250,000 people, had probably five living *juren*. Rural counties had even fewer, and most of these men probably did not stay in places with such limited cultural and commercial resources.[55] Although there were many degree holders in North China, they were likely to concentrate in a few major cities, notably Beijing and the provincial capitals, in contrast to the wide dispersal of gentry in the towns of the Lower Yangzi.

Several consequences derive from the weakness of county-level gentry on the North China plain. First, village elites were more likely to deal directly with the local magistrate's yamen than to work through gentry intermediaries as in Jiangnan. Some of the most important rural leaders in this area were either village brokers or subbureaucratic functionaries such as *lizhang* or *xiangbao* whose task was to communicate between village and county yamen on fiscal, legal, or other public matters.[56] Second, the power of the county government was greater than in Jiangnan or the southeast. North China elites had neither a strong economic base in land and commerce nor powerful networks to confront the imperial state. As a result, the state loomed larger in the north, and access to officials was, in itself, considered a mark of elite status. Thus one village informant in twentieth-century Shandong described the "village gentry" as those "who know the county magistrate."[57] Third, the weakness of a strong degree-holding elite in precisely those poor areas especially prone to disorder weakened the checks on the nongentry village strongmen/militia leaders/bandits who emerged as governmental power declined in the late-nineteenth and twentieth centuries.

Elites in the Middle and Upper Yangzi. We know much less about Yangzi valley elites above the delta, and the chapters by Rowe and Zelin in this volume represent some of the first detailed English-language studies of the subject. Structurally, Middle Yangzi elites looked like slightly less developed versions of their Lower Yangzi counterparts; the Upper Yangzi elites of Sichuan were perhaps even one step less developed—less urbanized, less uniformly commercialized, less culturally refined, and less successful in the examinations. The Middle Yangzi differed from North China in its stronger gentry and more widespread and complex patterns of landlordism, but we do not find the same development of large corporate estates as in the southeast. There were fewer degree holders compared to Jiangnan, and local elites retained more contacts with rural communities, continuing their considerable involvement in agriculture and water control and successfully rallying peasants into militia against the Taipings.[58] However, like the Lower Yangzi elite, the elite of both the Middle and Upper Yangzi relied increasingly on mercantile wealth as well as land.

There is a likely explanation for these patterns: the rebellions at the end of the Yuan and the Ming dynasties had a particularly devastating impact on the Middle and especially the Upper Yangzi, which reverted to frontier status at the end of the Ming. These areas went through several phases of economic development during the Qing. At the beginning of the dynasty immigrants were resettling and reclaiming the land, but by its end the core cities of the Middle Yangzi were starting to rival the Lower Yangzi as centers of modern development. Considering this later timetable of development, it may be best to conceive of these elites as an earlier stage of a single Yangzi valley prototype.

Local Elites in Peripheral Zones. The regional elites that we have been describing are mostly the elites of regional cores. We must not, however, neglect the distinctions between elites in core and peripheral zones. Certain common characteristics of peripheral elites, not limited to any one region, deserve further comment.

Most obviously, peripheries tended to be more violent and disorderly. Elites were more likely to command militia units, and their coercive resources were generally greater than those of elites in the cores. Government officials, important figures in the county seat, might have virtually no leverage in the countryside. Merchants, too, often entered rural areas as unpopular outsiders controlling long-distance trade. They were vital to the local economy but were not integrated into rural society. The multiple waves of immigration and the transfer of some mercantile capital into landholding could result in complicated, multilayered tenancy systems and the development of large-scale defensive organizations like lineages.

Second, the county seat and the district magistrate appear more important to the urban-oriented segment of elite society. Both the hilly topography and the focus of trade on the export of hill products, like tea and lumber, to the economic cores discouraged the growth of numerous linked marketing centers. Indeed the county city was also likely to be the local economic center. Elites congregating there included few upper-degree holders. Without the upper degrees and connections that gave core-zone gentry access to higher bureaucratic arenas, it was more difficult to circumvent the authority of county magistrates even though local men did acquire lucrative fiscal posts in the twentieth century.[59]

Third, the evidence regarding elite continuity is particularly contradictory. The instability of the Jiangxi periphery encouraged fluid elite structures with considerable downward mobility. On the other hand, there is contrary evidence for enduring local oligarchies in the Zhejiang periphery where some elite families remained locally prominent for centuries.[60] The key variable may be the degree of social strife in an area, with more settled peripheries like Zhejiang's able to support long-entrenched elites; but the question deserves further investigation.

Frontier Elites. On the edge of Chinese society frontiers, still less socially and economically integrated with the cores, were largely beyond the reach of state power.[61] Frontier elites had to establish their positions as leaders of settlements in rough, sparsely settled societies and lead their followers against indigenous non-Han natives and competing immigrant settlers. Leaders of minority peoples had to defend against the intruders as well as other minority groups. Hence military power was the most common resource of frontier elites—shared by strongmen on Taiwan, militia leaders in Guizhou, and Muslim elites in the ethnically divided, strife-riven northwest. In this respect, frontier elites were similar to those on the periphery; but because the power of the state was still weaker, elites relied more on their own local resources, whether material like landholdings or spiritual like the inherited charisma of the Muslim *menhuan* elites described in Jonathan Lipman's paper at the Banff Conference.

Frontiers developed through several stages in the Qing, starting with Han immigration in the seventeenth and eighteenth century, followed by mounting conflict with the indigenous populace, growing external commercial contacts, and increasing governmental efforts to pacify and control these societies in the late eighteenth and nineteenth centuries. The northwest also experienced rebellion and government suppression in the nineteenth century, although it did not follow quite the same pattern and timetable. As a result, a process of gentrification seems to have overtaken elites on widely separated frontiers toward the end of the nineteenth century. Despite its political and military weaknesses, the Qing state in its final years was proving unusually effective on the frontier and was serving as a catalyst for cultural integration. It is ironic that just as the Confucian consensus that had long sustained the cultural hegemony of the gentry was breaking down along China's coastal core, frontier elites began to gentrify.

The diversity of Chinese local elites illustrated by the eleven studies in this volume makes it clear that the image of a static and monolithic gentry society cannot encompass the range of elites in China. It is not enough, however, just to say that Chinese local elites were diverse. In the concluding essay we will return to factors behind this diversity. What environmental factors determined the nature of local elites and the basis of their local dominance? What resources did they rely upon? What strategies did they pursue? What structures did they build to maintain and bolster their power? What new attributes did they acquire during the period studied in this volume? Were there common characteristics amidst diversity? Answering such questions within the different historical and geographical contexts in which elites acted is a necessary prelude to addressing the broader comparison of Chinese and Western elites that dominated earlier studies of the Chinese gentry.

PART ONE

Late Imperial Elites

ONE

Family Continuity and Cultural Hegemony: The Gentry of Ningbo, 1368–1911

Timothy Brook

One evening in the fall of 1617, Wan Bangfu (1544–1628) and Zhou Yingzhi (*jinshi* 1580) were drinking with their friends at the Moon Society, a poet's club by the edge of Moon (or West) Lake in the southwest quarter of the city of Ningbo. The two men were celebrating the births of grandchildren. Zhou's daughter-in-law had given birth to a girl, Wan's to a boy, Wan Sinian (1617–93), who would become a leading scholar of the late seventeenth century. Well into their cups, Wan and Zhou decided that the newborns should be betrothed to each other to cement their own tie. The marriage took place as planned, nineteen years later.

Wan and Zhou were among the most highly placed members of the local gentry of Yin county, the prefectural seat of Ningbo, at the turn of the seventeenth century. The Wans had first risen to prominence through military achievements during the founding of the Ming dynasty in the 1360s, for which they had been awarded a hereditary guard commandership in Ningbo. The family was known even then for its literary cultivation: the daughter of the first commander had earned a local reputation for her studies and filial piety. Wan Bangfu's grandfather had been the first to transfer the family from military to civil eminence by becoming an outstanding Neo-Confucian scholar in the tradition of the eminent philosopher Wang Yangming (1472–1528). Wan Bangfu had similarly excelled in both military and literary skills, overseeing the defense of the Fujian coast while in office and composing poetry and penning calligraphy while out of office. He had married his son to one of the Xihu ("West Lake") Wens, a most respectable family from the fashionable Moon Lake residential district, and the new couple had produced Sinian.

In terms of family background, though, Zhou Yingzhi was the most eminent man in Ningbo in 1617. The Fushi Zhous were the leading gentry family of the county. They had recently acquired a new spacious residence by Moon Lake. As the senior member of his generation, Yingzhi was qualified to preside over elite society in all its forms, including the twenty-nine-member Moon Society where he and Wan celebrated grandfatherhood and tied the knot between their lines.

The betrothal of the infants was recalled many years later by their son, Wan Yan (1637–1705). Wan Yan was born the year after his grandfather, Bangfu, finally passed the provincial *juren* examinations. Like his grandfather and father, Wan Yan married well (a Shaoyaozhi Qian). Like them, too, he was active in literary societies with his friends, "the younger members of the great families of the county"—the Qijie Lis (to whom he was related by marriage), the Nanhu Shens, the Wanzhu Gaos, the Feng'ao Shuis, and others. At the center of much of this literary activity in Yin county was Huang Zongxi (1610–95), the outstanding intellectual of his generation. Huang had been a fellow-student with Wan Yan's father and during Wan Yan's own time was teaching in retirement in his native Yuyao county on the western border of Yin. "Our party" (*wu dang*), as Wan Yan called his friends, expressed their common moral and intellectual commitment and their regret for the fall of the Ming dynasty (1368–1644) by gathering around Huang. Later Wan Yan took Huang's concerns about Ming history to the capital by helping to compile the official dynastic history of the fallen Ming house on the basis of Huang's research notes. Wan Yan's in-law, Li Yesi, used the same expression, "our party," for the Ningbo gentry coterie that gathered around Huang. In Li's view the Wans in particular were preeminent in "our party." He called them "the model of the gentry lineage."[1]

This brief glimpse of the seventeenth-century social world inhabited by the upper levels of the Yin-county gentry touches on some ways by which this elite group established its hegemony in the late imperial period. Confucian social theory placed the gentry—those who distinguished themselves by entering the service of the throne via the examination system—at the top of a conventionalized four-tiered hierarchy above peasants, artisans, and merchants. The imperial political system, however, denied them a legitimate voice in the decision-making processes in their native places by empowering them politically only after they had passed the higher state examinations and left for a bureaucratic career elsewhere. This nonenfranchisement allowed the gentry to occupy the pinnacle of the social order at home only extrapolitically. To ensure their hegemony in that context, the gentry developed distinctive economic, social, and cultural strategies during the sixteenth and seventeenth centuries.[2] In this essay I do not challenge the institutional definition of the gentry in terms of state titles, but I do supplement it by arguing that sociocultural factors were not only part of the gentry's definition but also necessary to its constitution. I will focus on two strategies that, aside from the main forms of gentry economic dominance—that is, landlordism and the control of local surplus through marketing and usury—are essential for understanding the maintenance and character of local gentry control: family continuity and cultural hegemony.

YIN COUNTY AND ITS GENTRY

Yin county was the seat of Ningbo prefecture. The city, usually known by the name Ningbo, served as both county and prefectural capital. Located at the northeastern corner of Zhejiang province, Ningbo was outside the central Jiangnan core, but it was the region's main commercial city. As a maritime trading center it had been nationally prominent since the Song dynasty. The Yong River that linked it to the sea could carry ocean-going vessels upstream as far as the commercial flats east of the city wall, and a series of inland waterways leading west to Hangzhou made Ningbo the de facto southern terminus of the Grand Canal, the backbone of China's internal trading network extending all the way to Beijing. When the Song dynasty fell to the Jurchens and the capital was moved to Hangzhou in the twelfth century, Ningbo absorbed many northern elite families that chose to relocate to the region. Entering national politics by its proximity to the Southern Song capital, Ningbo gained a prominence it did not relinquish even after the political center shifted back to North China in the Yuan dynasty in 1279.

Yin enjoyed a flourishing agricultural economy based on a highly developed countywide irrigation system. The watercourses of the western half of the hinterland plain had been developed in the Song and Yuan; however, the hydraulic system of the eastern half achieved its maximum extent only by the latter half of the sixteenth century. Active commercial exchange between the hinterland and the coast combined with agriculture to make Yin a prosperous place in the Ming and Qing dynasties. Both internal grain circulation—wheat moving south, rice moving north—and foreign trade with Japan enriched the city. Designated a treaty port in 1842 and situated only 260 kilometers by boat from the emerging metropolis of Shanghai, Ningbo benefited from international commerce, although the rise of steam-shipping after the mid-nineteenth century led eventually to a modest eclipse in the city's prominence.[3]

The men of Yin county in the Ming dynasty could look back to the Southern Song for an impressive tradition of degree winning and office holding, and they proved themselves adept at continuing that tradition. Their success led to the rapid formation of a large titled gentry.[4] In the Ming, the highest metropolitan degree of *jinshi* was conferred on 293 individuals, a rate of slightly better than three per triennial examination session. The high tide of degree success in Yin came during the twenty-one *jinshi* examinations held at the capital between 1466 and 1526: Yin natives won this degree at the remarkable rate of five per session. Combined with those who gained only the provincial *juren* or the *gongsheng* degree, the number of people holding examination titles that qualified them for office in the Ming exceeded a thousand. With the exception of the two metropolitan counties where the provincial capital, Hangzhou, was situated, no county in Zhejiang could match this impressive record in the Ming.

The success with which Yin natives acquired degrees in the Ming suggests not only that they must have been well prepared to succeed in the examinations but also, more significant for our purposes, that examination titles were highly valued and aggressively sought by the county's leading families. It is usually assumed that men pursued degrees in the struggle to rise to power in Beijing. I would argue, however, that few proceeded through the exam system with this aspiration. Knowing the odds were formidably against them, they got degrees for another purpose. Titles from the examination system were an entrée into government service, but they were also a key resource in the local context, for they uniquely set apart those with claims to legitimate status. These titles can be viewed as proxies for other power—most notably that derived from wealth—because success in the examinations generally eluded those without considerable financial resources. Full elite status depended on acquiring a state title, not simply wealth; and the status these titles conferred—like wealth—was significant primarily in local, rather than national, arenas of power.

Yin's record in the Qing dynasty is far less impressive: only 131 *jinshi* for a period of roughly equal duration. Fully one-third date to the half-century after 1851, when degrees were made more available in provinces that had suffered during the Taiping Rebellion. Yin's pre-1851 rate of acquisition— little better than one per session—is therefore uninspiring. Given the well-known commercial and intellectual vitality of the region in the nineteenth century, this deterioration in the ability of Yin men to win degrees might be explained by their pursuit of other goals, such as accumulating landed or mercantile wealth. In other words, the decline in the number of higher degrees by members of Yin elite families possibly reflects a limited erosion of certain gentry-typical strategies within an elite that was being drawn more and more along other avenues of wealth and power, particularly commerce.

A diversification of strategies between gentry and mercantile goals may have been true in Yin to some extent even in the Ming. Mary Rankin has noted that commercialization and demographic growth in Zhejiang through the Qing propelled gentry and merchants toward an "incomplete fusion."[5] The scale of Yin gentry participation in this incomplete fusion in the Ming and Qing is hinted at in a few biographies of "filial and charitable men" (*xiaoyi*) in the 1733 Ningbo prefectural gazetteer.[6] Sun E, a provincial *juren* of 1489, was the son of a merchant who had gone off to Shaanxi province but failed to return because he had not made enough money to justify his absence. Sun's mother took charge of his education, and he gained his *juren* degree at the relatively young age of twenty. Thereafter he traveled north to find his father and bring him home; his own success canceled his father's failure. Sun's achievement was not the isolated luck of an individual, for a cousin had won his *juren* in the previous session of 1486. For unstated reasons, the Suns varied their strategies for success, at one time pursuing educational goals and at another following mercantile careers. Another local family, the Xihu Chens, shows the same pattern. Chen Shu (*jinshi* 1529) rose to the post of vice-intendant of education for Henan province; his great-grandson, orphaned and in straitened circumstances at the age of fifteen, gave up his studies to support his mother and later his own family by running a store. He was able to give his son an education, though his early death in turn forced the son to give up his studies and go into "textiles and grain."[7] Although neither of these families held a commanding position within the greater gentry, the county's preeminent historian of the Qing, Quan Zuwang (1705–55), regarded the Xihu Chens, and possibly the Suns as well, as belonging among Yin's "eminent lineages" in the Ming.[8]

The 1877 county gazetteer offers a few similarly brief references from the Qing: a 1765 *gongsheng* who "worked as a merchant when young in order to support his parents and younger brothers, and later in life turned to a career of scholarship"; an early nineteenth-century holder of the *shengyuan* degree whose elder brother was a merchant; another *shengyuan*, a wholesale dealer in firewood, was prevented from going on to a higher degree when his elder brother's death obliged him to stay in business to support the family; an 1832 *juren* whose great-grandfather had run a drugstore in Beijing.[9] To some degree, trade was permissible within gentry families that could not support themselves through more conventional gentry-style sources of income.

A significant portion of the Yin gentry nonetheless resisted this willingness to regard the commercial acquisition of wealth with equanimity, even as late as the end of the eighteenth century. Qin Jing, for example, started out as a promising student but decided to go into business to reverse his family's financial decline. (Growing rich through a bureaucratic career could only be a long-term strategy.) His father admonished him with the advice that he should "seek to be a gentleman, however poor, not a merchant, however rich." Persuaded by this appeal to gentry exclusiveness, Qin went back to his studies, winning his *juren* degree in 1798.[10] So long as the fusion between gentry prestige and merchant wealth remained incomplete, gentry ideals of a conservative mold were far from moribund prior to the nineteenth century. Indeed, we should probably read the lackluster performance of Yin natives in the exams compared with candidates from the more peripheral parts of Ningbo prefecture as evidence that the Yin gentry were neither expanding nor receiving large infusions from those outside their ranks,[11] such as mercantile families. The social context of elite life may have been changing as Ningbo was drawn further into coastal and international trade, but the upper echelons of the Yin elite continued to exercise their dominance in characteristically gentry fashion.

FAMILY CONTINUITY

Family identity is always a resource of dominance when social structure is relatively stable: The longer a family inhabits the elite, the stronger its elite identity. This principle has particular cogency for the late imperial Chinese gentry because gentry status strictly speaking cannot be inherited.[12] The full implementation of an examination-based bureaucracy in the Song dynasty led to forming a new elite largely composed of men recruited on criteria other than birth. The examination system provided a pathway to elite status that neither crossed the territory of prior privilege nor was hedged with legal barriers to talent in favor of birth. The Chinese political system, at least officially, did not condone the begetting of status by status.[13]

It should follow from this shift in the Song away from hereditary elites that the ability of elite families to continue to reproduce that eminence declined radically. The view that elite status could not be preserved in the manner of the old pre-Song elites became conventional wisdom within the gentry. As one late-Ming writer observed, "The son of a gentleman it not necessarily able to become a gentleman."[14] The myth of rapid upward and downward mobility became enshrined in popular sayings: "a gentleman's grace becomes extinct in five generations," or "a patriline has to migrate after five generations."[15] Previous studies of mobility in China, more concerned with national than local elites, have tended to accept this view of low-level continuity.[16] However, continuity and mobility, though parallel, are not the same; nor is the relationship between them exactly inverse. Low mobility certainly implies high continuity because the absence of newcomers will leave elite membership unchanged; but high mobility does not necessarily imply low continuity, for there can be considerable continuity of elite families at the same time that a substantial number of new people are entering the elite, particularly when the elite is growing in size, as it was throughout the Ming-Qing period. An exclusive focus on mobility may thus lead to conclusions about the flexibility or openness of a social structure without revealing much about long-term solidarity or stability.

Whether gentry families could withstand the vicissitudes of the post-Song system of political appointment and maintain their status over successive generations is critical for evaluating the centrality of gentry status to local-elite life. If we can detect a marked degree of continuity over time, then it becomes necessary to recognize that degree acquisition is affected by certain probabilities. Rather than an isolated foray into the realm of national political power, it appears as a general strategy for maintaining elite status over generations. Some recent studies have begun to suggest that many families

within the local elite continued in that status over considerably longer
stretches than the five-generation rise-and-fall pattern would suggest.[17] In
her study of Tongcheng county, Anhui, Hilary Beattie noted that there existed
"an elite group of families some of whose members were prominent in the life
of the county throughout most of the Ming and Ch'ing dynasties." Jerry
Dennerline found that the elite households in Suzhou's Jiading county in the
mid-seventeenth century "were from lines which emerged in the late fifteenth
or early sixteenth." Taking an even longer perspective, Robert Hymes in his
study of the Song dynasty local elite of Fuzhou prefecture, Jiangxi, remarked
that "specific Song or Yuan descent groups can be traced without difficulty
into the Qing." They "continue as identifiable social entities important
enough to be noted in examination lists and biographies, deep into the Qing
dynasty."[18] William Rowe's article in this volume reaches similar conclusions.

THE LINEAGE IN ELITE LIFE

By shifting our unit of analysis for the elite from the family to the lineage, we
begin to see that, with its ability to concentrate effort and resources within
certain lines or branches, the lineage could anticipate some measure of
examination success over generations. As Linda Walton observed in her
study of Yin county's Lou lineage in the Song, recognizing long-term elite
strategies through lineage allows us to see the late imperial elite "as a large
group of lineages who prepared candidates for the examinations and provided office-holders for the state, but who achieved, protected, and enhanced
their status locally through a variety of social and economic means."[19]

Studies of elite mobility conducted in the 1960s doubted the wisdom of
tracing elite continuity in terms of lineage. The principal objection was that
the privileges of an examination-degree holder extended only to his immediate kin and did not transfer laterally to other lineage members; one or two
branches might enjoy good fortune while the status or wealth of the lineage
as a whole declined.[20] Although some horizontal transfer did occur, rarely
did all members benefit from the success of one branch. The local elite mainly
formed lineages, not to transfer resources *horizontally* to living agnates, but
to limit collateral kinsmen's claims so that wealth and power might be husbanded for future generations.[21] This burden of sorting out such claims was
perceived as an issue within the Ningbo elite, for the county gazetteer of
1788 deplores the practice among the poor of making false kinship claims
on wealthy men of the same surname in the hope of extracting support from
them.[22] The goal of mobilizing lineage-wide assets was, therefore, not to
enable all members of a lineage to become gentry, but to invest in *vertical*
strategies to acquire or preserve gentry status (and the wealth that made
such status feasible) for some members of later generations. From what I

have seen in Yin sources, success did not scatter widely over a lineage but tended to concentrate within certain families or branches.

The obstacles to sustaining gentry status over successive generations were multiple: the division of family property through partible inheritance, the mortality of heirs, and the unpredictability of the examination system all militated against continuity. Through such institutions as shrines, schools, and corporate funding for education and other forms of advancement, lineages attacked the problem of mobilizing sufficient assets to invest in vertical strategies. The lineage was thus formed by its elite members around the principal descent lines to broaden the pool of resources and educated junior agnates that could be drawn upon in the difficult, recurrent effort to renew gentry status through the examination system.[23] For this reason the lineage is historically and analytically inseparable from the question of the Chinese gentry's continuity.[24]

Many historians of the region have observed that the lineage dominated the social, economic, and educational opportunites of the individual in northeastern Zhejiang toward the end of the imperial era.[25] A glance through Ming-Qing sources for Yin immediately confirms the importance of lineage. Certain "families" (*jia*) or "lineages" (*zu*)—the terms are largely interchangeable when referring to agnatic groupings among the elite—are featured repeatedly in accounts of gentry life. For instance, a popular mid-sixteenth-century jingle runs:

> The Tus rank tops this side of the Yong,
> One of the four great families of which Yin people boast;
> Just like the four great gentry lineages of the Song—
> Lou, Feng, Shi, and Zheng—who were likewise praised the most.[26]

The "four great families" were the Jiangbei Tus, the Jingchuan Yangs, the Chahu Zhangs, and the Xihu Lus. By pairing them with the four Yin families that were most successful in fielding bureaucrats in the Southern Song, the verse reminds us that participation in national politics, however much removed from the local scene, remained the key factor in establishing the highest elite status.

The only attempt to assess the continuity of elite status within gentry lineages in the late imperial period is Pan Guangdan's study of Jiaxing prefecture, located northwest of Ningbo across Hangzhou Bay. Pan places among the elite those lineages of which at least five members are named in the prefectural gazetteer of 1878. This admittedly mechanical principle of selection yields ninety-one greater gentry lineages, plus an additional group of sixty lineages of lesser status. Dating their periods of prominence from the generation of the first named member to that of the last, Pan finds that the ninety-one greater gentry lineages remained prominent for an average of slightly more than two centuries. Continuity among a secondary group of sixty lesser lineages was roughly one century. Given the gazetteer's incomplete and somewhat arbitrary reporting of names, this reconstruction in fact underestimates the actual degree of elite continuity. Pan thus concludes that the gentry lineages of Jiaxing were aristogenic in character, capable of reproducing themselves over time (in the manner of a hereditary aristocracy) and not completely hostage to the vagaries of status acquisition at each generation.[27]

My reconstruction of the elite gentry lineages of Yin county confirms Pan's general conclusion.[28] Reaching much further down into the elite of a single county rather than an entire prefecture, I have identified forty-eight lineages that had at least four members holding higher degrees, at least two of which are *jinshi* (table 1.1).[29] These criteria arbitrarily exclude lineages that, though less successful in terms of degree acquisition, may have won local prominence by other means; it also ignores lineages whose members have proven difficult to identify. The resulting sample, nonetheless, includes to my satisfaction the families of nearly all the most prominent individual gentry of Yin county through the Ming and Qing dynasties.

TABLE 1.1.   The Greater Gentry Lineages of Yin County, 1371–1904

Surname	Choronym	Degrees js	Degrees jr/gs	Dates of first and last degrees	Span of years
Fan	Chengxi (West Suburb)	13	48	1484–1874	391
Qian	Shaoyaozhi	9	6	1436–1658	223
Zhou	Fushi	8	11	1571–1776	206
Tu	Jiangbei (North Suburb)	8	7	1371–1865	495
Lu	Xihu (West Lake)	8	1	1433–1673	241
Yang	Jingchuan	7	6	1451–1639	189
Dong	Xicheng (West City)	6	27	1454–1867	414
Zhang	Chahu	6	13	1487–1646	160
Fu	Wuxiangqi	6	1	1472–1898	427
Bao	Wufeng	5	7	1371–1822	452
Shao	Zhuzhou	5	6	1484–1844	361
Zhang	Gaoqiao	5	1	1439–1620s	182+
Chen	Jiangshan	5	1	1445–1543	99
Xie	Liuding	4	6	1409–1852	444
Shui	Feng'ao	4	4	1586–1883	298
Shi	Guteng	4	4	1511–1713	203
Dai	Taoyuan	4	3	1420–1535	116
Li	Qijie	4	2	1523–1661	139
Shen	Nanhu (South Lake)	4	0	1568–1631	64
Zhao	Junziying	3	5	1571–1825	255
Huang	Guangjiqiao	3	4	1514–1706	193

TABLE I.I   (*Continued*)

Surname	Choronym	Degrees		Dates of first and last degrees	Span of years
		js	jr/gs		
Tong	Cuwuqiao	3	4	1805–1876	72
Quan		3	3	1522–1736	215
Chen	Longgu	3	2	1529–1771	263
Gao	Wanzhu	3	2	1574–1693	120
Wang	Yujiacun	3	1	1508–1711	204
Feng	Xihu (West Lake)	3	1	1436–1625	190
Huang	Wutaisi	3	1	1514–1696	183
Du	Guanjiang	3	1	1464–1600	137
Guan		3	1	1565–1670	106
Xue		3	1	1532–1619	88
Jin		3	1	1445–1517	73
Guo	Yinshan	2	11	1708–1873	166
Chai	Xiaowenfang	2	10	1517–1747	231
Wang	Zhuzhou	2	9	1807–1889	83
Huang	Qinghexiang	2	6	1579–1821	243
Lu	Huaishuzhen	2	5	1469–1852	384
Wan	Dingyuan	2	5	1520–1729	210
Yuan	Chengxi (West Suburb)	2	3	1487–1842	356
Wen	Xihu (West Lake)	2	3	1505–1736	232
Rong	Qingjiezhen	2	3	1649–1804	156
Wu	Lianghu	2	3	1453–1580	128
Mao	Chengxi (West Suburb)	2	3	1457–1528	72
Fan	Nanhu	2	2	1484–1874	391
Chen	Taoyuan	2	2	1505–1865	361
Xie		2	2	1406–1624	218
Huang	Jiajingxiang	2	2	1420–1506	87
Jiang	Heyi	2	2	1691–1771	81

SOURCES: *Ningbo fuzhi*, 17a; *Yinxian zhi* (1877), 23; *Yinxian tongzhi*, 1.
NOTE: Degree terms are abbreviated: js = *jinshi*; jr = *juren*; gs = *gongsheng*.

Eight families of outstanding distinction head this list of forty-eight greater gentry. They are led by the Chengxi Fans, holders of a remarkable total of sixty-one *jinshi*, *juren*, and *gongsheng* degrees. The family was known for its private library, Tianyige, which it bought in the sixteenth century from the Xihu Fengs, an eminent Song family then entering its decline; the library still exists as the repository of an exceptional collection of late imperial texts. Next to the Fans in number of *jinshi* are the Shaoyaozhi Qians, who became leading figures in the Ming loyalist fight against the Manchus; the Fushi Zhous, who through educational and patronage activities became associated with the finest in Ming gentry culture; the Jiangbei Tus, whose most noted member was the prolific and controversial essayist Tu Long (1542–1605); and the Xihu Lus, two of whom earned reputations for high-mindedness when they were flogged at court in 1522 for challenging the newly enthroned Jiajing emperor in the Great Rites Controversy. The Xicheng Dongs, known in the seventeenth century as an "eminent lineage," won only six *jinshi* but managed to garner an enormous number of lesser degrees over a period of more than four centuries, a span second only to the Tus. Among the eight, those with the briefest spans (less than two centuries) between their first and last degrees were the Chahu Zhangs, self-conscious spokesmen for Confucian orthodoxy in the late Ming; and the Jingchuan Yangs, who garnered six *jinshi* over three decades at the end of the fifteenth century, propelled four members into ministerial and vice-ministerial positions, and owned the finest residence in the city of Ningbo.[30]

Consistent with the selection criteria based on degrees, lineages with more degrees show longer spans of prominence. The average for the eight super-elite lineages is just over three centuries; only the Yangs and Zhangs collected degrees over a period of less than two centuries. At the next level down in Table 1.1, the average degree span is more than two and a half centuries; among lineages that acquired less than four *jinshi* degrees, the average is 190 years. These spans seriously underestimate the duration of a lineage's real prominence, for the first and last degrees do not necessarily indicate the lineage's entry into or exit from the elite. There would have been a preparatory period of several generations of lesser degrees leading up to the first higher degree; and at the other end, higher degrees had a sort of half-life that allowed their potency as status indicators to continue even beyond the holder's lifetime.

From Table 1.1 we see that the gentry elite of Yin county did not rise and fall with each title's acquisition and each title holder's death. Membership was relatively stable; the lineages that fielded the highest degree holders formed a small and well-defined group. As long as the imperial order remained in place, local prominence corresponded closely with membership in certain lineages. This should come as no surprise, for elite dominance by its very nature is sustained over time. The success with which the Yin gentry sustained their presence over generations must in turn be recognized as a key element in gentry hegemony and a powerful resource for the old aristogenic gentry families who peopled the county elite.

GENTRY CULTURE

The survival of a limited number of families within the elite over several centuries required more than carefully managing lineage resources; it depended equally on managing the symbolic capital that accrued to gentry status. I argue here that culture was one of the means most consistently (even though unconsciously) used to achieve a longevity of power.

In the analysis that follows, culture is regarded as a set of practices whose main effect is to project for all members of a society a sense of sharing common values that are good—in other words, a sense that the existing arrangements of class power and dominance are appropriate. Raymond Williams has characterized culture in this vein as "the lived dominance and subordination of particular classes." Culture is hegemonic because it saturates "the whole process of living—not only of political and economic activity, nor only of manifest social activity, but of the whole substance of lived identities and relationships."[31] The elite can pilot that hegemony by identifying and controlling key social activities that reinforce its status in the eyes of subalterns and make its authority appear inarguable.

We can sense how well this definition applies to the world of late imperial China and the practices of its gentry in the short story "Divorce" that Lu Xun, a native of the neighboring prefecture of Shaoxing, wrote in 1925. Aigu is fighting her husband's attempts to abandon her, and their conflict is brought to Seventh Master for resolution. Seventh Master is introduced as a man from the city who "exchanges cards with the magistrate."[32] At the beginning of the scene in which he presides over the divorce negotiations, Seventh Master deftly establishes his authority by examining and commenting upon a Han dynasty relic, an anus-stopper from a corpse. This parody of the taste for antiquities among the gentry only underscores the unassailability of the symbolic capital concentrated in the status display. Aigu launches into her complaint against her husband but is swiftly intimidated into silence by a second high-cultural gesture: Seventh Master has his servant fetch a (to Aigu) mysterious flat bottle the size of a tortoise shell and takes snuff from it. Without denying her claim, this lower-level gentryman is able to wield cultural symbols in meaningless display to cancel the conflict. Power in this context means the ability to be seen as powerful, a visibility that cultural affectation could establish with great force.

It should not be surprising to find Lu Xun illustrating the continuing potency of gentry culture as late as the 1920s, for gentry culture of the late imperial period was still alive in the Republic. Indeed, its characteristics proved singularly impervious to alteration. Despite incorporating mercantile elements into the elite through the Qing, gentry culture continued to determine the skills and idioms that elite men were expected to master. Wealth alone could not create status: it had to be mediated by cultural forms that rendered wealth acceptable. In part the gentry were able to dominate the gentry-merchant alliance that emerged in the Qing by supplying and controlling those forms. No member of the late imperial elite, either aspiring or arrived, could overlook the gentry's self-made styles and strategies. Not for lack of other terminology did the opponents of the early twentieth-century declining rural elites label them "wicked *gentry*" (*lieshen*), for they still clung to the fading aura of gentryhood for their paltry legitimacy.

The particular forms of cultural activity that gentry culture favored covered a wide range. Ritual, literary exercise, artistic appreciation, scholarship, philanthropy, and patronage were all regarded as appropriate activities through which both the crowning Confucian concept of benevolence (*ren*) could be realized and the gentry's priority at the top of the Confucian social order could be reaffirmed as unassailable. These cultural practices lent substance to gentry hegemony in several ways in addition to the sort of aggressive symbolic display caricatured by Lu Xun. The two I examine are the reinforcement of associational networks among the gentry and the creation of a recognized public sphere for gentry activism; both became part of the gentry's cultural identity.

Associational Networks in Gentry Culture. The key to the dominance that these old gentry families enjoyed in the county lies in their interaction with each other. They did not exist in isolated eminence; instead, they were consistently forming and reforming ties, building networks that favored men of equal status and disadvantaged lesser gentry and nongentry. Friendship, marriage, political commitment, and cultural pursuits all furnished opportunities for the elite to associate with one another. Through such social interaction, the leading families found a common identity and made entry into their charmed circle difficult. In this context, family continuity was critical, for it provided ready-made ties to other dominant families in the gentry elite's network. These ties could pass from generation to generation almost automatically, especially when members of the elite, like the betrothed newborns of the Wan and Zhou lineages, found themselves playing a part without any voice in the matter.

The intensity of the ties among the county gentry is reflected in another sixteenth-century jingle recorded by Li Yesi of the Qijie Lis:

> The Fu family of Huijiang and the Jiatang Wus:
> Their huge gates face each other, their buildings touching roofs;
> The Zhangs and Lus support each other like a pair of willows entwined;
> The Zhus and Chens, living together in one place, are likewise so inclined.[33]

The families in the first line are the Wuxiangqi Fus and the Lianghu Wus. Together with the Qijie Lis they were known as the "three great families of eastern Yin." In the third line appear the superelite Chahu Zhangs and the Xihu Lus. In the fourth are the Jiangshan Chens and possibly the Maodong Zhus, a family that had won two *jinshi* degrees in the latter part of the fifteenth century but by the late Ming was of little consequence.[34] All but the Zhus are found in Table 1.1.

The verse is silent on the types of ties we tend to look for in elite networks, particularly marriage ties, which are poorly reported in the available records for Yin. But it is revealing of one aspect of elite association—physical proximity. The Fus and Wus are pictured as living within sight of each other, the Zhus and Chens as neighbors. At first glance, the solidarity between the Zhangs and Lus would appear more symbolic than physical because the Lus lived in the city's exclusive Moon Lake area, whereas the Zhangs' native village was some six kilometers southwest of the city wall. "A pair of willows entwined," however, is probably not pure metaphor, for the Zhangs probably maintained a residence in town near the Lus. We have already seen that a family could maintain both a rural residence and a second house in town in the case of the Fushi Zhous, who acquired a property on Moon Lake in the sixteenth century.

Of the forty-eight lineages in Table 1.1, I have been able to determine addresses for forty-two. Twenty-four of these forty-two lineages were based either within the city of Ningbo or in its immediate suburban area. Another eleven, among them the Chahu Zhangs and the Fushi Zhous, identified themselves with villages west and southwest of the city within ten kilometers of the city wall. This area was the part of Ningbo's hinterland plain first drained and farmed during the Song dynasty. Of the other seven lineages, five were located on the eastern plain, and two were in major towns in the peripheral upland. If we restrict our sample to the nineteen lineages placed highest in Table 1.1, eleven lived in or adjacent to the city, and the rest lived on the hinterland plain. However the sample is determined, the distribution of elite lineages is skewed more heavily to the urban core of Yin county than is true for the population as a whole. As the Zhou family's possession of a second residence inside the city indicates, this survey underestimates the urban concentration of elite families. At the very least, it suggests a tendency for elite lineages to gravitate toward the political and commercial core of the county, adjacent not only to the center of power but also, and as important, to each other.

The concentration of elite residence in or near the city of Ningbo reflects the associational pattern of gentry life. This relationship is underscored by Wan Yan's reminiscence about the betrothed newborns that furnished this article's opening story.

> When I lived in Guangji ward in the prefectural capital, I was neighbors with many noted families. The Shens, the Huangs, the Zhangs, and the Gaos all lived there. My great-great-grandmother Wang was related to both the Huangs and the Zhangs, so I had cousins in both families.[35]

Wan further comments that in the winter of 1656–57 he and these cousins, thrown together during a period of civil unrest, formed a literary society, and that half the members were young men from the neighboring families.

Wan Yan's story brings us to the central issue of culture and its critical function in gentry hegemony. The connections between Wan and his associates, facilitated by residential proximity, were lent greater substance through a cultural practice unique to the gentry, the writing of poetry. The gentry came, in a sense, culturally equipped to exercise their hegemony over local society by the cultural expertise nourished by elite life-styles: a confident competence in the arts of reading and writing, an ability to interpret and manipulate the symbols of the Confucian order, an appreciation of complex artistic media through which elite values found expression, an understanding of courtesy and deference and their effective use in social encounters, a knowledge of acceptable models and precedents for decision making. These skills were automatically gained through neither classical study for the examinations nor acquisition of the wealth needed for leisure and cultural display, but they were polished through exposure to the practices and society of highly cultivated elites. Several generations might be required for the upwardly mobile to master these social and cultural marks of good breeding, without which they could not hope to be admitted to the upper levels of societies like that of Ningbo, where a mature gentry was firmly established.

Viewed from this perspective, family continuity was more than an empty symbol of established authority. By passing on the appropriate cultural orientation from generation to generation, a family steeped in gentry traditions was better positioned to train its young men to acquire and hone skills essential for succeeding in both serving the state and maintaining status at home. Culture should thus be thought of as providing a repertoire of activities by which the gentry could create and maintain networks of personal ties with each other and set themselves apart from those who had not mastered the nuanced language of elite life.

A good example of the mastery of this repertoire is Zhang Shiche (*jinshi* 1523). The Chahu Zhangs entered the sixteenth century with a reputation for living communally in accordance with the Confucian ideal of kinship harmony.[36] After three decades in bureaucratic office, in his years of retirement from the 1550s through the 1570s Zhang Shiche embodied the Confucian model of gentry responsibility by actively participating in a wide range of sociocultural activities. His name appears in numerous inscriptions, dedications, and publications connected with important projects in the region: Chongde Shrine, raised in posthumous honor of a Taoyuan Chen for lightening the tax burden of local peasants; the Donggang Sluice, built in neighboring Dinghai as part of a large gentry-sponsored hydraulic project to improve irrigation on Yin's eastern plain; the Dinghai county school; a private academy; four bridges, one of which was known as Minister Zhang's Bridge; and the prefectural gazetteer of 1560, for which he served as editor-in-chief.[37] Zhang Shiche was the mentor of the younger elite cohort of the 1570s, of whom Tu Long was the principal figure. We see him, for example, at a select reception for the Suzhou painter Wu Zhoushi when the latter visited Ningbo in the 1570s. In addition to his eldest son Bangren, this coterie included Tianyige library owner Fan Qin, the poet Shen Mingchen, two Jiangbei Tus, and two other eminent gentry.[38] Zhang Shiche's presence among these younger men in turn placed his own family in a central position within that generation, so that when Zhang Bangren published his collected poetry several decades later Tu Long wrote the preface recommending the work.[39]

Cultural pursuits thus were organized through the networks of elite society, and mastering cultural skills was necessary for those who sought access to those networks. Entry into the elite world of the gentry was difficult, even more so if one lacked formal gentry titles. Occasionally an interloper could break in by other means. A contemporary of Zhang Shiche, Lu Chuanmei, was a merchant whose father had come to Yin to escape pirate troubles elsewhere along the coast. Lu was annoyed at being unable to deal with the "powerful lineages" of his neighborhood. His lineage biographer says that he overcame their exclusion and came to their notice by cultivating "virtuous conduct."[40] Its exact meaning is not indicated, although Lu's mercantile wealth hints that he was buying his way into the elite. Entry into the gentry's world could thus be facilitated by strategically adopting gentry "virtues" (which could be measured by donations) as well as discouraged by ignorance of them.

Literary accomplishment was a key basis for signaling status and forming groups among the elite. Yin sources are particularly rich in information concerning poetry clubs, especially in the mid-seventeenth century when they provided Ming loyalists a refuge from the calamity of the Manchu occupation in 1645. The collapse of the Ming dynasty provoked a major crisis for the Ming gentry. Their legitimacy as the local elite rested on an agreement to serve imperial power in return for the highest tokens of status. Loyalty to a fallen dynasty, which such a contract demanded, essentially marginalized the existing gentry elite. They were not supposed to acquire further degrees or hold office under the new rulers, though some of course did. Bereft of public careers and further access to legitimizing state titles, the gentry in the immediate postconquest period turned to literary groups as the safest way to honor the fallen dynasty and display their own status. Indeed, the Yin elite achieved something of a reputation in this regard, for Quan Zuwang notes that "the gentry of Ningbo, whose distress had driven them into retirement, became nationally prominent after the fall of the Ming." The postconquest poetry clubs that Quan declares most noteworthy—like the "eight gentlemen of West Lake" and the "nine gentlemen of South Lake"—were highly exclusive. But he says there were many other "societies and gatherings" (*she hui*) besides these.[41] He describes in some detail the Discarded Silk Society (Qixu She), formed by his ancestor, Quan Meixian, who chose for its name the appropriately gloomy emblem of discarded silk to express how the late-Ming gentry perceived their prospects under the Qing dynasty. In addition to several Quans, the society's members included seven members of the most successful lineages listed in Table 1.1 and five men from other well-known families.[42]

Somewhat later, as their emotional response to dynastic collapse faded, some greater gentry of Yin sought to come to terms with the political crisis of transition by turning, as Wan Yan did, from the romance of the poetry of remorse to the labor of scholarship by attempting to reconstruct the causes of the Ming's decline. The intellectual tradition spawned by this reaction— from Wan Yan to his student Quan Zuwang and thence to his student Jiang Xueyong (*juren* 1771)—has been called the Eastern Zhejiang School of historiography.[43] The focal figure for this interest and its original inspiration was Huang Zongxi, living in retirement in the next county and presiding over a scholarly circle called the Society for the Discussion of the Classics (Jiangjing Hui).[44] This coterie arond Huang Zongxi, which Wan Yan and Li Yesi referred to as "our party," was based on existing networks among the leading families of Ningbo: a Dingyuan Wan, a Qijie Li, a Quan, a Shaoyaozhi Qian, a Longgu Chen, and a Qingjiezhen Rong, among others, were counted in this group. History neither excluded nor replaced poetry, however. Although Wan Yan says that the poetry group he formed with his neighbors in 1656–57 made a point of not talking about "historical records and the suppression of disorder," his presence in the Huang group indicates that the poets and the intellectuals did not move in separate worlds. Indeed, essentially the same elite families in Huang Zongxi's coterie can also be found gathering around Li Yesi in the Mirror Lake Poetry Society. By the next generation, poetry and history were fully combined in the Candid Society (Zhenshuai She), formed by Quan Zuwang and others in 1742. The network that existed among these men passed on through their families, for Li Yesi's son, Wan Yan's younger cousin, and the sons of several others in Huang Zongxi's circle met together at exclusive semiannual drinking parties later in the century.[45]

Nongentry elites appear to have had little place in the seventeenth- and eighteenth-century social networks that operated through these cultural associations; at least, local sources do not indicate their presence. Formal gentry status continued to define access to this cultural realm, and associational activity within this realm was the mantle of exclusiveness in which the elite wrapped itself.

Gentry Culture and the Public Sphere. The gentry's typical cultural practices served as mechanisms for not only bringing them together but also enlarging their presence in the public sphere of local society. This public sphere may be defined as the arena of nonstate activity at the local level that contributed to the supply of services and resources in the public good. It existed throughout the late-imperial period, but the types of activities pursued in this arena prior to the latter half of the nineteenth century were restricted because of the state's anxiety about local autonomy. Given the limited state resources available for local development, it was essential that the gentry adopt this role. As the state was forced more and more to rely on local decision making to maintain local stability, the public sphere grew gradually until, under the impact of the Taiping Rebellion and subsequent reconstruction, it expanded quickly to create a substantially new and greatly enlarged local political arena.[46] Prior to this enlargement, and to some extent even after it, the greater gentry occupied almost entirely the center of this public sphere in Yin county.

The historical origins of this public sphere are to be found largely in what Susan Mann has called the "liturgical" services that the state expected of the gentry. Max Weber derived the notion of "liturgy" from the Athenian practice of having the elite discharge various public responsibilities at private expense; similarly, in China local elites were expected to render services for the benefit of the local community, usually to ensure public order. Chief among gentry responsibilities were operating welfare services, supervising public works, and maintaining local institutions. In some areas, the gentry might also involve themselves in regulating local trade because, as Susan Mann has pointed out, "orderly markets and contented merchants were as important as schools and granaries to community well-being."[47] The Yin county gazetteer of 1788 contains an intriguing reference to "high-handed gentry" extracting payments from small-time merchants who traded in Ningbo's main commercial area on the river flats east of the city wall about 1640. The assistant maritime commissioner for the region stopped this practice by punishing the bond servants who were acting as the gentry's agents and forbidding them to enter the area.[48] The gazetteer presents this practice as extortion, although possibly the gentry's agents were simply collecting customary fees that both they and the merchants accepted as the price of liturgical supervision. Although problems inevitably arose, the state not only accepted but also encouraged gentry involvement in the public sphere, for it met needs for which state funding was inadequate or unavailable. For their part the gentry embraced the opportunity because this public service both heightened their social standing and more immediately augmented their incomes.

In some instances the gentry undertook activities in the public good at the behest of the state, whose practice of understaffing local administration made policy implementation impossible without help from some quarter. Famine relief particularly needed cooperation from local elites. The wealthy were called on to contribute grain, and the gentry were mobilized to manage its distribution, reinforcing the notion that the gentry should work in the public good. This division of labor is documented for a famine that struck Yin county in 1751:

During the Eastern Zhejiang famine of 1751, the magistrate deputed gentry to go to the wealthy people and encourage them to make donations. Li Changyu (*jinshi* 1754) and his friend Tu Ketang (*juren* 1752) rushed about encouraging people to forward grain and were successful in amassing the required amount. The magistrate suggested setting up a central soup kitchen, but Li Changyu pointed out the dangers of doing so. . . . [He argued that] the better method would be to draw up ward registers and distribute grain directly to the people [in their home areas]. . . . The magistrate agreed to his plan and thousands of lives were saved.[49]

Li Changyu's plan called for excluding yamen runners and involving the area's "wealthy households" as well as the local tax captains in overseeing the distribution of the relief grain, but it also held them doubly responsible for making sure that irregularities did not arise. The men of nongentry wealth whose grain made the relief effort possible were thus kept subordinate, subject to the gentry's managerial power. Mary Rankin has noted the role of welfare activities among the local elite in stimulating the growth of the public sphere during the post-Taiping reconstruction period.[50] Local-elite activism of this type was already found among the eighteenth-century gentry, however, though its influence in generating a public sphere was limited by the state's stronger supervisory presence.

According to this account, Tu and Li were able managers, but the motivation and justification for their activities rested on more complex cultural meanings. Active involvement in relief demonstrated commitment to general values, like benevolence toward social inferiors, with which the gentry were imbued. Men at the upper reaches of the Yin gentry could claim the moral credentials to take the lead in projects benefiting local society, and by doing so they would further enhance the image of moral responsibility with which the gentry associated themselves. By the same token, they could maintain their claims to superiority over elites with lesser cultural credentials.

Tu Ketang's ability to exploit cultural norms in this way is demonstrated in another context. When his father was, for reasons unstated, imprisoned and sentenced to a beating, Tu chose to embody the kind of filial behavior integral to gentry Confucian norms by begging the presiding official to allow him to be punished in his father's place. Such a grand gesture, with many historical precedents, was part of the lore of Yin gentry dedication during the difficult dynastic transition between the Ming and Qing.[51] A conventional Confucian official might be expected to accept the substitution, or, more magnanimously, to waive the punishment altogether, and Tu was probably hoping to alter the course of justice by this act. As it happened, his offer backfired; the annoyed official increased his father's sentence by forty strokes.[52] Despite the unsatisfactory outcome, Tu Ketang's attempt illustrates some cultural dimensions of the elite's public actions: moral motivation rooted in the Confucian tradition, dramatic public display, strategic appeal to basic norms, tension between the values of official duty and kinship solidarity, and the preservation of such gestures in gentry-controlled sources. Tu's part in the relief work of 1751 is integral to these strategies.

Far commoner among the gentry's liturgical duties than famine relief, and more central to their elite identity, was the funding of local institutions and local construction projects. Some of these, particularly larger hydraulic systems, involved at least the supervision if not the active involvement of local officials, but the gentry were the major source of support. All such projects had two aspects in common: they were accessible to the public (not restricted to an exclusive group, as in the case of a lineage shrine), and they were viewed as necessary to maintain the social fabric or economic infrastructure of the county. The number of institutions and projects that belonged to the public realm was great. They included schools, academies, city walls, granaries, bridges, ferry docks, hydraulic systems, orphanages, temples to state-sanctioned gods, shrines to local figures, even Buddhist monasteries.[53] Gentry involvement in these institutions was varied. Financial support was most common. From the seventeenth century onward the use of private wealth for public purposes became increasingly respectable, although private donors are infrequently named in Yin gazetteers. Choosing instead to reflect the gentry's persona as literati, these gazetteers far more consistently report essays, steles, and poetry written to commemorate the public projects with which the gentry were involved and to which they lent the prestige of their names.

Schools automatically attracted gentry support, given their direct link to the examination system by which gentry status was ratified. The local magistrate was responsible for supervising schools, but the gentry were conscious that it was largely their responsibility to keep the schools in operation so as to prepare local sons for the exams. The prefectural gazetteer of 1733 reports accordingly that rebuilding the county school in 1664 was accomplished by "the gentry of the county" under the direction of the county magistrate and further that its restoration in 1727 was financed by gentry contributions.[54]

In projects that served a larger constituency, the gentry were often assisted by "wealthy commoners," probably a polite reference to merchants. For example, "gentry and wealthy commoners" supported rebuilding the city wall in 1658.[55] Irrigation systems attracted the involvement of both "gentry and elders" (i.e., esteemed commoners), according to Zhang Shiche's text commemorating the building of the Donggang Sluice. As we noted in the case of the 1751 famine, the gentry considered the public sphere their particular domain and believed that their involvement should predominate over that of other powerful groups in society. A contemporary of Zhang's stresses that the management of hydraulic systems should be in the hands of "members of the families of gentry," who would be expected to monopolize appointments to the position of embankment captain (*tangzhang*). Respecting this claim, local officials in 1820 "called together the gentry to manage and complete" the reconstruction of the Fengpeng Sluice.[56]

Philanthropic activity was thus part of gentry life: It enhanced their reputations, justified their dominant position, and notified all that the public sphere depended on them. By mobilizing not only their wealth but also the accompanying educational and artistic skills, the gentry appeared essential to maintaining local society. The late imperial public sphere remained in their hands.

The gentry's domination of the public sphere does not imply total exclusion of lesser folk; rather it appears that the latter's contributions tended to go to more modest local institutions. The only full account I have found of charitable work by men outside the ranks of the greater gentry in eighteenth-century Yin is a full-page account in the 1733 prefectural gazetteer of the creation in 1730 of a charitable cemetery in the western hills. The account names nineteen men and one Daoist priest under the ambiguous epithet *shimin* ("gentry and commoners"). The greater gentry is not totally unrepresented: the list includes two Chengxi Fans, neither of whom earned a higher degree, though they had cousins who did. There is also someone named Chen Zhaoshen, whose brother Zhaojia won a *gongsheng* degree in 1731.[57] But the other sixteen are complete unknowns. This could signify that a public cemetery was not an institution the greater gentry considered worthy of their attention. But the more intriguing hypothesis is that being named in the gazetteer indicates that the Yin elite in the eighteenth century was obliged to acknowledge men who did not bear full gentry credentials but who, on the grounds of wealth, were asserting elite status in certain contexts and receiving public recognition for it.

TOWARD THE TRANSFORMATION OF LOCAL HEGEMONY

The gentry of late imperial China was never an aristocracy, but it was aristogenic in character; that is, the cultural conditions of elite life favored reproducing the same relatively restricted elite group over time. Deprived of any legal claim to long-term membership in the elite, gentry families nonetheless succeeded reasonably well in preserving their status from generation to generation. They strategically used the financial and human resources of their lineages to continue to win state titles through the examination system, using this continuity itself as a resource for securing future benefits in the social networks of marriage and friendship that bound them together. They also established long-term ties with other families by successfully manipulating the cultural resources that their training and elevated status made available to them. Associational practices such as proximate residence and the formation of literary and scholarly societies were important in setting this upper elite apart from the rest of the less prestigious or merely wealthy, who could enter the high ground of elite status only by assiduously cultivating gentry cultural skills and connections. The result was the hegemony of the gentry in the social processes of local life.

The cultural skills that helped make hegemony possible also provided this aristogenic gentry with the means to participate in the emerging public sphere, which during the Qing consisted of a range of infrastructural projects designed to guarantee social reproduction. These projects were at least formally in the purview of the state, and the gentry were often required to work in concert with state representatives. State power was the local elite's only major rival. As the public sphere grew in the nineteenth century, the waning ability of the state to intervene in managing local affairs enabled the gentry, long accustomed to some measure of involvement in the emerging public sphere, to move decisively into the gap.

The gentry's shift from junior to senior partnership in managing public resources within the local arena occurred as the ranks of the gentry opened wider to admit commercial elites and as gentry families themselves played more conspicuous roles in trade. The shifting basis of local power coupled with the erosion of the state's monopoly on political functions in the nineteenth century correspondingly weakened the legitimating ideology underpinning gentry hegemony; this in turn increased vulnerability to lower-level mercantile competition for elite status, especially in the nineteenth century, and began the end of traditional gentry dominance even before the fall of the imperial order.

The antitax uprising of Zhou Xiangqian in 1852 is emblematic of both this erosion and the limit to which it could go even in the nineteenth century.[58] Zhou Xiangqian was one of the Zhouhanzhen Zhous, a Sichuan lineage that in 1355 had changed its surname (originally Liu) and fled to Ningbo to escape the rebellion of Liu Futong, with whom they had become associated because of their common surname. Zhou Xiangqian had purchased the degree of *jiansheng*. He claimed relation to someone who had once served as a county magistrate in Shandong, though the identity of that person is not obvious from the surviving sources concerning this lineage. Perhaps the official was an affinal relation. The lineage clearly prospered in the eighteenth century, for it started constructing an ancestral shrine in 1795. Its prosperity probably derived from local marketing: Zhouhanzhen was the main market for the agriculturally prosperous south-central portion of the county, on the Yong River that linked Yin to Fenghua to the south, and the Zhous dominated it. The Zhous were thus a successful commercial-agricultural lineage, but their status as members of the official elite was marginal, propped up with only a minor title at the crowded bottom of the gentry where many a Yin lineage vainly sought entry into more substantive status.[59]

Zhou Xiangqian, like most nonprivileged landowners, was annoyed that the greater gentry were allowed by local custom to pay a lower tax bill on their landholdings because they could submit their taxes directly to the magistrate's office in a red envelope (and at a lower copper-to-silver conversion rate) instead of paying tax collection officials in white envelopes at a much inflated conversion rate. After discussing this inequity with other local nonprivileged landowners at a New Year's drinking party, Zhou decided to appeal to the local magistrate against what he regarded as an "inequity" (*bu gong dao*). He did so by working his way up through the gentry elite. He first approached a "powerful gentryman" in the city to present his complaint to the magistrate, but the man refused. He next sought support in Hangzhou, presumably from powerful Yin natives who resided there, in the hope of resolving this matter at the provincial level, but again his petition failed. Frustrated at his inability to find redress among those who did not consider him part of "our party," Zhou turned to his final option. He refused to pay the tax. Invoking as his ancestor the Three Kingdoms military hero, Liu Bei, Zhou led a broad popular uprising. The magistrate fled in terror. A second magistrate arrived on the scene and defused the crisis by persuading "the gentry inside and outside the city of Ningbo" to cancel the distinction between red and white envelopes.

This story leaves us with some suggestive observations about the state of nineteenth-century gentry hegemony. First, gentry titles, even as insubstantial as a purchased *jiansheng*, were still perceived as indicators of elite status among wealthy commoners. Otherwise Zhou Xiangqian would not have bought one, and it probably qualified him to assume leadership in this tax protest. In the next decade, the enormous number of *juren* degrees conferred on Zhejiang natives in the special "grace examinations" (*enke*), given out in compensation for the losses suffered during the Taiping Rebellion, attests to the continuing appeal of state titles.

Second, the greater gentry of Yin county in 1852 continued to enjoy hegemony over local matters that, like taxation, were properly within the jurisdiction of the state. They received preferential treatment at the hands of the state, and they alone could intervene in its administration. Zhou Xiangqian would otherwise not have approached certain members to intercede on his behalf. The hegemony of the upper gentry was further strengthened by formal organization, for the magistrate who resolved the issue says that he presented his propositions to the gentry at their office (*ju*) in the City God Temple.[60]

Third, however, the resentment of Zhou and others at the lower end of the local elite over their lack of access to privileges in the tax system indicates that the cultural construction of status based on gentry qualifications and privileges could be challenged. Like other lower gentry who led protests against unjust tax levies in the Qing, Zhou Xiangqian was moved to rebel less because of a generalized sense of injustice than because of his objection to being excluded from the tax favors enjoyed by the greater gentry.[61] This suggests that lesser elites were not always willing to sanction the full extent of gentry hegemonic practices in the local setting. Zhou's dilemma was that he could only look for politically influential support among the very men who benefited from the practices he sought to dispute.

Zhou Xiangqian was unsuccessful in shaking the aristogenic basis of gentry hegemony in Yin. He failed not simply because the state was stronger than the challenge he posed but because there stood, interposed between disgruntled lesser elites and their demand to redefine elite status on the basis of wealth alone, the very hegemonic structure they sought to overthrow. Gentry hegemony was still the order of the day among the elites of Yin county in the 1850s, but the challenges were growing. Social changes would accelerate as the empire drew to a close, though it would be another century before that hegemony had been completely transformed.

TWO

Success Stories:
Lineage and Elite Status in
Hanyang County, Hubei, c. 1368–1949

William T. Rowe

In 1946 the Han lineage of Jiangxia county (which included the Hubei provincial capital, Wuchang) published the fourth edition of its genealogy.[1]
Listed as general editor was one Han Jiwei, a graduate of Fudan University
in Shanghai. Immediately upon graduation, Jiwei had assumed the presidency of a small municipal technical college at Hankou, subsequently leaving to take a post in a local iron and steel firm, and eventually setting up his
own steel mill. He had done well, for at the time of his genealogy's compilation, he was general director of the Hankou Steel Trade Association. Han
Jiwei was a direct sixteenth-generation descendent of a man who in 1368 had
been installed as Wuchang prefect by the founding emperor of the Ming
dynasty.

The conventional picture of late imperial Chinese society as marked by
rapid social mobility, long doubted by some, has come under increasing
attack in recent years.[2] Yet a case such as that of Han Jiwei still seems somewhat startling, in the suggestion it offers of an hereditary local elite solidly
entrenched despite dramatic political, economic, and social change over
nearly six centuries. Was his an isolated case? The evidence presented in this
article argues that, at least in one local area, it was not. In this region of the
confluence of the Yangzi and Han rivers (map 2.1), almost precisely at the
geographic heart of China proper, *very* long-term continuity of local elite
lineages was not the exception but the rule.

In comparison to European or Japanese landed elites, those of late-
imperial China faced formidable obstacles to reproducing their status over
generations. China had no significantly widespread system of hereditary
aristocratic rank. Access to political office and its concomitant social and
economic rewards was in theory—and, within limits, in reality as well—
determined by merit rather than birthright. Most damaging of all was the

near universality in China of partible inheritance; when combined with the
pervasive legal principle of free alienability of land, this practice effectively
prevented preserving intact estates from generation to generation. Whereas
in much of Europe primogeniture and entail allowed landed elites to keep the
patrimony relatively undivided, Chinese elites with few local exceptions seem
not to have had recourse to any such "feudal" protections for their status.[3]
How then did certain elites remain so entrenched? In this paper I will suggest some tentative answers, by drawing a comparative profile of several
prominent lineages from a single local area.

The basic materials for this study are fourteen genealogies (*zupu*) from
lineages of south-central Hubei.[4] Nine of these lineages were from Hanyang
county; the remaining five were from contiguous counties.[5] The Hanyang
genealogies include all those known to exist today, incorporating all those
from the county listed in the standard bibliographies compiled by Taga
Akigōrō and by the Genealogical Society of Utah,[6] as well as others I myself
have discovered in China and the United States. Still, the sample presents
some problems. It is clear that only a small percentage of published genealogies from the area have survived and that only a minority of Hanyang's
prominent lineages are represented here. Among these, our group of lineages
is potentially self-selective because the very fact that they troubled to publish
genealogies suggests that they had a long local pedigree to advertise, which
indeed they did. Based on my broader reading of Hanyang county sources,
however, I have found no reason to believe that, in either their generational
depth or any other respect, this group of elite lineages was atypical of those in
the area as a whole.

Let me introduce at the outset several notes of caution regarding the relationship I wish to draw between lineages and elites. First, the membership of
the lineages studied here was far from exhaustive of the elite stratum in the
Hanyang area. Second, membership in these or others of what I have termed
"elite lineages" by no means *guaranteed* that a given individual would enjoy
elite status; within such lineages, component patrilines did better or less well,
and their fortunes rose and fell nonsynchronously over time. Third, the territorial arena within which these lineages or their elite members exercised
dominance was not precisely coterminous; as we shall see, for most this arena
was one or another subdistrict (*xiang*) of Hanyang, rather than the county as
a whole. Finally, it was not *necessarily* true that a given member of the local
elite would belong to any formalized lineage group, "elite" or otherwise,
although it should become evident that the individual would very *likely* belong to one.

With these cautionary notes in mind, however, I propose to argue, first,
that the lineage provided a considerable corporate resource to be drawn
upon by its members, in a wide variety of ways, to achieve and reproduce
personal or familial elite status. Second, in Hanyang at least, this powerful

instrument allowed members of certain advantaged lineages to maintain local elite status over many centuries in the late-imperial and Republican periods. Finally, and in light of the above qualifications rather less conclusively, our genealogical evidence suggests that in this area of China the idea that families might rise from local agrarian roots below into the local elite was little more than a myth.

THE LOCALITY

Hanyang county straddles the Han River just at its point of confluence with the Yangzi (map 2.1).[7] The terrain is flat and deltalike, laced with rivulets and dotted with backwater lakes and marshes. Although the hazards of flood are considerable, the soil is fertile, and the area's paddy-rice agriculture can produce handsome surpluses in nonflood years. Agricultural surplus and excellent water transportation, combined with the proximity of the great interregional trading center of Hankou, allowed Hanyang and its environs to develop after the late Ming into one of the most commercialized local systems in China. Its commerce entailed not only market gardening and fishing to feed the nearby urban population but also, increasingly, production of cotton and ramie to serve extraregional markets. Handicraft spinning, weaving, and other artisanal sidelines such as oil pressing were highly developed; consequently, nonadministrative market towns (*zhen*) proliferated, though not as intensively as in the hyperdeveloped Jiangnan.[8]

In the character of its local elite as well, Hanyang occupied a position somewhere between Jiangnan and the rest of the empire. Concentration of landownership was high, but not as high as in the richer Yangzi and Pearl river deltas. This landlord wealth was reflected in levels of academic achievement, which were among the highest in Hubei but still low enough to attract immigrants from Jiangnan seeking to capitalize on Hanyang's weaker competition for the local quota of civil service examination degrees. Based on the evidence of gazetteer biographies and lists of examination degree holders, the elite of the area seems to have been rather broadly based, including members of some thirty to forty prominent descent groups. As was true elsewhere in China, it probably also grew over our period as a percentage of the total population. Whether it was an open elite is another question.

FOUNDING THE LINE

The assignment by subsequent generations of the honored place as "founding ancestor" (*shizu*) to one rather than another lineage forebear was a decision complicated by many factors, as we shall see. Nevertheless, with certain exceptions, lineages in Hanyang most often dated their founding from the generation during which they had relocated to the county and declared it

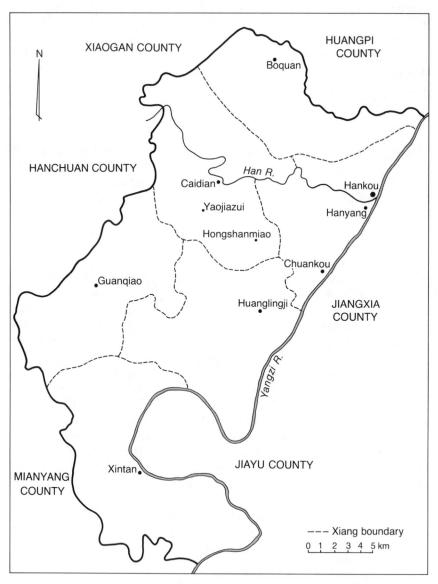

Map. 2.1. Hanyang County, c. 1880.
SOURCE: *Hanyang xianzhi* 1867; *Hanyang xian yutu* 1901; *Hanyang xian xiangtu* 1933.

TABLE 2.1. Establishment of Lineages in Hanyang and Contiguous Counties

Surname	New native place (county: locality)	Old native place (province: county)	Date of arrival	Comment
Zhang (1)	Hanyang: Boquan	Hubei: Macheng	c. 1644	Via Huangpi
Zhang (2)	Hanyang: Boquan	Jiangxi: Yugan	c. 1350	Via Huangpi
Lao	Hanyang: Hankou	Zhejiang	c. 1550	Via Hunan
Ling	Hanyang: Guanqiao	Jiangxi: Ji'an	1373	Via Hanchuan
Liu (1)	Hanyang: Lianhuati	Jiangxi	1466	
Luo	Hanyang: Hongshanmiao	Jiangxi: Taihe	1406	Via several localities
Yao (1)	Hanyang: Caidian	Jiangxi: Xinjian	c. 1368	
Yao (2)	Hanyang: Yaojiazui	Jiangsu: Jurong	1368	
Ye	Hanyang: Huanglingji	Jiangsu: Lishui	1750	Via Nanjing; owned property in Hankou since c. 1655
Zhang (3)	Mianyang	Jiangxi: Wan'an	c. 1368	
Feng	Mianyang	Jiangsu: Fengyang	c. 1368	
Han	Jiangxia	Jiangxi: Nankang	c. 1368	
Gui	Jiangxia	Jiangxi: Linchuan	1369	
Liu (2)	Mianyang	Jiangsu: Wuxian	1369	

their legal native place. *All* the lineages in our sample knew clearly how they had arrived in the area and could chronicle the generations of descent from the first immigrant in convincing detail. Table 2.1 depicts when and from where the local arrival took place for all lineages under consideration and reveals remarkable similarity between the cases. Of the fourteen lineages, eight had come from neighboring Jiangxi province, and all but one of the remainder from Jiangnan (southern Jiangsu or northern Zhejiang). They were thus part of the great westward population shift that has marked the Yangzi valley for nearly the past millennium. We might expect that many of these people had come following Zhang Xianzhong's devastations during the Ming-Qing transition, when, in Wei Yuan's famous phrase, "the people of Hubei filled up [the depopulated] Sichuan, and Jiangxi filled up Hubei." In fact, however, only one of our lineages arrived during this period, and it came only from Macheng county in northeastern Hubei. The Ming-Qing transition *did* see a considerable immigration into the Yangzi-Han confluence area, but these early Qing arrivals had come too late to establish themselves as leading lineages of the area. For the most part, the roles of dominant lineages had already long been cast.

The majority of our lineages arrived in the confluence area during the Yuan-Ming transition: fully half came almost precisely at the moment of the Ming founding, and two others slightly before or after that event. Why? Several lineages stated, rather conventionally, that their ancestors were "fleeing military disorder" in their former locality, and this must generally have been true.[9] However, no fewer than five of our kin groups acknowledged their descent from officers in the army of Ming Taizu, and two others also descended from officials of that same general era. The founder of the Caidian Yao, Yao Fulong, had come from Jiangxi to command the Xiang-Han Garrison; the Yaojiazui Yao founder, Yao Xingyi, commanded the Hubei courier detachment. Both changed their registration upon retirement from office and settled in Hanyang county. Feng Xingshan and Gui Fuyi held military posts and subsequently settled in Mianyang and Jiangxia counties, respectively. Han Yi, rewarded for his military service with the civil post of Wuchang prefect, moved his family permanently to Jiangxia. Liu Ben changed his registration to Hanyang county in 1466, after retiring from service as Hubei provincial judge. And the lineage with the longest demonstrable local pedigree stemmed from Zhang Deyi, who had moved to Hanyang while filling his family's hereditary military command under the Mongols and whose son moved almost immediately into a civil official post under Ming Taizu.[10] The founding of the Ming, in sum, seems to have been a pivotal event in forming subsequent local-elite society.

One final lineage among our sample represents something of a special case. The Ye owed their local roots to two men of the early Qing. Ye Wenji

(1636–1694), a native of Lishui (Jiangsu), operated a small general store in Nanjing and read medical treatises as a hobby. Sometime in the mid-seventeenth century he arrived at the great commercial port of Hankou and realized his ambition to open an herbal medicine shop and clinic. Apparently, Wenji had the good fortune to treat a Manchu prince who was bivouacking near the city, and the successful outcome brought immediate fame and fortune to his Hankou practice. More concretely, Wenji also hit upon two patent medicines, an eye drop and a medicated wine, which achieved tremendous local sales. Wenji eventually retired to Nanjing, leaving his Yekaitai Medicine Store in the care of an agent, and for three generations his descendents enjoyed a scholarly life-style there, based upon the profits of the Hankou store. On the death of Wenji's grandson Hongliang in 1750, however, the latter's three sons decided to divide their patrimony. One son, Ye Tingfang (1733–79), took as his share the Yekaitai store. Tingfang moved his family permanently to Hankou to more closely oversee the shop's operations, though he continued his literati life-style and remained aloof from daily business management. He was subsequently honored as founder of the Ye's Hanyang line.[11]

The Ye *were* somewhat unusual because their elite position in Hanyang county derived solely from a commerical windfall in Hankou. Yet their uniqueness should not be overstated. In subsequent generations most Ye households behaved as literati landlords, presenting themselves in local society with singular success as proper Confucian gentry. So successful were they, in fact, that one suspects their case was replicated, less dramatically but rather frequently, in the history of other prominent lineages both locally and elsewhere. In any event, the Ye did share with our other lineages the common feature of having entered Hanyang society at the top, pre-equipped with high status and considerable wealth. Whether this wealth was derived from commercial or bureaucratic sources, it is noteworthy that not a single prominent Hanyang lineage whose genealogy survives had achieved its elite status primarily on the basis of local agricultural success.

ECONOMIC BASES OF ELITE MAINTENANCE

The existing literature on maintaining elite status by lineages in late imperial China has emphasized two factors: landholding and bureaucratic service. Scholars have argued heatedly over the relative importance of the two in elite strategies, but for the most part the debate has considered these the only significant alternatives.[12] There are, of course, several good reasons for this. The records left by most elites stress their authors' mental conformity to the ideal of the "planter-scholar" (*gengdu*), and undoubtedly a fair amount of reality supported this idealized self-image.[13] Nevertheless, the evidence from Hanyang reveals that, beyond land ownership and official position, both commerce and military service played important—in some cases paramount—roles in maintaining wealth and social position.

Landholding. It is obvious, I think, that *most* component households of *most* lineages, however elite, subsisted on income from agriculture. It is thus no surprise that each of our fourteen lineage founders was credited with acquiring a sizable rural estate, which in almost all cases became the ceremonial center for the subsequent lineage organization. In the Luo, for example, the founder is depicted as wandering peripatetically through central China, fleeing military strife, until he reached the Chuannan area in southern Hanyang county. There in a dream he was told that if he broke ground at that spot he would have countless progeny; naturally, he did so.

The more common situation, however, resembled that of Yao Xingyi, who, when appointed to a lucrative military post in Hanyang, used the proceeds to procure tracts of paddy and mountain land in the county's south-central portion "in order to bequeath to his heirs." Similarly, Liu Ben in the mid-fifteenth century used his official salary to buy a large estate in the sparsely settled area of Lianhuadi, southwest of the county seat, from which his descendents spread out to acquire land throughout this Xiannan subdistrict (*xiang*).[14] The ease of acquisition of large tracts of property by lineage founders undoubtedly had much to do with the ready availability of land around the Yangzi-Han confluence at the start of the Ming, due to the devastations of peasant rebellion, the radical redistributionist policies of a new regime, and a still relatively undeveloped local agriculture.[15] Most of our genealogies suggest that their founding ancestors were pioneers in land reclamation. The two brothers who founded the Ling, for example, are said to have spent five years clearing and draining their new property in the Guanqiao area of western Hanyang before it could be successfully cultivated or even inhabited.[16]

This desire to root oneself in agriculture touched even the mercantile Ye. Shortly after relocating from Nanjing to Hankou, Ye Tingfang procured a large tract of rural land in east-central Hanyang, around the town of Huanglingji. Unlike contemporary England, where "commercial profits were rarely large enough to buy up whole estates, [and so] merchants were more likely to find close association with landowners through marriage,"[17] Chinese gentry-merchants by Qing times could easily buy into the rural elite. The Ye did this with a passion. According to a family account book from the mid-nineteenth century, Tingfang's descendents had by that time accumulated well over one thousand *mu* of land in both Hanyang and their former native county in Jiangsu.[18]

Although the Ye were extreme in being so clearly merchants first and landowners second, this pattern of ploughing commercial profits into land was hardly unusual during the Qing. The Yaojiazui Yao lineage, for example, around 1683 acquired the enormous rural estate that later became their official native place, using profits (reputedly more than a million taels) gleaned from the Liang Huai salt trade by two brothers of the thirteenth generation.[19] One cannot simply assume that capital acquired from commerce was invested in land for status rather than profit. By the 1860s one branch's rural property included substantial acreage in southern Hubei's booming Yangloudong tea country, which was so phenomenally profitable that the successful merchant Yao Lunzhi gave up his business in order to devote full time to his family's landholding accounts.[20]

Was landholding on a large scale thus sufficient by itself to maintain a lineage's elite status over several centuries? I think not. For some patrilines *within* lineages, such as that of Yao Lunzhi, landholding was certainly very lucrative. In the genealogy of our other Yao lineage, too, we are told that certain component lines were so wealthy from the proceeds of their land that they even chose to decline official posts.[21] Nevertheless, the general pattern of behavior of all our lineages, the Yao included, suggests unquestionably that in the long term landownership alone proved economically inadequate for maintaining status. Each sought and found additional avenues of support.

Bureaucratic Service. The socially approved complement to land ownership was office holding, and the approved route to office holding was via the civil service examination system. However, when one totals the number of examination successes enjoyed by our lineages, one cannot but be struck by how relatively unsuccessful they were. Table 2.2 presents the number of successes in the two upper-level examinations (*juren* and *jinshi*) achieved by the overall Hanyang county population and by several surname groups within that population. First, I list several surname groups for which we have genealogies, even though the successful examination candidates bearing those surnames were not necessarily from these lineages; then I list for comparison some other local surname groups that I suspect to be roughly comparable in size.

Although the sources do not provide data needed to disaggregate successful examination candidates by actual lineage rather than surname, it nevertheless seems clear that the relative success rate of groups under study was low indeed. This is even more striking when we consider the lowest recorded degree level, the *gongsheng*. While the Hanyang population as a whole enjoyed thousands of such successes over the 224-year period (1644–1867), the Lao surname achieved only one, the Ling none, the Luo nine, the Yao six, and the Ye six. Given the financial resources available to these groups for education, it seems fair to conclude that, ideology to the contrary, academic success was simply not an important strategy adopted by these lineages to ensure continued local prominence.

For persons of wealth, influence, and good breeding, of course, lack of an

TABLE 2.2.　Upper-Level Civil Examination Passes in Hanyang County, by
Surname, 1644–1867

	Juren	*Jinshi*
Hanyang county total	350	79
Surnames with surviving genealogies		
Lao　勞	1	1
Ling　凌	0	0
Luo　羅	4	0
Yao　姚	2	0
Ye　葉	4	2
Some other local surnames		
Jiang　江	10	3
Hu　胡	14	3
Wang　汪	10	1
Wu　吳	16	3

SOURCE: *Hanyang xianzhi* (Hanyang county gazetteer, 1867), ch. 16.

upper-level examination degree was no insurmountable obstacle to entering
bureaucratic service, and indeed each of our genealogies claims a handful of
ancestors who did hold bureaucratic posts. However, a pattern seems to
emerge here as well. Descended often from a founding ancestor who was
himself a middle-level bureaucrat, our lineages tended to produce a few distinguished officials in early generations, followed by several centuries of only
sporadic government service or none at all. For example, the Ling produced
two county magistrates in the early fifteenth century and no officials thereafter; the Luo, two magistrates and a subprefect in the Ming and none in the
Qing; the Caidian Yao, a magistrate, a prefect, and a senior secretary of the
Board of Rites in the fifteenth century and not a single civil administrator in
the next five centuries.[22] These histories suggest two stages in elite strategies:
An early period of zealous pursuit of public office effectively consolidated the
lineage's wealth and local prestige for many generations to come; subsequent
descendents turned their energies toward more inward looking husbanding
of this legacy and developing its material potential.

　　In its own way the Hankou Ye replicated this pattern at a later time.
Despite their commercial roots, the Ye, the most recently arrived of our
lineages, produced Hanyang county's most celebrated officials of the mid-
and late Qing. The Hanyang line's founder Ye Tingfang had himself been a
stipended scholar of his native district in Jiangsu. His son Weiwen became a
jinshi in 1788 and rose to become secretary of the Board of Punishments. One of
Weiwen's grandsons, Ye Mingfeng, was a *juren* of 1837, and another was the

famous and ill-fated Commissioner Ye Mingchen, a *jinshi* of 1835 and grand secretary after 1856.[23] After this brief fluorescence, the Ye never produced another examination success. In the late Qing and early Republic they purchased a number of local government posts, in some of which—notably fiscal posts such as domestic customs and salt bureau superintendencies— they actually served. Ye Mingchen's grandson, the restaurateur Ye Fengzhi, served as informal adviser to a warlord governor of Hubei, and his son Yong-zhai was a member of the Provincial Assembly.[24] But these were positions transparently designed to protect and enlarge family fortunes in a turbulent political era. Like the older Hanyang lineages, the Ye had reached and passed their peak of political glory early in their organizational life. After the generation of Ye Mingchen, the Ye devoted themselves primarily to direct management of their expanding commercial ventures.[25]

Indeed, only a single case among our lineages failed to follow the general pattern, and this exception was symptomatic of another set of status mainte-nance strategies. One Zhang lineage, descended from a line of Yuan military officers, produced only two important civil officials in its six-century history in Hanyang, but these could not have come at more opportune times. One, Zhang Rui, even though his father was a Yuan general, took and passed the *jinshi* examination the first time it was offered under the Ming (1370) and served in a succession of provincial posts. The second—the exceptional case—was Zhang Jing, a *jinshi* of 1618 who made an effortless transition from local official service under the Ming to similar service under the Manchus, rising eventually to become president of the Board of War.[26] Elite lineages of Hanyang were an extraordinary flexible group, and, as the Zhang demon-strated, this flexibility was not impaired by dynastic loyalism.

Military Service. We customarily think of the Chinese gentry, much like their English namesakes, as a thoroughly amilitary ruling class that had risen out of the ashes of an older military elite. Thus it comes as something of a surprise to find so many prominent local lineages owing their origins to mili-tary service. In part we may dismiss this as the short-term product of an anti-Mongol Han nativist rebellion and the turbulence of dynastic change. It is somewhat more difficult to explain an elite lineage like the Zhang, which could convincingly trace its origins to a line of hereditary military officers, but even here we can point to their good sense in adeptly moving from mili-tary to civil bureaucratic service when the alien and peculiarly militarized Mongol dynasty gave way to more familiar Chinese-style regimes under the Ming and Qing. Was the role of military service in maintaining elite status reduced to insignificance, then, after the fourteenth century? In at least one Hanyang case it most definitely was not.

The Caidian Yao lineage was described in a preface to its mid-nineteenth century genealogy as made up predominantly of "farmers and fishermen,"[27] and in numbers this may have been true. Yet as a general depiction of the Yao descent group in Hanyang it certainly conceals more than it reveals. The Yao were extremely diversified in both occupation and status. A key component of this diversification was military service, a tradition that went back to the circumstances of its founding in 1368. Unlike any of the other lineages surveyed here, and unlike the vast majority of Hanyang county residents, all Yao member households bore an hereditary military registration (*junji*). Legally, at least, they were soldiers, not ordinary commoners (*min*). This basic fact of the Yao's existence contributed to their maintenance of local-elite status in several ways.

First and foremost, it gave them land. The Yao's founding ancestor, Yao Fulong, had been appointed by Ming Taizu to command Hubei's Xiang-Han Garrison and transferred his native registration to Hanyang. We are told that he purchased a tract of private paddy land (*mintian*) in the heart of Hanyang's lake country around Mount Zha and then acquired a large stretch of military colony land (*tuntian*) near Zhaojiafan. Both of these he leased to tenants. Fulong then received an imperial commission to undertake massive reclamation of land along the lakeshores and Yangzi and Han riverbanks. All the property he purchased or reclaimed was reclassified as "military land" (*juntian*), a designation it retained into the 1890s, when the Qing government sought to resurvey the land and reevaluate its fiscal status.[28] Legally, military land fell into an ambiguous category between state and private. As hereditary military colony headmen (*tuntou*), Yao Fulong and his descendents held essentially stewardship responsibilities over this property, but, as was true throughout most of China, over time stewardship became effective ownership. Gradually during the fifteenth and sixteenth centuries regional officials handed over ownership rights to such land to its occupants, in return for assumption of somewhat modified land tax burdens.[29] It is uncertain whether the Yao received title to *all* the land accumulated by Yao Fulong, or whether this was divided between them and others of the original military colonists. It is clear, however, that they received the lion's share, which was thereafter subdivided as parts of various Yao patrimonies.

Second, the Yao had claims to a number of military or quasi-military posts in their home area, which gave them both income and local power. They were members of the hereditary officer class that, as Romeyn Taylor has shown, the Ming took over with few modifications from the Mongols.[30] The Yao's basic post was commander of a *wei*, a unit of some five thousand men, but with the move of the capital to the north during the Yongle reign (1403–24), Yao men were also charged with collecting tax grain from the local area and conscripting transport labor for the newly instituted northern grain tribute. By Qing times their military duties had essentially become those of local grain tribute administrators.[31] These duties were apparently onerous, and at some point the Yao obtained imperial approval to have their hereditary assumption of this post made voluntary. Thereafter, many Yao men shunned the job, but several, including Yao Yukui (1791–1861) and his son Wanchen, allegedly served with distinction, initiating important reforms in the management of transport personnel at the Hanko depot.[32]

When the duties of the grain transport service declined in the later nineteenth century due to commutation to cash payments, and when the structure of the Qing military establishment changed following the Taiping Rebellion, certain Yao men continued their lineage's military tradition in new ways. Although not a function of birthright per se, their achievement of these positions was certainly aided by their continuing possession of a military registration. For example, Lieutenant Yao Caishi (1842–1907) was awarded the Blue Peacock Feather for his work in combating riverine smuggling at the Xintan customs station in southern Hanyang. His cousin Yao Caihe became commanding officer of a Xiang Army detachment at Hankou.[33]

Finally, beyond the more tangible rewards of land and careers, their hereditary military status provided the Yao with access to a network of patronage and influence outside the normal channels available to other local elites. Let me cite but two examples. In the 1820s Yao Yukui found himself imprisoned by the Hanyang magistrate as a result of charges brought by antagonists in a lawsuit. Yukui sent his younger brother to ask a high grain transport official to intervene, citing his family's military registration and many generations in the transport service. This official sent a letter to the Hubei governor, who directed the Hanyang magistrate to overturn the charges against Yukui. Seventy years later, when the Qing sought to reassess military lands in Hubei, Yao Caishi used his connections with a local Xiang Army commander to have Yao lineage lands protected from any tax increase.[34]

How much of an anomaly was the military character of the Caidian Yao? There must surely have been other locally powerful lineages who also held military registration or participated regularly in the grain transport bureaucracy, but were they numerous enough to be statistically important? This is a subject for future research. Yet it is significant, I feel, that I had known of the Yao's existence for years with numerous references to their various activities in Hanyang county but only recently discovered their military registration. Not a few such lineages may lie similarly concealed.

Commercial Activities. In his seminal 1941 article, "The Rise of the Gentry," R. H. Tawney depicted this nonaristocratic English landed elite as an essentially "bourgeois" stratum; its power grew along with the market's expansion, and it largely maintained itself by a close relationship with trade. Although subsequent scholars have found Tawney's picture overdrawn, most would probably accept a more moderate version of his thesis.[35] By contrast, the gentry of China are commonly seen as avoiding any major participation in trade—other than investment in financial institutions such as pawnshops or Shansi banks—until the last decades of the nineteenth century. After all, the dominant Confucian tradition ostensibly despised commercial profits. The lack of primogeniture in China would also seem not to have provided the push necessary to get younger sons off the patrimonial estate and into trade, as happened in parts of Europe. The biases inherent in our most commonly consulted historical sources have systematically reinforced this view. For example, one would search in vain through the sanitized biographies of Grand Secretary Ye Mingchen and several of his kinsmen in the Hanyang county gazetteer for any mention of their economic dependence on commercial activity.[36]

The Ye were, of course, merchants first and foremost; what Chang Chung-li has termed a "gentry-merchant clan."[37] But others of our lineages, whose origins were not primarily mercantile, also participated significantly in commercial ventures. For some, involvement in trade may arguably have come rather late in their collective histories. The Liu of Lianhuati, for example, seem to have been primarily rural landlords until the 1870s, when several of their members founded leather goods and related firms in Hankou and Wuchang.[38] Others, like the Luo of Hongshanmiao, engaged in commercial activities since at least the late Ming, but they seem to have kept these secondary in their overall strategies of maintenance.[39] However, still others' commercial ties were both long-lasting and basic to their group interests. Both Yao lineages fell into this last category.

By the eighteenth century, if not before, members of the Caidian Yao lineage had begun to apply the financial acumen acquired as grain transport administrators and managers of their large rural estates to many mercantile ventures. Some became involved in the enormously profitable Liang-Huai salt trade; others opened a chain of old-style banks at Hankou; at least one became a porcelain merchant at the great industrial center of Jingdezhen in Jiangsi. In the second half of the nineteenth century they moved systematically into Hankou's interregional copper trade, with the Yaochunhe Store around 1870 and the Yaotaihe Store about 1890. Managed by two different branches of the lineage, the stores were at once spiritedly competitive and part of an overall Yao strategy for lineage enrichment; both were extremely successful. The Yaotaihe Store was destroyed during the 1911 Revolution, but it was rebuilt in the British Concession and subsequently opened numerous branches throughout the city.[40]

Our other Yao lineage, centered at Yaojiazui, made huge early profits in the Liang-Huai salt trade; beginning in the sixteenth century, it founded more than a dozen silk and cotton textile dealerships in local commercial centers throughout the river confluence area. In the nineteenth century they, like their namesakes from Caidian, gained a foothold in the empirewide copper and lead trade.[41] Though rural-based, they were by no means rustic literati landlords.

What percentage of lineage members were involved in trade? One suggestion is provided in the genealogy of the Luo, whose compilers fortuitously decided to list the primary occupations of some 135 member households that had moved out of the local area. Of these, 45 (exactly one-third) were listed as merchants, the remainder being distributed among farmers, scholars, and other callings.[42] Although it is likely that the proportion of merchants among those who moved away was higher than that among those who stayed at home, it is also clear that the Luo were far from the most commercialized of our lineage groups. Thus, if this one-third figure overstates the percentage of merchants among our elite lineage members, it may not do so by much.

Regardless of the actual numerical significance of merchants in our lineages, there is no doubt that the merchant component exercised a disproportionate degree of *influence* within the groups, just as it did within Hanyang society as a whole. In the case of the Ye and the Caidian Yao, for example, we have seen that the lineage estate itself was purchased and bequeathed by successful merchants. In the Yaojiazui Yao, Yao Mingli (1855–1906), the enormously wealthy founder of the Yaochunhe Copper Store, rebuilt the lineage temple in the early twentieth century, and the enterprising widow of Yao Zhongjie (née Li) not only expanded her late husband's Yaotaihe Store but also initiated and largely funded the 1923 Yao genealogy compilation. Around 1910 Luo Liangmo, scion of a small and relatively junior line within his branch of the Luo lineage, became head of that branch (*fenzheng*) by virtue of his commercial success. Similarly, around 1930 Hankou industrialist Liu Songping called together the heads of his lineage's several branches, reconstructed the lineage temple, rewrote the lineage rules, and commissioned the recompilation of the genealogy.[43]

In late-imperial and Republican Hanyang, then, the interpenetration of commercial and rural elites was rather thorough. As long as merchants played their Confucian roles well, they were not only accepted into elite society but actively welcomed. For their part, rural elites showed little aversion to engaging in commercial pursuits. They did so throughout our period but increasingly over time, as the profitability of trade became ever more apparent.

Modern Sector Careers. As seen in the story of Han Jiwei with which I opened this essay, the evidence of our genealogies far from supports the conventional picture of a tradition-bound local elite, gradually displaced in the years after Shimonoseki by a new, progressive-minded, Westernized elite drawn from different social origins. Rather, we see the same families and social groups that dominated Chinese local society for generations quite successfully adapting and maintaining their status following the dramatic changes of industrialization, republicanism, and abolition of the examination system. Not only did they adapt, but in many cases they also seem to have been at the forefront of change.

As was the case with English landed elites, those of Hanyang seem to have profited considerably from industrialization. Commissioner Ye Mingchen's grandson, Ye Fengzhi, for instance, operated a chain of electrical equipment dealerships in Shanghai and elsewhere, and in 1924 he cofounded the Han-Huang-Chu Steamship Company. One of Han Jiwei's kinsmen opened a modern printing firm in Wuchang in the 1930s, another an eyeglass dealership in Hankou, and a third a smelting plant in Hanyang city.[44]

More in keeping with their literati image, the generation born in the 1880s perceived the benefits of Western-style education and used these new skills to carve out for themselves important places within Republican China's new professions and rapidly growing technocracy. For example, Yao Fangxun of the Caidian Yao graduated from Hubei province's first Western-style secondary school and then from the Provincial Police Academy, becoming police commissioner of Jingmen county. His brother Fangchi, a graduate of Lianghu Normal College, became education commissioner of Yingshan and Jingshan counties. Yao Changxuan of the Yaojiazui Yao as a child received a classical education in preparation for the civil service exams, then adroitly shifted tracks to obtain a B.A. from Lianghu Normal College. Both his brother Changzong and his son Guangpu received degrees from Hubei Provincial Law School. All three served in numerous county and provincial posts, in such areas as legal administration, public security, and public works; Changzong in 1930 became Hanyang County educational commissioner. Zhang Qingyun, a Provincial Law School graduate, became a prominent lawyer in Wuhan during the 1920s.[45]

Such individuals were neither more cynically self-serving than modern professionals in other societies nor were they hypocritical in embracing Western-imported aspects of New China. Nevertheless, they quite comfortably retained strong elements of their inherited cultural and status group legacy. Indeed, their success in the new career arenas of twentieth-century China seems often to have heightened their attachment to this heritage. Barrister Zhang Qingyun and entrepreneur Han Benxu, for example, edited their lineages' genealogies, as did industrialist Liu Songping, founder of the "Wuhan Association for the Encouragement of Progress." Both the frequent compilation of genealogies in the twentieth century and the prominent role taken in this process by professional and entrepreneurial elites suggest that, as Morton Fried pointed out several decades ago, a surprisingly positive correlation existed between the rise of the industrial city and the resurgent appeal of old-style lineage organization.[46] Liu Songping himself offered one reason for the link when he argued that the way to construct an orderly, modern China lay in revitalizing its natural building blocks—the great corporate lineages.

RESIDENCE PATTERNS

The conventional depiction of Chinese lineages held that this type of "traditional" social organization was incompatible with urban life. For example, in her classic study of clan rules, Hui-chen Wang Liu based her case for a fundamental conflict "between the Confucian value scheme and the city mode of living" on lineage rules that cautioned members about the moral hazards of urban life.[47] As late as 1977, Hugh Baker argued that "in the face of opportunities for comparatively rapid individual economic advancement, the drive to a group unity of the kind afforded by the lineage seems to have been much less strong. City-based ancestral trust groups of the type found in the rural lineage were probably rare."[48] But this view, based on a forced dichotomy of urban and rural life-styles and attitudes, has been attacked in recent studies that stress instead the "continuity" or "continuum" between urban and rural in China.[49] Moreover, G. William Skinner suggests that lineages by no means shunned the city; they often thrived there. In Skinner's view, "The more urbanized the local system, the more favorably [the lineage] was situated to pursue advantageous mobility strategies and maximize profits from its corporate holdings."[50]

Information on residence contained in our genealogies supports this notion of the high compatibility of lineage organization with urban life. In general, the chief magnet for lineage members not actually working in agriculture was the nonadministrative market town (*zhen*). The most important (after Hankou) of Hanyang's many market towns was Caidian, a Han River port whose population around 1800 may have reached thirty thousand.[51] Several of our lineages were effectively headquartered there. One Yao lineage listed its native place as Yaojialin, a Caidian suburb; the Yaojiazui Yao lineage listed Caidian as headquarters of one of its branches; the Liu lineage listed the small village of Lianhuati as its native place, but actually its ancestral temple was in Caidian, where its most influential members dwelled. Others of our lineages were headquartered in other major *zhen*. The Luo lineage was centered on Chuankou, a medium-sized Yangzi River port upstream from Hankou, and the Ling at Guanqiao, the chief market town of western Hanyang county. Although the Ye was effectively centered in Hankou, its formal "ancestral home" of Huanglingji was the major market town of south-central Hanyang. A similar pattern obtained in counties surrounding Hanyang: the Han lineage was headquartered in Jinkou, an important Yangzi River port in Jiangxia county, and the Liu of Mianyang county were centered at Liujiahe, a suburb of the major Han River port of Xiantao.

When we look at relocation to the great regional metropolis of Hankou, we are no longer considering simply a step up the graded hierarchy of central places. Although located in Hanyang county, Hankou was oriented primarily to the national rather than the local economy, and its connection with its regional hinterland was at best tangential. Dominated economically and socially by interregional traders of non-Hubei origin, Hankou never provided a congenial place of congregation for rural landlord literati. It was entirely possible for local elites dwelling close to the great port to have no connection with it whatsoever; on the evidence of its 1876 genealogy, this seems to have been the case with one of our Zhang lineages. Clearly those elites who did establish themselves in Hankou, as did most lineages in our sample, did so out of a deliberate commitment to enter a qualitatively different sphere of activity and consciousness.

Numerous reasons, including civil or military official service, might call one to Hankou, but most people were attracted by commercial opportunity. For example, according to the genealogy biography of Yao Quan (1858–1914), the subject's immediate family had been severely hurt economically by the Taiping devastations, and its decline had been further hastened by the passion of Quan's father for literati pursuits and his corresponding neglect of family accounts. At the father's insistence, Quan spent his youth diligently acquiring a classical education, all the while chafing at his family's increasing impoverishment. Immediately upon the fathers's death, however, Quan hurried to Hankou to "study commerce" (*xuemao*); he eventually became a wealthy salt merchant.[52]

Most of our lineages similarly established a lasting Hankou connection. The Ye and the Lao, of course, were first and foremost Hankou people, and the two Yao lineages had particularly strong and enduring Hankou components. There was also movement by other groups:

The Guanqiao Ling. The genealogy records seven members who relocated to Hankou. The first of these, an eleventh-generation descendent, set up a raw cotton dealership there around 1750. Five more followed in the thirteenth generation and another in the fifteenth around 1820.

The Hongshanmiao Luo. At least six lineage members moved to Hankou. The first, a ninth-generation medical doctor, moved in the late seventeenth century. The remainder were all merchants, two moving in the eighteenth century and the others in the late nineteenth.

The Boquan Zhang. Two members established patrilines at Hankou in the third quarter of the eighteenth century; others followed in the early twentieth.

The Lianhuati Liu. Two brothers moved to Hankou in the 1880s, followed by numerous other kinsmen in the early twentieth century.[53]

The Mianyang Liu. Between the mid-nineteenth and the early twentieth century, at least ten lineage members from four distinct branches moved to Hankou and established flourishing patrilines there. All were merchants, many in the tobacco trade.

The Jiangxia Han. The genealogy shows no relocation to Hankou prior to

Han Benxu, a merchant who moved c. 1875. Many lineage members followed in the 1920s and 1930s.

The Mianyang Feng. Lineage members began to relocate to Hankou only in the early twentieth century.[54]

In sum, we find no movement to Hankou by any members of local elite lineages during the Ming, but a gradual process of relocation begins in the early Qing. The movement accelerated after the mid-nineteenth century and once again around the turn of the twentieth century. Our lineages, in other words, only slowly took advantage of the tremendous commercial opportunities offered by Hankou. I believe that this was due less to any basic aversion to commercial activity than to a well-grounded perception that Hankou, as the home of extraprovincial merchants with high levels of capitalization, was an alien and inhospitable place of business.[55] This changed in the mid-nineteenth century as a result of several factors, including the intensified development of export agriculture in the south-central Hubei region itself, the restructuring of commercial opportunities afforded by the Taiping razing of the Wuhan cities, and the new opportunities presented by opening Hankou to foreign trade in 1861. Finally, in the new economic and political climate created by the debacle of the Sino-Japanese War and the advent of rapid local industrialization after 1895, the last barriers to urbanization fell away. Many younger members of our lineages—including for the first time substantial numbers from counties beyond Hanyang itself—clearly came to feel that engagement in the new entrepreneurial world of Hankou was not only an opportunity but also an imperative to those who would assist in the great cause of national and lineage salvation.[56]

CORPORATE STRATEGIES OF STATUS MAINTENANCE

To this point, I have been speaking of "elite lineages" despite the fact that, after the first few generations, many if not most patrilines within such lineages had likely lost their individual claim to elite status. Is the notion of elite lineages then valid at all? I believe it is, for several reasons. Inclusion within the genealogical table of a descent group of long local pedigree, listing several prominent men, provided even the humblest households some measure of leverage in their dealings with neighbors and the local administration. More demonstrably, men of genuine wealth and power in Hanyang regularly felt the urge to establish, revive, or strengthen kinship ties and organization. Above all there is the simple, evident fact that a regular link uniting elites of one generation or century with those of another was membership in a common, purposely organized lineage group.

Steven Sangren has recently argued that we ought to think of Chinese lineages less in terms of kinship than of "corporation"; his point is that the lineage organization is not a simple accident of heredity but rather the deliberate adoption by a collection of economic actors of a group strategy that will, they believe, enhance their life chances.[57] A less charitable view, propounded most emphatically by Imahori Seiji, would see lineage organization imposed on a willing or unwilling rank-and-file by a leadership that foresees the possibility of turning to its own advantage the community ties thus created by granting the leadership control over collective material resources and allowing them to enforce the social harmony necessary to perpetuate their own superior position.[58] The two views, of course, are not mutually exclusive, and both are substantially supported by the evidence of our genealogies. In what follows, we will look first at the structure of lineage organization in Hanyang, and then at several potential advantages such organization offered, albeit differentially, to member households.

Group Boundaries and Group Structure. Genealogies, by their very nature, are produced after-the-fact by men who are making crucial decisions about just who are and who are not fellow lineage members (*tongzu*). The most critical, though by no means the only, decision to be made in defining group boundaries lay in identifying the proper lineage founder (*shizu*). The most common choice taken by our groups was to accord this honor to the first member of the line to move into the local area and change his legal registration, but this was far from the only available option. For several reasons a group might want to date its first generation prior to its arrival in the area: the desire to include within the fold wealthy or otherwise useful kinsmen still residing in the old home area, or the simple wish to establish for the lineage the cachet of greater antiquity than its neighbors. The corresponding disadvantage, of course, was the potential dilution of group solidarity. Even after the founding ancestor had been decided upon, the group was faced with a real choice whether or not to retain as lineage members kinsmen who had moved out of the local area, as well as their descendents. In other words, lineages in practice were not "natural" descent groups but deliberately crafted human artifacts.

Most lineages chose to root their corporate identity firmly in the county of current residence, thus adopting the kind of "localist strategy" Robert Hymes has seen as typical of Chinese kinship organization since the Sung.[59] Yet they did this in various ways. The Luo, for example, granted themselves an ancient pedigree by claiming knowledge of their family history since the Han; but they followed the common model in making the early Ming migrant to Hanyang their "founding ancestor" and including in their lineage only his descendents. A variant of this strategy was adopted by the Mianyang Zhang, who dated their origins to the Song and, unlike the Luo, opted to locate their founding ancestor in that distant era. They thus placed their migration to Hubei in the sixteenth, not the first, generation, and continued to claim their old home county in Jiangxi as their formal native place. Nevertheless, in practice they followed the common localist strategy by actually including in their genealogy only those persons descended from the first forebears to have arrived in their current home county.[60]

Only two of our fourteen lineages differ strikingly from the general localist pattern. According to the internal history of one Boquan Zhang lineage, founder Zhang Deyi had established his line in Huangpi county, north of Hanyang, around 1350. Thereafter some of his descendents had moved to Boquan in Hanyang and others to neighboring Xiaogan county. During the first half of the Ming the three separate county branches retained close ties but later gradually lost contact. Around 1723, however, leaders of all three branches were independently compiling genealogies when they "rediscovered" their common roots and decided to publish a single lineage history.[61] It is noteworthy in light of G. William Skinner's marketing model of Chinese social organization that the three counties making up the catchment area of the united Zhang lineage did clearly form a single integrated marketing system, linked by countless small rivulets ultimately converging on the Yangzi-Han confluence; yet precisely because their proposed lineage organization spanned county lines they were obliged to defend in detail their actions before a local administration wary of unduly large extragovernmental organizations. As it happened, the chosen scale eventually proved too broad to be practical for the Zhang themselves. Whereas the 1723 genealogy was chiefly compiled by, and gave honored place to, the senior Huangpi branch, the 1862 edition gave precedence to the Hanyang branch, by then clearly the most prosperous. By the time of the 1921 revision, both the Huangpi and the Xiaogan branches had dropped away, and *only* the Hanyang line was included, even though Zhang Deyi of Huangpi was still listed as founding ancestor and his generation as generation number one.[62]

Most unusual, and by far most suspect, is the Ye genealogical record. Although the Ye was in fact the most recently arrived of our Hanyang lineages (and perhaps *because* of this fact), it claimed greatest antiquity of all. It claimed as founding ancestor a step-brother of the founder of the Zhou dynasty (1122 B.C.) but modestly began the genealogical table only with Ye Yu (d. A.D. 44), a high official of the later Han, making those generations currently alive at the time of compilation generations number fifty-eight through sixty-one. Records of early ancestors are, not surprising, only spotty, but in fact a relatively continuous table of descent is supplied for generations after the thirty-third. This was the time of Ye Gui (b. A.D. 894), who was said to be part of a major migration from North China into the Huizhou area of Anhui province following the collapse of the Tang. Then in the fiftieth generation (sixteenth century), three Ye brothers moved from Huizhou to Lishui county in Jiangsu, which the Ye in the twentieth century still claimed as their native place.[63]

What prevents all of this from being dismissed out of hand as an *arriviste* merchant family's desperate search for ancient pedigree is the fact that, of all our genealogies, only the Ye did not restrict itself to descendents of the Hanyang line. They alone conspicuously abjured the localist strategy. Although Ye Tingfang had moved his legal registration to Hanyang in the eighteenth century and although his descendents in Hankou were by far the most prosperous patriline within the lineage and themselves undertook compilation of the 1873 genealogy, they portrayed themselves merely as a relatively junior branch of a much greater, nationally dispersed composite lineage. Tables of descent of numerous other branches, in the ancestral home Lishui and elsewhere, are included in the genealogy. Such detail convinces me that the Hankou Ye, if not actually tied by blood to these predominantly Lower Yangzi "relatives," had at least found sufficient economic cause to form a fictive kinship bond with bearers of their common surname in various downriver localities.

The Ye were exceptional; aggressive inclusiveness was not a usual lineage goal. Most groups, like the Boquan Zhang, eventually settled upon a fairly modest operational size, and it might even be said that an important goal of organizing descent groups into corporate lineages was specifically to *exclude* possible candidates for kinship. On the very first page of its genealogy, for example, the Luo stated there were many different Luo-surname families in Hanyang and that the work at hand was intended to differentiate those who were truly members of the Hongshanmiao Luo from those who were not. The preface to the combined Huangpi-Xiaogan-Hanyang Zhang genealogy of 1723, moreover, frankly admitted that the compilers' desire not to "admit indiscriminately" households into the corporate group had led to considerable squabbling with excluded parties.[64] This was especially important when more than one descent group sharing a common surname inhabited a common locality, as was the case with our two Zhang lineages from the town of Boquan or the two Yao lineages from nearby areas of central Hanyang county.

The deliberate nature of lineage construction is seen even more clearly when we turn from the question of boundaries to that of internal structure, the lineage's warp and weft: branches (*zhi*) and generations (*pai*). Our genealogies reveal the lavish attention that lineage elders paid to such questions, which were clearly seen as basic to the group's integrity. The compilers of a nineteenth-century Yao genealogy, for instance, complained in their preface that even though some symbols of common identity such as an ancestral temple had long existed, precisely because in the past "branches were not clearly sorted out and generational characters not clearly assigned," lineage consciousness could be said to have existed in only a very few members.[65] In looking back over the early history of a lineage one can usually spot a particular generation in which generational characters (*zipai*) were first adopted, and probably the agnates then first articulated their intention to act as a self-conscious descent group, if not a corporate lineage. In following successive editions of one genealogy, moreover, one sees the attempt by lineage elders to prescribe generational characters for succeeding generations, and later, in cases where for whatever reason these had been shunned in favor of other characters, to redraw the table to conform with historical practice.[66] In many cases, it should be noted, these generational characters were never used by the individual in real life situations; they were simply part of his so-called "genealogy name" (*puhui*), used only to locate him in his genealogical table.[67]

Deciding when to divide a lineage into collateral branches was usually a function of geographic movement out of the ancestral village, but when such movement occurred there was still a choice between remaining within the old branch and lineage, forming a new branch, or leaving the lineage altogether; the option chosen might strongly reflect political relations within the group and overall group goals. Mature lineages such as the Zhang or Yao might have respectively nine or ten branches, each associated with a particular locality within the home county.[68] The leaders of the branches would meet, usually annually, to take care of joint business and reaffirm intentions for future corporate solidarity. They were not always successful. The Liu of Mianyang, for example, had divided into eight branches in the fifth generation. The 1924 genealogy, however, recorded genealogical tables down to the current twenty-fifth generation for three branches only. One branch was said to have biologically died out, and the other four were recorded only to the twentieth generation, at which point they fell away from the composite lineage.[69]

Collective Property. Why such a determined effort to shape and maintain corporate lineage structures? One reason might be to serve as vehicles for ownership of property. Vesting ownership of the patrimony or a share of it in a corporate lineage group was one way to avoid the leveling influences of partible inheritance, akin to the entail systems of aristocratic Europe. Alternatively, the corporate lineage might be made proprietor of property accumulated after the fact, as in the "charitable estates" (*yizhuang*) advocated by Neo-Confucian social thinkers and actually created in many parts of China. Surveying evidence from the empire as a whole, however, Patricia Ebrey has recently argued that significant amounts of collective property were not the rule outside the southeast and may have existed for only a small minority of Chinese lineages, however formal their organization.[70] The evidence from Hanyang supports her judgment; ownership of income-producing property seems not to have been an essential rationale for the existence of any lineage group in our sample.

All of our lineages did own an ancestral temple, which was basic to their collective identity; most if not all also possessed lineage grave sites. Additional collective property was frequently vested in *intermediary* units between the individual and the lineage as a whole, such as branches and patrilines; the rural estate of the Hankou Ye family and the tea plantations of one line (*fang*) of the Yaojiazui Yao were just such cases. However, only six of our fourteen genealogies refer to income-producing property owned by the entire corporate lineage, and even in these cases the amount of such property seems to have been rather small.

Usually the property was referred to as "ritual land" (*jitian*), that is, land whose income went to finance the ancestral sacrifices and upkeep of the lineage temple.[71] Although this term might sometimes be used as a euphemism for lands held for other profit-making purposes, this does not seem to have been generally true in Hanyang; however, we do know that in the Caidian Yao and the Hongshanmiao Luo revenue from ritual land also financed a school for lineage members (*jiashu*).[72] None of our genealogies specifically refers to a "charitable estate," and only two refer to a portion of their collective property as "charity land" (*yitian*); in only the Caidian Yao do we have hard evidence that revenue from this land actually supported indigent lineage members.[73] Nowhere in any of our genealogies are we told of more general distribution of the proceeds of lineage lands to member households.

Corporately owned lineage land was a rather late development in Hanyang, and its amount rose over the course of our period. The Yaojiazui Yao ritual lands, for example, were first acquired in 1683 and added to nine times between 1799 and 1864. The Caidian Yao lands dated only from the early nineteenth century, and those of the Luo only from the post-Taiping era. Additions to corporate lands came either by contribution of wealthy lineage members (the Mianyang Liu property was augmented considerably in the 1920s by gifts of a Hankou merchant, Liu Zhongqi), or, in at least one case, by reinvestment of revenues from the lands themselves.[74]

Despite this growth, and although the economic importance of corporate holdings varied from lineage to lineage, in no case were they particularly extensive. One Zhang lineage, for example, stated in its 1862 lineage rules that whereas previously revenues from lineage lands had been negligible, the group was at that time acquiring property that would yield a total of six taels per year.[75] The holdings of the Yaojiazui Yao, which the owners claimed to be extraordinarily large in comparison to those of other area lineages, yielded a total annual rent of less than thirty taels.[76] Such figures are not insignificant, but they suggest that corporate holdings were miniscule compared to the personal wealth of many individual lineage members and the patrimonial estates of certain component lines. Thus, although it seems clear that collective property was a source of lineage pride and a symbol of kin identity, in the Hanyang area it served neither as a regular means of support for lineage members nor as a viable alternative to primogeniture for perpetuating intact hereditary estates.

Diversification and Distribution. If corporate organization on the part of Hanyang lineages was not intended primarily as a vehicle for capital accumulation and property ownership, it proved useful for providing a human unit of sufficient scale to allow the occupational diversification and geographic distribution necessary for husbanding and developing aggregate, not collective, group resources. We see occupational diversity encouraged in lineage rules; for example, the Yaojiazui Yao states: "Members of our lineage must select an occupation in order to earn their subsistence, whether as scholars, cultivators, artisans, or merchants. They are forbidden to waste their energies loafing, or in idle pastimes, excessive drinking, or gambling, thereby disgracing their ancestors and bringing harm to their home."[77]

Agricultural activity would ideally be combined with scholarship and official service. Lineages pooled resources in the hope of promoting a member into a position from whence he could dispense official patronage to kinsmen; the revenue from the Zhang corporate lands, noted above, for example, was used to help underwrite the educational expenses of promising lineage boys. More important in the Yangzi-Han confluence area, however, was the combination of agriculture and commerce. We have already encountered the case of Yao Quan, who left his rural home in the 1870s to "study commerce" with a kinsman in Hankou. This pattern, and indeed this phrase, recurs frequently in our sources; unlike Yao Quan, who defied his family to move into trade, in most instances the lad was specifically selected and ordered by his family to apprentice with another lineage member. It is significant that such apprenticeship relations were routinely formed across patrilines and even branches. Similarly, the various mineral dealerships of the Caidian Yao and textile dealerships of the Yaojiazui Yao represented different branches of the lineage, even while they acknowledged their mutual connections by repeating key characters in their shop names and introduced each other to valued extraregional (and eventually foreign) suppliers and customers.

Organization based upon kinship ties also allowed geographic distribution of group members. Lineages adhering to the localist strategy would theoretically drop from membership households that moved permanently to localities far from the home area, and such examples appear with regularity in our genealogical tables. Violations of this procedure could and did occur, however, when the dictates of commerce made lineage contacts in outports desirable. Groups such as the Luo and the Mianyang Liu, for instance, had members residing at most major commercial centers of Hubei, Hunan, and Jiangxi.[78] Most ambitiously far-flung was the Zhang of Mianyang, which maintained cadet lines in Chongqing, Guangzhou, and dozens of localities along the vast Yangzi-Han-Xiang river system, as well as at Chuankou in Hanyang, Babukou in Xiaogan, and other smaller ports of the immediate confluence area.[79] Most likely these lineages were affiliated with the "Han bang" (Han River guild), a loose confederation of merchants from the lower Han valley who shipped and marketed their region's produce—above all, cotton and ramie—throughout central and western China. In any case, members seem to have used their lineage ties as the basis of what Philip Curtin has called a "trade diaspora,"[80] a common enough phenomenon in late imperial China, most familiarly associated with the somewhat grander Shanxi, Huizhou, and Ningbo merchant families.

Internal Control. Hilary Beattie has convincingly argued that the impetus to impose formal lineage structures was felt by the elite most deeply in the wake of major social upheavals.[81] The chief instance she cites, that of the Ming-Qing transition, very likely did spark a surge of lineage building in Hanyang, as it did in Beattie's southern Anhui, but our surviving sources are silent on this point. We do, however, see a period of both frantic recompilation of lineage rules and reconstruction of lineage temples in the aftermath of the class warfare and local devastations of the Taiping Rebellion, and this activity is often explicitly identified as a response to the special needs of this era.[82] It is also surely no coincidence that seven of our fourteen genealogies date from the uncertain period between the effective collapse of central government in 1915 and the Japanese occupation of 1937 or that no less than three were compiled in the immediate postwar years (1946–48).

Lineage organization was a fundamental method of social control, in the interests of both the group as a whole and its leadership in particular. The lineage rules of one of our Zhang lineages, first drawn up in 1723 and reiterated several times through the 1920s, provide an example of the sort of solidarity lineage elders sought to impose on their kin. Members were enjoined to observe lineage exogeny and to refrain from filing lawsuits against kinsmen or hoarding grain when kinsmen were in need. In 1723, three lineage elders submitted this proposed code to the local magistrate, successfully requesting that he formally ratify both the code and the power of the lineage headman (*zuzhang*) to discipline the membership. They based their petition rather ominously on the need to "instruct in filiality" (*jiaoxiao*) bad elements *within the lineage*, who might otherwise routinely take advantage of weaker relatives.[83]

Lineage headmen in Hanyang enjoyed considerable disciplinary powers. The powers stipulated for the Caidian Yao head, for example, included not only the ceremonial (overseeing ancestral sacrifices and members' weddings and funerals) and the financial (collection of rents, payment of taxes on sacrificial lands, and support for lineage widows, orphans, and examination candidates) but also those powers to "admonish and reform" deviant lineage members.[84] In some cases headmen also enjoyed the power of proxy tax remittance (*baolan*) for the lineage group.

This tax power is seen most dramatically in the 1723 Zhang petition for lineage incorporation. In requesting the unusual privilege of incorporating across county boundaries, the petitioners proposed a system under which lineage headmen would collect grain tribute assessments from all lineage members and remit these directly to the authorities. They described this as an example of "rural community self-help." Though a cynic might simply see lineage leaders enriching themselves by exacting a commission as tax farmers, I think the chief motivation was otherwise. The petitioners appealed to the local magistrate to allow them this right, above all "in order to avoid the extreme vexation of runners and prompters coming at the end of the year."[85] In other words, the magistrate would get his money free from the profiteering of unsavory bureaucratic underlings (distaste for whom was shared by officials and local elite alike), and the wealthier members of the lineage would be spared the extortion of tax clerks who hitherto had held them responsible for defaults of their poorer kinsmen. By incorporating themselves the way the Zhang did in 1723 elites within the lineage undertook to guarantee payments by kinsmen, assuming the power to discipline defaulters, and by drawing up a clear genealogical table they conveniently excluded bearers of their surname with whom they did not acknowledge kinship and for whom they wished not to accept fiscal liability. In this as in many other ways, the internal imposition of discipline over lineage members was closely tied to solidarity versus the outside world, government and neighbors alike.

External Relations. In their relations with the outside world, Hanyang lineages apparently sought a balance between insularity and integration, between pursuit of narrow lineage and wider community interests. Lineage solidarity and group resources were crucial weapons in the contest for control of local material resources. The Caidian Yao, for example, engaged in a running feud over property rights with another locally powerful descent group, the Yu, which began in the 1750s under Yao Guanghan (d. 1805). In the early nineteenth century the feud was revived by Yao Yukui (1791–1861), who filed suit in the county yamen to guarantee access by Yao fishermen to lakeshores owned by the Yu. This so-called "lineage lawsuit" (*zusong*) dragged on for more than fifteen years, kept alive by repeated filing of charges and countercharges.[86] Such feuds provided useful means not only to pursue material advantages but also to deepen solidarity within the group. The Yao genealogy for instance makes a great point of the fact that Yao Yukui, not from a fishing household, was yet willing to suffer considerable personal hardship on behalf of poorer fishing kinsmen; it seems hardly coincidental that this same Yukui spearheaded the mid-nineteenth-century recompilation of the Yao genealogy and restoration of the group's corporate property.

While pressing such group claims, however, lineage elders usually took care in their relations with the wider community to assume leadership and philanthropic roles appropriate to Confucian local elites. Local Hanyang sources regularly list the contributions of members of our groups to county school construction, water control, flood and famine relief, repairs to altars of local tutelary deities, financing of river lifeboat services, and so on.[87] Not surprising, several prominent members of our lineages also played leading roles in organizing and commanding local militia resistance to the Taiping rebels in the 1850s.[88] The credit for such public service activism accrued to the individual, of course, but also in a more general way to the corporate lineage. For example, even the hostile history of the Ye compiled in the People's Republic emphasized that the ostentatious magnanimity of certain members was reflected in a positive local image of the group as a whole and in good public relations for its various business enterprises.[89]

Confucian social leadership could sometimes be turned to the advantage of the group in very practical ways. For instance the Yao-Yu feud just mentioned seems to have begun when Yao Guanghan succeeded in having himself placed in charge of a project he had devised to construct a Yangzi river dike protecting south-bank farmland. The Yu perceived the project as favoring Yao holdings at Yu expense. When, a century later, Yao Yukui had himself appointed by Governor Hu Linyi to conduct a cadastral survey for reassessing grain tribute obligations in the wake of the Taiping wars, the Yao genealogy unabashedly gloated over this opportunity to benefit their own lineage and correspondingly disadvantage the Yu.

More generally, social activism was useful in maintaining the lineage's cultural hegemony—the sense within local society that members of such lineages justified by their conduct possessing a greater than normal share of local wealth and resources, and that they were in some sense the common population's social betters. Championing local causes and displaying visible philanthropy (by no means necessarily devoid of genuinely felt moral imperatives) were means of perpetuating this charisma; so too was a public posture of cultural refinement and educational achievement. We have noted that members of our lineages on the whole were *not* unusually successful in the civil service examinations, yet they certainly did receive a better than average education in classical arts and letters, conspicuously displayed in such ways as patronizing local educational institutions. Yao Guangmei, for example, expended great money and effort to have the Hanyang county quota for stipended scholars raised around 1805, and Ye Zhaogang—not a scholar but a proprietor of the Beijing branch of his family's medicine store—renovated the hostel for Hanyang county examination candidates at the capital.[90] They also patronized promising nonkin local scholars, financed the publication of literary works, founded and participated in local literary societies, and collected rare books and art objects.[91] All these were ways of exemplifying through their life-styles the *gengdu* (planter scholar) ideal.

What was the geographic scale of our lineage members' social activism and the range of their influence? Studying the early modern British local elite, Alan Everitt has spoken of the "county community" as the basic component element of elite society.[92] In China as well, an interlocking, self-conscious local community seems to have played an important role in shaping elite lineages' behavior; but whereas the locus of this community in China as in Britain might at times be the county (*xian*), the evidence of our genealogies argues that more often identity was focused on a subcounty unit. At the very least, the Han River formed a clear boundary for lineage power; several of our groups speak repeatedly of their attachment to the area known as "Hannan" (that portion of Hanyang county lying south of the Han), and the two of our Hanyang lineages that did not hail from the area (the two Boquan Zhang lineages) seem to have moved in an orbit separate from the others.

But the spatial unit by far most commonly invoked in our genealogies is the subcounty administrative division, the *xiang*. Hanyang county had eight such subdistricts, each centered on a major market town (*xiangzhen*) such as Caidian, Huanglingji, Boquan, or Guanqiao. For most of our lineages the *xiang* was the social horizon—most member households dwelled within its borders, and the lineage headquarters was the *xiang*-level town. When elite activism extended beyond the immediate kinship group, it often explicity focused on the subdistrict community (*xiangdang*). Lineage leaders wrote routinely of "the people of our *xiang*," expressed concern over *xiang* problems, and participated in *xiang*-wide public projects.[93] Most Hanyang lineages, in short, seem to have been precisely the sort of *xiangzu* (*xiang*-centered lineage) identified by Fu Yiling as the characteristic Ming-Qing kinship group,[94] and their leadership the very type of the *xiangshen* (subdistrict gentry or—better—"local elites") so commonly encountered in late imperial sources.

Our materials allow us only to speculate on the degree of local dominance exercised by this subdistrict community of elites, but it may have been considerable. In the Qing, for example, the subdistricts were the major units of land-tax assessment and collection—Hanyang's twenty-one tax precincts (*li*) were directly subordinated to them in the fiscal hierarchy[95]—and the subdistrict elite must have enjoyed great leverage in the fiscal process. When, in the twentieth century, the *xiang* were transformed into units of "local self-government," with their administrative seats at the *xiang*-level market towns,[96] our lineage leaders would seem to have been ideally placed to derive maximum advantage from these currents of "modern" political change.

CONCLUSION

The collective profile we have drawn of elite lineages in Hanyang and adjacent counties above all presents remarkable long-term continuity. There was certainly some downward mobility within the elite; the 1867 county gazetteer reveals for example that the Cai—after whom Caidian had been named—"was in former generations a great lineage, but now has much declined."[97]

There was also from time to time a bit of new blood, as epitomized by the Ye. It is noteworthy, however, that the Ye entered the Hanyang elite through the back door, as it were, from outside the region via the interregional marketplace of Hankou. Whatever the limitations of our sample, the evidence of these fourteen genealogies suggests not only elite continuity but also nearly complete absence of promotion into the elite from local, rural roots.

The modern social hierarchy in Hanyang county seems to have been largely the product of a single revolutionary era, the first reign of the Ming dynasty. Other scholars have noted similar developments elsewhere. Looking at the origins of local elites in Hunan, for instance, Peter Perdue has remarked on the very high percentage who established themselves at the start of the Ming (in Hunan as in Hanyang most of these came from Jiangxi). Jerry Dennerline and Hilary Beattie have similarly noticed a lasting social hierarchy by lineage established during the Yuan-Ming transition in the Yangzi delta and in southern Anhui, respectively.[98] The evidence seems to be growing, therefore, for a new periodization of Chinese social history that would treat "post-Mongol China" as a discrete temporal unit.

Especially fascinating is the pattern displayed in our sources (and noted also for Hunan by Perdue) of frequent elite descent from soldier officials in the victorious army of Ming Taizu. One is even tempted to see in this something of an analog to European-style feudalism, with families of elites being essentially enfeoffed in return for military service. This impression is strengthened by the fact that two of our lineages, the Boquan Zhang and the Caidian Yao, were actually descended from lines of hereditary military office holders. In China, of course, such enfeoffment was hardly as widespread or as systematic as in Europe, but it may not have been wholly absent.

For most of our lineages, the cause of their rise was not the same as the means of their subsequent maintenance. Unquestionably, all benefited in great measure from the vast landholdings bequeathed by lineage founders. Yet, because no effective alternative to partible inheritance was found or apparently even sought, the adequacy of the landed estate as a basis for elite maintenance declined over generations with a cold mathematical logic. Thus the picture we observe is one of considerable flexibility, versatility, and adaptability in maintaining the economic bases of local status. One aspect of this adaptability was the capacity to transfer one's allegiance and political service from one regime to another. A second was the ability to fit quite comfortably into the new structure of economic and political opportunity offered by Western-inspired industrialization and state-building efforts in the late nineteenth and early twentieth century. Indeed, it might even be said that the very impossibility of maintaining status over generations on the basis solely of land gave the Chinese elite an advantage over its European counterpart in the face of major structural change, by having so thoroughly conditioned it to the need for constant flexibility and innovation.

Probably the most striking aspect of this flexibility was a diversified occupational portfolio, which gave an honored place to careers in trade. Corresponding to this was an apparently deliberate group strategy of geographic distribution, which included—even emphasized—urban residence. Like their British counterparts, members of our local elite were (in Namier's famous term) "amphibious"—equally at home in town and countryside.[99] Since very early in their histories most lineages had been centered in market towns, and over the nineteenth and twentieth century their urban membership grew in number, in the urbanness of their place of residence (more and more moving to metropolitan Hankou), and in their relative influence within the lineage. Well before the close of our period many of our lineage members might be classified as "pseudo-gentry," the term used by Everitt to describe the portion of the British elite that lived in cities, supported itself from neither a rural estate nor administrative office holding and yet by its cultured life-style and wide-ranging connections was popularly seen as belonging to the gentry stratum.[100]

Finally, our local elites displayed flexibility and versatility in using corporate lineage organization to maintain their status. Lineage structures were neither predetermined by heredity nor necessarily identical; rather, our actors used the rich cultural repertoire of organizational tools at their disposal (native places, generational characters, scales of branch and lineage organization, etc.) deliberately and creatively to fashion formal groups of maximum practicality. They were also able periodically to restructure such organizations as situations changed. Corporate lineage groupings varied in function as well as form, rendering futile any attempt to generalize too broadly about "why" lineages organized. For example, though collective property seems not to have been a critical factor underlying any of our groups, its importance clearly varied from one lineage to another. Other incentives for organization included those to diversify assets, to ward off predations of state functionaries, and to compete more effectively for local resources. The lineage group had many potential uses, and even within a single local area different groups organized for different sets of purposes.

To all, however, organization was useful in some way, and the evidence argues eloquently that the lineage group was a major vehicle for reproducing elite status over the course of generations and centuries. The primary effect of partible inheritance, then, and the chief difference between the Chinese local elite and their European counterparts, may have been just this: for the Chinese the more populous lineage, rather than the individual patriline, served as this vehicle. Lines rose and fell, but the lineage endured.

THREE

The Rise and Fall of the Fu-Rong Salt-Yard Elite: Merchant Dominance in Late Qing China

Madeleine Zelin

Shortly after the 1911 Revolution a transplanted native of Chengdu prefecture undertook to write a book about his new-found home, the capital of Sichuan's well-salt industry, Ziliujing. From the preface by the author, Qiao Fu, we can see that the following work was meant to be a cross between a traditional gazetteer and the guidebooks written for the benefit of travelers and merchants in the long-distance trade. Between its covers one could find highlights of Ziliujing's geography, history, products, and customs, as well as details of the salt trade, a description of Ziliujing's banks and messenger services, and suggestions for the best places to stay in town. Most striking for its absence was any discussion of local self-governing institutions and other traditional "gentry" concerns. Most striking for their inclusion were the frontispieces of the book. Following maps of the east and west salt yards were two pages of photographs of Ziliujing's most venerated women of the evening. It is almost as an afterthought that we find on the next page a crowded array of the region's less scenic, nonhuman sites.

Ziliujing and adjacent Gongjing together comprised a one-industry metropolis whose population reached several hundred thousand by the end of the Qing.[1] Although physically separated by only a few miles, administrative boundaries artificially limited the region's unity. The east yard, at Ziliujing, was under the jurisdiction of the Fushun magistrate and his superiors at Xuzhou prefecture, while the west yard, at Gongjing, was part of Rongxian and yet another prefecture, Jiading.[2] This division extended to the administration of salt production and distribution, despite the frequency with which both residents and outsiders spoke of the entire region as the Fu-Rong salt yard. Moreover, although many salt merchants had investments in both yards, it is clear from post-Liberation works of oral history and earlier biographical materials that individual merchant families tended to identify themselves with one or the other side of the river that ran through the two salt production areas.

Both Fushun and Rongxian lie in the hilly southwestern part of Sichuan province. Where the two counties meet, salt wells were arrayed in concentrated groupings; between them could still be found the agricultural fields upon which they increasingly impinged. Agriculture in Rongxian was generally poor, and the district could boast of few important products besides salt. Fushun, blessed by richer soil and superior water navigation, carried on a thriving trade in vegetables and fruit. Sugar, too, was manufactured in the vicinity of its own rich sugarcane fields along the Tuo and the Rongxi rivers. Nevertheless, by the time of the Qing, Fu-Rong's wealth, fame, and problems all emanated from the rich deposits of salt brine and natural gas below its surface. According to Qiao Fu, in its heyday, during the mid-nineteenth century:

> From Badian street up, the salt firms, extravagantly decorated in colors and gold, were packed together like the teeth of a comb. From the moment the sun went down in the west, [the singing girls] put on their makeup and took out their instruments and sang. The sound of their music overflowed, filling everyone's ear. The activity of the money markets, the flow of currency, could come to several tens of millions. Itinerant traders and retail merchants were all in close contact with each other in a town which was equal to the greatest commercial ports.[3]

This unembarrassed glorification of business and its by-products gives testimony to the spirit of the place. It was the third most important economic center of the Upper Yangzi region, following close behind Chongqing and Chengdu. But whereas Chongqing's prosperity rested on trade, and Chengdu's on farming, Fu-Rong was the archetypical early modern industrial town. Salt-well derricks dominated the skyline like the smokestacks of an English factory town. The vapors from the salt brine and gas wells were equally unhealthy and, according to Qiao Fu, were made worse by the unsanitary habits within Ziliujing's multistory urban dwellings.[4] The tens of thousands of buffalo that pumped the brine from Fu-Rong's wells also polluted its water supply and contributed to frequent outbreaks of intestinal disease.[5] It was a town where the elite—merchants and financiers—worked and laborers lived, where gambling openly flourished despite imperial prohibitions, and where a hierarchy of prostitutes served all levels of society, from the masses of unmarried male workers to the merchants who used the high-class bordellos as a place to make deals and grease the palms of local officials.[6]

The state demonstrated its desire to control this sprawling industrial center by dividing the two counties. Each county was assigned an assistant magistrate to its half of the yard, further evidence of the place's economic and political importance. But the heavy presence of government belied an independence of operations unknown to salt production areas outside Sichuan. By the early twentieth century Fu-Rong had a chamber of commerce manned entirely by prominent members of the salt-merchant community. However, this concentration of political and economic resources appears to have resulted in few manifestations of civic pride or local managerial effort. In Fu-Rong both the business of business and the business of society was salt.

Unlike the great Chinese merchant cities with which we are familiar, whose merchant communities made their fortunes in trade and finance, Fu-Rong society was centered on production. Brine was raised from deep wells and evaporated at furnaces fueled by coal or gas. During the last decades of the Qing, when the main gas-producing area was Ziliujing and the main brine production center was Gongjing, an elaborate network of bamboo pipes was laid to carry brine to the furnaces as far as twenty *li* away. Salt, supplies for the salt industry, and by-products of salt manufacture provided the main items of commerce and the main sources of wealth and employment in Fu-Rong. It comes as no surprise that the elite of Fu-Rong were merchants.[7] Members of this elite might make forays into the world of gentry-official politics, and they might even acquire and manipulate traditional symbols of elite status. However, we do not see the same interpenetration of gentry and merchant occupations as appear in Bell's discussion of the Jiangnan elite in this volume, and the story of the elite's rise and fall is as much economic as social history.

THE NINETEENTH-CENTURY SALT MAGNATES

The Business of Salt. Sichuan sits on salt. Salt deposits can be found throughout the rock layers deposited from about 900 to 65 million years ago. The most important are thought to have originated about 185 million years ago in an ancient epicontinental sea. Repeated inundation and evaporation in the basin produced thick accumulations of salt that are now preserved in rich subterranean deposits of rock salt and brine.[8] Evidence exists of its exploitation in shallow salt pits as early as the second millennium B.C. However, large-scale exploitation of salt wells appears to have dated from the Song (960–1279), with the invention of new drilling and pumping techniques that combined to produce the "lofty-pipe" wells (*zhuotong jing*), the basis for all well-salt production until the mid-Qing.[9]

During the Ming dynasty (1368–1644), the center of Sichuan salt production was the Shehong and Pengxi region of Tongchuan prefecture and Sui department in the upper Sichuan basin.[10] This lead was maintained during the early Qing until new deep drilling technology led to the rapid development of the richer salt resources in the Lower Basin counties of Jianwei, Leshan, Rongxian, and Fushun. Abundant coal deposits in Jianle gave it an advantage over the Fu-Rong yard until the Qianlong reign (1736–1795), when improved exploitation of natural gas in Ziliujing led to the rapid expansion of both Fu-Rong well excavation and salt-evaporation facilities.[11]

The physical destruction of Sichuan's economic substructure during the Ming-Qing transition, coupled with what one scholar has estimated to be as much as a three-fourths reduction in population,[12] made Sichuan a poor target for taxation by the new Manchu government. Even more important, the actual production of salt was left entirely in private hands. Not until 1686 was the province enrolled in the official salt gabelle, and salt sold to the more accessible parts of the province by specialized merchants authorized to purchase salt certificates (yin), entitling them to deal in a fixed portion of Sichuan's legal salt quota. By the Yongzheng reign (1723–1735), the expansion of Sichuan's salt market was deemed sufficient to warrant the institution of specified sales territories, encompassing Sichuan and parts of Yunnan, Guizhou, and Hubei. However, a system of flexible quotas (jikou shouyan) was installed to allow salt sales to grow with Sichuan's burgeoning population.[13] Supervision of this system was never tight, and less accessible areas continued to be served by petty merchants dealing in quantities deemed too small to be subject to tax. By the early nineteenth century, difficulties in meeting the legal salt quota and in controlling salt smuggling had led parts of Sichuan to eliminate the system of sale by yin and to absorb the tax generated by yin sales into the land tax.[14] At the same time, merchants in the more productive yards, like Fu-Rong and Jian-Le, both legally and illegally took over the quotas of the less efficient salt-producing areas.[15]

By the 1840s Sichuan's capacity to produce salt began to exceed the marketing limits permitted by the imperial salt administration. For the moment, those who suffered were the small producers outside the Lower Basin. However, with the advent of the Taiping Rebellion, salt producers throughout the province were faced with a vast new market, just waiting to be tamed.[16] As rebel forces cut Hubei and Hunan (Huguang) off from their designated salt suppliers to the east, Sichuan merchants moved in swiftly to take up the slack. The opening of the "aid to Huguang" (ji-Chu) salt territory marked a new stage in developing the Fu-Rong salt yard. To the exploitation of this market, the late Qing Fu-Rong elite, as both producers and wholesalers, traced their fortunes.

The Rise of the Fu-Rong Salt Merchants: Making a Fortune in Salt. By the end of the Taiping Rebellion four families had emerged as the leaders of the Fu-Rong salt community. Following in their wake, and no doubt aspiring to the enormous wealth and influence that these families had accrued during the years of war, were several hundred other large salt developers.[17] The strategies they pursued to build their fortunes were similar to those of the four great families, although in the case of the Lis, Wangs, Hus, and Yans, the results exceeded those of almost any merchant in the land.[18]

Wang Langyun was the architect of the Wang Sanwei lineage trust (*tang*) that would come to encompass much of the salt resources of nineteenth-century Fu-Rong. His ancestors are said to have emigrated to Sichuan during the early Ming from their ancestral home in Macheng county, Hubei.[19] At least as early as the Zhengde reign (1506–1521), Wangs were involved in brine excavation. During the warfare accompanying the Ming-Qing transition, Wangs fled to nearby prefectures like Chengdu, Luzhou, and Jiading and as far afield as Guizhou province. In the process, lineage records were destroyed, and the genealogical records compiled by the Wangs in the late nineteenth century go back only to the early Qing.[20] For most of the dynasty they remained a family of middling means set upon a conventional course of land management combined with attempts at official success. Wang Duanhu, the great grandfather of Wang Langyun, held a minor military rank. His grandfather, Wang Yuchuan, reached the position of expectant first class assistant department magistrate, while his father, Wang Kai, actually served in government as a legal secretary in a financial commissioner's yamen. During the first half of the dynasty, the Wangs accumulated a modest legacy in the form of agricultural and brine land, much of the latter apparently in the form of abandoned or relatively unproductive wells.

The Lis, whose fortune was incorporated during the nineteenth century as the Li Siyou lineage trust, had a similar history, although their ancestors were said to have come to the province during the late Yuan. Li Yuanqing, a native of Gushi county in Henan, first came to Sichuan in 1319. Residing in the capital of what was then Rongde county, his descendants took advantage of the depopulation of Sichuan during the Yuan-Ming transition by extending their holdings for a radius of several miles in what is now known as Jigong shan and Ziliujing.[21] Their involvement in salt production is said to have begun in the early Ming, and it continued to the end of the dynasty. In his biography of his grandfather, Li Jiuxia writes that in 1628, at the age of ten, Li Guoyu was already climbing the derrick to change the cable that drew up brine.[22] During the late seventeenth century, when Sichuan was under the oppressive rule of Wu Sangui, Li Guoyu is said to have often acted as a spokesman for salt industry interests—perhaps following a family tradition of local activism. The son of the founder of the Li lineage was a tithing head, and the family produced a number of lower-degree holders (*shengyuan*). The height of its academic success appears to have occurred in the mid-Ming when Li Shao earned the metropolitan degree (*jinshi*) and served as financial commissioner of Yunnan and later Fujian and Jiangxi. His son and grandson also achieved academic success, each earning the provincial degree (*juren*). Much of the Li's property seems to have been lost during the warfare accompanying the fall of the Ming.[23] However, with the restoration of peace, they quickly reestablished their stake in the salt industry. Until the early nineteenth century, the family pursued a mixed strategy, applying its energies to both farming and well drilling, while assuring that the children of each generation received ample education to achieve modest academic success. One of Li Guoyu's brother's sons earned the academic rank of *juren*, serving in several magisterial level posts. The next generation produced a *shengyuan*, a *juren*, and an instructor in the plain white banner, who later served as a magistrate. One cousin even presaged a pattern that was to be common among salt industrialists in the late Qing: he purchased the rank of prefectural registrar but never actually held a substantive post.

While the Wangs, the Lis, and probably the Yans grounded their fortunes in possessing land and cultivating traditional gentry roles, the founder of the Hu dynasty of Gongjing represents that other breed of immigrant so important to Sichuan's early economic development, the merchant.[24] Hu Liwei was born in Luling, Jiangxi, to a large but impoverished agricultural lineage. He and his kinsman, Hu Shiyun, came to Ziliujing in the mid-Jiaqing reign (1796–1820), lured by the already strong links between Jiangxi merchants and the salt-producing regions of this distant province. Liwei married in Sichuan but died soon after, leaving a wife and son, Hu Yuanhai, who were forced by poverty to return to Jiangxi. When Hu Yuanhai grew up, he borrowed some money from a relative and returned to the site of his father's dreams. Here he joined other members of the Jiangxi guild in selling cloth. Yuanhai made enough money to open a shop on Xinjie [New Street] in Ziliujing; soon after, the owner of the new Yuanhe shop married the daughter of a fellow provincial named Wang.

Together, Hu Yuanhai and his wife built a strong business, and with the money he made selling cloth he first entered a partnership to drill for brine. When this venture succeeded, he used the well's profits of more than eight thousand strings of cash to buy a piece of agricultural land yielding eighty piculs (about four thousand kilograms) of rice a year in rents. Far more important in the purchase was the apparently barren waste land and riverbank land that adjoined it. Here Hu Yuanhai opened his first gas and brine wells, and on the bank of the river, at the foot of Zhaizi hill, he moved his family and built his business offices.

In mid-century none of these families had sufficient resources to expand their operations on their own. With a prospering cloth business to fall back on, Hu Yuanhai was alone among the early salt giants to remain relatively independent in his business activities. After his first successful partnership, Hu tended to develop his wells on his own land. His method, using the profits from one well to build another well (*yinjing banjing*),[25] was a conservative business strategy ideally suited to an economy short of venture capital. Even if the new venture failed, the investor's original capital was safe. This same method protected another salt capitalist, Huang Zhiqing, from bankruptcy, despite an investment of almost seventy thousand taels in a well that was finally abandoned after drilling for eight years.[26] For Hu Yuanhai the method not only guaranteed profits but also promised to relieve him and his descendents of the complications that partnerships could bring. Nevertheless, it did limit the scope of his endeavors. Unlike his fellow magnates, most of Hu Yuanhai's wells produced low salinity yellow brine, albeit of good quality. The wells tended to be shallow and took relatively little time and money to drill. By the time of his death, Hu had accumulated an estate consisting of five brine wells and gas wells yielding enough fuel to evaporate thirty pans a day, agricultural land yielding two thousand piculs of rice in rents, and liquid assets amounting to several tens of thousands of taels.[27]

For merchants intent on a less cautious business strategy, extraprovincial investment capital and sophisticated partnership formation were the keys to economic success.[28] The most important sources of extraprovincial capital were merchants from Shaanxi. Shaanxi natives began exploiting Sichuan's economic opportunities during the late seventeenth century. Their earliest activities appear to have been in the wholesale marketing of Sichuan salt. When the salt gabelle was enforced during the early eighteenth century, licenses to sell salt were allocated to "honest" local merchants. However, few Sichuanese at this time had the requisite interest or experience in long-distance trade, and most salt distribution privileges were rented to Shaanxi merchants who took responsibility for paying the gabelle.[29] The stele commemorating the completion of repairs to the Xiqin guild hall in Ziliujing states that this guild of Shaanxi merchants had long been involved in shipping salt to Yunnan and Guizhou. They, too, engineered the early nineteenth-century revision of salt quotas that allowed salt-supply centers to shift to the more efficient salt yards in the southwest.[30]

During most of the Qing period, Sichuan's financial institutions were also dominated by merchants from the neighboring provinces to the north. According to Zhang Xiaomei, most pawnshops in early Qing Sichuan were owned by Shaanxi merchants who dominated the early development of native banking in the province. When the remittance business came to Sichuan, it too was controlled by outsiders, from Shanxi.[31] The Xiqin guild hall in Ziliujing, built between 1735 and 1752, was repaired in 1827 at a cost of several hundred thousand taels, with over 150 business establishments contributing to the repair fund.[32] The shops of the eight main Shaanxi merchant houses formed the backbone of the main street in Ziliujing, and the street itself was named after these establishments Eight Shops Road.[33] Such a strong economic presence could not but have had an influence on Fu-Rong's social life. However, during the first half of the dynasty, much of the money made by these extraprovincial giants appears to have been repatriated or used for business undertakings elsewhere in the country.[34] The sojourners were economically powerful at the salt yard but do not appear to have entered elite community activities. And neither the Fushun nor the Rongxian gazetteers highlight investment by Shaanxi or Shanxi men in county-level public welfare activities.

In the 1830s this pattern began to change, and investment by sojourners began to play an important role in expanding local industry and developing a local industrial elite. The possibility of larger markets and higher profits through exploiting the newly developed black-brine and gas wells began to lure Shaanxi merchant profits into the exploration of wells. This combination of Shaanxi (and to a lesser extent Shanxi) capital and native-owned land was responsible for the first phase of the "take off" in the salt industry at Fu-Rong. The effect on the composition of capital in the industry was dramatic. In one estimate, the Shaanxi merchant share in the total capitalization of salt production in Sichuan rose from almost nothing in 1830, to as much as 70 or 80 percent by the 1870s.[35] Although this may be an exaggeration, it is clear that an enormous increase in outsider investment did take place. The first major strike by salt evaporators was waged largely against the Shaanxi guild, which was said to own a dominant share in furnaces at the Fu-Rong yards.[36] Although we do not know the provenance of most investors listed in salt contracts, we do know that many wells featured in recent studies of late Qing Fu-Rong were also opened largely with Shaanxi merchant funds.[37] Indeed, at a well owned by Shaanxi guild members the first rock-salt well was dug.[38] Shaanxi merchant funds also helped transform the meager land holdings of the Wang Sanwei and Li Siyou lineage trusts into salt empires.

In the 1830s the fortunes of the descendants of Wang Yuchuan were on the decline;[39] they had few operating wells and only modest holdings in agricultural land. In 1838 one descendant, an enterprising and ambitious man named Wang Langyun, proposed that the property of the three existing branches of the lineage be divided and a small trust be maintained to support the triennial sacrifices to their common grandfather. Wang Langyun took over managing the trust and embarked on two projects that were to make his fortune and decide the destiny of his lineage.

With the meager resources of the lineage itself, Wang Langyun decided to redrill a well the family was already operating near Gaoshan jing. At the same time, Langyun signed a limited-tenure lease with a Shaanxi merchant to drill another black brine well on Wang land. The Wangs put up the land, and the lessee put up all the capital necessary to drill the well and build the pumping facilities. In return for their contributions, the Wangs received twelve shares in the well and the lessee-cum-investor received eighteen. All profits from the well were divided according to these respective shares. Thus, Wang Langyun and his relatives had nothing to lose if the well failed. If it struck brine the Wangs would enjoy two-fifths of the profits it produced. Even more important, after eighteen years the well and all nonmovable equipment would revert to their lineage trust.[40] By means of leases such as these the Wangs and other Fu-Rong landowners moved into the large-scale production of salt, and they may be considered a major strategy for the initial accumulation of resources by the Fu-Rong merchant elite. Many investors were outsiders looking for opportunities for the large profits from a successful black-brine or gas well. But at least a few partners in these new Wang ventures were local merchants, such as Yan Yongxing, who later became a salt magnate in his own right.

The early expansion of the Lis's salt holdings also depended on Shaanxi merchant wealth. As late as the 1820s the Lis had only four modestly productive brine wells.[41] When the profits from these wells were divided among the four sons of Li Shijin, little was left for investment in expanding the family business. In 1827–28 Li Weiji went to Chengdu to take the provincial examinations. There he chanced to meet a Shaanxi merchant named Gao who was involved in both the salt and tea trade in Sichuan. Gao became interested in the Li family's holdings and decided to invest three thousand taels to allow them to expand. Over the years, the Li-Gao partnership developed seven brine wells with a combined production of more than ten metric tons a day. Three more wells turned out to produce gas, giving them sufficient gas to evaporate approximately six hundred pans of salt as well.[42] With the addition of gas wells, the Li-Gao partnership was transformed from a net marketer of brine into a net purchaser, a factor that encouraged their further exploration of wells.

By the time of the Taiping Rebellion, families like the Lis, Wangs, Hus, and Yans were already becoming important producers of salt for domestic (*ji'an*) and border trade (*bian'an*). But the actual marketing of that salt still remained largely in the hands of the major Shaanxi salt firms (*yanhao*). When the Huguang market opened after the Taiping capture of Nanjing, this monopoly broke down. The dangers involved in shipping salt downriver before the trade was legalized made for an unmet demand for salt in Hubei and Hunan. Those merchants with stocks on hand and a bit of nerve had an unparalleled opportunity to amass thousands of taels in a short time through speculation in and export of Sichuan salt. Salt that cost only a few copper cash per *jin* (half a kilogram) at the Sichuan yards could be sold for ninety to two hundred cash per *jin* at the other end.[43] It was said that a man could sell a *jin* of salt in Hubei and come back with a *jin* of cotton, and indeed numerous salt merchants thus first became involved in the cotton trade. Many heroic stories circulated at the time, inspiring those with a sense of adventure and taste for wealth. At first this smuggled salt was beyond the constraints of the salt gabelle. Once legalized, the Huguang market for Sichuan salt was the only free market in salt in China, providing an outlet for excess productivity beyond the *yin* quota (*yuyin*), as well as *yin* quota salt that could not find a market in Sichuan (*jiyin*).[44] Anyone could get involved, and through this pirate trade the Lis, Hus, Wangs, and other salt producers became actively engaged in marketing as well as production.

By the end of the Taiping war, the Shaanxi commercial monopoly was broken, in not only the new Huguang market but also the domestic and border markets.[45] From then on, two marketing groups dominated the trade: the Chongqing group, largely extraprovincial and founded on control of financial resources in the economic capital of the province; and the Well group, whose ability to compete was based on their own enormous productive capacity at Gongjing and Ziliujing and their ability to buy up the product of many small Fu-Rong producers who could not market their salt themselves.[46] The leading salt merchants had made great fortunes as entrepreneurial risk takers. They dominated the industry as a whole and safeguarded the wealth upon which their elite status depended by combining a strategy of business integration and the merger of lineage and business structures.

Adaptation of the Corporate Lineage. The leaders of the four great salt dynasties of Fu-Rong, as well as those of many of the more modestly wealthy merchants families at the yard, skillfully adapted the institutions of the traditional charitable estate to the needs of early modern industrial development. Although they have taken many forms since the prototype was first suggested by Fan Zhongyan in the eleventh century, in general charitable estates (*yizhuang*) or lineage trusts (*tang*) served as a mechanism to preserve family property, ensure the education of talented youths, and provide a small income from which to maintain an ancestral hall and perform certain ritual functions connected with the ancestor cult. The salt merchants of Fu-Rong flexibly adapted this old form to construct a new institutional resource for furthering their business and protecting the family interests that depended so heavily on business wealth. They, in effect, turned the lineage trust into an analogue of the business corporation that evolved in the West during its early modern period. Application for and receipt of an imperial "charter" for founding such a trust provided an inviolate sanction against dissolution or division of its property. Whereas traditional trusts were largely based on agricultural wealth, in Fu-Rong the lineage trust was the structure within which business property was built, diversified, and preserved against the ravages of the tax collector, the creditor, and individual family members. Equally important, the trusts provided lineage elites with all the resources necessary for local economic and political dominance.[47] During the nineteenth century, it was within the lineage that the dramatic battles for power were fought and the managerial skills of the Fu-Rong elite were applied.

The lineage trusts of the great Fu-Rong salt merchants were established during the nineteenth century. In the case of the Lis, corporate identity preceded the establishment of a corporate trust. Genealogical records were maintained by the Lis at least as far back as the Qianlong reign (1736–95), and the Qianlong edition revised an earlier version of unknown date. A stone inscription marking the site of the family's ancestral hall was recut as early as 1694, further strengthening Li claims to earlier corporate identity.[48] However, it was the expansion of the family's salt holdings that led to the establishment of a lineage trust, named after the generational character, You, of the four (*si*) founders. Although we do not have a precise date for the founding of the Li Siyou *tang*, we do know that members of the Siyou generation reached adulthood during the early decades of the nineteenth century. Member Li Weiji first expanded the family's salt-related holdings in conjunction with the Shaanxi merchant Gao. During the first three generations of the trust's incorporation, all lineage resources were reinvested to build up its collective property. Even the potential for disputes among family members, which would soon plague the Wangs, was initially avoided by granting each branch of the lineage a fixed allowance of four metric tons of rice from agricultural rents and a cash allowance of no more than twelve hundred taels a year from the profits of the salt business. All other income from lineage enterprises was plowed back into production and sales.[49]

The Hu Yuanhe lineage trust also appears to date from the early nineteenth century. As the holdings of the family grew, its structure underwent a change specifically designed to meet the needs of a large salt conglomerate. In the early years of the Hu Yuanhe lineage trust, all positions of responsibility remained entirely in family hands. We know nothing of the family rules associated with the trust, but its structure was simple: a main office oversaw salt property, a separate department managed agricultural property, and another controlled all lineage business with the world outside. This latter office had the onerous task of cultivating useful connections for the lineage, as well as maintaining relations with businesses and officials associated with the salt industry. Each department was run by the husband of each of founder Hu Yuanhai's three daughters; therefore, control of the most important resources remained in the hands of the family of the trust's founder. Both the structure and the men who manned it remained largely unchanged until the 1890s, when Hu Yuanhai's son, Mianzhai, died and was succeeded by his second son, Ruxiu. Under Hu Ruxiu, the lineage rules were redrafted to include provisions that the family never live apart and that their property remain forever a corporate whole. However, in the event that a division should become necessary, a clause was added to allow equal distribution of wealth according to the number of lines in the present generation, not the three branches that had formed the original Hu Yuanhe lineage trust.[50] This would save the family from much of the bitterness and infighting that plagued the Wan Sanwei and Li Siyou lineage trusts when they finally dissolved.

At the same time, a set of management rules was incorporated into the regulations of the trust, establishing the complex corporate structure that would continue to run the personal affairs of the trust along with its many businesses. Besides a general manager in charge of the main counting house (*zhangfang guanshi*), there were managers (*guanshi*) with special responsibility for agricultural land, the family school, sacrifices to the ancestors, the family accounts, repairs to lineage property, feed for the lineage's buffalo, warehouses, and so on—twenty managers in all. This hierarchy continued downward for several levels and was devoted entirely to the private needs of the lineage members. A separate hierarchy was devoted to business affairs. Morever, in a radical departure from the usual practice, by the Guangxu period (1875–1908), most offices were manned by professional managers, not relatives.[51]

The lineage trust known as the Wang Sanwei *tang* was also formed specifically to meet the needs of a family in possession of a growing salt empire.[52] According to family tradition, Wang Langyun feared that his family would dissipate the property he had worked so hard to build up. Therefore, he incorporated the well and agricultural property that had grown out of an earlier sacrificial trust and set it aside as temple land to be maintained in perpetuity. The center of the new lineage organization was a recently built ancestral temple called the Yuchuan Ci. There the three branches with the hall name Wei pledged to follow the example set by Fan Zhongyan and establish a charitable estate. In 1877, presumably through the offices of the provincial governor, Wang Langyun requested and received the emperor's permission to have a stele carved and installed in the Yuchuan temple enjoining future generations to obey the regulations governing lineage property and its distribution.

In all, the Wangs put aside twenty operating wells and six hundred *mu* (one hundred acres) of agricultural land as a lineage trust.[53] This property was to pay for sacrifices, upkeep of ancestral graves, support of elderly lineage members, expenses of lineage members taking the examinations, and aid to relatives and neighbors in time of famine. To achieve the lineage's goals of wealth and influence, special provisions were made to support the examination success that would both extend the local status derived from the Wangs' great wealth to wider arenas and broaden political connections with officials and degree holders higher in the urban hierarchy. A school was established for all male progeny of the lineage; it was open to promising nonrelatives as well.[54] Each Wang son and grandson would be given twenty taels to help defray the costs of taking the provincial examinations and two strings of copper cash if he took the district or prefectural exams. Those who passed would be rewarded with one hundred taels; anyone fortunate enough to qualify for the metropolitan examinations would be given four hundred taels toward the trip to Beijing. And if someone was selected to enter the

Hanlin Academy or the Imperial University established during the last years of the Qing, the lineage would provide him with a stipend of four hundred taels a year.

The Wang Sanwei lineage trust also provided a pension of fifty kilograms of rice a year for any tenant on trust land who lived to the age of sixty, and put aside 240 strings of cash a year as payment for the man chosen by each branch to oversee ancestral sacrifices. The trust promised to request that a memorial archway be erected in honor of chaste widows and virtuous women among its female members, contributing fifty taels to the construction of every one for which permission was given. However, the most important passage, and that which set its governing rules apart from those of the traditional lineage trust, referred to the disposal of the huge surplus profits that the Wang Sanwei trust would undoubtedly produce. It was arranged that the entire lineage would meet annually to settle the trust's accounts. At this time, half the money remaining after the designated expenditures and upkeep of lineage property would be reinvested to add to the lineage's holdings. The other half would be used to buy more property for each branch, in accordance with its share of the lineage's corporate possessions.[55]

Corporate entities borrowing the structure of the lineage trust account for approximately 20 percent of all investors in the salt industry contracts collected by the Zigong Municipal Archives.[56] In other salt yards as well, the lineage trust became a crucial tool for managing industrial resources and insuring the integrity and continuity of business holdings. The lineage trust established by the Wu Jingrang *tang* of Jianwei developed into a major industrial empire in the twentieth century, controlling many modern industries as well as its holdings in salt.[57] Moreover, in Jian-Le as in Fu-Rong, although lineage trusts combined traditional gentry mobility strategies and business pursuits, increasingly the latter provided the resources necessary for the elite status of their members. We will, therefore, look further at how these families organized their businesses before considering the strategies they employed to cultivate symbolic status and social capital beyond the power and influence that flowed from great wealth.

THE ORGANIZATION OF BUSINESS RESOURCES

The key to the extraordinary business success of the Wang, Li, Yan, and Hu lineage trusts was the development of efficient management organizations that promoted expertise, centralized control of a large business empire, and allowed the expansion of the initial well business into a vertically integrated salt conglomerate. Although these practices were carried out to their fullest extent among the largest salt lineages, centralized hierarchical organization of diversified business interests was common to many families involved in the salt industry at this time.

The economic interests of all three lineage trusts about which we have information were based on a two-tiered management system. At the apex was a main office with supervisory control over the operation of each subsidiary business. At the Hu Yuanhe lineage trust this function was performed at the elaborate lineage hall known as the Shenyi *tang*, completed in 1867. The main office (*zong guifang*) was usually headed by a family member whose title was general director (*zong zhanggui*). Under him were five departments: (1) a counting house (*guifang*) run by a chief accountant (*zongzhang*) and two assistants (*bangzhang*) in charge of the overall productivity of the lineage's wells and furnaces; (2) a procurement department (*huowu gu*) in charge of purchasing all supplies needed for the daily operation of the wells and furnaces; (3) an external affairs department (*jiaoji gu*) in charge of buying brine for the lineage's furnaces and selling salt at lineage-owned retail shops; (4) a department of agricultural estates (*nongzhuang gu*) in charge of collecting rents and selling grain; and (5) a cash department (*xianjin gu*) in charge of daily cash expenditures and silver-copper exchange transactions.[58]

After a long period of unified management under the leadership of its founder, Wang Langyun, the Wang Sanwei lineage trust was almost destroyed by a period of fragmentation in the late nineteenth century. Individual family members, distrusting each other's intentions, took over operating groups of wells, furnaces, and other family businesses. Without violating the trust regulation that lineage holdings be maintained as an undivided estate, poor business practices, waste, embezzlement, and loss of the advantages of coordinating wells, furnaces, and wholesale enterprises left the family in debt for almost seven hundred thousand taels. The lessons learned in the 1880s and 1890s led to a renewed attention to centralized management, and during the height of its prosperity the counting house of the Jingfeng well regulated all income and expenditure, planning, and allocation of materials for the Wang Sanwei lineage trust's agricultural lands, wells, furnaces, wholesale firms, and brine pipes.[59]

Below the main supervisory bodies at each lineage trust was a separate management structure for each furnace, well, wholesale firm, and pipe. The literature on the Li Siyou lineage trust gives the fullest picture of how these management hierarchies worked.[60] Taking as an example the organization of furnaces, we find two layers of authority. Each furnace was under the overall charge of a counting house whose manager (*zhanggui*) received orders directly from the trust's main office. In reality, he had considerable freedom in running the furnace, with the aid of a head (*guanzhang*) and assistant accountant (*banggui*). Besides handling the furnace's books, the head accountant was the manager's assistant, in complete charge of the business when the manager was away. Together, these three men were the main decision-making group at the furnace, in charge of all purchases, sales, and planning.

Beneath the managers were supervisors in charge of specific operations at the furnace. In addition, most furnaces also employed a "master" or *shiye*; this man of education and some political sophistication was designated to handle the social obligations of the management. Social relationships played an important part in the highly competitive world of salt, and many of these men were probably chosen for the connections they would bring to the business. However, they also performed another function. Most masters were also high-level advisers to the lineage headquarters, not under the jurisdiction of the management of the enterprise itself. Probably they were also family spies, keeping an eye on operations and making suggestions when problems arose. At the same time, they undertook the task of training a number of apprentices who performed servile chores for the master while learning the ways of business, the use of the abacus, and the techniques for keeping accounts.

The elaborate centralized bureaucracies created under the auspices of the lineage trusts enabled strategically placed family members or their representatives to control large business empires; through them they could influence the fate of a large laboring population and the smaller businessmen with whom they competed and whose products they used at their wells. They also provided a route for upwardly mobile new elites. Like the hired managers of old-style banks, the managers of salt firm departments were well placed to make money for themselves and to acquire the knowledge and connections necessary to found their own companies.

Vertical Integration, the Key to Economic Success. The key to the economic and political power exercised by the large, lineage-based salt firms was vertical integration of salt industry holdings. By combining under a single management pumping brine, evaporating salt, wholesale marketing, and operating brine pipes, firms were able to guarantee dominance of a relatively unstable salt market.[61] By combining ownership of wells and furnaces, they could almost invariably guarantee their supplies of the key ingredients in salt manufacture: brine and gas. By controlling the main wholesale salt-distribution firms in the province, they insured that their salt was first to be sold in the major Sichuan salt markets. With the wealth accumulated in salt production they expanded into developing brine pipes, which gave them control over marketing a large portion of Gongjing brine and enabled them to hold the nonaffiliated furnaces of Ziliujing ransom to their needs. Their control of large capital reserves allowed them to buy up stocks of seasonal goods or items like coal, the price of which was lower in the winter, when the pits were operating at full productivity. Finally, they went on to diversify their holdings into almost every industry that served the producers of salt. At the same time, wealth and the ability to guarantee product delivery when others could not, gave them an advantage in dealing with the main buyer of salt, which, in the last four decades of the dynasty, was the state.

During the 1870s and 1880s, the Li Siyou lineage trust is said to have drilled hundreds of wells, although the names of only seventeen survive. While most of these were brine wells, the few gas wells in their possession were also highly productive, allowing the Li Siyou lineage trust at its height to evaporate more than eight hundred pans.[62] The holdings of the Hu Yuanhe lineage trust were far less extensive, reaching a maximum of twenty-six yellow- and black-brine wells. However, all but five of these were independent of outside investment, and at least ten produced gas as well as brine.[63]

At Shanzi ba, site of their first explorations, the Wang Sanwei lineage trust operated twenty-one brine wells, producing only about fifty metric tons of brine a year. However, early exploitation of the rock-salt layer kept profits from brine wells high. Far more important were the lineage's gas wells, producing sufficient gas to evaporate at least twelve hundred pans. Some of these were rented out, and some gas was rented from outside wells. In all, the Wang Sanwei lineage trust evaporated an average of seven hundred pans during the last years of the Qing. With this capacity, they and the Li Siyou lineage trust were responsible for approximately 23 percent of the licensed salt produced in Fu-Rong each year.[64]

The brine and gas holdings of the four great lineages would have been sufficient to guarantee them an important place in the economy of the salt yard, but they also controlled the pipes that transported Gongjing brine to the gas furnaces at Ziliujing. Each of the ten main brine pipes carried between 50 and 150 metric tons a day, compared to the total 150 tons a day carried at far greater expense by brine porters before the construction of the pipes. Well owners had to sell their brine to the pipe companies, which in turn sold all Gongjing brine to the gas furnaces. Pipe owners made large profits in these transactions and, moreover, enjoyed privileged access to the limited number of pipes in the yard. Their brine was the first to be sold in times of surplus, and their furnaces were the first to receive brine in times of shortage. According to one estimate, during the 1890s, 70 percent of existing pipes were owned outright or in partnership by Wangs and Lis.[65] A main pipe could cost as much as one hundred thousand taels to build, limiting their ownership to only the wealthiest merchants in the yard. More important to the large local lineages' dominance in pipe construction was the need to negotiate leases with the hundreds of individual landlords over whose property the pipes passed. Only large local landowners, with strong community influence, could put together such a deal—as many outside investors soon discovered.[66]

As important to the success of the large salt lineages was their operation of wholesale firms. The Wangs, Hus, and Lis each marketed their own and others' salt in the lucrative extraprovincial markets. The Wang Sanwei lineage trust's Guangshengtong company was the largest agent for the sale of

Sichuan's "aid to Huguang" salt; the Li Siyou lineage trust and the Wang Baoxinglong trust ranked second and third.[67] The Wang Sanwei lineage trust's Zhongxingxiang company and the Xiexinglong company (a joint Li, Tian, and Liu lineage operation) were the two main wholesalers of salt in the portion of the Guizhou market centered at Renhuai prefecture. More than seventy branches served the departments and districts between the company headquarters at Renhuai and the provincial capital at Guiyang. Each branch had a business office, salt warehouse, and living quarters for staff. Large agricultural holdings in the region yielded sufficient rents to pay for all operating expenses of the branch units. In addition, the firm trained and staffed its own antismuggling police (*yanjing*), who served as both escorts for their merchant shipments and personal guards for the firm's bosses.

The wealthy lineages also dealt in commodities other than salt. The Wang Sanwei lineage trust's Fuchangsheng company was a major purveyor of rice, broad beans, soy, rapeseed oil, and other basic provisions purchased in Luzhou and Jiangjing. They operated their own money shop in the center of Ziliujing and were among the first to use salt profits from Huguang to import machine-made cotton yarn. To guarantee their own stores of coal, the Wangs set up the Bianli Coal Yard at Gaotong, the main coal distribution point in Fu-Rong. At the same time, they established the Tianxintang Medicine Shop to purchase and retail herbal medicines, particularly those used in the treatment of water buffalo. The Hu Yuanhe lineage trust also dealt in white wax from Jiading and ran a pawnshop in Chengdu. The Lis were engaged in a number of retail businesses, including ownership of two medicine shops and their own lumberyard to supply materials for constructing wells, derricks, wheels, and salt-yard buildings.[68]

Finally, the main salt lineages were among the largest landowners in Sichuan. By his death in 1884, Wang Langyun had accumulated for his lineage agricultural lands spread over four counties and producing over 450 metric tons of rice in rents. By the turn of the century, Wang, Li, and Hu trusts produced rental incomes of 850, more than 250, and 380 metric tons, respectively. However, it would be incorrect to think of the accumulation of land as evidence that traditional investment strategies played a major part in developing the Fu-Rong elite. Land may also be seen as a liquid asset in an economic environment in which banking played a minor part. When the Wang Sanwei lineage trust ran into debt in the 1880s it sold off agricultural assets to shore up its industrial holdings. The same was true of many salt lineages in the early twentieth century.[69]

Business capital invested in land yielded comfortable returns in the form of rents, which could rapidly be converted into cash in the highly fluid land market of the late Qing. Land also played a part in the integrated salt business. We have already seen that the Li Siyou lineage trust used the income from its land holdings in those provinces to operate its wholesale salt firms in

Guizhou and Yunnan. The need to feed thousands of employees and buffalo at the wells was also a powerful motivation to invest in land. At its height the Wang Sanwei lineage trust kept a herd of between twelve and thirteen hundred buffalo. Even during the period of decline, their wells required maintaining at least six to seven hundred head.[70] Large well owners rented part of their landed holdings in nearby villages to tenants contracted to grow grass. Under one system of tenancy, the peasant had to agree to supply a certain well with an agreed quota of grass every day: periodic payment would be made to the tenant after deducting his rent. The landlord received his feed and a guaranteed rent. The tenant, tied to one buyer for his crop, was forced to sell at a low price.[71] Similar practices may have been imposed on peasants growing broad beans, another important component of the buffalos' diet and a major item of expenditure at the wells. In this way, business organization provided the structure through which these lineages dominated villagers throughout southern Sichuan, in addition to the more direct economic power they exercised over Fu-Rong's large industrial labor market.

THE CULTIVATION OF SOCIAL CAPITAL

To what extent did the Lis, Wangs, Hus, and Yans, whose local prominence in industrial Fu-Rong arose from their great wealth, also seek to enhance their status through the examinations or to enlarge their reputations through local community activity? Sichuan's Lower Basin produced more than one-third of the province's upper-degree holders during the Ming and early Qing. Families with a long history in the region, like the Lis, followed a mixed strategy, pursuing both academic honors and commercial or agricultural wealth. However, the depopulation and material destruction of the Ming-Qing transition created in Fu-Rong, as in much of early-Qing Sichuan, a frontier atmosphere that was reinforced by high levels of in-migration and sudden economic boom. Here bravado, conspicuous displays of wealth, and physical strength appear to have been more important than refined gentry politics.

Although the "wild west" character of Fu-Rong society receded by the mid-eighteenth century, the expansion of the Fu-Rong salt industry continued to steer local elites into nongentry strategies to acquire or preserve local dominance. As economic opportunities increased, both newcomers and established families concentrated on maintaining their burgeoning salt empires. Contrary to our expectations, they did not achieve great examination success soon after becoming rich. Perhaps the more tangible and accessible rewards of industrial development discouraged the pursuit of elusive examination degrees. In their formative years, when government involvement in salt distribution was limited, the Fu-Rong elite may not have valued the usefulness of degrees in forging contacts with the government bureaucracy. Moreover, until the mid-nineteenth century most often the large Shaanxi merchant firms controlled the salt distribution networks and dealt with Qing official-dom. This changed in the 1850s, when expanding economic opportunity, the threat of rebel military attack, and increasing government demands for rev-enue joined to forge a new outward-looking orientation among Fu-Rong's salt-yard elite.[72]

The Impact of the Taiping Rebellion. The event that so altered the political and economic fortunes of the Fu-Rong elite was the Taiping Rebellion. Sichuan's salt-producing regions were struck several times by rebels associ-ated with the Taiping, the worst of the fighting occurring during the uprising of Li Yonghe and Lan Dashun. Soon after the outbreak of the Taiping Rebel-lion, merchants in Fu-Rong began to construct fortifications in the hilly sub-urbs surrounding the yard.[73] Construction of Sanduo fort began in 1853 under the leadership of Li Ji'an, Yan Changying, Wang Kejia, and several members of the elite of neighboring Neijiang county. According to the obitu-ary of a descendant of the Li Siyou lineage trust, Li Tonggai, the merchant community raised over seventy thousand taels to build Sanduo fort. In 1860, Wang Langyun took the lead in constructing a stockade and hiring a force of mercenaries to defend the neighborhood of Da'an fort. An attack by one of the Li-Lan rebels' lieutenants, Mao Dexing, was launched before the for-tification was completed, but the merchant militia managed to survive. A second attack the following year resulted in a protracted siege during which many members of the salt lineages died, including Wang's own nephew, Wang Zhujun.[74] As a reward for his leadership in local defense the Sichuan governor general memorialized the court to award Wang Langyun the low rank of senior imperial bodyguard.

The need to defend their businesses and homes also drew the salt-yard elite into the local political arena. Acquiring honorary official titles placed the Wangs among the ranks of the new post-Taiping "irregular" bureau-cratic elite.[75] However, minor honors did not always help their changing relations with the state. The opening of the "aid to Huguang" market, which accompanied the Taiping Rebellion, not only created the opportunity for the meteoric economic rise of the Fu-Rong elite, but it also drew them into the legal trade in salt and left them increasingly vulnerable to government taxa-tion and regulation.

The first signs of government encroachment upon the profits of the newly developed free market in Sichuan salt came soon after the outbreak of war. The opening of the "aid to Huguang" market heralded the elimination of specified sales territories for *yin* salt as well as the "surplus salt" that had previously been sold freely within Sichuan. Officials in Huguang were simply instructed to set up tax collection stations at which merchants from Sichuan paid a single fee, set at between 10 and 20 percent of the market value of the salt, and received a certificate entitling them to sell their salt anywhere in the "aid to Huguang" region. Beginning in 1854 the *lijin* transit tax was also levied on salt shipments to Huguang. At first these imposts were collected at two key ports along the salt transport routes.[76] In 1855, checkpoints were established within Sichuan as well. At the same time, *lijin* bureaus were situated at the main salt yards for taxing both *yin* and surplus salt at the point of production. The most important bureaus were those at Wutong qiao in Jianwei, at Ziliujing and Douya wan in Fushun, and at Kangjia du in Pengxi.[77]

Unlike the *lijin* collected in the economic centers of eastern China, which became an important source of revenue for both government and elite activities, salt *lijin* was placed under strict bureaucratic controls from its inception. Moreover, much of the money raised in this way was exported to support the more intense fighting in other provinces and, later, to help pay China's growing foreign debt. For the large merchant conglomerates with interests in production and marketing, this new levy meant a double burden of taxation and they appear to have reacted swiftly, in swashbuckling frontier fashion.

Local legend holds that on an evening in 1863, the heads of the Yan Guixing and the Wang Sanwei lineage trusts led their workers to the local *lijin* bureau and razed it to the ground. There is no evidence of literati-style negotiation with the state prior to their act of protest, nor were past relations with the magistrate, who eventually arrested Wang Langyun, apparently cordial.[78] Indeed, it was from jail that Wang Langyun took his first real steps toward gentry politics. After several days incarceration he made an enormous donation to famine relief—some say seventy thousand taels—in exchange for which he received the rank of judicial commissioner, a second-class official button for his hat, posthumous honors for his ancestors extending back three generations, and his freedom.

The Move Toward Gentry Politics. The basic outlines of this story of prominent elites' violent resistance to government policies were resurrected frequently during the ensuing decades as government pressure on the salt industry increased. The most striking example of this phenomenon is offered by Manyin (pseudonym of a descendant of the Wang lineage) whose novel *Ziliujing* purports to tell the story of his illustrious family's declining years. In his version the entire episode took place in the 1870s; it was not an attack on the newly established *lijin* bureau but on the "official transport and merchant sale" bureau established in 1877.[79]

In fact, Wang and undoubtedly other members of the salt industry elite do appear to have opposed the system of official transport and merchant sale as soon as it was in place. However, protest against salt administration reform in the 1870s reveals the rise of a different leadership style among the Fu-Rong elite. Here, Wang Langyun and others voiced their dissent by establishing connections among officials in the capital in Beijing. The petitions their con-

tacts sent to the Board of Revenue and the Censorate may have been instrumental in sparking a debate that came close to successfully curtailing
official transport and merchant sale in Sichuan.[80]

The change in the strategy employed by the Fu-Rong merchant community in pressing their economic interests against those of the state reflects a
maturation of the salt-yard elite. The *lijin* protests demonstrated the ineffec-
tiveness of mere bravado in advocating merchant goals. In addition, the
peculiar position of the Fu-Rong yard encouraged attempts to cultivate connections at the centers of power, rather than nearer to home. The central
government's control of salt administration and the Fu-Rong yard's division
between two counties, themselves belonging to two separate prefectures,
made a concentration on metropolitan ties the most economical use of political capital. At the same time, governmental hunger for funds in the post-
Taiping period opened the door for men of wealth and local influence to
purchase the titles that gave them access to the regular elite beyond their
home communities. Li Shaotang's sons, Bichun and Yuru, each bought circuit intendant ranks at a cost of around ten thousand taels apiece. With these
passports into gentry society, both men spent most of their time in Chongqing, entertaining officials and degree holders and building connections for
the family among the province's nonbusiness elite. Li Xingqiao, who ran the
lineage firms between 1899 and 1911, also purchased the office of circuit
intendant and spent much of his time cultivating officials and degree holders,
both to protect the family against official pressures and to safeguard his own
position in the lineage. Only one member of the Li Siyou lineage trust
appears to have acquired a regular degree, giving that lineage one more
member of the examination elite than their fellow salt dynasties.[81]

Following his confrontation with the bureaucracy over *lijin*, Wang Langyun authorized the expenditure of lineage funds to purchase degrees for the
next generation of branch heads. Langyun's sons, Wang Dazhi and Wang
Huitang, each bought himself an expectant circuit intendant rank; the rank
of military defense circuit was purchased for a grandson, Wang Xingyuan,
whose father had died young leaving him in charge of his branch. Several
years later Wang Zuogan and Wang Yucai of the third generation also
purchased the rank of county magistrate.[82] Official connections served the
family well, when, in 1880, Sichuan Governor General Ding Baozhen decided to vent his anger on the most militant opponents of salt administration
reform. Having convinced the emperor that Wang Langyun was illegally
collecting salt fees and corrupting young girls, Ding issued an order to arrest
the head of the Wang Sanwei trust and bring him to Beijing. Connections in
the capital warned the Wangs, enabling Langyun to flee to Yunnan; he remained there for four years, returning to Fu-Rong only three years before his
death.

The Hu Yuanhe lineage trust appears to have been the most vigorous in establishing its members' credentials through purchased rank. Hu Ruxiu bought the rank of a board department director; Hu Shuliang, salt inspector; Hu Shizhong and Hu Tiehua each, second-class ministerial secretary; and Hu Xingsheng, Hu Jiyun, and Hu Zhongwen, ranks at level 9, the lowest bureaucratic grade. Like the Wang Sanwei lineage trust, the Hu Yuanhe *tang* established a lineage school at which numerous local degree holders were invited to teach.[83] Although there is no evidence that any member of the Hu lineage achieved success in the imperial examinations as a result of the investment placed in this school, it did develop links between the family and members of the local examination elite. Most important among them was Zhao Xi, who was to become the most prominent literati advocate of salt yard goals during the early Republican period.

The acquisition of official ranks continued to play an important part in the consolidation of elite standing within the salt yard community. In his survey of the Fu-Rong gentry during the late 1910s, Qiao Fu notes twenty title holders, all of whom were salt merchants. This resonates well with my findings for Chongqing, where at least 30 percent of merchants involved in lawsuits in the post-Taiping period appear to have previously purchased minor degrees.[84] A purchased degree or title was viewed as facilitating contacts with government in a period of considerable competition for economic dominance.

The decades following the Taiping Rebellion saw the consolidation of the business fortunes established during the heady years of the early nineteenth century. At the same time, the expansion of Fu-Rong's markets in Huguang and Sichuan, gains in output through deep-drilling technology, and renewed governmental interest in the revenue potential of Sichuan salt created new uncertainties and opportunities for new entrepreneurs. In such conditions the Fu-Rong elite began to jockey with each other for position in the social sphere as well as in the world of manufacturing and commerce.

Much nonbusiness activity of the salt-yard elite can be viewed in the context of image making and symbolic display. Wealth was demonstrated in both ostentatious marriage, funeral, and birthday rituals, and construction of sumptuous family mansions and gardens. All the leading salt lineages maintained large fleets of sedan chairs and corps of personal attendants.[85] To these rather crude expressions of economic power were now added various status-related behaviors designed to establish elite credentials within the larger local gentry community. As we have seen, at least one lineage mandated erection of memorial arches to chaste widows in its lineage rules. There is some evidence of intermarriage between salt-merchant progeny and prominent scholarly families,[86] and ties with the county-level elites of both Fushun and Rongxian were deepened when local scholars were employed as teachers at the schools salt merchants established for the children of their lineages.

A small portion of the great wealth accumulated by the Fu-Rong salt lineages was also contributed to the public welfare. Hu Mianzhai and his son, Hu Ruxiu, were major contributors to a late-nineteenth-century project to repave the imperial road between Weiyuan county and the outskirts of Chengdu. The Lis, Yans, and Wangs all contributed to the repair of bridges and roads in Fushun and in neighboring Rongxian.[87] During the early twentieth century the Hus, without charge, treated children in the yard for smallpox and established one of the first health clinics for the poor. The Lis, Hus, and Wangs founded schools, and Li Ji'an is praised in the gazetteer of Fushun for his sponsorship of scholars traveling to take the provincial exams.[88] These activities, too, should be viewed within the context of symbolic display. Focused on the local community, most fall within the kind of largess expected of local leading figures in late imperial China.

Two further examples of salt merchant activity in the public sphere deserve special attention. The most important outlet for extralineage philanthropy among the wealthiest families of Fu-Rong was famine relief. We have already noted Wang Langyun's not entirely disinterested activities in this field. During the catastrophic drought of 1884–85, the court rewarded Hu Mianzhai for providing low-cost sorghum cakes to the poor, a practice that later became an annual lineage event. And Li Ji'an was a major sponsor of relief programs in Sichuan and neighboring Hubei and Shaanxi.[89] Although a traditional expression of gentry largess, participation in famine relief also served the business interests of the large salt industry lineages. Achievement in famine relief and the contribution of money and rice to granary stores won predictable rewards in the form of official ranks and helped each lineage establish its credentials with the scholar elite and gain access to officials in Beijing.

The final arena for elite activism at the Furong salt yard, and the only one in which we can see sustained cooperation among members of more than one lineage, was local defense. The vulnerability of the salt yard to bandit attacks and, after the close of the dynasty, warlord attack resulted in the continued maintenance of merchant-financed armed forces. The fortresses or *zhai* constructed during the 1860s were kept up well into the Republic. A resident militia, commanded by Wang Hefu and Hu Tiehua, was an important feature of early Republican Ziliujing society.[90] Descendants of Li Ji'an are said to have maintained such a force at Sanduo fort until 1926, when a united militia joining forces from Weiyuan, Neijiang, and Fushun was formed. This was later expanded into a larger army, combining militias from forty-three counties. Li Tonggai, grandson of Li Ji'an, commanded one unit, and his son, Li Jingcai, commanded another. Individuals and lineages also maintained smaller military guards.[91]

In devoting their energies to communal defense, the elite of Fu-Rong were following a pattern common to the region. Defense-related activities formed the largest category of public service activities attributed to named individuals in the Fushun and Rongxian gazetteers. Almost all were carried out during or after the rebellions of the mid-nineteenth century.[92] However, the formation of higher-level militia during the early Republic was not matched by similar cooperative activity during the Qing. Between the independent exercise of local influence and the cultivation of Sichuanese officials in the imperial capital was a void that went unfilled until after the dynasty's fall. Besides joint efforts to establish academies and fight intruders, the only examples of collective mobilization we have for the Fu-Rong yard involve underground organizations. Both the Elder Brother Society and the Roman Catholic church provided alternative access to power, but their patrons were usually landlords and merchants who did not belong to the most powerful lineages.[93]

In summary, members of the Fu-Rong salt merchant community strove to enhance their status in two ways. First, and most important, they demonstrated wealth, military power, and to a lesser extent, ties to county-level literati through patronage, marriage, and purchased degrees. Displays in this sphere, while drawing money away from business, were aimed at establishing one's position in a local pecking order that included both native merchants and wealthy long-distance merchants from Shaanxi and Shanxi. Second, superficially related were activities like famine relief and the purchase of higher degrees, which also brought local prestige; but, more important, they linked Fu-Rong's elite and officials in Beijing and earned the salt merchants political capital that could be used in their never ending struggle to lessen the impact of government salt monopoly regulations on lineage profits.

The absence of intermediate-level political or community activity among the salt-yard elite prior to the twentieth century is striking. The activities described above could by no means be characterized by the term "elite activism" that is often applied to the expansion of the public sphere by both merchants and literati in regions like Jiangnan in the post-Taiping years. One obvious reason for this difference was that, unlike many areas of eastern and central China, Sichuan suffered little material damage during the period of the Taiping Rebellion, and military preparations in the late 1890s and 1911 were not matched by large-scale military activity. The massive work of reconstruction, which provided the basis for elite mobilization elsewhere during the late Qing, simply did not exist in Fu-Rong.[94] Equally important, the size and organizational complexity of the lineage-based salt firms to a large extent made cooperation unnecessary. Controlling both manufacture and marketing, the salt merchants did not need the complex brokerage, transportation, and banking relationships established among the commercial community of the Lower Yangzi and east coast. Their physical control of large parts of the yard, their ability to mobilize many workers and retainers, and their instant access to large reserve funds made independent action the most efficient and effective way to deal with the problems faced by Fu-Rong's salt merchant elite in the late nineteenth century. The most threatening of these was the salt administration. The fact that a central government institution decided their fate only reinforced the salt merchants' reliance on native officials and scholars in the country's capital.

STATUS MAINTENANCE IN THE EARLY REPUBLIC

The fall of the Qing marked the end of the self-contained merchant elite. On the one hand, the end of the dynasty brought an end to an easily defined and manipulated structure of authority governing salt and the salt yard. At the same time, changes in the technology of salt production, access to markets, and intralineage competition for lineage resources led to the economic decline of the old salt families.

By the late nineteenth century individual lineage members were already using corporate resources to build their own fortunes, often to the detriment of lineage-based business. However, the fall of the Qing was almost universally viewed as removing the authority that had sanctioned the formation of a lineage trust, and demands that the lineage trust be divided were frequently heard. Although the salt holdings of the Li Siyou lineage trust were not divided until 1948, those of the Hu Yuanhe lineage trust were divided as early as 1913.[95] An attempt to dissolve the Wang Sanwei lineage trust in 1911 was only thwarted by disagreement over distributing the spoils;[96] however, for many years it ceased to function as an integrated economic unit.

As lineage fortunes declined, only those members of the four lineage trusts who became involved in politics survived as important members of the Fu-Rong elite. Moreover, the outlets for political maneuvering increased as competition for control of the yard became more intense. Whereas the great salt merchants sometimes had to turn to politics to protect their business interests during the Qing, in the unstable political environment of the warlord period a focus on politics was critical to economic survival. Salt merchants dominated both the Zigong Provisional Assembly (*Zigong linshi yishihui*) and the chamber of commerce, founded shortly before the fall of the Qing.[97] Both organizations were lively advocates of free market policies in the administration of salt and during their short tenures proposed many economic reforms at the yard. But, if Qiao Fu is correct, they did little that could be labeled public service. Several members of prominent salt families left the salt yard to concentrate on political careers unconnected with salt. Hu Tiehua, guided by his mentor, Zhao Xi, became a leader in the Chongqing branch of the short-lived Progressive party. Several members of the Wang lineage moved to higher-level central places to seek their fortunes, and Wang Xinjiu was active in provincial politics as a director of the Sichuan-Hankou Railway Bureau.[98]

However, the most successful scions of the old salt lineages placed their futures in the hands of warlord patrons and tried to continue to exercise their power in the salt yard in which they were born. For example, Wang Zuogan served as an adviser to the Yunnan army brigade commander Liu Fakun, and his nephew, Wang Yuping, worked for division commander Gu Pinzhen. Li Jingcai developed close ties with the leading Sichuan warlord, Liu Xiang. The instability of the warlord regimes made such ties unreliable at best. Mere survival of a business was sufficient grounds for a new military ruler to suspect the owner of collusion with his enemies. During the first decade of the Republic, the Wangs, the Lis, and other lesser salt families suffered heavy losses in the form of fines, levies, and outright confiscations as their warlord governors changed from year to year. After an initial period of free market distribution of Sichuan salt, the new foreign-run Salt Inspectorate began to increase the gabelle and associated charges at rates several times those of the late Qing. Sichuan salt once and for all lost its competitive edge in the Huguang market. At the same time, banditry and warlord competition cut off Fu-Rong's markets at home and in the older Yunnan and Guizhou sales zones.[99]

The end of the free market system in the 1870s and the gradual erosion of Sichuan's designated market in Huguang had already meant diminished profits for the large salt wholesale firms. The Li Siyou lineage trust was the first to close its wholesale firm trading with Huguang.[100] With the introduction of "official transport and merchant sales," the lineage-based firms lost the advantage gained by preferential marketing of their own salt. With prices also fixed by the state, the profits that had helped finance conspicuous consumption, influence peddling, and other lineage businesses began to decline.

In the mid-1890s, the discovery of a layer of rock salt above the level of the black brine dramatically changed the structure of the industry at Fu-Rong. Rock-salt wells (*yanyan jing*) had to be irrigated by fresh water brought in from the outside. However, once water was introduced, salinity at these wells was far greater than that at either yellow- or black-brine wells. The volume of brine brought up each day was limited only by the capacity of the pumps with which a well was equipped. This inspired the introduction of steam-driven pumps, wide-mouthed wells, and metal tubes and cable, which increased the output from a single well as much as ten times.[101]

The advent of the rock-salt well was a boon to the salt yard as a whole, but apparently it contributed to the decline of the large lineage-based firms. First, the large lineage trusts in the nineteenth century dug mostly black-brine wells. Deeper than the new rock-salt wells, they had been opened at far greater expense, and represented a major commitment of lineage funds. By the turn of the century, many of these wells were drying up, and lineage finances were increasingly tight. Moreover, as brine supplies increased, they could not compete with the more productive rock-salt wells. Of the eighty-seven deep wells opened in Gongjing at the turn of the century, at least forty-six closed between 1910 and 1930.[102] Far more important for the lineage-based fortunes was the location of the rock-salt wells. Unlike the most efficient black-brine wells, at a considerable distance from the Ziliujing gas wells and furnaces, the rock-salt wells were in Ziliujing. The enormous power wielded by the large lineage-based firms, given their control of the brine pipes between Gongjing and Ziliujing, vanished almost overnight.[103] The erosion of their economic base was accompanied by the erosion of the elite status which was based upon it. Although they remained a presence at the yard until the Communist revolution, by the 1920s power and influence was passing to a new breed of men.

The introduction of rock-salt wells heralded another change in the balance of power at the yard. Before their large-scale exploitation, gas supplies far exceeded brine supplies, and untold quantities of natural gas were allowed to escape everyday for lack of a better use. As productivity at the rock-salt wells increased, gas became dear, and gas-well owners, many of them independents and newcomers to the yard, were able to set the terms of trade. At the same time, excess supplies of brine and the structure of the rock-salt wells themselves introduced a new-style entrepreneur. Men who controlled the irrigation of the wells, contracted to pump the wells, managed the growing number of credit institutions at the yard, and owned or rented furnaces were the economic powers to contend with in the second quarter of the twentieth century. Among the leaders of this new generation of salt merchants were several whose early careers had been spent as high-level managers for the large lineage-based firms. By the end of the 1920s, their former employers were deep in debt and no longer able to dominate the affairs of the salt-merchant community.[104] The new salt-yard elite would play an important role in reviving the salt industry, particularly after the Japanese invasion of eastern China made unoccupied China almost solely dependent on Sichuan salt. However, their interests would remain diversified in a way that the nineteenth-century integrated salt firms never were.

The great salt lineages of nineteenth-century Fu-Rong provide an important example of an early modern local elite whose dominance was based entirely on control of industrial and commercial wealth. The structures through which dominance was exercised were not unique to the salt yard, but rather they represented adapting universally available lineage institutions to the needs of locally based industry. The lineage trust integrated commercial and productive resources and, for a time at least, protected corporate industrial interests against the personal interests of individual family members. As such, the experience of the Fu-Rong lineage trusts represents an important transitional stage in China's early modern economic development. The lineage trust provided members of the Fu-Rong elite with economic advantages over smaller merchant operators, allowed a small number of firms to control a large portion of the labor market at the yard, and facilitated the exercise of traditional gentry roles. Even among those families with a history of degree and office holding, the salt business remained the focus of activity and the source of power and wealth.

Whereas changing economic conditions accompanying the Taiping invasion of eastern China helped propel the rise of an industrial elite in Fu-Rong, the political trauma that followed the fall of the Qing was a key element in its decline. The 1911 Revolution brought new opportunities for political participation and new threats to the markets won during the last years of imperial rule. For the twentieth-century salt-yard elite, the rules of the game had changed. Business relations became more complex, and the insecurity of trade under the post-Qing warlord regimes meant that few were willing or able to invest in the kinds of integrated salt empires that had been the strength of Fu-Rong merchants in the past. Politics now meant juggling a complex combination of ties to local warlords and militia chiefs, Guomindang officials, and officers of a Salt Inspectorate run under the auspices of foreign powers and a central government that had exerted little influence in local society. Business resources ceased to be sufficient determinants of status in the new Republican social arena. Even in this preeminently industrial Chinese city, access to these new political forces determined both business success and the maintenance of local elite dominance.

PART TWO

Local Elites in Transition

FOUR

From Comprador to County Magnate: Bourgeois Practice in the Wuxi County Silk Industry

Lynda S. Bell

One of the most difficult problems concerning local-elite roles in China during the late nineteenth and early twentieth century is the analysis of new industrial elites. Writing in the *Cambridge History of China*, Marie-Claire Bergère has presented one prevalent point of view on such men in Shanghai in the early decades of the twentieth century. Bergère argues that members of this group had the motivation necessary to develop a strong industrial order but lacked the government support necessary to accomplish their end. Chinese governments seemed more interested in taxing and controlling industrial enterprises than in developing sufficiently strong fiscal policies to support them. Moreover, as relative latecomers to industrial development, Chinese entrepreneurs depended on the world market to sell their new products, but they were unable to operate on an equal footing with their more advanced international competitors. As a result, China remained weak "as a nation" and failed to generate the necessary stage of "economic take-off."[1]

Although these last points suggest there may have been larger developmental dilemmas at work, the overwhelming impression left by Bergère's analysis is that the problems of China's modern industrialists were primarily political, as they dealt constantly with inept governments at home and aggressively dominant competitors abroad. These are significant issues, but to fully evaluate industrial elites I would argue that there is also a second set of problems to consider. These concern the socioeconomic position of such men, including their relationship to China's predominantly rural order.

Perhaps the easiest way to explore these equally important issues is to look at lower levels in China's economic hierarchy. The research I present here deals with events in a place of this type—Wuxi county, a semirural, semiurban district located inland from Shanghai, in the heart of the Jiangnan region.[2] Although there was no single critical event, the nineteenth and twentieth centuries were cumulatively a time of great change in Wuxi. Elites and peasants alike took part in changes in the local economy, including the introduction of modern technologies and participation in new international trade networks. Elsewhere I explore broader issues of economic development associated with these changes, but in this paper I am concerned particularly with new social relationships and stress how these were shaped by what I call "bourgeois practice."[3]

By using this concept, I try to pinpoint precisely what it meant to be bourgeois in early twentieth-century Wuxi. Industrialists' behavior included most activities that we associate with the bourgeoisie as defined in European or American contexts. They invested capital in industry, managed factories that employed wage labor, sold products in impersonal national and international markets, organized to promote their economic interests, and sought to influence officials in drawing up favorable economic regulations. But this was not the whole story of their bourgeois behavior. As we will see, new industrialists also built upon old patterns of economic and social dominance developed during Qing times by gentry-merchants of the Jiangnan region.

Given these observations, the twentieth-century industrialists of Wuxi may, in one sense, be considered hybrid types, somewhere between precapitalist merchants and the bourgeoisie of an advanced industrial society. Yet in another sense, they were also actors in a process that had no exact parallel in other national settings. This is why "practice" is also an integral part of my discussion. I use practice here in the sense that Pierre Bourdieu and Marshall Sahlins, among others, have used it. Bourdieu defines practice as social strategies that move through time, creating, recreating, or transforming hierarchical human relationships. Moreover, symbolic behavior is an important part of practice, constantly interacting with material life in different settings to shape unique patterns of dominance. Sahlins works from the same general assumptions but emphasizes that even in one culture practice does not always repeat itself. When historical circumstances change, evolving social strategies may fundamentally transform old patterns of dominance.[4]

Drawing on these discussions, I emphasize the unique historical process through which silk industrialists emerged in Wuxi and the ways in which they built their strategies of social and economic dominance. Members of this group did not accumulate wealth, power, and prestige through industrial investment alone; they also relied on elite-management activities and political styles developed in an earlier era. Moreover, behind relationships between new industrialists and peasants were significant changes in landlordism and the increasing importance of gentry-merchant roles within Jiangnan society. Because these developments had their roots in Qing times, I will begin by looking at the evolving nature of elite dominance in Jiangnan during that dynasty.

GENTRY DOMINANCE IN JIANGNAN DURING THE QING DYNASTY

The term Jiangnan means "south of the river," and it refers to the vast, rich expanse of alluvial plain situated on the central China coast at the mouth of the Yangzi River. This area, encompassing portions of southern Jiangsu and northern Zhejiang provinces, has a long history as one of China's most significant agricultural regions. Extensive development of Jiangnan began as early as the third century A.D., as the Han dynasty collapsed and nomadic tribes from the northern steppes began to push into China proper, setting off waves of southward migration that lasted for several centuries. In time, indigenous population growth combined with these patterns of immigration to make Jiangnan a densely settled and highly productive agricultural region. Accumulating wealth from agriculture fostered the development of commerce, cities, and intellectual life. Since the tenth century, a substantial proportion of successful examination candidates to staff China's sophisticated civil service administration came from the ranks of the Jiangnan elite.[5]

Although the agrarian development of Jiangnan was an ongoing, long-term process, crucial watersheds can also be identified. For the purposes of our analysis, we should pay careful attention to such a period in the seventeenth century, at the time of the Ming-Qing transition. The principal methods of achieving and maintaining elite status in Jiangnan in the late nineteenth century originated during this time. A brief review of the major findings of recent research on these issues will more sharply focus the interrelationships among changes in land tenure, patterns of commercialization, and new strategies for building local dominance.

A large literature deals with landholding patterns and changing land-tenure relationships in the late Ming and early Qing periods in Jiangnan. All the theoretical debates on the significance of these issues cannot be summarized here, so I will concentrate on the general contours of the process itself, something on which most scholars generally agree.[6] Landholding patterns during this important transitional period generally moved away from large estate-type holdings under the management of a single resident landlord toward small, fragmented holdings, farmed by relatively independent peasant households. Landlordism certainly did not disappear during the Qing period in Jiangnan, but it took on a significantly new form. There were several distinctive features of this new system: a high level of absentee proprietorship, with many of the largest landowning families moving permanently to urban settings; the collection of rent by bailiffs or later by organizations representing collective landlord interests known as "rent bursaries"; and finally, the shift from sharecropping practices to fixed rents, rent deposits, and permanent tenancy rights.[7]

On the one hand, it is possible to argue that the overall position of the peasantry improved during the development of this new pattern of land tenure and social relationships in Jiangnan. Growing commercialization reinforced the struggles of peasant farmers against various forms of legally defined servileness through which they won commoner status. Peasants also fought for owning "surface" rights to the land, a kind of permanent tenancy arrangement. By the eighteenth century, most land in Jiangnan had both "surface" and "subsoil" ownership rights. Landlords held the latter and hence had the right to collect rent on the land; tenants held a permanent claim to the former, in reality, a privilege to continuously use the land as long as rent payments were met. Both surface and subsoil rights could be freely bought and sold, so that, in any given locale, a complex and constantly changing pattern of land ownership emerged in which wealthier peasants benefited most. However, this system also made it increasingly difficult to dislodge any tenant farmer from his position as cultivator of a given parcel of land, and tenants as a group were now in a better position to resist rent payment when they judged a landlord's demands unreasonable. As a result, incidents of rent resistance increased as the period wore on.[8]

On the other hand, landlords responded to this situation with new methods of tenant coercion and control. For example, they increasingly required rent deposits, large lump-sum payments made at the beginning of a tenancy agreement. With the receipt of these deposits, landlords protected themselves from the possibility of rent default at a future date. As sharecropping gave way to fixed rental agreements, rent deposits also helped reestablish landlords' claims to shares of increasing surpluses generated by tenant farmers. Second, landlords benefited from a series of national tax reforms. Beginning in Ming times, these tax reforms involved the eventual merger of the land tax and converted cash corvée payments on individual, working-age males. By the eighteenth century, all taxes came only from landowners, causing local officials and landlords alike to view taxes as ultimately dependent on landlords' continuing ability to collect rent. The state thus had a clear interest in helping landlords resist rent default, using such means as sanctioning arrests of defaulters by the landlords' rent bursary organizations and incarcerating defaulting tenants in county-operated prisons.[9]

An important conclusion to be drawn from these observations on land tenure patterns is that both landlords and tenants developed new ways to assert their rights in the changing Jiangnan countryside. In the face of growing peasant independence, landlords struggled to assure their continued hold on elite status and, with state support, devised various new methods for doing so. A useful way to view this process has been suggested by Kathryn Bernhardt, who characterizes this trend as movement away from power built through tight patron-client relationships between individual landlords and their own tenants to a new more broadly based form of elite dominance that she calls "gentry hegemony." She uses this term not only to characterize the new situation in which the Qing state supported landlord economic rights vis-à-vis defaulting tenants but also to refer to a more generalized pattern of gentry dominance through active community leadership, in contrast with the previous more private and direct control of resident landlords over dependent peasants on their estate-type holdings. Under these new conditions, individual gentry members often took on new roles as organizers of communitywide irrigation projects and rural relief efforts. These activities further strengthened the elite's growing tendency to undertake multiple, nonparticularistic leadership roles, designed to enhance both community development and local social control.[10]

We have thus seen that new styles of gentry leadership emerged in Jiangnan against the backdrop of important changes in land tenure and shifts in relationships among elites, the state, and rural society at large. As a final step, we must also consider two other equally significant trends—the commercialization of Jiangnan's rural economy during Qing times and the continued expansion of elite functions via gentry-merchant roles.

The general contours of late imperial commercialization in Jiangnan are well known. As population increased, land productivity also improved, a process fueled by development of a wide range of labor intensive agricultural techniques. Peasants further enhanced land productivity through localized crop specialization; for example, they converted portions of land from grain production to cash crops, such as cotton or mulberry trees to feed silkworms. These developments also spurred the growth of peasant household-based cottage industries, especially cotton and silk yarns and textiles. By the eighteenth century, these converging trends in population growth and commercialization resulted in Jiangsu and Zhejiang provinces becoming grain deficient. To pay for grain imports, Jiangnan sold its handicraft products outside the region, contributing to the nationwide escalation of long-distance, interregional trade.[11]

Within this evolving economic context, the possibility for individuals to accumulate private fortunes through commerce multiplied. In addition to long-distance trade, commercialization led to widely dispersed marketing within the Jiangnan countryside, with permanent, intermediate-level marketing centers emerging.[12] At this lower level of the economic hierarchy, locally important gentry families began to assume new merchant roles. Ping-ti Ho has presented evidence, for example, that local "official" families in Jiangnan engaged increasingly in commerce throughout the Qing period.[13] As Mary Rankin has further demonstrated, by the late nineteenth century, this strategy was widely used in many Jiangnan locales, as commercial and manufacturing opportunities grew at an even more dizzying pace.[14] Moreover, this volume's essays by William Rowe and Madeleine Zelin suggest that such gentry strategizing was an empirewide phenomenon, emerging during Qing times in commercialized areas of Hubei and Sichuan as well.

Overall, then, the changing nature of landlordism, the proliferation of state-sanctioned elite management of community-oriented public institutions, and the development of gentry-merchant roles created a complex and highly diversified pattern of expanding elite functions during the late imperial period. However, we should also underscore that throughout this process achieving degree-holding rank—the legitimate claim to gentry status—remained the ultimate mark of social pedigree within the system as a whole. Perhaps the best evidence to support this claim is that men who made their initial fortunes through commerce either continued to purchase degrees or provided classical educations for family members who might eventually succeed in the more regular examination route to degree-holding status.[15] Thus commercial wealth was one way to bolster family fortunes but was insufficient in and of itself to legitimate elite status. Although it was now possible to enter the informally defined, lower ranks of elite society through activities geared toward local development and social control, these patterns of social change had not produced an alternative to gentry degree holding as the principal criterion for upper-elite status. For instance, the type of gentry networks and associational activities that Timothy Brook describes in this volume for Ningbo persisted throughout Jiangnan during Qing times, despite the growing interest in trade among many gentry members.

The result of this particular trajectory of regional social change in Jiangnan was that, as elite functions diversified, they also tended to concentrate within a relatively small number of degree-holding or potential degree-holding families. Late Qing local histories often refer to a strata of local notables known as *shendong*, a term we usually translate as "gentry managers." Everyone could identify these men—a small core of local leaders with power to mobilize their communities at large for any and all forms of social, political, or economic activity. Many gentry managers were degree holders, but this was not an absolute prerequisite for entry into this locally defined functional elite. Literacy and wealth seemed far more important, yet most wealthy, literate families also aspired to have, or already had, a member with degree-holding status. Thus, our picture of local-level elite society in late Qing Jiangnan is that of domination by a small, self-contained group of prominent families, engaged not only in landownership and degree seeking but also in assuming a multitude of new local managerial roles.[16]

COMMERCIALIZATION AND THE WUXI COUNTY ELITE

When industrialists appeared on the local scene in Wuxi in the late nineteenth century, they built upon elite strategies already at work, developing their bourgeois practice by combining leadership of new industrial enterprises with other forms of local social management. A brief look at commercialization in Wuxi will provide a clearer picture of how the local socioeconomic environment fostered this trend.

The eighteenth century was a period of substantial commercial development in Wuxi. The main impetus came from two sources: Wuxi's role as a key marketing center in the growing interregional rice trade and the involvement of local peasants in cotton textile production. We have already seen the general contours of the rice trade for Jiangnan as a whole, so it remains only to point out that Wuxi became a major transshipment point for rice within Jiangnan during the eighteenth century. Strategic positioning made this development possible. Not only did Wuxi sit on the northern shore of Lake Tai, a major transport link between southern Jiangsu and northern Zhejiang, but the Grand Canal also passed directly through the middle of the county, only a few kilometers south of its confluence with the Yangzi. Many smaller canals and rivers also converged in Wuxi, making it one of the best water-based transport hubs in the entire Jiangnan region.[17] Rice imports came down the Yangzi River to feed Jiangnan's burgeoning population, and requisitions of "tribute grain," a supplementary tax assessment levied on central China's most prosperous rice-producing provinces, also passed through Wuxi on their way north via the Grand Canal to Beijing. The combination of these two trends led to a substantial rice market in Wuxi, where officials responsible for meeting tribute grain quotas as well as merchants involved in the long-distance rice trade congregated.[18]

Concomitant with these developments in the rice trade, peasants in Wuxi also began to produce cotton textiles for market. Although it is difficult to map this trend with any great precision, population growth probably contributed to this new stage of intensified labor efforts by Wuxi peasant households. Throughout Jiangsu as a whole, population doubled from the early eighteenth through the early nineteenth century, and gazetteer figures suggest that the rate of growth may have been even faster in Wuxi.[19] In response to both declining land-per-person ratios and the increasing need to purchase additional grain supplies, many peasant families in Wuxi began to spin and weave cotton during slack agricultural periods to make goods that they could sell at market or keep for home use and pawn when money was needed. Although Wuxi peasants did not grow cotton themselve   cotton imported from surrounding counties provided the raw materials necessary for this new sideline activity.[20]

Trade in rice and cotton provided two key components of countywide trends in commercializing Wuxi during the eighteenth century. Not entirely clear, however, is exactly when gentry members began to participate in merchant activity. Jerry Dennerline has gathered evidence in the form of local folklore suggesting that gentry members began to sponsor market-town development in southeastern Wuxi as early as the sixteenth century. Dennerline also points out that even rather small landlords developed local granaries and sold their surplus rice at market.[21] In lieu of more comprehensive work on merchant communities in Wuxi during Qing times, Dennerline's observations allow us to suggest that as population grew and land available for purchase declined, even before the eighteenth century some gentry families turned to commerce as a supplement to their land-based income-earning capacity.

To enhance their long-term staying power in a rapidly changing economic environment, prominent families also built lineage organizations, a trend that seems to have gained momentum in Wuxi during the eighteenth century. Again, Dennerline's work gives us some insight into this process. Branches of the Hua and Qian families, living in the vicinity of the important market town of Dangkou, each organized lineage-based charitable estates in the eighteenth century, pooling some wealth from several agnatic kinsmen. On the one hand, these estates built their corporate presence by purchasing land that then became the permanent property of the estate. At least in part, this was a response to the problems generated by increasing population, partible inheritance, and a rapidly evolving land market. From the viewpoint of those lineage members who were also part of the local gentry-elite, a corporate estate provided a means to keep ownership of a core of landed property within the control of a kinship-based group that they themselves could lead. On the other hand, these estates provided local charity and relief, enhancing the moral reputation of local lineage leaders.[22]

In the nineteenth century, as subordinate branches of the original Qian and Hua lineages began planning to organize their own charitable estates, a new strategic twist materialized. A group of Huas in Dangkou who wished to found a new estate had no degree holders among them; instead, they were "local merchants, manufacturers, and purveyors of the wine and soy sauce for which Dangkou was known."[23] However, by the time that Hua Hongmo, son of one of the original four brothers who had proposed the estate had formally organized it in 1873, Hongmo himself had passed the prefectural and provincial examinations. Under his directorship, the "New Hua charitable estate" amassed landholdings of nearly four thousand *mu* (one *mu* = one-sixth acre) but also developed an important new method for increasing its corporate wealth. Hua Hongmo's own private rice warehouses in Wuxi city were turned over to the charitable estate, thereby "channeling revenues earned from storing the grain of inland merchants en route to Shanghai into the Huas' Dangkou projects."[24] Thus, in Hua Hongmo, we have a classic case of how multiple roles in social management built elite position. Not only did Hongmo seek and receive degree-holding status, but he also fashioned his local career through managing substantial landholdings on behalf of his lineage organization. Meanwhile, he made a private fortune via the increasingly lucrative Wuxi grain trade. By turning his warehouses over to the charitable estate, he assured that the source of this fortune would not be divided among his heirs upon his death but would remain intact, a means to promote the economic well-being and local prestige of the Dangkou Huas at large.

This was the tradition of elite strategizing, increasingly merging careers in commerce, scholarship, and gentry management, into which local industrialists entered in late-nineteenth-century Wuxi. We should turn now to that story itself—the world of the local silk industry elite.

THE ORIGINS OF BOURGEOIS PRACTICE

The late nineteenth century was a tumultuous time in China. To analyze elite roles in industrial development, at least three major events must be noted. These are the Opium War (1839–42), the Taiping Rebellion (1851–65), and the New Policy reforms (1902–11). Trends set in motion by these events had a substantial impact on the economic activities and political orientation of Jiangnan local elites.

Of these events, perhaps the relationship between our story and the Opium War is most obvious. The Treaty of Nanking, signed at the conclusion of this war, made Shanghai one of five "treaty ports" open to foreign business and trade. This marked the beginning of Shanghai's development as a major new commercial city as well as China's most important center of new-style industry. Early industrial efforts were usually financed with foreign venture capital, but Chinese investors soon became active as well. By the turn of the twentieth century, a large proportion of Shanghai's new industry was Chinese-owned. Moreover, by that time, a kind of "spin-off" effect was also at work: men who began their careers as comprador agents for foreign firms in Shanghai began to return to their homes to develop industry there as well.

The relationship of the Taiping Rebellion to the story of industrial elites in Jiangnan is at first glance, not so apparent. However, for Wuxi, the Taiping period marked a crucial watershed for evolving gentry management in the Jiangnan region. Because wartime devastation in many Jiangnan locales had been so severe, rural rehabilitation efforts led by gentry members were essential in the post-Taiping period. The pace of gentry management escalated, and its scope expanded; thus, in many places, new patterns of commerce and industry also became part of overall plans for the region's economic reconstruction.

To complete our picture of shifts in elite behavior during these years, we must also consider the political impact of the New Policy reforms. These reforms marked a critical period in rethinking political structures, especially at the local level, and had important ramifications for the range of political activity undertaken by local elites. Perhaps the most important events within the context of the reforms were abolishing the examination system in 1905 and restructuring local-level recruitment into political service. Provincial assemblies and local "self-government" bureaus now served as recruiting grounds for men to move into higher levels of government service. However, locally based, interest group–oriented organizations, including merchants' and industrialists' guilds, which had increased throughout the Qing, and chambers of commerce, which appeared in the New Policies period, also emerged at the local level. As commercialization and industrialization escalated, these sorts of organizations developed in many locales, serving as vehicles of self-regulation and self-protection for local businesses and also acting as collection agencies for commercial and industrial taxes. With the New Policy reforms, these organizations received official sanction to undertake new quasi-governmental roles.

Clearly, these major events of the late-nineteenth and early-twentieth centuries affected local elite behavior, especially in the rapidly developing Jiangnan region. However, it is difficult to assess exactly how these new developments differed from past elite activity. A case study based on one industry in a single locale cannot provide a definitive answer. However, the silk industrialists of Wuxi are an important example because they represent a group at the forefront of the most advanced types of local-level change, both economic and political, during this period.

Based on what we will see of the activities of the silk industry elite in Wuxi, I will argue that even the most progressive industrialist among them, Xue Shouxuan, built upon previous patterns of elite behavior to create a familiar style of local dominance. Because he used commercial links to the peasantry to build a fully integrated silk industry, the continuation of a peasant family–based rural order dominated by local elites was essential to his goals. In the political sphere, although the examination system had long since been eliminated, we will see that Xue also continued to build upon local practices linked to gentry management, constructing his own network of personal political relationships from the county level upward. Despite these continuities, Xue's behavior differed in its content. The kind of commerce he promoted brought the peasantry into an international marketing system for raw silk, and his filatures used the most advanced technology and management practices available. His total repertoire of economic and political activities thus assumed a hybrid form as they grew out of and built upon existing patterns of local social dominance. The results of this combination were powerful. Industrial development resulted in a high degree of commercial dependency among the peasantry, as Xue built a system of economic control that was unusually tight, even by Jiangnan standards. To make these arguments, I must begin with the early stages of silk industry development in Wuxi, namely the establishment of commercial links between local elites and peasantry via the cocoon-marketing system.

GENTRY, PEASANTS, AND COMPRADORS IN EARLY
WUXI SILK PRODUCTION

Two principal activities occurred in the first stages of silk industry development in Wuxi. First, peasants switched from cotton handicraft production and began to raise mulberries and rear cocoons for sale to Shanghai's new steam-powered silk filatures. Second, comprador agents began to establish commercial firms that acted as cocoon purchasing agents for Shanghai filatures. Cocoon marketing was based not only in Wuxi but also in other areas new to sericulture, including several counties to its west and north.[25] However, because Wuxi was so favorably located in terms of water transport and had such extensively developed commercial networks, it emerged as the most important point of both new cocoon production and trade within the Lower Yangzi region.[26]

The introduction of sericulture and the development of the comprador-based cocoon-marketing system were inseparably linked in Wuxi; both developed through encouragement and initiative of members of the local gentry elite. To demonstrate these linkages, we must turn now to a step-by-step breakdown of the early years of silk production in Wuxi. Elsewhere, I explore in detail the motivations of the Wuxi peasantry for engaging in sericulture.[27] Here, I emphasize the local gentry's role at each stage of silk industry development.

Sericulture Promotion in the Post-Taiping Period. In the decades following the Taiping Rebellion, many counties in the Lower Yangzi region required substantial agricultural rehabilitation and development. Wuxi fell within the area hardest hit by depopulation through death, flight, and agricultural devastation.[28] Local gentry members were concerned that land be resettled and that peasants become productive again as rapidly as possible. These plans were usually rationalized through typical Confucian morality. Simply, it was the duty of elites to promote the people's livelihood following a period of social and economic upheaval. However, reconstruction also made good economic sense because both tax and rent collection depended upon a fully flourishing agrarian sector. Such elite efforts were not unique to Wuxi; Mary Rankin has detailed the general parameters of agrarian rehabilitation of Taiping-devastated counties in northern Zhejiang and has demonstrated that these conditions allowed increased elite management activity throughout Jiangnan in the latter decades of the nineteenth century.[29]

An important aspect of post-Taiping rehabilitation in Wuxi was the introduction of sericulture. Although Wuxi bordered the traditional silk handicraft areas of southern Jiangsu and northern Zhejiang, there had been no substantial mulberry cultivation prior to the Taiping period.[30] This situation changed rapidly after 1870, with the development of the new Shanghai-based filature industry. Under these circumstances, gentry members, behaving as traditional elites promoting agricultural improvement, introduced a substantially new form of mulberry cultivation. In contrast to the older sericulture districts south of Wuxi, where mulberry trees were grown on scattered embankments between rice fields, gentry members in Wuxi now encouraged cultivation in relatively large tracts.[31] Moreover, these gentry-sponsored innovations linked the peasants who cultivated these trees to a new chain of production relationships, dependent ultimately on the Shanghai trading sphere and the international market for Chinese filature silk.

Memoirs of two elite members of Wuxi society discuss how they promoted new-style sericulture. The first case is Yan Ziqing, a Wuxi native, who had served as a county magistrate in Shaanxi province. Yan returned to his native town of Zhaimen in the northeastern Wuxi subdistrict of Huaishang in 1871. A posthumous collection of his writings records that one of his first projects upon returning home was to import three thousand mulberry saplings from Jiaxing county in Zhejiang, an area long famous for sericulture and the production of handicraft silk. Yan had these saplings planted on a thirty-*mu* plot and erected a large residence next to it. He proclaimed his hopes for the success of this endeavor with a stone engraving above the door of the residence, calling it the "Cottage for the Study of Mulberry Cultivation."[32] The second case is Hua Guanyi, designated simply as a "large landowner." In a letter written to his daughter-in-law in 1873, Hua recounts the planting of three thousand mulberry saplings on fifteen *mu* of land. He also discusses the importance of establishing the ideal ratio of trees to land, in the case of his land, about 230 to 240 trees per *mu*. At this ratio, Hua knew that peasants could harvest about twenty *jin* of leaves per tree (one *jin* = one-half kilogram) and that each *jin* could be sold for 1.30 to 1.40 Chinese *yuan* (dollars).[33]

Due to the efforts of men like Yan and Hua, sericulture spread rapidly in Wuxi during the next several decades. In the 1881 revised version of an important Wuxi gazetteer, a new entry for silk added to the category of local products stated:

> In the past, silk was produced only in the subdistrict of Kaihua. From the early years of the Tongzhi reign period [1862–74], conditions have been in flux with much vacant land and many people [coming to resettle it]. This has created an ideal situation in which to begin the planting of mulberries and the rearing of silkworms. Sericulture has begun to flourish, and has spread to every subdistrict.[34]

By the 1920s, one-third of all arable land in Wuxi was devoted to mulberry, and virtually all peasant families were involved in cocoon rearing as a subsidiary cash-earning occupation.[35] Despite the positive gentry role in promoting sericulture, elite efforts alone did not cause this dramatic shift in agrarian production patterns. Factors related to the structure of peasant farming in Wuxi were also at work, helping to rapidly integrate sericulture into the overall peasant family work effort.

Sericulture and Small-Peasant-Family Farming. The overriding consideration for Wuxi peasants when they opted for sericulture was the promise of sub-stantial cash earnings.[36] In turn, this search for new income led them into a new form of dependence on the marketplace and the elites who controlled it. Detailed data from three villages in the early twentieth-century countryside in Wuxi demonstrate that peasant families relied on sericulture for at least 50 percent of their families' cash incomes.[37] In the 1930s, such income was essential to maintain basic peasant livelihood in Wuxi because rice and wheat farming alone was insufficient to feed the existing rural population. Nearly all peasant families purchased grain to supplement their own produc-tion of rice and wheat and they needed cash income from cocoon sales and other subsidiary occupations to do so.[38]

Behind these circumstances were factors traceable to the situation in the post-Taiping Wuxi countryside. Population statistics reveal that Wuxi lost as many as one-half to two-thirds of its people during the Taiping period.[39] However, repopulation was rapid in the immediate post-Taiping years, given Wuxi's reputation as a rich agricultural region; this proved a powerful pull for in-migration from surrounding counties. Especially likely to immigrate were peasants from north of the Yangzi, an area much less fertile and productive than counties south of the river.[40] Moreover, peasant farming families were also drawn to Wuxi by the attractive opportunity to earn cash through cocoon rearing. Via such subsidiary work, they could use the chronically underemployed labor power of peasant women to boost living standards and long-term prospects for economic well-being.[41] By the 1920s, Wuxi's population had been restored to pre-Taiping levels, resulting in the second highest person per land ratio in all Jiangsu, with 1.29 people per *mu* of available farming land.[42]

Ironically, the rapid repopulation of Wuxi under conditions of sericulture expansion undermined peasant expectations for new levels of prosperity. In three villages for which we have extensive household data, the average size of farming units was only 2.54 *mu* in 1940, approximately one-half acre.[43] Because landholdings were small, peasants depended on cash income from cocoon sales to purchase additional grain. Although they were able to augment their grain supplies in this way, these peasants, on average, still fell only within the lower range of grain consumption patterns observed throughout China as a whole.[44] Moreover, there was no guarantee that potentially pro-fitable sericulture would always provide even this rather basic level of secu-rity. Climatic conditions in Wuxi constantly worked against the peasantry's cocoon rearing efforts.[45] Frequent rain and high humidity during spring and

summer often wreaked havoc with silkworm crops, causing bacterial infec-
tions to grow at a rapid rate and wiping out the entire season's efforts. Facing
these conditions, peasants in Wuxi, who had enjoyed favorable land-tenure
conditions during the labor shortage of the post-Taiping years, gradually fell
into patterns of subordination typical of poor peasant life—often mortgaging
their land and seeking loans from wealthier members of their communities.[46]

Thus by the early decades of the twentieth century, Wuxi peasants had
replaced cotton cloth production with sericulture. In their hopes for prosperity, they actually committed themselves to continuing sericulture to ensure
their basic subsistence. This situation created a new form of dependence
between peasant farming households and the Shanghai-based filature industry. Commercial dependency in this new form was a step beyond what
peasants had experienced before. Not only was sericulture a relatively risky
enterprise ecologically, but it also put them in contact with the international
luxury market for raw silk. They were therefore subjected to boom-bust cycles
of demand over which neither they nor Chinese filature owners had much
control. At the local level, this relationship between peasants and filatures
was mediated by a new cocoon-marketing system, run by elites who did business in Shanghai but who, in many cases, came originally from Wuxi.

Development of the Cocoon-Marketing System. Cocoon *hang* were merchant
firms that purchased cocoons from peasants on a contractual basis for early
Shanghai filatures. Cocoon firm facilities consisted of a building or set of
buildings in which cocoons were gathered twice a year, in spring and fall,
and then dried before shipment to their final filature destination. The firms
operated in market towns, buying cocoons from peasants living in villages
that fell within the town's marketing scope.[47] In Wuxi, cocoon firms were
first organized in the 1880s, making use of Wuxi's position at the center of an
extensive canal and river system, which proved ideal for cocoon transport.
After 1904, with the completion of the Shanghai-Nanjing railway as far inland as Wuxi, the firms developed at an even more rapid rate. By 1909, Wuxi
had seventy to eighty cocoon firms. British, American, Italian, and Japanese
firms all sent comprador agents to Wuxi, with the Japanese firm of Mitsui, as
well as the British firm of Jardine, Matheson, and Company, among the
earliest promoters of cocoon-marketing activity.[48]

The careers of four early cocoon firm agents demonstrate how Wuxi men
with important ties to new urban-based commercial networks developed this
enterprise. These men were Zhou Shunqing, a newly rising man of comprador backgound; Xue Nanming, son of the nationally prominent upper-degree
holder, Xue Fucheng; and, finally, Rong Zongjing and Rong Desheng,
brothers who started their careers in commerical positions established by
their father and who became two of China's most important new industrialists.

Zhou Shunqing made his initial fortune as a comprador in the Chinese iron industry. Working first as manager of the British-backed Shengchang iron brokerage firm, he later became sole owner of the firm and opened branch operations in several cities. Zhou then began to follow more traditional routes to elite status. First, he purchased official rank through a personal contact he cultivated with an uncle of the Guangxu emperor. Through this connection, Zhou solicited deposits from members of the imperial court to found one of China's first modern banks, the Xincheng, with branches in Beijing, Tianjin, Nanjing, and Wuxi. When the dynasty fell, the bank closed, and depositors lost 4 million *yuan*; yet Zhou survived the crisis, salvaging private reserves of 1.2 million *yuan*. Second, with his profits in comprador and banking activity, Zhou entered more traditional forms of elite activity, becoming a large-scale landowner in his home county. In the name of his lineage organization, he bought more than three thousand *mu* of land at very low prices from peasants forced to sell in the drought-plagued northeastern section of Wuxi. He also purchased land for himself in the vicinity of his native village of Dongze in the southern part of the county, an important new sericulture district. He then single-handedly turned Dongze into a bustling market town by building facilities for shops, various local marketing firms, and pawnshops. He called his new creation Zhouxin *zhen*—"Zhou's new market"—and built Wuxi's first silk filature there in 1904. Among his many early business ventures in Wuxi, Zhou operated seventeen cocoon firms.[49]

While Zhou's career began with comprador activity and led into more traditional, locally based elite activity, Xue Nanming's career took the reverse route. Born into a bureaucratic, landholding family, only later in life did Xue invest in new commercial and industrial ventures. Xue's father was Xue Fucheng, a holder of the highest level *jinshi* degree, who had achieved national prestige and position in late Qing times, serving first as adviser to Zeng Guofan and later as ambassador to England, France, Italy, and Belgium. Xue Fucheng, a substantial landholder, also owned a large private granary. Xue Nanming began his own prestigious career in 1888, when Li Hongzhang appointed him to serve in Tianjin as a judge in court cases between foreigners and Chinese citizens. However, upon the death of his father in 1894, he returned to Wuxi and subsequently declined to resume office in Tianjin. Beginning in the late 1890s, Xue Nanming concentrated his efforts on the family's landholdings and new investments in silk production. In 1896, he collaborated with Zhou Shunqing in a brief filature venture in Shanghai. During this period, he also established ten-odd cocoon firms on behalf of Italian filatures.[50]

The Rong brothers had more modest claims to traditional forms of elite prestige. However, they, too, chose Wuxi as a primary base for new-style investment activity after sojourning careers in commerce. Their father, owning only about ten *mu* of land, furthered family fortunes by traveling to

Guangdong in 1883, where a relative working in Zhang Zhidong's administration helped him become a collector in two different locations for new *lijin*,
transit taxes on internal trade. He sent his elder son, Zongjing, to Shanghai
at age seven to study in a firm manufacturing iron anchors. Soon after he
arrived, Zongjing fell ill and returned home, but at age fifteen he went again
to Shanghai to study old-style banking. He subsequently was a collection
agent in Shanghai until the company for which he worked suffered financial
difficulties at the time of the Sino-Japanese war. The younger son, Desheng,
was apprenticed to a Shanghai old-style bank, and later worked under his
father in the Guangdong Sanshui *lijin* bureau. Father and son returned to
Wuxi in 1895, but in 1899, Rong Desheng briefly returned to Guangdong as
an accountant in the provincial tax bureau. In 1900, he returned once again
to Shanghai. At that point, he worked in an old-style bank that he and Zongjing had founded in 1896. Rong Desheng also set up a branch of this bank in
Wuxi. Together, the brothers established several cocoon firms with funds
borrowed from the Wuxi branch bank, on which they paid no interest as
owners. They favored their native market town of Rongxiang *zhen* as the
location for their first cocoon firm ventures.[51]

As the first cocoon firm agents in Wuxi, Zhou, Xue, and the Rong
brothers set the stage for the pursuit of business practices that would become
increasingly bourgeois. Within a matter of years, each became an industrialist, although not necessarily a filaturist. Zhou and Xue took this route,
but the Rongs organized flour processing plants and cotton mills. For our
evolving analysis of silk industry elites, most important at this stage is that
as comprador agents for the cocoon trade they first combined old-style commercial management with new content: filature-solicited cocoon marketing.
As they did so, they set an important precedent for other elites who followed.
By expanding their economic activities at home to take advantage of changing times, they established the cocoon-marketing system, an important new
commercial network with which all Wuxi peasants would eventually reckon.

INDUSTRY, COCOON FIRMS, AND GENTRY-MERCHANT ROLES

Comprador agents with ties to Shanghai initiated cocoon marketing, but
without the cooperation of lower-ranking members of the elite social hierarchy in Wuxi cocoon firms could not have been established. These firms
needed managers familiar with local marketing conditions who would actually supervise the purchase of cocoons from peasants and oversee the first
stages of cocoon processing. Through contractual arrangements with such
men, comprador agents could assure the effective organization of cocoon
marketing. As the years passed and filatures were built in both Wuxi and
Shanghai, compradors became less important, and local cocoon firm owners
became predominant in the Wuxi cocoon-marketing system.

The activities of Wuxi cocoon firm owners are significant for exploring the expanding role of local elites in the course of silk industry development. These men not only ran cocoon-marketing establishments but also formed the core of a new political organization, the cocoon merchants' *gongsuo*, or guild, which played an important role in both local and provincial politics.[52] In these capacities, members of the Wuxi local elite became progressively more bourgeois, while also using traditional styles of gentry management to build the cocoon-marketing network.

It is difficult to determine the precise social origins of cocoon firm owners in Wuxi, but a few general descriptions of their backgrounds do survive. Japanese investigators visited cocoon-marketing sites in Jiangsu in 1916 and described the owners of cocoon firms as "local wine-makers or wealthy men."[53] While these designations are somewhat vague, they suggest the sorts of local gentry-merchants previously engaged in an expanding array of commercial and managerial activities within their home locales. These men were ideal candidates for cocoon firm investment—close enough to rural marketing structures to be able to tap immediately into the system, but worth enough financially to afford the initial venture. The Japanese researchers further observed that to build the largest and most up-to-date cocoon firm facilities in the late teens took an investment of "several tens of thousands of *yuan.*"[54] Although this figure was probably inflated, it clearly implied that only men of some substance at the local level could either have invested money for such a venture or have been in a position to borrow funds to support it.[55]

Local men of economic substance were solicited by comprador agents via a complex contracting system to build and operate cocoon-marketing facilities.[56] A surviving cocoon firm contract from 1887 demonstrates the dimensions of such a relationship between comprador and local cocoon firm owner. This contract—between two individuals, Gu Mianfu, a comprador agent dispatched from Shanghai, and Sun Boyu, a local Luoshe landlord—served as the legal basis of operation of the Renchang cocoon firm with three sites in Luoshe *zhen*, a major market town in the northwestern part of Wuxi. The signing of the contract was witnessed by a county official so that it could also serve as the official license, establishing local government recognition of the business and sanctioning its operation.[57]

Ideally, we would like to know how much land Sun owned and what role cocoon marketing played in his overall economic situation in order to place him more precisely in the local social hierarchy. But profiles for nondegree-holding local notables like Sun are more difficult to develop than for men of higher social standing. The identification of Sun as a landlord at the market-town level came via independent discussions with two informants who had known Sun's son in the early 1960s. The informants, men with extensive experience of their own in the Jiangnan silk industry, insisted that men like

Sun Boyu, a landholder who also had commercial interests centered in his market-town environment, were the main builders of cocoon-marketing facilities.[58] An article published later by one of these informants stated that cocoon firm owners were men of "local gentry standing."[59]

As the economic power of cocoon firm owners grew, so, too, did their need for political organization to protect and develop their evolving interests. They responded by organizing the cocoon merchant guild, an organization that performed the all-important task of "self-regulation," imposing basic rules governing the conduct of the cocoon trade in Wuxi and acting as a self-collection agency for new tax revenues. The second form of guild activity was "self-protection," an area that could be further subdivided into three main protections: from other merchants who bought cocoons in the region; from the consequences of adverse government policies; and from the wrath of unhappy peasants when prices or other aspects of the cocoon-marketing process did not meet with their satisfaction. Given the breadth of these activities, I will concentrate here on only two aspects: the social origins and economic activities of guild managers, and their resulting relationships with the peasantry.[60]

There was at least one precursor of the countywide cocoon merchant guild—the *wenshe*, or "culture association," of Kaihua subdistrict. Although this name is often translated as "literary society," I believe the translation "culture association" comes closer to its organizers' original intent to promote and enhance the general culture, broadly defined. Clearly, the name also had symbolic value, drawing upon what Pierre Bourdieu would call the "symbolic capital" of gentry culture.[61] By using this name, gentry managers marked themselves as men of refined social status who also were interested in serving society at large via such organizations. The designation "culture association" was commonly chosen by gentry managers for their locally run community-service organizations, but in the early twentieth century its symbolic significance could also be used to enhance the legitimacy of entirely new activities.[62] For example, a core group of Republican army officers who began the 1911 Revolution in Wuhan also called themselves a "culture association." Likewise, the first seven members of the Kaihua group were still firmly within the gentry-literati social world—all held the lowest examination degree of *shengyuan*—but the association's main tasks revolved around newly developing cocoon-marketing activities within the subdistrict.

The economic activities of the Kaihua Culture Association began informally in the early 1880s, with the seven *sheng-yuan* acting as troubleshooters of a sort, paying visits to the parties involved in disputes and suggesting ways of resolving problems that had arisen. One such issue involved a dispute between a local cocoon merchant and peasants over prices; a second involved setting the licensing fee for cocoon firms so that it would be on a par with the fee already existing for handicraft silk-buying establishments in the area.

They also had the capacity to solicit local government support for their efforts and summoned official county militia to assist cocoon firm owners in dealing with unruly peasants. Once these sorts of state-backed military actions materialized at the behest of Culture Association members, peasants realized, much to their initial surprise, that local gentry planned to use traditional means of coercion to promote a commercial activity as new and strange as cocoon marketing. Local peasants sometimes referred to these men as *yangshang*, "foreign merchants," a reflection of their growing awareness of the complex intertwining of old-style gentry managerial functions, elite-peasant marketing relationships, and the new international market for Chinese filature silk.[63]

In 1886, the Kaihua Culture Association received county government recognition as the principal organization within the subdistrict involved in the regulation and protection of the cocoon trade. The original seven *shengyuan* formed its core managerial group, retaining their troubleshooting function and becoming the official tax collectors for *lijin* charges on the cocoon trade. There were now more than twenty members, including a clerical staff of an accountant, a manager, and a secretary. The core group of seven, headed by *shengyuan* Zhuang Hao, continued to make major decisions affecting cocoon marketing.[64]

The Kaihua Culture Association set important precedents for elite organizing to develop and defend local cocoon-marketing networks. In the 1890s, this kind of activity spread throughout the county, as Shanghai and Wuxi merchants involved in cocoon firms began to meet during the spring cocoon-marketing period. At Shijinshan temple, located in a northwest suburb of Wuxi city, they decided matters related to cocoon marketing. Following a decade or so of such meetings, a countywide cocoon merchant guild was formed in 1902, with a permanent office at the temple.[65] With this act, although they abandoned the literati-linked symbolism of the culture association, the members of the successor cocoon merchant guild substituted an obvious symbol of spiritual authority of still greater significance to the community at large: their temple-based guild organization thus underscored the legitimacy of their new commercial roles. Once again, in Pierre Bourdieu's terms, this move was a skillful use of "symbolic capital"—a means to convey their own moral consensus that cocoon marketing was good for the community and, crucially, that they were the ones controlling it.

In subsequent years, the seasonal regulation of cocoon-marketing operations became the task of guild managers, a hired staff who actually ran the organization. As in the case of the Kaihua Culture Association, the newly founded guild chose its managers from the ranks of gentry society. The first permanent manager of the countywide guild was Sun Xunchu, who soon thereafter left Wuxi to begin a tour of duty as an official in Hubei province. The guild then selected Zhang Dingan as its new manager. Zhang was son-in-law of Zhou Shunqing, the comprador-turned-degree holder from Kaihua subdistrict already noted as a comprador agent involved in early cocoon firm development. Zhang Dingan managed various commercial endeavors in Zhouxin *zhen*, the location of Zhou Shunqing's new silk filature, cocoon firms, and pawn shops. Zhang was also the headmaster of a special school organized by Zhou to teach business skills. Upon Zhang's death, *shengyuan* Hua Zhisan became guild manager. Thus, among the first three managers of the Wuxi cocoon merchant guild, two were lower gentry and one had family ties to Zhou Shunqing, a rapidly rising figure in the upper tiers of elite society.[66]

Gentry managers of the cocoon merchant guild in Wuxi also developed their links to county government, carrying out basic licensing and tax collection activities on its behalf.[67] With state support, guild managers organized ever more elaborate systems of protection for the cocoon firm network. To this end, a primary duty of guild managers was to prepare formal petitions each spring to the county and provincial governments, asking for naval police to protect boats used for cocoon and silver cash transport.[68] Although such protection was essential to guard against random banditry, we have seen that armed force could have a significant psychological effect on the peasantry. As in the case of the Kaihua Culture Association, when local gentry summoned county militia to defend cocoon firm interests, the cocoon merchant guild continued to rely upon the coercive force of government to extend the power and influence of the cocoon-marketing system.

Although few accounts of the actual marketing process survive, those extant confirm the growing power of cocoon firms backed by their guild organization. The following description of a cocoon-marketing situation in Wuxi is taken from an English translation of a Chinese journalist's account:

> At the time when cocoon collecting was at its height, the cocoon collectors deliberately spread rumours of political unrest, impending civil war, slump in cocoon prices and even suspension of cocoon collection. These rumours were quite sufficient to trap the peasants, but there were also many other ways by which the collectors could get the better of the peasants. The peasants often had to bring their cocoons a long distance to the door of the collectors and, in spite of the crowd, the collectors would delay weighing for many hours. During the weighing the collectors would sham depression and poor business, thus deliberately lowering collection prices. Finally the peasants, exhausted by fatigue and hunger from early dawn, were forced to beg in pitiful tones for a little better price, which when granted only meant about ten or twenty cents extra. In addition, the Chinese system of "big" and "small" money [that is, silver and copper cash], gave the collectors a further opportunity to cheat the peasantry [through manipulation of the exchange rate]. At the end of the day there would still be peasants who had not sold their cocoons. They often made a great noise cursing the collectors, calling for fire from heaven, without realizing that the

collectors' property was insured and that such a burning would be of actual benefit to the collectors.[69]

Other journalists' accounts confirm that factors such as fear of political turmoil or uncertain weather conditions frequently caused cocoon firm owners to lower prices offered for cocoons.[70] Because peasants depended upon cash income from cocoon sales to purchase grain for family consumption, they sometimes took drastic measures, forming villagewide groups to protest the arbitrary lowering of cocoon prices.[71] Sporadic, random violence also occurred over price issues, and local officials were called upon to arbitrate these disputes.[72]

Despite defensive actions on the part of the peasantry, we have seen that cocoon firm owners also asserted themselves, using multiple methods of gentry authority to establish the growing power of the cocoon-marketing system. On the one hand, these practices and tensions were familiar in the highly commercialized rural society of Jiangnan. On the other hand, gentry interests were now channeled into an economic system related to new technology and an international marketing network for raw silk. These developments set the stage for a powerful new form of bourgeois practice. As it emerged in its full form in the 1920s and 1930s, we shall see that bourgeois practice in Wuxi was built not on a thoroughgoing transformation of productive relations but rather on a skillful merger of past and present methods of social and economic dominance.

XUE SHOUXUAN AND THE MODERN SUBSTANCE OF ELITE CONTROL

By the 1920s, fifty filatures and more than two hundred cocoon firms operated in Wuxi.[73] Several events in China and abroad contributed to this increase. The fall of the Qing dynasty and the establishment of a new Republic caused political uncertainty, but Chinese entrepreneurs on the whole seemed to prosper, gaining increased social prestige within the new system. Careers as businessmen became more acceptable in their own right, and new governments recognized that modern development was both necessary and desirable. World War I also changed the economic environment, hampering the foreign competitors of Chinese industry in both domestic and international markets. Economic recovery after the war provided an especially favorable situation for such products as Chinese silk because Western customers once again were able to purchase luxury consumer goods. From the mid-twenties onward, falling silver prices in world markets also favored China, which elected to remain on a silver standard while the rest of the world used gold. The relatively cheaper Chinese products made possible a more favorable balance of payments and accumulating supplies of silver. Finally, the establishment of the Nationalist government in Nanjing in 1927 brought commitment to a series of national policies to foster and promote industrial growth.[74]

In this milieu, a single entrepreneur emerged as the most powerful force shaping Wuxi silk production. Xue Shouxuan, son of Xue Nanming, was one of Wuxi's earliest investors in the silk industry. His career is worth exploring in some detail, for it illustrates how bourgeois practice matured by linking traditional styles of economic and political maneuvering at the local level with new industrial management.

As the grandson of Xue Fucheng and the son of Xue Nanming, Xue Shouxuan began his silk industry career as a well-placed member of the Wuxi elite. Xue Fucheng had been a *jinshi*-degree holder and a high-ranking official, putting the family within the ranks of the late Qing upper gentry. Xue Nanming expanded family fortunes through land management at the local level and also by building five local silk filatures.[75] Xue Shouxuan continued all aspects of the family tradition, retaining family landholdings, further developing the family's silk filatures, and also engaging in political activity at the highest levels possible by becoming an important participant in new Nationalist government committees for silk industry development.[76] He solidified his position via marriage ties as well, a common practice among elite families, by marrying the daughter of Rong Zongjing, who had become one of China's most prominent cotton mill owners.[77]

In the mid-1920s, Xue Shouxuan took over the family's silk filatures in Wuxi and began reshaping the management and investment patterns that had prevailed under his father's direction. Xue was educated at the University of Wisconsin, an experience that gave him insights into the organization of American business and also made him a representative of an emerging western-trained portion of China's twentieth-century elite.[78] Upon his return, Xue's first important innovation was to end a system of organization in the family filatures called "split ownership/management" (*shi/ying ye*), under which the majority of Wuxi and Shanghai filatures operated. This system created major problems because filature organizers did not operate the filatures themselves. Instead, they rented them annually to a separate stratum of filature operators, and neither owners nor operators took responsibility for filature maintenance or renovation. As a result, the output of Chinese filatures fell behind the Japanese in both quantity and quality, compromising Chinese competition in the world silk market.[79] Xue aimed to change this situation by instituting a system of personal management under his direct control. To this end, he hired several men as his assistants in managing the family filatures; with their help Xue Shouxuan set about orchestrating a new phase of silk industry growth.[80]

Although Xue first concentrated on introducing new filature equipment and instituting training programs for both male and female workers,[81] he soon extended his work into sericulture as well. In 1930, Xue organized a sericulture affairs office under the direction of the Yongtai filature and built two egg breederies in Wuxi and Zhenjiang. The Yongtai office also began to organize sericulture cooperatives, promoting extension work in the country-side and the sale of Yongtai egg cards to local peasants. Under this system, the breederies prearranged contracts with peasants to purchase cocoons raised from Yongtai's improved egg cards. Xue's goal was not only to im-prove the quality of cocoons available to Yongtai but also to raise the quan-tity of cocoon output, thereby eliminating chronic problems the filature in-dustry faced in maintaining an adequate cocoon supply.[82]

With these ambitious efforts underway, Xue capitalized on his growing stature within the Wuxi silk industry even during the darkest days of the depression, when virtually all filatures in both Shanghai and Wuxi were forced to close because of the collapse of the world silk market.[83] Not surpris-ingly, Xue's position as a well-connected member of the local elite gave him his initial maneuvering edge. As a first step, Xue turned to his powerful businessman father-in-law, Rong Zongjing. With Rong's personal introduc-tion to the general manager of the Bank of China, Xue arranged loans to keep his filatures operating.[84] Xue also became one of a select group of new busi-ness advisers to the Nationalist government in Nanjing. Their first project was a government bond program in 1931–32 to make loans to filature owners to assist industry recovery.[85] This program set an important new precedent by involving the most prominent filaturists within central China in directly supervising and managing government programs to assist the silk industry. Among this group, Xue gradually emerged as the most prominent new leader, earning the title, China's "silk industry magnate."[86] This title reflected not only Xue's political influence but also his growing economic position within the central China silk industry. By the mid-1930s, Xue either owned or leased approximately forty of Wuxi's fifty filatures.[87]

To achieve this new stature, Xue continued to use his strategy of alliance with Nationalist government leaders. During 1934–35, the Nationalists established an elaborate system of governmental commissions designed to supervise both agricultural and industrial development, especially in central China. A Commission for the Administration of Sericulture Improvement was formed in Jiangsu to devise new regulations for cocoon firm operation and silkworm egg breeding, to be implemented in county-level model silk districts and sericulture development districts.[88] Wuxi was made one of two model silk districts, and county magistrate Yan Shenyu was appointed its first head. There was one other government-appointed bureaucratic man-ager of this organization, Vice-head Cai Jingde, but the other fifteen mem-bers of the model silk district committee in Wuxi were all businessmen from within the Wuxi silk industry itself. This group was headed by three promin-ent filaturists: Qian Fenggao, Cheng Bingruo, and Xue Shouxuan.[89] Xue

Shouxuan clearly wielded the most influence, serving also on the sericulture commissions of the provincial and national governments.[90]

At this point, Xue's rapidly growing political influence, built from within the county and outward, affected the way his activities as an industrialist impinged upon rural society in Wuxi. Xue had not divorced himself from the traditions of old gentry society, in which locally based, multiple strategies for dominance were employed with the best connected, wealthiest, and most talented individuals emerging to serve at higher levels in the bureaucracy. By the 1920s and 1930s, the old mark of social pedigree, degree-holding status, had been eliminated, but the tradition of local power brokering within elite circles had not yet faded. Xue built on this tradition and changed it by using it to pursue modern industrial development. His actions had ramifications vis-à-vis both cocoon firm owners and the peasantry in Wuxi, as seen through initiatives that were part of the model silk district program.

New measures for cocoon firm control were the first aspects of model silk district policy in Wuxi that Xue Shouxuan used to his advantage. Regulations stipulated that all new cocoon firms must install in their drying rooms Japanese-style hot air blowers, the most modern equipment available.[91] Small cocoon firms of four drying rooms or less, likely to be least technically advanced in their equipment and methods, were no longer allowed to operate.[92] Both these measures were designed to guarantee higher quality cocoons by drying them under optimal conditions, thus insuring a more complete and uniform drying process. For Xue Shouxuan, however, who already had the most advanced drying machines, these measures meant that he would now have an advantage over his competitors.[93] By maneuvering these restrictions he developed a plan to control cocoon marketing throughout the Lower Yangzi region.

Evidence of Xue's ambitions can be seen in neighboring Jintan county where Xue rapidly expanded his influence over cocoon marketing under the model district program. It is somewhat surprising that Jintan became the second model silk district; it was not a major producer of cocoons when the program was established.[94] However, when we realize that Xue Shouxuan had important personal connections in Jintan, the rationale for granting model district status becomes clear. Xue cultivated close friendships with the head of the Jintan police bureau and also with the county magistrate who served simultaneously as vice-head of the model district. Assisted by these two county-level officials, Xue's agents were able to rent many cocoon firm facilities in Jintan. Once these facilities were rented, under model district guidelines, Xue renovated the existing drying rooms, installing new drying equipment. Although this required a substantial capital outlay, when the facilities were rented and the machines in place, Xue quickly established the capacity to buy and process a large proportion of Jintan cocoons. At the time he started this system in Jintan, Xue also began to cultivate friendships with the magistrates of Yixing and Liyang counties, having similar plans for developing their cocoon trades.[95]

Xue also used the model silk district restrictions on the selling of silkworm egg cards to peasants to his advantage. These provisions halted selling egg cards by private breederies—a new industry rife with speculation and abuse, that had arisen in Wuxi in the late 1920s.[96] Now private breederies could continue to operate only under one condition: if a breedery was willing to take the time and effort to establish egg-rearing cooperatives with peasants, instructing them in new techniques and lowering the risk of cocoon crop failure, then it could retain the right to sell its improved egg cards.[97] Under this provision, Xue Shouxuan's Yongtai and Huaxin filatures, which already had such a system of cooperatives, continued to run breederies that sold egg cards directly to peasants. In 1934, the Huaxin filature prepared female extension workers to organize new contractual cooperatives, where filature staff sold egg cards and required that the cocoons raised from those cards be sold back to filature-controlled cocoon firms.[98] In 1935, the model district extension program sent out one hundred workers, but Yongtai and Huaxin also sent out another one hundred in Wuxi and surrounding counties to set up contractual co-ops.[99]

The ultimate benefit reaped by Xue from this cooperative program was the ability to monitor all aspects of cocoon rearing and marketing in the Wuxi countryside, including the important matter of prices. Although the cocoon merchant guild had long been responsible for setting a cocoon price at the beginning of each marketing season, prices ebbed and flowed daily, sometimes even hourly, at the actual cocoon-marketing sites.[100] Thus, it was to Xue's advantage to control more closely the price paid to peasant producers for their cocoons, and the cooperative system helped accomplish this end. An account of the resulting situation appeared in the Chinese press, relating that cooperative members had to carry cocoons from their households to the filatures, no matter how far the distance. Peasants were given certificates of the weights received but without a stated price. At least a month later the filatures announced their cash payments for cocoons divided into three grades. Prices for the relatively small portion of cocoons in the first grade were set slightly above the market, but Xue filatures paid well below the market for the second and third grades. If the market price for the first grade was thirty *yuan* per *dan* (one *dan* = fifty kilograms), the filatures would pay thirty-one or thirty-two *yuan*, but the second grade invariably brought one or two *yuan* less than the market price, and the payments for third grade cocoons were not much more than twenty *yuan* per *dan*. Only a small proportion of the cocoons were classified as first grade, so Xue's filatures, on average, paid substantially below market price by using this cooperative system.[101]

Other press reports confirm that cocoon prices remained low in Wuxi throughout the mid-1930s—a situation caused by both the lingering effects of the depression and Xue's power to influence prices. In 1936, the Nationalist government's Commission for the National Economy, on which Xue served as a silk industry adviser, announced that it would decide each year on a uniform nationwide price for cocoons based on raw silk prices on the international market and average production costs for Chinese filatures. For the spring season of 1936, the commission decided that the price offered to peasants for their cocoons would be thirty *yuan* per *dan*.[102] Although raw silk prices had recovered to 74 percent of their 1929 level by that time, this suggested price for cocoons was only 42 percent of predepression highs.[103] When the Wuxi cocoon industry association met on May 31, it merely reaffirmed the thirty *yuan* price. Hua Shaochun, one of Xue Shouxuan's personal associates, headed this association, accounting for the rapidity with which the organization agreed to the new system.[104] Whether Hua had been installed by Xue or cultivated by him after assuming his position, the effect was the same—a decision that clearly favored Xue and his filatures by assuring that cocoons could be bought at lower prices.

In the final analysis, Xue Shouxuan used multiple methods to build a more fully integrated silk industry. He oversaw a partial reshaping of the cocoon-marketing system and in the process raised quality standards for Chinese silk production. However, the price to be paid for these advances was a silk industry increasingly dominated by Xue's personal networks. In addition, peasants found themselves with a diminishing capacity for price bargaining within the cocoon-marketing system. Xue thus combined old elite strategies with bourgeois leadership of modern industry and government programs designed to support it. At the level of local society, this combination comprised a powerful new system of social dominance linked to industrial modernization.

BOURGEOIS PRACTICE IN A CHINESE CONTEXT

Traditional form, modern substance: these were the social dyad that shaped bourgeois practice in the context of the Chinese Republic. In the late nineteenth century, members of the Wuxi gentry elite expanded their commercial initiative, bringing the peasant economy into contact with a new international system of mechanized silk production. The trajectory of social change already underway in Jiangnan created an environment suitable for these developments. Patron-client landlordism had waned during Qing times, and gentry members developed new strategies to build or maintain their local social dominance. As commercial activity became an important source of income, new economic relationships between elites and peasants resulted.

The story of Xue Shouxuan demonstrates the culmination of these trends. I have outlined the parameters of his bourgeois practice, emphasizing the social power resulting from this new hybrid form behavior. Xue built his modern silk industry by using strategies of the earlier gentry. To maintain his symbolic capital, he carefully cultivated relationships with selected local officials and elites, as well as high-placed acquaintances in Nanjing, and provided essential markets for peasant producers even while depressing the prices they received for their cocoons. When one adds the eminence of his family background to the aura derived from his business success, Xue still appears as a prestigious patron-broker as well as an aggressively successful capitalist. His status in higher arenas reinforced his local dominance over dependent peasants, and his local prominence contributed to his stature in national circles.

However, Xue's political style was derived from the tradition of gentry-merchants before him, and his industrial activities occurred within a rural society that, though evolving, was still substantially within the late imperial framework. In the early twentieth-century context, Xue's activities neither simply recreated nor totally transformed the previous relationships between gentry-merchants and peasants. He modified elite dominance by introducing new technology and factory organization, but he did not try to displace or transform peasant society by divorcing his suppliers of cocoons from their rural households. The resulting pattern of development differed substantially from those we think of as constituting classical capitalist modes. Peasant family farming was not eliminated as part of this process, but rather it became an integral link in a chain of new production relationships serving modern industry.

Further studies of early industry in China might well begin here—with an examination of how modernizing elites linked industry with the existing rural order. Until we have more studies that examine evolving relationships such as these, we will be unable to argue conclusively about either the nature of the Chinese bourgeoisie in the early decades of the twentieth century or their roles in promoting early industrial growth.

FIVE

Power, Legitimacy, and Symbol: Local Elites and the Jute Creek Embankment Case

R. Keith Schoppa

During the last two decades analyses of Chinese local elites have concentrated on identifying functional elites; delineating their social, political, and economic groupings; and describing their functions. The focus on identification was in part a necessary reaction against the long-held view that local society was dominated simply by the traditional gentry (i.e., civil service degree holders). Important studies have spelled out a range of more apposite functional elite categories (in the late Qing, for example, scholar-gentry, gentry-merchant, merchant, gentry-manager; and in the Republic, a much wider array, including militarist, capitalist, educator, landlord, and bandit chief). The study of elite groupings (lineages, associations, parties) has provided a fuller sense of key collective actors in local society. Examining spatial contexts for elite actions has suggested variations in patterns of elite organizations and political culture. In treating elite functions, scholars have detailed changes over time and space in their nature or mode.

Because of the paucity of detailed sources, however, relatively few studies concentrate on the processes and discourse of local decision making and of changing local power relationships, studies that might offer insights into elite stratification and patterns of dominance vis-à-vis lesser elites and nonelites. One generally well-documented case that provides such evidence is the struggle during the last years of the Qing dynasty and the early Republic over the Jute Creek Embankment (*Maqi ba*) in Tianyue subdistrict (*xiang*), Shanyin county, Zhejiang province in the Lower Yangzi macroregion.[1] In a series of crises relating to local dominance, the episode reveals elites in a core subdistrict struggling to continue domination over elites in a backwater subdistrict and the latter's paramount leader maneuvering to maintain his control over the subdistrict's lesser elites and nonelites. Furthermore, an analysis of the affair's context and course provides considerable insight into the wide range of resources for local-elite legitimacy and power and the strategies for their maintenance.

THE SETTING

Tianyue Subdistrict. Contiguous to Xiaoshan county and to the flourishing Puyang River port of Linpu, Tianyue subdistrict was located in the southwest corner of Shanyin county, which was merged with Guiji to form Shaoxing county in 1912. The area's political agenda was dominated by flood control issues. Situated along the narrow-channeled and precipitously sloping Puyang River, both Linpu and Tianyue frequently had to fight rampaging floodwaters after storms in the mountains to the south. Before the mid-fifteenth century, the Puyang turned to the east immediately before it reached Linpu to join the Little West River in Tianyue (map 5.1).

With mountains on three sides and the Puyang to the west, the subdistrict had traditionally been divided into three sections: upper, middle, and lower—designating placement along the Puyang River and delimiting its varying topographical orientation (map 5.2).[2] Upper Tianyue, south of Dayan Mountain, sloped to the west with its streams flowing directly to the Puyang. Lower Tianyue, north of Qinghua Mountain, also sloped to the west with its streams flowing to the Little West River. Between the two mountains was Middle Tianyue, sloping to the northwest and drained by Jute Creek, a stream which joined the Little West River east of Linpu. The land at the foot of the mountains in Middle and Lower Tianyue was very low, in the words of the subdistrict's gazetteer, "sunken like the bottom of a pan." Floods were a continual problem; the area reportedly experienced natural disaster nine out of every ten years, becoming commonly known as "the barren subdistrict."[3] The plight of Lower Tianyue and sites down the Little West River in northern Xiaoshan and Shanyin counties was especially tragic during floods; the river did not empty into Hangzhou Bay until it reached the Three River Outlet, northeast of the prefectural capital of Shaoxing. Large areas along its channel were frequently flooded.

To deal with these problems, in the reign of the Chenghua emperor (1465–1488), the prefectural government sponsored the diversion of the Puyang River through the excavation of a new channel northwest of Linpu and the construction of the Maoshan sluicegate where the Puyang River had previously turned east. From that time, the main force of the Puyang River flowed west along the southern edge of Linpu on its way to join the Qiantang River.[4] For Lower Tianyue and the northern part of Shanyin county, the river's diversion meant freedom from the floodwaters of the Puyang.

In its fervor to end the flooding problem, the prefectural government also constructed an earthen embankment across Jute Creek to check the runoff from the mountains to the east of Middle Tianyue. Although this construction

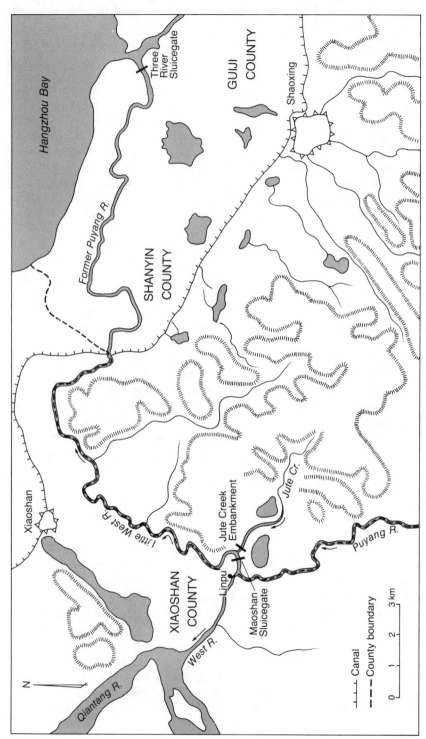

Map 5.1. Major Rivers and Streams in the Three-River Drainage System, Xiaoshan and Shanyin Counties, 1911

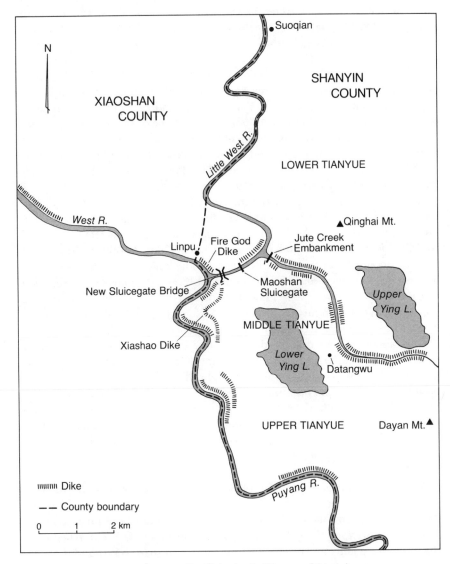

Map 5.2. Waterways and Water Facilities in the Tianyue-Linpu Area

made water problems farther downstream even less likely and theoretically provided Middle Tianyue with a reliable irrigation source, in reality it
consigned much lowland in that part of the subdistrict to swamp. Not only
did storms in the mountains to the east send cascades down to submerge the
crops; but also, when dikes broke along the Puyang River to the west,
floodwaters pouring into the area could not be drained off. Forty-eight villages were, to use the gazetteer's language, "abandoned like entrenchments
on the frontier" to face the ravages of flood unprotected, "outside the embankment."[5] Whether the prefects and their advisers had foreseen the unfortunate
results, they did nothing to correct the situation. Once the embankment was
in place, the rest of the county declared its efficacy and refused to counte-
nance any change. There appeared little recourse for redress.

The political impotence of the forty-eight villages is shown by the very
phrase "within the embankment," which came to stand generally for the
lower reaches of the Little West River. By any objective evaluation, however,
Middle Tianyue was "within the embankment," a fact that had turned it
into the flooded realm of "fish and turtles." The language of description was
infused with the perspective of the dominant. Productive farm land was soon
covered by two lakes, Upper Ying and Lower Ying, which in turn had to be
diked to prevent even further inundation of farm land. The 1588 reconstruction of the embankment included an opening to be used for irrigation "within
the embankment" in case of drought, but it was narrow and low, and
moreover the Middle Tianyue elites did not hold the prerogative to open the
watergate.[6] As time passed, the forty-eight villages came to be marked by
both bleak poverty and outbursts of banditry and unrest. Although generally
surrounded by the flourishing inner core of the late imperial Lower Yangzi
region and bounded by the flourishing economic center of Linpu, Middle
Tianyue remained, in fact, peripheral—poor, troubled by social unrest, and
embittered at being held hostage to nature.[7]

The World of Linpu Town. The people of Middle Tianyue were, in part,
unable to change such a disastrous situation because of the subdistrict's
dichotomous orientation. Administratively it was under the jurisdiction of
Shanyin county even though it was separated by a mountain watershed from
the rest of the county and oriented naturally to Xiaoshan county and the town
of Linpu. Shanyin county treated Upper and Middle Tianyue like unwanted
stepchildren. Linpu created yet another problem of identity because its
administration was divided between Xiaoshan and Shanyin counties. Its
main market area, to which Tianyue sent rice and paper products, was
located not in Shanyin, but in the Xiaoshan section of the town.[8] The subdistrict's natural and administrative status cast it into a political no-man's-
land where local inhabitants were often forced to handle problems (like water
control projects along the Puyang River) that in other areas the state might

help to solve. This sense of isolation only exacerbated the problems of unrest spawned by the area's poverty and banditry.

The presence of the important entrepot of Linpu so near to the peripheral pocket perpetuated Tianyue's poverty and stimulated continual awareness of its powerlessness. A flourishing market already in the Song,[9] the town had apparently been seen by administrative decision makers as potentially too wealthy, and therefore powerful, to function as a single administrative unit. Its administrative duality, however, was a source of continual political and economic problems, making it harder, not easier, to control.[10] One of Zhejiang's six great rice markets, in 1912 Linpu had sixty rice firms (*hang*), most of which participated in the town's powerful rice merchants' guild (*miye gonghui*). The price of rice in the three-county area (Xiaoshan, Shanyin, and Guiji) depended on the Linpu market, which operated under the direction of rice and shipping firms, brokers (*yahang*), and large numbers of outside merchants.[11] Because the three-county area had to import large quantities of rice annually, many merchants from Jiangxi and Hunan represented so-called "long route" (*changlu*) rice firms in those provinces; present also were large numbers of shippers from Ningbo and Shaoxing prefectures who delivered rice along the region's canals. The presence of large numbers of sojourners contributed to the wide open atmosphere of Linpu, where opium dens and brothels flourished.[12]

When industries (rice-husking mills, oil presses, breweries) were established in the late nineteenth century, rice merchants played major roles in their operation, thereby expanding their share of the local wealth.[13] In the Republic, the Linpu merchant "establishment" compiled an infamous record of hoarding and corruption.[14] Officials sometimes plotted with commercial elites: in 1920 the Linpu police force became involved in a bribery and kickback scheme that became one of the county's most notorious twentieth-century scandals.[15] Perhaps not surprising in such a situation, frequent social outbursts resulting in injury and death against the merchant-official establishment are recorded: rice riots (May 1911; March and April 1925); a salt riot (April 1917); and a riot against paper taxes and charges (August 1921).[16] For these reasons, merchant militia units were active in Linpu; and in September 1914 the town became one of only five sites in Zhejiang for the establishment of a subsidiary county yamen.[17]

The unrestrained commercialism of Linpu and the poverty of Tianyue seemed two different worlds. The subdistrict's geography and administrative location virtually invited exploitation. Linpu rice merchants moved aggressively into Tianyue and attempted to make killings on rice purchases by taking advantage of desperate farmers in those reputedly exceptional years of decent harvests.[18] The sense of being exploited led to social explosions like the 1921 riot against paper stamp surtaxes, when an estimated five thousand Tianyue people involved in the manufacture of paper attacked and destroyed the Linpu paper firms and demanded the abolition of the new tax.[19] Although this collective violence may have had a class dynamic, the rioters' locale-determined identity pointed again to the perceived subordinate status of the subdistrict.

TANG SHOUCHONG AND SUBDISTRICT ELITES: SOURCES OF LOCAL DOMINANCE

The leading figure in water control projects undertaken in Tianyue and at Linpu in the first five years of the Republic was Tang Shouchong, a resident of Datangwu, a village located at the approximate center of Middle Tianyue subdistrict and the Tang lineage home since the twelfth century. The village was about 4.5 kilometers southeast of Linpu and 3.0 kilometers from the Jute Creek Embankment in an area of low ricelands and bamboo- and tea-producing mountains.[20] In addition to the Tang's agricultural base,[21] the lineage also had strong financial interests in Linpu, where Shouchong likely had a subsidiary residence. A list of Linpu contributors to the 1922 reconstruction of lake dikes in Tianyue shows that at least eight of the town's twenty-one individual contributors were from the Tang lineage.[22]

Tang Shouchong himself clearly straddled the worlds of agriculture (Tianyue) and commerce (Linpu). In his role as the Tianyue subdistrict manager (*xiangdong*) in the late Qing self-government structure, he was active in various local issues in addition to water control.[23] In Linpu, where his management of waterworks repair was predicated on a channel's significance as a merchant thoroughfare, he was codirector on the Fire God Dike project with Lu Zumei, head of the town's chamber of commerce branch.[24] He was personally involved in the ownership and/or management of the Yuantai old-style bank (*qianzhuang*) in Linpu.[25] In constructing public service institutions apart from water works, Tang focused not on the subdistrict but on Linpu. There in 1905 he established a school with three other elites from nearby Ruluo subdistrict in Xiaoshan county; in contrast, the earliest recorded school establishment in Datangwu was 1931.[26] In 1910 Tang also established an orphanage in Linpu at substantial personal expense.[27]

Sources do not disclose whether the subdistrict's population resented Tang's public works focus on Linpu; whether they distrusted Tang's close relationship with Linpu commercial elites who often took advantage of the subdistrict; or even whether Tang himself may have been involved in underwriting the financial activities of rice merchant exploiters of Tianyue. We also cannot tell whether in the case of a conflict, his interests in town affairs perhaps weakened his will to defend subdistrict interests. But we do know that some people in the area considerably resented Tang.[28] It is certainly safe to say that, as in any dominant-dependent relationship, subdistrict residents experienced ambivalent feelings—resentment and antagonism as well as appreciation and admiration—for Tang.

The Tang lineage also straddled the world of native place and the world beyond. While Tang Shouchong took Linpu and neighboring Tianyue sub-district as his stage, his elder brother Tang Shouqian strode into the provincial and national arenas.[29] Shouqian, a *jinshi* or metropolitan graduate of 1892, headed the Zhejiang Railway Company in the first decade of the century, taking a popular nationalistic stance that catapulted him to the governorship of Zhejiang in the aftermath of the 1911 revolution. Although he was appointed minister of communications in the provisional Nanjing government, once Yuan Shikai assumed power, Tang left for Southeast Asia to visit overseas Chinese, never again taking an official position.[30]

Sources indicate that the nationalistic fervor and activity of Shouqian had a great impact on Shouchong and his Linpu allies. They purchased more than five thousand *yuan* of railroad stock from proceeds of the land set up to finance the school that Shouchong had established with others in 1905.[31] Because the brothers' relationship was reportedly very close, their conversations on Shouqian's visits home doubtless dealt with the elder brother's activity in the railroad affair, in the Society to Prepare for Constitutional Government, and in other nationalistic and reformist efforts.[32] Some later developments in the Jute Creek episode reflect Shouchong's own absorption of the spirit of nationalism and political change. In any event, the prestige accruing to the lineage and its local leaders, particularly Shouchong and his younger brother Shouming, from the accomplishments of Shouqian was undoubtedly great, enhancing their other bases of local power.[33]

Among lineages in Tianyue, the Tang had cast a dense marriage net.[34] In Middle Tianyue, circumscribed by mountain and river, the lineage had marriage connections with at least thirteen of the twenty-one major lineages.[35] A frequent Tang liaison was with the Ge lineage of Shantoubu, less than 2.5 kilometers east of the Tang lineage home; the mother of Shouchong and Shouqian was a Ge. From the end of the Qianlong reign, the Tang lineage produced only one upper-degree holder—Shouqian. Ties to the Ges, however, linked the Tangs to the most prolific degree-attaining lineage in Middle Tianyue from 1796 to 1912.[36] In the closed defensive society of the subdistrict, the Tangs were able to utilize marriage ties to solidify their leadership position and link themselves to the subdistrict's other most powerful lineage.[37]

Joining Shouchong in the Jute Creek Embankment case and other water-control work were Ge Bilun, Kong Zhaomian, and Lu Luosheng. Ge of the Shantoubu lineage, resident in Tianyue since the Yuan dynasty, was a scholar who chronicled the events of the early Republic for the county gazetteer.[38] Kong, whose lineage home was established in the fifteenth century about two kilometers southeast of Linpu, was the only one of the four with an upper-level degree (a *juren* or provincial graduate of 1894).[39] Though he was his lineage's only upper-degree holder after 1777, his lineage played important roles in the locality into the Republic. A brother, for example, served as dike administrator on the first section of the West River Dike near Linpu in the late 1920s.[40] Lu, a scholar who also chronicled events of the times, represented a lineage that was not particularly distinguished, but its village was the closest (less than half a kilometer) to the Jute Creek Embankment.[41] Like Tang, Ge and Kong served in local self-government positions in the late Qing and early Republic: Ge, in the Shaoxing county assembly from 1912 to 1914, and Kong, as the subdistrict council chairman (*yizhang*).[42] Heading the new self-government institutions apparently added little substantial power to their roles, but the positions officially confirmed their preexisting local power.[43]

An analysis of Tang's local social and political dominance by 1912 shows his success emanating from an ability to operate in several dichotomous but complementary spheres: Tianyue (agriculture, periphery) and Linpu (commerce, core); local (leader of a lineage with strong socioeconomic base) and beyond (ties to provincial and national affairs through Shouqian); private (voluntary managerial roles) and public (self-government position).[44] In addition to operating effectively in these spheres, he had obvious expertise and energy in the field of local water control. He directed all the major repair work in the area from 1911 to 1916. His appointment by the county assembly in September 1912 as honorary inspector of the West River Dike noted his public-spirited enthusiasm and the seriousness with which he undertook water conservancy responsibilities.[45]

It should be noted that Tang's power in the locality derived in the main from resources legitimated by traditional cultural values.[46] His social status as gentry-manager, his reliance on lineage-marriage ties, and his fraternal connection to higher places were social resources based on cultural patterns that lent legitimacy to his leadership position.[47] His self-government leadership invested him with officially recognized legitimacy. His expertise brought what one writer has called "competent authority."[48] With the latent political power of Tang's wealth undergirding his social, political, and personal legitimacy, his local leadership position appeared secure. Yet, power has been defined as "legitimacy put to the test of social action."[49] The case of the Jute Creek Embankment not only tested Tang's power but also began to erode his legitimacy.

THE JUTE CREEK EMBANKMENT CASE:
SUOQIAN ELITES VERSUS TIANYUE SUBDISTRICT

When proposals to change the embankment into a bridge reached the government in 1911, it was not the first time. As early as 1643, the subdistrict's cause was championed by local native Liu Zongzhou (1578–1645), philosopher, Donglin adherent, and teacher of the philosopher, Huang Zongxi.[50] Liu, whose pen name (*hao*) was Jishan, advocated demolishing the embankment, pointing out that the Maoshan sluicegate provided the security from floodwaters that Lower Tianyue and points farther downstream needed.[51] Such a move was strongly opposed by the spokesman for downriver sites in Xiaoshan county, Ren Sanzhai, who credited the Jute Creek Embankment with preventing serious floods in the preceding two centuries—a curiously myopic view that discounted the Maoshan sluicegate, which had actually prevented floods.[52] In the views of Ren and others, the issue of the embankment constituted a zero-sum game: "They speak of [Middle] Tianyue not having half its land [because of floods]. The only question is who is going to have the difficulty."[53] Though nothing came of Liu's effort, the people of Middle Tianyue remembered him with respect and appreciation while their situation festered. In 1881 Tang Shouchong's father, Tang Pei'en, resuscitated Liu's suggestion by setting down principles of a Ji [shan] Society to remember Liu's spirit.[54] Although there were no immediate tangible results, a decade later the Shaoxing prefect broached the idea of changing the embankment to a bridge. Despite the fact that neither he nor his successors followed up the suggestion, Middle Tianyue villagers invoked the proposal in subsequent years.[55]

In fall 1911 the subdistrict's bitterness expressed itself in the Tianyue self-government council's petition, drafted by Tang and Kong, to the provincial assembly in Hangzhou.[56] Although the petition came during a barren harvest period in the aftermath of two serious floods, this calamity alone doubtless did not catalyze local elite action because countless others had not. More likely, elites were activated by the establishment of local self-government districts and institutions. In that year, because of its elites' arguments, Lower Tianyue had been separated to form an independent subdistrict named after its main village of Suoqian, the first administrative recognition of the separation wrought centuries earlier by the embankment's construction.[57] Whether this decisive action motivated the petition, it seems apparent that, though self-government titles added little to the actual credentials of local leaders, the idea and institution of self-government began to transform local political processes. Local leaders quickly grasped the utility of this new institution for handling local matters.

The petition had two goals: demolishing the embankment (to relieve at last the flood-stricken Middle Tianyue) and attaining provincial assistance in repairing river dikes in Middle and Upper Tianyue (now called simply Tianyue). In their presentation, Tang and Kong set forth the plight of their native place: through the existence of the embankment, "evil gentry" in Lower Tianyue (now Suoqian), motivated by their own private advantage (*sili*), continued to prey on the subdistrict's people.[58] The embankment was a "question of life or death."

By pointing to the area's economic poverty, the petitioners had in mind not only the recurring pattern of cropless years but also the recurring use of

scarce private funds for repairing and maintaining dikes—amounts traditionally contributed by households whose fields were thereby protected. In
part, lack of any outside support stemmed from the county's general inatten-
tion to this area and to what the petition pointed out as the political and
cultural poverty of the subdistrict: very few people were literate; and the
subdistrict produced no officials, no *muyou* (the private secretaries and legal
advisers that made Shaoxing both renowned and reviled in the empire),[59]
and few gentry. There was some exaggeration here: Tang Shouqian was an
important outside "connection." But the main thrust was true enough. The
thirteen subdistricts of Shanyin county in the Qing dynasty produced 2,032
upper-degree holders, an average of 156 per subdistrict. Although Middle
Tianyue contained 59 per cent of Tianyue subdistrict's population, its villages produced only 18 (0.8 percent) of the county's total degree holders.[60] In
sum, in Tianyue there was an obvious paucity of local leaders legitimized by
upper degrees and possessing outside connections who might be able to effect
desired changes. In contrast, Suoqian subdistrict had no chronic flooding
problem (thereby escaping the financial burden of continual dike expenses),
and, the petition noted, the subdistrict had many "connections" to officialdom.[61] From the subordinated's point of view, Suoqian's main instrument
of continuing dominance was its connection to officialdom, a tool Middle
Tianyue felt deprived of by its political poverty. Although not specifically
mentioned in the petition, we may surmise that Suoqian's newly independent
administrative identity further enhanced its political visibility and influence.

The provincial assembly reacted to the petition by asking the governor to
investigate the situation, but the coming of the 1911 Revolution frustrated
this effort. Before the revolution Tang and Kong had served as Tianyue (i.e.,
former Middle and Upper Tianyue) self-government leaders. After the
revolution, as evidence of renewed determination to solve the problem, the
forty-eight villages in former Middle Tianyue elected Tang, Kong, Ge Bilun,
and Lu Luosheng as representatives (*daibiao*) to bring the issue to a conclusion. Probably the impetus for the election of "representatives" and for the
designation itself came from Tang and his allies, an evidence of the constitutionalist ethos common at the time among core elites and perhaps specifically
of the oppositionist mobilization of the railroad movement.[62] Its use at the
moment of elections for a national parliament was symbolic of Tang and
the others' absorption of the new ethos, which, in turn, might impart some
measure of legitimacy to their effort.

By early 1913 Tang, the acknowledged subdistrict leader, had assumed
two social roles vis-à-vis the farmers of Tianyue in the embankment case.
In his position as long-time gentry-manager in the subdistrict, he acted as
patron to subdistrict residents. In exchange for his expenditure of political,
instrumental, and economic resources in the community, he expected support and loyalty from the farmers for whom he acted with paternalistic

authority.[63] A second role was as *representative* of the subdistrict's forty-eight villages, a role in which Tang's authority at least theoretically came from subdistrict residents. Although Tang's relationship to the state was defined by his self-government role,[64] his relationship to the villagers was defined by both patron and representative. The dynamics of the latter roles, however, were sharply different. We know neither how the villagers perceived Tang's role nor the depth of their understanding of representative forms, but it is likely that in their view he remained primarily "patron."

In November 1912, the four representatives called for the embankment's end in letters to the Shaoxing county assembly, military governor Zhu Rui, and the provincial assembly.[65] The arguments in these letters emphasized the increased possibility of action following the recent revolutionary change to a republican polity. The spirit of the time, they alleged, was one of change and innovation.

The counterattack by Suoqian subdistrict and the rest of Shaoxing county nonofficial elites was multifaceted. Their past dominance over Tianyue had been based simply on political power and the legacy of the past. With their control now challenged, the elites quickly devised a host of methods in an effort to maintain their pattern of outright domination over the elites and masses of Tianyue. The county assembly chairman, Ren Yuanbing, who had close connections to Suoqian elites, stonewalled, not answering the Tianyue letter, not introducing it for discussion in the county assembly, not investigating or soliciting other subdistrict opinions. At the same time, he sent telegrams to powerful Shaoxing figures outside the county, claiming that the "scoundrel (*gunpi*) Tang lineage" was trying to destroy the crucial dike.[66] To the cabinet in Beijing, Ren specified the villain to be none other than Tang Shouqian.[67] Suoqian subdistrict leaders sent the provincial assembly a specious map of the area to make it appear that the danger to Suoqian would be acute if the embankment were destroyed.[68]

Stonewalling, deception, ad hominem attacks were the defensive reactions of elites "within the embankment." In addition, the moral discourse of those upholding the status quo was similar to that used by those placed on the defensive in other local crises of the rapidly changing late Qing and Republican periods.[69] It should be obvious that in elite culture there may be an inherent contradiction between the particularistic sectional interests of elites and the universalistic moral values they are seen to represent.[70] When sectional interests are being promoted or protected, discourse on the basis of general moral values both masks the struggle for dominance and enhances the legitimacy of the cause. Thus, in contrast to Tang's invocation of innovation in the political symbolism of the revolution, Suoqian elites retreated to the legitimacy of the traditional social symbols—the morality of the group and its harmony—to combat threatened change. Suoqian and seven other

Shaoxing subdistricts claimed that the issue was one of private (*si*) advantage for Tianyue subdistrict: if the embankment were destroyed, the other subdistricts could never again be defended against serious flooding; the morality of the collective opposed the immorality of private interests.[71] Jin Tanghou appealed to the graves of ancestors (the group's past) and warned of the likelihood of outright struggle between Suoqian and Tianyue subdistricts (the value of harmony).[72] The chairman of the Suoqian subdistrict council, Lou Kehui, even threatened staunch resistance to the government if it decided to destroy the embankment.[73]

Whatever the merits of the case, the arguments were couched in categories of traditional moral symbols that purposely lent legitimacy to the cause. Nowhere was there discussion of the political, economic, or ecological facts of the situation; nor was the argument placed in current spheres of discourse (such as the growing debate over the meaning of public and private, or the trend in water-control controversies to investigation by outside conservancy organizations).

Winter 1912–13 brought several provincial and county investigators to the scene.[74] In December two deputies of the provincial government reported that removing the embankment would have no harmful effect for those downstream. While the magistrates of Shaoxing and Xiaoshan delayed a formal recommendation until spring, Civil Governor Qu Yingguang was dispatched in January to meet with the magistrates and representatives of both sides (for Tianyue, Tang, Kong, Ge, and Qiu Shaoyao, leader of another Tianyue lineage; and for the downstream sections of the Little West River, two representatives of the Suoqian subdistrict council, the subdistrict manager from Ruluo [north of Linpu], and the vice-chairman of the Xiaoshan county assembly).[75] Unfortunately, there is no record of these discussions. From what we know of later events, it is unlikely that the Suoqian elites yielded at all in their resistance to change. The burden of Tang and other Tianyue spokesmen was to demonstrate to officials and elites that the situation was *not* (as Ren Sanzhai in the sixteenth century had depicted it) a zero-sum game. For the discussions to have continued at all, compromise must have been pursued. Whether Tang was willing to make concessions or whether Governor Qu, serving as broker, was able to effect the compromise, we do not know. But, at the conclusion of the discussions, the governor announced his support for changing the embankment in some fashion.

When the Ministry of Agriculture and Forestry authorized proceeding, Military Governor Zhu Rui dispatched another deputy to discuss the methods. Pressed by elites from the two sides, the provincial government compromised: the embankment would not be demolished, but the opening installed in the late sixteenth century would either be widened and heightened or another would be cut in the embankment to allow better and faster drainage. Projected expenses would determine the method.[76] In March Zhu Rui announced the decision to widen the existing opening.

Unable to accept any change in the status quo, Suoqian elites and their county allies, acting through the Shaoxing assembly, wired their opposition to the Ministry of Agriculture and Forestry. In almost immediate response, the ministry and its agricultural affairs office ordered Zhu Rui to delay any action.[77] The source of such a rapid, favorable response to the assembly was almost certainly long-held connections, a reminder that, despite the Tang lineage, Tianyue still suffered from poverty of appropriate connections. Noteworthy also are the connections of county and Suoqian elites to Beijing bureaucrats revoking decisions by the provincial officials. The decision seemed to perpetuate the dominance of the downstream areas over Tianyue. Government ultimately responded to the most powerful and best connected, not to those stricken by economic, political, and social poverty, however just their cause.

THE JUTE CREEK EMBANKMENT AND AFTER: TANG SHOUCHONG AND TIANYUE SUBDISTRICT

For the Tianyue subdistrict, the imposed indefinite delay on any action meant that Tang Shouchong, despite his considerable resources for local power, simply could not parlay his local legitimacy into influence beyond the Tianyue-Linpu area. Even more significant, however, because of his unsuccessful efforts to persuade Suoqian and county elites to assent to changes in the embankment, Tang lost the support of those subdistrict farmers whom he represented. It is unclear whether the expectations Tang raised among the farmers caused their discontent with his leadership; but the sources do make clear that, once the decision to delay action became known, Tianyue farmers applied unremitting and antagonistic pressure on Tang and the other three representatives to insure a favorable solution. The four representatives, caught between immovable official delay and growing pressure from the subdistrict, reportedly had no alternative but to resign from their positions in the spring. Tang and Kong also resigned their self-government posts.[78]

Perhaps the elites meant the resignations as a ploy: by resigning Tang and Kong, able leaders in an area without many educated or outward-looking elites, may have been trying to signal the government about the urgency of positive action. It did not work: Zhu Rui responded that according to self-government regulations,[79] they could not resign. Whether or not their resignations were legal, there is no record that from this point they actively fulfilled self-government functions. The resignations of the four "representatives" of the villagers may also have been a ploy directed against the farmers of Tianyue subdistrict. Threatened or actual resignations, they may have thought, would lead the farmers to see that their able, prestigious representatives (and patrons) would be unable to continue in the face of such unremitting pressure from below. This approach implied that the four men believed the subdistrict depended on their ability for future negotiations. If that was their other strategy, it also did not work: within a short time, the farmers had formed their own Forty-eight Village Association (hereafter called the Association) under the leadership of Qiu Shaoyao.[80]

Although Tang's recently established relationship to institutions of state as a self-government deputy brought a certain mechanistic impersonality in social exchanges, his mode of domination over Tianyue farmers remained largely one "in which relations [were] made, unmade, remade by interactions between persons."[81] The necessary "continuous creation" of dominance as patron required more than Tang's economic preeminence in the area and his claims to traditional cultural legitimacy. It may have included personal characteristics—demeanor, voice, habits, dress—which enhanced his dominance in any situation. But it definitely entailed his continuing success and expertise in the day-to-day "practice" of water control. Undoubtedly word had reached the villagers that their initial demand for demolition of the embankment had been compromised. There may thus have been some suspicion of the role of the patron/representative even before the word to delay had come from Beijing: had the case not been argued forcefully enough? What role did Tang's long-time friendship with He Bingzao, negotiator on the opposing side, have in the deliberations?[82] These doubts likely contributed to the subdistrict farmers' willingness to choose another spokesman when Tang was unsuccessful, for Tang's role as patron had been badly damaged when defeat in the larger political arena drastically depleted his symbolic capital.[83]

Little is known about the Qiu lineage or the leader of the Association, Qiu Shaoyao. With a lineage base since the Southern Song in two villages within two kilometers of the Ge lineage home, the Qiu produced no upper degree-holders during the Qing.[84] The Qiu were also not included in the 1937 county gazetteer's list of nine important subdistrict lineages. Circumstantial evidence suggests that the Qiu, however, may have been one of the most significant Tianyue lineages whose arena of action was limited to subdistrict boundaries. Although there is no evidence that any Qiu served beyond the subdistrict in any capacity, in the 1922 subdistrict repair of the Ying Lake dikes no fewer than seven of the nineteen managers were from the Qiu lineage.[85] These repairs only benefited area farmers, in contrast to the broader commercial implications of water projects in which Tang was involved.

Although Shaoyao had no recorded degree, he was obviously literate. The Association met three times from its inception in the spring until July 1913. Following those meetings, Qiu petitioned the authorities requesting rapid action on the embankment case and an end to the officially imposed delay.[86] During that three-month period, spring and summer rains had once again broken the Puyang River dikes, flooding the land in Tianyue. With the embankment opening insufficient for rapid drainage of the area, crops drowned or were felled in the mud by the force of the floodwaters. The Association wrote to Zhu Rui saying that "unless the outlet is widened, there will be no end in sight to the flood-caused famines"; the letter was signed "the men and women refugees of the forty-eight villages."[87]

In the face of continued government silence, on the night of July 17, 1913, the families—men and women, old and young—of the forty-eight villages, armed with shovels and hoes, demolished the embankment. When police and troops arrived from Shaoxing, no one was at the site. Jute Creek flowed unobstructed into the Little West River for the first time since the mid-fifteenth century. As late as November 1913 Shaoxing elites requested restoration of the embankment, but heavy rains in late summer showed clearly that the river system could handle the additional water without a problem.[88] There was general agreement that the river should be dredged and its banks should be made higher as a precaution. At the site of the former embankment, construction of a bridge began in December 1913 and was completed in July 1914.[89]

Farmers, acting on their own authority, had ended the crisis. Qiu had clearly been their leader in communications with the government and had probably been involved in planning the demolition—though the sources list no leader of that episode. The government's choice neither to investigate the act nor to prosecute anyone involved indicates its probable satisfaction that the social and political tension had been relieved. Why did the Tianyue farmers act only at this time after over four centuries of bitter acquiescence to Suoqian elites? I would suggest that the rhetoric of change accompanying the 1911 Revolution and the active leadership of Tang and his allies raised hopes as never before that change would come at last. When these hopes were unexpectedly dashed, the long pent-up frustration exploded. Perhaps the widespread local political and military mobilizations in the aftermath of the revolution provided models for the farmers' response.

The main losers in the episode were Tang Shouchong and his Tianyue-Linpu allies.[90] They had failed to prevail against outside opposition to the relatively minor change of widening the outlet, only to be rejected by embittered local farmers who then illegally solved the problem by destroying the dike. By spring 1914, Tang's local leadership credentials had been further diminished and discredited. The self-government system that had officially legitimized Shouchong's local leadership position was abolished in February. In April his brother Shouqian, former nationalist symbol and garnerer of prestige for the lineage, was also discredited, becoming in effect an added liability to Shouchong. Shouqian had at last assented to nationalizing the

Shanghai-Hangzhou-Ningbo Railway; he had vigorously opposed that action during the last decade of the Qing, and it now aroused considerable hostility. Shouqian's decision followed a 20,000 *yuan* bonus bestowed by the government: many interpreted that as a bribe, and Tang used the bonus to help make up a large cash deficit in a Hangzhou native bank of which he was the largest stockholder.[91] Two weeks after Shouqian's decision, a telegram reached Shanghai that Shouchong had been assassinated at the Linpu native bank with which he was associated. Although the report was false, the reporter attributed a spate of such rumors to those who were "nursing grievances" (*xiechou*) against Tang.[92]

RESTORING LEGITIMACY: THE JI SOCIETY

In this context of the rapid decline of his personal and lineage prestige, Tang Shouchong espoused a powerful local symbol from the past to reestablish his legitimacy and strengthen his damaged clientelist relations with Tianyue villagers in water control matters.[93] He resurrected his father's idea of a Ji[shan] Society to revere and do obeisance to the spirit of Liu Zongzhou, the first advocate of changing the embankment into a bridge and relying solely on the Maoshan sluicegate.

The timing of the founding of the Ji Society—and its leadership, goals, and roles—indicate that it was primarily a vehicle to recoup the local standing of Tang and his allies and their authority in water-control matters. As for timing, Tang did not establish the society in the crisis of 1912–13 when the legacy of Liu might have been used as a rallying point for the subdistrict. Nor did he establish it during fall 1913, when the county and even the civil governor toyed with the idea of erecting another embankment. He organized it instead in spring or summer 1914,[94] when the embankment was already destroyed, the bridge almost completed, and the area already totally dependent on the sluicegate. Such timing suggests more than simply remembering Liu for his particular water-control proposal.

Tang clearly dominated the society. Of eleven original "disciples" (*houxue*) of Liu who joined in establishing the society, there were five Tangs (including the three brothers, Shouqian, Shouchong, and Shouming); Linpu Chamber of Commerce head Lu; Ge Bilun and Lu Luosheng, earlier representatives of the forty-eight villages; Tong Zhaolin, a close friend of Shouchong; and two representatives of the Xu and Hua lineages.[95] At least nine of the eleven were close personal allies or relatives of Shouchong. Notably not involved was Qiu Shaoyao, who had led the Association in summer 1913. That Tang did not choose to organize a modern association or club (then fashionable in the core zones) is significant. In a time when Tianyue farmers had taken matters into their own hands—an obviously disconcerting episode for elites not in control—and in a place where Tianyue and Linpu lawlessness had bred outright unrest and rumors of assassination, Tang's claim to legitimacy and his opportunity for social and political dominance lay in reasserting not ideas of change but values of traditional cultural morality.

Specifically his goal was unifying the subdistrict community around a cult of Liu, a symbol of its past unity (albeit one produced by shared poverty and weakness) to heal the breach between key subdistrict elites and villagers.[96] The old temple to Liu at the site of the Maoshan sluicegate was repaired; a new room was constructed to house a newly inscribed tablet and a portrait of Liu. Rites were held on the second day of the fourth month to observe the day of Liu's birth; essays were written to commemorate the founding of the society and celebrate Liu's significance.

If rituals "express in a condensed dramatic way the meaning of the shared values that bind a community together and, in the very act of expressing these shared values, deepen the community members' commitment to them,"[97] Tang clearly hoped to deepen the subdistrict commitment to values he and his allies felt especially significant. Delineated on the temple tablet and in Ge Bilun's record of the society's establishment, the central values were reverence and gratitude for Liu's past contribution.[98] Recalling the common heritage embodied in Liu's efforts was further designed to foster the subdistrict's sense of community, especially important at a time when the changed environment (the removal of the dike) would physically open the community to greater contact with areas downstream and likely provide challenges to old social arrangements and situations. A third value, the indispensability of social harmony, focused on Liu's renowned sense of morality as a salutary antidote to the threat of lawlessness in the Linpu-Tianyue area in general and the spirit of illegality that had given rise to the dike demolition in particular. Ge began his account with an implied comparison of the decline in morality and the threat of disorder during Liu's life at the end of the Ming with the situation of the early Republic. But, just as Suoqian elites had earlier utilized traditional symbols to maintain control over the embankment, Tang and his allies now used symbols of morality and harmony to restore control over their former clients.

Finally, but very important, in an emphasis that reveals Tang not only as keeping the traditional symbols but also as manipulating those symbols for change, the founders of the society stressed Liu's love of country, a value from Liu's own life that had never been central in the subdistrict's remembrance of his importance. In the past Liu was revered for his concern for the people of the subdistrict. In his commemorative essay, Ge stressed emulating the spirit of Liu's patriotism—he had starved himself to death out of loyalty to the Ming in the wake of the Manchu victory. This manipulation of the past had clear meaning for the present.

The perceived arena of the Ji Society was the world of the subdistrict *and* the world of the nation beyond—the worlds of the elites who founded it; it

was not solely the world of Tianyue led by the Qiu lineage. The society and
the Liu cult were efforts to coopt the leadership of Tianyue water issues from
Qiu, restore fully the leadership of Linpu *and* Tianyue to the Tang and their
allies, and help redirect the vision of Tianyue farmers to the outside world.
This nationalistic reemphasis on the meaning of Liu suggests that much
subtle but important change could be effected amidst the continuity of old
forms. As keepers of the Liu cult's symbols, Tang and his allies dominated
not only the old forms but also the meaning of the past and the movement to
new thought patterns and attitudes.[99]

With the repair of the temple came renovation of the temple grounds. A
large plum orchard was planted where there had once been a fish pond; to
one side of the temple a new lotus pond was formed. These symbols of the
new productivity of the subdistrict followed the dike's demolition. Whether
the first year of the remodeled temple brought vandalism, we do not know.
But in late 1915, Ji Society members petitioned the Shaoxing magistrate to
give official protection to the temple and its grounds. Their stated concern
was that ignorant rustics would cut down newly planted trees, harvest
lotuses in the pond, and harm the temple structure itself. The Shaoxing
magistrate ordered the desired protection, thus underwriting the concerns
and dominance of the elite organization. One elite petitioner, it should be
noted, was Qiu Shaoyao; he was now brought into the society, his leadership
of the villages coopted.

Tang Shouchong dominated the reconstruction of water projects after the
establishment of the Ji Society. Having tapped the subdistrict's reservoir of
historical respect for Liu and having officially subsumed Liu's remembrance within the society, Tang could use the society to mask his own leadership and circumvent possible opposition. In 1914, for example, the Ji
Society announced the establishment of a Forty-eight Village All Elder Society to discuss rebuilding the New Sluicegate Bridge near the Maoshan
Sluicegate.[100] Nine men were named directors of the project; only one, Tong
Zhaolin, was a close associate of Tang. Yet the sources make very clear that,
even though one Hua Xuchu was chosen head of the project, the superinten-
dence and financing of the affair were completely in the hands of Tang
Shouchong. He and Tong Zhaolin reportedly worked day and night, totally
controlling the project. Given the unfriendly climate for Tang and his allies
during the first half of 1914, the mechanism of the society allowed him to
reassert his legitimacy and control.

In 1915, Tang's reputation had apparently been revived sufficiently to
permit him to act on his own without reference to the Ji Society in calling
together elders from the forty-eight villages to discuss the nature and cost of
repairs on the Xiashao dike, southeast of Linpu.[101] Once again, Tang managed the whole project, reportedly at great personal sacrifice. Although this
effort was a personal success, Tang used the authority of the society to

announce regulations on dike maintenance from the stage of a dramatic performance at the April rites for Liu. With the power of ritual and symbol supporting the regulations, Tang and the Ji Society leaders undoubtedly hoped to impress their import more deeply into the minds of the people.

The Ji Society did not play any specific role in water projects after 1915. Tang managed major work on Linpu's Fire God Dike in 1915–16 and 1922 without reference to the Ji Society, which had always applied more directly to Tianyue subdistrict.[102] In the repairs of the Ying Lake dikes in 1922, however, the society also was not a factor; in this effort, the Qiu lineage once again emerged as the major actor. As its last known act, the Ji Society published the documents concerning the embankment from the late Ming until its demolition in 1913. It thereby imprinted its domination of both the distant and recent past onto the future by selecting and arranging the materials that would constitute the historical record.[103]

CONCLUSION

Two struggles for dominance in the Jute Creek case occurred within Tianyue subdistrict: the first between elites in former Lower Tianyue and elites and nonelites in Middle Tianyue; the second between upper-ranking elites (with bases in Linpu and Tianyue) and lower-ranking elites and nonelites within Middle Tianyue itself. In the two episodes, the nature of the elites and their patterns of dominance—specifically, the nature, mode, and application of dominance—differed.

The historically developed social ecology of the subdistrict is crucial in understanding the dynamics of the first episode of contention. While Lower Tianyue (Suoqian) had continued from the Ming period to thrive in a core region with close ties to Shaoxing via the Little West River, a flourishing artery of trade, Middle Tianyue had been relegated by political decision to a waterlogged periphery, isolated from direct water ties to the rest of the Three-River system. In addition to Suoqian's productive agricultural lands, the intermediate market town and salt entrepot of Suoqian provided lineages there with an opportunity for economic diversity through trade.[104] The wealth of Suoqian was in sharp contrast to the poverty of Middle Tianyue, which, although oriented to the central market town of Linpu, most often found itself the town's exploited target rather than advantaged satellite.

More important were the social and political results of the economic situation in both areas. In the Suoqian case there was reportedly a greater diversity of elites, including wealthy farmers, commercial magnates, and larger numbers of degree holders. Many looked beyond the locality, and many had connections to elites in Shaoxing and beyond. In the Middle Tianyue periphery, there was a greater homogeneity of elites. Most were farmers, a few were involved in Linpu trade, and a small number were degree holders.

Connections to elites beyond the subdistrict were few, though Tang Shou-qian was, at least at times in his roller-coaster career, a formidable "connection." In the end, the openly confrontational and antagonistic domination of Suoqian elites was both guaranteed by social ties that could tap political power at the capital for their purposes and continued (until the dike's demolition) through direct political orders to provincial officials to desist in their actions.

The dynamics of the second episode—the effort of Tang Shouchong to reestablish his domination over other Tianyue elites and nonelites through water control—were sharply different. Here the issues were patron-client ties and their sociocultural base. Tang exploited the culturally symbolic Liu cult and Ji Society to restore his symbolic capital and reassume the subdistrict's paternalistic leadership. In the culturally and socially homogeneous subdistrict, Tang reapplied his domination over the populace subtly and indirectly, using personal and value-based methods. If, following Bourdieu, we consider any application of domination in society to be "violence," then it can be said that Tang used the Ji Society to "euphemize" his "symbolic violence" against the people of the subdistrict.[105]

Why did the people of Middle Tianyue accede to Tang's domination? The answer lies in the basically pragmatic, self-interested reactions of nonelites within their general social acculturation of submission to elite dominance. Throughout the episode, the farmers pursued their own interest as they saw it. Despite several centuries of inaction in the face of the calamity wrought by the embankment, their quiescence was not necessarily permanent. Specific circumstances finally motivated them to act: heightened anticipation that the problem would at last be solved led them to pressure Tang to reach a favorable conclusion. When Tang resigned, they formed the Association; when it too failed, they demolished the embankment. But just as it would be misleading to see the farmers as an always quiescent mass, it is equally incorrect to see them as a continuing interest group aggressively intent on forcefully directing their affairs on their own initiative. In subsequent water work, the villagers were again at the beck and call of Tang.

Their willingness to follow Tang over Qiu or other Tianyue elites undoubtedly came from his superiority in material and moral resources and their perception of that superiority.[106] A simple comparison of Tang's and Qiu's resources makes the point obvious. In any sort of synthetic status ranking of their resources,[107] Qiu, whose credentials were those of a literate lineage leader respected by Tianyue villagers, comes up short. In comparison, Tang was a wealthy and literate lineage head with a creditable record in public works, business involvement in Linpu, and connections to Linpu elites and his famous brother. Qiu could not transmute his degree of local legitimacy to permanent power equal to that of Tang any more than Tang could transmute his local legitimacy and dominance to power equal to that of even better credentialed elites at a higher level.[108] Pragmatic township residents could easily see Tang's advantages and the greater likelihood of his long-term success in water conservancy leadership. In this sense, Tang could fully re-establish his dominance because the villagers were willing to be dominated.

The general categories of elite dominance—economic wealth and diversity, political status and position, social status and connections—provide the bases for understanding in general the relationship between contending elites or between elites and masses. But in every time and place, the specific "practice" of dominance differed according to the issues and people involved. In the Jute Creek case, the ultimately decisive tools of domination were either based on or attained legitimacy through cultural values. I have argued that Tang regained his leadership and attempted to maintain local dominance through cultural symbols, ritual, and personal suasion. It should also be noted that the social connections bringing Suoqian elites temporary dominance were, in their origins, a cultural phenomenon (sharing a native place where respective ancestors were interred), objectified into a potent sociopolitical mechanism. In addition, in both episodes, the discourse of dominance was often symbolic, tied for import to cultural ideals. These episodes indeed illustrate that "domination is as much a matter of cultural and psychological processes as of material and political ones."[109]

Finally, these episodes point to the fluid means of dominance in a society where, even in "objectified" state structures, social relationships (including the dominant-dominated nexus) formed a continually evolving dynamic core. In Tang's dealings with the township, the continuous maintenance, if not creation, of relationships was the means by which his legitimacy was established and dominance maintained. Suoqian's long-term dominance, upheld by government decree, was overthrown overnight by rebellious Tianyue farmers grown exceedingly weary and upset by the unyielding outside domination and the failure of their own patronlike leaders to bring satisfactory results.[110] In the study of local history, it is finally the matters of human relationships—their continuities and discontinuities, their timing and expectations—amid the full array of contexts, contingencies, and processes that complicate the analysis of patterns of elite dominance. Undergirded by the very particularity of social and cultural norms amid which all Chinese acted, these relationships pose analytical challenges for the social scientist and the humanist alike.

SIX

Local Military Power and Elite Formation: The Liu Family of Xingyi County, Guizhou

Edward A. McCord

In his path-breaking study of militarization in nineteenth-century China, Philip Kuhn identified the control of local military forces, specifically militia, as a key component of local-elite power in the late Qing and early Republican periods.[1] There is, however, a paucity of supporting studies showing how militia leadership functioned in practice for specific elite families in the establishment, maintenance, or expansion of local power.[2] In this article I attempt to meet this deficiency with a case study of the role of local military power in the rise of one family, the Lius of Xingyi county in Guizhou province, to a position of local, and eventually provincial, dominance.

The most renowned member of Xingyi county's Liu family was Liu Xianshi, military governor of Guizhou province from 1913 to 1920 and again from 1923 to 1925. As Guizhou's preeminent warlord, Liu Xianshi played a leading role in the political struggles and civil wars that ravaged southwest China in the early Republican period. Contemporary and historical accounts of Liu Xianshi's rise unfailingly note one distinguishing feature of his background: the militia base of his family's power. Both Liu Xianshi's grandfather and father, as well as three of his uncles, were actively involved in militia organization in the mid-nineteenth century; through militia leadership the Liu family originally established itself in a position of importance in Guizhou society. Heir to this family tradition, Liu Xianshi also led militia in Xingyi county in the last decade of the Qing and used this local force as the military base for his climb to provincial power.

One advantage to Liu Xianshi's notoriety as a warlord is that it has increased available historical materials on his family. With these materials it is possible to trace the family's use of local military power for a period extending from the mid-nineteenth century through the early twentieth. This history shows not only that military power played an essential role in determining and advancing the social and political power of the Liu family but also that the control of local military force was most effective as a medium for expanding elite power within specific contexts. The successful upward mobility of the Liu family depended, in the long run, on a family strategy that adjusted to both military and civil opportunities in the changing social and political milieu of nineteenth- and twentieth-century China.

THE SETTING: XINGYI COUNTY AND THE LIU FAMILY

Xingyi county is located in the southwest corner of Guizhou province precisely at the point where the province's border meets Yunnan and Guangxi provinces (map 6.1). To a certain extent, the county resembles the rugged, underdeveloped frontier areas often found along the borders of Chinese provinces. In terms of the core-periphery paradigm applied to China by G. William Skinner, Xingyi falls within the periphery of the Yun-Gui macroregion. Because the Yun-Gui macroregion was one of the most backward and least integrated in China, many of Xingyi's frontier features actually characterize the entire region.[3]

Although most of Xingyi, like most of Guizhou, is covered by mountains, the terrain here is particularly rugged even by Guizhou standards.[4] The rivers of southwestern Guizhou flow southeast into the West River system, which enters the sea at Canton, but they are not navigable until well into Guangxi province. Therefore, until the twentieth century, all transport to and from Xingyi went by human bearers or pack animals along well-worn paths. As for much of the Yunnan-Guizhou region, Xingyi county has only a small amount of level, arable land. Nonetheless, rich soil and plentiful rainfall make this land extremely fertile. Xingyi's county seat is located on a rich, irrigated plateau, one of the larger stretches of level ground in the province.[5]

Despite its location, Xingyi county was not as isolated as many peripheral areas. Xingyi city was established at the site of a preexisting market town, Huangcaoba, that marked the juncture of two important interprovincial trade routes: one, with Huangcaoba at its center, linked Guizhou's provincial capital, Guiyang, with Kunming, the capital of Yunnan; the second went southeast from Huangcaoba into Guangxi where it tied into river transport systems ending in Canton. In the eighteenth century, Huangcaoba was already a well-established marketing center for local products from the forests and mines of southwestern Guizhou and eastern Yunnan. Raw domestic cotton imported into Xingyi in exchange for these products helped supply a local weaving industry. During the nineteenth century, the content of this interprovincial trade underwent some important changes. Opium was introduced to southwestern Guizhou at the end of the eighteenth century and

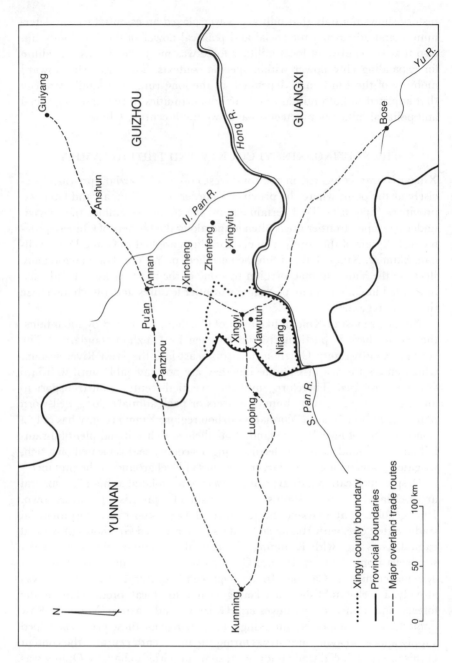

Map 6.1. Xingyi County in Relation to the Provinces of Yunnan, Guizhou, and Guangxi

eventually became the main product exported out of Huangcaoba. Penetration of foreign goods also increased in this period, and by the end of the nineteenth century foreign yarn from Canton steadily replaced domestic cotton as a main import into the Xingyi area.[6]

Despite the large volume of trade carried along these interprovincial routes, the level of commercial organization in Xingyi county remained relatively low. In the 1890s, a visiting British consul described the bustling market at Huangcaoba as a rather wild and unregulated "free mart." According to his report, Huangcaoba had no banks, and very little money actually changed hands in the market. Most commercial transactions were conducted by barter, with opium serving as the most frequent medium of exchange.[7] This low-level monetization reveals the relatively underdeveloped and peripheral character of Xingyi's economy.

Until the late eighteenth century most of southwestern Guizhou's inhabitants were members of non-Chinese, primarily Miao, ethnic groups. As in many parts of Guizhou, these ethnic groups came under increasing pressure from Han Chinese immigration in the eighteenth century. Because of its important trade routes, the Xingyi area was a particular target for Han settlement.[8] The ethnic balance in the Xingyi area began to swing in favor of the Han Chinese following the harsh suppression of a major Miao rebellion in the late 1790s. As Miao and other ethnic groups involved in the rebellion in southwestern Guizhou were pushed into more remote areas, a new wave of Han immigration flowed into the Xingyi area. By the mid-nineteenth century, Han Chinese guest people (*kemin*) were estimated to make up 70 to 80 percent of Xingyi county's forty thousand inhabitants.[9]

One characteristic Xingyi shared with much of the Yun-Gui region was a low level of social and political integration. In fact, only after the defeat of the Miao rebellion in 1797 was Xingyi county officially established as an administrative unit as part of a larger reorganization designed to strengthen bureaucratic control over Guizhou's southwestern border.[10] Nonetheless, the county retained a reputation for independence as a place "where the room [distance] of officials has been preferred to their efforts at government."[11] The Xingyi area also had relatively few of the higher-degree holders or retired officials that formed the upper social elite in more settled areas of the country. One mid-nineteenth-century source noted that because of Xingyi county's position on the "Miao frontier," it was only beginning to produce degree graduates qualified for assignment to official posts.[12] For the entire period from 1796 until 1854, Xingyi prefecture as a whole produced only fourteen provincial degree holders (*juren*) and one metropolitan degree holder (*jinshi*); of these, only one provincial degree holder came from Xingyi county.[13] Although no exact correlation can be made, the comparative weakness of the state and the thinness of traditional gentry elites may have contributed to the extraordinary rise of the Liu family to a position of local power in Xingyi county.

Although the arrival of the Liu family in Xingyi county cannot be precisely dated, it appears that they were part of the wave of Chinese immigration entering Xingyi at the end of the eighteenth century. Liu Xianshi's great-great-grandfather, Liu Taiyuan, a traveling peddler of literary supplies from Hunan, made the move to Xingyi county (figure 6.1). Liu Taiyuan settled in Nitang, a remote village on Xingyi's southern border, where he gave up his previous occupation to establish a tung oil extraction business. Thus, like many other immigrants into southwestern Guizhou, Liu Taiyuan had been attracted not by land but by commercial opportunities. Under Liu Taiyuan's son, Liu Wenxiu, the family oil business expanded to the point of hiring nonfamily labor. Real prosperity, however, was only achieved when Liu Wenxiu's son, Liu Yanshan, moved the family business from remote Nitang to Xiawutun, a village in a fertile irrigated valley only a few miles from Xingyi city. With greater access to the Huangcaoba market and the assistance of four able sons, Liu Yanshan's business flourished. In a short time, the Lius had become one of Xiawutun's richest families.[14]

The Liu family's prosperity was accompanied by a shift in their economic interests. After moving to Xiawutun, Liu Yanshan began to use his commercial profits to acquire agricultural land. In the end, he and his sons abandoned the oil trade entirely to concentrate on managing their landholdings. By the mid-nineteenth century, the Lius had gone from being a leading merchant family to one of richest landlord families in Xingyi county.[15] Given the success of the Lius' oil business, it seems unlikely that this shift to agriculture was simply economic. Although the sources are silent on this matter, one can assume that the family may have been responding to traditional values that emphasized the prestige and security of landholding over commercial activity.

Within traditional Chinese society the next logical step for the Lius might have been to seek advancement into the ranks of the scholar-gentry by competing for degrees in the state-sponsored examination system. In some regards, the Lius were already poised for such a step. According to one account, the Liu family established a private school at their original home in Nitang.[16] Liu Yanshan's four sons, and most likely Liu Yanshan himself, were literate and well versed in the classics on which the examination system was based.[17] Whether or not the Lius intended to pursue this route to educational advancement, they were soon distracted by more pressing concerns. Beginning in the 1850s, a number of increasingly serious rebellions began to erupt in different parts of the province. When the Lius stepped forward to organize local defenses against these rebellions, they embarked on a path that would bring them greater rewards than they could have hoped to gain through the examination system.

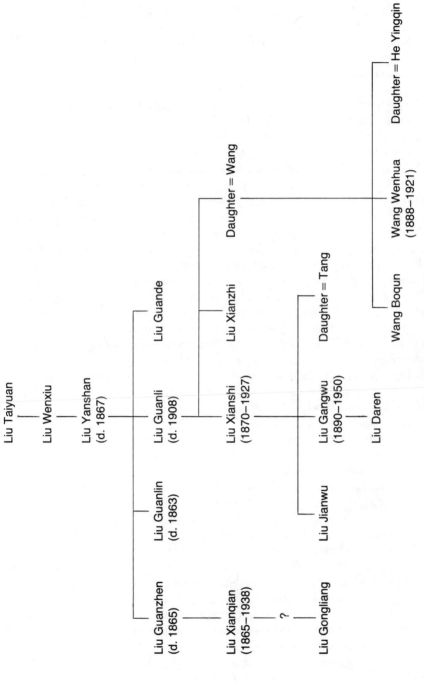

Figure 6.1. The Lius of Xingyi

THE MILITARY BASE OF ELITE POWER

Although coinciding somewhat with the outbreak of the Taiping Rebellion in neighboring Guangxi in 1851, Guizhou's rebellions had indigenous roots in increasing ethnic tensions and economic inequities. From 1850 to 1875 there was always at least one, and usually more than one, rebellion active in some part of the province. Before the end of this twenty-five-year period over 90 percent of Guizhou's administrative cities would fall at some point to rebel forces, and at the height of the rebellions more than 60 percent of the province would be under rebel control.[18]

For the first half of this period, Xingyi county, apparently escaping much disorder of these rebellions, may have even prospered. According to one account, the market at Huangcaoba flourished during the rebellions, "keeping the peace in its own streets and selling opium, arms, and foreign goods to all who could pay for them."[19] War finally came to Xingyi with an ethnic Hui (Muslim) rebellion that arose along the Yunnan-Guizhou border in 1858 and sparked other local ethnic and secret society uprisings. In 1860 the county seat of Pu'an directly north of Xingyi county became the first in a chain of administrative cities to fall to the rebels. By 1862 the rebels had advanced to take Xingyifu, the administrative seat of the Xingyi prefecture, less than sixty miles from Xingyi city. As the rebellion spread, local officials, following precedents established elsewhere in Guizhou and other provinces, encouraged local communities to organize militia for their own self-defense.[20]

The Lius were one of many families in southwestern Guizhou who stepped forward to manage local self-defense when they saw their own localities threatened. In 1860 Liu Yanshan and his four sons led local residents in constructing a stone fortress and then began to train local residents as militiamen. The Lius' defensive efforts at Xiawutun came none too soon. Six months after the fall of Xingyifu, Xingyi city also fell to rebel forces. The fortress at Xiawutun, which became a place of sanctuary for the local refugees, was soon besieged. After seven desperate months, the Lius were finally forced to negotiate a token surrender to the rebels.[21] Despite this questionable tactic, by successfully guiding Xiawutun through this particularly difficult period, Liu Yanshan and his sons established their reputations as local military and community leaders.

The Liu family's militia leadership provides a case in point for Philip Kuhn's observation on the inadequacy of defining the local elite solely in terms of degree-holding gentry; not only local degree holders but also many wealthy or influential commoners assumed militia leadership, clearly an elite function.[22] In a study of Sichuan province in the 1850s and 1860s, Keith Schoppa has also shown that the majority of the men who performed conventional elite functions in local defense, education, and philanthropy were not degree holders.[23] Thus attention to elite activities instead of status categories

both provides a more accurate picture of local elites and particularly identifies nondegree-holding elites such as the Lius of Xingyi county.

Once degree holding is no longer the sole criterion for elite status, an
examination of elite activities presents a more dynamic picture of change
within the structure of local-elite power. The Lius, emerging as a wealthy
landlord family, must at least be considered members of the village elite of
Xiawutun, but prior to the 1860s the scope of their influence was limited.
Before this time, for example, there is no sign that the Lius had assumed any
community leadership roles. Likewise there is no indication that the Lius
functioned as power holders in the tradition of "local strongmen" often seen
in frontier areas.[24] The Lius' landholdings, after all, were located in one of
the county's more settled areas and did not require private armed retainers
for their protection. Only in their organization of local defenses in the 1860s
did the Lius begin to act as community leaders and become local strongmen;
also as militia leaders the Lius extended their influence beyond the borders of
their own village. Militia leadership therefore provided the Lius with a
means for upward mobility unavailable to them in more peaceful times.
Thus, militia organization served as an arena for not only elite activity but
also elite formation.

In the years following the siege of Xiawutun, the Liu family became involved in local defense and militia activities on an ever wider scale. While
Liu Yanshan guarded the family's base at Xiawutun, his sons led militia in
campaigns against various rebel strongholds in both Xingyi and neighboring
counties. There are no exact records on the size or organization of Liu family
forces, but at different times estimates of the Liu brothers' command ranged
from several thousand to more than ten thousand men. Three times (1864,
1866, 1868) militia led by the Lius helped retake Xingyi city from rebel
forces. Subsequently, the Lius also participated in recovering other important cities in southwestern Guizhou, including Xingyifu and Xincheng. The
Lius' militia activities were not pursued without some family losses. Liu Yanshan's second son, Liu Guanlin, was killed in an assault on Xingyi city in
1863, and his first son, Liu Guanzhen, was killed in a feud with neighboring
militia leaders in 1865. Liu Yanshan himself died, apparently of natural
causes, in 1867. After this, Liu Yanshan's third son, Liu Guanli, assumed
primary leadership of the family's military forces, assisted by his younger
brother, Liu Guande.[25]

The activities of the Liu family in this period, however, were not limited to
commanding militia forces; to support their forces, the Lius were also active
in collecting funds and provisions. No doubt benefiting from Xingyi's wealth
as a commercial center, the Lius not only supplied their own forces but also
supported regular army units campaigning in southwestern Guizhou and
provided funds to obtain the services of militia from neighboring areas to
assist in their own campaigns. Liu family leadership and fund-raising skills

were also applied to community construction projects, primarily defensive. Besides the stone fortress they built at Xiawutun, the Lius aided in constructing ten other forts in neighboring areas. After the third recovery of Xingyi city, Liu Guanli and Liu Guande led efforts to rebuild and strengthen the walls of the county seat. Finally, after the death of Liu Guanzhen, the Lius directed the construction of a loyalty temple (*zhongyi ci*) to commemorate him and other local "martyrs." When this temple burned in 1875, the Lius again contributed to its reconstruction.[26] The Lius' attention to this temple no doubt reflected its symbolic importance to the family, a concrete reminder of their community leadership.

The position of local leadership attained by the Liu family in suppressing rebel forces of the 1860s and early 1870s was enhanced by the receipt of official titles and brevet offices. Liu Guanzhen was awarded an army rank of major (*youji*) for his role in the first recovery of Xingyi city. After his death, this title was passed on to his younger brother, Liu Guande. Liu Guanli received the honorary rank of subprefect (*tongzhi*) for his role in the second recovery of Xingyi city. His military abilities were also recognized by appointing him with official authority over all militia in Xingyi prefecture. After the recovery of Xingyifu, Liu Guanli was further rewarded with a prefect's rank (*zhifu*) and the right to wear a peacock feather.[27] In a society where the state had always claimed the right to determine the criteria for social status, such titles and awards were not considered empty honors. Indeed, the paucity of regular upper-degree holders in Guizhou made these awards even more valued, something officials sponsoring militia realized and used to their advantage.[28] The titles received by the Lius were important, then, because they both legitimated their positions as local leaders and considerably advanced their community status. In the eyes of the state and society, the Lius' official titles removed them from the category of commoners and placed them within the ranks of the gentry.

The Lius also found ways to translate their newly acquired local power as militia leaders into more material benefits. First, the family no doubt gained from the plunder of territories recovered from rebel hands.[29] Second, the Lius were not above using their new authority to consolidate their family landholdings by intimidating other landowners into selling or ceding to them prime lands around Xiawutun.[30] Finally, the Lius benefited from their access to funds and provisions collected for support of their military forces. Sources sympathetic to the Lius attributed their effectiveness in obtaining contributions to the high esteem in which they were held by the public.[31] But charges brought against the family for illegal exactions and embezzlement suggest that these contributions were often more coerced than voluntary and that the Lius were not averse to pocketing part of the proceeds for their own gain.[32]

Although the original purpose in raising militia had been to aid in suppressing rebellion, the Lius also used their military power to better the family's position in struggles with other "loyal" forces. Contrary to views of elite solidarity in the face of rebellion, conflicts over manpower, funds, or the command of military operations often led to feuds and even open warfare among various militia leaders. The death of Liu Guanzhen in 1865 was the result of one such feud between the Lius and another group of Xingyi militia leaders.[33] Such conflicts with militia rivals intensified after 1866 when Liu Guanli attempted to assert his authority as general militia head for Xingyi prefecture. Sometimes these power struggles even brought the Lius into conflict with local officials and regular army units. One such case occurred in 1866 when Liu Guanli initiated an attack on the forces of a neighboring militia leader who refused to accept his authority. Liu's adversary, however, received the support of Xingyi's prefect and a local brigade-general who sent official troops to repel Liu's assault. Only after a new prefect, a previous military ally of the Liu family, was appointed, was Liu Guanli able to defeat this opponent.[34] In another instance, the Lius reportedly attacked Xingyi city to force the flight of a magistrate who had sought to curtail their growing local power. After gaining access to the city, the Lius proceeded to massacre a number of gentry families who had supported the fallen magistrate.[35] Although eagerly accepting official recognition for their role in the suppression of rebel forces, the Lius could and did use their military power to challenge official authority when their own interests were at stake.

In these local power struggles expedient alliances with rebel forces could also blur the distinction between orthodox and heterodox forces. For example, one weak militia leader caught between powerful rebel forces on one side and aggrandizing militia leaders, including the Lius, on the other, changed sides no less than five times within a three-year period.[36] Despite their own questionable surrender to rebel forces during the first siege of Xiawutun, Lius were not reluctant to use charges of rebel collaboration, true or not, against their enemies; thus Liu Guanli finally avenged his brother's murder. Labeling these enemies rebel collaborators, Liu attacked their forces, pillaged their villages, and massacred their families.[37] Through such tactics, the Lius eliminated possible militia competitors while expanding their own military power by absorbing rival forces into their own.

As can be seen from these cases, the military conflicts of this period were hardly limited to the war between elite forces of order and armies of rebellion. The organization of militia, although meant to combat rebellion, also introduced military force as a new element in determining elite power, and elite power structures had to be reconstituted to incorporate this new element. To some extent, then, the conflicts between militia leaders, and between militia leaders and officials, were the violent manifestations of readjustments in the hierarchy of local-elite power.

Abuses of power and disregard for authority by militia leaders were naturally matters of official concern.[38] While rebellions still flourished, however, the government was often willing to overlook the transgressions of important militia leaders such as the Lius in exchange for their support. Nonetheless, in the early 1870s the Qing court finally felt compelled to respond to the accumulating charges and complaints against the Lius and ordered Guizhou's governor to investigate officially the family's activities. Because military resistance to a court order would have placed the family irrevocably in rebellion, this challenge demanded a political rather than a military solution. Liu Guanli immediately departed for the capital of Yunnan to seek higher-level protection from the governor general. Liu Guande, meanwhile, remained in Guizhou to oversee the bribery of local officials. In the end, the governor general interceded on the Lius' behalf, and the investigation was dropped. Furthermore, on the recommendation of his new benefactor, Liu Guanli was even appointed expectant intendant (*dao*) and was retained for a time on the governor general's staff.[39] The generous application of wealth and the careful cultivation of official patronage enabled the Lius to emerge from this affair not only unpunished but also even more secure in their position.

Although the Lius of Xingyi may have originally assumed militia leadership as a matter of self-defense, militia power helped the family do more than simply survive. Before the rebellion the Lius were already a prominent and wealthy landlord family, but by commanding local militia the Lius gained new status and influence as community leaders and local strongmen. By applying military force, the Lius increased their family wealth and eliminated local rivals. As a result of their military achievements, the Lius gained official honors that gave them status equivalent to the degree-holding gentry and established valuable official contacts that extended as far as the governor general's office in Kunming. In the course of their military campaigns their influence grew beyond the confines of their own village; by the end of the rebellions they were considered the most powerful family in Xingyi county and one of the most important families in all southwestern Guizhou. For the Lius, then, militia leadership served as a medium for a remarkable leap in local status and power. However, the family's escape from official prosecution also attests to limits on the uses of military power. Ultimately, maintaining the Liu family's elite position would depend on the extent to which they could be more than military strongmen.

GIVING UP THE GUN

Conditions in southwest Guizhou had changed considerably when Liu Guanli returned from Yunnan in 1875. The previous year, the last of the Hui rebel strongholds had been taken by government forces, and the Muslim rebellion had ended. Although scattered bands of ethnic or secret society rebels continued to trouble parts of Guizhou until 1880, by and large the major rebellions had by this time been defeated. Liu Guanli responded to the restoration of peace by announcing that he would retire from government service to devote himself to the care of his ailing mother. After fifteen years of almost continual fighting, Liu then proceeded to disband all his family's military forces.[40]

Given the importance of militia leadership to the expansion of Liu family power, Liu Guanli's willingness to dissolve his family's military forces appears at first glance almost quixotic. Nonetheless, Liu's response to restoring peace was not all that unusual. There is considerable evidence that most elite-led militias raised throughout China to combat midcentury rebellions were disbanded in the more peaceful postrebellion period.[41] The only question that requires further examination is why militia leaders such as the Lius abandoned so willingly the control of local military power that had been for a time so essential to their elite positions.

One of the most important reasons for Liu Guanli's decision to disband his family's militia was certainly his recognition of the risks in attempting to maintain military power after the rebellions ended. As the government's military strength recovered, officials were better positioned to curb the excesses of militia leaders, especially those whose activities had been too blatantly illegal or whose loyalty had been too inconsistent. The Lius had participated in enough campaigns against "rebellious" militia commanders to know how easily this label might be applied to themselves.[42] There was also a lesson to be gained from the family's costly struggle to defend itself from prosecution in the early 1870s. Their strong-armed self-aggrandizement had antagonized local officials and many members of the local elite. Continuing to behave as local military strongmen would allow these antagonisms to fester and might make the government more attentive to their enemies' complaints. With the restoration of peace, the best hope for maintaining the family's position lay in abandoning, not preserving, their militia power.

Liu Guanli was perhaps also willing to give up militia leadership with few hesitations because to do so by this time detracted little from his family's local power. Through militia leadership the family had gained new power "resources" that, once acquired, did not depend on military force to be maintained. One resource was Liu Guanli's expectant intendant rank, which gave him both community status and access to high officials. Another hidden strength was Liu's former position as general militia head for Xingyi prefecture. Through this position Liu could claim a superior-subordinate relationship to most militia commanders of southwestern Guizhou who, like the Lius, emerged from the period as important local community leaders.[43] Marriage ties also helped solidify these relations. Liu Guanli married his daughter to the son of Wang Peixian, who, after the Lius, was perhaps the most important militia leader in Xingyi county and one of the Lius' closest allies.[44] The Lius' influence with such men helped balance the enemies they had made among other members of the local elite. Finally, the Liu family had emerged with more wealth and property than they had had before the rebellions. The political advantages of wealth were readily evident in the bribery that helped the family avoid prosecution in the early 1870s. In the years to come, the Lius continued to use their wealth to cultivate official goodwill by generous "gifts" to local and provincial officials and their staffs.[45]

The dissolution of the Lius' military forces thus had little effect on the Lius' local power. Indeed, in the postrebellion period they continued to be recognized as the dominant family in Xingyi county, and to a certain extent in southwestern Guizhou as a whole.[46] The Xingyi magistrate reportedly would not act on any issue without first consulting with Liu Guanli, and Liu's opinion generally settled any local affair, big or small. As a result of his far-reaching power following the rebellion, Liu Guanli was pictured as heading a "small court" in Xingyi with influence over the entire Pan River watershed of southwestern Guizhou.[47]

From the case of the Liu family alone it is impossible to determine the extent to which state power may generally have devolved into hands of local elites in the postrebellion period. In the 1890s the British consul Frederick Bourne reported that the Xingyi county magistrate had candidly acknowledged that he had little authority in the county.[48] But Bourne saw this as merely continuing government weakness inherent in the region. Nonetheless, the relative scarcity of upper gentry in southwestern Guizhou through the mid-nineteenth century suggests that the rise of the Lius to a position of such influence was an elaboration of elite power that, at the very least, changed the structure of Xingyi society. Although the state's position may not have been any weaker than it had been before the rebellion, the power of the Liu family in Xingyi county may have helped thwart any attempt to strengthen government authority.

The Liu family's continued domination of Xingyi local society was not, however, simply the result of its achievements from the period of militia leadership. Viewed over time, elite power in local society appears not as a static construct but as a set of relationships in a constant process of formation and reformation. The Lius' activities in the postrebellion period seem to show an awareness that the maintenance, let alone enhancement, of their position and influence required that they seek out new means of renewing their power as local elites. The particular strength of the Lius as elites was their flexible response to changing circumstances and opportunities. Just as they adapted to possibilities for elite power found in militia leadership during the period of rebellion, the Lius turned their attention to civil potentialities for elite power in the peaceful period that followed.

Traditionally, education served as the main channel for status enhancement in Chinese society; and in the last quarter of the nineteenth century Liu Guanli focused his public efforts in this field. Although the titles Liu had received as a militia leader placed him officially at a level equal to the upper-degree holding gentry, ranks attained through military achievement were viewed in practice as inferior to those acquired through education. The power the Liu family wielded in local affairs would not necessarily translate directly into social acceptance within the ranks of the scholarly elite. Thus, Liu's attention to education at this time not only revived family interests that had been interrupted by their military activities but also initiated a strategy to transform his family's social status for more peaceful times. As a militia leader Liu had made many enemies among the local elite by his bullying, but in his new guise as educational patron he presented a more cultivated image by being "courteous to the wise and condescending toward the scholarly."[49] Personal behavior and public activity thus combined to reflect the Liu family's gentrification along more socially acceptable lines.

Liu Guanli's educational pursuits involved many traditionally approved activities. He established an academy in Xingyi county and filled it with the books needed for a classical education. He also provided financial assistance for the education of promising local students. Finally, to raise the quality of local education he provided generous stipends to bring prominent scholars from the provincial capital to Xingyi either to supervise the county's educational programs or to lecture in its schools.[50] Largely through Liu's efforts, Xingyi county became, despite its peripheral location, something of a regional educational center.

Besides the reputation Liu Guanli gained as a patron of local education, his activities had even more concrete benefits. His assistance to young local scholars established patron-client relationships with the men most likely to emerge as the next generation's social elite. Likewise, Liu established social contacts with the provincial elite through the scholars he brought to Xingyi to assist in his education projects. This same end was achieved by generous gifts sent to promising scholars in Guiyang.[51] By assuming the role of a patron of men of talent, Liu solidified his social influence within the Xingyi area and extended it to the provincial capital.

Liu Guanli's goals in promoting local education were not, however, simply limited to enhancing his own reputation. Liu was also providing for the educational advancement of his own sons and nephews. While he and his brothers had their educations interrupted, Liu Guanli could hope that the younger generation might contribute to the family fortunes by succeeding in the traditional examination system. In the mid-1880s the family achieved some success when Liu Guanli's elder son, the future warlord Liu Xianshi, and his nephew, Liu Xianqian (the son of Liu Guanzhen), both earned the lowest level degree (*shengyuan*).[52]

The year 1875 therefore was a turning point in the history of the Liu family whereupon they shed the military power that had made them southwestern Guizhou's preeminent strongman family in favor of pursuing civil status through educational promotion and advancement. For the Lius, military and civil activities were not exclusive categories of community leadership; rather, the sharp contrast between the family's activities before and after 1875 appears determined primarily by the different contexts of the two periods. Indeed, when changing conditions at the turn of the century offered new opportunities for community leadership in both military and civil fields the Lius responded with alacrity in both areas.

THE REVIVAL OF FAMILY MILITARY POWER

After a quarter of a century of relative peace, Guizhou in the first decade of the twentieth century was again beset by periodic local disturbances and ethnic rebellions. By one account, a total of seventy-three separate uprisings occurred in the province in this period.[53] With official approval, Guizhou's local elites again responded by raising militia for local self-defense.

For Xingyi, the main threat came not so much from local uprisings as from a series of secret society rebellions that began in neighboring Guangxi in 1898 and produced roving rebel and bandit bands that harassed Guizhou's southern border.[54] In the face of this threat, Liu Xianshi gave up his studies to devote himself to militia work, accepting a position as manager of Xingyi county's General Militia Bureau (tuanfang zongju).[55] The greatest danger to Xingyi came in 1902 when a large rebel army crossed the river that formed the county's border with Guangxi. At this point Liu Guanli also stepped forward in response to official appeals to help organize the county's defenses. Because the county's own garrison troops had been called away to quell rebel forces in Yunnan, the Lius first attempted to use their militia to defend Xingyi city. They soon found themselves outnumbered and abandoned the city to defend their own fortress at Xiawutun. For six days Xiawutun itself was then besieged by the rebel army. Before they could be forced to surrender, though, government troops fought their way back into the county, and the Lius reemerged from their fortress to join the offensive. The Lius then helped government armies recapture Xingyi city and push the rebels back into Guangxi.[56]

As a result of this action, the Lius revived their military reputation and gained new official rewards for their military services. First, in the course of the campaign the militia units led by the Lius were officially given an irregular army designation as the Border Pacification Battalions (Jingbian ying). Liu Guanli was appointed general commander (tongling), and both his son, Liu Xianshi, and his nephew, Liu Xianqian, were given battalion commander (guandai) posts.[57] According to one source, Liu Xianshi was also rewarded with the honorary rank of a county magistrate.[58] Later, in recognition of his military abilities, Liu Xianqian became the commander of the Guangxi governor's personal guard.[59] Thus, militia leadership again reinforced the Liu family's standing by helping its members acquire new official titles and posts.

Although the original rebel problem had been handled, the unsettled conditions in Guizhou as a whole argued against the complete disbandment of the Liu's militia. With Liu Xianqian's departure for Guangxi, the Border Pacification Battalions were reduced from two to one. But, Guizhou officials continued to see the Lius' forces as an important element in southwestern Guizhou's defenses and encouraged their maintenance. Thus, Liu's battalion was not included in a 1906 reduction of old-style irregular military forces carried out by Guizhou's governor in order to provide funds for a modern new army. Instead his unit was one of twenty battalions of these old-style forces retained for incorporation into a new standardized patrol and defense force system (*xunfangying*). Liu Xianshi's battalion was renamed the second battalion of the West Route Patrol and Defense Forces, and Liu Xianshi retained his position as its commander.[60] It should be noted, however, that as one of the poorest provinces in China, Guizhou had no funds for the extensive reorganization and retraining required by national orders establishing the patrol and defense force system. Thus, to some extent recognizing Liu's force as a patrol and defense battalion was merely an attempt to create the appearance of compliance with military reform requirements at minimal cost to the provincial treasury. For all practical purposes, Liu's battalion remained a militia unit under Liu's personal control. In this instance, the patrol and defense force reorganization simply provided further legitimation for the Liu's local military forces.

Prior to assuming militia leadership Liu Xianshi appeared prepared to seek advancement through the degree system, but, as a result of his role in suppressing the Guangxi rebels, he obtained a military office and established a military reputation. Because of his later emergence as a warlord, Liu Xianshi's military activities are often seen as the most salient feature in his background. But, in fact, despite his retention of this military post, much of Liu Xianshi's attention after suppressing the rebel army was taken up with civil not military matters. Proceeding naturally from Liu Guanli's previous educational work, the Liu family became actively involved in the new educational and reform programs that were among the most important features of elite activity in the years immediately preceding the 1911 Revolution. These civil activities in the end proved as important as the Lius' renewed military power in Liu Xianshi's eventual emergence as a warlord.

LATE QING REFORMS AND EXPANDING ELITE POWER

The Liu family's connections to late Qing educational reforms had early beginnings. In 1897, Yan Xiu, an eminent scholar with ties to Kang Youwei's reform party, was appointed as Guizhou's educational commissioner.

Arriving in Guiyang, Yan established the Statecraft School (Jingshi xuetang), the first Guizhou educational institution to introduce Western elements into its curriculum.[61] Only a select group of forty talented students was enrolled in the new school; among them was Liu Xianzhi, Liu Xianshi's younger brother. In the following years, Liu Guanli's program of inviting prominent scholars to lecture in Xingyi schools also brought leading reformers into contact with the Liu family.[62] Despite Xingyi's peripheral location, these educational contacts kept the Lius well informed of the reform programs emerging in the provincial capital. The Lius quickly realized that these programs were creating new arenas for expanding elite power, and they moved to confirm and enhance their own local leadership by introducing these reforms into the Xingyi area.

The Lius' own participation in reform activities began with locally implementing the modern educational system mandated by the court to replace the civil service examination system in 1905. Liu Guanli actively promoted educational reform, but due to his ill health (he died in 1908) his son, Liu Xianshi, acted as the effective head of the family in these matters. Thus, although Liu Guanli supported the establishment of a Xingyi educational promotion office (*quanxuesuo*) to oversee the county's educational revitalization, Liu Xianshi actually took the lead by serving as its general manager. Many of Liu Xianshi's efforts in this post were directed toward setting up modern schools in accordance with new educational directives. The private academy originally founded by the Lius was converted into an upper-level primary school (*gaodeng xiaoxue*). At the same time, Liu assisted in establishing about twenty lower-level primary schools within Xingyi and others in surrounding counties. Finally, Liu Xianshi was also involved in founding other educational institutions, such as a girls' school, a teacher training institute, a military school, and a public reading room.[63]

The Lius also continued to foster their patron-client relations with other Xingyi families by encouraging and supporting the education of their sons. The Lius paid special attention to promising students, helping them attend the higher-level professional or technical schools that were beginning to be established in Guiyang, and the family even provided stipends to help more than twenty students seek advanced education in Japan.[64] Among these students was He Yingqin, the scion of a prominent Xingyi family who would later gain fame as a Guomindang general and Nationalist China's minister of war. He's military education in Japan was supported by Liu Xianshi, and his ties to the Liu family were later enhanced by marriage to Liu Xianshi's niece.[65] Naturally, as in their previous efforts, the Lius did not fail to insure that the younger generation of their own family would also benefit from these new educational opportunities. For example, Liu Xianshi's younger brother Liu Xianzhi, his eldest son Liu Gangwu, and a nephew

Wang Boqun (the grandson of Wang Peixian) were among a number of family members sent to pursue higher education in Japan.[66]

Although concentrating on education, Liu Guanli and Liu Xianshi also responded quickly to other types of elite reform. In the economic field, Liu Guanli supported a proposal for constructing a Yunnan-Guizhou-Sichuan railroad and encouraged Liu Xianshi to set up forestry companies. In politics, Liu Xianshi headed a Xingyi association to prepare for local self-government. In support of social reforms, Liu Xianshi even helped establish a society for the elimination of footbinding.[67] In regard to the content of their activities, the Lius remained imitators rather than innovators. All the reforms the Lius introduced into Xingyi followed precedents established in the provincial capital. Still, their role in diffusing reform programs belies the usual perception that late Qing reforms were the preserve of urban elites in more advanced core areas.

One important result of the Lius' participation in reform activities was the enhancement of their reputation with and connections to members of the emerging provincial, and even national, reformist elite. The Lius' efforts to bring eminent scholars from Guiyang to Xingyi continued, in this period, to help the Lius establish personal relations with members of the provincial elite. Liu Guanli's reputation in educational affairs had already been established, and Liu Xianshi's assumption of leadership in reform activities helped him gain the respect of Guizhou's educational and constitutionalist leaders in his own right. Equally important were the contacts made by the younger members of the Liu family while attending new schools in Guiyang or higher institutions abroad. For example, while attending the Statecraft School in Guiyang, Liu Xianzhi's teachers were Guizhou's most prominent educators, and many of his classmates were the children of Guiyang's eminent families. After going to Japan, Liu Xianzhi entered the circle of reformers that gathered around Liang Qichao, and he even served for a time as Liang's aide. Upon completing his education in Japan, Liu was invited to take up a position on the Yunnan governor-general's staff.[68] By achieving this post Liu Xianzhi illustrates the opportunities for elite advancement that many found in the new educational system. At the same time, the contacts he made while pursuing his education also contributed to his family's broader social connections at provincial and national levels.

The most telling sign of the social standing the Liu family had achieved in the first decade of the twentieth century was the marriage of Liu Xianshi's daughter to the son of Tang Eryong, a provincial degree holder (*juren*) and the scion of one of Guizhou's eminent families.[69] As the founder and head of Guizhou's provincial educational association, Tang Eryong was the single most powerful man in Guizhou educational circles and a leading member of the provincial reformist elite. The matchmaker who arranged the Tang-

Liu marriage had some reason to boast that it marked "the reach of Tang Eryong's power out into the province and the advance of Liu Xianshi's power toward the center."[70]

Even though reform programs became the main focus of the Lius' public activities in the last years of the Qing, they did not abandon their local military concerns. Indeed one of the Lius' educational projects, their military school at Xingyi, helped bolster the family's military power by training a cadre of officers for Liu Xianshi's local military force. No matter how pressing his other activities, Liu Xianshi also continued to inspect his troops regularly and insure their loyalty by personal attention to their needs.[71] Even after the death of his father in 1908 Liu Xianshi did not give up his military post but rather moved his battalion headquarters into the family residence so he could continue to oversee its affairs while in mourning.[72] In terms of the Lius' total influence, however, their educational and other reform activities, not their military power, projected the family into a wider social and political arena. Although Xingyi county remained the Lius' main power base, this base stood at the center of an emerging network of elite relations that prepared the family for a new outward extension of power during the 1911 Revolution.

THE MAKING OF A PROVINCIAL WARLORD

One of the most important factors influencing the course of the 1911 Revolution in Guizhou was an antagonistic split in the province's reformist elite over the control of Guizhou's public organizations. One faction, organized as the Self-Government Study Society (Zizhi xueshe) under the leadership of Zhang Bailin, successfully won a majority in the first Provincial Assembly elected in 1909. Their opponents, the Constitutional Preparation Association (Xianzheng yubei hui) led by Tang Eryong and Ren Kecheng, based their power on control of the province's educational institutions.[73] At the beginning, the division between the two factions was primarily personal and political not ideological. Over the course of their struggle, however, Zhang Bailin's group slowly became more inclined toward a revolutionary republican program. When news of Hubei province's successful revolutionary uprising against the Qing dynasty reached Guizhou in mid-October 1911, Zhang's "revolutionary" faction, not their more conservative "constitutionalist" (i.e., constitutional monarchist) opponents, set about plotting a similar uprising in Guizhou.[74]

The outbreak of the 1911 Revolution in Hubei found Guizhou's governor, Shen Yuqing, in a precarious position. Although new to his office (he had only arrived in Guizhou in April 1911), Shen was well aware of growing revolutionary sentiment in the province. He was particularly concerned, quite rightly as it turned out, that Guizhou's modern New Army, which served as his capital's main garrison, might follow the lead of Hubei and other provinces and carry out a revolutionary coup. In the face of this danger, Shen turned for advice to Ren Kecheng, head of the constitutionalist faction. Besides suggesting that the leaders of the Self-Government Society be rounded up and executed, advice Shen declined to follow, Ren proposed that Liu Xianshi be called upon to lead a force of local troops to Guiyang to defend the capital against a possible New Army uprising. With his personal military experience and his family's long history of loyal military service, Liu Xianshi was a logical candidate for this assignment. At the same time, given his family's strong ties to the constitutionalist faction through Tang Eryong, political considerations no doubt also influenced Ren's recommendation. In any event, Shen accepted Ren's advice and sent an urgent message to Liu Xianshi asking him to lead five hundred men to Guiyang. As a "sweetener" to insure Liu's speedy compliance, Shen offered to supply Liu's men with new guns from the provincial arsenal. Upon receiving this message Liu showed no hesitation and immediately set out for Guiyang at the head of five hundred men.[75]

Guizhou's revolutionary plotters, meanwhile, were emboldened by the news that a successful New Army uprising had taken place on October 30 in neighboring Yunnan. At the same time, they learned of Liu Xianshi's advance toward Guiyang and decided their own plans could no longer be delayed. On the evening of November 2, New Army soldiers and military students rose in support of the Revolution. With no reliable military forces at hand, the governor was forced to surrender to the provincial assembly, and on November 3 the assembly declared Guizhou's independence. While a Japanese-educated new army instructor, Yang Jincheng, was elected military governor, the real power in Guizhou's revolutionary regime was a policy-making cabinet (*shumi yuan*) headed by Zhang Bailin.[76]

Liu Xianshi and his army had only marched halfway to Guiyang when they received news of the uprising. Although Liu's chance to be a counter-revolutionary hero had been snatched from his grasp, he was unwilling to miss an opportunity to play some role in the events at Guiyang; therefore, instead of retreating to Xingyi, he sent a bold message to the new regime proclaiming, "Although I have approached the capital this time under the orders of Governor Shen, for a long time my heart has inclined toward the revolution you gentlemen have supported."[77] Liu then asked that he be allowed to proceed to Guiyang to bolster revolutionary military power. Because his own contacts had been strongest with the constitutionalist faction, he sent this message in the hands of a young nephew, Wang Wenhua (Wang Boqun's brother), who had become close to several members of the Self-Government Study Society while studying in Guiyang and was known to have revolutionary sympathies.[78]

Neither Liu's message nor his messenger was sufficient to allay the doubts of some revolutionaries over his supposed change of heart. Zhang Bailin called a meeting of revolutionary leaders to discuss Liu's offer; some felt that Liu should be ordered to return to Xingyi with his men, and others argued that the only safe course would be to arrest and execute him. In the end, though, the decisive factor in this issue was Zhang Bailin's conviction that the strength of the new regime required healing the antagonism between Guizhou's two reformist factions. In pursuit of this goal, several prominent constitutionalists, including Ren Kecheng, had been offered posts in the revolutionary cabinet. These men supported Liu Xianshi's entry into Guiyang and argued that his military experience could be useful to the new regime. As a sign of conciliation, Zhang overrode the objections of his colleagues and welcomed Liu Xianshi into Guiyang.[79]

Liu Xianshi's opportunistic jump from counterrevolutionary to revolutionary ranks paid off handsomely. Upon arriving in Guiyang, his unarmed band of five hundred men received the new guns originally promised by Governor Shen. Liu's men were then recognized as a regiment (*biao*) in Guizhou's new revolutionary army, and Liu himself was allowed to retain his command. Finally, Liu was also given a place on the revolutionary cabinet and was appointed head of the new government's military affairs section.[80] Thus Liu was allowed to combine actual military command with an active role in the regime's military administration and policy making.

Zhang Bailin's attempts to reconcile Guizhou's competing elite factions proved a failure. After his entry into Guiyang, Liu Xianshi became the constitutionalist faction's main military ally in an ongoing and increasingly bitter struggle with revolutionary leaders for control of the provincial government. The revolutionaries were weakened by the departure of Yang Jincheng, with most of Guizhou's best troops, for the revolutionary front in central China. On February 2, 1912, Liu and his allies incited a dissatisfied military commander to lead an attack on revolutionary leaders in Guiyang. Liu's main military opponent, the head of a revolutionary force organized from secret society followers, was killed, and Zhang Bailin was forced to flee the city. When Zhang attempted to gather a military following in west Guizhou to fight his way back to Guiyang, Liu ordered his cousin Liu Xianqian, who had returned to Xingyi after Guangxi joined the Revolution, to lead a militia unit from Xingyi to attack Zhang's rear. Zhang was defeated and forced to flee the province.[81] Even at this point, however, revolutionary forces in Guiyang remained sufficiently powerful to prevent Liu from eliminating them. To achieve this end, Liu and his allies sought military assistance from the Yunnan army, an action in which Liu family connections again played an important role.

From the beginning of the 1911 Revolution, Liu Xianzhi, from his position on the governor-general's staff in Yunnan, had been alert to the Revolution's opportunities for extending his family's power. When news of the

Hubei uprising reached Yunnan, he had urged the governor-general to have Liu Xianshi lead a force from Xingyi to Kunming to help defend the city from revolutionaries. Before anything could come of this, however, Yunnan's new army had successfully seized Kunming in the name of the revolution. Despite his original opposition to the revolution, Liu Xianzhi was protected by Cai E, Yunnan's new military governor, because of Liu's strong ties to Cai's mentor, Liang Qichao. On the basis of this connection, Liu was even given a staff position in Yunnan's new government. Unaware that Liu Xianshi had already set out for Guiyang at the request of Guizhou's loyalist governor, Liu Xianzhi then proposed that a detachment of Yunnan troops be despatched to join up with Liu's troops in Xingyi in order to march on Guiyang in the name of the revolution. This plan was also abandoned once the news was received of the successful uprising of Guizhou's New Army.[82] After Guizhou's revolutionary government was established, Liu Xianzhi, along with other Guizhou men connected to the Liu family on Cai's staff, became a secret channel of communication between Liu Xianshi and the Yunnan government.[83] Following long negotiations, Cai was finally convinced to send a military force led by Tang Jiyao to seize control of the Guizhou government.

On February 29, 1912, Tang's forces arrived in Guiyang where they were welcomed by the revolutionary government, which had been deceived into believing they were simply passing through to relieve other revolutionary forces in central China. On March 2, Tang Jiyao joined with Lu Xianshi to carry out a military coup. Revolutionary military forces were surrounded and disbanded or in some cases disarmed and massacred. The military governor who had replaced Yang Jincheng was forced to flee. Other revolutionary leaders who still held military or civil posts were killed or forced to flee the province.[84] Thus, with Tang's aid, Liu and his allies were finally able to defeat their revolutionary rivals.

The price for Tang's military assistance was his assuming Guizhou's military governorship. At the same time, Tang recognized that he required an internal base of support to rule in Guizhou. Thus, Liu Xianshi's civil allies were allowed to control the province's civil administration. Liu himself was rewarded with the post of provincial minister of war, placing him even more firmly in administrative control of Guizhou's military forces. Besides his own original unit, which he was now allowed to expand, Liu was also placed in command of a new Citizens' Army consisting of reorganized patrol and defense force units. Certainly, the Yunnan occupation to some extent limited Liu's military power. Nonetheless, with Tang's assistance, Liu completed the elimination of revolutionary or otherwise unreliable military forces, effectively removing all his Guizhou military rivals.[85] Although Liu's army remained small in relation to Tang's army, Liu had become, by default, Guizhou's most important military leader.

The final reward from Liu Xianshi's Yunnan alliance came in October 1913 when Tang Jiyao returned to Yunnan to succeed Cai E as Yunnan's military governor. Having proven himself a useful ally, Liu was allowed to take over Guizhou's military governorship. Liu quickly undertook a large-scale expansion of his army to insure his military control of the province. As was often the case with Republican military governors, Liu also dominated Guizhou's civil administration, using the same civil elites who had been his political allies since 1911. Finally in 1916 he ended any pretense of a division between civil and military powers and directly assumed the post of civil governor. By establishing his control over Guizhou's military and civil administrations, Liu Xianshi joined the ranks of China's Republican warlords.

The political upheaval of the 1911 Revolution provided an ambitious Liu Xianshi with the opportunity to transform local into provincial power. There was no question that his rise to become Guizhou's preeminent warlord would have been impossible without his family's local military base and his experience as a local military commander. At the same time, this local military power alone does not explain Liu's success. The crucial points of Liu's advance—Governor Shen's request for Liu's military assistance, Liu's admission into Guizhou's revolutionary government, and the procurement of Yunnan's military assistance—all depended not so much on Liu's own military power as on the broader network of social and political influence established by Liu Xianshi and other family members in the decade before the 1911 Revolution. The civil as much as the military aspects of Liu family power helped Liu Xianshi exceed the limits of his family's original local power base.

THE LIU FAMILY IN THE REPUBLICAN PERIOD

After Liu Xianshi's 1911 march from Xingyi county to Guiyang he no longer functioned as a member of the local elite. From this point on, Liu Xianshi's attention was not focused on Xingyi's local affairs but on the broader struggle for provincial and national power. Only in 1925 did he finally retire to Xingyi after being forced from power by a military rival, and less than two years later he was dead. Although Liu's career as a warlord is beyond the scope of this study, it is perhaps fitting to look briefly at the effects of Liu's political success on his family and its Xingyi power base.

One of the most obvious effects of Liu Xianshi's rise was the opportunity it gave him to obtain official posts for other family members. The loss of effective central control over local and provincial appointments after the 1911 Revolution opened the way for a degree of nepotism by Republican period power holders that would have been unimaginable under the imperial system. Liu Xianzhi, on his brother's insistence, was "elected" as a Guizhou national assemblyman and served for many years as his brother's political representative in Beijing.[86] Liu Xianqian held a series of high Guizhou military posts as well as important civil positions including a circuit intendancy and even, for a time, Guizhou's civil governorship.[87] Wang Wenhua, the nephew who acted as Liu's intermediary during the 1911 Revolution, rose under Liu's patronage to the position of division commander in the Guizhou army.[88] Wang's brother-in-law, He Yingqin, also held a number of posts in the Guizhou army including brigade commander and chief of staff.[89] Wang Wenhua's older brother, Wang Boqun, held a circuit intendancy in Guizhou after the 1911 Revolution and then served as Liu's official emissary on a number of political missions.[90]

Although Liu Xianshi's patronage was essential for the initial posts received by his relatives, many of them used these positions as stepping stones for official careers independent of Liu's direct influence. Liu Xianshi's son, Liu Gangwu, made contacts within the Nationalist Party while serving as his father's emissary to Sun Yatsen, and, after his father's death, obtained a series of posts in the Nationalist government.[91] After leading a Guizhou expeditionary force into Sichuan, Wang Wenhua emerged as an autonomous warlord in his own right. He Yingqin eventually left the Guizhou army to take a post as an instructor at the Whampoa Academy in Canton and then became a leading Nationalist general. As a result of extensive social and political contacts made early in his career, Wang Boqun obtained many posts from the Nationalist government in the 1920s, culminating in an appointment as minister of communications.[92] It is highly unlikely, however, that any of these men would have achieved these positions without the original impetus of their relationship to Liu Xianshi.

In traditional Chinese society, elite families saw official posts as a means to replenish family wealth and status. Under the imperial system, however, the direct combination of official and local family power was prevented by the "law of avoidance" that kept an official from holding an office in his home province. This principle was abandoned after the 1911 Revolution, as exemplified in Liu's own rise to provincial power, and this change added an extra dimension to the benefits of officeholding in the Republican period. In the late Qing, the Lius had to apply much money and effort to cultivate relationships with provincial officials to protect their local position. Once Liu Xianshi assumed control over provincial administration, however, his family's local interests were not only freed from official interference but also placed under official protection. Indeed, to watch over the family's power base, Liu Xianqian often held west Guizhou military or civil posts, which gave him direct authority over the Xingyi area.[93] While Liu Xianshi remained in power, his family's dominant position in Xingyi was unchallengeable.

The manner in which Liu Xianshi's official position could be used to protect local family interests, however, suggests a subtle change in the importance of the Lius' local base to their family power. In the late Qing, the Lius'

Xingyi base was the family's main source of both military and economic power. After 1911, more important sources of power came from outside Xingyi. For example, the family's military power originally came solely from its Xingyi-recruited forces. In the Republican period, family members in Xingyi still maintained their local military power, at times using this power to bolster the family's broader political interests; for instance, Liu Xianqian's 1912 attack on Zhang Bailin with Xingyi militia forces. Another example can be seen in 1923 when Liu Xianshi recovered Guizhou's governorship with Yunnan assistance after a two-year fall from power: a local force from Xingyi, led by one of Liu's nephews, joined the vanguard of Yunnan troops escorting Liu back to Guiyang.[94] Nonetheless, while Liu Xianshi ruled as governor he had the military resources of the whole province at his disposal. In this period, this greater military power, not the family's local militia, contributed more to the family's overall position.

A similar change in the sources of Liu family wealth can also be seen in the Republic period. By 1911 the Liu family was already one of the wealthiest landlord families in southwestern Guizhou. In the Republican period, however, the family's total landholdings exceeded four thousand *mu*, making the Lius possibly the largest landlord family in all of Guizhou. Given the extravagant life-style of the Liu family in Xingyi, reported in the Republican period, it is unlikely that this leap in landed wealth came solely from the frugal reinvestment of the profits from previous holdings.[95] Rather, it suggests new external sources of wealth that no doubt also derived largely from office holding. In the Republic, as under the empire, official wealth came not from salaries, which remained quite low, but from graft. For warlords like Liu Xianshi, authorities unto themselves, the opportunities for personal profit were in general limited only by the size of the public treasury. Although records on this type of graft were seldom kept or made public, some reports reveal the sums the Lius were able to extract from their public offices: During a 1916 political crisis, Liu Xianshi sent more than four hundred thousand *yuan*, reportedly taken from the Guizhou treasury, to Shanghai to serve as a personal emergency fund in case he lost power.[96] In two separate cases, Liu Xianzhi and Liu Xianqian were each accused of embezzling two hundred thousand *yuan* in public funds.[97] Even granting some bias in these reports, they suggest the amount of wealth the Lius were able to acquire from their positions. There is no question that much of his wealth eventually found it way back to Xingyi, where it was invested in the family's growing estates.

Liu Xianshi's fall from power in 1925 did have some impact on the Lius' local power base in Xingyi because it removed the political shield of invulnerability that his position had provided for family interests. There had been no such danger to the family's Xingyi base in his earlier loss of power from late 1920 to 1923 because in that case he had been ousted by troops loyal to his nephew, Wang Wenhua, in what was to some extent an intrafamily conflict.[98] In 1925, however, Liu was forced out by an unfriendly rival who decided to establish a military presence in Xingyi county under the guise of a bandit pacification campaign. The Liu family tried to resist this intrusion into their base with disastrous results. The Xiawutun fortress fell to the invading army, and the Lius' military forces were disarmed and disbanded. A large store of weapons the Lius had hoarded at Xiawutun (enough to arm two regiments) was also confiscated, along with a large quantity of the family's accumulated "loot."[99] Liu Xianshi's 1925 fall thus meant the decline of not only the family's provincial political influence but also its local base.

In the end, however, the Liu family landholdings were so extensive and its social status so high that even the 1925 disaster was only a temporary setback that could not undermine the family's dominant position in Xingyi county. Of course, some members of Liu family, such as Liu Gangwu (who never returned home after his father's death), had official careers that drew them more or less permanently away from the Xingyi area. But other members of the family remained in the county to husband the family's interests and continue the family's tradition of local leadership. For example, several of Liu Xianshi's nephews later held district head (*quzhang*) posts in Xingyi and thus maintained the family's influence over local administration. In the 1930s and 1940s, Liu family leadership in Xingyi was primarily assumed by one of Liu Xianshi's nephews, Liu Gongliang, who had become Liu Xianshi's trusted secretary in his last years as governor and had followed his uncle back to Xingyi after his fall. There he upheld family traditions by his involvement in many local affairs, including a special emphasis on local defense. During the Red Army's passage through the area in 1934, Liu Gongliang helped organize an anticommunist defense committee, directed the construction of fortifications throughout the county, collected arms and funds for local defense, and trained local militiamen. Much like descriptions of the Liu family's "small court" in the late Qing, Liu Gongliang came to be seen as Xingyi county's "de facto magistrate."[100] Only the coming of the Communist revolution in 1949 ended the Liu family's century of local power.

CONCLUSION

The history of the Liu family of Xingyi illustrates the manner in which local military force could function in Chinese society, forming and enhancing local-elite power. Through the organization of militia in the mid-nineteenth century the Lius rose from the ranks of village landlords to become a dominant elite family in southwestern Guizhou. Likewise, the family's local military power later provided the base for Liu Xianshi's emergence as provincial warlord. Nonetheless, the Lius as local elites were never simply military strongmen. Indeed, in the last quarter of the nineteenth century the Lius gave up their militia leadership with no appreciable loss in elite status. Instead the family concentrated on enhancing their social position by more traditionally approved forms of elite behavior, notably educational patronage and network building. Although they revived a local military base at the turn of the century, in the following decade they also sought to perpetuate and expand their local power by introducing reform programs into the Xingyi area. The long-term maintenance of the Lius' position as local elites ultimately depended on both military and civil activities.

The case of the Liu family suggests that the real key to understanding the role of military power in local elite formation is to identify the context in which it was applied. In the mid-nineteenth century, militia leadership served as the agency for the Liu family's remarkable rise to a position of local dominance, but the condition of widespread rebellion and social disorder ultimately made this rise possible. Likewise only the special conditions of the 1911 Revolution in Guizhou gave Liu Xianshi the chance to parlay his family's local military power into provincial military domination. For the Lius, then, extraordinary times had presented extraordinary opportunities to benefit from local military power; in peaceful times the Lius switched just as easily to civil means of enhancing their social position. The Lius' particular success lay in the ability to adjust their social strategies to new conditions and to employ their military and civil resources in ways that took best advantage of changing circumstances.

PART THREE

Republican Elites and Political Power

SEVEN

Patterns of Power:
Forty Years of Elite Politics in a
Chinese County

Lenore Barkan

In recent years scholars have revealed much about the nature of China's early twentieth-century local leaders and the ways in which they interacted with state authorities. However, major questions concerning pre-1949 politics in the Chinese countryside remain unresolved. Most important, what was the overall pattern of change in the composition and activities of twentieth-century local elites as well as their relationship to the state and other social and political groups, and why did this pattern emerge?

Through a study of local leaders in North Jiangsu's Rugao county from the beginning of the twentieth century until the late 1930s, this essay addresses these questions. The evidence from Rugao suggests that early twentieth-century China witnessed neither consistent local-elite growth and expansion nor persistent local-elite disintegration. Instead, this period of rapid change saw China's local leaders both reacting to and capitalizing on ever new sets of political relationships within a constantly changing national context.

Initially, historians portrayed the late Qing dynasty as a period of social turbulence and governmental decay.[1] Moreover, they argued that there was further disintegration after the 1911 overthrow of the Qing and the subsequent inauguration of the Republic. China became politically fragmented, and because military concerns dominated governmental thinking, other programs for education and economic development got short shrift. Only with the Communist revolution of 1949 was China again united.[2]

The portrayal of local elites during this period was equally unflattering. Chinese and Western writers frequently referred to local leaders as "rotten gentry" or as "evil gentry and local bullies."[3] Later historians, particularly those writing about the turbulent North China plain, characterized local leaders as selfish, violence-prone individuals solely interested in enriching their private coffers and increasing their personal power. Moreover, the

historians claimed that local elites' pursuit of individual advantage contributed to the increasing fragmentation and disintegration of both local
society and national polity.[4]

Kuhn, Mann, and other scholars subsequently challenged or modified
this unpromising picture in a number of ways. They argued that after the
devolution of power, a by-product of gentry involvement in suppressing mid-
nineteenth-century rebellions, there was a long-range trend toward governmental reassertion of control over local elites. Begun by the Qing, and
continuing unevenly under the Republic, this effort was characterized by
growing central fiscal control and extended state bureaucracy at the district
and even village levels. Often cited manifestations of the trend include the
organizations established by New Policy reforms at the end of the Qing, such
as local educational associations and chambers of commerce and the elected
assemblies and councils set up in name of "local self-government." These
scholars further proposed that a second phase of state assertiveness occurred
after the Nationalists seized power in 1927. Through reforming the tax system, particularly the abolition of *lijin* and the imposition of a business tax,
abolishing *dibao* (local constables), and establishing subdistrict government
offices, the Nationalists sought to strengthen the central government's administrative and fiscal control over local leaders still further, albeit with
somewhat disappointing results.[5]

Other historians stressed the local elites' progressively stronger initiatives
that resulted in a new "public" sphere of activity, neither fully autonomous
nor completely controlled by higher-level officials. In post-Taiping Zhejiang
province, Rankin argued that an increasingly active, commercialized, and
differentiated local leadership ultimately challenged the imperial dynasty
and contributed to its overthrow. In Nantong county, Jiangsu province—
next to Rugao—Bastid found that county-level gentry, led by the well-
known reformer Zhang Jian, were reform-minded rather than conservative
and were genuinely concerned with the well-being of the entire society rather
than their own personal security and power. Similarly, Schoppa drew a picture of Lower Yangzi valley elites who in the first decades of the twentieth
century sponsored a complex process of association building, social management, and elite participation in local politics.[6]

A still more complex picture was drawn by those writers who carried
questions concerning the nature of local leadership into the 1930s. I found
that although local leaders continued to engage in many of the same activities as their earlier counterparts, the considerable services performed by local
leaders narrowed, and the importance of security activities, particularly at
the subcounty level, increased.[7] Geisert expressed doubts about the Nanjing
government's progress in implementing its plans for local reorganization,[8]
and Duara suggested that what amounted to incomplete state making had a
deleterious effect on rural communities by encouraging the rise of entre-

preneurial, subadministrative "state-brokers" who profited at the expense of both government and peasants.[9]

Such findings partly reinforced the older view of an increasingly violent local elite and a progressively deteriorating local society. But they also made it clear that it is difficult to discern consistent patterns of growing elite leadership capacity, increasing state control, or advancing social disintegration amidst the rapid changes of the first half of the twentieth century. Instead, they indicated the importance of viewing both state and local societal actors not as isolated entities, but as parts of a larger network of social and political relationships in which a change in one area produced variations in others. On the basis of my study of Rugao, I would suggest that these changes be grouped into five periods:

Period I (Early twentieth century until 1915): Local elites between state and society. Local leaders concerned themselves with reform, but were very sensitive and responsive to issues raised at national or provincial levels. Because the central state still existed (in fact until 1911, and as an ideal until 1915) the most prominent local leaders directed much of their attention toward reform at central or provincial levels rather than reform originating in their own areas. Many local changes were mandated by the center or province, but as state control weakened, local elites had some latitude to take increasing initiative and sponsor reform in their local domains.

Period II (1915 to 1924): Local-elite triumph. This was the golden age of local-elite leadership. The central state had almost totally disintegrated leaving local leaders on their own, and opposition to local-elite rule had not yet appeared at the bottom of the system. As a result, local-elite leaders devoted their energies to building up their local areas. The result was a burst of road building, hospital construction, land surveying, new business ventures, and other projects.

Period III (1925 to May 1927): Rise of the opposition. Now instead of being threatened from the top of the system, local leaders, for the first time, were threatened by disaffected elites forging ties to the masses outside existing social channels. As students, Communists and Nationalists organized; they criticized both local leaders and their programs, putting local leaders increasingly on the defensive.

Period IV (May to October 1927): Attack and retreat. During this period local leaders, under attack by Communists and Nationalists, resigned local leadership posts and withdrew from public affairs. In addition, the newly installed Nationalist government in Nanjing attempted to substitute its officials for local leaders.

Period V (October 1927 to March 1938): Local leaders return. The Nationalist government defeated the left-wing opposition. However, because the new officials proved ineffective, the Nationalists were forced to rely on local leaders. Although local leaders became increasingly powerful, they were neither as innovative nor as independent as in the late 1910s and early 1920s; they were no longer concerned with social change and made no new local investments. Instead, confronted with both pressure from the Nationalist government above and potential opposition inside local society led by continuing Communist and student movements, the local leaders worried about their own security. Consequently, a bifurcated power system, split between local leaders and the Nanjing regime, became an obstacle to effective local government.

This periodization of local elites reacting to and operating within a larger political environment aims to resolve the apparent conflict between those scholars who portray early twentieth-century China as a country marked by disorder, violence, and instability and those who discern either growing state control or increasing local leadership capacity. It also emphasizes that throughout the first several decades of the twentieth century, local leaders were only one of several forces active in Rugao. In Period I, the Qing state was still an effective force; however, in Period III, revolutionary elites in the united Communist and Nationalist parties challenged the existing local-elite establishment. After the spring of 1927, Communists, acting alone, continued to exert revolutionary pressure while the Nanjing regime attempted to gain political control through the Nationalist county government.

If one thinks of each of these as groups occupying a political "arena," then the relationship that existed between these arenas during each period can be illustrated as in Figure 7.1. To describe the character and activities of local elites through these five periods, I will focus on two of the most important members of Rugao's twentieth-century elite: Sha Yuanbing, one of the most active pre-1927 local leaders, and Sha Yuanqu, one of the most important post-1927 political actors. Examining the changes in the lives of Rugao's notables and the context in which they operated also provides information relative to three more general questions: First, what were the social and economic characteristics of local leaders during the late Qing and Republican periods, and in what types of activities did they engage? Second, what kind of relationships did local leaders have with higher levels of government, as well as other locally active social and political groups, and what was the resulting pattern of elite-state and elite-society relations? Third, how did the characteristics of local leaders and their relationship to both the central state and other social and political groups change over time?

RUGAO COUNTY, JIANGSU PROVINCE

Rugao county is located in North Jiangsu. Stretching between the Yangzi River and the Yellow Sea, in the 1920s and 1930s it was on the periphery of the Lower Yangzi macroregion.[10] Thus it was close enough to Shanghai for

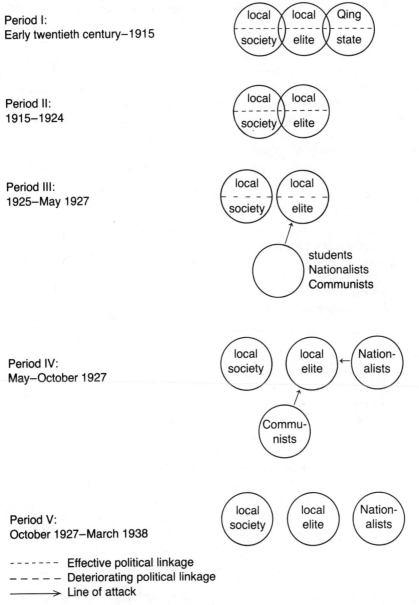

Period I:
Early twentieth century–1915

Period II:
1915–1924

Period III:
1925–May 1927

students
Nationalists
Communists

Period IV:
May–October 1927

Period V:
October 1927–March 1938

- - - - - - - Effective political linkage
- - - - - Deteriorating political linkage
⟶ Line of attack

Figure 7.1. The Relationship Between Political Arenas in Twentieth-Century
Rugao County

news of its affairs to be printed frequently in Jiangsu and Shanghai news-papers but far enough away from major urban centers to have retained its traditional rural character.

In 1930 Rugao reported a population of 1,356,777 individuals, of which, based on 1929 figures, at least 183,268 were urban residents.[11] A few years later Rugao was said to be home to more than 1.5 million people, making it both Jiangsu's and China's most populous county. About 70 percent of the population engaged in agriculture. Of these, the vast majority were tenants (75.4 percent). Only a small minority were either half-owners and half-tenants (7.7 percent) or owner-cultivators (16.9 percent). Moreover, plots were not large: 50 percent of the households cultivated between five and ten *mu* (one *mu* equals one-sixth acre), 30 percent between ten and twenty *mu*, and 15 percent between twenty and thirty *mu*; 5 percent tilled between thirty and fifty *mu*, and only a very few over fifty.[12]

Although little use was made of machinery or chemical fertilizers, farmers in Rugao were relatively productive and prosperous. In an average year, the county was self-sufficient in food grains. Until the early 1930s, the biggest crops were rice and cotton. Barley, wheat, beans, corn, and sweet potatoes were also important. In the early 1930s, when weather conditions changed, farmers substituted more drought-resistant crops (like cotton, corn, soy-beans, and peanuts) for rice. By 1934 "very little" rice was grown in Rugao.[13]

Rugao produced abundant cotton, but unlike neighboring Nantong, the county never developed permanent facilities to process this raw material into finished or even semifinished goods.[14] Rugao's two best-known agricul-tural specialties were turnips and processed ham. But every August, with clockwork regularity, the turnips caused massive outbreaks of typhoid and other serious diseases when they were eaten raw after being washed in con-taminated water. The hams were good but definitely inferior in quality to those produced in Zhejiang and Yunnan.[15]

In political terms Rugao was no more distinguished. Under the Qing dynasty it was part of a prefecture dominated by its more influential neigh-bor to the southeast, Tongzhou.[16] By 1927, even though it was China's most populous county, the Jiangsu government still considered it a county of lesser status than Nantong, the new name of Tongzhou.[17]

RUGAO'S LOCAL ELITE: THE OLDER GENERATION

Because scholars disagree over what constitutes the local elite, it is impossi-ble, when studying a particular area like Rugao, to start with an a priori definition of the local elite and then use it to identify the particular indi-viduals who meet the definition's requirements.[18] Instead, I will define the Rugao local elite as those individuals considered elite by contemporaries who lived in or wrote about the county. According to this criterion, it quickly becomes apparent that several families, including the Shas, the Mas, and the Zhus, dominated Rugao politics from the later Qing until the Japanese occupation and that among these the Shas were preeminent.[19]

The Shas were a well-established kinship group, some of whose members had been part of the Rugao gentry since at least the early Qing. Although not among the most successful in passing the examinations, by 1873 Sha family members had acquired various *gongsheng* degrees and purchased other degrees or honorific titles. Several had served as magistrates or held other low-ranking official posts, and some had local reputations as scholars or poets. The 1860 establishment of a home for chaste widows (*jingjie tang*) in a Sha family building probably indicates that Shas were involved with locally managed public institutions. Finally, the incorporation of the top family members into district gentry networks is demonstrated by the presence of a Sha in the compilation committees of both the 1837 and the 1873 Rugao county gazetteers.[20]

By the early twentieth century the most notable local leader in Rugao was a member of the Sha family named Sha Yuanbing. Contemporary newspaper articles refer to Sha Yuanbing in more adulatory terms than anyone else in the county, and later materials reinforce this impression of Sha as the most highly esteemed early twentieth-century Rugao leader. Even current Rugao residents still regularly refer to Sha not only as a "local gentry" (*difang shenshi*) but as a "big gentry" (*ju shen*) or an "old gentry" (*lao shen*). Several writers state unequivocally that Sha Yuanbing was the most prominent among Rugao's pre-1927 gentry.[21]

Sha Yuanbing was born in 1864. He passed the *jinshi* examination in 1894 and entered the Hanlin Academy. Throughout his adult life, Sha continued to pursue learning. He maintained a large, locally famous library of several hundred volumes, collected paintings and calligraphy, and belonged to a local literary society that often met at the Sha house. Sha's son reports that during the day his father involved himself in public affairs, but after he returned home he always had a book in his hand and never stopped reading.[22]

Steeped in traditional scholarship, Sha nonetheless was open to new ideas, including those from Japan and the West. During the 1898 reform movement, he was part of the Shanghai Agricultural Society (Nong hui), which met for five years under the direction of reformer Luo Zhenyu. Members translated foreign magazine articles concerning agriculture and published them in the journal *Nongxue bao* as well as other periodicals.[23]

In addition to promoting new learning, Sha set a high moral tone for the county. He vigorously opposed the use of even ordinary tobacco, and in 1924 led a local gentry association called the Society to Prohibit Smoking (Jinxi zhiyan hui). The Society disliked cigarettes "because they cost so much, were a drain on the local economy, and had no redeeming value." Sha also hated gambling, to the extent that people close to him did not dare gamble publicly and other gamblers, seeing him coming, would quickly hide their gambling devices to avoid being chastised.[24]

Sha's credentials as a local leader in the early twentieth century thus rested on several foundations: He enjoyed the status conferred by possessing the highest examination degree; he was a man of landed wealth, and he had a high reputation for learning and probity. These attributes were not affected by the abolition of the traditional civil service examinations in 1905, and until his death in early 1927 they provided him with the symbolic capital that underlay his local influence and legitimized his socially derived authority.

Other prominent Rugao leaders referred to as gentry during the later Qing and early Republic had similar characteristics. Like Sha, many came from well-established local families and were Qing degree holders who, even after the fall of the dynasty, remained active in education. Huang Qiwu, leader of the 1911 Revolution in Rugao, was a *xiucai* who in 1904 went to Japan to study medicine. While in Tokyo he met Sun Yat-sen and became active in Sun's Revolutionary Alliance (Tongmeng hui). After returning to China he spent four and a half years teaching in a Nanjing normal school before returning to Rugao, where he continued to teach in the Rugao Normal School and became known for his calligraphy. He also is listed among the investigators (*shen cha*) of the 1933 gazetteer.[25]

Similarly, Mao Guangsheng was the offspring of a venerable Rugao family that dated to the end of the Ming; its members frequently appear in the pages of Rugao's gazetteers.[26] After obtaining a *juren* degree during the first decade of the twentieth century and studying herbal medicine, Mao read Rousseau, developed an interest in political reform, and became a follower of Liang Qichao.[27] Still others include Zhang Fan, holder of a *gongsheng* degree, who helped found the Rugao Normal School and was one of its assistant principals;[28] and Deng Pujun, a *shengyuan*, and also a noted calligrapher, who became an expert on Buddhism after retiring from politics and traveled to many counties to instruct prisoners in its doctrines.[29]

RUGAO'S LOCAL ELITE: THE YOUNGER GENERATION

Those gentry active during the 1910s and the 1920s were mostly men of broad learning who cultivated widespread intellectual interests and could act in many different realms. Their descendants, however, received more technical educations and had narrower bases of authority. Many of this latter group were graduates of normal schools. Sha Yuanqu, a younger relative of Sha Yuanbing and an active post-1927 leader, graduated from the Nantong Normal School, one of the most progressive schools of its day.[30] Following his graduation, Sha Yuanju, like Sha Yuanbing, became active in running Rugao's schools, but he never became as preeminent as the older Sha. The existing sources contain neither a single mention of his participation in literary or cultural activities outside the realm of his official duties nor any reference that would make him appear a model of social and civic virtue. Thus, after 1927, even though a small group of relatively highly educated individuals such as Sha Yuanqu continued to dominate Rugao, symbolic capital derived from traditional cultural pursuits was apparently replaced by new and perhaps less symbolically potent authority derived from technical expertise.

Another group of local leaders received a legal education, and most of Rugao's early lawyers became important local leaders. Zhang Xiang, active in both local and provincial affairs, was one of the first five lawyers in Rugao along with He Sen, Hu Zhaoyi, and another probable member of the Sha family, Sha Xunyi. Less admired, but nevertheless powerful, was Xu Guozhen, a blind lawyer, who, after his fertilizer factory went bankrupt, fled to Rugao's sandbars where he continued to amass both wealth and power by managing reclaimed land.[31]

Cong Peigong, a poor *gongsheng* at the end of the Qing but a powerful Rugao local actor by the 1920s, got his start in a technical class. Cong graduated from the Rugao Normal School's special training course in surveying. He then was appointed to the Grand Canal's North Jiangsu Engineering Office (Jiangbei yunhe gongcheng ju). Later, a friend introduced Cong to a past Jiangsu governor by falsely claiming that Cong's father and the governor had received *juren* degrees in the same year. With the governor's support, Cong was appointed head of the county surveying office (*qingzhang ju*) in 1921. Subsequently he was put in charge of building Rugao's first public roads. Although he developed a "great reputation" in these posts, it was largely as a wealthy technician.[32]

Similar changes can be seen in other families like the Mas, who, in the twentieth century, gradually moved away from their gentry origins. The nineteenth-century Mas were literati. At least one Ma was a *gongsheng* and an elementary school teacher, and another was a *juren*, who with Sha and others, helped set up the Rugao Normal School.[33] The most locally prominent was the wealthy *gongsheng* Ma Jinfan, who participated in compiling the 1873 Rugao gazetteer and helped raise money for educational and religious institutions as well as various public works. He also set a moral tone for the community through his efforts on behalf of the blind and the orphaned.[34] The prestige Ma derived from his moral stature and community activities was much the same as that enjoyed by Sha Yuanbing about three decades later.

Aside from their scholarly interests, the Mas were among both Rugao's largest landowners and those wealthy families who owned and rented out about one-third of the buildings in Rugao city.[35] Mas also became active in the chamber of commerce founded at the end of the Qing. The man from this kin group who was best known for public activities in the twentieth century,

Ma Jizhi, had less impressive credentials than his older relatives. He held numerous political offices but was known for neither his learning nor his devotion to public service. Widespread and detailed contemporary sources never mention any educational achievements. More recent writers describe him as avaricious with a gift for political trickery; furthermore, they accused him of using one of Rugao's long-established charitable institutions "to carry out small favors and to fish for fame and compliments" and called him Rugao's "number one evil gentry."[36]

From the above examples, one can see that the abolition of the Qing examination system and the demise of classical education that supported it changed the characteristics of Rugao's gentry. Prior to 1905, Rugao's local leaders were trained as generalists and could easily wield authority in many areas. In contrast, after 1905, Rugao's local leaders were much more likely to be trained in a profession like teaching, law, a technical field, or business.[37] Although local-elite members continued to come from the same few families, the change from generalist to specialist reduced each individual's symbolic capital and divided authority into much more discrete arenas, making collective elite domination of a particular locale more difficult. Consequently, the entire system of local-elite domination became more vulnerable to challenges from either the top of the system (i.e., the state) or social groups whose members previously had not held local power.

This shift from generalist to specialist was not sudden. Gentry members trained under the old examination system such as Sha Yuanbing, Huang Qiwu, Mao Guangsheng, and Deng Pujun continued to dominate the county until the mid-1920s. Simultaneously, throughout the 1910s and 1920s, the number of specially trained modern school graduates only increased slowly. Not until after the arrival of the Nationalists in 1927 did elites with these new credentials dominate Rugao. The coincidence of the Nationalist's arrival with changed local leadership made the late 1920s a more significant watershed in Chinese local history than it might otherwise have been.[38]

Because generalists continued to dominate Rugao through the mid-1920s, the gradual change in the characteristics of Rugao's local leaders is important. If local leaders are generalists, changes in programs and policies, even when involving western ideas and modern technology, can be made without changing personnel; the same individuals can merely alter their activities. Because change does not threaten their power or authority—quite the contrary, it often enhances it—generalists promoting the overall well-being of their particular local area can be receptive to new ideas. Prior to 1927, by supporting the establishment of modern schools and businesses, China's degree-holding gentry could add to their symbolic capital and hence their local prestige. Therefore Sha Yuangbing's combination of high traditional status, interest in Western-style reform, and, as we shall see below, impor-

tant outside connections made him a logical leader in establishing new institutions in Rugao.

However, if local leaders are specialists, new programs or policies neces-
sitate a change in personnel and threaten local-elite dominance. As a result,
existing leaders are likely to oppose such change. After 1927, any call for
innovative organizations and programs meant that a new group of individuals appeared on the local scene to challenge local-elite control. That Sha
Yuanqu and others like him became conservative upholders of the status quo
should not be surprising.

Thus, the changing characteristics of Rugao's elites partially explain why
Rugao's pre-1927 elites appeared more receptive to new ideas and its post-
1927 leaders more hostile. That explanation is not sufficient, however. By
following Sha Yuanbing and Sha Yuanju through the five periods of local
politics we can see how outside forces also affected Rugao's leaders.

PERIOD I: LOCAL ELITES BETWEEN STATE AND SOCIETY

From the 1898 reform period until two years after the 1911 Revolution,
Rugao's local leaders both reacted to and were involved in reforms generated
at the central and provincial levels. Sha Yuanbing, although not the only
reform-minded Rugao gentry, was clearly the leader of these efforts. Sha's
extralocal ties dated back to his success in the metropolitan examinations
and appointment to the Hanlin Academy. At that time he formed one particularly crucial personal relationship. The major Jiangsu reform leader,
Zhang Jian, also passed the examination in 1894 and was also a Hanlin.[39]
This "same-year" (*tongnian*) tie presumably was the basis of Sha's long association with Zhang and his projects. As a friend and close associate of
Zhang Jian, Sha was a member of the Shanghai-centered Jiangsu provincial
reformist network, which interlaced with networks of elites in adjacent
provinces to become a vigorous political force in central China. Zhang Jian
was the central, best-known figure in the Jiangsu network, although he was
surrounded by other high-status, wealthy gentry and merchants. Like Sha,
these men were not only involved in joint projects in Shanghai or Nantong
(Zhang Jian's home and the center of his reform projects) but were also
active in other macroregional associations in Shanghai and presided over
organizations in their native areas.[40]

Sha's earliest reform activities were concentrated in education. He and
Zhang Jian met with Zhang Zhidong in Nanjing to discuss schools in 1902.
During the first decade of the new century Sha set up Rugao's first major
modern educational institutions: the Rugao Normal School (*shifan xuexiao*),
the Rugao Middle School (*zhong xuexiao*), and the Yizhong Commercial
School (Yizhong shangye xuexiao). The quality of these schools was compar-

atively high, and the Normal School became relatively well known throughout the province. In addition, Sha's schools—all located in the county seat—were important because they produced modern trained personnel who were sent to work in other, more backward areas of the county.[41]

Sha also became active in both provincial- and national-level political movements. He was part of the Jiangsu railway movement, a nationalistic effort by Jiangsu gentry members to raise private Chinese capital for provincial railway construction as an alternative to foreign loans.[42] He belonged to the Shanghai-based Society to Prepare for Constitutional Government (Yubei lixian gonghui), founded in 1906 by reformist gentry and merchants from several provinces and the Jiangsu Educational Association. In 1909 Sha's many progressive provincial-level activities and similar efforts in Rugao led the small number of Rugao county voters, which probably included many of his close associates, to elect him to the newly established Jiangsu Provincial Assembly. In the years following the 1911 Revolution he was reelected to the 1913 assembly, whose members selected him as assembly president, and in 1914 he was chosen an alternate Jiangsu representative to the lower house of the National Assembly.[43]

Sha's close association with Zhang extended to business affairs as well. He was one of a small handful of gentry who supported Zhang Jian's early industrial projects, including the Dasheng cotton mill in Nantong. Because of these and other commercial ventures, Bastid places Sha among the most active Jiangsu provincial-level entrepreneurs. Eventually, Sha's reputation earned him a position on the Shanghai chamber of commerce.[44]

Within Rugao itself, prior to 1911 Sha headed Rugao's local self-government association and the Rugao chamber of commerce. Shortly after the 1911 Revolution, he was one of thirty people who made plans to set up a Rugao agricultural association (Rugao xian nonghui).[45] In 1911, his local political prominence convinced other local leaders, such as Huang Qiwu, that Sha's support was essential if Rugao was to join the revolution. Subsequently, Huang persuaded Sha to support a declaration of independence from the Qing dynasty and to become involved in the revolution in Rugao.[46]

In November 1911 after the last Qing magistrate left the county, Sha gathered together the county's prominent citizens (renshi) for a meeting. They decided to follow the example of other counties and set up a temporary military government general headquarters (Rugao xian linshi junzheng zong siling bu). Sha was put in charge of political affairs and subsequently served briefly as county magistrate (xian zhishi).[47] However, presumably because he became involved in higher-level politics, Sha soon gave up his Rugao post. Although he continued to be politically active and to hold many lesser positions, Sha did not again officially head the county government.

Although probably the most distinguished, Sha was not the only Rugao gentry member to be drawn into the vortex of both district and higher-level political events during the first decade and a half of the twentieth century. Large numbers of Rugao's local leaders were benefactors of the mainly privately funded modern schools. Many of these same individuals, especially those with Qing degrees, also joined the schools' faculties. Moreover, provincial and national organizations such as the Society to Prepare for Constitutional Government, and the Jiangsu and national political assemblies all had several members—in addition to Sha—who were from Rugao.[48]

In sum, opportunities opened up by the 1898 reforms, the constitutional movement, the 1911 Revolution, and the creation of the provincial and national assemblies incorporated Rugao's local leaders into overlapping movements for political change at the national, provincial, and local levels. Whether confronted with the state-initiated late Qing reforms and the constitutional assemblies or with the 1911 Revolution against the state, Rugao's leaders consistently showed that they were responsive to outside movements and willing to implement new ideas in their local arena.

The gentry have been called the link between the traditional Chinese state and the society it governed.[49] In the early part of the twentieth century, even though the programs formulated in Beijing and elsewhere changed dramatically, Rugao's gentry, showing impressive flexibility and adaptability, continued to function effectively as the link between center and locality. Only when the political structure changed did the role of the gentry alter significantly.

PERIOD II: LOCAL ELITE TRIUMPH

Following the 1913 failure of the Nationalists' Second Revolution and Yuan Shikai's consolidation of control in Beijing, the political power of the Chinese central state declined dramatically. Between 1913 and 1915 Yuan abolished the representative assemblies, breaking the last major structural link between national and provincial capitals and their constituents in the hinterland. Without formal functions at higher levels, Rugao's gentry, like Sha Yuanbing, returned to their home counties. Because no activist national or provincial government competed for their attention or demanded their services, for the next ten years Rugao's leaders concerned themselves almost exclusively with building up their local area—including politics, water conservancy, education, taxation and finance, land surveying, road building and maintenance, electrification, newspapers, small-scale industry, and charity. As might be expected, Sha Yuanbing was a leader in these efforts.[50]

Starting in 1914 Sha headed Rugao's Water Conservancy Committee (Shuili hui). Given water's importance to both Rugao's agriculture and its transportation, this may have been one of Sha's most important positions; he often either mediated among Rugao's citizens or negotiated with outside bodies on behalf of Rugao residents.[51] Likewise, Sha was instrumental in bringing electricity to Rugao. In 1916 Sha, along with Zhang Jian, raised 50,000 *yuan* and built the first electrical generating station in Rugao. Sha was its director. Several years later, at least in part as a result of disputes with Zhang Jian, the company neared bankruptcy; Sha saved it by personally buying one thousand shares at 100 *yuan* each. Until his death in 1927 Sha continued to head the reorganized company, which made a small profit under better management.[52]

Sha also concerned himself with the county's finances. Although there is no evidence that he managed county funds directly, after the 1911 Revolution Sha was heavily involved in land resurveys and land tax reassessment projects carried out in the hopes of increasing county collection of tax revenues. In 1914 Sha and others set up a surveying office (*cehui ju*) within the county government to survey all of Rugao's topography. By 1917 the work of the office was completed. Subsequently, from 1921 until his death in 1927, Sha headed the office that supervised land surveying and land tax adjustments (*qingzhang ju*).[53]

To improve community health, Sha actively supported both Chinese and Western medicine. In 1922 he was made honorary chairperson of the newly established Rugao Traditional [Chinese] Medical Society (Zhongyi gonghui). He founded and headed the Rugao public hospital that treated local citizens using Western techniques. And, in 1926, shortly before his death, Sha made fund-raising plans to acquire land for hospital expansion.[54]

In the commercial realm, Sha was no less innovative. Although most studies of the Nantong area have focused on the well-known entrepreneur Zhang Jian, they have failed to note that Zhang was only one of a larger group of gentry, some in outlying counties like Rugao, who throughout the 1910s and 1920s raised capital locally to invest in larger factories in major cities such as Shanghai, as well as in new commercial ventures in their own areas. Sha's investments were widespread. In addition to helping capitalize Zhang Jian's Da Sheng Weaving Mill in Nantong, he invested in a drugstore, a ham factory, an oil pressing mill, a flour mill, an iron foundry, a Shanghai steamship company, a local steamship company, a local old-style bank (*qianzhuang*) and several land reclamation companies along the coast of Dongtai county north of Rugao. One of Sha's ventures, the Kuang Feng Ham Factory was very successful; its product was sold in Shanghai and the United States—perhaps through its own storefront in San Francisco—and received a prize at an international fair in Honolulu. Although it later went bankrupt, this company laid the foundation for what is still one of Rugao's major industries: the curing and processing of ham and other types of sausage.[55]

Sha also effectively linked Rugao and the remaining higher levels of government. For example, in 1915 the provincial government approved a petition by Sha and another gentry member for an addition to the local land tax.

Later, in 1926 Sha turned over to the provincial governor a Rugao grain merchants' request that a particular tax be abolished. Again, Sha's wish was granted and the tax abolished.[56]

In short, after returning to Rugao, Sha engaged in various activities including politics, public works, finance, medicine, and commerce. Several characteristics of Sha's activities are notable. First, he never concentrated on one type of endeavor but spread his energies over a broad field. Even when innovative, Sha remained a generalist. Second, Sha took part in reform efforts and consciously brought new ideas, organizations, and technologies into Rugao. As a result, in the 1910s and 1920s under the leadership of its traditional gentry, Rugao started to move into the modern world.

Third, there is no evidence that Sha moved from progressive civil activities into the more coercive and militaristic ones that have been said to mark the twentieth-century decline of China's gentry class. Because Rugao escaped the depredations of the Taipings in the mid-nineteenth century, as well as those of marauding warlord armies in the early twentieth century, Rugao remained peaceful during Sha's lifetime. Undoubtedly, Rugao's lack of involvement in military affairs allowed Sha's reforms to proceed apace and protected him from having to worry about security affairs. He did not have to raise a militia or personally control troops.

In conclusion, a description of Sha's Rugao activities provides further evidence to support the image of elite activism in late nineteenth- and early twentieth-century China. Like his Zhejiang counterparts studied by Rankin and Schoppa, Sha Yuanbing increasingly engaged in activities outside the fields of traditional learning, including commercial and industrial affairs. Also like his contemporaries, Sha's widespread efforts in areas like public health, water conservancy, and finance created a new and expanding "public realm," in which initiative and control lay with local leaders, not the state.

The question remains, what effect did Sha's activities have on the relations between local elites and the state? Did they increase the power of local-elite leaders or add to the authority of the state? Sha's many public offices and private enterprises were all officially sanctioned. However, the impetus for Sha's activities came less from the state than from the reformist networks centering about Zhang Jian and the still larger complex of overlapping gentry-merchant networks linking activists in Rugao, Nantong, Shanghai, and other part of Jiangsu and beyond.

In other words, when the central state organization disintegrated, gentry such as Sha Yuanbing could no longer link that organization and the Chinese populace. Instead, after 1915 Sha's local prominence derived from his high-gentry status, his outside connections, and the particular context of the last years of the Qing and the beginning of the Republic. That period first favored the rapid expansion of the "public realm" through the new reformist associations and organizations and then, when central power disintegrated, allowed elites in districts such as Rugao to continue their activities locally. Whether such social mobilization might build into a force able to create a new Chinese state depended, however, on a favorable environment continuing, unlikely in the volatile political climate of the Republic.

PERIOD III: RISE OF THE OPPOSITION

Starting with the 1919 May Fourth Movement, and gaining momentum in the mid-1920s, new ideas and organizations traveled up the rivers and canals of North Jiangsu from Shanghai and Nanjing, to Nantong, and then on to Rugao. Spread initially by students, and later by the Nationalist and Communist parties, these increasingly radical ideas and organizations welled up to challenge the power of China's local leaders.

The first challenge came in May 1919 when students at the Rugao Normal School, in response to requests from their Beijing counterparts, formed a Rugao student association and announced a boycott of Japanese goods. Gu Dengzhi, a local gentry member related by marriage to Sha Yuanbing and chief stockholder and manager of Rugao's largest purveyor of foreign products, the Datong department store (Datong shangdian), failed to comply. Much to the surprise of local residents, the students confiscated and burned his store's large stock of foreign goods.[57]

After 1919, despite threats to withhold their degrees and the dismissal of their principal, most of Rugao's students continued to acquire radical publication and agitate for change. In 1922 Rugao students attending schools and universities in Nanjing and Beijing set up the Common Peoples' Society (Pingmin she), which included many future members of Rugao's Nationalist and Communist parties. One of its goals was to "attack corrupt gentry." In both the newspapers and the courts, the association accused many of Rugao's local leaders—including Li Yaqing, Yu Dasan, Mao Jie, Fang Ziying, Pan Shushen and Sha Yuanqu—of unscrupulous and illegal behavior.[58]

In 1925 the nationalistic May Thirtieth Movement echoed throughout Rugao, leading to student-staged demonstrations not only in the county seat but also in many other towns. Local leaders, especially those involved in merchandizing foreign goods, were among the movement's targets. In neighboring Nantong, a Rugao student, Xu Jiajin, was selected to head the Nantong joint student association coordinating demonstrations and other related events. After the excitement of May 30 died down, Xu, now a Communist Party member, took part in the 1927 Nanchang and Guangdong uprisings and then returned to Rugao to join its newly organized Communist Party.[59]

Xu was not atypical. In the wake of the May Thirtieth Movement many Rugao students and teachers, initially in places like Shanghai and Nanjing, later in Rugao itself, joined the Communists. As a result, the Communist

Party became increasingly active, first within Rugao city where it encouraged a worker's movement and after 1925 in the Rugao countryside where it started to organize peasants.[60]

The party members typically were graduates of a normal school, in Rugao or elsewhere, who had been introduced into the party during their studies. After being assigned to teach in or head an elementary school, often in a remote part of the county, they quickly founded party branches and started to recruit new members among the school's other teachers and students. The first such party branch was set up in summer 1925. A year and a half later, on New Year's Day 1927 the Rugao County Communist Party Committee (*xian wei*) was formally established.[61]

Simultaneously, while the two parties were joined in a united front, many Communists participated in local Nationalist party politics. Starting in 1926, in alliance with left-wing Nationalists, they set up Rugao Nationalist Party branch organizations and in January 1927 the Rugao county party head-quarters (*xian dangbu*).[62] Both Nationalist and Communist Party programs called for exposing and removing Rugao's "evil gentry."

Initially, Rugao's local elite reacted aggressively to the rise of societal opposition. Following the May Fourth Movement, Sha Yuanbing successful-ly had the progressive head of the Normal School replaced by a local leader, Pan Shusheng, who opposed student activism.[63] After the establishment of the Common Peoples' Society, Pan made a special trip to Nantong to talk with Zhang Jian about ways to counter the society's influence. As a result, a rival Silence Society (Jing she) was set up under the aegis of the county education department. It tried to dissuade students from becoming interested in politics or interfering in societal affairs.[64]

Following the May Thirtieth Movement, however, the local-elite response began to change. Instead of continuing to struggle with their increasingly organized and active opponents, many previously influential individuals withdrew from public life. Several others died. Just months before National-ist armies reached Rugao, depressed because his favorite son had died of scarlet fever, frustrated by the difficulties of his various financial enterprises, and angered because students in the schools he had founded were demanding reforms he opposed, Sha Yuanbing turned to Buddhism for solace. He spent his last months secluded in his residence where he died in February 1927.[65]

In the mid-1910s, the link between local leaders and the state was broken, but that between local leaders and local society remained intact. During the late 1910s and early 1920s, due to their reformist activities, local leaders appeared to strengthen their bonds to local society. However, after the mid-1920s, as a result of escalating attacks from below and the natural attrition within the aging local elite, the link between local leaders and local society weakened. In May 1927 when the Nationalist armies reached Rugao, they confronted an increasingly isolated local leadership. Moreover, for the first time the leadership consisted primarily of individuals educated in modern schools; thus, the leadership lacked the accumulated status, prestige, and symbolic capital of its forebears.

PERIOD IV: ATTACK AND RETREAT

As they swept across the countryside of central China, the Nationalists, often in alliance with the Communists, attacked many local leaders. As a result, it appeared that the Nationalists might sunder completely the ties between rural elites and the Chinese population, and that without connections to either state or populace, these heirs to China's gentry would lose their political and social importance.

In Rugao, Nationalist attacks on the local elite began shortly after the revolutionary army arrived in the county and quickly became widespread. Beginning in the second half of 1927, the Nationalists and others associated with them accused local-elite members in many districts of misappropriating public funds, squeezing and oppressing the people, or colluding with the forces of Jiangsu warlord, Sun Chuanfang.[66]

After a particular individual was labeled an "evil gentry" (*tulie*), a request was sent to the county government for his arrest. If incriminating information surfaced in a government investigation, police then apprehended the individual and held him for trial. Cases started in the county courts but were frequently appealed to higher levels, including the province's most important judicial body, the Jiangsu High Court. During this time, sometimes two or three years, the accused languished in county or provincial jails. Bail appears to have been unknown.

The case of He Sen, a well-known gentry member and district (*qu*) head from Lifa, was typical. In July 1927 sixty people accused He before the county government of being an "evil gentry" because, they alleged, he had given money to an officer of Sun's army. Several days later He was arrested and jailed. At the same time a county party representative posted a notice saying that if the general public had any evidence against He, it should be reported immediately. In July 1928 the case went to trial. He was found guilty, sentenced to four years in prison, deprived of ten acres of his land, and stripped of his civil rights.[67] In another case, Cong Peigong received similar treatment.[68]

But not all gentry members had their cases tried in court. Some were subjected to much more spontaneous and sometimes harsher treatment. After the arrival of the Nationalists, Deng Pujun got together with a priest and organized a Buddhist Study Society. Apparently for a while the society successfully obtained recruits among Matang's "shop clerks and young women." But Deng's success angered the area's "students" (probably a euphemism for young Nationalist Party followers). They gathered in front of

Deng's gate shouting slogans like "Down with Deng [and others] . . . who kill people, set fires, and do not have good hearts." Deng was scared. He closed his doors and refused to emerge, sending someone else to negotiate with the students. These negotiations apparently involved the provincial party's propaganda department, as well as the provincial party headquarters.[69]

Although some county-level leaders such as Mao Guangsheng, Zhu Guangyue, and former Jiangsu Governor Han Zishi were accused of being evil gentry and/or arrested, most Rugao elites attacked by the Nationalists, like He, Lu, and Deng, were district-level, not county-level, leaders. Most local leaders within the county seat were too well protected, either militarily or politically, to be attacked. Others probably had sufficient funds to buy their safety. Outside the county seat, local leaders in the villages and towns were more vulnerable. As a result, subcounty rather than county elites were attacked more often by Communist or other left-wing members of the Rugao Nationalist Party, and the attacks were more severe.[70]

However, the arrival of the Nationalists affected even county-level leaders who escaped persecution. Because the Nationalists set up a new county government organization and staffed it with appointees from outside the county, many county leaders lost their posts. Sha Yuanqu resigned as head of the education department, and Ma Jizhi lost his post as Rugao city's chief official, although he may have been replaced by a relative.[71] Others, such as Fang Ziying, were ordered arrested for conspiring against the Nationalists and fled to Shanghai.[72] Existing sources do not reveal their fate, but after March 1927 the names of many of Rugao's leading gentry disappear from the public record, presumably because their social and political responsibilities passed to other hands. Thus, the events of 1927 left few of Rugao's pre-1927 local leaders untouched and gave the Nationlists a potential opportunity to forge a completely new link between state and society that bypassed members of Rugao's pre-1927 elite.

PERIOD V: LOCAL LEADERS RETURN

The year 1927 and the few years following may well mark one of history's more significant "missed opportunities." In February 1928 Rugao's Nationalist Party, more concerned with ideological purity than organizational effectiveness, purged all leftists and radicals from its ranks. The remaining party members preoccupied themselves with intraparty feuds, rather than reforming society. During the remainder of the Nanjing Decade, the numerically insignificant Rugao party failed to play an important role in local politics. Similarly, China's Nationalist government made many apparent far-reaching organizational reforms after 1927, but in localities like Rugao it failed to back up these reforms with the necessary money, personnel, and determination to implement them.[73] Therefore, neither the Rugao Nationalist Party nor the Rugao county government became an effective agent for the provincial and national governments they were supposed to represent. Nor was either a visible link between the Nationalists and rural society. The Nationalists' failure to establish their presence at the local level enabled Rugao's local leaders once again to dominate Rugao's countryside.

The first indication that Rugao's local elite was winning their battle came in February 1928, when the Communists left the Nationalist Party organization and legal accusations against local-elite members dropped precipitously. By mid-1930 new legal charges against local leaders were uncommon, and old cases were being dismissed.[74]

Between 1928 and 1930 bandits or Communists sometimes physically attacked members of the local elite, particularly those who lived or were traveling in Communist-controlled areas outside the county seat. Sometimes these attacks were isolated events directed at one or two individuals;[75] other times, the local elite and their lands were part of bandit or Communist battlefield objectives.[76] But the Nationalists' defeat of the Rugao Communists in fall 1930 apparently ended even this threat to local leaders. Few other organized attacks on the local elite occurred throughout the remainder of the Nanjing Decade.

Perhaps the best example of what happened to county-level local elite members after the arrival of the Nationalists is provided by Sha Yuanqu. As we have seen, by December 1927 Sha no longer headed the education office, but this dismissal did not mean that Sha was no longer active in educational affairs. Quite the contrary; in that month Sha was appointed one of nine members of an education office executive committee (Jiaoyu xingzheng weiyuanhui), a post he presumably used to watch over his old domain.[77]

Moreover, Sha moved quickly to expand his power. A year after he lost his education office post, Sha, at the request of the county magistrate, agreed to set up and run a county relief organization (*jiuji yuan*), a traditional local-elite function. Eight months later, on August 1, 1929, he became head of the public property management office (Gongkuan gongchan guanli chu). Finally, in February 1932 he regained his old job as head of the Rugao education office.[78] The comeback of at least one member of the Rugao local elite to the position of power he had occupied before 1927 was now apparently complete.

Ma Jizhi, prior to 1927 the head of the Rugao city executive committee, followed a similar, though not identical, path. In August 1927 Ma helped raise money for an emergency medical clinic. A year later he became one of the five directors of the Rugao chamber of commerce and a year after that (1929) the head of the School of Commerce run by the association. In May 1931, when the chamber of commerce was reorganized, Ma still maintained his place on its executive committee and in 1936 he was publishing a local newspaper. Although Ma never regained his original post, clearly he continued to play an important and influential role in Rugao affairs.[79]

Many other members of important Rugao families also continued their activity in local affairs. However, the resulting pattern of elite dominance was distinctly different than that existing previously. Most conspicuously, local-elite members no longer controlled Rugao's formal political structures. In late 1927 and early 1928 the Nationalists abolished many elite-dominated institutions and replaced them with new bureaucratic offices. The pre-1927 executive committee and county governing committee, as well as all the district governing committees and executive committees, ceased to exist. After mid-1927 all power, in theory, belonged to the magistrate's yamen and the new series of specialized subordinate offices, such as the finance office and the reconstruction office. At the district level all authority was vested in a district office head appointed by the magistrate rather than in the chair of an executive committee chosen by local leaders.

With a few exceptions, like the reappointment of Sha Yuanqu to the education department, the Nationalist government did not appoint old local elites to these new institutions, particularly at the district level. The lists of district heads from between 1927 and 1929 contain very few names of individuals whose careers can be traced back before the arrival of the Nationalists.[80] But the old local-elite members did not simply vanish from the scene when the Nationalists cut their official government ties; instead, many stayed on, performing the same functions that they had before 1927. Often they successfully competed with their official government counterparts for power and prestige.

The most obvious example of such competition was the rivalry between the county government's new finance office and the local elite-controlled public property management office. In theory, the finance office oversaw the collection and disbursement of county funds. However, all cash collected from supplemental taxes (and in Rugao supplemental taxes yielded eighteen times more silver than the regular land tax) went to the public property management office, an officially established but elite-run organization with a broad and vague mandate to "manage public funds and public property and make sure that benefits accrued from their collection and expenditure." Although the provincial government initially made significant attempts to reform the finance system, it never brought the public property management office under county government control or even obtained a part of the supplemental tax revenues for county government use. When a major public project was undertaken, the project's organizers frequently appealed both to the county government and to the management office to provide the funds. Usually, the latter came forward with the most cash. Finally, in 1933 the provincial government recognized the status quo. It abolished the county finance office, unambiguously leaving control over local funds in the hands of the "upright gentry" rather than of government officials.[81]

Moreover, local elites were no longer reformers. Although they continued to help collect funds—albeit at significantly reduced levels—to support education and other public services, they rarely attempted to initiate institutional change. When innovations were introduced, they were usually short lived. For instance, an old local-elite leader opened and ran a dog pound, which for several years reduced the incidence of rabies in the county; after he died, the dog pound closed, and rabies once again increased. Neither the government nor another local leader moved in to fill the gap.[82]

Members of Rugao's elite also no longer appeared to promote new commercial ventures. Instead, younger men specifically interested in new business opportunities and only peripherally concerned with the other policy areas in which old members of the local elite had played a vital role, became business organizers and managers. For example, in April 1933 a new, larger electrical plant opened outside Rugao city. The stockholders of the company were "all enterprising local young men," a different group from that which had owned the old electric company and chosen the venerable Sha Yuanbing as its chair in 1926.[83]

Similarly, in spring 1928 a "local person" started raising capital to buy a steamboat that would ply the canal waters between Rugao city and the coastal town of Juegang. He planned to raise 14,000 yuan by selling 140 stock certificates worth 100 yuan each. By December, the cash had been raised and the service started. At no point is local elite involvement with this enterprise ever mentioned.[84]

Furthermore, in direct contrast to their decreased participation in formal political organizations, after 1927 the local elite took increasing responsibility for local defense. After the Nationalists arrived in Rugao the number and size of local militia, generally at the subcounty level, increased dramatically for two primary reasons: the Nationalists appealed to local-elite members to organize militia against Communists and bandits; and local elites feared that the only way to protect themselves and their lands was to organize their own military forces.[85]

After the defeat of the Communists, at least some locally organized militia remained, possibly even increasing in size. Prior to 1927 weapons were controlled by either the provincial soldiery or the county police. Local gentry had to appeal to either county or provincial officials if they wanted military support. During the 1930s these officials depended on the militia controlled and funded by the local elite, particularly to maintain order outside the county seat.

Finally, Rugao's rural leaders appear to have had fewer ties to elites in other areas such as Nantong and Shanghai and to have been less able to work out arrangements with officials to solve local problems. Unlike Sha Yuanbing, Sha Yuanqu had no known connections to well-known personages such as Zhang Jian. He was not part of a Lower Yangzi elite network and did not participate in Shanghai organizations.

Probably because Sha Yuanqu lacked outside connections, there is no record of requests for him to intervene with higher-level officials on behalf of others in the county. Without effective elite brokers and mediators, local turmoil increased. Under the Nationalists, disputes over water rights that had been successfully handled for hundreds of years suddenly became major issues resolved unfavorably for the people of Rugao. Although Rugao was always known as a litigious county, the number of lawsuits filed under the Nationalists reached alarming proportions. The traditional gentry-centered system of dispute resolution had broken down.

In sum, the role of the local elite in formal political organizations, public service institutions, and commercial efforts declined, while the local elite's responsibility for public security—not a traditional area of Rugao local-elite strength—increased and local-elite activities outside the official realm took on new significance. Whereas from about 1915 to 1927 the only effective claimants to power and authority in Rugao were generalist local leaders whose hegemony rested on displays of traditionally sanctioned elite culture, wealth, outside connections, and actions on behalf of their communities, the local leaders after 1927 had to compete with the similar claims of modern school graduates, new-style businessmen, students, Communists, and Nationalist government officials. Although their quasi-official control over areas like county finances, coupled with control over some means of coercion gave Rugao's local leaders more power than any of their competitors, it left them with only a weak claim to legitimate political authority.

Because the Nationalists neither drove this local elite completely from power nor incorporated them fully into official government organizations, a bifurcated power structure resulted—one official, the other unofficial—that in part immobilized both sides. On the one hand, the Nationalists commanded an organizational network incapable of implementing their programs. On the other hand, because the local elite were now fragmented and unable completely to insert themselves into the formal Nationalist political structure, their links with both higher levels of government as well as Rugao's population were broken and their effectiveness as local leaders curtailed.

CONCLUSION

Most peasants living under Rugao's local leadership from the 1898 reforms until the Japanese invasion probably concluded that over forty years not much changed: the gentry-led reforms of the 1910s and 1920s were largely confined to the major towns; the small local Nationalist government apparatus and party had little impact outside the county seat; and Rugao's major families like the Shas, Mas, and Zhus continued to be the county's largest landlords and most powerful—and to the peasant most visible—social and political actors. Moreover, no major structural change in landlord-tenant relationships appears to have disrupted peasant lives. From 1927 to 1930, in the southwestern part of the county and along the coast, Communists and bandits created disturbances and challenged the local power structure. But because the Communists undertook military actions rather than programs for social change, their impact was also probably negligible from the peasants' point of view.

However, from the standpoint of local leaders, much had changed between 1898 and 1938: they received specialized training in Western knowledge rather than a generalized education in the Chinese classics. Because of this training, as well as competition from other societal groups, they engaged in a different mix of activities than their predecessors and had far fewer interactions with individuals and officials outside the county. Local leaders continued to hold sway in their own increasingly circumscribed local arenas, but as a result of the changes generated by the late Qing reforms and the pressures applied on them by students and Communists as well as Nationalists they became both more conservative and more isolated and ceased to function as an effective link between state and society.

From the peasant point of view, the revolutionary war of the late 1940s was the first watershed that significantly altered their lives; from the local-elite point of view the divide was the events of the mid-1920s. Until 1925 local elites—sometimes in response to provincial and central initiatives, sometimes acting on their own—ultimately determined what happened in China's local arenas. After 1925 local leaders' ability to act was restricted by forces at both the top and the bottom of the system.

Just as the impact of abolishing the examination system was not felt until twenty years after the event, so the importance of the increasing attacks on China's local leaders was not immediately apparent. However, the difficulties encountered by local leaders under the Nationalists, under the Japanese, and ultimately under the Communists fragmented local leadership. Some fled; at least one, Ma Jizhi, committed suicide; and several others, including Huang Qiwu and Mao Guangsheng, supported the Communists. By the time the Communists permanently occupied Rugao in 1948 very few local leaders held unchallenged positions of power and prestige.

What then can one say about state building during this period? Generally I would say that it did not take place. From 1911 to 1927 counties such as Rugao had capable leaders who might have participated in a state-building enterprise, had there been an effective, legitimate central and provincial leadership with whom they could connect, but this leadership did not exist. Although the lack of higher-level leadership initially gave local leaders the freedom to experiment, its absence ultimately deprived them of any way to maintain their fragile enterprises without government resources and protection. Although the Nationalists provided a more unified organizational structure, the failure of this higher-level national system to generate effective local leaders similarly precluded success.

In other words, for state building to occur, both central and local components must be effective and present. During the warlord period an effective local, but an ineffective national, structure existed. During the Nationalist era the national structure was potentially effective, but the local structure was not. Only in 1949 did the Communists integrate local and national political organizations and begin modern Chinese state building.

EIGHT

Mediation, Representation, and Repression: Local Elites in 1920s Beijing

David Strand

Capital cities are necessarily well supplied with elites and individuals with elite aspirations and pretensions. Late imperial and early Republican Beijing attracted and held its share of power seekers. In addition to thousands of men with official positions in the central political apparatus, tens of thousands of others journeyed to the city as examination candidates under the empire and as politicians and aspirants for public office under the Republic. Over four hundred hostels for natives of particular provinces or counties stood ready to receive politically minded sojourners.[1] In 1922, a Beijing newspaper complained about a superabundance of unsavory gentlemen or "bureaucratic gangsters" (*guanliao liumang*) with outsized ambitions who hung about the city angling for a post in the Republican governmental apparatus.

> [They] all live outside Qian Gate in various big hotels and inns. Most are southerners or men from Tianjin. They are on prominent display in theatres, public parks, restaurants and even cheap amusement areas, impersonating the relative of some official or calling themselves the friend of some politician. They have taken over the brothels, parks and restaurants where they hold big gatherings, throw money around or cheer on favorite actors and actresses with gifts and applause.[2]

Until 1928 when the Nationalists moved the capital to Nanjing, the city remained "clotted with government and crowded with bureaucrats."[3] In a population of over one million, approximately eight thousand individuals held official and support staff positions in ministries and bureaus.[4] As many as one hundred thousand others, of the sort caricatured above, sojourned in Beijing in the hope of capturing a job or sinecure.[5]

Within this mass of office holders and seekers, the weight of which gave

Beijing a "heavy official atmosphere," lay a harder kernel of administrative and political elites.[6] These ministers, political faction leaders, and generals attempted to control and use the government and the city as the regime's immediate physical and social foundation to further their own political ends.[7] In addition to struggling to dominate cabinets, ministries, parliaments, and military strongpoints in the capital's vicinity, power holders based in Beijing appointed police chiefs, invested public and private funds in economic ventures, subsidized and intimidated the local press, extracted and extorted money from city residents, and manipulated public opinion. The logic of the situation invited local economic and social notables to become the simple agents of higher elites.

However, the picture of a strong state dominating a weak or compliant society, in this case the local-level political field encompassing the city of Beijing, distorts the actual relationships between state and society and higher and lower elites prevailing during the Republican period. The last Chinese dynasty, the Qing, had been overthrown in 1911 by a diverse revolutionary coalition that immediately lost control of the Republic to strongman-bureaucrat Yuan Shikai. After Yuan's death in 1916, the Beijing-based regime hosted a succession of short-lived warlord governments. In 1926 Nationalist armies, led by Chiang Kai-shek, marched north with their Communist allies from Guangzhou in a drive to defeat the warlords. In the midst of this Northern Expedition, Chiang purged the Communists. By summer 1928, the Nationalists had succeeded in unifying the country from their new capital in Nanjing. Beijing ("northern captial") had been renamed Beiping ("northern peace"). (For events after June 1928 described below, I use Beiping rather than Beijing.)

The Republican regime based in Beijing in the 1910s and 1920s had weakened with each passing crisis. Heir to late Qing policies favoring bigger and more expensive government and yet unable to govern either Chinese society or itself, the Republic succeeded mainly in provoking the ire of citizens reluctant to cede it taxes, loyalty, or simple obedience.[8] The Nationalist successor regime in Nanjing formally resolved the contradiction between centralizing bureaucrats and rebellious citizens by creating a one-party state that both administered and mobilized. In practice, the Nationalists added to the factionalism and immobilism of the early Republic a remarkable capacity to lead popular rebellions against themselves and punish natural allies among the monied and propertied classes.[9] Local elites who looked to Republican regimes for authority and guidance were rewarded with contradictory displays of power and impotence, advancing and collapsing government agencies, and support for and attacks on the existing social order.

Republican regimes, in short, showed "the combination of power and fragility" that distinguishes the contemporary third world state.[10] Power based

on modern military organization and bureaucracy was sufficient to intimidate domestic challengers who lacked these assets. Yet both Beijing and
Nanjing succumbed to foreign threats and to active and passive resistance by
domestic forces. Under these circumstances, local elites, although rarely in a
position to challenge higher-level political authority directly, were often able
to blunt or parry that power. This "politics of accommodation" at the local
level is a natural by-product of the confrontation between a "weak state" and
"strong society" in which "social control is vested in numerous local-level
social organizations" and where the local rules of the game are "dictated by
critically placed strongmen—landlords, caciques, bosses, money lenders"
and other local elites.[11] In the process, local elites can be found "simultaneously embracing and foiling the state."[12]

The strength of local elites in Republican Chinese cities depended on their
ability to entangle and deflect higher-level power and maintain proprietary
control over wealth, status, and position in the community. In the Republican period not only insistent pressures applied by ministers and warlords but
also the general politicization of urban residents complicated these tasks.
Local elites were forced to fight a two-front political struggle with higher
elites and politically conscious subaltern classes at the same time that they
competed among themselves for patrons and supporters. If efforts by local
power-holders to alternately, or simultaneously, "embrace" and "foil" the
direct agents of the state was an old theme in Chinese political life, then the
emergence of politically active citizens as the object of elite control was a new
theme. Elite politics at both higher and intermediate levels would never be
the same once the fate and interests of a powerful minority or elite were
coupled to the existence of mass political participation. Lenore Barkan shows
similar sets of pressures on county-level elites in Jiangsu, but those elites
enjoyed more autonomy, faced less formidable opponents, and had more
room to manuever than could be found in the circumscribed but highly
politicized public arena of Beijing.

SOCIAL NETWORKS AMID POLITICAL TURBULENCE

Local elites occupy an intermediate zone between higher elites above and
everyone else below because they are richer, more powerful, or better connected than most people in their communities. All things being relative in
these matters, elite credentials are likely to vary from person to person and
community to community. In a large city like Beijing undergoing rapid social
change, the bases of elite power were inevitably diverse. By the 1920s,
modern educators, journalists, financiers, political cadre, and social activists
had joined the older pool of "gentry and merchant" elites predominant in the
late imperial city. Although diversification meant that no one's wealth-

status-power portfolio was likely to be complete, for some individuals these endowments tended to be cumulative.

For example, Meng Luochuan and Meng Jinhou, owner and manager respectively of Beijing's famous Ruifuxiang silk and foreign goods shops, drew strength from wealth, positions held in local organizations, and connections to individuals richer and more powerful than they. Both what they had and what they lacked suggest changing and prevailing community standards for local elites and provide a baseline against which to compare other individuals of weight and substance in Republican Beijing.

Meng family patriarch Meng Luochuan and his kinsman, Meng Jinhou, established their first shop in Beijing in 1893.[13] The Meng fortune had its genesis in the family's home area of Zhangqiu county, Shandong, where landholdings and business ventures provided a base for commercial expansion to major cities in North China. Even though the family's wealth was enough by 1800 to permit educating sons for the official examinatons if that had been the family's wish, the Mengs continued to produce merchants and landlords rather than examination candidates. As a result, the clan was known in Zhangqiu for "having wealth without honor" (*youfu wugui*).[14] Meng Luochuan carried on this reputation for single-minded devotion to business matters. Despite the fact that he acquired an official degree (probably, as was common among merchants, through purchase rather than examination), people said that Meng Luochuan's only books were account ledgers. Late Qing reforms brought honor and a more fitting title to the Mengs when Luochuan was appointed the first president of the Shandong chamber of commerce by Governor Yuan Shikai.[15] As pioneer business professionals in the midst of a Confucian culture that normally persuaded even hard-nosed business types to mimic the life-style of scholar-officials, the Mengs were about to find their metier in a world reshaped to be more congenial to their acquisitive instincts.

In 1900 the Boxer uprising and the foreign invasion that followed devastated much of Beijing, including the business district outside Qian Gate where the first Ruifuxiang store was located. Meng Jinhou, who was responsible for managing the shop, happened to be in Shandong at the time. Despite the danger, he rented a mule cart and rushed back to Beijing to salvage what he could of the family business. Finding the shop in ruins, he recruited employees from clerks and apprentices still left in the city and raised new capital in order to reopen. Meng Jinhou's intrepid behavior in guiding Ruifuxiang to a quick recovery reaped great profits for the Mengs and made expansion into additional stores and trades possible. By the 1920s the Ruifuxiang stores, with hundreds of employees, were reputed to form the largest single business enterprise in the city.[16] The impressive wrought iron facade and spacious display rooms of the firm's flagship store can still be seen on Dazhalan Street in downtown Beijing.[17] Meng Jinhou also rebuilt Ruifu-xiang with an eye to withstanding future disorders. The "thick doors and high walls" of the new stores protected the business from looting in the 1912 troop riots that accompanied Yuan Shikai's rise to the presidency of the new Republic.[18] Later in the 1910s and 1920s, when other merchants hesitated to unshutter their shops because of threatened war, riot, or revolution, Ruifu-xiang kept on doing business.[19] By 1925 Rufuxiang's five Beijing stores were turning over a volume of 600,000 taels a year selling silk, cloth, leather, tea, and foreign imports.

Not only did Meng Luochuan and Jinhou guard their investments with thick doors and high walls, but they also drew a protective thicket of polit-ical connections around their business activities. When Yuan Shikai became president, Meng sought to capitalize on his earlier association with the polit-ical strongman. Reportedly, Yuan offered Meng an important post as a local official but, leery of the demands of office, he declined. Nonetheless, Meng Luochuan's dealings with Yuan Shikai initiated a period of close association between the Meng family and early Republican VIPs (*daguan guiren*).[20] An editorialist probably had in mind the Ruifuxiang stores when in 1922 he mentioned complaints that "a certain silk shop outside Qian Gate caters to rich and powerful officials and treats them with great respect while treating ordinary people or country people with contempt."[21] Meng strength-ened these political ties with marriage alliances. A daughter married police reformer and future president Xu Shichang, and a grandson wedded future president Cao Kun's granddaughter.

Ruifuxiang manager Meng Jinhou also cultivated high-level political con-nections including militarist Zhang Zuolin and his son, Xueliang, as well as numerous other northern warlords. Meng Jinhou had a special reception hall built in one of Ruifuxiang's warehouses where he hosted powerful friends and acquaintances; it was said that one banquet alone could consume the daily receipts of all five Ruifuxiang shops. In return Ruifuxiang was able to cater to the conspicuous consumption of politicians like President Cao Kun who, near the end of his inglorious tenure in office in 1924, held 10,000 gold *yuan* worth of unpaid-for Ruifuxiang goods in the Zhongnanhai presidential palace. As Cao's position wavered in 1924, and in spite of the close ties be-tween the Mengs and Cao, Meng sent agents to Zhongnanhai to repossess the goods unless payment was forthcoming. The threats paid off, and Ruifu-xiang extracted most of Cao's debt before he was driven from office.

The Mengs systematically approached the accumulation of wealth and power. An enterprise that began with one shop and one (albeit exalted) official patron developed into a chain of stores with a convention annex to accommodate an increasingly promiscuous approach to higher-level connec-tions. This was a necessary adjustment if the Mengs, for profit and protec-tion, were to keep track of a political elite splintered by factionalism and buffeted by political and military competition. Ruifuxiang's wealth and the assiduous cultivation of connections gave the Mengs great influence in the Beijing chamber of commerce and other elite arenas.[22] The wealth of the silk and foreign goods trade made Ruifuxiang or silk guild representatives welcome in any enterprise involving local fund raising.[23] Although Meng Jinhou never ran for office as a chamber director or officer, he was given the honorary status of "special director."

The Mengs realized that vertical ties could radically enhance one's prospects and position. Placing a trade or business under the "protective aura" (*menqiang*) of a noble or high official had been a common practice under the Qing. Trades as diverse as the lumber, jade, artificial flower, and book businesses relied on various forms of official patronage.[24] In the past, few fortunes could be made or protected without ties to official Beijing. Construction firms specializing in erecting and repairing palaces, temples, and other official buildings routinely bribed courtiers and officials to win contracts.[25] To gain easier access to the court and officialdom and to make coming and going in mansions and offices more natural, builders purchased degrees.

The Mengs simply pursued this strategy with exceptional vigor through a period in which status hierarchies were in flux. Of course, one need not be a capitalist among bureaucrats to realize the advantages of this kind of patronage. Other economic and political entrepreneurs came to the same conclusion in settling on means to promote projects ranging from welfare reform to Communist revolution.

One such example occurred in the early 1920s. A consortium of charities, the Metropolitan Welfare Association, divided over the question of whether to modernize its established practice of dealing with hunger and poverty through directly distributing food and clothing at soup kitchens and temporary aid stations.[26] A maverick social reformer named Liu Xilian decided that a casework approach would better serve the city's indigent. The established charities opposed Liu's "scientific" methods, insisting that soup kitchens were indispensable. The old distribution system, organized around a seasonal "winter defense" (*dongfang*), served those who entered the city in search of food, whether famine victims or war refugees, and gave high visibility to the philanthropists involved. Elites sometimes visited the soup kitchens to pass out copper coins or show their public concern through other personal donations. But the hundreds who starved and froze to death each winter while convocations of elites ponderously arranged for the opening of the kitchens attested to the traditional system's inadequacy.[27]

Liu temporarily overcame opposition to welfare reform in winter 1922–23 by securing a patron to tip the balance in his favor after failing to persuade his fellow association members to endorse his plan. Warlord Zhang Zuolin, who was looking for ways to build popular support in the city, personally contributed a large shipment of grain to Liu, allowing him to commence his social experiment. However, although Liu implemented his pilot program, he never abolished the old welfare system.

Similarly, Communist leader Li Dazhao placed the groups of intellectuals and workers he organized in Beijing in the early and mid-1920s under the protection of two, successive North China warlords in the hope of boosting the power of "mass" politics.[28] As Communist setbacks in the 1920s suggested, this was a risky strategy; a patron could always disown a client or suffer defeat. The need for higher-level protection against predatory and repressive political forces was acute, but the reliability of such ties was often difficult to gauge given the instability of factional alignments and the power of political ideologies to bind and split people against the grain of personal connections. A staff member of a radical newspaper recalled having dinner with prominent Nationalist Party member Wang Jingwei in 1925, at a time when he feared his paper might be closed down by police. Wang assured him that "things were already arranged" with the police chief. The following day the newspaper was banned, and the unfortunate fellow spent months in jail.[29]

Would-be patrons could also find that their efforts to mobilize support based on personal ties were problematic. A radical student from Hunan recalled being propositioned in 1925 by a fellow provincial on behalf of the besieged Hunanese education minister Zhang Shizhao. Zhang sought allies in the student movement to defuse protests against his policies. The student, however, repaid the overture by using access to Zhang's household to obtain damaging information from the minister's wife on her husband's personal life.[30] When the high-level backers of the Beijing Streetcar Company recruited employees in the mid-1920s, they pointedly hired former district police commander Deng Yu'an, thinking that his connections in the police force and his understanding of Beijing society could protect the interest of the enterprise "from below." Instead, the former police officer's attempt to do just that by recruiting fellow policemen for company jobs created bad feelings among police left out of the scheme, and these tensions made the utility more, not less, vulnerable to criticism and opposition.[31]

A personalistic approach to protecting and expanding one's influence could be expensive (requiring the kind of venture capital invested by the Mengs or the streetcar company) or dangerous (risking sudden exposure when abandoned by one's patron). But the appeals of clientelism for local elites went beyond a simple calculus of these costs measured against the benefits from the quick resolution of a problem through the right connections. Vertical mobilization, as a general principle, operated throughout Beijing society from Republican political elites down to neighborhood charities and militia or labor gangs.

The spatial and social structure of the city supported connections, based on deference, between elites and ordinary residents. The city contained great extremes of wealth and poverty and yet little by way of class-based residential segregation. Neighborhoods, with a few exceptions, were mixed in character; mansions, hovels, courtyard residences, and courtyard tenements stood in close proximity.[32] As a matter of status and self-interest, the monied, propertied, and degree-holding classes had reason to lead and support projects to care for and control the poor who lived just beyond their courtyard wall or gathered outside their shop doors. Thanks to the efforts of late Qing reformers concerned about threats from assassins and rebels, Beijing had a large police force. But social control on the streets still depended in part on militia and other communal and private security arrangements that required elites' courage and aura to function.[33] In addition, the social organization of the workplace favored small shops where owners, managers, masters, workers and apprentices lived and worked side by side. Liberal reformers criticized the amount of personal authority exercised by shop owners who applied patriarchal principles, "Households have a rod for punishing children and servants; Shops have shop rules."[34] But even during the Republic, personal authority and custom continued to be as important as law and formal organization in regulating relations between social classes.

Classified from a broadly comparative point of view, a "traditional notable" is someone "embedded in a network of personal and family obligation" who parlays those ties into becoming "a kind of paterfamilias of the community."[35] This role is likely to be more passive than active, insofar as community interests are concerned. One is a notable not so much because of what one does as because others recognize who one is. That solidity on the part of individuals of substance, no matter how old-fashioned in appearance, has practical value in a turbulent, moderizing age when the question of who is responsible for whom is urgent.

In principle, a modern state, the kind the Republic was supposed to be, was responsible for ensuring the protection and welfare of its citizen.[36] In reality, and because the state itself was as dangerous as it was helpful to individuals and communities, local elites continued to take responsibility for employees, fellow guildsmen, neighbors, and the larger community. In nineteenth-century Europe, even after feudal privileges had been abolished, a "deference society" persisted based on the community's "habitual respect" for the nobility.[37] In China, even after the state ended new examination honors in 1905, deference as a basic principle of social organization continued, not merely as a residue of gentry culture but as the active element in a whole range of old and new organizations like guilds, labor unions, and chambers of commerce. Many city residents would probably have agreed with a statement made in 1928 by the directors of the Beijing chamber of commerce. Confronted with the sudden resignation of their president and vice-president, they declared, "As we face the precarious moment, the chamber cannot be one day without someone to take responsibility."[38] A resident observing the activities of press gangs in the city during one of Beijing's periodic military crises similary remarked: "Soldiers were seizing everyone who had a strong back and a weak master."[39]

ASSOCIATION AND MEDIATION

The pursuit of personalistic strategies by local notables does not exclude the presence of civic incentives derived from broader loyalties.[40] The Mengs' family prejudice against office holding did not prevent them from accepting positions and honors based on their wealth and prestige. But their coolness toward public service stands in striking contrast to the alacrity with which other local elites, including chamber of commerce leaders, built reputations and power through active involvement in public affairs. The Chinese pater-familias leaned in that direction naturally, through a "self-image of public responsibility—a sense of service or 'cadredom'—which characterizes local leadership in Chinese culture."[41] Animated by popular and elite expecta-tions concerning community leadership or galvanized by political and social turbulence, a local notable could be pitched toward activism even though "embedded" in a personal network that seemingly valued order and stasis above all else.

This civic activism and a related devotion to formal organization and ideology owed a great deal to a grass-roots tradition of urban management and to late Qing reformist ideals and practice.[42] In Beijing, merchants and gentry cooperated in neighborhood order-keeping bodies like *shuihui* ("water" or fire-fighting societies), which had been organized in the mid-nineteenth century to remedy government neglect of local affairs. In sharing responsibility for maintaining social peace at the local or neighborhood levels, degree holders and merchants joined to produce "a blurring of roles and the emergence of a local leadership class" with a dual merchant-gentry identity.[43] Fire-brigade charters explained that the brigades had assumed quasi-governmental tasks in city neighborhoods because "fire, flood and rob-bery were rampant."[44]

> Whenever there was a fire, [the government bureau in charge] was unprepared to put it out. As a result, criticism arose during the Xianfeng reign [1851–1862]. In those years fire brigades were established so as to have fire-fighting equipment at the ready. At the same time "calamity relief" neighborhood groups took responsibility for catching thieves.[45]

After 1900, government reformers at the highest levels took a series of actions that allowed this associative tendency to develop more fully.[46] Both a kind of officially "licensed participation" by elites in government-sponsored profes-sional associations (*fatuan*) like chambers of commerce and a more autonomous participation through elected assemblies accompanied the state's drive for greater bureaucratic control.[47]

David Johnson, in a recent essay, applies Antonio Gramsci's notion of "hegemony" to explain the pervasive influence of the ruling ideas associated with Confucianism in the late imperial period.[48] He also argues, however, that "Gramsci's distinction between the private institutions of 'civil society' and the public institutions of the State has little relevance for China, where a single elite controlled all national institutions."[49] During the late Qing and early Republic Gramsci's distinction does become relevant. A "civil society" represented by new and newly independent associations and institutions became visible in China's cities, and the political roles played by local elites were transformed.[50] Official hostility and elite ambivalence toward developing an autonomous associational life reflected a powerful residue of the hegemonic culture to which Johnson refers.[51] But other elites defended the integrity of the organizations they directed.[52]

One of the clearest statements of local elite confidence in the value of public associations was made by Beijing jeweler An Disheng in 1920 as he struggled to regain the post of chamber of commerce president, which he had lost in a scandal earlier that year when he was falsely accused of embezzling chamber funds.[53] An had been instrumental in pushing the Beijing chamber toward the kind of activism pursued a decade earlier by sister organizations in other cities. Blaming his ouster (with good cause) on the machinations of higher-level elites hostile to his independent leadership of the chamber, An appealed to fellow notables ("*junzi* [gentlemen] of various circles [*jie*]") not because of the personal humiliation he had suffered but because of the "libel directed against the group [*tuanti*]" he represented, the merchants of the city.[54] An Disheng—a former member of the Hanlin Academy, an inventor of a new process for manufacturing cloisonné for export, and a participant in the late Qing and early Republican self-government movement—was an outstanding example of the spirit of cadredom carried by the merchant-gentry class. He took credit for both breaking with the subservient role for professional associations favored by Qing and Republican officials and giving the chamber a sense of "group autonomy" (*tuanti zidong*). He blamed his current difficulties on the "Anfu Clique" at the national level for directing a great chain of conspirators in and out of the chamber to unseat him. Faced with a swarm of plots and personal attacks, his only defense was the power of law and public opinion. He addressed his appeal for help to "various provincial assemblies, educational associations, chambers of commerce, agricultural societies, unions, lawyers' associations, student federations, newspapers and professional associations"—that is, to politically active groups in civil society. Despite the sharp distinction An Disheng drew between his own civic activism and his opponents' dependence on connections and private intrigue, it must be noted that even before he went public with his troubles his friends from the jewelers trade and from his native county in Hebei had tried to mobilize support on his behalf.[55] It is also true, however, that An Disheng consistently supported the rights of professional associations, self-government, republican virtue, and democracy.

Ideological coherence linked to a clear plan for institutional reform surfaced in other forms in the 1920s and met with some of the same difficulties self-government activists like An faced. When your enemies came for you with trumped-up charges and guns, legal niceties and civic traditions had limited utility. The liberal variant of reform assumed a stable constitutional order that did not exist. The one-party systems advocated by Nationalists and Communists assumed an organizational monolith yet to be built. Under the circumstances, neither the manic networking of the Mengs nor the principled association building of An Disheng was as appealing to some as a balanced approach; this recognized that the intermediate zone one occupied as a local elite was defined by both status hierarchies and what Gramsci describes as the "powerful system of fortresses and earthworks" representing the institutions and institutionalized beliefs of civil society.[56]

In his study of grass-roots politicians in France and Italy, Sidney Tarrow argues that when a personalistic approach proves outmoded and civic-minded administration is unrealistic, a local elite is likely to assume the role of a "policy broker" who takes "initiatives at the local level to direct policy goods toward particular communities and to capture resources from the state."[57] The role Tarrow describes emerged in modern Europe as a result of a constant stream of programs and projects emanating from the center. Under conditions prevailing in Republican China, local elites could hardly expect to enjoy that kind of official largess. With the exception of minor anomalies like Liu Xilian's welfare reforms, the heyday of government-sponsored or- directed change in Beijing came during the New Policies reforms in the last decade of the Qing. By the 1920s the problem for local elites was often exactly the reverse of what Tarrow describes: how to prevent representatives of the state from capturing local resources for use at the center or as part of a political struggle to seize the center.

From 1916 to 1930, the total tax burden on Beijing residents, excluding tribute extorted by warlords, increased more than two and one-half times.[58] With few exceptions, including funds for support of the local police, higher taxes did not reflect or lead to enhanced services. The taut relationship that existed between regimes and organized local society often had less to do with efforts to bend state policy in a particular direction than with a tug of war over taxes. Tax protests were practically continuous in response to the ingenuity of government agencies in seeking new or increased revenues. Taxes on commodities and services, including flour, stock transactions, restaurants, fish, horses, charcoal, coal, butchery, and vegetables, triggered strikes, marches, and petitions. As Susan Mann has suggested, the practice of tax farming, which began in the late Qing and continued into the Republic in competition with a directly bureaucratic approach, was a "temporary phase in the state-building process" during which time an expansionary state was "met, matched and thwarted by local interests."[59]

Meeting and thwarting the state required brokers, in Tarrow's sense of the term, who were effective because they could mobilize both networks of supporters and the resources of formal organization. One such defensive broker was three-time chamber of commerce president Sun Xueshi. Sun, who defeated An Disheng's bid to recover the presidency in 1922, owned a chain of roast duck restaurants. He led the restaurateurs' guild, had connections based on his Shandong provincial background, maintained close ties to Beijing brothels, and headed a fire brigade located in the midst of the merchant district outside Qian Gate.[60] Sun was reputedly at his most effective in the "realm of social intercourse," which included rounds of banqueting for which he was obviously well-placed.[61] However, when necessary, Sun presided at public meetings, attended self-government rallies, and used his formal position as professional association leader to participate in citywide convocations of elites. To the extent that Sun articulated an ideology, it was based on the old notion of "people's livelihood" (*minsheng*), which justified protection of markets and jobs. When local elites like Sun pursued these defensive strategies they slipped into the role of paterfamilias, a posture that earned Sun the reputation of being the "*taidou* (the worthy everyone looks up to) of Beijing's merchant circles." Such a posture at once disguised and legitimized the contrived, political nature of what he was attempting to accomplish: hold together a diverse, quarrelsome constituency of guilds and modern enterprises.[62]

In the 1920s, liberals like An Disheng, dependent on the success of coherent plans, could be displaced by a traditionalist like Sun, whose strength lay in his command of social networks and his ability to evoke a sense of communal solidarity often against the plans of bureaucrats, warlords, and capitalists. Sun Xueshi played the role of broker in a style that resonated with the traditional mediating function of the gentry.[63] But he also faced a modernizing state and armed himself with the modern political weapons available to professional association leaders.

Sun Xueshi's skills in this regard were tested during the occupation of the city by warlord Zhang Zuolin. Before he abandoned Beijing in 1928 to oncoming Northern Expedition armies led by Chiang Kai-shek, Zhang instituted a luxury tax on various commodities sold in the city ranging from gold to sugar. The chamber under Sun Xueshi's leadership was made responsible for collecting it.[64] For months after the initial demand for revenues Sun and his vice-president, Leng Jiayi, played the role of broker between regime and the merchant community. Zhang's agents demanded 100,000 dollars a month. Sun and Leng offered 50,000 on the condition that the city's livestock tax be suspended.[65] When the government pushed too hard or chamber members balked at paying, Sun and Leng submitted their resignations and retired to their residences until chamber and government representatives persuaded them to return.

The delicacy of Sun and Leng's maneuvering derived from calculated displays of indispensability. They, in effect, balanced their personal prestige against the institutional weight of the chamber, for which one director claimed a popular mandate as "the only professional association in the capital that genuinely represents city people."[66] As political theater it was familiar and transparent. But by portraying themselves and their leadership roles as fragile and liable to break, they effectively buffered the potentially dangerous collision between violent men like Zhang Zuolin and their own contentious and cost-conscious followers. Everyone had to tread softly so as not to hurt their feelings, wound their pride, or drive them from their responsibilities. In this context, it made sense for a local strongman like Sun to appear weak and for merchants to organize their collective defense around someone who retreated in the face of superior force. If elite culture as a "process is partly ideological, partly dramaturgical; partly collective, partly individual," the individual and small-group dramas that arose when local elites found themselves caught in the middle protected corporate rights and collective interests.[67]

In performing these brokerage functions and in self-defense local elites frequently resigned, fell ill, or otherwise absented themselves from their positions—all sensible strategies in an era of scathing public debate, insurgent masses, and sojourning armies. Although this softening of institutions charged with protecting civil society might be construed as a sign of weakness, "underdevelopment," or retrogression to the posture of gentry-broker, the practical value of a politics of accommodation was widely recognized.

REPRESENTATION AND REPRESSION

Dominance by local elites depended not only on wealth, position, and social connections with higher elites but also on maintaining the active support of followers and constituents. Without a sense of reciprocity and a means of representing the views and interests of elites and nonelites, it would have been difficult for organizations like the chamber of commerce to perform certain tasks, for example, extracting small sums from thousands of contributing shops to pay predatory regimes. It was impossible for the Mengs of Ruifuxiang to be inconspicuous, and other elites like An Disheng and Sun Xueshi chose not to be. However, the small-scale nature of Beijing economic activity and residential life made passive withdrawal from citywide responsibility an option for many notables and their dependents. Local elites and their constituents might agree that strong or shrewd leadership in defense of community interests made sense, but at the same time they might evade the costs and risks involved in producing these "public goods."[68]

A commitment to mediation and consultation was critical not only because it protected elite and community interest but also because public display of mediation celebrated the notion of reciprocity as a general principle at work in operating social and economic organizations at every level. E. P. Thompson has argued that elite hegemony "can be sustained by the rulers only by the constant exercise of skill, of theatre and of concession."[69] In Beijing society, mediation was an art widely practiced by street policemen, guildsmen, elder statesmen, and even casual passersby who happened upon fights and quarrels. A Japanese visitor to Beijing drawn into a minor quarrel between a shopkeeper and a tourist over broken merchandise was impressed by the performance of a police officer called upon to adjudicate the matter. With a fine sense of ceremony the policeman declared that "the task of the police is to 'mediate disputes.' In other words, our task is to resolve disputes, not entrap people in crime."[70] In guild disputes between rival factions, mediators appeared physically to separate the combatants at the risk of injury to themselves.[71] When quarrels on the street or in shops or residences became violent, press accounts blamed the escalation on bystanders who either "looked on without lifting a finger" to mediate or reported that the wildness of the fray meant that "mediators dared not come in."[72] Elite activists could draw on broad popular support for the role of mediator to justify their actions as broker or buffer between hostile parties like warlord armies and the merchant community.

Elites like Sun Xueshi had a superior grasp of this kind of moral showmanship; however, this quality was not proof against attacks when norms of deference and reciprocity broke down. One of Beijing's most prominent fixers and mediators was the elder statesman Xiong Xiling. Xiong had retired or "descended" from national politics after a brief tenure as Yuan Shikai's prime minister in 1913–14 following a career that suggested a "progressive yet malleable" nature.[73] By the 1920s Xiong, using his extensive political and social connections, had built an impressive network of philanthropic and commercial ventures in the city, ranging from an orphanage to a bus company.[74] Xiong's sociable nature and broad human sympathies, which compromised his effectiveness at the higher levels of Republican politics, made him ideal as a pivot for intermediate-level brokerage activities. But in 1929 when Xiong attempted to rescue a failing factory for poor bannermen by merging it with one of his own philanthropic enterprises, he was bitterly criticized by the city's Manchu Advancement Society even though the mainly Manchu officers and apprentices of the factory supported Xiong.[75] (It did not help Xiong's case that he had been involved in a scandal involving the theft of Manchu treasures in the 1910s.)[76] Later that year rickshaw men, who resented competition from the bus company he had started to connect his orphanage at Xiangshan with Beijing, marched in protest against him.[77]

Even someone as practiced at the art of local politics as Sun Xueshi faced periodic leadership crises. In 1922 Sun was opposed for reelection as chamber president because of dissatisfaction over his aggressive support for the rickshaw men who feared competition from a new streetcar system. He kept his position by threatening to resign "to protect his reputation" and then hosting a series of banquets to rebuild support.[78] In 1928, several guilds belonging to the chamber joined a local Nationalist Party "merchants union" and led a campaign against Sun for dunning merchants to pay costs incurred in "protection" payments to Northern Expedition armies.[79] Local elites were both celebrated as protectors of group and community interests and attacked as dictators, embezzlers, and frauds. The record of local politics in 1920s Beijing shows that respected local elites like chamber of commerce presidents, guild heads, and labor union leaders could suddenly find themselves sued, jailed, slandered, conspired against, and deposed.

For local elites this "small politics" of reputation is just as important in generating and destroying status and prestige as the connections and positions available in the larger world.[80] In his study of the politics of reputation F. G. Bailey suggests that people invariably ask two questions at the micropolitical level: "How can you bring back into line a leader who is showing signs of becoming a despot? How, in [a] particular culture, do you signal to the leader that he is reaching the point of no return?"[81] Beijing residents continued to ask precisely these questions of chamber leaders, union officials, school administrators, party cadres, factory owners, and labor bosses. Even as civil society developed, tensions created by applying old expectations to new social and political situations gave rise to intense, sometimes violent disputes; the conflicts were both weighted with personal drama and freighted with larger social and political significance.

Staple items of local news in 1920s Beijing were tales of social disorder centering on a politics of personality or reputation marked by what Georg Simmel described as the "particular bitterness which characterizes conflicts within relationships whose nature would seem to entail harmony."[82] In one case an apprentice bit off the ear of a flour shop owner (who had destroyed the family business through profligacy) who beat him.[83] In another, carpet factory workers, led by their labor bosses, denounced their newly appointed manager's corruption and set in motion a series of violent confrontations with the manager and his personal retinue.[84] Managers, officials, and school administrators suddenly found themselves locked in battle with their workers, employees, students, or followers. Leaders, or "responsible persons," were labeled tyrants, dictators, or thugs after having begun their tenure in office with a fund of deference and respect. Mobilizing resources related to founding guilds and unions and providing new services to constituents created the impetus for many unpleasant incidents.⁸⁵ The elaboration of a civil society through association building at this time intensified the small politics of reputation beyond the capacity of mediators to maintain social peace. Cobbled together by opportunistic elites and counterelites, the politics of reputation took on an ideological tone with powerful organizational consequences.

Local elites could find themselves in a tight position when confronted by a second "front" of mass politics generated from within their own domains and strengthened by alliances with outside cadres and publics. This potential for internal opposition became difficulty—manifested in 1928 with the arrival of Northern Expedition forces. Having shed much of their commitment to popular mobilization following the bloody break with the Communists, Chiang Kai-shek and his conservative allies in the Nationalist regime emphasized social order to the exclusion of party-led mass participation. However, non-Communist party activists retained their local positions and their enthusiasm for organizing workers, peasants, merchants, students, and women. While Chiang attempted to unify the country by defeating or coopting rival warlord armies, local party activists mobilized city residents to win higher wages, abolish unpopular taxes, promote social and cultural change, combat foreign influences, and establish popular organizations at the expense of professional associations and guilds, which they judged elitist and inimical to the revolution. As a result, in summer 1928, local elites faced the challenge of a divided, even schizophrenic regime, with the higher levels behaving like regional militarists or conservative modernizers and the local or intermediate levels acting like revolutionaries.

Mass mobilization by Nationalist cadres was an immediate success. By the end of 1928, the Beiping Federation of Trade Unions (FTU) numbered twenty-six unions with more than fifteen thousand members.⁸⁶ Nationalist union organizers in Beijing began as local representatives of the Grand Alliance (Da tongmeng) faction recruited by leftist party figure Ding Weifen on the basis of school and Shandong native place connections.⁸⁷ Factional ties gave a handful of cadres in the Grand Alliance the ability to emerge as leaders from the thousand or so Nationalist Party members in Beiping. In the process of building the FTU, the Grand Alliance then established an organizational base. By late 1928 the faction's leaders, especially a former university student and brilliant orator named Zhang Yinqing, began to act like brokers as they mediated between the unions and higher-level authorities, represented the interests of their constituents, and repressed any challenge to FTU and Grand Alliance power. Predictably, given the political trajectories of other elites who made a similar progression, during 1929 insurgent unions and party allies of Chiang Kai-shek attacked the "old faction" of the FTU. The incumbents, criticized for "clutching the unions in a monopolistic grip," were finally toppled.⁸⁸

More fundamental limitations to the labor movement in Beiping were revealed by the FTU's inability to penetrate most wholesale, retail, and craft shops where the bulk of the city's laborers held jobs. Attempts to unionize shop employees brought into the open the conflicting interests of the city's laborers and business elite. Elite paternalism and brokerage no longer sufficed to maintain social dominance when labor organizers as representatives of the workers pressed demands. Employer-employee relationships were politicized, and the contentiousness of civil society was revealed as its new associations clashed rather than coexisted. Challenged by unions from below, the local-elite leaders united within their most powerful organization, the chamber of commerce, to seek to repress their employees with help from governmental elites who shared the goal of social order but who proved uncertain allies of local-elite organization.

These sociopolitical fissures were dramatized by the shop clerks' movement of 1929. Most of the thirty thousand shops in the city had fewer than five employees, and the lion's share of clerks and craftsmen were attached to these small-scale enterprises.[89] Many shops doubled as residences, with much of the firm's business conducted on the street.[90] Larger shops boasted ornate facades and a number of rooms for business transactions, manufacturing, storage, and living quarters. The wealthiest establishments outside Qian Gate, like the Meng family's Ruifuxiang silk and foreign good shops, employed as many as several hundred persons in elaborate hierarchies of salesmen and apprentices.[91] The familylike character of the traditional shop did not exempt it from conflict between owners and workers. But the small scale and the appeals and threats embodied in shop-based paternalism, combined with the double-cloaking effect of guild and chamber of commerce organization, offered formidable barriers to labor organizers.

In 1928 the merchants' union, sister organization to the FTU, had failed in its attempt to create a mass base among shopkeepers to rival the chamber of commerce. In 1929, the merchants union shifted tactics from winning over guild leaders to undercutting merchant authority by mobilizing shop employees; the merchants launched a campaign to organize a shop employees' or clerks' union. By mid-February, the local press reported that "in the last few days, young shop clerks in the big shops, with the encouragement of the Nationalist Party branch and the merchants' union, have organized branches of the Beiping Clerks Association (Dianyuan gonghui)."[92] Eight or nine of the more famous shops in the city were immediately affected, and the clerks themselves were said to be in "high spirits."

At the main Ruifuxiang store, manager Meng responded to unrest among his clerks by arranging a theatrical party for the workers. At the gathering Meng explained his views on unionism and tried to convince the workers that the firm could not afford the extra $240,000 in wages they were demanding. Most clerks present were reportedly swayed by Meng's arguments and his display of paternal concern for their interests; but a minority, citing Sun Yat-sen's Three People's Principles, declared that they must be allowed to organize. Meanwhile, against the chance that the workers might not be persuaded, Meng had given orders that all stock be cleared from his stores and the buildings locked. When the clerks found out what had happened, they angrily accused the Ruifuxiang management of antinationalism. Outside the locked and shuttered shops, merchant union leaders led the clerks in chanting "Down with Meng!" As the clerks movement spread throughout the crowded merchant quarter, many owners followed the lead of Ruifuxiang and closed their businesses. In other shops, clerks either convinced employers to allow them to organize or took over the stores themselves. Posters appeared in store windows declaring the right of workers to organize. In all, as many as one thousand workers joined the movement in the first days of agitation.[93]

Long-standing grievances soon surfaced in the movement, giving the lie to the ideal of elite paternalism. The clerks movement showed class and ethnic solidarities normally suppressed by the regime of social hierarchy. In the tea trade, the managers of shops were mostly from the same county in Anhui. Many tea-store clerks who joined the movement claimed that workers who were not natives of that area had long suffered discrimination. They were paid less than one-quarter of what the others earned and were "treated like animals." But the pressures exerted by the clerks' association also stimulated internal reform in some shops where managers raised wages and lightened work loads to prevent organizers from gaining a foothold. Signs announcing that "this shop's clerks have organized their own association and will not join any other group" were tacked to the front of some stores. While guilds and guildlike bodies limited the nature and comprehensiveness of worker demands and grievances, the nested hierarchy of shops, work groups and gangs, and citywide umbrella-organizations like the chamber of commerce offered a framework for expressing and resolving grievances through mediation and reciprocity.

The chamber of commerce called a special meeting in late February 1929 to consider what to do about a movement that, as an outgrowth of the merchants' union, directly threatened its control over the commercial sector. The chamber created a ten-man committee to try to mediate between the clerks' association and affected shops. It also authorized formation of a merchants' militia in the event mediation failed. Militia were typically deployed only in time of war or serious social turmoil, and the chamber's action suggests that the body viewed the new movement as a greater threat to its interests than the rise of either the FTU or the merchants' union in 1928. Many trades represented in the chamber were accustomed to yearly rounds of labor negotiations. But these disputes typically pitted merchants against craftsmen organized either in their own guilds or informally in bodies led by labor bosses. Until 1929, retail and wholesale shops themselves had been immune from union organizing.

In the smallest shops, where home and workplace were practically identical, there would have been room for a small politics of rebellion and feud but not for the ideologically militant worker or labor organizer. Conflict remained personal and factionalized within the narrow compass of the owner and a few employees. In larger shops, where the division of labor was better defined and where the binding strength of native place ties was missing or fractured, there was room for organized dissent. In the Ruifuxiang stores managers and apprentices were linked through Shandong native-place bonds. On the one hand, because managers themselves rose from apprentice status, a strong sense of master-apprentice relations pervaded the firm's social organization.[94] On the other hand, shop clerks were divided into "inner" and "outer" employees with the latter serving as temporary or contract workers. The outer clerks had higher wages and lower status and might not even be invited to the customary end-of-year banquet to celebrate shop solidarity.

Faced with the growing power of the clerks' association, the chamber appealed to both regional power holders and Nanjing for help in suppressing the movement. Representatives of Chiang Kai-shek and North China militarist Yan Xishan obliged by denouncing the organization as illegal.[95] The merchants' union defended its creation by arguing that it was an "association" rather than a "union." However, the Beiping Branch Political Council, which represented the alliance of Nanjing and the northern warlords, rejected the argument out of hand and ominously referred to the bloody repression of the "poor clerks" in southern cities. The mayor and the police chief informed the chamber of commerce that shop owners whose employees had been organized by the clerks' association should call on the police for help in disbanding it. Policemen went to stores occupied by militant clerks and ordered that political placards be torn down. With the backing of the chamber, the police, higher-level Nationalist officials, and regional militarists, shop owners were emboldened to fire workers who had joined. The Ruifuxiang stores alone dismissed over one hundred clerks. Finally, under pressure from police and military authorities, the merchants' union itself disowned the organization. Clerks who had joined the movement were ostracized by the merchant community. Months later they were still out of work and living off alms from sympathetic party officials.

The dismal performance of the clerks' association stood in sharp contrast to the success of the labor movement and the temporary inroads made by the merchants' union. The FTU had withstood Yan Xishan's attempt to break the union movement the previous August. Workers had held firm, and union leaders had exploited divisions between Yan and Chiang Kai-shek, benefiting from local-elite apathy. The initial success of the merchants' union in 1928 stemmed from its ability to divide chamber members and win several guilds to its side by exploiting resentment over chamber collection of extra taxes to feed Northern Expedition armies encamped around the city. In the case of the clerks' rebellion, however, the chamber remained unified and found common cause with regional and national military and bureaucratic elites. Conflict between guild leaders over the issue of protection money or disagreements between local elites and Nanjing over taxes did not prevent elites from protecting a principle central to the functioning of Beijing's social order—the exclusive power of the shopkeeper over workers and apprentices.

CONCLUSION

Local elites in Beijing practiced a politics of accommodation throughout the warlord period. They were neither so weak that they needed to bow habitually to the demands of higher elites nor so strong that they could elevate acts of defiance into an independent municipal politics. The frustrations of warlord Zhang Zuolin when denied the revenues he craved by the tightrope artistry of Sun Xueshi and the bitter defeat of insurgent shop clerks at the hands of the Mengs suggest the outer limits of local-elite power. They ruled a realm bordered by clashing militarists and restive mass constituencies. A few individuals, like An Disheng, believed that the autonomy bequeathed local organizations by Qing reformers and reluctantly confirmed by Republican politicians could be the stuff of a liberal politics. New legal statuses of professional association and citizen grafted onto traditional prerogatives exercised by gentry and merchant elites would make the state dependent on civil society for legitimacy, rather than the other way round. The utopian nature of An's idealism allowed him to see that a window of opportunity had opened for this kind of project, if local elites had the courage to challenge a weakened, though still dangerous, state. An Disheng's more pragmatic confederates and adversaries refused to be drawn into risky enterprises of the sort An favored. They either broadened their involvement in local affairs to fill the paterfamilias-cum-broker role of a Sun Xueshi or narrowed their approach to the specific defense of individual or group interests like the Mengs.

The real threat to the baroque structure of the local elite, with its old dome of gentry and merchant activism embellished by the 1920s and the addition of new professionals and cadres of various hues, was central state power combined with mass mobilization. This kind of radical circumvention and subversion of local-elite power, alien to the thinking of Qing reformers and early Republican power holders, was considered and finally rejected by the Nationalists. It turned out to be the key to future Communist success.[96]

PART FOUR

Village Elites and Revolution

NINE

Corporate Property and Local Leadership in the Pearl River Delta, 1898–1941

Rubie S. Watson

Scholars of late imperial China have long debated the relative openness of Chinese society. In the 1950s and 1960s these debates focused on the nature and extent of elite continuity and tended to emphasize questions of personnel rather than structure. Few would disagree with the view that later imperial society was divided into status groups and classes. At issue has been the movement between these groups. For many scholars, China provides an example of an agrarian society with an open, highly fluid system in which families entered and left the elite with considerable regularity. According to this view the division between China's late imperial elite and the ordinary population was guarded not by a closed door but by a revolving one.

In recent years, studies of elite mobility rates have been combined with a concern for the institutions, structures, and mechanisms that affect those rates. The advocates of openness maintain that China's competitive examination system and the custom of equal inheritance among sons made it difficult for a family to retain its status for more than two or three generations.[1] Because access to the bureaucracy and the economic benefits of office holding were determined by examinations, scholars have argued that families could not easily pass their status on to their sons and grandsons.

These arguments for an open elite have been criticized by other scholars who maintain that the mobility advocates have predetermined their results by their definitions and methodology.[2] Early mobility studies, they contend, focused on the office-holding elite and measured mobility by the number of higher-degree holders whose fathers, paternal grandfathers, and paternal great-grandfathers all lacked examination degrees.[3] Critics have argued that imperial degrees and offices are too narrow criteria on which to build a model of social stratification. As long as elite status is defined solely in terms of office and degree holding, and as long as the measurement of mobility is restricted to three generations of direct descent in the patriline, it is statistically quite easy to demonstrate high rates of mobility, the critics contend. Robert Hymes and Robert Hartwell, it should be noted, have found that mobility rates are significantly lower if the measurement of mobility includes collaterals and affines in the universe of potential office-holding relatives.[4]

Elite status, many of the critics argue, is not simply a matter of degree holding; more attention, they urge, should be given to the interlinkages of wealth, lineage organization, local leadership, and scholarly achievement. Recent studies, which have tended to focus on one particular locale, have found considerable continuity of the local elite, with the patrilineal descent group providing a powerful bulwark against downward mobility.[5] Hilary Beattie's work on Tongcheng county, Anhui, during Ming and Qing times is an excellent example of this approach. In her book, *Land and Lineage in China*, Beattie argues that private landowning, cohesive lineage organization, and joint property constituted a powerful set of safeguards that protected families from the four-generation rags-to-riches-to-rags scenario so prevalent in the Chinese folk tradition and the writings of mobility scholars.[6] In a study of status in the Song, Linda Walton summarizes the critics' position:

> A new picture has begun to emerge in which the elite of late imperial China can be seen as a large group of lineages who prepared candidates for the examinations and provided office holders for the state, but who achieved, protected, and enhanced their status locally through a variety of social and economic means, such as marriage alliances with other elite families, and the establishment of the institutions of joint property.[7]

Scholars who argue for high rates of mobility point to the examination system as the institution that kept the elite open to new blood, while partible inheritance produced unavoidable pressures for downward mobility of older elites. There is, of course, much merit in the view that partible inheritance directly effected rates of social mobility in late imperial China,[8] and I have no particular quarrel with this argument. However, there is a danger that explanations of this sort may make us think that we understand more than we do. In fact, the asserted link between partible inheritance and high rates of mobility remains largely unexplored in China. In Europe, for example, equal inheritance did not inevitably lead to a highly fluid pattern of stratification. Late marriage, nonmarriage, status endogamy, cousin (or "close" kin) marriage, and high rates of infant mortality contributed to retaining wealth under regimes of equal inheritance.[9] Perhaps China specialists have too easily accepted the dogma that equal inheritance leads to an open social system.

The landlord-merchant elite described in this chapter was embedded within a large, highly-segmented lineage. Unlike some members of China's late imperial and Republican elite, the group discussed here enjoyed considerable staying power. For more than 250 years a single patriline (the descendants of a mid-eighteenth-century ancestor) dominated political and economic affairs in the village of Ha Tsuen and its hinterland. I explain how it was possible for a single line of agnates to maintain a position of wealth and power in a society known for its downward mobility.

In this essay control over both the lineage's organizational machinery and corporate property are seen as mainstays in the arsenal of formal and informal supports that made elite domination possible. I argue that a high ratio of corporate to private property is likely to affect local political organization, the ways in which elite and nonelite are linked, and the continuity of local elites. Half or more of the land belonging to the residents of Ha Tsuen was not subject to partible inheritance but rather was tied up in indivisible corporate estates. The role that corporate lineage estates played in diminishing the effects of equal inheritance and in creating political capital for the people who controlled those estates is examined in detail. In Europe, late marriage and high rates of celibacy appear to have reduced the pressures of downward mobility in at least some areas where partible inheritance was the norm. Is it not possible that corporate estates may have a similar effect on elite continuity in China?

In this article I enlarge on themes developed in previous work and situate the Deng lineage of Ha Tsuen in a larger regional context.[10] By placing the Ha Tsuen material in a comparative perspective it is possible to clarify at least some of the links between corporate property and class structure. Whether the patterns described here fit the Tongcheng model so ably described by Beattie remains to be seen.[11] There were, to be sure, some significant differences between the lineages of Guangdong and those Beattie describes for Anhui. The question of regional variation will be taken up in a later section of this chapter.

SETTING: HA TSUEN AND ITS ELITE

This article covers the period from the British takeover of Hong Kong's New Territories in 1898 to the Japanese occupation in 1941. Changes in village politics in the postwar period are detailed elsewhere.[12] This discussion is based on data collected in the village of Ha Tsuen, located in the northwestern sector of the New Territories. Prior to 1898 this area was part of Xin'an county in Guangdong province. At the time of my fieldwork in 1977–78, the village had a population of twenty-five hundred; all were Cantonese speakers. The males of Ha Tsuen share the surname Deng and trace their descent from Deng Fuxie, an official who settled in the Hong Kong region during the twelfth century. The Deng controlled a hinterland consisting of an administrative subdistrict, or *xiang*,[13] containing fourteen satellite villages inhabited by dependent (non-Deng) tenants. Until the early 1960s, most villagers were engaged in double-crop rice production. By local standards the village was a powerful and wealthy community; it was dominated by a small group of landlords and merchants who until recently lived off the rents they collected from their agnatic kinsmen and unrelated tenants. These landlords lived in Ha Tsuen but had extensive interests in shops, businesses, and factories outside their home village.

The landlord-merchants described here rank well below the national elite of Qing or Republican times. The China historian is unlikely to have seen much of this local elite in the archival record. Ha Tsuen never boasted a *jinshi* or *juren* degree holder, although their agnatic kinsmen in Kam Tin (six miles from Ha Tsuen) did produce an occasional scholar-official. The Ha Tsuen Deng seem never to have been very concerned with education. A few men sought the trappings of literati status, but their efforts were never crowned with any real success.

These people did not travel in the power circles of Guangzhou or Beijing. However, their agnatic ties linked them to wealthy and powerful men from other Deng communities in Xin'an and neighboring Dongguan counties. In 1709, five Deng settlements joined to establish a lineage hall (Duqing *tang*) in Dongguan City. Members of the Duqing *tang* were bound by their common descent from their twelfth-century founder, Deng Fuxie. The guiding force behind this hall was a Kam Tin Deng named Deng Paosheng, a *jinshi*, but we know little about Ha Tsuen's involvement in this higher-order-lineage except that they were members of the Duqing *tang* and did, according to my Ha Tsuen informants, take their turn at organizing the ritual sacrifices commemorating the founding ancestors.[14] From interviews and genealogies I know that the Ha Tsuen and Kam Tin Deng shared a particularly close relationship. Until the Second World War they had mutual responsibility for the care of graves belonging to a number of shared ancestors. Ha Tsuen was in fact an offshoot of Kam Tin; Ha Tsuen's founders had moved from Kam Tin in the ninth generation (in the mid-fourteenth century). The Ha Tsuen Deng are proud of their close links to Kam Tin whose elite have for generations been considered the cream of local society.

Beyond their connections to agnates in the region, the Ha Tsuen elite's extensive economic interests also took them out of their village into the *xiang*, the standard market town of Yuen Long, and the intermediate marketing networks of the region. Some of these contacts involved kin; others did not. In the eighteenth and nineteenth century Ha Tsuen's elite owned and operated cargo boats that serviced parts of the Pearl River delta, Western District on Hong Kong Island, and the coastal area as far north as Swatow. In the latter half of the nineteenth century two brothers, members of Ha Tsuen's wealthiest line, established a pawn shop and match factory in Yuen Long Old Market, the standard market town that serves Ha Tsuen. Members of this line were also the original shareholders in Yuen Long's new market (established in 1916), which eventually eclipsed the older market. Beginning in the mid-nineteenth century men of this patriline built or expanded a sugar-processing factory in Ha Tsuen and in the 1880s added a peanut oil factory.

That the marriage networks of this elite should mirror their expansionist economic outlook is not surprising. According to a survey to twenty elite women covering the period from about 1900 to 1978, all wives who married into this line came from beyond the immediate *xiang*, some from as far away as urban Hong Kong and the county administrative center at Nantou.[15] For Ha Tsuen's landlord-merchants affinal ties were an important resource. Their mercantile activities and their role as political brokers depended on an extensive interpersonal network. The members of Ha Tsuen's local elite were never simply lineage or village personalities; their influence depended on extravillage ties as well as a solid economic and political foundation at home. As I have argued elsewhere,[16] there is little doubt that affinity and ties to maternal kin helped to create and sustain the external relations that were so important to maintaining elite status.

No single factor can account for the privileged position of the local elite described here. Their ownership of important resources was certainly crucial, but their roles as merchants, political intermediaries, and managers of lineage institutions were also significant. Chinese rural elites were sustained by various institutions, many of which had little to do with everyday politics. In this chapter I examine in detail the relationship between control over lineage (corporate) resources and elite power.

CORPORATE PROPERTY

The list of corporate property types in China is extensive. There was, for example, temple land, temple association land, voluntary association estates, lineage land, and lineage segment land.[17] Under these last two categories there were many subtypes: for example, charitable estates (*yizhuang*), scholar estates, service land (*yitian*), ritual land (*jitian*), and ancestral estates (*zu, tang*).[18] Estates were formed by pooling resources or reserving the private property of a deceased ancestor (turning a private holding into a corporate holding). Here I focus on ancestral estates. The rents from these estates provide offerings for the estate's focal ancestor; leftover income is shared on a per capita basis among the estate's membership (i.e., the descendants of the focal ancestor or the descendants of those who formed the estate).

Clan or lineage estates in China are often seen as a form of charity in which benefits are provided for needy kin. The famous Fan estate founded by Fan Zhongyan is an example of a charitable estate, or *yizhuang*.[19] That there is a benevolent, charitable aspect to many lineage estates is undeniable, but in the area I studied ancestral estates (*zu*) are the primary form of corporate property, and they have little to do with charity. They were religious, economic, and political institutions. Here I stress their political role.

In 1905 the first land survey of the New Territories shows that about half of all Deng-owned land belonged to corporate ancestral estates. Corporate landholdings were extensive and central to the local economy. When one asks villagers why they tie up so much of their valuable property in corporate estates, they do not answer by pointing to their charitable natures or the needs of their kin. Rather they say that they establish estates in order "to honor their ancestors" (a filial rather than a charitable act). No doubt their ancestors are indeed honored by these estates; *zu* rents guarantee that proper offerings and proper rites are carried out, giving their ancestors a kind of immortality. However, the formation of ancestral estates, especially large ones, also had the very practical effect of keeping land out of the cycle of family division and fragmentation that was so common in rural China. Estate land is inalienable, and those who share in it (the descendants of the ancestor) remain a group in both an economic and a political sense. As the number of descendants grows over the generations, the economic utility of the estate may decline, but its political significance may in fact increase.

Thus, in a society that practices equal inheritance among brothers, the formation of corporate ancestral estates is one strategy for avoiding or minimizing the disintegration of family property. I do not mean to imply that ancestral estates solve the problems of population pressure on the land; obviously this is not the case. Given a limited technology, the more people who have rights to the income from a piece of land, the less income each shareholder receives. However, in Ha Tsuen I found that members of well-endowed estates rarely shared equally in estate property. Some estate members controlled a disproportionate share of estate income and assets; some also monopolized the estate's political benefits.

Parallels with the use of "entail" among the English elite are striking. (See also Rowe in this volume.) From the mid-seventeenth to the nineteenth century entail was commonly employed as a strategy to preserve property for future generations.[20] There are of course differences between entail and ancestral estate property: the *zu* is established in perpetuity, the entail for only a few generations (usually three). However, both were part of the strategic repertoire that protected property from sale, division, and fragmentation. Comparisons of entail and *zu* are particularly useful because they take the latter out of the lofty realm of the ancestral cult and place it on the more prosaic terrain of property holding, inheritance, and elite continuity.

EXTENT OF CORPORATE PROPERTY IN HA TSUEN

According to the 1905 land records, 377.64 acres of Deng-owned land were tied up in corporate estates. Of this total, 369.69 acres were owned by ancestral estates (*zu, tang*) and the remaining 7.95 acres belonged to hamlet or religious associations. According to my estimates, about 50 percent of land located in Ha Tsuen *xiang* and owned by the Ha Tsuen Deng was incorporated into ancestral estates. This figure is comparable to other estimates of corporate property ownership in the area. For example, a survey of the standard marketing region of which Ha Tsuen is a part found that 44 percent of the land was "lineage owned in 1905."[21] Two dominant lineage villages in the New Territories have a similar proportion of corporate to private property. Baker gives a figure of 52 percent corporate ownership for the Liao lineage of Sheung Shui,[22] and J. Watson estimates a rate of 65 percent for the Man lineage of San Tin.[23] All these figures, however, are much lower than Potter's reports for Ha Tsuen's near neighbor, Ping Shan. According to Potter, one of Ping Shan's eight hamlets (Hang Mei) registered a staggering corporate rate of 93 percent in 1960.[24] Perhaps one reason Potter's figure is so much higher than those reported for neighboring lineages is that he based his calculation on the wealthiest hamlet in Ping Shan, the one that contains nearly all the community's large ancestral halls and many of its richest residents. (In the land records ancestral estates are listed under the hamlet where their managers live.) In surveys made of Guangdong province in the 1930s, Chen Han-seng calculates that what he calls "clan land" (presumably referring to lineage estates) made up about 35 percent of the total cultivated land.[25] If only the Pearl River delta is considered, Chen's estimate climbs to one-half. Compared to these figures, Ha Tsuen is not unique in its percentage of estate land.

There is great variation in the size of Ha Tsuen's ancestral estates;[26] the largest estate (Gouyue *zu*) owns 40.96 acres, and the smallest has a miniscule 0.02 acres of poor hill land (table 9.1). Potter found a similar but more glaring pattern of difference in Ping Shan where 37 percent of the estates he surveyed (N30) owned less than 1 acre, and 50 percent owned from 1.1 to 15 acres. The largest owned 178.4 acres of land, an enormous holding for the area.[27] To keep landholding in perspective, two facts are helpful: the largest private landholding in Ha Tsuen in 1905 was 71 acres, and about 1.5 acres of good paddy land supported a household in the period under discussion here.[28]

Because a significant proportion of property in lineage-dominated areas was corporately owned, ancestral estates were important sources of rental land. According to my estimates, in Ha Tsuen in 1905 the landless rate was about 55 percent, and 97 percent of Deng households rented some of the land they farmed. Of those households that did own land, 84 percent had holdings of less than one acre.[29] No doubt a considerable amount of valuable land was tied up in ancestral estates, which were often cast in the role of landlord. In Ha Tsuen some villagers said that their rents were reduced if they were tenants of their own *zu*, while others claimed that they paid the same rent as nonmembers. For the Pearl River delta village of Nanching, C. K. Yang reports that there was "no practical difference in the type of tenancy and the amount of rent charged" between private and ancestral land.[30] Although there were no general restrictions on renting estate land in Ha Tsuen, some villagers claimed that members tended to have an ad-

TABLE 9.1.   Major Ancestral Estate *Zu* and *Tang* Landholdings for 1905 in
Ha Tsuen Subdistrict

Zu and Tang	Acres
Gouyue *zu*	40.96
Juren *zu*	38.28
Jiarong *zu*	28.79
Yaozong *zu*	27.59
Zhuoqing *zu*	26.10
Hanzhang *zu*	22.15
Yougong *tang*	16.00
Zongcheng *zu*	14.96
Zuhou *zu*	14.51
Youshan *tang*	14.06
Sile *zu*	13.18
Niaozhang *zu*	12.94
Total	269.92

SOURCE: This table is adapted from a table that first appeared in Rubie Watson, *Inequality Among Brothers: Class and Kinship in South China* (Cambridge: Cambridge University Press, 1985), 71.
NOTE: There were eighty-two estates in the Deng lineage in 1905. Seventy *zu* and *tang* had less than ten acres. Of these seventy, sixty-three had less than five acres.

vantage over nonmembers in competing for tenancy rights. There appear to be, however, no significant distinctions in terms of rental arrangement between lineage and private holdings.

It is clear that some estates produced large rents. However, few Deng could afford to live off the proceeds of ancestral estates without some other source of income. In 1905 the largest landowning estate in Ha Tsuen, Gouyue *zu*, had nearly 41 acres (see table 9.1) and in 1978 a membership of more than eight hundred men. During recent generations, rent from this estate produced a surplus after expenses that was sufficient to pay only a token cash dividend to members. In 1905, of course, a few estates produced large amounts of rent shared among a small membership. These estates were all recent in origin; two of the largest estates, with a combined holding of 51.34 acres, were formed in the 1880s and had only a few members. Until recently the yearly dividends from these estates were considerable, but it is unlikely that members lived solely on estate proceeds, for in 1905 these men were among Ha Tsuen's wealthiest landlord-merchants.

THE BENEFITS OF CORPORATE PROPERTY: ESTATE MANAGERS

In two recent articles concerning charitable estates in nineteenth-century Wuxi, Dennerline discusses the role that *yizhuang* played in political life.[31] Although Dennerline is not primarily concerned to detail the exact processes that connect *yizhuang* to political leadership, his discussion does make clear that local power and its exercise were inextricably bound to the control of charitable estates. Dennerline is no doubt correct in stressing the communitywide benefits of *yizhuang*, but he also states: "Once an estate was established, to control the management of it was a major political objective." He concludes that "charitable estates were . . . tools by which the most powerful men in rural society exercised both their own influence within the lineage and the lineage's influence within the community."[32]

The estates that Dennerline describes are not the same as those I found in Hong Kong's New Territories.[33] Wuxi's charitable estates had an important welfare role (certified by the state), an insignificant aspect in the case of Ha Tsuen and, to my knowledge, other estates in the Pearl River delta. I place special emphasis on the unequal way in which corporate benefits were apportioned and the advantages estates gave to those who controlled and managed them. I do not deny that corporate estates offered important benefits to poor agnates; I do argue, however, that the wealthy benefited far more than did Ha Tsuen's smallholder-tenants.

I have already noted that ancestral estates make it possible to maintain a sense of group unity and purpose often endangered by the normal cycle of family division. Figure 9.1 represents the pattern of lineage segmentation among the Ha Tsuen Deng in 1905, and Table 9.1 provides a list of all Deng estates with more than ten acres of first- and second-class land. Ha Tsuen's landlord-merchants, it should be noted, were descended from ancestor Jingwu (generation 14). Taken together, Figure 9.1 and Table 9.1 make it clear that nearly all the largest ancestral estates in Ha Tsuen were clustered in the Jingwu line. Not only were Ha Tsuen's landlord-merchants members of the lineage's wealthiest estates, but they also managed these estates.

Ordinary villagers may have recevied a few dollars each year from their share of corporate holdings, but they were nearly always alienated from active control over the large estates. The real benefits were firmly in the hands of the wealthy, who served as estate managers (*sili*). Managers handled, and continue to handle, the business affairs of the estates. They also act as the estates' legal representatives; in the words of a 1910 ordinance, the manager acts "as if he were the sole owner . . . [of the estate land], subject to the consent of the Land Officer."[34] In Ha Tsuen, once selected, managers usually retained the position for life. Often managers were the sons of previous managers, a pattern that is still repeated. Even today there is no formal procedure for choosing a manager, although the colonial administration has established guidelines for performing managerial duties. Nearly all the men who became managers, especially of the large estates, were members of the local elite. Potter notes a similar pattern in Ping Shan, "The last surviving gentry member of Hang Mei village, who died in 1920, was said to have been the manager of all important ancestral land estates in the village."[35] In 1977–78

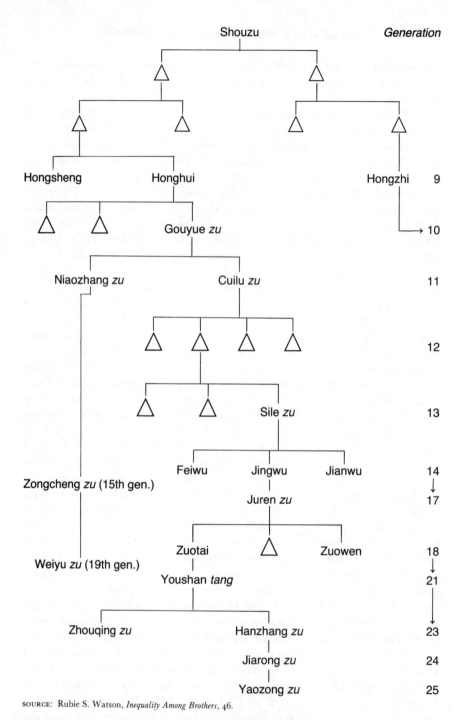

SOURCE: Rubie S. Watson, *Inequality Among Brothers*, 46.

Figure 9.1 Outline of Major Segments of the Deng Lineage

managers of Ha Tsuen's largest estates were political leaders or wealthy men; often they were both. Among the Deng, managers have always been members of the estates they control.

The usual requirements for becoming an estate manager, especially of a large estate, were literacy, knowledge of the world outside the village, and wealth. Personal wealth, it was believed, ensured a minimum of honesty because the manager's private property could be confiscated if he strayed too far from acceptable behavior.[36] The importance of wealth in choosing estate managers also ensured that a few men, mostly landlords and merchants, monopolized this source of local power.

Once a wealthy man became a manager he increased his opportunities for making money and acquiring influence.[37] In Ha Tsuen, managers were especially powerful because they served life terms.[38] Potter notes that in Ping Shan a manager could take advantage of his position by loaning cash from the estate fund. At the end of the year when the accounts were due, he collected and put the principal back in the estate coffers and kept the interest for himself.[39] Ha Tsuen residents report that managers often received "gifts" of money from prospective tenants or lessees of estate property who wanted to secure the tenancy of badly needed agricultural land. According to villagers, estate managers often acted toward tenants much like private landlords. At harvest time managers measured and determined the rent just as private landlords did, and, to the disgust of the villagers, they too used nonstandardized baskets (*douzhong*) to measure the grain rents, keeping the extra for themselves.

It is no secret that on occasion the community of Ha Tsuen, and some of its ancestral estates in particular, have been badly served by their managerial elite. Many Deng believe that Ha Tsuen lost valuable property and suffered a general political decline through the corruption or incompetence of past leaders and estate managers. In particular, villagers point to the eclipse of their local market, darkly suggesting that at best their leaders were outmaneuvered by a group of outsiders and government officials or at worst their acquiescence was for sale.[40]

Nearly seventy-five years after the event villagers are still upset by an area of marshland in front of the village that was usurped and leased by the colonial government to a consortium of overseas Chinese developers. The marshland reclamation, which created about five hundred acres of land, began in 1915 and set in motion a series of ecological changes that are still causing the Deng serious problems. Most notably and immediately affected was the narrow channel through which cargo boats serviced Ha Tsuen Market. Soon after the reclamation began, this channel became hopelessly silted and had to be abandoned, thus hastening, according to the Deng, the decline of their market. A number of villagers believe that the manager of the Yougong *tang* (the *tang* with responsibility for administering general village affairs, see below) either refused to make a case for Ha Tsuen's rights over this marshland and/or accepted a payoff from the developers to let their arrangement with the government proceed unchallenged.

Ha Tsuen villagers also continue to feel bitter over the perceived betrayal by the manager of the Duqing *tang*, the estate of the Deng higher-order lineage. In 1892, in anticipation of commercial development in the area, the Duqing *tang* obtained rights (in the form of a reclamation certificate) from the Qing government to about 117 acres of coastal land near the present-day city of Kowloon. In 1894, before improvements were made, a Kam Tin Deng, a *juren* and manager of the Duqing *tang*, claimed personal possession of the certificate by taking it on lease (in perpetuity) apparently without the knowledge of other Duqing *tang* branch members. Palmer reports in his study of New Territories land tenure that after serving as both lessor and lessee in this transaction, the manager then proceeded to inform the five member branches, including Ha Tsuen and Kam Tin, of the new arrangement. He confessed that he had mortgaged the certificate to Fuk Tin (Futian) Company of Hong Kong, a commercial land enterprise owned by Li Sheng, a native of Xinhui county and a member of Hong Kong's trading and manufacturing elite.[41]

The Deng eventually brought this case before the new Colonial Land Court which, to their great anger, decided in favor of Fuk Tin Company's rights to the disputed land. The court took the view that the Duqing *tang* had made no improvements in the land while it was in its possession and therefore had no right to the reclamation certificate. Villagers in Ha Tsuen still smart from this loss in which, once again, the local elite was hoodwinked out of their rights by what they consider the duplicity of a corrupt manager and the greed of a new class of commercial land developers. It is certainly worth noting that both these cases involve the victory of urban entrepreneurs over a traditional elite, two groups that for much of Hong Kong's history have remained highly suspicious of each other.[42]

The 1905 land records include the names of the managers of each of Ha Tsuen's ancestral estates. An examination of these records shows that one man, landlord-merchant Deng Zhengming (a pseudonym), managed eight estates; during his lifetime he controlled, as either private owner or estate manager, a total of 193.75 acres in Ha Tsuen *xiang*. Zhengming's personal wealth included 68 acres of *xiang* land, a partnership with his brother involving at least three local factories, a money lending business, and a cargo boat company. Zhengming was the second largest landowner in Ha Tsuen; his brother was the largest, with a private holding of 71 acres.

Of the twelve ancestral estates in Ha Tsuen with more than 10 acres, Zhengming managed six, and of the nineteen estates with more than 5 acres he managed eight; thus, in his role as manager Zhengming controlled 52 percent of all ancestral land. According to my own calculations, the Deng owned approximately 750 acres in Ha Tsuen subdistrict,[43] which means that Zhengming either privately owned or managed more than 27 percent of Deng land in the area. Zhengming's philanthropy, his abilities as judge, and of course his wealth are still remembered; he remains a very popular figure in Ha Tsuen although he has been dead for nearly eighty years. Figures like Zhengming illustrate the complexity of managerial dominance. Resting in part on control of important resources, such dominance also relied upon the prestige that came from able management and the symbolic and political capital that prominent managers accumulated through their public and charitable activities.

POLITICAL ORGANIZATION IN HA TSUEN

Chinese rural political organization in the nineteenth and early twentieth centuries must be understood in the context of a waning Chinese state and, in the case of Ha Tsuen, a colonial regime noted for its methods of indirect rule. As Ha Tsuen and other New Territories villages moved from Chinese to colonial control, changes were inevitable. There is little doubt that local commerce and manufacturing were directly affected by colonialization, but the British, like their Qing predecessors, continued to allow a considerable amount of local autonomy in the conduct of village political affairs. In the New Territories this remained true until the Japanese occupation.[44]

The nature of local autonomy is well documented for this period. Hsiao Kung-ch'uan and Philip Kuhn have provided detailed studies of the mechanisms of local control in late Qing society.[45] Although Mary Rankin focuses her analysis on Zhejiang, her characterization of rural political organization applies to areas well beyond the Jiangnan region. In Zhejiang she writes that the locally prominent dominated key public institutions, creating "the familiar end-of-dynasty pattern of autonomous control over peasants by socially conservative local oligarchies."[46] Cole refers to lineages in Shaoxing as "mini-states" filling as they did a power vacuum at the local level, and Mann has utilized Max Weber's concept of liturgical governance to define and analyze these extrastate institutions and structures.[47] There can be little doubt that liturgical forms of governance were widespread, and in this respect Ha Tsuen and other lineage-dominated areas were in no way unique.

There were no formal political offices and no formal arrangements for selecting community leaders in Ha Tsuen until the 1950s, when the colonial authorities introduced the Rural Committee system.[48] Prior to this time there were, however, men who wielded great power and influence among the Ha Tsuen Deng. Elsewhere I have argued that lineage elders as a category did not play a decisive role in community affairs.[49] Leadership fell not to the aged but to those with experience and economic influence.

Until the 1950s, community affairs and lineage affairs were not clearly differentiated; politics was embedded in the structure of the lineage. Lineage institutions like Ha Tsuen's Yougong *tang* (Hall of Friendship and Reverence) served various functions. Yougong *tang*, founded in 1751, was one of two institutions that cut across hamlet and segment affiliations (the other was the village guard, which I will discuss below). Ha Tsuen's main hall (or *da zu tang*) was at once religious center, meeting hall, administrative office, and symbol of Deng success and unity. In the absence of formal political organizations, it provided the framework for local decision making and administration. The term *tang* has a dual meaning in Chinese, referring to both the physical hall in which ritual offerings to the ancestors are made and the corporate estate, or "trust," of lineage property. In Yougong *tang* we see a structure of both religious and economic dimensions, but it functioned above all in the realm of politics.

During the period under discussion the manager of Yougong *tang* was expected to play a leading role in local affairs. Although formally charged with the duty of administering the hall's corporate property, he was far more than a mere accountant. The position of manager carried no inherent political powers, but in the hands of a forceful individual it placed the incumbent in a powerful position. Ostensibly the manager of the Yougong *tang* was selected by lineage elders. However, because it was essential that the manager be literate and possess business skills and independent wealth, there were few possible candidates. The selection was further restricted by the fact that the manager usually held the position for life. Considering all these limitations, the freedom of the elders to choose a manager was more apparent than real; they were, however, entrusted with the right to legitimize the manager's authority. This was done when the elders gathered with village notables for a special banquet that marked the installation of a new manager.[50]

In 1905 Deng Zhengming managed the Yougong *tang*. Zhengming was a descendant of Jingwu and Zuotai and therefore a member of Ha Tsuen's elite patriline (Figure 9.1, generation 18); at the turn of the century he was a leading figure among this group. Wealth, philanthropy, political acumen, and knowledge of the world are the qualities that the Deng themselves mention when speaking of Zhengming. Personal confidence and wealth allowed Zhengming to enter the political arena, but it is important to stress that his ability to dominate local decision making did not rest on his charisma or money alone. Zhengming's role in local politics and the role of other members of the elite (all drawn from the Zuotai patriline) were supported by their wealth *and* their institutional control over Yougong *tang* and the village guard. These two institutions were closely linked; the manager of Yougong *tang* was in fact entrusted with overseeing the local security corps. Members of the local elite had no direct role in the village guard organization, but nevertheless they had considerable influence through the oversight function of the hall manager.

As manager of the Yougong *tang*, Zhengming was also in a position to dominate many economic activities. The manager administered Ha Tsuen's market and therefore had an important voice in determining market fees and licenses. He also oversaw the maintenance of the channel that linked the cargo boat traffic of Deep Bay to Ha Tsuen's market pier and had overall responsibility for collecting the fees charged for the use of that pier. Community projects such as the construction of public paths and public wells were largely in the manager's domain. Finally, and perhaps most significant, the Yougong *tang* manager (together with the elders) organized the bidding process by which the leader of Ha Tsuen's village guard was chosen.

MANAGERS, LANDLORD-MERCHANTS, AND THE VILLAGE GUARD

The village guard was a local security force; it was neither responsible to nor directly linked with the formal apparatus of the state. In the case of Ha Tsuen, the guard was firmly controlled by the local elite during the half-century discussed here. Because of their coastal location, the Deng had two guard organizations, a "water guard" (*shuixun*) and a land-based patrol group (*xunding*). James Hayes, in a discussion of the Hong Kong region from 1850 to 1911, notes that dominant lineages "got a sizeable revenue from leasing fishing stations and beaches to villagers and boat people."[51] Among the Ha Tsuen Deng, this sizeable revenue was protected by their special water guard.

The water guard was responsible for watching over the Deng's coastal fishing stations and oyster beds whereas the land guard protected *xiang* households. The organization of Ha Tsuen's two guards was very similar. Both had their own written constitutions that set out the responsibilities of guardsmen and specified the procedures for selecting members. Each year a new leader for the land-based security force was chosen by an auction held at Yougong Hall. The leader of the water guard was selected every three years. As organized by the hall's manager, the bids for both offices were sealed, but, according to villagers, this did not protect the process from favoritism or manipulation. The manager who organized the auction retained considerable control over the selection. The bids were often substantial, amounting to as much as one thousand Hong Kong dollars in the 1930s. Villagers report that in the past landlord-merchants often staked potential guard leaders to the money they would need if their offer was accepted.

The highest bidder became the head of the guard, and the cash he bid went into the coffers of Yougong *tang*. Each new leader was then formally confirmed by the manager and the lineage elders. After putting their seals to a paper signifying their public acceptance of the new leader, the elders were treated to a banquet hosted by the newly installed guard head. As long as each of Ha Tsuen's eleven hamlets was represented by at least one member, the leader had the right to choose the guardsmen who served under him. The land guard maintained a force of up to fifteen men, and the water guard had twelve members. Guardsmen were usually poor tenant farmers. All were of the Deng lineage; no outsider has ever served in either of Ha Tsuen's security forces.

Although the guardsmen did not receive salaries, they shared in the fees they collected from all households located in Ha Tsuen *xiang*. The leader of the guard received the largest share and derived his profit from the fees he collected in excess of his original bid. The income for the water guard came from their right to take 18 percent of the value of all oysters harvested along the Lau Fau Shan coast. The water guard had a more clearly defined commercial role than that of the village guard. Water guardsmen kept track of the ownership of individual oyster beds and restricted collection to only those who had the rights to use Lau Fau Shan's lucrative fishing stations.

Ha Tsuen's village guard, like that of other communities, must be seen in the context of the endemic violence along the coast during the nineteenth and early twentieth century.[52] Village guard organizations were important and useful. They provided farmers with a primitive form of insurance; if guardsmen could not retrieve stolen or lost goods, they were required to replace them. The guard also defended the community against bandits, pirates, and encroaching neighbors. In the New Territories each dominant lineage had its own village guard organization that presented a united front against the security forces of neighboring *xiang*. The Ping Shan Deng and Ha Tsuen Deng were often at odds over land, water, public thruways, and control over satellite villages. On occasion their antipathies spilled over into open confrontation and violence. In 1978, Ha Tsuen villagers recalled with pride their once bellicose reputation when their guard brooked no challenges.[53]

Obviously Ha Tsuen's guardsmen served the entire *xiang*; there can be no doubt that their regular patrols did deter criminals and unfriendly neighbors.[54] This was no small matter in an area where local people could count only on the support they themselves could muster. It is clear, however, that the Deng had more to gain from the guards' actions than did their dependents. Because the guardsmen themselves received direct rewards from their activities, they had a vested interest in maintaining the hegemony of the Deng. In effect, their fee-taking privileges depended on their ability to maintain the local status quo. Prior to the 1950s, migration out of Ha Tsuen was the only escape from landlord-merchant dominated politics. Because bids for the guard monopoly were large relative to an average householder's income and members of the local elite often staked guard leaders to the funds they needed to make their bid, it is not surprising that the heads of Ha Tsuen's guard organizations were usually closely associated with local landlord-merchant families. As late as 1978, during my fieldwork, the leader of the water guard was in fact a close political ally of one of the village's elite families.

Ordinary villagers did receive some advantages from the guard and its activities, but there can be little doubt that those who gained most from security activities were those who had the most to lose. Ha Tsuen's water and land guards provided the force that stood behind the economic and political power of the local elite, and as such they were important factors in the maintenance of the landlord-merchant elite. This force, it should be remembered, was guided by the manager of Yougong *tang* and the members of his family and line.

COMPARATIVE PERSPECTIVES

As noted in the introduction to this essay many scholars have viewed high rates of social mobility as characteristic of late imperial and Republican China. In comparison to the caste hierarchy of India or the rigid status boundaries of Tokugawa Japan, China appears to have been a society in which mobility was not only tolerated but also expected. Two main reasons are usually given for this fluidity: China's system of bureaucratic examinations, and the practice of equal inheritance among brothers. Together these institutions are seen as central to creating an open society in which family background did not predetermine status or the opportunity for advancement.

Discussion of the influence of these two institutions has focused on two populations at opposite ends of the social hierarchy: the small bureaucratic elite at the top, and the peasantry at the bottom. We have already noted some shortcomings of the mobility literature focusing on the degree-holding elite; now we must turn our attention to China's villages, for many scholars have found significant evidence for mobility there as well. Mark Elvin, for example, has argued that "Chinese rural society in the nineteenth and twentieth century was . . . one of the most fluid in the world."[55]

The most sophisticated work on rural social mobility has focused on the peasantry of North China. For the authors of these studies, inheritance practices play an important role in rural mobility patterns. Philip Huang, writing about rural Hebei and Shandong, argues that "few rich households maintained their status for more than a generation or two." He concludes, "The main reason for downward movement was the division of family property among sons"; according to Huang a single partition could drive a rich household down to middle- or poor-peasant status.[56]

Clearly the North China countryside described by Huang and others (including Duara in this volume) differed markedly from the New Territories village discussed in this article. Although in Ha Tsuen a small group of landlord-merchants maintained dominance over many generations, on the

North China plain, owner-cultivators predominated, landlords were often absent from the local scene, and villages exhibited low levels of internal stratification and considerable mobility.[57] In contrast to the aggressively self-protective, single-lineage village I studied, Ramon Myers has noted the lack of a strong sense of village identity in North China.[58] He argues that "the influence of clan [lineage] management in village affairs and farming was very small" and concludes by pointing out that the composition of the village elite "constantly changed from one generation to another and was not based upon hereditary succession." These changes "very much approximated," Myers argues,"the rise and fall of households in the village."[59]

Myers's discussion of local political organization is supported by Sidney Gamble's survey of northern villages, conducted in the 1920s and including communities in Shanxi and Honan as well as Hebei and Shandong. In striking contrast to the oligarchic forms of leadership characteristic of villages like Ha Tsuen, Gamble found that most surveyed villages operated a system of regularly rotated leadership positions.[60] One should not, however, conclude that northern villages were little democracies led by meritorious community servants. Property qualifications for leadership positions were not uncommon, and Gamble mentions cases in which leadership passed from father to son or circulated among a small number of "local worthies."[61] In general, however, the leadership patterns described by Myers and Gamble are a far cry from the gentry-led politics of Zhejiang or the landlord-merchant-dominated regimes of villages and towns in Guangdong's Pearl River delta.[62]

Studies based on 1920s and 1930s land surveys of North China show that the majority (sometimes 75 percent or more) of peasant households owned the land they farmed and few cultivators were landless (20 percent or fewer by some counts).[63] In a survey of land distribution figures for pre-1949 China,[64] Esherick cites a rate of landlessness for China as a whole (32.1 percent of peasant households) that, while slightly higher than some estimates,[65] is far lower than those reported for many communities in the southeast. Not surprisingly tenancy rates as well as landlessness rates tended to be low in the North. In Hebei and Shandong, for example, rates vary from the Guomindang Land Commission's estimates that 15 percent of farm households were tenants or part-tenants to the National Agricultural Bureau figure of 28 percent tenant and part-tenant for Hebei and 26 percent for Shandong.[66] Many southeastern villages do not fit this owner-cultivator model.

Rates of landlessness and tenancy are extremely high in southeastern China.[67] Unfortunately there are not a great deal of data on landlessness in the Pearl River delta region during the first two decades of the twentieth century, but the available data from a slightly later period suggest that Ha Tsuen's landless rate of 55 percent and its tenancy rate of 97 percent are not improbably high. Based on a survey of a number of Pearl River delta villages,

Chen Han-seng found tenant rates in the 1930s that ranged from 70 to 90 percent;[68] he also discovered that "nearly half of the peasant families [in Guangdong] are entirely landless."[69] Reporting on the Pearl River delta village of Nanching in the 1940s Yang notes that "we did not encounter a single peasant who did not rent some land from others."[70] In a study conducted thirty years later, Potter found that of the forty-two Ping Shan farmers he surveyed 83.3 percent rented all the land they farmed and only 11.9 percent owned part of their farms.[71] Potter does not give any estimate of landlessness for Ping Shan as a whole, but his extremely high rate of tenancy suggests that the vast majority of Ping Shan farmers were without land.

One way to account for high landlessness and tenancy rates in Pearl River delta villages like Ha Tsuen is to remember that 50 percent of agricultural land was held by corporate estates,[72] and of the remaining 50 percent available for private ownership 36 percent was owned by six Ha Tsuen landlords. In total, about 86 percent of Deng-owned land in Ha Tsuen *xiang* was held by estates or a few large private landlords. It is not surprising, considering these statistics, to find that many Ha Tsuen farmers were without land. Although it is easy to appreciate that extensive corporate holdings have an effect on landownership patterns, it is far more difficult to know what political and economic significance to attach to these patterns.

The contrast with the Lower Yangzi region is interesting in this regard. Beattie's work on Tongcheng and Dennerline's work on Wuxi support the view that lineage organization and corporate property were important factors in establishing elite leadership patterns and in preserving elite status.[73] On the surface the Deng lineage of Ha Tsuen and those described by Beattie and Dennerline appear similar in form and content, and it is tempting to conclude from these similarities that the relationship between lineage and elite was the same in each case. There is, however, considerable evidence to suggest significant differences in the ways in which lineage organization and landownership patterns combined in these two areas.

In this paper I emphasize the importance of corporate property and management more than Beattie does, but the differences between the Ha Tsuen and the Tongcheng data exceed matters of emphasis. Two factors are especially important in distinguishing these two areas: (1) the ratio of corporate lineage property to private property, and (2) differences in the types of landed estates established. Both Beattie and Dennerline report low rates of lineage property (as does Rowe, in this volume, for the Middle Yangzi). Beattie does not provide exact figures but notes that corporate holdings were not large in Tongcheng.[74] Dennerline estimates that in 1881 only three percent of Wuxi land was owned by lineage corporations.[75] In 1931 this figure had risen to 7.81 percent,[76] but even this higher proportion is a far cry from the 50 percent corporate property rate reported for Ha Tsuen.

According to my reading of Beattie's and Dennerline's work, the charitable estate (*yizhuang*) was the primary form of incorporating lineage property in their two regions. As noted above, charitable estates, unlike the ancestral estates (*zu*) described for Ha Tsuen, functioned primarily as welfare institutions. In Ha Tsuen, income from *zu* resources were available only to the descendants of the founding ancestor (however designated). After proceeds paid for sacrifices at the founder's grave, the remaining funds, which were often considerable, were divided among the membership. Some families in the Pearl River delta received substantial personal incomes from estate property.[77] In contrast, *yizhuang* profits were generally reserved for lineage widows, orphans, and the poor. In Ha Tsuen there were immediate and direct economic benefits from estate membership; in Tongcheng and Wuxi benefits to ordinary and even wealthy individuals and families were far less tangible.

In both areas, however, lineage estates played an important organizational role, and the wealthy men who managed them were assured a voice in local decision making.[78] In Ha Tsuen economic benefits and political advantage tended to be closely linked, but in the cases described by Beattie and Dennerline the links seem less firmly established. In fact, from Dennerline's evidence there appears little overlap with political advantage accruing to the managerial elite and economic benefits going to the weak and poor.[79] Before making a final judgment on the extent to which *yizhuang* financially benefited local elites, more information on managing these charitable estates is required. For example, did the overseers of such estates obtain direct economic advantages from their managerial role? If charitable estates did strengthen elite political control and economic dominance, what mechanisms made it possible to achieve these ends? And, finally, how important was lineage property in preserving landholdings from the fragmenting tendencies of partible inheritance? At this point the evidence suggests that *yizhuang* played a different economic role than the *zu* and *tang* estates of the Pearl River delta.

There were high rates of tenancy in both the Lower Yangzi region and the Pearl River delta.[80] According to Perkins, provincewide tenancy rates for the early 1930s (tenant farm families as a percentage of total farm families) ranged from 46 percent to 33 percent for Jiangsu and 65 percent to 44 percent for Anhui. The same surveys found rates of 49 percent to 52 percent for Guangdong.[81] Based on a 1930s survey of Wuxi, Buck calculates a 6.6 percent landless tenant rate and a combined rate of 52.5 percent for part-owners and tenants. For Tongcheng, Buck finds that 43.4 percent of county farmers were landless tenants and 86.8 percent were part-owners and tenants.[82] Based on these figures it is clear that half or more of the farmers in each of these areas depended on rented land for their livelihood. In contrast to Ha Tsuen, which had both a higher tenancy rate (97 percent by my estimate) and a substantially larger portion of rented land in the form of corporate estates, lineage property in Tongcheng and Wuxi appears to have made up only a small portion of the available rental land.

In Ha Tsuen—where half of Deng-owned land was tied up in corporate property, where more than a third of the remaining land belonged to a small number of locally resident landlords, and where more than half of the better endowed estates were managed by one of these landlords—tenant farmers had few choices but to deal with Ha Tsuen's elite. In Tongcheng and Wuxi, farm families also depended on rented land, but, because corporate property did not make up a significant portion of this land, farmers were not forced to rely on lineage estates and estate managers as much as their counterparts in Ha Tsuen. Control over corporate property in Wuxi and Tongcheng does not seem to have had the economic significance that it did in Ha Tsuen. That is, tenant farmers in these areas were far more dependent on private land-holders, including presumably both agnates and nonagnates, than on corpo-rate ones. In this sense Tongcheng and Wuxi managers appear not to have wielded the same kind of economic power that was the stock-in-trade of Ha Tsuen's managerial elite.

In Ha Tsuen the peasant farmer depended on the village guard for his security, on intermediaries for dealing with the outside world, and on the small elite of landlord and estate managers for access to land. Among the Deng the roles of guard overseer, intermediary, and landlord-manager were monopolized by members of a small, tightly-knit group whose ancestors had dominated local society for more than two hundred and fifty years. The ties that bound Deng peasant to Deng landlord were complex and compelling, allowing great durability and cohesion to lineage communities like Ha Tsuen and giving them organizational advantages over villages where centraliza-tion was more difficult to achieve.

There are interesting similarities between the lineages of Guangdong and the Lower Yangzi region: in each case the political role of the lineage was a factor in establishing and maintaining elite control. There were, however, significant differences in the realm of economic control. One suspects that the contrasting ratios of corporate to private property, along with the differing forms of corporate estates (*yizhuang* versus *zu/tang*), may have created dif-ferent patterns of elite domination and continuity in these two areas. Whether the discontinuity between the lineage's weak economic power and strong political power in Tongcheng and Wuxi established a less cohesive and more permeable elite formation remains to be seen. Differences in the nature of elite control were, of course, not simply due to corporate property rates or the differences between *yizhuang* and *zu/tang*. Factors like land concentration, elite residence patterns, and the proportion of office holders also affected elite control. There can be little doubt that the extent of commercialization and industrialization in these two areas also played a key role in the political and economic life of local elites. In Ha Tsuen, the lives of ordinary villagers were encompassed by the lineage; in Tongcheng and especially in Wuxi this appears not to have been the case.

As noted in the introduction, one case study does not allow us to draw general conclusions about rural elites in China. But the Ha Tsuen material is fully consistent with data collected from the New Territories and other Pearl River delta sites. It certainly leads us to ask whether the presence of well-endowed lineage estates created a more rigid, more hierarchical, and less permeable class structure than existed in villages where corporate property was unimportant. Furthermore, the existence of major estates may well have allowed for more political centralization in lineage-based communities. The Ha Tsuen data support the view of those who claim that the corporate land-lordism of southeastern China produces a social formation that differs from the owner-cultivator regimes of the north and, I submit, the private land-holding complexes of the Lower Yangzi region.[83]

TEN

Elites and the Structures of Authority in the Villages of North China, 1900–1949

Prasenjit Duara

It has long been observed that rural society in North China was very different from that of South China, reflecting as it did a very different ecology. The prosperous rice-growing economy of the southern regions supported a highly stratified society where rural elites exercised domination through individual and corporate control of material and symbolic resources. In the north, rural elites at the village level were much less sharply differentiated from the bulk of the peasantry. This was certainly the case by the twentieth century, and it is unlikely that these elites had ever, since the early modern period, been able to attain the levels of wealth and power of their southern counterparts.[1] In many ways the more sharply stratified rural society of South China conforms to the typical image of agrarian societies: relationships of dependency between landlord and tenant exist at the heart of all social arrangements. In the north, where dependency relationships were not quite so dense, the elite's grip over the structures of local authority was correspondingly weaker.

This chapter investigates the special relationship between the status of the rural elite and the structures of authority in North China through a study of customary law in four villages in Hebei during the Republican period. Each village was studied by Japanese investigators in the 1940s, and the four revealed a range of village elite types. Hou Lineage Camp (Houjiaying) is located in northeastern Hebei, near Manchuria, where many of its villagers worked as sojourners. Sand Well (Shajing), considered by its investigators to be an average North China village, is located just north of Beijing. North Brushwood (Sibeichai) in the cotton-growing district of south-central Hebei represents a village where commercialization led to an impoverished village elite and an unusually large role for absentee landlords and moneylenders. Finally Wu's Shop (Wudian), south of Beijing, had been frequently ravaged

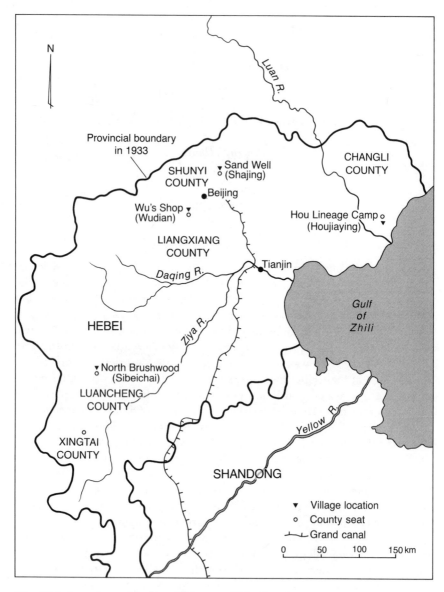

Map 10.1. Locations of the Four Villages in Hebei Province
SOURCE: Prasenjit Duara, *Culture, Power, and the State* (Stanford, 1988).

by warlord armies, whose depredations led to the flight of the village elite (map 10.1).[2]

Despite their marked differences, all these villages on the North China plain shared many characteristics of that entire region. Its ecology produced what Philip Huang has characterized as "a conjunction of low-yield, disaster-prone dry farming with high population density that laid the basis for severe scarcity."[3] Not only did these conditions make large-scale land-lordism an unprofitable venture (at least until extensive commercialization of agriculture in some areas in the twentieth century), but the absence of significant amounts of corporate property also made it difficult for elite families to avoid diminishing their wealth at each successive generation through the practice of partible inheritance.[4]

Historically, the area had been the theater for wars of succession to the imperial throne in Beijing. During the Republic, it was once again devastated by the battles between warlords and then by the Japanese invaders. Moreover, in spite of the political confusion, the peasants and elites of the region were subjected to the pressures of somewhat less than successful, but nonetheless intrusive, attempts at statebuilding by the successive regimes of the twentieth century. These efforts are too complex to evaluate in detail here. They include the state's attempts, for instance, to appropriate community religious properties for purposes of "modernization" and to force village leaders to pursue unpopular policies such as implementing land investigation or supervising the deed-tax payment that the rural folk had evaded for as long as they could remember. Most of all, state penetration involved heavy and unpredictable taxes on the village community to finance the expanding administration and its many programs at all levels—county, province, and center. Such unpopular state policies often led elites to evacuate leadership positions in the villages.[5]

Under these conditions, the opportunities and incentives for local elites to exercise authority in the villages began to recede still further. In this essay I explore how, under these circumstances, an elite that did not directly control the means of production—land, labor, credit, and markets—managed to establish and exercise its authority in rural society, and further study the implications for a community in which the elite was unable to control the structures of authority.

ELITES AND THE NATURE OF AUTHORITY IN RURAL CHINA

I follow Max Weber in defining authority as legitimate domination,[6] and by *structures of authority* I signify the means used to stabilize a social structure by guaranteeing the distribution of its material and symbolic resources. In advanced industrial societies, authority is formally located in the state and its legal system. Elites do not necessarily dominate, or otherwise participate in, these structures of authority; they find other means to reproduce or extend their privileges.[7] In small-scale societies such as the rural society of tradition-al China, however, local elites often dominate these structures, for reasons arising from the needs of both the elites and the community. It is easy enough to understand why these elites sought to monopolize the structures of author-ity. In a society where the state's reach was limited and the means available to maintain and expand resources were constrained by the absence of pri-mogeniture, elites needed to ensure peasant compliance, or at least acquies-cence, if they were to obtain their goals and maintain their position in society.

More interesting, however, are the ways in which communities might have needed elite participation in structures of authority. In China, various social roles—for example, sponsor and manager of religious societies and festivals, lineage leader, mediator with the outside world—typically conferred authority. However, in China's relatively commercialized peasant society, community tasks often required wealth, leisure, and influence for their effec-tive performance. Structures of authority in this society gained credibility through elites participating to "make these structures work." To secure benefits for the lineage, for instance, village leaders in South China had to maintain informal networks among officials and county elites at a scale beyond the horizon of peasant capacities. Thus, authority derived from the performance of roles that were seen to maintain or bring collective benefits; but the effective performance of such roles often required elite resources.

Although participation in structures of authority was important to elite status, elites need not be synonymous with "persons in authority." I will, therefore, define *elites* only in terms of the first two attributes of the usual triumvirate of wealth, power, and prestige; the third might be acquired by nonelites as a result of the authority they derived from assuming community roles. Genealogically senior lineage members, ritual specialists, and others who did not necessarily have wealth and power might thus command pres-tige at the expense of richer and stronger elites. In practice, elites were likely to monopolize genuinely authoritative village roles precisely because of their wealth and power. Nonetheless, we shall see that prestige from community activity could under certain circumstances confer authority upon people who would not otherwise be considered elite and, therefore, might follow a dy-namic other than wealth and power.

We see this most clearly in studies from the Canton delta region of South China. Although genealogically senior elders in Hong Kong's New Terri-tories played a ritually important role in the lineage, the powerful lineage members—the elite of the community—dominated both lineage and com-munity life.[8] Rubie Watson's study (in this volume) of a New Territories village shows that a small number of wealthy landlord-merchant families of the Deng lineage managed to dominate the bulk of tenant-smallholders from the same lineage for centuries. The elite dominance in landownership was reinforced by their control of the market and credit and their marriage alliances to other wealthy and powerful families.[9]

The many-stranded relationships between landlords and tenants in the New Territories required elite domination of the structures of authority. For an economic elite that rented out land and lent money to ordinary peasants, authoritative roles ensured, for instance, that rents and interest were paid. However, even if the elite's aim was simply to protect its own interests, this elite could gain authority only by promoting, or appearing to promote, the general interests of the community. It was not enough for village landlords to exercise great power over their tenants and debtors; to gain legitimacy they also had to be responsible kinsmen and social leaders. Watson argues that the ideal of brotherhood within the lineage justified elite domination. But she makes it equally clear that lineages did not automatically confer authority to these elites; they needed to build up their symbolic capital within the lineage by engaging in philanthropy and other community tasks.[10]

Unlike their southern counterparts, village elites in the north had neither the ability nor the compelling need to control local authority structures. Because these elites dominated neither landholding nor moneylending, their efforts to control the structures of authority were not as effective as those of the southern elites; nor was their desire to dominate so directly motivated by the need to preserve their economic interests. At the same time, rural North China was not a simple, self-sufficient society; this complex commercialized society required relatively strong leadership and authority figures—often stronger than available—to fulfill the peasantry's demands and coordinate community tasks. Genealogically senior lineage elders and ritual specialists were not especially powerful here and were hardly able to address its complex community needs. Who, then, would perform these roles? Who would be able to sustain credible authority structures, especially during the Republic, at a time of great stress in rural society?

Traditionally, authority in these villages derived from both effectively managing such community tasks as crop watching and religious activities and protecting or securing the villagers' interests through such roles as middleman in the innumerable contracts into which villagers entered. Such functions legitimated elite domination—that is, according to our definition, they gave elites authority. But this does not mean that there was no coercive basis for elite power. Occasionally, such coercive powers were built into community activities; for instance, the crop-watching associations were among the most popular and important village-level associations in Hebei during the Republic. Outsiders often assumed that these associations were meant to protect village residents' crops from outside bandits and robbers. In fact, the crop guards would hardly have been able to take on a band of robbers; rather, the crop-watching system was designed to guard the crops from the local poor, including the poor members of the village itself. Nonetheless, many poorer landowners also benefited from this protection. The militia in some localities may have worked in a similar way. However, in the villages studied here, the militia were organized by higher-level offices, often by the ward (*qu*) of state administration.[11] Whatever the local variation and despite our focus on legitimacy and acceptance of domination, we can hardly over-look the fact that, in peasant society, this domination was inevitably tied up with some threat of coercion.

The remainder of this essay focuses on the authority that accrued to village middlemen operating within the realm of customary law and convention. Peasants relied on these middlemen to arrange contracts for many purposes, from securing loans to partitioning family property. The middlemen often indicated village authority more clearly than did managers of community activity. Not only were middleman functions vital to peasants' livelihood, but other community roles traditionally performed by village leaders, such as managing village religious ceremonies, were diminishing in importance in the twentieth century.[12]

ELITES AND MIDDLEMEN IN CUSTOMARY LAW

Ramon Myers and Fu-mei Chen have demonstrated the crucial role of cus-tomary law in facilitating the informal market for land, labor, and credit in rural North China.[13] Here I focus on three kinds of contractual arrange-ments: taking out a loan, leasing land, and selling land. All three types of contracts were critical to the life of the commercialized agricultural society of North China, and all required a middleman (*zhongren, zhongbaoren*).

Loans were perhaps the most frequent type of contract in North China, and peasants acquired credit by mortgaging property or providing a guaran-tor. For loans based on mortgaged property, the middleman mainly acted as a witness to ascertain the contents of the contract—in particular to investi-gate any competing claims on the pledged or mortgaged property—and to mediate disputes. Then, if the loan was not repaid, or more commonly, if interest payments were not forthcoming, it was his duty to either arrange for an extension or dun the debtor. The middleman for a guaranteed loan, in addition to performing these tasks, also undertook to guarantee the repay-ment of the loan.

In the villages I have studied, guarantors were not usually required for rental contracts, probably because tenures were short or unspecified in many villages.[14] Under these circumstances, nonpayment of rent meant certain eviction and difficulty in finding another tenure. The importance of the middleman lay in his ability to locate a tenure, to gain favorable terms for the tenant, and intercede when rent payment was contested. In a land sale transaction, the middleman had several functions. He was usually ap-proached by the seller to seek out a buyer and negotiate a favorable price.

He was responsible for ascertaining the quality and the size of the plot. More important, he had to determine, by inquiring of neighbors and the lineage, whether there were any competing claims on the land. Finally, he ensured that payments were properly made and mediated all disputes.

All contracts required middlemen, but not all contracts required that the rich and influential elite play this role. Probably only loan contracts requiring guarantors needed propertied middlemen; in practice, it was distinctly advantageous for villagers to employ a man of wealth and influence as the middleman. Wealthy and influential middlemen often had extensive connections, and they could contact people interested in seeking credit or purchasing land from a much wider radius than could an ordinary villager. Even more important was the credibility such men brought to their authority as middlemen.

What authoritative roles was the middleman expected to play? In case of a dispute over a contract or a violation of its terms, the authority and responsibility to mediate fell upon the middleman. Moreover, a contract was almost always embedded in an unequal power relationship, and the middleman's authority was crucial not only to prevent the violation of the contract terms by a stronger party but also to negotiate and renegotiate the terms on behalf of a weak party. This was not an uncommon scenario and took place, for instance, when a villager entered into a contract with an absentee landlord or moneylender from the city.

Whether to prevent violations, mediate disputes, or negotiate the terms of a contract, the effectiveness of the middleman's authority was considerably shaped by his "face." For example, in one village, Hou Lineage Camp, a price dispute broke out just as a land transaction was about to be completed. After many attempts to find a mutually agreeable price, the buyer finally resigned himself to the seller's price, saying, "I agreed because it is difficult to do the job of the middleman. If I decided not to buy it, it would affect the middleman's face."[15] The mere presence of a third party known to two contracting strangers was thus itself a means of facilitating negotiations because it added a personal element to the contract. Similar considerations worked to discourage contract violations. The ties of personal obligation to a middleman weighed much more heavily upon a would-be violator if the middleman had considerable "face." Moreover, the higher the status or "face" of the middleman, the more successful dispute mediation was likely to be.

When the middleman introduced a villager seeking a contract to a powerful figure, it was believed that the more "face" the middleman had, the greater was his ability to negotiate terms favorable to the villager. If the middleman was of sufficiently high standing, there was said to be no need for a written contract. A middleman with "face" could fetch a good price for property, get a loan for a longer period, arrange for its extension, negotiate the interest rate, or get the lender to forgive part of the interest.[16] Elites, particularly declining ones like Zhang Yueqing of North Brushwood, took pride in what their face could obtain. Zhang, a village headman for many years, remarked, "If a seller wants to return a deposit [having changed his mind about the transaction] and the buyer refuses to accept it, there is no hope for the seller if his middleman is a poor man. On the other hand, if I was the middleman, I would use my 'face' and ask him accept the deposit."[17]

Thus, what seemed to count in the exercise of authority, in customary law at least, was what the Chinese call *face* (*lian, mianzi*), a subject that deserves more attention than it has been accorded. In his study of Taitou, a Shandong peninsula village near Qingdao, Martin Yang observed that everybody had face, although one person may have more or less than another. His notion of face brings it close to ideas of honor and shame. In his discussion of village conflict, Yang reveals that gaining, preserving, or causing the loss of face was the object of much social interaction and strategizing. The gain or loss of face was shaped by a highly complex matrix of social variables, including not only the statuses of the people involved but also their relationships to other people. Yang gives us an instance of this social complexity:

> Another kind of circumstance in which face is involved is when a youngster offends a senior member in the village. When the offended man is about to punish the boy, other villagers may pacify him by saying: "For his parents' face, you may forgive him." Then the senior member may say: "All right you are old neighbors. For your face and for his parents' face, I forgive him this time."[18]

Yang could have added here that, had no one witnessed the event, the older man might have let the matter slip, and the whole question of losing face might never have arisen. But had the event been witnessed by a different set of villagers, with less status and thus less ability to plead the boy's case, the boy might have indeed been punished, and his parents might have lost face. Thus the social context of an event was also important.

Yang's analysis of face as an object of social contestation helps us understand the concept as a desired cultural goal that people both aspired to attain and valued in others. It enables us to understand, for instance, why an elite that did not control the means of production in a peasant economy was still motivated to undertake various seemingly thankless public tasks with remuneration only in prestige. However, Yang's analysis only illuminates one dimension of a manifold phenomenon. To acquire face was also to acquire authority, and nowhere was this connection clearer than in the realm of customary law. In this sense, face was not just an attribute everybody possessed; rather, some people possessed more face than others, and, moreover, possessed a kind of face that was efficacious: it could get things done without the overt use of wealth or power.

Although face did not always give people of wealth and influence authority, often the face of the elite was authoritative. Consider, for instance, the matter of trust. Several peasant informants equated effective face with trust. Trust was not something particularly associated with elites, but in economic matters the trustworthiness of an individual was not easily separable from his wealth and standing in the community. Indeed, wealth and trust were the two sides of a face whose authority was judged by its efficacy in obtaining practical results. In a loan contract, for instance, the size and duration of the loan and even its rate of interest could be determined by the face of the middleman. A moneylender who made a loan to a villager whose middleman was an ordinary person, not particularly known for his trustworthiness or standing in the community, had to consider the higher risk involved. He might, therefore, loan out a smaller sum for a shorter period and charge a higher rate of interest than if the middleman's ability and reputation ensured repayment.

Of course, face did not always work according to strict economic logic. Probably the face of an elite middleman would be more successful in pressuring a powerful figure than the face of a common peasant, if for no other reason than because the elite was likely to be part of a more elaborate network of reciprocal obligations with other elites than the peasant. Thus, when villagers sought middlemen with face, these middlemen were often—though by no means always—elites with wealth and power in rural society. For a member of the elite, gaining face represented a mechanism for converting wealth, power, and influence into prestige and authority. By gaining face, he was accumulating what Bourdieu has called "symbolic capital," which might be re-deployed at some later time in the service of politics or honor.

One qualification is in order. Face was only relevant within the middleman's arena, defined both territorially and organizationally. Nonelites could exercise influence within the village or with outsiders when they had some special connection. Village elites might have been able to drive a bargain not only with other clients in the village but also with clients and business partners in lower-level markets; however, they may have been completely powerless at higher-level marketing centers where some absentee landlords resided—those of a class with few ties to the village elite. In the following analysis, we see how the arena in which villagers conducted their business varied from village to village, and the ability of the elite to control the structures of authority also depended in some measure on the arena in which they operated.

ELITES AND MIDDLEMEN IN FOUR VILLAGES

Hou Lineage Camp. This village, located in Changli county in the northeastern corner of Hebei, had become increasingly prosperous through the first third of the twentieth century, mainly given increased incomes of so-

journing workers and traders who went to Manchuria. Of the approximately
110 households in the village in 1940, about 11 percent (or 12 households)
owned between 60 and 150 *mu*, while about 70 percent owned less than 30 *mu*.
This 70 percent had to supplement their income by leasing part of the land
belonging to the 12 or 13 households with surplus lands. The presence of a
small, visible elite, which controlled part of the land cultivated by other villagers, makes Hou Lineage Camp more similar to the southern villages of the
Canton delta than any other village studied here. However, differences in
wealth between the ordinary peasant and this elite did not even begin to
approach the sharp differences between elite and peasant in the Canton
delta.[19]

This village elite undertook most middleman roles for loans and land
transactions;[20] with its large circle of friends and acquaintances it could
negotiate a good deal. The middlemen were never paid for their services,
but, if they performed special favors, their client would bring over a gift for
their children as a token of this gratitude.[21] The most common type of loan
taken out by villagers requiring guarantors was often made by merchants
from outside the village. Such loans placed heavy responsibilities on the
guarantor-middleman, and five of the most prestigious and powerful village
leaders were said frequently to play this role. Four of them were wealthy
villagers with face, unquestionably part of the village elite.[22] Let us look
more closely at these elite middlemen, in particular at the careers of Xiao
Huisheng and Liu Zixing.

Hou Lineage Camp had a tradition of elite participation in community
activities. Three plaques awarded by villagers to their leaders attest to this
tradition. One recipient of such a plaque worked in the county tax office. The
plaque, dated 1870, noted that he often advanced money to villagers unable
to pay taxes or requested the magistrate to grant extensions. Another plaque,
from around the turn of the century, had been granted to the first modern
headman of the village and hung on the outside wall of his son's home. It
represented a token of the villagers' gratitude for his various services, such as
mediating disputes, giving aid to the poor, and assisting people entangled in
legal suits.[23]

The third plaque, inscribed "ardent in public service" (*rexin gongyi*), was
granted to Xiao Huisheng, undoubtedly the most influential leader in the
village. Although the leaders of Hou Lineage Camp had promoted the idea of
a plaque, it was presented to him in 1937 by the residents of thirty-eight
villages—all within the fourth ward of Changli county. The villagers were
grateful for his mediating disputes that might have become ruinous legal
suits, especially when he was director of the county telephone bureau from
1934 until 1937. Later he was awarded yet another plaque, this time by his
fellow villagers only, to acknowledge raising money for the village school.

Underscoring the practical value of face, plaques were apparently granted to benefactors during their lifetime to enhance their face.[24]

Despite some similarity between Hou Lineage Camp and Canton delta villages, a leader like Xiao could probably never have emerged in the lineage-dominated society of the south. Not only did Xiao have no lineage in this village, but also he had not even been born there. Xiao's father had settled in Hou Lineage Camp, the native village of his business partner, after the two men's business had failed in Manchuria. Xiao grew up in the village, attended school in the county seat, and graduated from a university in Manchuria. He returned to the county and headed up the telephone bureau of the county government. He was said to be well versed in the law and able to arbitrate disputes before they became legal suits; but it was also said that once a dispute became a legal case he never tried to influence the decision. He had many friends and extensive contacts at the county level, which he appeared to use generously for the villagers. For instance, he could get loans for villagers without collateral, and he often acted as a middleman in contracts. He had sixty *mu* of land when he returned to the village in 1937 and served as the assistant village headman and a member on the school's board of trustees.[25]

Although Xiao managed well without a lineage, Hou Lineage Camp was not without lineage politics. Lesser-elite leaders relied on combinations of kinship bonds and patronage to build bases of support. Liu Zixing (sometimes known as Liu Zixin), the leader of the Liu lineage, had been village headman twice, once in the early 1920s and again in the late 1930s. Among the richest men in the village with 170 *mu* of land, he himself lent money at interest. In the late 1930s, he began to accumulate more and more land by foreclosing mortgages. At the same time, however, he often guaranteed contracts requiring no collateral, thereby undertaking the risk to pay for a peasant should he become bankrupt.[26]

As the leader of the Lius, Liu Zixing had been deeply involved in lineage feuding. In 1921, when he was village headman, the village undertook a survey of all village lands for tax purposes, and Liu was found to be one of those with concealed land. His Hou lineage rivals on the council threatened to take him to court. The matter was ultimately dropped because Liu, like most people, had concealed only a few *mu* of land, and nobody in the village really cared. But the Hous had achieved the purpose behind their threat to go to court: Liu was made to resign from office and taught at a county school until 1929. Thereafter he served on the county education board but returned to live in the village.[27]

When Hou Dasheng became the village headman in the early 1930s, Liu got his opportunity to exact revenge. Hou Dasheng ignored village councillors in decision making and misused public monies, following an increasingly common pattern in the late Republic when the pressures of warfare, heavy taxation, and increasing government intrusion into village affairs made it extremely difficult for responsible leaders to stay in office. Finally, in the mid-1930s, a group of villagers reported the matter to the county magistrate, and Hou Dasheng was forced to resign.[28] The principal leaders of the opposition included Liu Zixing, who probably took the matter to the magistrate himself. As a member of the board of education, he had access to the county authorities. In 1939, several years after the incident, he became the headman of the village and remained in the post until 1941.[29]

From these plaques and biographies, we see how face and authority came to those with wealth and influence only if they utilized those resources for the benefit of the community. Needless to say, this would hardly prevent these elites from also using their prestige to pursue their own personal goals—as we glimpsed in the career of Liu Zixing. Nonetheless, the fact that village authority rested with this kind of elite is underscored by the official posts in the village that most of them held at one time or another in their careers.

The fifth middleman, Kong Ziming, did not fit this pattern. Kong was not rich and owned less than twenty *mu* of land, but he was educated and enterprising. We do not know how much education he really had, but he was highly regarded in the village because he could quote the Confucian classics and talk smoothly (a skill he learned as a shop assistant in Manchuria). This, of course, made him an adept mediator and an invaluable middleman during negotiations. He mediated the conflict between the Lius and the Hous in the village. Kong also initiated the move to grant the plaque to Xiao Huisheng. In 1940 he became the assistant village headman, and in the same year he leased fifty *mu* of rice land from a Japanese company and farmed it with two hired laborers. Kong's successful career reveals that one did not need to be wealthy to command authority in the village; clearly education and resourcefulness went a long way in rural North China. It would probably have been rare for this kind of person to command authority in the Canton delta where generations of domination by a few elite families made it extremely difficult for one who was not wealthy, and especially one who, like Kong or Xiao, was not from the dominant lineage, to break into this monopoly.[30]

Sand Well. Located in Shunyi county, approximately thirty kilometers north of Beijing, this was considered by Japanese interviewers to be an average North China village. In the late 1930s, there were seventy households in the village. There were no large landlords employing many tenants, but several managerial landlords owned more than seventy *mu* and employed wage labor. Distribution of land was unequal: 60 percent of the households owned 14 percent of the land, and 15 percent owned 52 percent.[31]

In Sand Well, the wealthy had actively participated in middleman roles, locating partners for land and credit contracts and serving as guarantors and mediators. Here grain loans requiring guarantors were made by the store in the nearby market town or by speculators on the grain market. The well-respected village headman, Yang Yuan, had extensive contacts in the market town and often acted as the guarantor.[32] Yang Yuan was descended from a line of wealthy village councillors, and two of his brothers were also councillors. He owned a handicraft store in the county seat; for villagers this was their most important opening to the commercial world of the city. Here Yang introduced his fellow villagers to prospective moneylenders, to landlords looking for tenants, and to those seeking to buy or sell land.[33]

By our standards, the Yangs might seem corrupt. He and his brothers concealed more land than most others in the village, and he doubtless used his position as village headman to sell off some infertile land to the village government. However, the villagers did not seem to care a great deal; they seemed reasonably tolerant of people who pursued personal gain from public office as long as these people contributed to the welfare of the community. As an indication of his standing, he was an important mediator in disputes both between villagers and between villages. Although in 1940, after eight years of service, Yang was keen to give up the post of headman, which had become an especially high pressure job under the Japanese occupation, he was clearly regarded as a local leader. He was, for instance, appointed principal of a school established jointly by four villages around this time.[34] Yang Yuan was a typical elite leader whose authority was built upon his role as the gatekeeper of his small community, protecting its interests from, and securing its needs in, the outside world.

In Hou Lineage Camp we saw, in Xiao Huisheng, the rise of an elite patron and the growth of his authority; in Sand Well, we see the decline of elite patrons. Two elite members who had frequently served as middlemen actually lost some property as guarantors. Zhao Tingkui came from a line of wealthy and prestigious councillors. His father had owned 130 *mu* of land, but he himself had inherited only 70 *mu*. By 1940, his property had dwindled to 19 *mu*, in part because he had to pay for a defaulter; the person he had stood for as guarantor had died, and the family was simply unable to repay the loan.[35] Du Xiang, himself a councillor, was also descended from a family of councillors; his uncle was said to have owned 700 *mu* of land.[36] In the early years of the Republic, Du Xiang owned 54 *mu* of land. During these years he was an active middleman arranging loans and rental tenures for the villagers. Once, he acted as a guarantor for an affine who was unable to return the loan, and Du lost 10 *mu* of his own land. For various reasons he lost more and more land. By the 1930s, although he still acted as a middleman, Du Xiang did not have the same face that he had held earlier.

Yang Yuan and Du Xiang were still the most commonly used middlemen in Sand Well, especially in loan contracts with outsiders.[37] Villagers also turned to friends and relatives, often in neighboring villages, to serve as middlemen in land transactions and land tenure contracts.[38] By the 1930s, however, another very different type of middleman had appeared in the village. An impoverished peddler, Fu Ju, settled in Sand Well in the early 1930s. His job took him all over the area and secured him a wide range of contacts, which he put to good use. In the late 1930s, he became a tenant of a powerful landlord living in the county seat and frequently used this connection and his other contacts to act as a middleman. In particular, he arranged for villagers to mortgage their land to landlords in the county seat. Unlike elite middlemen in the village, Fu charged a commission for his services, although he denied it. By the late 1930s, Fu Ju served as the middleman for most land tenure contracts and many land transactions in Sand Well.[39]

North Brushwood. The circumstances of the two remaining villages, North Brushwood in Luancheng county and Wu's Shop village in Liangxiang county reveal a picture of elite activity quite distinct from the other two villages. By the late 1920s and 1930s, these villages had become so thoroughly poverty-stricken that one could scarcely speak of a village elite any more. At the same time, absentee landlords from the county seat became significantly involved in the market for credit and land; thus, the arena in which peasants were involved to secure their needs was widened considerably. But these new participants in land and credit markets came from social strata so distant from the world of the village that what remained of the village elite could scarcely exercise influence on them. As a result, this elite became increasingly irrelevant to the life of the village.

The peasants in North Brushwood principally grew cotton. In this region of south-central Hebei, cotton began to outstrip millet cultivation sometime between 1910 and 1930. The county gazetteer of 1871 registers the land owned by the villagers of North Brushwood between 2,400 and 2,500 *mu*.[40] A number of bad harvests during the early 1920s and early 1930s, together with the depressed prices for cotton, had rapidly impoverished the village.[41] By the early 1930s, over 1,600 *mu* of peasant-owned land had shifted to the hands of big absentee landlords in the county seat. However, 627 *mu* of this land had been mortgaged and could still be redeemed. With the rise in agricultural commodity prices in the late 1930s, many peasants might have been able to redeem their land, but they still had to clear rent arrears before they could do so.[42]

The poverty of North Brushwood is indicated by the fact that the average family owned less than ten *mu* and cultivated a total of less than fifteen *mu* in an economy in which a family of five needed twenty-five *mu* to make ends meet.[43] Only about ten families in the village were able to manage without taking out loans in a normal year. Stratification was not very sharp within the village, and only three households owned as much as thirty to forty *mu*. The one large landowner, Zhang Yueqing, had mortgaged forty-eight of his eighty *mu* to landlords in the county seat.[44]

In terms of property relationships, North Brushwood seemed less like a northern village populated by peasant proprietors than a poorer version of a Lower Yangzi village, with the bulk of the peasants cultivating land owned by large absentee landlords. Three landlords in the Luancheng county seat controlled 723 *mu* of the total of 1,372 *mu* of land leased by the North Brushwood villagers.[45] Much of this land had been mortgaged by the villagers to landlords who kept them on as tenant-cultivators on their own mortgaged land. Relations between the mortgagor-tenants and the moneylending landlords were not harmonious, and they worsened after the Japanese invasion. Even before 1937, tenants delayed rent payments and landlords frequently had them arrested. Tenants retaliated by burning the homes of the landlords. The turmoil accompanying the Japanese invasion made it difficult for tenants to harvest their crops and pay their rents, as bandits and soldiers pillaged their fields. In 1940, when the Japanese army gained fuller control of the region, the landlords began to demand these rent arrears in current prices, which were much higher as a result of the wartime inflation. Apparently backed by the county government, they refused to allow tenants to redeem their mortgaged lands unless these arrears were paid.[46]

Some evidence suggests that in earlier periods an elite in the village included individuals who owned two hundred to three hundred *mu* of land.[47] However, by the late 1930s, scarcely a person in North Brushwood had wealth and connections comparable to those of the elites of Sand Well or Hou Lineage Camp. The single partial exception was Zhang Yueqing, a former village headman of fourteen years' standing who was descended from wealthy village councillors. But Zhang's wealth had also diminished, and he too had mortgaged forty-eight of his eighty *mu*. Part of Zhang's financial problems arose because, as village headman, he had advanced money to pay the heavy irregular taxes demanded by the Nationalist government in the late 1920s, and the wretchedly poor villagers had been unable to pay him back. He resigned from the village headmanship soon after but returned to the position again in 1934. Following the Japanese invasion in 1937, he was kidnapped by bandits who demanded a ransom for his release. After that experience, he gave up his post permanently.[48]

Despite his reduced circumstances, Zhang strove to retain his status as a community leader. He still worked as a traditional doctor in the village, dispensing free services, and ran a traditional-style school in his home. He claimed that he was still the most effective middleman in negotiating loans because of his "face"—as he put it—and he was an expert at measuring land in the village.[49] But Zhang was fighting a losing battle. As the urban moneylenders' power over the village increased, his influence began to dwindle, and villagers turned to other middlemen. Zhang himself had mortgaged more than half his property to the biggest moneylender, Wang Zanzhou; because Zhang too had incurred rent arrears in 1937, Wang refused to let him redeem his lands. Not unexpectedly, Zhang was North Brushwood's bitterest critic of these moneylenders and a vocal champion of the rights of the mortgagor-tenants: he was losing more to these outsiders than just his land.[50]

It is easy to see how the absentee landlords were increasing their power over the villagers. Mortgaging property to these landlords had become the principal means of acquiring credit in North Brushwood. Villagers also depended on these landlords to allow them to continue cultivating their lands as tenants. They were beholden to them for additional loans based on the increased value of their mortgaged land, for extensions on rent payments, and the like. As the hold of these landlords tightened, there was little room for an independent patron to provide access to credit, land, and labor markets on terms favorable to the villager. Instead, to communicate their needs to the absentee landlords villagers became entirely dependent on a different kind of person—one who did not necessarily represent their interests.

Two such individuals, Zhao Laoyou and Hao Laozhen, lived in the village. Like Fu Ju in Sand Well, neither owned more than a few *mu* of land; nor did they have prestige or authority in the lineage. Nonetheless, they were the middlemen in all negotiations with the three big landlords. Villagers approached these men when they wanted to sell or mortgage land, and these middlemen checked the productive capacity of the prospective mortgagor. Before they leased out the land, the money-lending landlords wanted these middlemen both to see that the mortgagor and prospective tenant had adequate labor, implements, and farm animals to work the farm and to determine that the tenant's own property was not so great that it would absorb all of his productive capacity. Landlords also used these middlemen to dun tenants for arrears and act as witnesses when legal action was brought against the tenant.[51]

It would be difficult for such middlemen to acquire face in village society. Indeed, it was claimed that they were agents of the landlords, receiving money secretly for each transaction and keeping an eye on each mortgagor-tenant to see that he did not secretly sell off the land. They themselves received interest-free loans from the landlords and were allowed to lease 80 *mu* and 60 *mu* under the best conditions of tenure. Villagers often wined and dined Zhao and Hao in hopes of obtaining favorable terms from the landlords, but the evidence suggests that the two always protected and promoted the business of their patrons.[52] Zhang Yueqing captured the difference between this type of middleman and the community-oriented elite-patron:

> If the mortgagee feels that he has already lent out too much money and does not wish to raise the value of the loan, he tells that to the middleman who simply communicates that to the mortgagor. But as long as I am the middleman I would never simply communicate [but rather negotiate] such a decision because I would incur a loss of face.[53]

These new middlemen were a far cry from the village elite-patrons who sought to enhance their status by employing their face to secure favorable terms for the villagers. In fact, villagers often did not know these new men personally and had to approach them through a relative or friend—in effect using a middleman to secure a middleman. Men like Zhao and Hao performed their brokerage roles as clients of the big landlords or as specialists who charged a fee for their services. The decline of previous village elites seems to have been spurred by the increased tax demands of the expanding state and by the disorder and warfare of the twentieth century. But the accelerated commercialization of the rural economy in the cotton-growing regions of Hebei also had a clear impact on North Brushwood. As falling prices pushed more peasants into poverty, absentee landlords secured a grip on land and credit markets. The face of the older village elites was inadequate to deal with such men, and a new group of specialists—tied to landlords as clients—monopolized middleman functions.

Wu's Shop Village. Located just south of Beijing, the village was squarely in the path of armies battling their way to the capital. Like North Brushwood, the villagers here depended on absentee landlords, but here the cause of poverty had more to do with the depredations of warfare and weather than the price of crops. In the late Qing period, Wu's Shop residents cultivated some two thousand *mu* of land; by 1941, the residents cultivated only eleven hundred *mu*, of which six hundred *mu* were owned by landowners living outside of the village. Although some absentee landowners were Wudian residents who had fled to the county capital in the 1920s and 1930s, most of the decline represented villagers' sale of land to landlords living in the county seat, some of whom were officers in the county government.[54]

Poor harvests, the frequent disorder, and excessive taxation beginning in the early 1920s explain the impoverishment of this village.[55] In the late 1930s, 77 percent of the fifty-seven families in the village owned less than twenty *mu* in an economy where twenty-five *mu* was the minimal standard of living.[56] Although these peasants supplemented their incomes by working as tenants and wage laborers, most were still compelled to borrow at the end of the year. Thus they were caught in a cycle of debt, the distress sale of land, and further debt.[57]

In late Qing times, the village elite had managed temple festivals and other public activities such as the crop-watching association. But the demands of the Republican era warlord-armies for taxes and requisitions of food and draft animals were so intolerable that many elite fled to the city. Warlord battles began to ravage the area as early as 1919: first, the battles between Wu Peifu and Duan Qirui, and then three successive battles between Zhang Zuolin and Wu Peifu in the early 1920s. With the Japanese invasion in 1937, the last two village families of some substance also left the village.[58] From that time on, village office, especially that of headman, was occupied mainly by reckless villagers who felt that they could squeeze some personal gain from an otherwise unrewarding role.

In Wu's Shop, as in North Brushwood, the need for a guarantor for loans often posed a problem because, by the 1930s at least, it was difficult to find villagers with sufficient property to play the part. Moreover, the precarious financial condition of the villagers made the guarantor's role truly perilous. But life had to go on, and ordinary relatives and friends acted as middlemen in all contracts and even guaranteed small loans for one another. Needless to say, these guarantors were often unable to pay when called on to do so, and cases often ended up in the county courts. According to a former headman of Wu's Shop, the state did not enforce the guarantor provision very strictly, and sometimes let both the borrower and the guarantor off the hook.[59] Such occasional acts of state paternalism hardly addressed the basic problems of this hapless village. Unlike North Brushwood, where the decline of old elites was at least accompanied by the rise of specialists or professional agents, however slight their value to the peasants, most residents of Wu's Shop had no place to turn but to their own diminishing resources.

A TYPOLOGY OF MIDDLEMEN

We have identified three types of middlemen employed in rural contracts: the elite patron, the professional-agent, and relatives and friends. The elite patron with face was propertied, well-connected, and involved in various community tasks. As a middleman, he could often secure a contract in terms favorable to the villager, and for this he did not expect a material reward. The elite middlemen in Hou Lineage Camp and Yang Yuan in Sand Well exemplify this type. It is likely that elite middlemen existed in all four villages until as recently as the 1911 Revolution, and Zhang Yueqing of North Brushwood presents a poignant example of a declining elite patron.

It is not easy to distinguish the particular causes for the decline of elite middlemen in the individual villages. In Sand Well, Du Xiang and Zhao Tingkui probably represented downwardly mobile families in a society where, historically, elite families circulated fairly rapidly. Not many families in the villages of North China could prevent the diminution in their fortunes through the equal partition of family property over a few generations. But in North Brushwood and Wu's Shop the causes of elite decline seemed part of a more secular trend of social change resulting from warfare, commercialization, and state building. We see here the disappearance of elites per se, not the replacement of individual elites by other village elites.

What does this tell us about elite domination over the structures of authority? In Hou Lineage Camp, apparently the elite continued to guarantee the basic needs of the community, and thus maintained the patronage relationships upon which their authority rested. In Sand Well, although Yang Yuan, the headman, continued to perform important middleman roles, the few other elite men in the village stayed away from these roles, possibly mindful of the fate of the two who had lost money as guarantors in this village. By the late 1930s, the peripatetic peddler, Fu Ju, was handling most land tenure and mortgage contracts. Given that elite involvement in middleman roles in this village was languishing by the 1930s, we may conjecture that the community-centered authority structures of this village were weakening.

In North Brushwood, elite participation in brokerage roles had declined by the early 1930s, and the type of middleman had clearly changed. The domination of the village by powerful absentee landlords living in the county seat led to the emergence of contracts secured by professional agents. The professional-agent middleman may have appeared as a response to the accelerated monetization of the region's cotton-based economy in the twentieth century. Indeed, in this respect, this type of middleman resembled the professional middlemen of the Lower Yangzi valley. A study of the middlemen for absentee landlords in Suzhou indicates that they were full-fledged professionals whose job it was to seek out tenants and sellers of land from a catchment area often covering several counties.[60] Middleman services there had clearly developed into a depersonalized, contractual business, with little room to exercise or develop one's personal authority. Perhaps, people like Fu Ju and the North Brushwood professional-agents, who had little authority in the old world of paternalistic elites, might have come to establish new contractual relationships appropriate for an economy in which depersonalized contracts were replacing face-to-face relationships. Meanwhile, however, peasants continued to view them as agents of powerful outsiders and insensitive to villagers' needs. This made for a very ambivalent relationship.

In Wu's Shop, heavy tax demands and warlord battles left the village with hardly any prestigious or substantial figures to play the roles of elite middlemen. There is not even much evidence of professional agents of the absentee landlords, although they possibly did exist. In the absence of alternatives, friends and relatives performed the roles of middlemen, especially in loan contracts, as best as they could. We can find examples of friends and relatives serving as middlemen in the other villages, especially North Brushwood, where old village elites were also weakening. However, the impartiality of such a middleman who was particularly close to one party in an agreement was always suspect, and he was unlikely to be as successful in his efforts as the elite patron. Aside from the suspicion of partiality, poor friends and relatives did not have the kind of face that elite middlemen could bring to the bargaining table; and their thinly scattered individual connections could not compare with the special access to the market that the professional agent could boast.

CONCLUSION

This essay has sought to illuminate two themes: the manner in which an elite with no direct control over the means of production establishes its dominance over the structures of authority; and the implications for a community where the elite's exercise of authority is weak or nonexistent. Both phenomena were found in the villages of North China. The peculiar ability of the elite in parts of South China to dominate authority structures came from their direct control over the ordinary peasants' means of livelihood. While northern elites had no such direct control, they were still in a position to significantly affect the livelihood of the peasantry by, among other means, performing the role of middleman in contracts. Peasants' gratitude and obligation for these brokering elites conferred on them a certain authority, exemplified, for instance, in the cultural ideal of face or in the awarding of plaques. In a word, these elite figures were patrons.

S. N. Eisenstadt has analyzed the kinds of societies dominated by patron-client relationships, and the rural society of North China fits his typology.[61] Patron-client relationships are marginal in developed capitalist societies where the market, backed by the legal code, governs access to resources. They are also marginal in societies where closed corporate groups completely control access to these resources. Patron-client relations typically occur in societies where the market, a major agency regulating the flow of resources, is imperfect and poorly integrated. Perhaps one of the greatest imperfections of the market is the absence of an effective civil or commercial code. This lack reflects the inability or disinclination of the state to guarantee the rights of partners in an economic exchange, thereby allowing their regulation by the authority structures of local systems.

As a consequence of the imperfect market and legal system, the individual peasant or village household often depends upon a powerful local figure, a patron, to ensure the fulfillment of a contract, to provide access to the market on terms not impossibly weighted against him, and to protect him from predatory local government functionaries. In return, the patron receives expressions of gratitude and loyalty upon which he builds a stock of political capital. Thus the relationship between patron and client is marked by reciprocity; though as Alvin Gouldner has reminded us, reciprocity should not be mistaken for equality.[62] Indeed, in many societies the patron exercises considerable domination over his client, and the attitude of the client toward his patron is correspondingly ambivalent.

In many ways, the principal characteristics of this type of society—an imperfect market and a weakly developed system of formal legal guarantees—were found in North China into the twentieth century. We see this most clearly in Hou Lineage Camp where elite figures played the role of patrons and no doubt used the support of their clientele in contests for power and office in the village. We see it to a lesser and diminishing extent in Sand Well, but by the 1920s and 1930s we hardly see this phenomenon at all in North Brushwood and Wu's Shop. The reasons for the impoverishment and evacuation of the elite from these villages can be found in complex inter-related factors involving economic decline, dependency, warfare, and state building. What happened to these villages when they were deprived of pa-trons who could secure their needs, especially in the world outside the village? What was the fate of the structure of authority, embedded, for instance, in the middleman's role, in places lacking elite patrons to lend their weight?

People, of course, continued to use customary law and enter into contrac-tual arrangements to satisfy their needs. They were able to do so because of the nature of customary law in China, which did not absolutely require the regulating authority of a powerful local figure for its operation. The very act of contract violation would make it nearly impossible for the violator to obtain the services of a middleman in the future. Thus we can see whole communities managing to get by without influential elite patrons, but many peasant families probably did not get by very well or very long. Given a society where peasants often faced powerful forces in the markets and polit-ical centers, the appeal to elite paternalism could make a crucial difference in their ability to obtain tax remissions or delay rent payments.

In a world with few other subsistence guarantees for peasants, the dis-appearance of the village elite or the renunciation of its responsibilities could ultimately lead—as it often did—to rebellion or banditry. If so, what might this tell us about elites and the peasant revolution sweeping across the North China countryside in the 1940s? To the extent that powerful elites outside the village were at least partially responsible for the weak position of the peasan-try, class interests were an important element in creating revolutionary con-ditions; but to the extent that communities were without elites who might have been able to shore up the authority of the old system, the absence, rather than the presence, of class differences within the village made for rev-olutionary conditions. Any explanation of China's peasant revolution will have to consider this shifting nexus of community and class in rural society.

ELEVEN

Local Elites and Communist Revolution in the Jiangxi Hill Country

Stephen C. Averill

In May 1930 Mao Zedong accompanied the Red Army on one of its sweeps through the hill country of southern Jiangxi. While the army carried out mass mobilization activity in the countryside, Mao remained around the capital of Xunwu (formerly Changning) county for nearly two weeks gathering information on conditions there through conversations with revolutionary cadres, local merchants, and peasants. Mao's long survey report of what he considered a typical part of the Jiangxi-Fujian-Guangdong border region constitutes by far the richest and most detailed contemporary description available of the economy and society of this area during the early stages of the Chinese revolution.[1]

By this time Mao had already begun to familiarize himself with the life of the hill-county peasantry, and he now wished to learn more about the elites and market towns that mediated peasant access to the outside world. His "Xunwu Investigation" therefore devoted only one section to the conditions of the local peasantry, and barely mentioned the bandits, sworn brotherhoods, and feuds that were an important part of the hill-country social scene. Instead, it provided a rare and painstakingly thorough delineation of the county's trade routes and marketing conditions, and of its mercantile and landlord elite community.

By combining Mao's account with information from other sources, it is possible to obtain a revealing picture of conditions in a peripheral region quite different from the prosperous and sophisticated Yangzi valley areas that have figured so prominently in scholarship on modern Chinese society. In the following pages I examine the local elites of the region during the early stages of the Chinese revolution. More specifically, I trace the transmission of the electrifying impulses of radical political change from their urban origins to their ultimate point of discharge in the Jiangxi hill-country hinterland and explicate how these impulses affected and were affected by the complex and highly stratified local-elite society through which they passed.

XUNWU COUNTY AND THE JIANGXI HILL COUNTRY

Xunwu is located deep in the Nanling mountain ranges of southernmost Jiangxi, astride the administrative and economic divide separating the Gan Yangzi macroregion to the north from the Lingnan macroregion to the south. The county, in fact, has a foot in each region: its northern parts drain into the Gan River, while streams in its southern half feed into Guangdong's East River system and flow into the South China Sea. At some point, merchants (probably outsiders) had taken advantage of these divergent waterways to establish a trade route through Xunwu linking the major regional city of Ganzhou in Jiangxi with cities of the Guangdong coast. In the late nineteenth century the county's modest mercantile community still depended heavily on this route.[2]

Most of Xunwu's inhabitants were Hakka (guest people) peasants whose ancestors had settled in the region several centuries earlier, and their customs, dialect, and life-styles were similar to Hakka elsewhere in the Jiangxi hill country. Most supported themselves through terraced paddy rice cultivation along valleys and in mountain basins or by the manufacture or growth of a variety of handicrafts and mountain products such as timber, tea oil, and grass cloth. The little agricultural land available in this mountain region was widely but inequitably held: most peasants had at least a little land, but few had enough to support themselves fully, and the bulk of the land was owned by a few individuals, lineages, and associations. Probably most of these wealthy people and groups were from the major market towns of the county that were strung along the river valley trade route. Certainly this was the common pattern elsewhere in southern Jiangxi, where long-established valley communities used their wealth, locational centrality, and historical headstart to dominate more peripheral and recently settled mountain hinterlands.

Lineages were as common in the Jiangxi hill country as they were in nearby Fujian and Guangdong, and they appear to have had the same organization and activities that scholars (including Rubie Watson in this volume) have found in the coastal provinces. Massive, multisegmented lineages with thousands of members and extensive corporate property were common throughout the hill country, especially in established local (*bendi*) communities and among Hakka living in the triprovince border region (including Xunwu) known as the Hakka heartland. Coexisting uneasily and often servilely alongside these behemoths were many smaller and weaker lineages.

Deep in the mountains, a few Hakkas and non-Han minority peoples lived scattered in small multisurname hamlets with little or no apparent lineage organization.[3]

The assorted pressures of living in this difficult environment, the legacy of conflicts engendered by earlier migrations, and the area's general inaccessibility had long combined to make Xunwu and the rest of southern Jiangxi an extremely violent and anarchic region. Bandit gangs, Triad sworn brotherhoods, gambling societies, and sectarian groups were endemic to the area, and massive lineage feuds frequently mobilized thousands of people against each other for years at a time. Traditions of resistance to governmental authority were so deeply ingrained that yamen runners, feared as oppressive "tigers" in many parts of China, were frequently beaten and killed in this area. Even county magistrates dared not venture into the countryside.[4]

Into this hard, wild country had begun to creep by the early twentieth century, a variety of institutions, products, styles, habits, and inclinations—largely Western in origin or inspiration—that, for lack of a better term, we may call "modern" and that in various ways were altering the lives and attitudes of the region's people. We will discuss a few of these changes, such as a new school system, but most we must pass over, though Mao took obvious delight in discussing the changes at great length, including such minutiae as the introduction of new shoe styles and haircut fashions.[5] Both trivial and significant changes notwithstanding, by the early 1920s the main structures and processes of Jiangxi hill-country society—particularly rural society—remained essentially intact, and life for most people went on much as it had for centuries.

STRATIFICATION OF HILL-COUNTRY ELITES

Presiding over this conflict-ridden society was a remarkably multilayered, many-faceted, and socially volatile group of local elites, whose diversity and rapacity reflected their environment.[6] These elites were themselves stratified over a rather broad continuum, with members varying substantially in power, prestige, and sophistication. Before examining elite involvement in arenas of particular relevance to the growth of the Jiangxi revolutionary movement, let us first subdivide the elite continuum into several broad strata, each crudely, but for our purposes sufficiently, defined by the locus and range of activity of its members.[7]

At the upper level of the local elite in a given county stood a small group of "great households" (*wanhu*) whose influence or reputation extended throughout the area and sometimes beyond. At least in very rural areas such as Xunwu, these households almost by definition were large landowners, defined by Mao as those having land producing more than five hundred *shi* (about 45,000 kilograms) of grain per year,[8] but they also engaged in such a range of other activities that perhaps they are better viewed as small-scale conglomerates rather than simply landlords. In Xunwu almost all heads of the twenty great households resided in the county, though it is difficult to determine precisely where. Presumably most lived in or near the county capital or largest market towns, though they also typically maintained a strong presence (complete with fortified dwelling) on their respective rural "turfs."[9]

The Xunwu family of Pan Mingzheng indicates the contours of this group and illustrates the range and extent of its members' influence. Pan himself was by far the largest landlord in the county; his yearly ten thousand *shi* (900,000 kg.) of grain production ranked him well above the other great households of the county. In addition to his paddy landholdings, Pan also controlled mountain and forest lands, houses and several stores in the nearby market town of Jitan (the county's commercial center). All told, his assets were said to have totaled nearly three hundred thousand *yuan* (dollars). Moreover, Pan's individual holdings were only part of those controlled by the important lineage to which he belonged: at least six other households in the lineage had individual holdings greater than one hundred *mu* (one *mu* equals about one-sixth of an acre), and numerous others had lesser amounts. The lineage had formed an association known as the Rongyang Hall (*tang*) to handle its affairs, and Pan's family almost certainly played a major role in administering its corporate property.

Beyond controlling these immediate economic resources, Pan and his relatives wielded influence in other aspects of local life. Though an elderly and stubbornly conservative man himself, Pan had personally run one of the several middle schools that functioned briefly in Xunwu after 1911. One of his sons ran another school, and several of his grandchildren went outside the county, or even the country, to study "the new learning." Two of his sons (one of them a Qing lower-degree holder) also at different times headed the office of financial administration within the county government, and one of them later successively headed the county militia force, joined the Guomindang (GMD) county committee, and in 1930 acted as county magistrate. Various members of the family were also connected through marriage to other important figures within the county's upper elite.[10]

In the multiplicity of his interests and the range of his contacts, Pan was typical of the upper layer of the local elite. This stratum of great households included the largest landlords and merchants and leaders of the most powerful and prosperous lineages. Even when, as in Pan's case, their initial power probably stemmed from landholding and lineage leadership on a rural "turf," almost all the upper layer of the local elite also established a presence in county capitals or strategically located market towns where they developed extensive and varied networks of influence. From these bases they moved to build up ties with elites from other parts of the county and sometimes extended their influence to still higher levels of the central-place hierarchy.[11] Often, of course, the main attributes of elite status suggested by these examples—wealth, family pedigree, official position, educational accomplishment, and military strength—were interlocking, overlapping, and mutually reinforcing. Wealthy landlords might simultaneously be important lineage leaders and merchants, their sons prominent educators or local administrators, and their daughters wives of other important elite figures.

Often connected in various ways with the "great families" of this upper elite, but considerably more limited in their resources and connections, was a much larger stratum of middling elite individuals and their families. This stratum included medium-sized landlords, defined by Mao as those with lands producing two hundred to five hundred *shi* (18,000 to 45,000 kg.) of grain per year, merchants, principals, and teachers of Western-style upper-elementary or middle schools, many members of the county bureaucracy, and some militia and police leaders. Although members of this stratum of the local elite had much less impressive reputations than leaders of the "great families," they were often well-known and important individuals within more limited arenas.

One such Xunwu elite figure about whom we have some information is He Zizhen. He's father had begun in humble circumstances, as a clerk in the county yamen's punishment office and later as a geomancer. Then he reaped a minor bonanza by somehow (probably through his old yamen contacts) being awarded local tax-farming rights for the cattle tax. The income from this license was sufficient for He's father to buy paddy land that produced "several tens" of *shi* in rent.

These resources were sufficient to send He Zizhen to middle school in nearby Pingyuan, Guangdong province, and then to a mining school in Henan. Following his education, He taught school in Xunwu for eight years, during which time he also organized a night school for adults and an association for Xunwu students who had studied in Guangdong. Later he served for a time as county police chief and used the proceeds of his work to buy land of his own. His wealth grew further after he followed his father's lead and in 1927 took up tax farming, in this case obtaining a license to control the sale of beans in the county seat. By this time he had also become a member of the GMD's county committee. Thus, He's family had worked its way to a position of considerable influence.[12]

In other cases we can see clusters of related middle-elite families that mark the fission products of the breakup of great households. Such, for example, was the case with many relatives of the Chinese Communist Party (CCP) leader Gu Bo, from Tangbei village in the southwestern part of Xunwu. Gu's great-grandfather was apparently already wealthy, though sources provide no details. At any rate, his grandfather was wealthy enough to give land producing one hundred *shi* (9,000 kg.) of grain to help provide an educational endowment for the county and to marry into a large landlord family. An amazing total of twelve men in Gu's father's generation attained the rank of *shengyuan* (lowest degree) before the imperial examinations were abolished; in 1930 eleven of them were still alive (out of a total of about four hundred *shengyuan* in the entire county), giving this village of approximately a hundred families by far the highest concentration of such degree recipients in Xunwu.[13]

Whether degree holders or not, in the late 1920s several direct descendants of Gu's great-grandfather were well-established members of the middle elite. For example, Gu Lesan and his unnamed older brother together owned land producing three hundred *shi* (27,000 kg.). The brother was a *shengyuan* who had twice served as a member of the provincial assembly, while Gu Lesan had formerly served with a warlord officer of Jiangxi origin and had been a local official in Guangdong. Among their relatives, Gu Guangrui was an upper-elementary school graduate with land producing more than two hundred *shi* (18,000 kg.) and a son who had graduated from middle school in nearby Meixian county. Other family members were small landlords or, like Gu Bo's own father, local school teachers. Although this cluster of families (actually probably a branch of a larger Gu lineage) could clearly not match the much more extensive and powerful networks of a great household like Pan Mingzheng's, they were nonetheless a comfortable, respectable community with considerable aggregate resources that doubtless exerted substantial local influence.[14]

As these examples indicate, the middle stratum of the local elite engaged in diverse occupations and activities but on a somewhat more limited scale than the upper elite. The examples of He Zizhen and Ge Lesan's brother show that members of the middle elite could be well traveled and well educated and could tap into extensive and significant networks of power and influence at the county level or beyond. The other Gus, however, are perhaps more typical of this group in their predominantly rural power base and localistic orientation. Although they were often connected through clientelistic ties with upper-elite local power holders, the primary locus of activity of mid-elite figures was the local market town and its hinterland, and their power was based primarily on local land ownership, kinship ties, and government service.

Coexisting with the middle stratum of the local elite in the countryside, and often even more confined in their sphere of activities, was yet another, much larger, group of local elites. The members of this lowest layer of the elite resided largely in villages and small market towns in close contact with the peasantry. In this rural setting they held various leadership roles: heads of small or branch lineages, militia captains, traditional local school teachers, or village elders. Economically this stratum was quite diverse but generally much less secure than their counterparts in the upper-elite strata. Many of this group were small landlords, though as was true of the middle-elite figures cited above, such small landlord households could have quite different origins. Mao took pains to divide Xunwu small landlords into two major groups. The first was the "declining households" (*poluo hu*), descendants of large landlord families now reduced in wealth and status after dividing family estates. This group (nearly one-third of all landlords) Mao further subdivided into three segments: families that still had a surplus beyond their needs; families that were occasionally forced to sell or mortgage property to survive; and families that were en route to real destitution. The second landlord group was the "newly emerging households" (*xinfa hu*), aggressive and hard-nosed families just risen from the ranks of the peasantry or small merchants. Many members of this group, too, were not well off; indeed, some Communist cadre preferred not to consider them true landlords at all but rather a special subgroup of rich peasants they awkwardly termed "rich peasants of semilandlord character" (*ban dizhu xing de funong*). Whatever their precise character, Mao estimated that the newly emerging households comprised almost half the entire landlord stratum.[15]

Whether small landlords or rich peasants, almost all members of this elite stratum necessarily relied upon activities other than landowning to provide at least part of their livelihood. Around 10 percent of the small landlords in Xunwu, for example, also managed small businesses in local market towns, and the "newly emerging" households were notorious for the rapacity of their money-lending operations. Other lower elites either made money by participating in governmental or quasi-governmental activities such as dispute mediation or proxy tax-remittance (*baolan*) or served as collection agents for larger landlords. Some also colluded with bandits and sworn brotherhoods, set up gambling houses, grew opium, or engaged in other illegalities.[16]

Although the resources of the "great households" were far greater and their reputations far broader than those of lower-elite households, the latter arguably had the greatest cumulative impact on the mass of the population. Certainly in peripheral counties like Xunwu, where great households were fewer and poorer than their counterparts in core regions, lower elites were in much closer contact with the peasantry, and their actions and attitudes were more influential in shaping popular perceptions of elite culture.

The very nature of the lower elites' position on the ambiguous and shifting boundary between the elite and the mass of the population, as well as the limited extent of their power and prestige, has meant that little detailed information has survived about their lives and careers. As one brief example from the upper echelons of this stratum, however, one might cite Yan Guo-xing, a small landlord-cum-merchant in southwestern Xunwu who had land producing about one hundred *shi* (9,000 kg.) of grain, ran a small drygoods store in the market town of Gongping, and acted as a minor paper merchant. Yan obviously had considerable influence in the local merchant community, for he persuaded them to loan him several thousand *yuan* for an abortive electoral campaign for the provincial assembly; in 1930 he was still mired in debt.[17] Another example might be Gu Bo's father, Gu Guangming, a "bankrupt small landlord" who taught at the local village school (*sishu*) and had to rely on wealthier relatives to finance his son's middle-school education.[18] Many other members of this lower-elite stratum, lacking the business or familial connections of Yan or Gu, were forced to rely much more upon their own meager resources.

How large was the local elite in a county such as Xunwu? The question is complicated by gaps and inconsistencies in Mao's data and the lack of population estimates for the county, but by extrapolating from the available information, I have roughly estimated the elite at about 3.5 to 4.0 percent of the population. This figure is probably at the low end of the scale for southern Jiangxi counties.[19]

In sum, local elites in Xunwu (and by extension, the entire Jiangxi hill country) were a small, diverse, three-tiered collection of families combining considerable access to the outside world with an emphatically localistic orientation, strong emphasis on landowning with substantial commercial activity, and commanding collective dominance with remarkably insecure individual tenure. If in the 1920s some elites sought election to the provincial assembly, sent their children out of the county or the country for "modern" educations, and (as we shall see) joined national political movements, plenty of others were still ignorant of the outside world—men disparaged as "old mountain rats" (*shan laoshu*) by impatient Xunwu youths.[20] Although local elites had hopelessly blurred the traditional distinction between landlord and merchant, they were still in far closer contact with the countryside and its peasant inhabitants than many of the Jiangnan elites on whose lifestyles so many stereotypes about Chinese elites are based. And if the elite as a whole controlled a grossly disproportionate amount of land and other resources in the hill country, that was little consolation to the nearly one-third of all landlords who made up the "declining households," as they plunged through the lower layers of elite society toward reentry into the peasantry.

ELITE POWER AND CONFLICT

As the foregoing description of elite stratification indirectly indicates, local elites in the Jiangxi hill country maintained social dominance through intertwined webs of power whose important strands included educational achievement; wealth earned through land, commerce, and usury; access to state authority and resources; and private control of the means of coercion. Elite dominance was likewise typically exercised through a variety of institutions,

many of which had a long history in the region. All these various sources and
expressions of elite dominance constituted limited resources to which elites
had differential access, and keen competition over them often led to violent
conflict. It is impossible to discuss here all the ramifications of elite power.
Nevertheless it is important to highlight certain aspects of the structures and
uses of elite power and of the strife they generated, for it was amid these
entrenched institutions and nagging insecurities that the revolutionary
movement eventually emerged.

   The Maintenance and Exercise of Elite Power. Lineage ties constantly entered
into social calculations, and lineages are one of the first arenas to consider
when examining how elites maintained dominance. Lineages in Jiangxi,
like those elsewhere in southern China, often served as the institutional focus
for many activities other than defining and perpetuating kinship relations.
Thus lineages commonly owned and managed collective property, ran local
schools, helped finance higher education for worthy members, established
and enforced codes of social behavior, mobilized armed forces, and sometimes helped the state collect taxes, spread its ideology, and maintain local
order.[21]

   Although these functions were carried out in the name of the collective
good, elites within the lineage frequently gained disproportionately from
them. Most lineage land and other collective property, for example, was
managed by elites, who habitually used their positions to profit financially in
various, mostly illicit, ways. Elites likewise appear to have received disproportionate benefit from lineage-run schools and scholarship funds because
their children were more likely than peasant youths both to attend school and
to seek advanced education outside the community. Lineage codes of conduct generally expressed sentiments congenial to, and were interpreted and
enforced by, lineage elders who were usually also local elites; they also mobilized and directed (often for their own purposes) armed lineage forces and
served as intermediaries between lineage members and the state. Controlling
the means of coercion and opportunities for mediation further enhanced the
power and prestige of local elites.[22]

   Whether in lineages or other arenas, elites differed among themselves in
how and why they exercised power. Money lending provides a clear example
of these differences. Hill-country elites of all strata made loans, but their
ways and purposes differed. The few upper and numerous middle elites who
made loans wanted either safe investments or (in the event of default) the
chance to acquire property used as collateral. Therefore, they loaned relatively large amounts at moderate interest rates, mostly to lower-level elites
rather than directly to peasants. Lower-level elites, particularly the aggressively entrepreneurial "newly emerging households," sometimes sought such
loans as capital for small-scale commercial enterprises. More often, however,
they sought interest income and so reloaned the money at moderate interest

rates to other lower elites or in small amounts at high rates to peasants. Lower elites who controlled small lineage trusts or other collective property also often loaned part of the resources they managed to peasants, expropriating part or all of the proceeds. The variable amounts and interest rates in this elite loan "industry" were doubtless based primarily on relative investment security, but they probably also helped strengthen patron-client links among elites of different strata; they certainly helped perpetuate overall elite economic domination of the peasantry.[23]

Similarly differentiated patterns of elite activity almost certainly existed in other institutional contexts—such as management of different public bodies (*gonghui* or *gongtang*) or relationships to the state—though it is difficult to determine their precise extent. Merchants and landlord/merchant hybrids, for example, often dominated the management of temple associations and other organizations in market towns. Members of the middle and upper elite probably managed most large lineage and social welfare associations, and small branch-lineage associations appear frequently to have been dominated by lower-level elites.[24] Likewise, upper-stratum or urban-oriented elites doubtless had much better access to benefits provided by the state (and may therefore have reciprocated with greater support) than did the more rural lower-stratum elites.

How does this pictures of elite structure and power relate to recent scholarly emphasis on the long-term stability and continuity of the local elite?[25] According to this scholarship, elite power and status were more frequently and reliably attained and maintained via landholding, lineage development, and other localistic methods than through the rewarding but unpredictable route of examination success and high bureaucratic office. Lending support to this view we see in Xunwu (and doubtless other southern Jiangxi counties as well) that some surname groups persisted for centuries in the elite-centered historical record despite the county's poor overall record in the examinations and despite the underrepresentation in the degree-holder lists of some of the county's most powerful and well-known surnames.[26]

However accurate the general argument for continuity may be, the frequent references to "former great households" now fallen in wealth and status that fleck Mao's accounts of the Xunwu middle elite, and the large number of "declining households" he found in the county's lower elite, suggest that we must be wary of viewing the complex question of elite continuity too simplistically. Most analyses of elite mobility have studied imperial rather than twentieth-century elites and dealt with lengthy time spans. They have also focused on prosperous core regions, and their authors have been forced by the nature of their sources to give more exclusive coverage than does this essay to the great-household stratum of the local elite. Mao's comments remind us that in more peaceful times and more prosperous areas, some rise and fall of elite households must have occurred, even within the

most dominant and enduring lineages or patrilines. In troubled times and
out-of-the-way places, and among the volatile lower elites whose lives are so
much less well-documented, both the actual occurrence and (equally important as a factor in elite behavior) the subjective fear of downward mobility
must have been a constant fact of life.

Intra-elite Factional Conflict. As one might expect given the complex classification of hill-country elites and the intense pressures to obtain scarce resources and avoid the disastrous consequences of family fragmentation, elite
relationships were often characterized by competition and strife. Although
information on it is limited, this intra-elite conflict is important to our understanding of political behavior in the hill country and demands at least a few
remarks.

Let me again begin with some examples. In Chongyi county, in southwestern Jiangxi, two major elite cliques struggled with one another during the
1920s. Adherents of one clique lived in the vicinity of the county capital and the
market town of Yangmei. According to the Communist reminiscence
that is our main source on the subject, this group had long "colluded" with
county magistrates and had a firm grip on all "public property." The other
clique was based in a group of market towns on branches of a river system
separated from the county capital by a range of hills. In the mid-1920s this
clique, considered more progressive than its rival, supported the local GMD
organization.[27]

In Yudu county north of Xunwu there were also two cliques, the Changcun and the Yushui factions, named after the middle schools that served as
their headquarters. According to another CCP leader, the Changcun faction
was based in parts of the county—largely in the east and north—where
lineages were large and strong, and its adherents were the large landlords
and "local despots" (*tuhao*) who controlled these lineages. The Yushui faction had its strength in the county capital and in the western and southern
sections of the county, where lineages were relatively weak. This faction
included many middle and small landlords who were also engaged in commerce. Around these cores, each faction gathered various "poor intellectuals" and students, presumably recruited from their respective middle
schools. Both cliques competed for influence within the county government
and access to profits from proxy remittance and pettifogging.[28]

In Xingguo county just north of Yudu, factional conflict also revolved
around different middle schools. Here a coalition of elites from around
the county capital controlled the county's public middle school, while
rural elites, organized into a body called the Federated Township Self-
Government Assembly (Lian xiang zizhi huiyi) controlled a nearby private
middle school. The city elites had better access to successive county magistrates and with their support obtained a larger share of local spoils and

forced the rural elites to pay a disproportionate share of local government costs. As in Yudu, students in the local schools became involved in the factional struggle started by their elders.[29]

Several points emerge from these examples. First, elite conflict focused on the county capital and government, most obviously because the magistrate's yamen and the center for such government functions as public security, tax collection, and education were in the capital. Elites interested in obtaining government office, profiting from tax collection or litigation, or protecting their private activities from government functionaries or other local elites had good reason to compete for influence with the county bureaucrats. For their part, officials also inevitably became more involved in local elite politics. Because Qing magistrates could not be regularly appointed to serve in their own provinces, magistrates serving in Jiangxi were unfamiliar with local conditions and perforce relied upon local elites to help them govern. After the fall of the Qing, people often served in their own provinces, but magistrates in Jiangxi were rarely assigned to their home counties and still required local advice. Magistrates lived and worked in the yamen, so they were naturally most likely to come in contact with members of the elite who lived nearby, a fact that gave such elites definite advantages in local factional struggles.[30]

Second, economic and social centrality of the county capitals and their immediate surroundings also made them the focus of factional strife. Although some county seats in Jiangxi, including Xunwu, were not the largest commercial centers in their counties, the majority were. Virtually all were well located along transportation routes, surrounded by fertile and densely populated lowland paddy lands. By contrast, much of the remaining hill-county territory consisted of rugged mountain country, with difficult access, low productivity, and sparse population. Moreover, the county capital was generally the site of the region's largest temples and lineage halls and its most prestigious schools. The vicinity of the county capital was thus likely to be both a base of important elite interest groups and a prize to be competed for. In many Jiangxi hill counties, elite conflicts also replicated and intensified general and long-standing divisions between urban and rural or between established communities and later-arriving "guest people" (Hakka) immigrants.

The Yudu county example also indicates another type of intra-elite competition, namely interlineage factionalism and feuding. That such feuds were often really disputes between the respective lineage leaderships rather than the mass of lineage members is underlined by a conflict in Ruijin county, where in 1923–24 two upper elites quarreled over whether to establish new local transit-tax stations and eventually mobilized more than a thousand men from each lineage to settle the issue through armed conflict.[31] At least as common as open fighting between leaders of large lineages, however, were situations similar to the Yudu case: one or more large lineages and their leaders seeking to dominate surrounding areas inhabited by many small lineages.[32]

The Yudu case is particularly intriguing because social and economic attitudes seem linked to elite type, with large lineage leaders representing older, more "feudal," landlord attitudes and the small landlords-cum-merchants opposing them embodying more modern "bourgeois" sensibilities. Agriculture and handicrafts in the Jiangxi highlands had been highly commercialized well before the twentieth century, and elites at all levels were substantially involved in trade; thus, we must be careful not to overdraw such distinctions. Nevertheless, as we shall see shortly, elite attitudes toward revolution were often affected by their economic and social circumstances, and it is plausible that some such factors influenced earlier elite factionalism as well.

NETWORKS OF INFLUENCE FOR ELITE REVOLUTIONARIES

Although elite factionalism was surely influenced by socioeconomic distinctions between urban and rural elites, or landed versus commercial wealth, it is notable that education was a key arena for political conflict in both Yudu and Xingguo. This politicization of conflict in education was quite natural. Education and scholarship had long been linked to elite status and political activity in China. Moreover, in the modern era, most early CCP members were intellectuals from elite families, politicized during the student activism of the May Fourth era. Back in the hill country, these revolutionaries exploited connections within the factionalized elite "educational circles." But they also came to rely upon quite different networks of influence—hill-country bandit bands and sworn brotherhoods. With these connections in mind, let us first investigate the role of elites in hill-country education and then discuss elite ties to bandits and brotherhoods.

Hill-country Education. Although Jiangxi hill counties produced few successful candidates in the imperial examinations, traditional education there had many of the same social effects as in other parts of China. Mastery of the Confucian classics, measured by success in the imperial examinations, was for centuries a major criterion of elite status, and a large, ramified, and conservative institutional apparatus had grown up at all levels of society to support the quest for examination achievement. Moreover, education in imperial China, as in most other societies, provided young people with opportunities to expand their intellectual and social horizons. Aspiring students had to travel periodically to county, prefectural, and provincial capitals for examinations, and most spent some time in local or regional academies (*shuyuan*). Both gathering for examinations and attending academies normally involved boarding away from home in company with other wealthy and/or bright young men from different localities, and the experience frequently led to lifelong friendships and student-teacher ties.

Abolishing the examinations in 1905 and developing a new Western-style educational system significantly affected existing elites. With a few strokes of the bureaucratic brush, the Qing leadership abandoned the entire formal process by which many of its own members had been selected and threatened to negate the educational efforts of millions of younger Chinese currently involved in the system. Within a few years, Western-style schools became disseminators of new ideas and incubators of political agitation instead of guardians of intellectual orthodoxy.[33]

The important new impact of the Western-style schools, however, should not blind us to the many institutional and attitudinal links they maintained with the past. Many of the first new schools were simply renamed academies, located on the grounds and inheriting the endowments of their predecessors. Like the academies, the most successful and prestigious of the new schools remained clustered in the largest administrative centers. After the imperial examinations ended, teaching in the new schools was one of the few remaining respectable job opportunities for many Qing degree-holders, and some of them remained influential in local educational establishments well into the 1920s.[34]

Moreover, although the avowed aim of education changed from preparing students for the examinations to teaching them the skills that had made the West strong, the main concern for most people continued to be education's role as a route to individual and family—not national—wealth, power, and prestige. Possession of a modern school degree still brought special community respect; and modern schooling was either an important passport out of the hill country or a route to acquiring important jobs in one's own county bureaucracy or educational establishment. Moreover, a school degree, unlike land, was a portable resource that could be used in different places and arenas of elite interaction. It might well be that in the twentieth century school degrees became more easily renewable from generation to generation than were landholdings, enhancing the effectiveness of education as an elite strategy to help ameliorate the effects of partible inheritance.

Management and certification of education had, however, changed. No longer did the government set tight quotas on the number of students per province who could receive, say, a middle-school degree or determine the subject matter to be studied. Although there was still some governmental regulation of education (particularly of provincially run middle schools) and many schools still had entrance examinations, now school leaders themselves much more firmly controlled education.[35] Greater local control over access to a still-important educational process appears to have been at least as significant as the prestige of a scholarly vocation in explaining the continuing power of educators in local-elite affairs during the 1920s.

Control over educational access was aided by well-developed networks based on school experience and student-teacher ties. Ties of this sort had been important under the imperial examination system, but their influence was perhaps even greater during the Republican period. Local educators who had graduated from prestigious urban middle schools facilitated their brightest protegés' entrance into the same schools and then frequently hired them for county and subcounty schools after they graduated. Even when students pursued different occupations they often maintained contact with their old teachers. Through these networks of contacts both within and without the educational system, local educators could exert influence on, or call for aid from, people in a wide variety of places and occupations.[36]

The value of education as a route for career advancement, the position of local educators as brokers controlling access to influential networks of personal connections, and the important role played by schools and scholars in the political discourse of the late nineteenth and early twentieth century together made educational circles a prime arena for the widespread elite contention and factional struggle previously noted.[37]

By the 1920s, then, local schools throughout Jiangxi were ambiguously modern institutions in which new concern for Western culture and the abhorrence of Western imperialism coexisted with older conceptions of the function of education in the social order and the role of educators in local politics. In the southern Jiangxi hill country these diverse currents were accentuated by problems of peripherality: the region's distance from better-developed centers of culture and communication enhanced the importance of local schools as one of the few sources of information about new ideas and trends and one of the few routes out of the hill country for ambitious young people seeking rewarding personal careers and new resources to maintain elite status.

Ironically, the deficiencies of the hill-country schools themselves enhanced their importance as links to the outside world. The overall poverty of the hill country meant that it was difficult to find funds to build and maintain schools, especially higher-level, Western-style schools. The density and quality of such schools in a given area was therefore generally low, and students were forced either to use them as stepping-stones to further training elsewhere or to bypass them entirely. Most children still began their education in old-style village or lineage schools (*sishu*), often taught by aging Qing lower-degree holders; education beyond this level was mostly confined to children of local-elite families. Only a few counties in the Jiangxi hill country were able to maintain local middle schools during the 1920s. In Xunwu, for example, four middle schools had opened before 1930, but all had closed quickly (three within a year of opening), and most students seeking a middle-school education either went to Ganzhou or crossed the border to Meixian or Pingyuan in Guangdong.[38]

According to Mao's research, elite attitudes toward the new schools varied somewhat depending on age, geographical location, and position on the continuum of elite wealth and status. Most patriarchs in upper- and middle-elite families were willing to manage new schools, serve as county educational officials, and send their children away to middle schools, but they were motivated more by desire of personal power and profit than by enthusiasm for the new education. Those upper elites who lived close to major market towns or near the riverine trade route connecting the county with Guangdong, Mao found less conservative—as were the children and grandchildren of conservative stalwarts like Pan Mingzheng. Given the substantial resources of most upper- and middle-elite families and the length of time they could afford to wait before receiving benefits from their children's education, it is not suprising that three-fourths of the county's university graduates and two-thirds of those who studied abroad had this sort of background.[39]

Mao also found that attitudes toward education varied within the lower stratum of the elite, depending on whether a familiy was "declining" or "newly emerging." Declining lower-elite households embraced the new education almost desperately. Sometimes they were following family traditions: the bulk of the county's surviving lower-degree holders were apparently small landlords and/or village schoolteachers. Often, however, creating an educated "man of talent" was viewed as a last chance to revive sagging family fortunes. A high percentage of children from such families therefore attended upper-elementary and middle schools. If the declining families looked fearfully to the future, newly emerging elite households anxiously recalled their recent past; they tended to retain the aggressive, single-minded pursuit of short-term profit that had just enabled them to scrabble a bit above their former fellows, and they saw more immediate and certain return on their hard-earned capital from today's usury than from tomorrow's middle-school graduate. Children from this group were thus educationally underrepresented in the county.[40]

As we shall see shortly, these differing elite attitudes toward education paralleled their differing stances toward revolution. Before we can properly discuss the interaction between education and revolution, however, we must consider briefly a very different arena of elite concern, equally important for the eventual growth of a revolutionary movement: the world of "the brothers of the greenwood," the bandit gangs and sworn brotherhoods endemic in the hill country.

Bandits and Brotherhoods. For all that the schools of the Jiangxi highlands suffered by comparison to their counterparts in higher-level urban centers, they were still indisputably part of the respectable mainstream of hill-country elite life. The bandit and sworn brotherhood gangs that swarmed through the hill country, on the other hand, seemed clearly and unambiguously to belong to the world of the peasants, and to its most disreputable segment at that. After all, the gangs were primarily composed of peasants. To the desperately poor, banditry offered a last chance to make a new life or prolong a miserable existence. To the able and ambitious, banditry constituted one of the few routes for social mobility open to those starting without wealth and family connections. And to peasants exasperated and discontented with the arbitrary injustice so prevalent in their lives, banditry provided an opportunity, however limited, to strike back at their oppressors. In each function, banditry remained apart from, and potentially antagonistic to, the elite political system.

Yet there were connections as well. Hill-country bandits and brotherhoods by no means totally divorced themselves from local society, including its elites. Economically, hill-country bandits supplied their everyday needs, fenced their plunder, and spent their profits in local market places. Socially, they remained in close contact with family and friends in their home communities, even while they (or at least their leaders) acquired the wealth and power that set them apart from the populace. And politically, the gangs organized armed forces that intervened in factional disputes and occasionally vied for control of local government.[41]

In all these areas the gangs interacted with the elite power structure. Indeed, southern Jiangxi elites sometimes had such close and symbiotic ties with the region's bandit and brotherhood organizations that officials found the two groups difficult to distinguish. Some elites established sworn-brotherhood or patron-client relationships with bandit leaders, covered for sworn-brotherhood gambling operations, sold goods to and fenced booty from gangs, enlisted gangs to browbeat the local populace or intimidate rival elites, or recommended gang leaders for bureaucratic appointment.[42]

As with other aspects of elite behavior, relationships among elites and gangs varied according to the situation and the self-interests of the elite members involved. Upper and middle local elites—wealthier, further removed from the countryside, and more sympathetic to official concerns than the lower elites—tended to be more antagonistic toward "heterodox" groups. Their persons and their property were, after all, prime bandit targets. Lower elites, on the other hand, were often much closer to bandit leaders in sympathies, activities, and origins. Both lower elites and bandit leaders were often recently, and only barely, removed from the peasantry; both were, to use Eric Hobsbawm's phrase, "men who made themselves respected."[43] Lower elites themselves sometimes became bandit leaders, while particularly effective bandit leaders might be rewarded with militia commands and other perquisites of elite life.[44]

Nevertheless, despite the attempts by local groups to draw gangs into their orbit and under their control, to coopt gang leaders and profit from their activities, bandit and brotherhood activity in the Jiangxi hills remained at least partially distinct from the elite-dominated political and economic system. It is precisely this ambiguous quality of gang activity, simultaneously associated with and yet separate from elite life, that compels our attention here. Just as educational circles addressing both long-standing needs and new concerns served an important transitional function that facilitated a nascent revolutionary movement's entry into local elite society, so the hill-country "bandit world" later played a corresponding role in facilitating the revolution's movement out of elite society and into the wider peasant world. As powerful peasant-based armed bodies outside the mainstream of elite life, yet tantalizingly susceptible to elite manipulation, bandits and brotherhoods were logical objects of attention by Communist cadres of elite background seeking to enter and transform rural society.

ELITES AND THE ORIGINS OF REVOLUTION

In 1921 the young teacher, He Zizhen, formed a Guangdong Schools Alumni Association (Liu Yue xueyou hui) in Xunwu to organize the many local youths who, like himself, had studied there.[45] Gu Bo, once He's student in elementary school, joined the group later while attending middle school in Guangdong, where he also became a Communist. In the mid-1920s Gu and other young radicals split with the alumni association to form a separate organization that eventually emerged as the core of the county's revolutionary movement. This group, rather misleadingly named the Xunwu Common People's Cooperative Society (Xunwu pingmin hezuo she), recruited more than one hundred followers in Xunwu's educational circles, founded the Zhongshan (i.e., Sun Yat-sen) School, and began mass movement activity. In response, He Zizhen and several conservative associates formed a rival body known as the Young Revolutionary Comrades Association (Qingnian geming tongzhi hui) and founded the Xinxun (New Xunwu) School to compete with the Zhongshan School. People referred to these groups as the Cooperative Society Clique (sometimes called the Zhongshan clique) and the New Xunwu Clique.

These groups were formed during the 1923–27 Guomindang-Communist Party United Front that culminated in the Northern Expedition and the nominal unification of China under the Nationalist government of Chiang Kai-shek. Events in the hill country unfolded against the backdrop of this national revolutionary upsurge and the accompanying conflict within the United Front that led in 1927 to the GMD's break with the CCP and the suppression of radical elements.

Competition between the two groups heated up as the alliance between the CCP and GMD gradually deteriorated. By mid-1927 the conservative New Xunwu Clique appeared to have the edge, aided by the spreading "white terror" that had violently suppressed mass movements and purged radical leaders across the province. Nevertheless, the Cooperative Society

Clique retained control of the Zhongshan School, and its members for a time operated relatively openly as they sought to make the transition to a more rural stage of the revolution.

As part of the transition, the radicals established several rural branches of the Zhongshan school, which they used to propagandize among the peasantry and contact a local Triad sworn brotherhood known as the Three Dots Society (Sandian hui). After Gu Bo and other CCP leaders themselves entered the brotherhood, its lodges around the country joined the schools as centers of secret preparation for an armed uprising that occurred in March 1928; students and brotherhood forces coordinated attacks on the Xunwu School and the government yamen in the county capital, and other Communist-led forces attacked elites in the southern part of the county where Gu Bo's family lived. Although initially successful, the uprising was soon crushed by government troops and forces of a local bandit working in collusion with threatened local elites.

Despite its failure, the attack clearly marked the transition of the struggle between conservative and revolutionary elites in the county from a conflict waged largely by factional groups based in the mainstream elite educational institutions to a violent civil war with widespread peasant participation. Following their defeat, Communist forces retreated, reorganized, and built a base in the southern part of the county. By the time Mao visited in 1930, most of the county was in Communist hands, land redistribution and other radical reforms were well underway, and the stage was set for the eventual incorporation of the region into the emerging central soviet.

Even this brief account of events in Xunwu sufficiently reveals the close but complex relationships between the emerging revolutionary movement and several enduring institutions and processes—the educational system, bandit and sworn brotherhood gangs, factional strife—important to local elites. To explore these relationships more fully, however, it is necessary to move for a time beyond Xunwu to discuss these and other aspects of elite society in the context of the revolutionary movement in the hill country as a whole.

A distinct Communist-led revolutionary movement in Jiangxi first appeared during the mid-1920s in the province's elite-dominated school system, following and building upon the earlier use of local educational circles for disseminating radical ideas and forming new political organizations. After the May Fourth incident of 1919, students throughout Jiangxi had formed study groups and associations to further both their understanding of the "new culture" and their ability to exert local political influence. Later, as vague radical sensibilities were channeled into formal party affiliations, many early CCP leaders returned as teachers to organize party branches in the local schools from which they had graduated or in new schools established in small towns and villages. Evening classes at some of these same schools provided opportunities for early efforts to organize the peasantry. Eventually after the collapse of the GMD-CCP alliance in 1927, schools also functioned as way stations for Communist cadres seeking to reenter hill-country society, centers for propaganda and recruitment, and headquarters for armed uprisings.[46]

If the elite-dominated school system thus nurtured the revolutionary movement, then the pervasive factionalism afflicting hill-country elite society also simultaneously shaped it. In the 1920s, factionalism in education generally took the form of school-centered struggles between young and liberal "new cliques" (*xinpai*) and "old cliques" (*jiupai*) dominated by more conservative and elderly educators. During these struggles, smaller factional groups similar to the Cooperation Society often formed within the larger ill-defined cliques, coalescing on the basis of hometown, kinship, or school ties, common ideological interests, or patron-client connections to a particular leader. Over time such groups became both the scaffolding within which even smaller party branches could be organized and the institutional vehicles for some early assaults on the established power structure.[47]

At this point, communist attacks on elite powerholders were still well within accepted parameters of elite activity and still largely indistinguishable from the background clutter of local-elite factionalism. But factional tactics were not merely calculated ploys used by the Communists to disguise their intentions and cover their tracks. They were also expressions of a deeper and less conscious style of elite political behavior absorbed from the environment in which the young CCP leaders had grown up, and as such continued to manifest themselves from time to time throughout the early history of the revolutionary movement. The CCP leaders' temporary alliances with armed local powerholders after 1927, the continued influence of distinctions like urban/rural or large lineage/small lineage on the development of base areas, and the numerous internal disputes that plagued the communist leadership, all reflected the revolutionary movement's persistent tendency to both expand and fracture according to patterns of political interaction typical of hill-country elites.[48]

Other institutions important to the conduct of elite politics—bandit gangs, sworn brotherhoods, and lineages—also became involved in similarly complex ways in the emerging revolutionary movement. In its initial stages gangs and brotherhoods that had habitually colluded with established elite power holders frequently continued to support their erstwhile patrons by helping to attack Communist party branches and mass movement organs. Especially after 1927, however, the dynamics of the situation changed: conservative elites relied more on government troops and personally raised militias, and communist leaders found alliances with gangs among the few available alternatives to the now-disbanded peasant associations.[49]

Communists recognized that in addition to military striking power the gangs also provided useful and familiar routes for contacting the peasantry and ready-made organizational nuclei around which peasants could be mobilized. Many CCP cadres, therefore, went beyond simply negotiating alliances with gang leaders—a method that produced quick but often impermanent results—and sought to win over gang members from within. They became initiated into gangs and brotherhoods themselves and assigned CCP political agents to the gangs to help "reorganize" them. In this way cadres both established close ties with potential peasant recruits and helped mitigate the dangers of intrigues and mutinies by gang leaders. Eventually most gangs were fully incorporated into the rapidly expanding Red Army, with their original leaders either firmly committed to the Communist cause or (more frequently) replaced by people who were.[50] CCP leaders also tried persistently, though with only moderate success, to curb the power of lineages. Generally larger, more cohesive, and more permanent than gangs, lineages were also solidly rooted and widely ramified institutions of elite dominance. Any revolutionary restructuring of Jiangxi rural society required destroying, or at least neutralizing, these centers of elite power. That Communist cadres made some progress toward this difficult goal is clear, but the scarce available sources do not clearly reveal their methods.

It is reasonably certain, however, that CCP cadres initially sought whenever possible to accommodate and take advantage of lineage ties rather than force any immediate confrontation. Thus cadres sometimes commanded attention, obtained protection, or appealed for support on the basis of their prominent surnames. They might also use their status as scions of elite families with major lineage branches, or, conversely, arouse relatives to redress wrongs done to their own poor lineage by some nearby giant oppressor. This latter practice was apparently particularly effective. Cadres united numerous small lineages to oppose, under the banner of the revolution, the largest and most dominating lineages and their elite leaderships.[51]

Because hill-country elites played such a prominent role in the early stages of the revolution, we must ask where, within the highly stratified local elite, support for the revolution was strongest and where resistance to it was most determined. The answer to these complicated and different questions appears essentially the same: the lower stratum of the hill-country elite.

We have seen that members of different elite strata differed markedly in their access to public bodies and bureaucratic officials, their connections with bandit gangs and brotherhoods, and their attitudes toward education. We might, therefore, assume that many lower elites would also support at least some measure of political challenge to an upper-elite power structure from which they derived relatively little profit. Mao supports and elaborates on this hypothesis in his "Xunwu Investigation," asserting that elite attitudes toward the pace of political change in hill-country society paralleled their attitudes toward the new education. Those with substantial wealth and considerable security were basically conservative, though most would accept or even promote some change if it worked to their own advantage. Lower-level elites just emerging from the peasantry had little time for politics but clung like bulldogs to every shred of economic and social advantage they had accrued within the existing system. And declining lower-elite families were most anxious to see changes, political or otherwise, that would arrest their downward social slide.[52]

Mao's assertions receive empirical support from both the evidence he provides on the differing memberships of the New Xunwu and the Cooperative Society cliques in Xunwu and biographical information collected on other Jiangxi revolutionaries. Mao confirms that members of the Cooperative Society were predominantly scions of declining families from the local elite's lower stratum, leavened with a few progressive middle or upper elites.[53] Less detailed biographical data on other Jiangxi revolutionaries generally supports this picture of a revolutionary leadership drawn mainly from the lower-elite stratum, especially its "declining households."[54]

If the declining households provided much early elite support for the revolution, the newly emerging households of the lower elite appear later to have become its most stubborn and effective opponents. The revolutionary movement originated in the intellectual ferment and factional strife of the Jiangxi educational system, an arena that lay, both by choice and circumstance, largely beyond the purview of the newly emergent elite households. This situation changed, however, once the revolutionary movement percolated into the countryside. With their hard-won and tenuously held positions now directly threatened, and lacking the resources that made flight a viable option for higher-level elites, the newly emergent elites had little choice but to fight, and their resistance was widespread and tenacious.[55]

In sum, the lowest of all the elite strata was simultaneously the most open and most resistant to change: most open because its many declining households were willing to tamper with a status quo that offered them little prospect but further decline; most resistant because its newly emerging households were unwilling to jeopardize the smallest morsel of their hard-won gains. The dual nature of the lower elite—both facilitators of and obstacles to change—made dealing with this group one of the most delicate and exasperating problems facing the Jiangxi revolutionary leaders.

CONCLUSION

Most studies of the Chinese revolution have given little systematic attention to the role of local elites, dismissing as a minor irony the fact that numerous Communists came from prosperous families and treating elites almost exclusively as targets of the revolution.[56] As we have seen, however, elites in southern Jiangxi instigated as well as obstructed social change: revolution was disseminated via elite-dominated schools, structured in elite-run organizations, shaped by elite-centered patterns of factional politics, and aided by elite-influenced bandits and brotherhoods. Of course, few elites fully supported the revolution throughout its course; some resisted from the start, and many others joined the opposition as the movement's challenge to the established order deepened. Nonetheless, the growth of the revolution in rural Jiangxi—and elsewhere in China—depended far more and far longer than commonly realized on a support structure provided by local-elite society.

In contrast to many China experts, scholars of comparative revolution have long recognized the importance of elite action, but they have generally discussed elites only in macrosocietal terms, as abstract, largely undifferentiated groups acting on national or even international stages.[57] This essay, however, has looked at revolution in a local context and emphasized elite diversity rather than uniformity. Elites in southern Jiangxi were far from the unitary social category still often implied in discussions of "the local elite." They were, in fact, a diverse, multitiered collection of people who varied considerably from one another in resources, attitudes, and roles in the established power structure. Recognizing these differentiated layers allows us to appreciate more clearly the nature of the interlocking, highly articulated elasticity of local-elite society that for so long absorbed the shocks and transferred the energy of contacts between the peasantry and the outside world.

Understanding local-elite differentiation in Jiangxi also invites closer attention to the pivotal role played by Chinese elites occupying the liminal social terrain near the imprecise boundary separating elite from peasant. In the 1920s and 1930s, Communists looking at Chinese society from the bottom up frequently spoke of "rich peasants of semilandlord character"; officials viewing the same scene from the top down talked of "local bullies and rotten gentry" (*tuhao lieshen*); this essay has described both "declining" and "newly emergent" elites. Although these various terms are imprecise and by no means synonymous, there is certainly much overlap in the groups they represent; their zone of convergence largely encompasses those members of the lowest, largest, and most volatile stratum of the local elite, whose attitudes and actions were crucially important to all who sought to change the contours of Chinese rural society.

Mao Zedong was just such an individual; and more than the simple curiosity of an admittedly avid observer and analyst of Chinese life, the pressing, practical worries about revolutionary policy doubtless motivated his inquiries in Xunwu in May 1930. Nonetheless, his concern then was, on one level, much the same as ours is now: comprehending the rumbustious society of the Jiangxi hill country, and most particularly the jostling, arguing local elites who wrapped the region in such strong but anxious embrace. The "Xunwu Investigation" is testament to the significant progress he made in this effort, and it remains today a vivid and valuable record of a vanished way of life.

CONCLUDING REMARKS

Mary Backus Rankin and Joseph W. Esherick

The eleven chapters in this volume provide a picture of diverse and changing Chinese local elites. Clearly we cannot capture the essence of these elites in such simple static definitions as "gentry," "scholar-officials," or "land-lords." But if we conceive of elites as the people exercising dominance in local arenas, we can describe a coherent range of different patterns of dominance as a variety of elites adapted their strategies to the available resources. That provides a broader basis from which to consider the questions raised in the introduction. How much mobility was there in traditional elite society? What were the natures and resources of late imperial Chinese elites? What strategies did elites use to dominate other groups in local society? We can then move to questions of how these elites changed over time and to the still critical issue of elites and the state in China.

Although the local focus calls attention to diversity, the articles in this volume do not inspire images of endless fragmentation and disorder. Instead they suggest that social patterns in China were shaped less by the political center and woven more in local society than the usual picture of a uniform gentry-elite suggests. Local patterns varied markedly, but the elites in this volume, following their own routes and using the available resources, created institutions, expressed cultural values, used symbols, and interacted in ways generally accepted in Chinese society. The emphasis thus shifts from the question of how government controlled local leaders and unified society to issues of how local elites, acting within Chinese historical and cultural con-texts, dominated local arenas and interacted with elites in other arenas in ways common to the larger society and culture. Most institutions under local leadership—lineages, poetry clubs, guilds, or militia—were not neatly linked to hierarchies ending up in the capital but were shaped at home and joined to other localities and to government in looser and messier ways. By examining elites in their local contexts, we can work from the bottom up to identify the resources and strategies they employed to maintain their dominance.

One fundamental factor shaping the strategies of Chinese elites was their relative insecurity. Elites in China had few reliable long-term guarantees of their status compared to old-regime elites in Europe or to elites in caste societies like India. The European nobility, especially on the continent, was a hereditary status group with legal guarantees, rights to landholding, and tax privileges that far exceeded those available to the Chinese gentry.[1] Although recent research suggests that the long-accepted contrast between primogeniture among European elites and partible inheritance in China has been overdrawn,[2] there is little doubt that rather strict Chinese adherence to the practice of dividing property equally among sons made it more difficult to maintain the family patrimony than in societies with such customs as entail and "strict settlement."[3]

Acquisition of at least the lowest examination degree, with its attendant legal privileges, was the surest reasonably achievable route to elite status in late imperial China. But this status was marginal in many areas—a *shengyuan* degree per se provided little prestige in prosperous Jiangnan, with its abundance of higher-degree holders—and it could not be passed on to heirs. Furthermore, and again unlike caste or estate societies, status in China was not an effective substitute for wealth because in the long run it depended on wealth—to educate heirs for the examinations, cultivate connections, and maintain an appropriate life-style. The cultivated gentry life-style set elites apart from commoners. Although the examination system and gentry networks were important in spreading the social practices of the literati throughout China, these life-styles could mark a family as elite through long periods without any examination success.[4] The styles were remarkably uniform throughout the country, spread by both the examinations and officials and the sojourning merchants and scholars. By the end of the nineteenth century even the frontier elites of Taiwan, Sichuan, and Guizhou were adopting such ways of life.[5]

To determine the success of Chinese local elites in devising strategies to maintain their dominance we must distinguish between the continuity of elite personnel and the social continuity of elites. Continuity of personnel means that specific families maintain their elite status over long periods of time even though the nature of the elite they belong to may change. Social continuity refers to the persistence of a particular elite type, although the families belonging to that elite may change over time.[6] Previous studies of Chinese gentry have emphasized its social continuity. We later argue that the late imperial elite was changing in important ways, but the persistence of characteristic, elite-identifying life-styles through the nineteenth and even into the twentieth century indicates that in comparative terms there was re-markable social continuity of the Chinese elite. Influential studies have also suggested that the Chinese gentry elite maintained its dominance in part because the examination system kept it open to the talented and ambitious, allowing it to absorb potential rivals. Thus social continuity was linked to discontinuity of personnel.[7]

Recent research, however, has seriously questioned the earlier work on elite mobility, suggesting substantial continuity of elite personnel as well.[8] The work of Beattie on Anhui, Meskill on Taiwan, and the articles by Rowe, Brook, and Watson in this volume strengthen the argument for elite contin-uity at the local level.[9] Local dominance could be maintained for long periods of time without relying on degrees and office, and it is time to recog-nize that there was both mobility in the scholar-official elite and continuity in the local elite.

How can we explain the combination of social continuity and continuity of local elite personnel in China? We might expect that landed wealth was the essential foundation for Chinese elite status, but the landholdings of the Chinese elite were comparatively very small. Twentieth-century surveys indicate that landlords, comprising 3 to 4 percent of the population, owned only about 39 percent of all cultivated land in China as a whole,[10] and given the enormous number of petty landlords, local-elite families probably owned less than half that amount. In late nineteenth-century England, by contrast, thirty-five hundred to forty-five hundred great gentry families owned be-tween 70 and 75 percent of the land.[11] In Russia, nobles and the crown essentially monopolized landholding. France was more similar to China, but ecclesiastical, noble, and bourgeois landholders still owned roughly 60 per-cent of all land on the eve of the French Revolution.[12]

The Chinese elite could not maintain its status simply through officeholding and links to the state, for that entailed unbroken success in the examinations, which no family could guarantee. Nor were the comparatively limited land-holdings of the elite adequate to explain its persistent dominance. Rather it was the flexible application of a broad repertoire of strategies relying on multiple resources that enabled local elites to preserve their positions. Chinese local elites became masters at dealing with ambiguous mixtures of security and insecurity; their multiple resources allowed options in deal-ing with new situations. This flexibility served them well. When marked and rapid social discontinuities occurred in the twentieth century, a signif-icant number of elite families maintained their social standing in the face of changes that had little precedent in the Chinese historical experience. To understand this flexible elite repertoire we must look more closely at the nature of the late imperial elite and the resources and strategies it employed.

STATUS, CLASS, AND STRATIFICATION OF THE
LATE IMPERIAL ELITE

Insecure status in late imperial China and the interdependence of status and wealth produced a different interaction between the principles of status and class than one finds in other parts of the world. In seventeenth- and eighteenth-century continental Europe, separate status and economic stratifications developed in which rich bourgeoisie outranked less wealthy merchants but could not move in the same circles as the nobility at the top of old estate hierarchies.[13] In China, merchants were not kept apart by rigid status boundaries, and commercial wealth interacted with status throughout the Qing period. The Chinese social structures contrast differently with India and Japan: in India, wealth and caste stratifications fitted increasingly poorly during the nineteenth and twentieth centuries, but local caste lines remained intact; in Japan, despite blurring of barriers toward the end of the shogunate, relatively firm status and legal lines led to a merchant-urban culture distinct from that of the samurai elite.

The flexibility and interchangeability of status and class in China by no means indicates that distinctions were absent. First, a clear consciousness of class and status existed both among elites and between elites and masses. This situation appears similar to E. P. Thompson's description of eighteenth-century England.[14] There was strong consciousness of social distinctions and a certain degree of tension, but no strong class cohesiveness based on common relationships to the means of production or other economic factors. Superiority was demonstrated through life-styles, honor, and cultural display, all of which required both wealth and a cultural mastery that could not simply be bought. This consciousness permeated relationships in which social differences were small (as between a long-established great family and a recent arrival in elite society) as well as the greater gap between elites and masses.

It is also important that, despite the strong consciousness of social distinctions, Qing society was on the whole distinguished by weak personal dependency between elites and nonelites. Legally dependent, serflike bonded tenants began to disappear during the late Ming in the face of commercialization and peasant uprisings. The Manchu invasion and consolidation of Qing rule further disrupted the remnants of manorial society. By the eighteenth century, agricultural bondage was rare, although it occasionally persisted in places like Huizhou, Anhui, where tenants continued to till corporate property, living in a house provided by the master and bound to the land; even they, however, enjoyed security in return for their small obligations and were allowed to sublet their land.[15] Such holdovers were unusual, and so-called feudal relations between landlords and tenants rested on informal, possibly oppressive practices, underlining peasant inferiority but without legal standing. Bell's article gives examples of how gentry land-lords could get official support to force peasants to pay rent or meet other obligations, but elites could not always rely on the backing of a government that also wanted to prevent lower-class uprisings.

If neither legal privilege nor the relation to the factors of production, nor personal social ascendancy seems adequate by itself to account for elite domi-nance, then were relations with the state the key? The state was the source of the degrees, titles, and honors held by the gentry. Stratifications of Chinese elites in terms of degree holding have been made familiar through the works of Chang Chung-li, Ho Ping-ti, and Ch'ü T'ung-tsu so often cited in this volume. Lines are drawn between upper-gentry *jinshi, juren,* and *gongsheng* who could hold office, lower-gentry *shengyuan* and *jianshen* who had some legal privileges but did not qualify for office, and commoners who had no degrees and no legal protections against official power. Philip Kuhn has recently and powerfully argued that Chinese views of hierarchy embodied in Confucian theories of social relations were strongly reinforced by the hierarchy of degrees and state office and that the distinction between rulers and ruled overwhelmed social divisions, dividing the state sector from all others.[16] State-certified status was certainly of great importance, but this still seems too much a view from the center. Examination and office were not the only sources of the hierarchical perceptions that seem ingrained in Chinese culture. Such perceptions were also nurtured within family and local social systems not constantly impinged upon by the state.

The other main approach to stratification, described in Bell's paper, has focused on economic relationships between landlords and tenants and the effects of the Ming-Qing commercial expansion in Central and South China. It suggests growing class distinctions between wealthy landowning gentry living in towns and cities, small landlords and wealthy cultivators in the villages, and poor peasants and wage laborers at the bottom of the social hierarchy. Averill's article in this volume introduces Mao Zedong's division of the local elite into three layers based essentially on the size of their landholding.[17]

These approaches through state-conferred status and economic position have not been systematically related to each other, and neither in itself seems to offer a comprehensive model. Scholars have, therefore, begun to look for broader alternatives. David Johnson's nine-part model plotting education/literacy (with its associated legal privileges) against dominance widens the degree-based criteria into a more general one that can be applied from the top to the bottom of society.[18] Others like Min Tu-ki have elaborated upon earlier work on distinctions within the gentry.[19] Jerry Dennerline, in partic-ular, has examined the interactions of such factors as kinship, marriage, lineage organization, local philanthropy, and network alliances in estab-lishing social stratification.[20]

The articles in this volume provide much material to support a more complex view of stratification, and they suggest that, rather than focus on degrees
or land, it is better to start by looking at the arenas dominated by local elites.
The possibilities of the arena approach are particularly illustrated by Averill.
Starting from Mao Zedong's economic classification of the elites in Xunwu,
he draws in the many other factors that defined family position in the Jiangxi
hill country. The result is a map of power and status in the county. At the top
were a few great households, based in the district seat or biggest market
centers, who had the highest reputations, broadest connections, greatest influence, and the most resources. Below them were middle-elite families, often
in smaller towns, who commanded smaller quantities or a smaller range of
the same resources and whose influence did not extend as far. At the bottom
of the elite were insecure families whose resources were barely adequate to
warrant their inclusion in the upper reaches of society. The categories of
classification are necessarily vague because what ultimately counted was the
reach of a family's power. Yet the identities of the dominant families were
common local knowledge, and local people would have had no difficulty
ranking elite families within county or subcounty arenas.[21] Still, no single
factor defined elite status, which leads us to consider the diversity of elite
resources and their uses in dominating local arenas.

LOCAL ELITE RESOURCES

We may think of local elites in China as competing for a limited store of
resources that were generally effective in Chinese society. The relative
importance of each resource varied with the context of local arenas and
geographical regions. They also served different functions in acquiring or
maintaining elite status. The most basic of these resources are to be found in
the familiar list of education and office, commercial wealth, military power
and land.

Education was surely the most prized resource—as a means to gain examination degrees during the late imperial period or to acquire school or
university degrees and professional expertise during the Republic. A high
examination degree under the old system not only allowed entrance to
bureaucratic office and a chance to enter national circles of power, but it also
guaranteed access to the local magistrate simply on the presentation of one's
calling card and insured that officials would treat the holder with appropriate
courtesy and respect.

Education thus functioned as a stepping-stone to higher and broader
arenas outside the locality. It put elites into official positions or gave them
contacts they could use to act as patrons for kin and community. Within the
local arena it increased community status, broadened social alliances and
marriage prospects, and conferred the prestige that was such an important
factor in local dominance.

Even though education was one of the most important values in elite society, its importance as a local resource, and especially the importance of degree holding, varied markedly. Except on the most unruly frontiers, elites sought to educate their children; but the fruits of this education in the form of upper degrees were unevenly distributed across the map of China.[22] As a result, *jinshi* and *juren* degree holders were so numerous in the core zones of the Lower Yangzi that a lowly *shengyuan* degree conferred little status. Even in provinces that produced the most upper-degree holders during the Qing—Jiangsu and Zhejiang in the Lower Yangzi, and Hebei (Zhili) and Shandong in North China—there were enormous differences in the number of upper-degree holders from core and peripheral counties.[23] The *gongsheng* degrees, conferred for protracted but unsuccessful efforts to pass the provincial examinations, and the lower *shengyuan* degrees could be effective local resources on peripheries or areas like the North China plain where higher-degree holders were rare, but they provided negligible access to higher arenas.[24]

The diligent scholar from a poor family who succeeded in the metropolitan examinations was a persistent, but seldom realized, ideal in late imperial China. In reality, it was difficult for a family to leap into elite status through the examination system. Some wealth was needed to support a boy through years of study, so a degree, especially an upper degree, was likely to be a return on previous generations' economic resources that had already moved the family to at least the lower local elite. Degree holding was, however, effective in maintaining elite status. Once examination success and office holding had established a family in the local elite, the family was well-placed to garner resources to educate sons and win more degrees in future generations. Even if a family did not win more degrees, the prestige from one major success could, as Rowe points out, maintain elite standing for generations to come. Upper-degree holders usually came in the middle of a cycle of rise and decline. As Brook observes, they were likely to be preceded by several generations of more moderate success in the prefectural examinations and followed by another period when the family only acquired lower degrees but was still locally recognized as part of the elite. Given the competition in the imperial examinations, upper degrees were the most prestigious, but also the most uncertain, resources of late imperial elites.

Wealth from trade was perhaps even more important to the rise than the maintenance of elite families, although it was often vital to both. References to "raising one's family through trade" abound in the biographies of elites in local gazetteers. Commercial wealth was such an important resource because of the growing opportunities in the Ming and Qing periods and also because this wealth could be so easily converted into the resources of status—in the form of education, degrees, or life-styles—or into landholding. Multiple strategies of family maintenance based on commerce, education, and landholding became well established in the Lower Yangzi during the Ming.[25]

Chapters in this volume repeatedly illustrate the impact of commercial activity on local-elite societies from the coastal cores of the Lower Yangzi and the southeast to the peripheral hill country of Jiangxi and the southwest.[26] Zelin shows that a local elite far removed from cultural centers might even be defined by mercantile resources, and Rowe suggests that commerce was an effective alternative to upper degrees in maintaining local lineages in the relatively developed Middle Yangzi county of Hanyang. Commercialization made mercantile wealth a widespread, basic resource for gentry and military men as well as traders during the Qing, and in a few places even before.

What, however, of military power in a society where soldiering was theoretically even more disparaged than trade? Military degrees, in contrast with civil-service degrees, brought little status in core areas, although they had more weight in peripheral zones with few civil-degree holders. Nonetheless, the articles in this volume add to the evidence that military power was, in certain places and times, an important resource. Coercive power was most important on frontiers or peripheries not firmly under governmental control. Elites of core zones were more likely to use their greater rapport and influence with officials to obtain protection from governmental forces. In certain other areas, like parts of Guangdong and Fujian, piracy, banditry, and lineage or village feuding were common over protracted periods, even though the areas had left their frontier origins behind.[27] The village guard that Watson describes in Ha Tsuen originated in such circumstances, even though its relative importance as a resource seems to have declined in the twentieth century. In other places, like the North China plain, control of local forces became increasingly vital with spreading banditry and warlordism during the late nineteenth and twentieth century.

In general, military force was more useful in acquiring than in preserving elite status. The founders of several Hanyang lineages in Rowe's article rose as officers in the Ming armies during the Yuan-Ming transition, but they quickly used their military resources to acquire land and begin the pursuit of education and civil degrees. Military power did not have the legitimacy to sustain elites over long periods. As a more practical matter, although the government could not discipline unruly elites everywhere, even the declining Qing state proved in the northwest during the 1870s that it could smash local forces if its power was focused on a particular area. Thus even frontier strongmen needed and acquired more reputable resources to maintain their positions in the long run.[28]

Military power tended to be a temporary resource that assumed importance in troubled times of rebellion or dynastic transition but diminished in importance once order was restored. Local societies might become militarized as Philip Kuhn showed for Hunan and neighboring provinces during the Taiping Rebellion, but it is more problematical whether that condition persisted.[29] McCord's material on the Liu family suggests militarization was likely to be a temporary response to specific conditions that favored military power. The Liu's progress toward acquiring gentry educational resources was interrupted by mid-nineteenth-century rebellions in Guizhou. As militia leaders they rose more rapidly than they could have done by more conventional routes. Once that crisis had passed, they again began building up their educational resources but returned to military pursuits when disorder increased at the beginning of the twentieth century.

Finally, land was the most commonly acquired resource of local elites and was the ideologically approved source of wealth in Confucian China. Land ownership demonstrated status and brought wealth through rents or direct management, more stable sources of income than trade. The image of the gentry landlord is particularly associated with the Lower Yangzi, but peripheral elites also bought land to establish their positions, and Rowe points out that several of his Middle Yangzi lineages were able to buy large tracts of land after wars and rebellions. Merchants in these lineages invested large amounts of their profits in land. They also reclaimed flooded land—a common way of acquiring land in the southeast and Yangzi valley.[30]

Landholding was probably more useful for maintaining status than for entering the elite, though Rowe suggests that wealth from land alone was not enough to maintain elite families over long periods. It was possible for peasants gradually to improve their economic positions and build up their landholdings, and Averill's chapter indicates that such progress did occur. However, to buy land a family needed money, and it was difficult to accumulate such wealth from agriculture alone. The wealthy merchant acquired more land than the diligent peasant. Furthermore, land was a scarce resource in China, and growing population pressures made it particularly difficult to accumulate. Large tracts could be acquired on frontiers or in areas depopulated by rebellion. But in most times and places, land was accumulated only slowly, in small pieces and scattered plots. Even when large holdings, by Chinese standards, were acquired, they were not impressive in European terms. Nor was land always safe: records of ownership could be lost or destroyed in times of war or rebellion.

Unlike other elites in the world, Chinese elites were not defined by a few key resources—land, caste status, or inherited titles. In one sense they might be considered weaker than an elite with an unassailable claim over a basic social resource. However, they compensated for their lack of monopoly by a remarkable flexibility in using various resources selected according to the opportunities available in their local arenas. Mercantile wealth, particularly important in commercialized regions like the Yangzi valley and the southeast, could be significant in some peripheries and frontiers as well. Landed wealth was more common in the fertile south than the north; education was more useful in peaceful cores, and military power in troubled peripheries. But the resources of elites were not all internal to their local arenas. In fact, a crucial aspect of elite power was access to external and overlapping arenas.

THE SPAN OF ELITE ACTIVITY:
LOCALITY AND OVERLAPPING ARENAS

Frequent reliance on combined outside and local resources was basic to local-elite strategies. Their interests were not limited to their home turf, and we need to ask what forces pulled elites away from their home areas. Joan Vincent pointed out at the Banff conference that anthropologists working on other parts of the world have found that external resources are essential if local elites are to maintain their dominance for extended periods of time. In a closed local system, leveling processes will gradually narrow elite-mass distinctions.

Both outside resources and outwardly directed strategies appear particularly significant to understanding late imperial and Republican Chinese elites. Indeed, as Philip Kuhn provocatively asked at the Banff conference, were there any genuinely local elites in China at all? Were they not all culturally bound to a China-wide system defined by the Confucian state, which offered every well-educated boy a hypothetical chance to pass the civil service examinations? Did other factors also pull elites away from home? These questions raise important issues about the articulation of local and wider arenas.

From their local arenas in village, subdistrict, town, county, and city, elites ventured into what can be conceived as both wider (extending over larger geographical areas) and higher (focusing on a higher level in administrative or commercial urban hierarchies) arenas. Participation in these higher and wider arenas typically required more resources (higher degrees, greater wealth) and sometimes different resources (education rather than land) and brought greater opportunities for power. Some successful local elites permanently moved up and out of their original arenas, often migrating to other provinces, but during the late imperial period it was more typical for them at least to maintain contact with a home base. Many also brought outside resources into their home localities and returned home during and at the end of sojourning careers that had increased their families' resources and local power. For this reason it is often difficult to draw clear lines between local, provincial, and national elites in China because the same person might appear in each role as he moved back and forth between arenas at different points in his career. In such cases, patterns of local dominance typically had an outside dimension.

The outward pull of the examinations and the bureaucracy and the externally derived status from state-conferred office of degrees directed elite interests toward the center and caused the often-noted circulation between national and local elites. But this is only part of the picture. G. William Skinner introduced the concept of marketing systems with ascending orders of central places grouped into macroregional economic systems.[31] The completeness of this economic integration varied markedly with the levels of development in different parts of the country, but it increased decidedly during the late imperial period. Through this system trade fostered outside elite interests as much as did bureaucratic office. The form of urbanization in China, which dispersed small towns throughout the countryside in an interlocking hierarchy of central places, influenced the nature of local elites' external strategies. With urban activities scattered over the levels of this hierarchy rather than concentrated in a central megapolis,[32] official control over elite movements and interests was much more difficult. After long-distance trade increased, and major manufacturing centers developed; traders established regional and interregional networks and associations with others from their locality. The growing numbers of scholars in places like the Lower Yangzi also formed their own provincial or regional networks outside the bureaucracy.[33]

Skinner has called attention to the importance of sojourning in late imperial China, suggesting that as a key family strategy it also served to bring resources into otherwise disadvantaged areas.[34] In areas like Huizhou, Anhui, and certain Shanxi and Shaanxi counties, sojourning merchants brought back wealth to buttress their local position; and the clerks and private secretaries from Shaoxing county in Zhejiang did much the same thing, relying upon their bureaucratic connections.[35] By the nineteenth century, sojourning had become a pervasive phenomenon. Scholars as well as merchants, the poor as well as the elites, people from wealthy areas as well as those from peripheries found employment away from home. Significant for our purposes are the elite families' links to wider commercial, bureaucratic, or academic arenas from which they derived resources to enhance dominance at home.

Articles in this volume provide numerous examples of such external links. The salt elites in Sichuan initially relied on venture capital provided by Shaanxi merchants; the elites in Rugao had contacts in both Shanghai and Nantong. Hanyang lineages extended trade and kinship networks, and Jiangxi hill-country elites also had outside commercial links. In Schoppa's chapter, superior contacts to higher bureaucratic arenas helped the elites of one locality to force unfavorable water-control arrangements on a neighboring subdistrict. The importance of contact with people outside one's home arena also helps explain why brokerage between arenas and patronage by elites with access to higher arenas were so essential to local elite activity. Above all, local elites' transactions, mediations, and gatekeeping roles between intersecting arenas required them to face two directions: in toward their local arenas and out toward nonlocal determinants of their local power; and they carefully cultivated connections and developed strategies in this double context.

LOCAL ELITE STRATEGIES

All elites must plan and maneuver to some extent to preserve their status. Early modern European elites rigorously husbanded their economic resources, carefully arranged advantageous marriages, and practiced strict family discipline including birth control.[36] In China, the insecurity of elite status and the comparative scarcity of local elite resources required them to plan carefully for the future. These strategies were frequently devised in a context of intense competition for scarce resources.

Such elite competition was exacerbated by divisions based on such factors as kinship, ethnicity, locality, networks, and differential access to markets, productive resources, water, or political power. We see competition to win examination degrees or dominate markets, divisions between old and new money or local people and outsiders, fights among militia leaders and different religious groups. This competition could become violent, particularly in the peripheries and frontiers but also sporadically in more settled regions.

If elite strategies often assumed social conflict with other elites as well as other classes, they also illustrate some ways in which conflict was tempered through expected patterns of behavior that fostered civility. Cultural ideals of harmony reinforced unities arising from community or kinship, resistance to outside threats, common education, experiences, and associations.[37] Elite strategies were crucially divided between those that tended to enhance elite competition and conflict and those that tended to unite elites as a self-conscious dominant class.

A catalog of the many strategies pursued by local elites would be long indeed. They constructed marriage alliances, sent sons into different occupations to diversify resources, and carefully cultivated connections with their equals and superiors. Such strategies might be pursued by families seeking either to rise within the elite or to maintain their positions. We have already indicated that certain strategies were particularly useful in bringing new families into the elite. During the Ming and Qing trade became the preeminent strategy for upward mobility. Men could also rise to prominence by commanding military force, but strongmen had to broaden their strategies to retain power for long periods. Marriage served as an avenue both to enter the elite and to remain there, and it deserves further study. Education-based strategies to acquire upper degrees offered the possibility of moving beyond the local level into the highly prestigious national scholar-official elite. But because a family could not expect to remain in those circles for many generations, degrees were also symbols to demonstrate family status within local arenas.

The topic of this volume is local elites rather than social mobility, and we are moreover persuaded that—despite fluctuating family fortunes, regional variations, and particularly unstable lower boundaries between elites and nonelites—significant social continuity in the late imperial period extended to a lesser extent into the Republic. Therefore, we will here stress certain strategies that the articles in this volume suggest were particularly important in maintaining elite status and dominance: husbanding assets and extending local political power through lineages; defining local elite circles through horizontal networks and associations; creating vertical networks of obligated clients through patronage; and enhancing their prestige and community standing through essential functions of mediation and brokerage. Most of these strategies assume elite status. Together they illustrate how elites used basic resources to create social organizations and relationships to protect their social positions and extend their dominance over others.

Shaping Lineage Organization. Chinese lineage organization, a particular focus of anthropological and historical study, plays a central role in a striking number of articles in this volume.[38] We see lineage not just as a kinship organization but a socioeconomic institution growing out of elite strategies to maintain local power. Lineages were defined by locality as much as by genealogy. Rowe points out that lineages often date their founding from the patriline's relocation to the locality, and Watson shows how the coincidence of lineage and territorial community could result in locally powerful social organization. Lineages were also closely associated with elites, particularly in South and Central China—their founding typically followed a family's rise to elite status.

Lineages thus play an important role in the "localist strategy" Hymes sees emerging among Southern Song elites. Lineage formation tended to come in waves, and peaks tended to come in periods of devolving state power, such as the late nineteenth century, when elites were turning their attention more to maintaining themselves in their locality than to advancing through the national bureaucracy. This was not, however, the only factor governing the growth of lineage power. Beattie's study of Tongcheng, Anhui,[39] and Rowe and Watson in this volume all note that the accumulation of lineage land took place in the wake of major social disruptions and depopulation: the Yuan-Ming transition in the Middle Yangzi, the 1660s relocation of coastal populations in Guangdong, and the rebellions of the Ming-Qing transition in southern Anhui. Some late-Qing growth of lineage landholding in Jiangnan may have resulted from the availability of land in the wake of the Taiping Rebellion, and it certainly reflected the increasing initiatives taken by Lower Yangzi elites in this period.[40]

When newly wealthy merchant families formed lineages, they may have been claiming membership in the local elite, but lineage formation appears above all as a defensive strategy to protect resources, particularly in contexts of competition, uncertainty, and change. Official permission was needed to establish charitable and other lineage estates, which nearly made gentry connections a necessity. However, the variety of lineage forms and uses makes it clear that lineages evolved in local settings and beyond any unifying governmental direction.

The resources accumulated in lineage organization benefited the whole lineage, and the charitable estates of the Yangzi valley, in particular, indicate genuine concern for the well-being of relatives. Watson clearly shows, however, that lineage structure also helped perpetuate the position of the elite managers. It is useful to distinguish between elites in a lineage and the more problematical concept of elite lineages—that is, those with unusual local power or many degree holders. Elite lineages included many nonelite members, but certain families or branches used the lineage as a resource to maintain their status. Then they might not only act as patrons for nonelites in the lineage, but they might also dominate nonelite lineage members, whose interests might not coincide with their own.[41] Thus lineages both defended group interests and enhanced elite power within them.

This they did in various ways. Zelin's and Watson's chapters underline the nature of the lineage as a corporate body with institutions that could assume various economic roles. Zelin most dramatically illustrates how the lineage estate (*tang*) could be adapted to function as a business corporation. In his comments at the Banff conference, Rowe further suggested that in the nineteenth century, lineage, welfare, or commercial *tang* all acted like "trusts": legal entities with designated uses and limited liability.[42] Whatever the exact nature of these trusts, they clearly demonstrate the institutional flexibility of lineages. They combined a measure of sanctified inviolability, by virtue of their association with an ancestral legacy, with a capacity for corporate action that was easily adapted to business requirements. Traditional legitimacy and economic rationality seem effectively combined in the trusts of the salt-well merchants of Fu-Rong.

The lineages described by Brook and Rowe fall into the different pattern of the Middle and Lower Yangzi valley, where lineages were also widespread and numerous but owned less land in their charitable estates (*yizhuang*) and did not go into business.[43] Even without huge assets they were corporate organizations for the primary lineage purpose of defending against the progressive fission of family wealth through the custom of partible inheritance. These lineages thus functioned much as entail did in Europe, producing an undivided and inalienable patrimony.[44] Brook succinctly sums up lineage formation in Ningbo as a strategy for transfering elite family resources from generation to generation. Lineages limited the claims of collateral kinsmen on elite family wealth while providing a "somewhat broader pool of elite resources and junior agnates" for the difficult, recurrent task of succeeding in the examinations. Rowe further points out that even though his Middle Yangzi lineages did not have sizable corporate estates they still husbanded the "aggregate resources" of their members to protect their interests and increase their opportunities. Jonathan Lipman's paper at the Banff conference showed that elite strategies to adapt kinship forms transcended religious and ethnic boundaries: The saintly patrilines (*menhuan*) of Muslims in the northwest sought to confine sanctified charisma to a single patriline, thereby excluding others from claiming socioreligious power.

Scholars have found evidence of kinship solidarity, transmittal through patrilines, and even lineages, within North China,[45] but these lineages were usually much smaller and weaker with little or no corporate property or organization. If any organization existed, it usually focused on the ritual honoring of ancestors. Elites on the North China plain simply lacked the resources of land, wealth, and education to support the kind of lineages seen in the south. In North China weaker kinship organization contributed to the rarity of the kind of elite continuity seen in the Yangzi valley and the southeast. Northern elite families tried to preserve their wealth through the patriline and rose and fell more rapidly.

The Construction of Networks. Lineages, in general, protected existing resources and excluded outsiders from access to them. At the same time, elites also had to look outside their own kin group to preserve their local positions, and for this purpose networks were important. Whereas lineages were constructed to exclude even kin who might drain resources, networks included selected useful outsiders; whereas lineages were especially useful in elite competition, networks enhanced elite cooperation and solidarity; whereas lineage protected existing resources, networks expanded resources; whereas lineage activity often focused on the local arena, networks reached beyond locality. Networks, pervading all societies, have been defined as "quasi-groups," unbounded social fields with no clear leaders and organization linking friends, neighbors, affinal relatives, and occupational associates.[46] Both horizontal networks between approximate social equals and vertical networks linking inferiors and superiors were essential components of Chinese social relations.

Certain characteristics of late imperial society encouraged Chinese local elites to form horizontal networks: the linkages between local and larger political, commercial, and social structures; the connections and support systems originating in the academies and examinations and continuing through government service; the lack of firm status guarantees, which put a premium on support from personal allies; the weak legal protection for real and mercantile wealth, which made powerful connections always useful; and imperial prohibitions on formal associations with any political implications. Networks were an important vehicle for *guanxi* (connections, relationships), a pervasive element in Chinese social interaction. In the absence of the firm criteria and guarantees of elite status (estate, caste, class) found in some societies, the bonds of *guanxi* were constantly created and recreated through elite social practice and extended through ongoing networks.

Brook's article in this volume gives the fullest picture of an elite subcommunity defining itself within the local arena of Yin county, Ningbo, where an aristogenic upper gentry provided its own social certification, creating a long-lived upper class held together in horizontal networks. If not completely impermeable, this status-conscious social network maintained its identity against less prominent elites by a dense web of interconnections. Marriage alliances were a particularly powerful form of social connection, and the Chinese principle of *mendang hudui* (literally: "the gates are matched and the households paired") favored marriages between social equals. Affinal ties, poetry clubs, historically oriented scholarship with links back to dead heroes of the anti-Manchu resistance, and the organization of local relief were among the many activities through which this Ningbo group defined its exclusive membership and reaffirmed its social solidarity.

Seemingly inconsequential and often ephemeral literati associations like the Discarded Silk Society and the Mirror Lake Poetry Society were intimately tied up with the networks. The clubs had little organization beyond the personal connections of their members; but they provided members a reason to meet, thus solidifying and demonstrating elite cohesion. Because the Qing effectively banned any political organization until the end of the dynasty, such organizations might also provide a place to discuss local or national affairs, discussion that could easily take on political overtones. On a less exalted level, government-sanctioned, but locally run, community schools in Guangdong province during the eighteenth and nineteenth centuries also served as meeting places for elites to discuss local affairs.[47] Bell shows that similar associations could be used for economic dominance. Through the Culture Association, established in late nineteenth-century Wuxi county, a group of lower gentry sought to control silk marketing and peasant producers.

In addition to forming networks to solidify their position within the local arena, local elites were also linked outward by both vertical and horizontal networks. Gentry, especially upper gentry, cultivated friendships with upper-degree holders and scholars in other arenas or with officials in the bureaucracy. Outward-reaching literati networks were particularly visible in the Lower Yangzi where dense commercial networks and a large community of upper-degree holders fostered broad contacts among local elites and with their friends in government. Barkan's chapter shows that ties formed through the metropolitan examinations and office in Beijing were instrumental in bringing Sha Yuanbing into reformist networks of prestigious scholars and wealthy merchants in Jiangsu province after he retired from office. Elsewhere, Kuhn has noted the networks of militia formed in Hunan during the Taiping Rebellion, networks that sponsored the rise of a powerful group of provincial officials in the late nineteenth century.[48] Networks also linked sojourning merchants to one another and to their native arena. Long-distance trade gave rise to highly visible associations of merchants from Huizhou, Shanxi, Shaanxi, Fuzhou, and Ningbo. Common place of origin was a principle about which networks were frequently established, and when enough people from the same locality sojourned within a given town or city, they gave institutional expression to such ties by forming native-place associations (*huiguan*).[49] Thus, the vehicles for networking varied with the resources available to the elites of a particular area at a particular time, but the propensity to form networks was widespread, encouraged both by culture and the overlapping arenas.

Vertical Networking and Patronage. Vertical networks linking men of unequal wealth and status were equally common. Many of these were not strictly authority structures. Thus the Liu family studied by McCord increased its power by making connections at higher administrative levels and becoming part of provincial reformist networks. Others incorporated unequal patron-client relationships that provided one side with loyal supporters and the other with access to influence, employment, or reflected glory. Late imperial society was replete with such patronage ties, linking civil service examiners and successful candidates, teachers and students, wealthy merchants and artists, elites at different levels of the administrative hierarchy, military commanders and subordinate officers, lineage elites and ordinary members, shopkeepers and apprentices. Such ties continued easily into the Republican period. Averill, for instance, notes in the Jiangxi hills the importance of school ties between local educators and the protegés they helped enter middle schools. Vertical networks might also link elites of that area downward to marginal figures like the bandit leaders who provided occasional military muscle in return for protection and markets.

Patronage was a pervasive phenomenon in China. As in other partly commercialized agrarian societies, village-level patronage was encouraged because peasants did not have the power, knowledge, or contacts to affect outside decisions impinging upon their lives.[50] The role of patron ideally fell to a powerful member of the community—landlord, lineage head, or manager—who would be trustworthy in representing the community and effective in pressing the interests of its members. Thus Watson says the manager of the major lineage trust in Ha Tsuen was chosen because his wealth, knowledge of the world, and connections would make him an effective patron; such credentials implied that the patron was well-educated and wealthy, with status relative to others within the community. As Duara suggests, however, the community credentials of patrons varied with the village social structures of different regions. In North China villages—with few landlords, less resources, and relatively undeveloped kinship structures—patrons skillful at arranging affairs might rise from quite humble circumstances and, in striking contrast to village elites in the southeast, from outside the dominant kin groups of a village.

Above the village level, patronage was equally important. If imperfect market development made patrons and middlemen necessary for economic transactions, the imperfect political integration of the late imperial polity made patrons necessary for bureaucratic access and official appointment. The law of avoidance banned men from holding office in their home province and made local officials always outsiders. The best access to such outsiders was through men who shared their culture and life-style—the gentry. Because the powerful upper gentry of core areas also had links to higher levels of officialdom, which could be utilized to overturn an unfavorable decision by a magistrate, gentry, when locally available, were particularly desirable patrons. A successful examination candidate was virtually expected to act as patron for his home area and community by providing introductions, encouragement, and sometimes jobs and by using his connections in government to promote and defend local or kinship interests. In his account of the dispute over the Jute Creek flood-control embankment, Schoppa shows that access to such outside spokesmen was crucial to the ability of elites in wealthier towns to advance their interests at the expense of poor villages in a disadvantaged geographical location upstream.[51] At still higher levels, the great surplus of degree holders seeking office in the Qing meant that official appointment also depended on patronage networks, which inevitably worked to the advantage of core areas with prestigious and well-connected elite families. Nongentry elites also used patronage to enhance their status and further their own and community interests. Frontier strongmen might patronize young scholars, thus building clientage networks that could later be used to enhance their elite status. As commercialization fostered the practice of sojourning during the late imperial period, sojourning merchants also became patrons providing jobs for relatives or people from their home area.[52]

Patronage implies paternalism and reciprocity, but patron-client relations were unquestionably asymmetrical, particularly when clients were from lower social strata. An act of patronage underlined the patron's superiority, conferred or confirmed authority, and offered a step in building a useful clientele. Aside from providing material advantages to both sides, patrons dealt in symbolic capital. Through patronage they enhanced their own reputations, made these reputations available to their clients, and often increased the legitimacy of their claims to superiority by softening the more direct dominance they exercised as landlords, usurers, or merchants.

Brokerage and Mediation. Brokerage was closely linked to patronage, for successful patrons often performed brokering roles. But patrons had particularistic ties of mutual obligation to their clients, ties brokers often lacked.

Like patrons, brokers were most effective if they had the wealth, status, and reputation that tended to make brokerage an elite function. Conversely, however, because brokering was an empowering role, in areas where elite brokers were weak or unwilling to serve, nonelite individuals could rise to perform brokerage roles and thereby gain power over local arenas.

Duara's article provides the fullest analysis of brokerage's impact on elite dominance in China. Brokers were needed because buyers and sellers had to be brought together in incompletely integrated market systems; also, business discussions through intermediaries, reflected in the customary legal practice of middlemen guaranteeing agreements, was culturally preferred. Brokers acted between two arenas, and precisely the constant intersection of overlapping arenas made their role so common. The ideal broker was a community patron with outside contacts and some wealth relative to the other villagers. Even if he lacked significant material resources—as many North China brokers did—this ideal broker possessed "face" that inspired trust on both sides. The prestige associated with face enhanced influence in both the local community and the external arena to which the broker gave access. In the resource-poor northern villages with weak kin structures, this symbolic capital might be enough to bring a man into village elite circles.

It is striking that although brokerage, like patronage, might indicate incomplete integration, both economic development and attempts at state building in the Qing and the Republic probably *increased* the need for brokers. Compradors rose as brokers between foreign traders and Chinese merchants or producers. Tax farmers became more visible in the nineteenth and twentieth centuries, inserting their own interests while brokering between a revenue-hungry state and reluctant taxpayers. Middlemen purchased handicraft products or raw materials from peasant households for factories in China or resale in urban or foreign markets. Third-party introductions continued to be necessary in many social and political situations, and, as Strand points out, the breakdown of order during the Republic created a need for patron-brokers who could defend their arenas against the incursion of coercive state power.

If brokerage connected two different arenas, mediation was a community function that required a person of some local stature. Traditionally, dispute settlement fell to those with demonstrated authority derived from status and wealth; but new state initiatives, such as the creation of modern police, bureaucratized some twentieth-century mediating roles. The cultural value placed on harmonious relationships, coupled with the hesitancy to submit to corrupt judicial processes, placed a premium on informal mediation of the very frequent disputes within Chinese society. One apparent distinction between the powers of the old nobility of England and the Chinese gentry is that the former had local judicial authority denied to Chinese elites by the state. This difference narrows, however, if one considers the social authority possessed by a mediator: his powers were not legally secured; his aim was reconciliation, not judgment or punishment; and the sanctions at his disposal might include censure or fines but rarely any corporal punishment or confinement. Nonetheless, the social authority derived from mediation, like that from brokerage and patronage, enhanced the influence of elite leaders.

This discussion of networks, patronage, brokerage, and mediation indicates the extraordinary importance of interpersonal relations in defining and preserving elite status in China. The brokers in North China villages illustrate how people with very few material resources could claim elite status by performing certain structurally necessitated roles. The theoretically autocratic imperial state monopolized authority but possessed limited power. As a result, most local governance was worked out in the local arena through informal arrangements. To guarantee and maintain these arrangements required patrons and brokers who could reach agreements with local officials, negotiate tax rates and remissions, guarantee loans and land sales, and mediate disputes between competing interests. Over time, performing these roles came to be regarded as elite functions, and the behavior patterns associated with patronage, brokerage, and mediating roles—serious demeanor, cultivated bearing, proper regard for ceremony, broad community concern, and apparent impartiality tempered by a respect for human feelings— became integral parts of elite culture. To the extent that these roles were necessary and the behavior associated with their performance was accepted as proper, the elite could use them to maintain its cultural hegemony over the rest of the population.

CULTURAL HEGEMONY AND PATTERNS OF DOMINANCE

We began our discussion with the notion that elites are defined by their dominance in local arenas, and we have explored the resources and strategies that individuals and families employed to attain and maintain elite status. We must now focus on the strategies employed by these elites to dominate nonelites in local arenas. The resources used for domination were much the same as those for defining social position, but here the issue is their use in exercising sociopolitical power over others.

We have noted above that ties of personal dependency—of bondservants and servile tenants—were rare after the Ming dynasty. In general, the Qing and Republican elites dominated free men and women. Coercive resources available to elites were designed for use against outsiders or in outside arenas, but militia could equally well be used against peasants at home; and the knowledge that elites commanded such force deterred insubordination. Such military resources were certainly important on peripheries, frontiers, and the southeast coast, but, except in times of rebellion, they were far less important than the economic resources of elites in core areas. Landlords demanded half the harvest in rents, merchants controlled markets and manipulated prices, and moneylenders extracted usurious interest payments. Despite community norms that might restrain collections causing excessive hardship, and even though rather secure tenancy rights were won by peasants in more commercialized areas, such relations were clearly unequal and the threat of coercion was large. If elites and peasants were, as Watson observes for South China, often bound together by many-stranded ties, the patterns of coercion and symbolic violence embedded in these ties were also many-stranded and reinforcing.[53]

Economic forms of domination by landlords and merchants were no doubt increasingly important as commercialization intensified and spread across China, a point well-illustrated in Bell's chapter. What place was then left for cultural hegemony as economic relations became increasingly prevalent?[54] An answer is suggested by further exploring patron-client relationships. These were not undermined by the commercial economy. On the contrary, the roles of middlemen or guarantors required by commercial transactions often had to be filled by well-connected elite patrons. The resulting patron-client ties subordinated more than just tenants: freeholding peasants might especially require such services, for they (unlike tenants) had to deal with local functionaries who collected their land tax and validated their land deeds. The patron, whatever his actual shortcomings, could display wealth, education, and knowledge of the world to justify his dominance; acts of patronage demonstrated status and increased legitimacy. When a patron was successful as protector and broker, he added still more to his symbolic capital and created bonds of obligation and loyalty among his clients. Cultural symbolism could be turned into networks of power without usually resorting to open coercion. At the same time, the implied threat in these unequal relationships—that the patron could withhold benefits or turn his power against an ungrateful or insubordinate client—was greatly reinforced when patrons held other power over the resources of their clients. Mutually reinforcing ties, to some degree reciprocal, lent stability to unequal relationships within a community setting, but they did not eliminate the coercive underpinnings of dominance.

As patrons, elites maintained support by, as Strand points out, conveying a sense of reciprocity and mutuality in personal relations. The benefits from elite patronage, brokerage, and mediation were tangible justifications for elite claims to superiority, as were their other community functions like welfare, education, and contributions to maintain buildings and roads. At the Banff conference Robert Forster pointed out that the English gentry was more successful than the French nobility in retaining the deference of the lower classes because in England the upper classes retained administrative, legal, and judicial functions that enabled them to play a paternal role, whereas in France the local elite had little to justify its claims to superiority after such functions were assumed by the developing state. Although the functions of Chinese local elites were different, they were clearly more like the English gentry in this respect—an example of why the term gentry was originally borrowed from English society. Elites, or some of them, were quite continuously engaged in performing the functions that justified their authority, and, as Duara shows, they might invest considerable time and effort in cultivating the relationships necessary to maintain hegemony.

The most essential relationships to cultivate were those with other elites in shared or higher arenas, for through those relationships local elites could make the deals requiring their patronage and brokering. Thus the very same strategies of resource accumulation and network building that brought men acceptance among their elite peers also earned them deference from the wider population. It follows that elites came to be much concerned with displaying their elite status, for that very display validated their status and indicated that they might successfully perform elite roles. The theater of symbolic display allowed them to broadcast and justify their claims to their social equals and superiors and to legitimize their power over inferiors.

For such an exercise of cultural hegemony to be effective required shared values that would induce the populace to accept the elites' claims to superiority. The state examination system played an important part by encouraging respect for education and the educated and by spreading hierarchic Neo-Confucian values in the learning appropriate to examination success and at lower levels of education as well. The examinations, monthly Confucian lectures under the *xiangyue* system, handbooks of family instructions and almanacs spread values like unity, harmony, hierarchy, and respect, which benefited both state and elites.[55]

Another range of values—including reciprocity, magnanimity, and community—were less exclusively related to, although present in, orthodox Confucianism, and they were more closely intertwined with Buddhist concepts of charity and the communal orientations of agrarian society. These norms were ingrained more by social practices than by state policies. The diffusion of cultural norms thus flowed from several sources, and values were not shaped solely by one Confucian elite that controlled national institutions and the "media of indoctrination" and consciously integrated Chinese culture on the basis of a single ideology.[56]

When we move from the values themselves to the ways in which elites used them to inspire respect and create power, culture appears even more an active process of people expressing values rather than a code of predetermined meanings.[57] Late imperial elites gained legitimacy by demonstrating that they were bearers of Confucian gentry culture, but they did not follow any one script in translating values into life-styles that marked them as elites and into symbols that conveyed their superiority. Confucian learning was almost always important, but so was local service and conspicuous consumption, especially in ritually important matters like weddings and funerals. Nondegree-holding lineages might use such cultural symbols even more effectively than families with many degree holders,[58] and the masses were familiar with these symbols even if they did not interpret them exactly as elites did. Life-styles then played a critical role in converting the basic resources of status into the stuff of social domination. Cultural hegemony could under many circumstances replace more overt, forceable, and illegitimate dominance while ensuring that elites retained their privileged positions.

Probably the most famous picture of the life-styles of the highest national elites is in the novel, *The Dream of the Red Chamber*, which describes the refined pleasures and sorrows of the Jia family within the confines of its opulent mansions and lovely gardens. We sense the many dimensions of display when scholar-friends show off their knowledge of poetry in suggesting names for features in the new garden created for the visit of a daughter who was an imperial concubine; when thousands of townspeople line the streets to view an elaborate and costly funeral procession for a family member; and when a woman in the household is told to hire a new maid to keep up the number of servants at a time when parvenu families were adding to theirs.[59] Few could match the Jias, but the historical record is full of accounts of cultural display in the life-styles of the rich and famous. Brook and Rowe in this volume argue that elites in local settings were defined by criteria of education, refinement, opulence, and pedigree—not simply examination degrees. Scholars communicated with each other through poetry more than through classical scholarship, and literati networks like those in Ningbo (or even the far more modest local leaders studied by Schoppa) kept alive local intellectual traditions that might not be entirely approved by the state. These cultured life-styles spread from the economic cores to the frontiers, and Meskill's book is an excellent illustration of elite families on Taiwan slowly shedding their military strongmen's garb and donning the robes of the Confucian scholar.[60]

Life-styles and high culture became part of the symbolic capital of elites operating within specific arenas, and the symbols of status required public display. Thus gentry wore scholars' robes and buttons on their caps to indicate their rank. They rode in sedan chairs and built elaborate ancestral halls. Weddings cementing alliances between elite families and funerals demonstrating filial piety were carried out with lavish and expensive ceremony. Such symbolic display was composed of a host of individual acts, which together formed a holistic, culturally infused image that elicited deference and respect. The expense involved in such display ensured that elite status would be available only to those of some wealth, but simpler behavioral patterns were equally important to the elite image. These are captured by Barkan's portrait of Sha Yuanbing: a stern but just man, intolerant of moral laxity and ignorance, but concerned over the affairs of district, province, and nation; a learned scholar sitting in his library surrounded by books. This image, not just his prestigious *jinshi* degree, contributed to Sha's community prominence for two decades after the end of the imperial examination system.

Symbolic capital was created in another way through welfare activities benefiting the community. Such activity reflected the value placed on magnanimity in China as in India and other agrarian societies. Other forms of periodic largess, like paying for major religious feasts also reflected this value, and served to establish wealthy elites as a force in the community.[61] Such charity was always offered in a highly public manner. Soup kitchens made good works visible to all, and the names of temple donors were carefully recorded on the walls or a specially carved stone stele. The eighteenth-century English gentry may have been masters of theatrical display,[62] but Chinese elites more than matched them in this respect.

Such symbols and behavior created capital in the form of obligations of deference, respect, service, or favors through social intercourse. Cultural symbols thus opened the way to future material rewards through opportunities to gain wealth or amass a following of clients.[63] What F. G. Bailey calls the "small politics of reputation" pervaded social relations.[64]

Cultural symbols were used most obviously to maintain hegemony, although Duara shows that symbolic capital, in the guise of face, could in itself establish authority in the social structures of North China villages. During the Qing, cultural hegemony often maintained the unequal balance of elite-mass interests in uneasy and periodically punctured equilibrium. Late imperial elites and the masses shared the "field of force" that E. P. Thompson saw encompassing upper and lower classes in eighteenth-century England. Higher and lower poles were held together by certain shared values, similar views of the proper social scheme of things, and a sense of limits beyond which it was impractical or improper for power to go.[65]

Elites in both city and countryside often, as Strand notes, lived side by side with the poor. This proximity made their cultured life-style more visible and, at the same time, inspired—or forced—them to assume responsibility for poor neighbors. They easily fell into the role of patrons to the potential clients next door—a role that expanded into continuous involvement in local philanthropy during the Qing. It was also easier for the poor to evaluate the rich and, as suggested by both Schoppa's account of the Jute Creek embankment dispute and Watson's article, to set forth terms for their continued deference.[66] Because the status of Chinese elites was not entirely secure, and because expectations of magnanimity were as widely diffused as those values that directly reinforced hierarchy, the Chinese poor were periodically able to hold their superiors accountable. Rioting was one way to do so when circumstances had surpassed the poor's tolerance, and this is just what happened when local elites were unable or unwilling to get rid of the Jute Creek embankment that periodically flooded the fields in their home area.

The limited latitude for disorder in still basically ordered society also reduced social tensions by providing an outlet for the energies and grievances of the lower classes that stopped short of full social conflict.[67] Chinese elites did not necessarily approve, but mainly tolerated, disorderly festivals, unorthodox sects, and minor riots that were more likely to target the state than themselves. Sometimes they also participated in unrest. A stock figure in Chinese history and literature is the disgruntled *shengyuan* who led or joined the masses in protest. Lower-class riots might even be useful to more locally dominant elites in their conflicts with other elites or officials. Schoppa shows that subdistrict leaders tolerated the community riot that destroyed the Jute Creek embankment and then worked to restore their social authority. The inhibitions on indiscriminate use of power created by the interaction of elite and lower classes were reinforced by the power of the Qing government, which had its own interest in social equilibrium.

The centrality of the patron image in legitimizing power and exercising dominance is revealed in situations where it was inoperative or broke down. Much of the social conflict in China, as in premodern agrarian Europe, occurred between different localities. Such conflict not only directed we-they consciousness away from inequalities at home but also reinforced the patron-client nexus by increasing the need for elite leaders capable of defending the community. A more serious threat to elites came from the portion of the masses with whom they could not form patron-client relationships. Sectarian bands and the geographically mobile underclass, including laborers along transport routes, peddlers, miners, seasonal workers, disbanded soldiers, beggars, and criminals—all of whom escaped the vertical networks of local dominance—presented a more fundamental problem. Traditional elites were not very successful in developing strategies—other than exclusion or periodic philanthropy like the "winter defense" distributions of food and clothing—to meet this kind of challenge as it escalated after the mid-nineteenth century.

Esherick's study of the Boxer uprising illustrates just how destabilizing the unrooted poor might be in an area where community ties were eroded and local elites lacked material and symbolic resources to maintain control.[68] But the itinerant lower fringes of society did not often invade the structures through which elites maintained dominance. This kind of challenge only arose during the Republic, when left-wing and revolutionary elites began to organize groups in the old vertical structures of authority. Strand describes how, in the 1929 campaign to unionize shopworkers and clerks in Beijing, long-standing grievances surfaced that gave "the lie to the ideal of elite paternalism." Class solidarities and conflicts were revealed as Beijing shopowners co-operated to suppress the movement. The still more forceable reactions of landlords to the first Communist attempt to organize peasants in Haifeng county, Guangdong, during the early 1920s suggests a rural version of the same class conflict.[69] Elites did not want to pay higher wages, accept lower rents, or give up land. These economic interests alone do not seem to explain the strength of their resistance, however. Organizations like peasant unions threatened the very structure of patronage and denied the symbolic capital upon which so much elite authority rested. At that point conflict, not paternalism, dominated elite-mass social relations, and the stakes escalated to matters of life and death.

CHANGES IN ELITES OVER TIME

The resources and strategies discussed in the previous section may be considered the stock of an elite repertoire of practices. Actual practices varied as conditions changed, and Chinese elites changed as well during the entire period from Ming to Republic. The chapters by Brook and Rowe indicate that periodic political crises of rebellion, war, and dynastic change destroyed old families and created conditions favoring social mobility. They find that the Yuan-Ming transition in the fourteenth century was probably even more disruptive in this respect than the seventeenth-century transition from Ming to Qing.[70] In the nineteenth century, the Taiping Rebellion again loosened elite social structures in large parts of China; this time when the character of social institutions was beginning to change. The more fundamental transformation was, of course, part of larger processes of economic, social, and political change: commercialization, increased foreign trade, militarization, functional specialization, growing and politicized voluntary associations, and the shifting political context of republican China. During most of the late imperial period these processes changed the elite without fundamentally altering the elastic social structures. Toward the end of the nineteenth century they began to transform social structures as well. Here we consider various dimensions of these changes, their impact on Chinese elites, and their effect on elite relations to the state above and the general populace below.

The Growing Importance of Commerce. Although some have traced China's commercial revolution to the Song,[71] the really dramatic growth in local markets, handicraft production for the market (especially cotton textiles), interregional trade, and a vigorous money economy began during the Ming. Population growth, new crops (corn, sweet potatoes, tobacco), an extended reign of peace, and the influx of silver from the New World fueled this expansion. The new commercial activity affected Chinese elites in several ways. It provided an important new avenue to elite status. Some merchants like the Fan family of Shanxi and the salt merchants from Huizhou made enormous fortunes during the seventeenth and eighteenth century through government monopolies in salt, copper, and other commodities.[72] More fortunes were made in trade beyond strict government supervision: first in grain, then in handicraft products (especially cotton cloth and silk), and, in the southeastern coastal provinces, in foreign trade with Japan, Taiwan, and Southeast Asia.[73]

In the sixteenth and seventeenth centuries, references to parvenu merchants are often colored by classical Confucian disdain for profit making—the attitude that formally relegated merchants to the lowest stratum of the social hierarchy. Some literati certainly felt compelled to protect their status against the challenge of commercial wealth,[74] but literati disdain for mercantile activity eventually became more pro forma than real. Already in the Ming sumptuary laws were breaking down, merchants were purchasing degrees and interacting with gentry, and gentry families were rising from merchant backgrounds.[75] By mid-Qing times gentry families commonly engaged in usury and trade, and merchant families supported Confucian academies and gentry publishing projects. The cultured sons of merchants were accepted into the gentry elite, and merchants eagerly assimilated the norms of the literati, bought land, and joined in philanthropy and other public works.[76] The social/cultural fusion of merchant and gentry elites was largely accomplished in the commercialized zones by the end of the eighteenth century, setting the stage for broader political collaboration in the nineteenth.

In the nineteenth century, trade with the West opened up further commercial opportunities, which were effectively exploited by some established trading families. The merchants of Foshan, west of Canton, provide an interesting example of the elite transformation that resulted from this process. With backgrounds in handicraft production and trade with Southeast Asia, these merchants were among the first licensed by the Qing to trade with the British in Canton. When the treaty ports were established in 1842, following China's defeat in the Opium War, such men had skills and connections to work as compradors for Western firms.[77] Ambitious men from Canton and other coastal entrepots like Ningbo followed opportunities for foreign trade in Shanghai. Although these treaty ports were marginal to Chinese society as a whole, many successful Chinese business-elites escaped marginality by acquiring official titles, purchasing land, and becoming patrons and philanthropists in their home towns; some advised officials on the new problems of intercourse with the West. Such men were strategically located to insert themselves into a changing nineteenth-century elite, which required men with particular specialized expertise as well as the classical cultivation that had traditionally qualified one to rule.[78]

The gradual erosion of literati exclusiveness was further illustrated by the massive sale of examination degrees in the late nineteenth century. As a result of the Qing's desperate efforts to raise revenue, one-third of the gentry class had purchased their degrees, and two-thirds of the official establishment had qualified by the "irregular" route of purchase.[79] As merchants routinely purchased examination degrees and official titles, and as venality of office undermined Confucian assumptions about bureaucratic qualifications, merchants and gentry were increasingly drawn together in various local arenas where they were routinely identified by a newly popular term: *shenshang*, or "gentry-merchants." Bell's article shows how, in the twentieth century, this new hybrid class became an integral part of an emerging business elite, engaging in bourgeois practice but also relying on well-established elite strategies of networking and local management.

This changing relationship of merchant and gentry elites in China is particularly important for comparative history. Robert Forster provocatively noted at the Banff conference that trade and commerce appeared more respectable in China than in Europe before 1900; this observation is an important corrective for those still believing in the efficacy of classical Confucianism's anticommercial bias. There is no question that the Chinese gentry was more open to mercantile wealth than the nobility of continental Europe, but the parallel to England—where the purchase of a country house and the assumption of a proper life-style could qualify wealthy merchants for gentry status—is striking indeed. Because this allegedly "open" English elite is often credited with both England's political stability and the country's economic modernization, it is fair to ask why a seemingly comparable Chinese elite had the former effect, but not the latter.[80] We suggest three things that seem to distinguish the Chinese and English cases.

First, the type of trade accorded proper status differed in the two countries. The 1700 edition of Edward Chamberlayn's *Angliae Notitia*, the standard reference of the day, dropped all disparaging comments on "shopkeeping" and proclaimed that "in England as well as Italy to become a merchant of foreign commerce, without serving any apprenticeship, hath been allowed as no disparagement for a gentleman born, especially to a younger brother." But domestic wholesale or retail trade was clearly beyond the pale.[81] By contrast, the Ming and Qing dynasties periodically restricted and prohibited foreign trade. The prohibitions were demonstrably ineffective and not seriously enforced for long periods by the Qing, but they still left those engaged in foreign trade open to disparagement as "criminal merchants and sly people . . . [who] secretly trade with foreigners in prohibited goods."[82] But because China was a single empire, long distance domestic trade was comparable to foreign trade between the countries of Europe—and was also capable of producing great wealth that brought high status. The Chinese in effect *reversed* the European evaluations of domestic and foreign trade, which certainly inhibited the sort of overseas trade that fueled so much of Europe's early modern expansion.

Second, the greater Chinese acceptance of domestic commerce may also be related to the structure of Chinese commercial enterprises, which maintained a reasonably firm separation of ownership and management. We see some of this among the salt merchants described by Zelin, but they seem perhaps more involved in day-to-day management than many Chinese merchants, especially those with gentry aspirations.[83] Xue Shouxuan in Bell's article deliberately sought to end this separation as part of his new "bourgeois practice." Because earlier Chinese "merchants" left most direct commercial dealings to their managers, they were less tainted by money grubbing and freer to pursue the cultivated life-style of the gentry.

Finally, the economic geography of merchant-gentry relations was different in England and China. The landed gentry who ruled England through the mid-nineteenth century were always closely tied to London, where they maintained townhouses, rubbed shoulders with the great merchants, invested in banking and overseas ventures, and formed the connections which made England "a nation of aristocrats and squires ruling in the interest of bankers and overseas merchants."[84] In effect the structure of elite power in England concentrated capital and influence in London, where it fueled the nation's economic modernization.

In China, a different structure prevailed. The most powerful commercial interests in China were not concentrated in the nation's capital, nor did they derive from the Jiangnan economic heartland. The typical Chinese merchant was a sojourner. Merchant groups from Huizhou (in the hills of southern Anhui), from Jiangxi, and from the interior northern provinces of Shanxi and Shaanxi dominated much trade in the early and mid-Qing. They were joined by Fujianese and Cantonese from the southeast. Later, Ningbo merchants rose through coastal and foreign trade and banking during the nineteenth century. Thus, the Chinese merchant was always something of an outsider, who met the gentry on the latter's ground and, almost inevitably, on the latter's terms. As an outsider, the merchant was also relatively dependent on bureaucratic favor, which left him vulnerable to sometimes extravagant demands for "contributions." The wide range of sojourning also meant that investments were not concentrated in one or a few centers.[85] Sojourning merchants might sometimes trigger the rise of local entrepreneurs, but they also remitted a substantial portion of the profits of commerce back to widely separated, and in some cases peripheral, areas from which they had come.[86] In fact, the differing merchant-gentry interaction in China deflected the London-style concentration of wealth by returning some capital to the hinterland.

In this context the sort of entrepreneurial elite described by Bell in Wuxi and epitomized by Zhang Jian in Nantong is so important. In the twentieth century, these local gentry-merchant elites began operating their own enterprises in the economic heartland. Not only were profits kept in areas of potential economic development, but money also began flowing from land to commerce; most critical, this all happened in a context where commercial and industrial elites were not outsiders, but the dominant elements in the local political arena.

Militarization and the Rise of Military Elites. In the mid-nineteenth century, the threat of rebellions throughout China led to organized militia for defending the established order. Philip Kuhn has studied this process of militarization in the Middle Yangzi valley, and in this volume Edward McCord has documented the phenomenon in Guizhou. In provinces like Hunan, the gentry under Zeng Guofan seem to have maintained firm control of militia networks, but McCord shows that in Guizhou militia networks were an avenue for new men to enter the elite. The same was probably true in Anhui and in North China—where the orthodox gentry were weaker than Hunan, and the state had to rely on new elements to combat the threat of rebellion.[87]

The militarization of local society was not a continuous process. McCord shows that the Liu family abandoned much of its original militia base in the late nineteenth century to concentrate its power on patronage networks and promote educational and other reforms. Elsewhere, he has demonstrated the discontinuity of local militarization between nineteenth- and twentieth-century Hunan.[88] However, clearly by the early twentieth century the status of military men was rising significantly, as nationalistic ideology preached the need both to train a new core of military professionals and to spread military training and values among the general population.[89] This late Qing rise of the military was the foundation for the rise of the men who would dominate China during the warlord era and (to a somewhat lesser extent) under Chiang Kai-shek's Guomindang.

How much did the militarization of national and provincial elites affect the nature of local elites? Here the record is surely mixed, with military power playing a fairly minor role among the Lower Yangzi elites. On the frontiers, where coercive resources were always important, they seem to have become even more so in the twentieth century. On the peripheries and in North China,[90] where gentry and commercial elites were weak, local elites did become significantly militarized. In an era when modern rifles were readily available from foreign suppliers and provided a weapon to check or challenge the state or other rivals that was infinitely more threatening than the swords, spears, and flintlocks earlier dissidents could wield, local military elites became a serious force to be reckoned with. This greater power of military technology did not, however, normally increase the status of local militarists. The small-scale local commanders were too close to bandits and "local bullies"—and their use of coercive power was too destructive to the fabric of local societies—to be legitimate. When militarization occurred in once relatively settled societies it had a different social impact than did the military force integral to newly forming frontier societies or long incorporated into peripheral community structures. In the twentieth century, externally triggered militarization was likely to erode communities rather than strengthen them. The character of elites, new or old, was also compromised as they substituted more direct forms of domination for cultural hegemony.

Functional Elites. The twentieth-century rise of business and military elites was the most visible example of a process wherein discrete functional elites arose alongside (or in place of) the old gentry elite. But the process was not simply elite functional specialization creating a pluralist society; occupations were not that separate. Averill refers to his great households as "small-scale conglomerates." Xue Shouxuan, described by Bell, was not only an industrialist but also a landlord, a scion of a prominent gentry family, and a member of the new Nationalist regime. Functional categories do not show how elites diversified to protect their interests. They underplay the importance of networks and associations linking elites together and may overstate the social distinction between merchants and gentry in the late Qing and Republic.

Nonetheless, increasing evidence of specialization clearly begins before the twentieth century. Benjamin Elman has argued that the eighteenth-century complex of academies, libraries, and printing houses in the Lower Yangzi supported a prestigious group of professional academics.[91] The medical profession provided respectable employment for upwardly mobile men or sons of gentry families who would or could not follow the standard examination route—much as the younger sons of English gentry families became attorneys in the seventeenth and eighteenth centuries.[92] Merchants specialized in particular trades or in banking. Local management, another respectable career, might involve special skills in water control, famine relief, or philanthropic activity. Law and administration required more and more specialists during the Qing, including respectable occupations such as private secretaries in the bureaucracy, less respectable jobs such as clerks, and clearly disreputable callings such as the pettifoggers (*songgun*) who serviced the everyday lawsuits of ordinary citizens.[93] Specialization was slowly redefining the acceptable range of elite occupations, but on the whole it elaborated established gentry and merchant roles. Skill in certain approved occupations might bring social approbation, but it did not markedly improve status unless combined with other factors—birth, education, social connections, personal rectitude—that were commonly accepted social markers.

There are, however, serious indications that elites were becoming more functionally specific in the twentieth century; certainly professional elites were becoming more prominent and more *organized*. Various "worlds" (*jie*) of educators, merchants, industrialists, journalists, lawyers, and financiers emerged as publicly identified and frequently organized contenders for influence in the new China. The elite functional repertoire broadened, and the required level of expertise increased with greater specialized training. More important, functional competence was gradually becoming an independent source of status. In the seventeenth and eighteenth centuries, elites may have been significantly involved in commerce, but such involvement did not per se contribute to elite status. Commerce provided the wealth a family might use to seek status through scholarly or philanthropic activity or education for the exams. By the twentieth century, with the formation of chambers of commerce and the official encouragement of trade, commercial or industrial prominence alone was likely to earn one a position among the local elite. As this shift took place during the late Qing New Policies and the early Republic, one finds hybrid cases in which upper-degree holders like Barkan's Sha Yuanbing, with local standing and presumably also business interests, headed chambers of commerce and other new organizations influential in local affairs; thereby they conferred status on these institutions while simultaneously receiving influence from them.

As the Republic progressed and elite functions proliferated, more and more elites were defined by their competence in functional roles rather than by their embodiment of gentry cultural ideals—that is, by their jobs and occupations rather than by their backgrounds and behavior. We see this at the village level in the new "professional" brokers described by Duara; in the villages, these new elites do seem to be new men—upwardly mobile hucksters. We see it at the county level in the silk industrialists of Wuxi and the succession of Shas of Rugao. At the county level it is striking, as Barkan, Bell, and Rowe all indicate, that new functional elites were drawn so often from old elite families. Now more occupations conferred elite status and more routes provided upward mobility, particularly through the army. New men appeared, but elite, or at least near-elite, families were often best positioned to acquire new skills. Long-established patterns of elite flexibility and adjustment to changing conditions meant that even when the nature and institutions of the elite changed, there was still continuity in personnel. Though the *social* continuity of the old elite was broken, the *biological* continuity of elite families was often preserved. Averill describes a particularly interesting variation of this process: young men who were able to challenge the old order due to the respectability and status they commanded from their family positions within it.

Finally, we should note that in many cases, this emergence of functional elites in the twentieth century is described as the rise of less legitimate, less prestigious elite types. This is certainly true, and the new men out to make their fortunes were likely to be more openly exploitative than established elites. Even so, legitimacy is a normative judgment, and not all change represented social erosion. Normative standards are always slow to change, but they do, in time, catch up with social realities. We should remember that it was late in the nineteenth century, one hundred years after the onset of the industrial revolution, before English industrial elites were regarded as respectable.

The Emergence of a Public Sphere of Local Elite Activity. The imperial state had always been extremely suspicious of independent elite associations, though in the late Ming, the Jiangnan elite had managed to transform scholarly and cultural networks into organizations for quite overt political activity. The Qing cracked down severely on any associational activity that looked at all political, but they did not prohibit all organized gentry activity on the local level. Philanthropic associations—including foundling homes, societies providing support for widows, and famine-relief bodies—were the most im‍portant types of local elite organization. Angela Leung has pointed to the seventeenth-century emergence of united welfare associations (*tongshan hui*), as local gentry and merchants took over responsibility for moribund governmental institutions in Lower Yangzi cities and towns. Although the Qing reasserted state interest in welfare in the eighteenth century, the resulting united welfare agencies (*tongshan tang*) were run by local elites under official supervision.[94] Even during the height of Qing state power in the eighteenth century, local elites were gradually outstripping bureaucratic authorities in other arenas as well, such as the small, but important, community-oriented water control projects of the Yangzi valley and South China.[95]

State policy did much to encourage this tendency toward extrabureaucratic elite initiative. Madeleine Zelin has shown how the eighteenth-century Qing government pulled back from giving county magistrates adequate funds to run local government and fully control local arenas.[96] In the nineteenth century, the Qing further compromised its authority by delegating certain tax collection powers to local gentry, merchants, brokers, and guilds.[97] Commercial taxes in particular were collected outside the bureaucracy, and, as they became increasingly important, the fiscal power of merchant and gentry groups expanded.

The mid-nineteenth century certainly represented a major watershed in the growth of autonomous local-elite power. Philip Kuhn has shown how elite autonomy was enhanced by militia building in this period. Though the militarization may not have been permanent, Susan Mann's work on taxation, William Rowe's on Hankou guilds, and Mary Rankin's on elite initiatives during the postrebellion reconstruction further demonstrate the emergence of increasingly autonomous structures of local-elite power in the last half century of the Qing.[98] Rowe and Rankin have analyzed this process in terms of a growing, community-focused "public sphere" of organized elite activity between the official bureaucracy and the private sphere of families, kin groups, and business enterprises.

If the Qing actively discouraged any overt *political* role for local elites before the 1890s, the 1902–1911 New Policies of the Qing government explicitly permitted elite political mobilization in local assemblies and councils and also gave them larger powers in education, economic development, and public security. Elite mobilization of this period built upon the "public sphere" activities and networks of the nineteenth century, but the new political context of the reform period fundamentally altered the import of elite behavior. China's defeat in the Sino-Japanese War of 1894–95, the threat of partition in the 1897–98 Scramble for Concessions, and foreign occupation of the capital and of Manchuria in the wake of the Boxer Uprising gave rise to an unprecedented wave of nationalist sentiment. The rise of the Chinese press fanned this sentiment; general politicization of elite activities followed—a politicization that soon promoted hostility to the Qing dynasty. Provincial assemblies, local chambers of commerce and educational associations, study societies, and political associations, really proto-parties, provided powerful institutional bases for political opposition and helped bring about the republican revolution of 1911.

Republican elites controlled even greater organizational resources in private associations and quasi-governmental professional associations (*fatuan*). These resources could, as proposed by Strand in this volume, lead to the appearance of a "civil society," a more autonomous successor to the public sphere, in which independent groups might organize, explicitly pursuing the interests of their members. A new type of local politics emerged in this civil society, a constituency politics of associations as interest groups, which threatened to replace the old politics of networks and personal relations. This politics developed in the cities of core areas, but as Averill's article indicates even the peripheries were ultimately affected by the new politics, with revolutionary consequences.

At the same time a new mass politics emerged, capable of threatening elites from below but using the same organizational forms that elites devised to press their interests against the state. Whereas the Qing had quite successfully prohibited open political activity for some 250 years, politics dominated the twentieth century; the genie was out of the bottle, and the forms, structures, and discourse of elite politics changed irrevocably. Once the public pursuit of private interest was legitimized, once elites began to function as representatives as well as patrons, once appeal was made to progress and change as well as harmonizing accommodation to cultural norms, the polity began to be transformed in ways that presented both new opportunities and new challenges to local elite dominance.

The Fragmentation of the Elite. The late imperial gentry elite was arguably the most unified (though not uniform) elite in the world. Even while it included more than the degree holders who had passed the state-administered examination system, those degree holders set the behavioral norms and defined the life-styles that set the elite apart. The examination system unified the gentry nationally, guaranteeing a comparable number of lower degrees to each county and providing preferential quotas of upper degrees for isolated and underdeveloped provinces on the frontier.[99] No clerical, aristocratic, or military elite challenged the dominance of the gentry; and the commercial elite imitated, joined, and slowly transformed the gentry—but did not compete with the gentry for local power as a separate group.

The late-nineteenth- and twentieth-century transformation of the elite placed unprecedented strains on elite unity, however. The emergence of a public sphere of elite organization provided a growing number of local arenas for elite activity. Elites came increasingly to focus on their separate local arenas as much as on the national examination system. But the environments, the resources, and the interests of these local arenas differed markedly, encouraging differences in elite behavior as well. Both Rankin and Schoppa have noted a widening gap between economic cores and peripheral zones. The cores benefited more from the commercial expansion of the nineteenth and twentieth century and recovered more quickly from the rebellions. When new schools were established to replace the examinations abolished in 1905, official funds favored the provincial capital. Core elites demonstrated the will and the resources to finance schools in their own communities, and the peripheries fell further and further behind. The same was true of other associational activity. Core elites organized more quickly, more extensively, and more effectively and managed to press their agendas in higher political and economic arenas.[100]

Although Rankin and Schoppa have stressed the gap between core and periphery, others have stressed the rupture of urban and rural elites. Esherick has emphasized the role of an "urban reformist elite" in the 1911 Revolution, and Kuhn has written of a modernizing "new urban elite that found it increasingly hard to identify itself with the problems of rural China."[101] In fact, there is substantial overlap between these urban-rural and core-periphery cleavages. The major urban centers were all in regional cores, and the elites of these cities diverged most markedly from those in peripheries. The urban elites were more commercialized, more functionally differentiated, more likely to be trained in modern schools and affected by Western culture, and more committed to models of economic modernization that favored the cities and the cores. These characteristics often put them at odds with the elites of less developed rural hinterlands, who were more concerned with protecting their own security against a rising tide of bandit attacks and communist insurgency than they were with the core elite's fancy blueprints for economic development and political reform. To the hinterland, the urban elites were "false foreign devils"; to the cities, the rural elites were "local bullies and evil gentry."[102]

Just as important as these broad social fissures in the elite were more particularistic splits that came with the functional differentiation of the elite and its politicization. Warlord struggles could make bloody affairs of such divisions in the elite; and the ideological polarization of the 1920s tended to color a wide variety of local factional quarrels. With different functional groups represented by their own associational structures, and with political groups forming factions to compete for political advantage, it was inevitable that the old elite would lose some of its former cohesion. We should not over-state those divisions, however. Broad consensus still existed on who the elites were and what qualified them to rule; but the challenge to that consensus was growing, and the internal solidarity of the elite was not as strong as it had once been.

LOCAL ELITES AND THE STATE

All these changes in Chinese elites affected their relationship to the state—a relationship that has been a central concern of scholarly inquiry on China. The early work on Chinese elites stressed the state-conferred examination degrees as authentic cachets of elite status and the role of the local gentry in defending the imperial order. Although more recent work, including the chapters of this volume, has focused on the local sources of elite power, almost all scholars agree that only in relatively limited portions of the frontier can Chinese elites be considered totally apart from the state. The critical question from our perspective is the transformation of this elite-state rela-tionship in the modern period.

First we must confront the problem—complicated by changes associated with the dynastic cycle—of a baseline from which to chart the process of change. In many respects, the late Qing looks like the late Ming, where historians have found expanding social organization, elite political initia-tives, and weakened governmental efficacy. But the early Qing state reversed most of these trends, and it makes some sense to begin our account in the eighteenth century, which appears as the most effective era of Chinese bureaucratic governance. In the monographs of Peter Perdue and Pierre-Etienne Will and the survey by Susan Naquin and Evelyn Rawski, we see a state capable of impressive initiatives in land reclamation, resettlement, water control, and famine relief, but its powers are increasingly circumscribed by local interests as the century progresses.[103] In Perdue's work in particular, the devolution of state power to local elites that Philip Kuhn associated with the mid-nineteenth-century rebellions can be seen as a process beginning in the eighteenth century.[104]

It is also clear, however, that the process involved more than the devolu-tion of state power. We have just reviewed a series of initiatives, dating back to the late sixteenth century, through which local elites gradually established a public sphere for their activities in philanthropy, education, local defense, water control, public works, fiscal affairs, and, in the twentieth century, in professional associations, journalism, political organization, economic de-velopment, and local self-government. Local elites were doing more than just stepping in to fill gaps left by a disintegrating state. They were developing

new strategies and new institutions to protect their positions and to guide
political developments in accord with their interests and ideals.

By 1911, provincial and local elites perceived their interests and ideals to
be incompatible with the Qing state. The symbiosis of imperial state and
gentry elites had come to an end, and the latter joined the Republican revolution. But the revolution was not simply a triumph of local elites over the
state; and the Republican period was more than just the political disintegration of the state.[105] Most important, the modern competition between state
and local elites was not a zero-sum game. At the same time that local elites
were organizing in new ways and increasing their resources, the state was
doing the same. Beginning with hesitant nineteenth-century reactions to
foreign imperialism and internal rebellion, the state was enlarging and modernizing its armies, increasing its fiscal resources with new commercial taxes,
and improving its communications with telegraphs, steamships, and (by the
1890s) railways. In the first decade of the twentieth century, the Qing state
took on an impressive range of economic development activities through the
new Ministry of Agriculture, Industry and Commerce and the Ministry of
Post and Telecommunications, plus the new Bank of China and all their local
appendages. The new army and the police greatly strengthened the coercive
forces of the state; and the campaigns to eradicate opium demonstrated that
the Qing was willing to use its new powers.

Under the Republic, economic development projects expanded to include
the efforts at cooperative formation and sericulture improvement described
by Bell. The social reforms broadened into widespread attacks on footbinding or popular "superstition," which could be dramatically intrusive even
when sporadic. Tax increases and the conscription of corvée labor unquestionably brought the weight of the state much more directly to bear on the
average peasant. Duara shows the impact that such changes could have on
village society as old elites with status in the community were replaced by
new and more exploitative parvenus connected to the bottom rungs of the
new state apparatus.[106] Even if it was not very effective, a process of state
building was certainly going on, and local elites were involved in it and reacting to it.

One local-elite reaction was simply to distance itself from the state,
increasingly separating local and national elites. In Schoppa's article the
absence of the nationally prominent Tang Shouqian from the struggle over
the Jute Creek embankment, so important to his home village, symbolizes
this separation. Local elites found few positive qualities in the predatory
national warlord governments of the late 1910s and 1920s. In her Banff conference paper, Helen Chauncey described how some retreated defensively to
pursue independent reformist aspirations at home; others, with a military
following, became local strongmen or regional warlords protecting their
own turfs.

It is probably best to think of elite-state relations in the late Qing and the Republic as reflecting the conjuncture of a cyclical devolution of state power with secular trends of state building and elite self-mobilization. The competitive expansion of both state and elite power, in a context of increasing elite organization and politicization, resulted in a more profound conflict between elites and the state than was characteristic of the late imperial period. Authoritarian/bureaucratic/militarist governments failed to build a broad constituency for modernizing state building but kept elite associational politics from developing into a serious bourgeois democratic alternative. Expanding state resources were not effectively translated into control or legitimacy; and the most effective republican era government, the Guomindang's Nanjing regime, showed, in Strand's words, "a remarkable capacity to... punish its natural allies" among the local elite. As the Guomindang shifted from a mobilization to a bureaucratic style of state building at the end of the 1920s,[107] it found that it could neither replace local elites nor win their loyalties. Barkan's work on Rugao indicates that, far from successfully establishing a corporatist state,[108] the Nationalist government vitiated locally run services without providing effective substitutes. For example, Western-educated Xue Shouxuan in Bell's article cooperated closely with the Nationalists, but he used the official sericulture agencies so profitably in Wuxi that one may ask whether the state brought him into the fold or whether he captured a bit of the state.

The changing elite relationship to the state, and what it meant for local dominance, can be illustrated by looking again at brokering roles. In areas like North China or regional peripheries, where elite material resources in land and commercial wealth were limited, the elite's privileged access to the magistrate and local bureaucracy was one of the most important foundations of its influence in the community. The literature on the late imperial gentry has stressed this role as intermediary between the state and rural society. Local elites were brokers: acting between the official world and the local community, participating in both and (in a sense) not belonging totally to either.

F. G. Bailey has written insightfully about brokers on the basis of fieldwork in South Asia. The broker "must make the villagers believe that he can communicate with and manipulate clerks and officials in a way that the ordinary villager cannot." This may require him at times to deliver "an authoritative, if mystifying and unhelpful, lecture" on some particular administrative procedure about which a question has been asked. Above all, he must prove his efficacy, and this entailed a "complex task of presenting himself to the world." He must wear "a normative mask of devotion to the public weal, which had, however, to be sufficiently transparent to allow clients to see his skill at maneuvers which were normatively condemned."[109]

This description does not readily fit the gentry or community-rooted brokers of the Qing, who had the symbolic capital, and sometimes the genuinely high status, to justify their credentials in both arenas. It certainly seems to apply to the new type of village brokers described by Duara, however, and it may apply to the new county elites of Barkan's and Bell's chapters as well. Duara's new middlemen are recognized as necessary, but often, it seems, despised; and as Bailey notes, "the middleman is despised in proportion to the disparity of the two cultures" between which he must operate.[110] Seemingly the process of state building increased not only the extractive demands of the state but also the cultural distance between it and rural society. Those who served as brokers to the new state were indeed increasingly looked upon with contempt. Respectable members of the community drew back from such tasks; and a new brokering elite stepped in. Where the imperial state had served as a source of legitimacy for local gentry, the Republican state helped both to foster and to delegitimize a new brokering elite.

Thus on the one hand the devolution of state power left locally entrenched oligarchies unchecked by the central state. Such unchecked power was likely to be used abusively, and the repeated complaints against "local bullies and evil gentry" indicate that this was indeed the case.[111] At the same time, equally disreputable men rose to act as brokers for the expanding governmental activities. The appearance of such unchecked, illegitimate, and exploitative parvenu elites increased social tensions and created constituencies for the radical young intellectuals, described by Averill, who returned home to promote revolution. Because governmental power was most important in North China, both the devolution of state power and the rise of state-brokerage roles should be most important there too. The revolutionary forces grew in the north and the peripheries, where local yamens were a more important focus of elite activity and independent networks of elite cohesion were less developed. That revolution might have been crushed had the Nationalists created a more effective coalition in the rest of the country, but in the core areas the stalemate between Guomindang state making and local-elite organizing left both groups incapable of mounting an effective counter-revolutionary effort.

These changes in modern Chinese elites relate more to context and structure than to behavior and strategy. The behavioral continuities across fundamental changes in twentieth-century economic structures and technology are extremely important. They suggest that the most distinctive characteristics of Chinese elites are to be found in behavioral patterns rather than static attributes such as those associated with the degree-holding gentry. This interpretation suggests new ways to look at the interaction of structure, practice, and change in Chinese society.

Flexible reliance on multiple resources was one of the most important characteristics of late imperial elites, who were never guaranteed enough of any one resource in education, land, commerce, or military power to be defined by that single attribute. Because they had long since learned to exploit changes in the available resources, they readily adjusted to the new opportunities and challenges brought by the forces of "modernization" intruding from the West and Japan. As a result, many twentieth-century Chinese elites came from the same families that had dominated their localities for generations.

The social resources, constructed in shifting contexts by elites themselves, were the most resilient. Dense networks of human relationships (*guanxi*), cultural symbols, and behavioral norms held elites together. Aware of their social superiority, Chinese elites set out to construct webs of influence to protect their status. Such social relationships proved an enduring social resource during the process of China's modern transformation, as preexisting connections facilitated elite control of twentieth-century institutions. This same continuity also insured that modern forms of association were regularly infused with the status- and display-conscious norms of older elites.

Networks were fostered by the larger context of Chinese society. Neither economic integration nor bureaucratic rationalization had progressed to the extent that patrons, brokers, and middlemen could be dispensed with. Such roles were particularly important for activities that crossed arena boundaries, and China was replete with intersecting arenas: between levels of the economic and administrative hierarchy, between state and society, between upper and lower classes. Particularly in the political realm, the combination of formal integration and informal delegation of state power left unusual room for elites to exercise their patronage and brokering roles. These roles existed in dialectical interdependence with the elite's cultural hegemony; hegemony supported their monopoly of these roles and was reinforced in turn by successful performance.

The Chinese elite's exercise of dominance through cultural hegemony, while hardly unique, was certainly striking. Cultural symbols and behavioral norms identified these elites, gave them social cohesion, and advertised their superiority. It is important to understand that the infusion of the norms of gentry society into almost all sectors of the late imperial elite represented more than the hegemony of Neo-Confucian values and ideals. Culture given living interpretation in elite daily life was basic to the ways in which elites defined themselves locally and legitimized their dominance. Elite culture meant literati activities, to be sure, but also included patronage, philanthropy, mediation of social conflicts, avoidance of physical labor, mastery of courteous social intercourse, and public and ceremonial display of affluence. These forms of behavior proved remarkably adaptable to the social requirements of modern life, and many were found among the practices of republican as well as late imperial elites.

These few characteristics—elite flexibility, reliance on networks and other social resources, and cultural hegemony—can assist us to understand the interplay of unity and diversity among Chinese local elites and the *historical* processes of elite transformation in late imperial and republican China. Unlike static conceptions of gentry society, they help explain the flexible adaptations that sustained many elite families in the hybrid elite society of the twentieth century. They also allow us to focus on those structural changes that fragmented the modern elite, fundamentally altered its relation to the expanding state, and ultimately left it prey to the revolutionary forces that united a new stronger state above and mobilized the masses below. With that new combination, the cultural hegemony of the old Chinese elites was brought to an end, but it remains to be seen how many of their behavioral norms might still survive.

NOTES

Full citations of all cited works appear in the Bibliography.

NOTES TO THE INTRODUCTION

1. Mencius, 117.

2. There were a few exceptions to the principle of open access, namely certain base groups such as actors and entertainers, Guangdong boat people, Jiangnan beggar communities, and Anhui bond servants who were disqualified from the examinations. Ping-ti Ho 1962, 18–19.

3. Weber 1951, 107–108.

4. Balazs, 6.

5. Weber 1951, 13–20; Balazs, 66–78.

6. Hsiao-t'ung Fei 1953, 74.

7. Eberhard 1971, 71–75. Eberhard is unusual in seeing this much continuity in the Chinese elite. Most scholars see a significant shift from an aristocratic to an examination-based elite beginning in the mid-Tang dynasty (618–906); and usually the term "gentry" is reserved for the late imperial elite of the Ming and Qing dynasties.

8. T'ung-tsu Ch'ü, 2. This figure actually includes 1,282 counties (*xian*) and 154 departments (*zhou*). Because departments were virtually undistinguishable from counties in size and administrative level, we will normally refer only to counties. "County elites" means "county or department elites."

9. This figure was supplied by Robert Forster at the Banff conference. For a general picture of the French state under the ancien régime, see Mousnier, esp. vol. 2.

10. Wittfogel (1953), on the contrary, advanced the idea of a supremely strong Chinese state in his theory of "Oriental despotism" built on Marx's notion of an "Asiatic mode of production." Wittfogel's state based its power on control over waterworks and dominated a fragmented peasant society. Eberhard (1970) directly challenged this exaggeration of state power, pointing out that local leaders took responsibility for much of the water control.

11. T'ung-tsu Ch'ü, 168.

12. Chung-li Chang 1955, 71–141. The distinctions between upper gentry, lower gentry, and commoners have been debated by Chang, Ping-ti Ho and T'ung-tsu Ch'ü. For a summary of views on this issue and of the Chinese terms translated as gentry, see Min Tu-ki, 22–32.

13. Ping-ti Ho 1962, 52.

14. Marsh, 187–188.

15. *Huang Ming tiaofa shilei zuan* (Categorized substatutes and regulations of the Ming dynasty), cited in Oyama Masaaki, 130–131. On gentry landownership, see also the articles by Tanaka Masatoshi, Tsurumi Naohiro, and Shigeta Atsushi in Grove and Daniels. Mori Masao (1975–76) provides a quite comprehensive introduction to this literature. For more recent English summaries, see Mori Masao 1980; Grove and Esherick. Skocpol (p. 49) observes that competition between imperial states and landed elites to control peasant labor and surpluses from agriculture and trade occurred in Russia and France as well as China.

16. Shigeta Atsushi, 335–386. Shigeta treats essentially the same problem as English historians of the eighteenth century: how did the ruling gentry class maintain its dominance as a wage economy eroded the personal dependence inherent in more paternalistic relations between masters and manual laborers? (See E. P. Thompson 1974). We shall return to this problem in the concluding chapter.

17. Mori Masao 1980, 35–37, 47; Shigeta Atsushi, 337, 351.

18. Hymes 1986a.

19. Kuhn 1970, quotes from 213, 223.

20. Wakeman 1975a, 4, 8 and passim.

21. Mann 1987.

22. For a classic example, see Kung-chuan Hsiao.

23. Lapidus, 42.

24. Yung-teh Chow, 158–172, 220–225. Cf. Hsiao-t'ung Fei 1953; Hsiao-t'ung Fei and Chang Chih-i.

25. Beattie 1979a, 4.

26. Meskill 1979.

27. Schoppa 1982.

28. Rankin 1986.

29. Among the many collections of articles on capitalist sprouts are Nanjing daxue lishixi, ed. 1981 and 1983. More recent articles stressing the limits of capitalist development and a consolidation of the merchant and gentry classes include Huang Qichen and Ye Xian'en 1987. On some socioeconomic effects of Southeast Asian trade on Fujian and Guangdong, see Lin Xiangrui and Luo Yixing.

30. Naquin and Rawski; Ping-ti Ho 1954.

31. Gates, 241–281.

32. See Weber 1958, 180–195.

33. E. P. Thompson's (1978, 146–150) comments on class in eighteenth-century England would seem to apply very well to China.

34. Swartz, 6, 8–10. The concept of "arena" is sometimes used interchangeably with "field" in the anthropological literature.

35. Bourdieu 1977, 171–183.

36. For an introduction to recent thinking on these matters in social anthropology, see Ortner, esp. 130, 145; and Vincent 1978 and 1986.

37. Kuhn 1970, 64–87, 102–104, chap. 4.

38. See Skinner 1977c. In a revision of this original scheme, Skinner (1985, 273) split Jiangxi from the Middle Yangzi to form a macroregion in its own right.

39. Detailed accounts of eighteenth-century society in each of Skinner's macroregions appear in Naquin and Rawski, 138–216. For a theoretical discussion distinguishing economic cores and peripheries, see Schoppa 1982, chap. 1.

40. E.g., 23.6 percent of all *jinshi* came from the two Lower Yangzi provinces of Zhejiang and Jiangsu during the Ming and Qing. Ping-ti Ho 1962, 227–228, 246–247.

41. Gu Yanwu, *Rizhi lu* (1695), 10: 15a, cited in Oyama Masaaki, 103. Tenancy rates were lower in other parts of the Lower Yangzi, but still usually well above 50 percent.

42. For a picture of the Jiangnan elite of the Ming, see Wakeman 1985, 92–126. For the Qing, see Naquin and Rawski, 55–72, 147–158.

43. Wakeman 1985, 99n; Naquin and Rawski, 151; Ebrey 1983 and (for an earlier period) Walton.

44. Rankin 1986, 2–8, 45–46, 61–62.

45. Ibid., 3, 92–135; Mann, 94–120.

46. Rankin 1986, 202–309; Schoppa 1982.

47. The Japanese literature on this process is extensive. See especially Muramatsu Yūji; Suzuki Tomoo. A forthcoming study by Kathryn Bernhardt will soon introduce this subject in English.

48. See Imahori Seiji 1956.

49. The classic works on this area are Freedman 1958 and 1966. On frontier conditions and lineage formation, see Freedman 1966, 162–166; Pasternak, 551–561. On the influence of official Confucian models, see Faure, 142–144, 149–165.

50. Lin Xiangrui, 61–72.

51. Rubie Watson 1985, 90.

52. Freedman 1966, 68–76, 82–85; Faure, 23–26, 111–113, 128–140.

53. Jing Su and Luo Lun, 106–153.

54. E.g., *Shan xianzhi*, 2:77a–77b.

55. For a discussion of the Shandong gentry, see Esherick 1987, 28–37. Sources for this calculation are indicated in that volume on pp. 347–348, n. 11. Life expectancies for *juren* are based on Chung-li Chang 1955, 122–125. For a similar calculation for the eighteenth century, see Naquin 1981, 29–32.

56. Philip Huang, 224–233; Esherick 1987, 238, 242.

57. Niida Noboru, et al., eds., 4:506. A communist organizer in Shandong similarly stressed ties of the local elites to the county officials during the war against Japan. Wang Yu-chuan, 87.

58. Perdue 1987, esp. 168–170, 226–227.

59. In twentieth-century Zhejiang local magistrates often pressed innovations in the periphery in contrast to elite leadership in the cores. Schoppa 1982, 102, 132–134, 187.

60. Ibid., 130–131; *Yongkang xianzhi*, 2:20b, 3:8a–11a.

61. For a breakdown of types of frontiers and frontier cycles of development, see Von Glahn, 215–220. See also Rowe 1985, 251–252; and for the eighteenth century, Naquin and Rawski, 199–205, 226–227.

NOTES TO CHAPTER ONE

1. Wan Yan, 1:16a–b, 27a, 31b, 35a–36a; Li Yesi, 3:1a, 21a, 33b; *Ningbo fuzhi*, 17:49a, 19:26a–27a, 20:62a–b, 29:4b; Hummel, 353–354, 803–804.

2. The political context of gentry hegemony is skillfully analyzed in Shigeta Atsushi, 335–385.

3. On Ningbo and its history, see Davis, 21–31; Shiba Yoshinobu 1977; Tsur. Other details are from *Ningbo fuzhi* and *Yin xianzhi* 1788.

4. My principal sources for degrees were *Ningbo fuzhi, juan* 17 (note that the first two names in the 1565 cohort were Yin natives, though not marked as such); *Yin xianzhi* 1877: *juan* 23; *Yinxian tongzhi*, 1:319b–530b; Rankin 1986, 314.

5. Rankin 1986, 7.

6. Mann (1987, 90) has noted that the gazetteer section on filial paragons was where editors might place biographies of merchants, whose occupation did not recommend them for public commendation under any other category: an "umbrella of historical respectability shielding entrepreneurial offspring who stayed home to mind the family store."

7. *Ningbo fuzhi*, 24:12a, 24a.

8. Quan Zuwang 1803, 2:4b. The two Sun lineages are listed on 12b–13a, although I have not been able to identify conclusively Sun E with either of them. I am grateful to Mi Chü Wiens of the Library of Congress for providing me with a photocopy of this work.

9. *Yin xianzhi* 1877, 43:20a, 46b; 44:12b, 20b.

10. Ibid., 43:40b.

11. Yin men are not conspicuous in commercial circles: none of the most prominent Ningbo merchants who were active both at home and in Shanghai in the nineteenth century was a native of Yin. The merchants came from outlying counties like Zhenhai (Jones 1974, 84–85). In such places one finds families simultaneously pursuing banking and business interests and examination degrees; e.g., the Fangs: *Shanghai qianzhuang shiliao*, 733–734; *Zhenhai xian xinzhi beigao*, 27:14b.

12. The one institution that overrode this principle was the *yin* privilege granting office to first- (and sometimes second-) generation progeny of high officials. Although much restricted from its use in earlier dynasties, the privilege was conferred on members of twenty-three Yin lineages in the Ming (*Ningbo fuzhi*, 17b:46a–49a). On the *yin* privilege in the Song, see Davis, 16–17.

13. Robert Hartwell (1982, 419) has warned against overstating the openness of the elite in the Song, pointing out that elites manipulated the examination system to favor established families.

14. Ai Nanying, 7:26b. Ai (1583–1646) made this remark in an encomium to an acquaintance who was setting off to become registrar of Dinghai *wei*, a military district on Ningbo's offshore islands in the Zhoushan Archipelago.

15. Pan Guangdan, 94. The translation of the former is from Ping-ti Ho 1962:166.

16. E.g., Ping-ti Ho 1962; Marsh 1961.

17. In a parallel fashion, scholars of early modern Britain have argued that there was a high degree of continuity within the British elite. Membership in the elite changed considerably in certain areas of Britain, but elite families outside the

immediate political and commercial orbit of London tended to survive for many centuries (Holmes, 12, 231). The Civil War, once considered a major catalyst for the emergence of new gentry and the decline of old, may in fact have had only negligible impact: in south Wales three-quarters of the leading gentry families entering the eighteenth century had dominated local political office under the Tudors (Jenkins, 29, 42). High continuity among the greater English gentry into the nineteenth century has been most energetically argued in Stone and Stone. Their methodology and conclusions have been questioned in Spring and Spring, who argue that lower-level gentry pedigrees and marriage mask nouveaux-riches origins.

18. Beattie 1979b, 88; Dennerline 1981, 113; Hymes 1986b, 132, 133.

19. Walton, 36.

20. Ping-ti Ho 1962, 166–167.

21. Ebrey 1986, 41–42.

22. *Yin xianzhi* 1788, 1:18a.

23. For the role of the gentry in creating lineage institutions during the Ming, see Brook 1988, 73–75, 78.

24. Early modern European elites by contrast sought to sustain their continuity through a wide range of strategies—law, marriage, entail, bachelor- and spinsterhood, birth control, and careful management of their fortunes. But they lacked the extended kinship ties that made the Chinese lineage, and its status-conscious strategies, possible. For Chinese elites, entail through primogeniture was unavailable and fertility restriction unacceptable. We are grateful to Robert Forster for pointing out this contrast.

25. Shiba Yoshinobu 1977, 434; Tsur, 18–19, 36–37; Cole 1986, 160; Zhang Xingzhou, 237.

26. *Yin xianzhi* 1788, 29, 31a, from an anthology of local verse by Li Yesi. On the four Song lineages, see Walton for the Lous and Davis for the Shis.

27. Pan Guangdan, 94–110.

28. My reconstruction is based on Quan Zuwang 1814 and the comprehensive lineage tables in *Yinxian tongzhi, juan* 1. On the basis of these sources plus inferences from local writings, I have identified 198 lineages with Ming or Qing holders of the *jinshi* or *juren* degree. This survey is not complete because I have been unable to identify roughly one-quarter of Ming-Qing *jinshi* by lineage. A few surnames were particularly resistant to lineage identification (Chen, Wang, Xu, Ye, Yuan, Zhang, and Zheng).

29. I have excluded the Yingfang Chens and the Haohe Lings, each of whom garnered three *jinshi* plus several *juren* and *gongsheng* degrees, during and immediately after the Taiping Rebellion when degree quotas were eased; also the Geluo Mas, the Dali Wangs, and the Junziying Zhus, whose degrees were acquired within less than sixty years.

30. The data on these families are from Quan Zuwang 1803, 8:566, 589, 687; *Ningbo fuzhi*, 20:46a, 59b, 78a; 24:33b.

31. Williams 1977, 110.

32. Lu Hsün, 217. I thank Jonathan Lipman for calling my attention to this story.

33. *Yin xianzhi* 1788, 29:31b–32a.

34. A lack of genealogical data concerning the Zhu surname makes it difficult to

distinguish Zhu lineages. The Zhus in this verse are probably the Madong Zhus, Madong being just south of Jiangshan (the Chens' home village) in the southern part of the county.

35. Wan Yan, 2:70a. For another reference to the importance of proximity in sustaining gentry friendships see *Ningbo fuzhi*, 26:31b.

36. *Yin xianzhi* 1788, 18:10b.

37. *Ningbo fuzhi*, 7a:26b, 30a–b; 7b:21a; 10:10b; 35:36a; *Yin xianzhi* 1788, 25:7a; *Dinghai xianzhi*, 6:10a (see also 12a, 15b).

38. *Ningbo fuzhi*, 20:45a; *Yin xianzhi* 1788, 27:39b.

39. Tu Long, 4: 14a.

40. *Yongshan Lu shi Jingmu Tang zongpu*, 3:2b.

41. Quan Zuwang 1803, 8:577.

42. Ibid., 8:600. The Discarded Silk Society also *excluded* those who collaborated with the new regime. Chai Degeng, 102.

43. *Yin xianzhi* 1877, 43:24a; Jiang Xueyong was a Heyi Jiang. For the "Eastern Zhejiang School," see Struve.

44. Concerning the Jiangjing Hui and Huang's relationship with the Dingyuan Wangs, see Elman, 115–117.

45. Wan Yan, 2:70a; *Ningbo fuzhi*, 26:26b; *Yin xianzhi* 1877, 41:32b.

46. Kuhn 1970, 215–216; Rankin 1986, 93–97; Min Tu-ki, chaps. 4–5. Kuhn has shown how the mobilization of local militias (*tuanlian*) against the Taipings made the power of the local gentry less informal. Gentry in Yin also formed anti-Taiping *tuanlian* (*Yin xianzhi* 1877, 44:33a).

47. Mann, 83. Gentry operation of markets in eighteenth- and nineteenth-century Shandong was confined to lower gentry, mainly *shengyuan* and *jiansheng*. Yamane Yukio, 558.

48. *Yin xianzhi* 1788, 29:27a.

49. *Yin xianzhi* 1877, 43:7a.

50. Rankin 1986, 106.

51. Zhou Rong, the leading Ningbo poet of the mid-seventeenth century, offered to take the place of his patron captured by pirates. The pirates accepted, then crippled Zhou to prevent him from escaping, which he later did anyway (*Ningbo fuzhi*, 26:26b).

52. *Yin xianzhi* 1877, 43:9b.

53. Gentry patronage of Buddhist monasteries is treated in Brook (forthcoming). Shiba Yoshinobu (1977, 423) points out that most non-Buddhist urban temples and shrines in Yin were under the patronage of commercial and residential groups rather than the gentry.

54. *Ningbo fuzhi*, 9:35b.

55. *Yin xianzhi* 1788, 2:4a.

56. *Ningbo fuzhi*, 35:28a, 36b; Zhou Daozun, 4:12b.

57. *Ningbo fuzhi*, 10:6b; *Yin xianzhi* 1877, 23:23b. Zhaoshen (cemetery benefactures list) could be a typographical error for Zhaojia (degree list).

58. Sasaki Masaya, 185–299; Liu Guangjing, 354–359; *Yinxian tongzhi*, 1:447b–448a.

59. By the nineteenth century, a lineage possessing one or two lower degrees had little hope of rising into the greater gentry. The term gentry is stretched too far if one includes, for instance, a family in a 1927 genealogy that shows the lineage had acquired no more than one or two *shengyuan* degrees every few generations since its most recent *juren* degree in 1489. *Yongshang Leigongqiao Wu shi jiapu, juan* 3.

60. Liu Guangjing, 359. After the magistrate left Yin for a subsequent posting, local people raised a shrine in his honor. It was also the site of sacrifices in memory of Zhou Xiangqian, whose uprising had prompted the magistrate to deal with the tax inequity.

61. Kobayashi Kazumi (223–224), commenting on the involvement of lower elites in tax resistance, uses Zhou as an example of "rectifying the unfairness of the tax assessment administered by the county magistrate," although he does not mention Zhou's personal interest.

NOTES TO CHAPTER TWO

Abbreviations

Feng (1946)	*Feng shi zongpu*, 1946
Gui (1935)	*Gui shi zongpu*, 1935
Han (1946)	*Han shi zongpu*, 1946
Lao (1755)	*Lao shi zupu*, 1755
Ling (1883)	*Ling shi zongpu*, 1883
Liu (1924)	*Liu shi zongpu*, 1924
Liu (1932)	*Liu shi zongpu*, 1932
Luo (1918)	*Hongshanmiao Luo shi zongpu*, 1918
Yao (1923)	*Hanyang Yao shi fangpu*, 1923
Yao (1930)	*Yao shi zongpu*, 1930
Ye (1873)	*Ye shi zongpu*, 1873
Zhang (1876)	*Zhang shi sanxiu jiapu*, 1876
Zhang (1921)	*Hanyang Zhang shi zongpu*, 1921
Zhang (1948)	*Zhang shi zongpu*, 1948

1. Throughout this chapter I follow Ebrey and Watson in using the term "lineage" to refer to a collection of agnates who were both conscious of their common descent and participated in some formal organizational structure on that basis. Although, as we shall see, all lineages discussed here had other organizational attributes as well, for my purposes the existence of a genealogy is itself sufficient demonstration of both collective consciousness and a minimal degree of organization. For my purposes the decision of the group to refer to itself as a "*zu*" or a "*zong*" (sometimes translated as "clan") is irrelevant. See Ebrey and Watson, "Introduction," 5–6.

2. See, for example, Beattie 1979b; Odoric Wou, 69–88.

3. Not all European elites practiced primogeniture, to be sure, and even in some regions where primogeniture predominated parents regularly found means to provide for daughters and younger sons, thus partially dividing their estate; see Goody, Thirsk, and Thompson, eds., 1976; Spring, ed., 1977. Nevertheless, it seems clear enough that partible inheritance was a far more general practice among the Chinese than the European elite. For one apparently exceptional area of China, see Rubie Watson's chapter in this volume.

4. The genealogies from adjacent counties are *Feng* (1946), *Gui* (1935), *Han* (1946), *Liu* (1924), *Zhang* (1948). The remaining nine, listed under "Abbreviations," are from Hanyang.

5. Except where specified, "Hanyang county" refers to the *xian* as it was constituted prior to the twentieth century. That is, it incorporates the city of Hankou, which was subsequently detached to become first a "special municipality" and then part of the combined metropolis of Wuhan. It also includes the area north of the Han River, which was detached in 1901 to form Xiakou county.

6. Taga Akigōrō 1960; Genealogical Society of Utah, ed., 1983.

7. This section is based on a wide range of evidence, some of which is reported in Rowe 1984 and Rowe 1989.

8. A late nineteenth-century source lists twenty-three important markets (*shiji*) in Hanyang county itself; *Guangxu Hubei yudi ji*, 5:22–23. For an enumeration of the major market towns in the broader Yangzi-Han confluence area as of 1800, see Zhang Xuecheng, 24:23–24. Representative of the burgeoning recent scholarship on lower Yangzi market towns is Fei Xiaotong, et al., vol. 1.

9. For example, *Ling* (1883), *juan* 3; *Liu* (1924), *juan* 1; *Luo* (1918), 20:1.

10. *Yao* (1923), 15:2; *Yao* (1930), 2:1; *Feng* (1946), *juan* 1; *Gui* (1935), *juan* 1; *Han* (1946), *juan* 1; *Liu* (1932), preface, 11; *Zhang* (1921), 1:9, 12, 22.

11. *Ye* (1873), 4:25, 32; 15:7; 16:1. On the history of the Ye, I am also able to draw upon two manuscript studies produced in the People's Republic based upon locally held family records: Wuhan Municipal Commercial Industrial Alliance, undated, and Wuhan Municipal Commercial Industrial Alliance 1965.

12. For a survey, see Beattie 1979b, chap. 1.

13. For a discussion of this term, which appears throughout our genealogies, see Johnson, 60. Johnson is possibly correct in viewing this term as a reference to a specific social type, but it is clear that it also more generally described a behavioral ideal.

14. *Luo* (1918), 20:3; *Yao* (1930), *juan* 1; *Liu* (1932), 1:24, 29. Similar stories appear in *Feng* (1946) and *Gui* (1935).

15. On the state of the agrarian ecology in this Hubei "interior delta" at the start of the Ming, see Will 1980b, 261–287.

16. *Ling* (1883), 1:9.

17. Mingay, 106.

18. "Jiahuitang," cited in Wuhan Municipal Commercial Industrial Alliance 1965.

19. *Yao* (1930), 2:1. For a case from Shanxi province at least as extreme as the Ye in this regard, see Rawski, 245–273.

20. *Yao* (1930), 6:6. For examples from western Europe, see Wilson, 145–172; Forster 1980.

21. *Yao* (1923), 4.1:11–13.

22. *Hanyang xianzhi* 1867, *juan* 16; *Yao* (1923), 3:2.

23. *Ye* (1873), 6:1–15; *Hanyang xianzhi* 1867, 18:60–61, 20:27; Hummel, ed., 904–905.

24. Ye Fengzhi was a purchased expectant Shaanxi daotai; his brother Mengzhi was expectant Nanjing daotai and domestic customs superintendent at Changsha; Ye Yongzhai was director of the Hubei Salt Bureau. See Wuhan Municipal Commercial Industrial Alliance 1965.

25. Ye descendents' return to direct management of commercial interests coincided with a second boom in store profits, following a Yekaitai employee's discovery of a means to package traditional herbal medicines in the form of Western-style pills. In 1896 three of Ye Mingzhen's grandchildren divided their patrimony: Mengzhi took control of medicine store operations; Xingzhong invested his share in a salt dealership; Fengzhi became a famous restaurateur and entrepreneur in Hankou and Shanghai. *Ye* (1873); Wuhan Municipal Commercial Industrial Alliance, undated.

26. *Zhang* (1921), 1:22, 1:23–27.

27. *Yao* (1923), 16:6.

28. *Yao* (1923), 14.1:7–8, 15:2–3.

29. Ray Huang, 287–288.

30. Taylor, 23–40.

31. *Yao* (1932), 14.1:7–11. On the general background of this evolution, see Hoshi Ayao.

32. *Yao* (1923), 14.1: 41, 15:3.

33. *Yao* (1923), 14.1:4–6, 32.

34. *Yao* (1923), 14.1:42–43, 15:2–3.

35. Tawney, 1941. For differing perspectives, see Mingay, 106, and Wilson, 152.

36. *Hanyang xianzhi* 1867, 18:60–61, 20:37. The biography of lineage founder Ye Tingfang, for example, cites as the reason for his move to Hanyang his inheritance of some "income-producing property" (*chanye*) there, neglecting to specify that this property was a commercial firm at Hankou.

37. Chung-li Chang 1962, 181.

38. *Liu* (1932), preface: 11–12, and "Shishiji," 15.

39. *Luo* (1918), *juan* 4, 5, 15.

40. *Yao* (1923), 14.1:7–8, 33, 37–40; *Hanyang xianshi*, 2:20.

41. *Yao* (1930), 2:1, 6:1–11.

42. *Luo* (1918), *juan* 5.

43. *Yao* (1923), 14.1:37–40; *Luo* (1918), 15:58; *Liu* (1932), preface, 3:29.

44. *Han* (1946). On the English case, see David Spring 1971, 16–62.

45. *Yao* (1923), 14.1:6; *Yao* (1930), 7.3:33; *Zhang* (1921), 4:1.

46. Fried, 287.

47. Hui-chen Wang Liu 1959a, 84.

48. Baker 1977, 500–501.

49. Rankin 1977; Mote, 103–116.

50. Skinner 1977b, 239–260.

51. *Hanyang xianzhi* 1818, 7:21.

52. *Yao* (1930), 6:10–11.

53. *Ling* (1883), *juan* 3, *Luo* (1918), *juan* 5, 11:54, 15:41, 20:34; *Zhang* (1948), 3:195–196, 7:188; *Liu* (1932), *juan* 1.

54. *Liu* (1924); *Han* (1946); *Feng* (1946).

55. Hankou was founded only in the 1460s, and a recent Chinese study has argued that a peculiarly repressive local administration prevented its significant commercial development until the Qing conquest. See Fan Zhiqing, 156–163.

56. Zelin (1986, 583) has noted a comparable phenomenon in the commercial metropolis of the Upper Yangzi, Chongqing. She writes: "The wealth generated in Chongqing city seems to have had surprisingly little impact on the rural economy of the Baxian hinterland before the 1890s. . . . The interpenetration of rural and urban elites seems to have been small. This is perhaps explained by the dominance of extraprovincials in Chongqing's export trade." In Chongqing, of course, the opening to Western trade, industrialization, and the national survival movement were all telescoped into a considerably shorter period of time than they were in Hankou; thus, the opening to rural elites in that city probably appeared more suddenly.

57. Sangren 1984.

58. Imahori 1953.

59. Hymes 1986b.

60. *Luo* (1918), 1:1–13; *Zhang* (1948), 1:55–60.

61. *Zhang* (1921), 1:9–11. The Zhang described their transcendent lineage as one of "common surname with different branches" (*tongxing zhiyi*) and "linked lineages under a single ancestral clan" (*hezu zuzong*). In Ebrey and Watson's terminology, the group was a "higher-order lineage."

62. *Zhang* (1921), 2:10, 4:1.

63. *Ye* (1873), 1:110, 2:1, 11, 3:6, 14, 4:1.

64. *Luo* (1918), 1:1; *Zhang* (1921), 1:10.

65. *Yao* (1923), 15:2–3.

66. Compare *Zhang* (1921), 1:12, with the same work, 2:10. For comparable cases from the Lower Yangzi, see Ueda, esp. 129–138.

67. For example, a Yao man whose *ming* was Xichong and *zi* was Shaolung, was listed in the genealogy as Yao Caishi, inasmuch as "cai" was his prescribed generational character.

68. *Zhang* (1876), *juan* 1; *Yao* (1930), *juan* 4.

69. *Liu* (1924), *juan* 1.

70. Ebrey 1986, 40.

71. In the absence of such land, a lineage might meet ritual expenses either by contributions or by regular assessments on member households; see *Liu* (1932), "Jiagui ji" (lineage rules), 2.

72. *Yao* (1923), 15:3; *Luo* (1918), *juan* 28. In typical fashion, the Luo school was converted in 1918 into a so-called "lineage-founded national modern school" (*zuli guomin xuexiao*).

73. Biography of Yao Guanghan in *Hanyang xianshi* 1867, 20:8–9.

74. *Yao* (1930), 5:1–3; *Yao* (1923), 15:3; *Luo* (1918), *juan* 28; *Liu* (1924), 16:27.

75. *Zhang* (1921), 2:10.

76. All estate lands were rural and located in Hanyang county. There were some thirty tenant households, whose average rent, payable in mixed cash and kind, amounted to less than one tael. About one-third of the tenant households were themselves Yao lineage members. *Yao* (1930), 5:3.

77. *Yao* (1930), 1:3.

78. *Luo* (1918), *juan* 5; *Liu* (1924).

79. *Zhang* (1948).

80. Curtin, 59–66.

81. Beattie 1979b:93–94, 114–115.

82. *Zhang* (1921), 2:10; *Liu* (1924), *juan* 1; *Yao* (1923), 15:2–3.

83. *Zhang* (1921), 1:10–11.

84. *Yao* (1923), 15:2–3.

85. *Zhang* (1921), 1:10–11. A similar instance from the Lower Yangzi is described in Dennerline 1979–80.

86. *Yao* (1923), 14.1:7–8, 41–46.

87. For example, *Hanyang xianzhi* 1867, 20:8–9, 16, 24; *Hanyang xianshi*, 2:20.

88. Lao Mouji, Ling Yulin, and Yao Yukuei, among others. *Hanyang xianzhi* 1867, 19:29–32.

89. Wuhan Municipal Commercial Industrial Alliance 1965.

90. *Hanyang xianzhi* 1867, 20:9; *Hanyang xianshi*, 2:14. The strategy of the mercantile Ye for acquiring cultural refinement is illuminating. Upon acquiring a rural estate near the market town of Huanglingji, they established a relationship with a local family named Hu of modest wealth but impeccable scholarly credentials. Thereafter, generations of Hu scholars served as household tutors for Ye children, in both the market town and Hankou.

91. *Ye* (1873), 16:1; *Yao* (1923), 14.1:33; Wang Baoxian, 2:11–15, 4:26–28.

92. Both Everitt (1966) in discussing the British "county community" and Hymes in discussing the "localist strategy" among Chinese elite lineages make their cases largely on the basis of marriage alliances among local elite families. Jerry Dennerline (1986), too, has spoken of the "community of affines" as a key element in local elite community. That Hanyang elite lineages similarly engaged in a pattern of systematic intermarriage is not unlikely, but our sources do not provide adequate data to draw meaningful conclusions on this subject.

93. For example, *Liu* (1932), preface; *Ling* (1883), *juan* 3; *Yao* (1923), 14.1:4, 39, 16:6. For a graphic example from another province of the *xiang* as horizon of collective action, see Winston Hsieh 1974.

94. Generalizing from local studies of Fujian, Fu Yiling has over many years developed an argument that elites, acting through lineage organizations at the *xiang* level, perpetuated local particularisms and exercised almost total domination over local society. Although my sources do not suggest anything like the level of severe exploitation implied in Fu's model, several factors he identifies as crucial to *xiangzu* hegemony—such as major roles in land reclamation and water conservancy projects—had clear parallels in Hanyang. See, for example, Fu Yiling 1982. For a summary and critique of Fu's ideas, see Mori Masao 1985.

95. *Guangxu Hubei yudi ji*, 5:23.

96. *Hanyang xian xiangtu* 1933.

97. *Hanyang xianzhi* 1867, 20:32.

98. Perdue 1986, 170, 173; Dennerline 1986, 177, 181–182; Beattie 1979b, 26–27.

99. Cited in Cannadine, 30.

100. Everitt, 70–72.

NOTES TO CHAPTER THREE

1. Yan Ruyi, 10:7.

2. This extreme administrative bifurcation was implemented in 1730. *Fushun xianzhi*, 1:7b. However, the Gongjing saltyard appears to have been under independent administration from time to time during earlier dynasties as well.

3. Qiao Fu, 2.

4. Ibid., 205.

5. Jiang Xiangcheng and Luo Xiaoyuan, 108, 125.

6. Luo Xiaoyuan 1984, 63–64. Qiao Fu (187) claims that the best sing-song girls were leaving Chongqing for Fu-Rong because business was better there.

7. In his chapter on Ziliujing's "gentry" (*shishen*), Qiao Fu (185) makes this explicit: "There is no distinction made between merchants and gentry at Ziliujing. There are many illustrious gentry, too numerous to name them all. Today I will just name a few representative ones." A list of the most powerful merchants of his day follows. The gazetteers of Fushun and Rongxian label powerful members of the salt-yard elite as *changshen* or "yard gentry."

8. Zigongshi dang'anguan, 22–23. Special thanks to Douglas Rankin for clarifying this process.

9. Ran Guangrong and Zhang Xuejun 1984, 1–3. For a discussion of the technological breakthrough embodied in the "lofty pipe" wells, see Paul Smith (57–58) and Liu Chunyuan.

10. Ran Guangrong and Zhang Xuejun 1981, 541.

11. Brine wells dug to between 1,200 and 1,300 Chinese feet were known as "yellow-brine" wells and produced brine with a salinity of approximately 13 percent. The shallowest "black-brine" wells, at least 1,600 feet deep, could run as much as 2,800 feet. These wells produced brine that was 18 percent salt. Li Rong, 230–231; Xu Dixin amd Wu Chengming, eds., 591. For a detailed discussion of technological improvements in the salt industry during the Qing period, see Ran Guangrong and Zhang Xuejun 1984; 53–78; *Sichuan yanfaxhi, juan* 2 and 3.

12. Entenmann, 59.

13. G. William Skinner has estimated that Sichuan's population grew from at the most 3 million in 1673 to 28.5 million in 1853 because of both natural increase and large-scale immigration, primarily from Hunan, Hubei, Jiangxi, and Guangdong. Skinner 1987, 62–66.

14. Zhou Xun, *juan* 1.

15. Jian-Le was a combined appellation for the neighboring Jianwei and Leshan yards. Increased *yin* quotas in more productive areas and legalized transfer of *yin* quotas belonging to other yards (*zengyin gaipei*) were originally introduced in response

to the drying up of northern Sichuan wells. Yan Ruyi, 13. By the end of the nineteenth century Fu-Rong was producing more than 58 percent of Sichuan's total official quota of salt. Figures given to Alexander Hosie by the Sichuan salt commissioner placed taxed salt from Fu-Rong at 137,100,000 kilograms a year as compared to 234,743,610 kilograms for the province as a whole. Estimates of smuggled salt range from 10 percent to 50 percent of the legal total. Hosie, 181–182.

16. Fu-Rong appears to have been the main beneficiary of the opening of the Huguang market, although smaller salt yards, some of which had been threatened with closure during the early nineteenth century, were able to reopen and serve domestic Sichuan needs. Lu Zijian, 80. By the 1860s, production in Fu-Rong had expanded to such an extent that both Huguang and many domestic markets switched to purchase of its salt.

17. According to Li Rong's *Ziliujing ji*, several hundred families were prominent in the salt business in the late Qing. Li Rong, 234.

18. A popular ditty in Fu-Rong during the Qing went, "If you're not named Wang, if you're not named Li, then old man, I'm not afraid of thee." Qiao Fu, 186.

19. According to Entenmann (161), 94 percent of lineages that emigrated to Sichuan during the Ming came from Huguang, and two-thirds of these came from Macheng.

20. *Fushun Ziliujing Zhenzhushan Wangshi Baoshan ci sixiu jiapu, juan* 1.

21. *Lishi jiapu, juan* 1.

22. Li Zilin et al. 1962, 145–146.

23. *Lishi zupu, juan* 4. This state of affairs is implied in the biographical section of the Qianlong genealogy: the Lis rebuild their home and drill new wells on land that had previously belonged to someone else. In at least one instance, the return of the original landlord forced the family to relocate and begin drilling anew. *Lishi zupu, juan* 9.

24. Very little information exists on the Yans. A number of surviving funerary inscriptions describe the founder of the lineage hall, Yan Changying, and his brother as experts in locating brine deposits and drilling on what may have been their own land. Song Lanxi, 36–37. For the Hus, see Hu Shaoquan, 49–51

25. According to a former manager at the Gongjing yard, Hu Yuanhe was the only Gongjing salt merchant to own and operate wells without partners. Ji Runqing, 187.

26. Lai Minqin et al., 39. Luo Xiaoyuan, one of the great twentieth-century salt magnates, used this method to develop furnaces. A tael was approximately one ounce of silver.

27. Hu Shaoquan, 50.

28. For a detailed discussion of partnership contracts at Fu-Rong, see Zelin 1988.

29. Wang Shouji, *juan xia*.

30. The text of the stele is quoted in Xu Dixin and Wu Chengming, eds., 603. Yan Ruyi, *juan* 10:13.

31. Zhang Xiaomei, ed., 4:50, 52. See also Tian Maode 56–72, and Ouyang Yuemou et al., 146–155.

32. Some individual contributions were over 3,000 taels. See the stele com-

memorating these repairs, now in the Zigong museum of the history of the salt industry housed in the old guild hall. Cited in Ling Yaolun, 80.

33. Ran Guangrong and Zhang Xuejun 1980, 31.

34. There is little evidence of how profits were used. The 1937 edition of the *Santai xianzhi* (*juan* 12) notes that both pawnshops in the district were opened by Shaanxi merchants in 1697 and that "they took high interest. Every year the amount they sent back to Shaanxi was unlimited." There is also some evidence that they invested in land in the province.

35. *Qingchao xuwenxian tongkao*, 37:9.

36. Shu Wencheng et al., 39–40. The date of this strike is not given, but from internal evidence it must have been sometime in the 1850s.

37. In tracing the history of various districts within the Fu-Rong yard, Huang Ziqing and Nie Wufang (251–257) have identified numerous wells established by Shaanxi merchant investment. See also Ling Yaolun, 81.

38. Huang Zhiqing and Nie Wufang, 256.

39. This discussion is based largely on information in Luo Xiaoyuan 1963.7 and 1963.8 passim.

40. Well-drilling partnerships based on the lease of land to individual and group investors was common by this time. The earliest surviving limited tenure lease of a well site in Fu-Rong is dated 1779. Zigongshi dang'anguan, ed., 309–310. For a detailed study of the evolution of brine-well partnerships and the gradual reduction in the power of the landlord in these arrangements, see Zelin 1988.

41. According to a memoir of this lineage's history, these wells produced no more than several tens of *dan* a day each. (A *dan* was approximately 50 kilograms.) Li Zilin et al. 1962, 147.

42. Ibid., 147–148.

43. For salt sales, see *Sichuan yanfazhi*, cited in Lu Zijian, 78. For salt-cotton trade, see Luo Xiaoyuan 1963, 7:167.

44. Lu Zijian, 77.

45. The role of the Taiping Rebellion in altering the nexus of commerical power in China's main economic centers deserves far more attention than it has received. One of the best treatments of this issue is found in Rowe 1984, 78, 118–120.

46. *Sichuan guanyun yan'an leipian*, 34:21, cited in Lu Zijian, 79.

47. For an excellent discussion of the role of much older lineage trusts in the establishment of elite dominance, see Rubie Watson's essay in this volume. William Rowe's essay in this volume provides a counterexample of merchant lineage trusts whose interests continued to be linked to traditional goals and whose properties were limited and largely restricted to land.

48. *Lishi zupu, juan* 15.

49. Li Zilin et al. 1962, 146; 1963, 193.

50. Hu Shaoquan, 51, 56–57.

51. Ibid., 56.

52. An ancestral hall was founded in 1759, but it appears poorly endowed and served largely ritual purposes. *Fushun Ziliujing Zhenzhushan Wangshi jiapu*, preface.

53. The provisions of the lineage trust rules as outlined in the memorial to the emperor may be found in Luo Xiaoyuan 1963, 7:176–177.

54. The Santai academy (*shuyuan*) was one of five academies in Fu-Rong during

the Qing period. A separate and considerably smaller school, the Yucai Academy, was established during the early Guangxu reign to educate members of the Wang lineage. Hu Shanquan and Luo Xiaoyuan 1984, 198–190.

55. Luo Xiaoyuan 1963, 7:176–177.

56. This estimate is based on a survey of the signatories to 845 contracts in Zigongshi dang'anguan, ed. According to these editors, approximately 3,000 contracts, many of which are duplicates, are in the Archives.

57. For the history of the Wu Jingrang lineage trust, see Zhang Duanfu 1979, 1980.

58. Aspects of the business management structures described here were probably adapted from those utilized by the Shaanxi merchants, whose presence was so strong at the salt yard. Hu Shaoquan, 56.

59. Luo Xiaoyuan 1963, 8:185–186, 191.

60. Li Zilin et al. 1962, 152–154.

61. This instability was less a product of consumer demand than of politics. During the Taiping Rebellion a relatively free market existed for Sichuan salt. Following its suppression and the restoration of communications between Huguang and eastern China, an effort was made to restore the Lianghuai salt producers' control over the central Chinese market by demarcating salt territories and differentiating taxation. At the same time, rebellions in Yunnan and Guizhou continued to disrupt salt sales there. In 1872, a new system of salt administration known as *guanyun shangxiao*, official transport and merchant sale, interposed a governmental purchasing agency between producer and wholesaler; this truncated the Sichuan salt market, with a deleterious effect on the large lineage-based salt firms. For a detailed discussion of the system of official transport and merchant sale, see Wu Duo 1971.

62. Li Zilin et al. 1962, 151–152.

63. Hu Shaoquan, 78–79.

64. Luo Xiaoyuan 1963, 8:187–188, 189. For a discussion of the role of gas rental in allowing furnace operators to respond quickly to changing market conditions, see Zelin 1988.

65. Luo Xiaoyuan and Jiang Xiangcheng 1983, 135, 139.

66. Lin Zhenhan, 2, 9:248; *Sichuan yanjing shi, juan* 3, *pian* 2, *zhang* 10, *jie* 1:69 and *jie* 2:79; Luo Xiaoyuan 1981, 187.

67. The Wang Sanwei lineage trust was authorized to sell approximately 12 percent of the quota of licensed salt in this market. Luo Xiaoyuan 1963, 8:190.

68. For the Wangs, see Luo Xiaoyuan 1963, 8:190–191. For the Hus, see Hu Shaoquan, 53. For the Lis, see Ma Fangbo, 274.

69. Luo Xiaoyuan 1963, 8:187. The lineage regulations of the Wang Hele lineage trust, one of the largest landlords in the Jianwei yard, stipulated that its members could sell the land under its wells and furnaces, but not the wells and furnaces themselves. Ran Guangrong and Zhang Xuejun 1984, 232.

70. Luo Xiaoyuan 1963, 8:187.

71. Jiang Xiangcheng and Luo Xiaoyuan, 119.

72. The Lis, with the longest history of continuous residence in Fu-Rong, counted among their number many officials and degree holders during the late Ming and early Qing. However, by the mid-Qing, they, too, appear to have concentrated family resources largely on profits from salt. Rowe (this volume) notes a similar phe-

nomenon in Hubei. This retreat from examination-based status among the most successful merchant families may have affected the performance of the region as a whole.
Whereas the Lower Basin produced an average of 35.6 percent of Sichuan's *jinshi*
during the Ming and early Qing, between 1706 and 1814 (the last year for which we
have complete provincial figures) that share fell to 21.7 percent. See Smith, 22. On
the increase in the number of upper-degree holders from this region after 1865, see
Fushun xianzhi, juan 10.

73. *Fushun xianzhi*, 8:20a–34b.

74. Luo Xiaoyuan 1963, 7:170. The nephew was also granted a posthumous
hereditary rank of a low order.

75. For a discussion of the effect of the Taiping on the composition of the
bureaucratic elite in China, see Chang Chung-li 1955, 71–141.

76. *Sichuan yanfazhi, juan* 11:6. These were Yichang and Sashi in Hubei.

77. Wang Shouji, 20–22.

78. For a full account of this protest, see Luo Xiaoyuan 1963, 7:171–173.

79. Manyin [pseud.], 18–19. In this version Wang Langyun donates 200,000
taels to help China build a modern navy and 10,000 taels to famine relief.

80. Luo Xiaoyuan 1963, 7:174–176.

81. Li Zilin et al. 1963, 195, 200. This Li Siyou member was Li Xinzhu, a *juren* of
1874. *Fushun xianzhi*, 12:53b.

82. Luo Xiaoyuan 1963, 8:185–186.

83. Hu Shaoquan, 59, 60–61.

84. For the Fu-Rong gentry, see Qiao Fu, 185. The Chongqing figure is based on
a survey of merchant lawsuits housed in the Baxian archives, Sichuan Provincial
Archives. Although I was not able to see all the merchant lawsuits available for the
period, a random sample of more than four hundred cases reveals a distinct pattern of
degree purchase among resident urban merchants. These men were by no means as
wealthy as the salt merchants discussed here.

85. Luo Xiaoyuan 1963, 7:173, 196; Hu Shaoquan, 63–67; Li Zilin 1963, 195–
196; Qiao Fu, 201.

86. E.g., a daughter of Wang Dazhi is said to have married a *jinshi* degree holder
from Fushun. Luo Xiaoyuan 1963, 8:196. Available genealogical records for the Li
and Wang lineages do not give sufficient data to undertake a detailed examination of
marriage strategies.

87. *Fushun xianzhi, juan* 3, 12; *Rong xianzhi, juan* 2.

88. Hu Shaoquan, 65; *Fushun xianzhi*, 12:53b.

89. Ibid.

90. Qiao Fu, 36.

91. Wang Roude, 24; Qiao Fu, 201. Among the salt merchants known to have
had personal guards ranging from several dozen to over a hundred men were Wang
Sufeng of the Wang Sanwei *tang*, Li Xingqiao of the Li Siyou *tang*, Wang Hefu of the
Wang Baoxinglong and Zhang Xiaopo and Huang Dunsan.

92. Keith Schoppa (1973, 17–20) has shown that a majority of those involved in
public service were nondegree holders like the merchants examined here.

93. The most striking example is Li Bozhai, discoverer of the rock-salt layer,
whose son was a leader of the Ren banner of the Elder Brother Society and who
himself joined the Catholic church at the turn of the century. Luo Xiaoyuan 1981,

94–97. Secret society membership appears to have gained in importance during the Republican period when the means to political authority ceased to be as clear as during the Qing.

94. For an excellent treatment of reconstruction as the foundation for later elite cooperation and mobilization, see Rankin 1986, 93–135.

95. E.g., Li Zilin et al. 1963, 193–194, 210; Hu Shaoquan, 70.

96. Luo Xiaoyuan 1963, 8:196.

97. Zhang Xuejun, 12; Wang Roude and Zhong Langhua, comp., 1985, 93–96.

98. Hu Shaoquan, 68; Luo Xiaoyuan 1963, 8:195.

99. Zhang Xuejun 1983, 12–16.

100. Li Zilin et al. 1962, 166–167.

101. For a discussion of the rock-salt layer, see Lai Mingqin, 3–52. Brine pumped from rock-salt wells had an average saline content of 25 percent; Xu Dixin and Wu Chengming, 591. On the pumps, see Yang Duxing et al., 148.

102. Ji Runqing, 189–190.

103. The large lineage trusts continued to control pipes within Ziliujing. In the 1920s, with the help of the Li Siyou lineage trust, newcomer Zhang Xiaopo constructed a new pipe that operated by charging well owners a simple fee for transporting their brine. Other pipe owners were forced to follow suit, allowing direct dealings between brine producers and gas furnace operators. This marked the end of brine-pipe power in the economy of the yard. Luo Xiaoyuan and Jiang Xiangcheng 1983, 141–142; Luo Xiaoyuan 1981, 188–189.

104. By the 1920s most Wang Sanwei lineage trust holdings were being operated by the Chongqing-Shashi credit group, to which it owed almost 650,000 taels. Luo Xiaoyuan 1963, 8:201. The Li Siyou trust alienated most of its salt holdings by 1931 in order to clear debts and provide an income for its members. Li Zilin 1963, 208–210.

NOTES TO CHAPTER FOUR

Abbreviation

Mantetsu   Minami Manshū tetsudō kabushiki kaisha, Shanghai jimusho chōsashitsu (Shanghai Research Office of the South Manchurian Railway Company)

1. Bergère 1983.

2. The Jiangnan region and Wuxi's place within it are described in detail below.

3. For the relationship between social structure and economic development in Wuxi, see Bell, draft ms.

4. Bourdieu 1977; Sahlins 1981, 1985. See also the review of recent anthropological theorists by Ortner 1984.

5. A useful summary of these developments in the Jiangnan region is found in Elvin 1973.

6. The following discussion of changing landholding patterns and land tenure practices in Jiangnan in the Ming and Qing periods is based on some of the most important interpretative articles published by Japanese scholars; a summary and

review of much of this literature written by American scholars Linda Grove and Joseph Esherick; and an extensive reevaluation of Qing land tenure patterns by American scholar Kathryn Bernhardt. See notes 7–10 below.

7. Shigeta Atsushi, esp. 350–366; Grove and Esherick, 404–408; Bernhardt, chap. 1.

8. Oyama Masaaki, esp. 136–147; Grove and Esherick, 404–408; Bernhardt, chap. 1.

9. Shigeta Atsushi, 336–379; Oyama Masaaki, 147–150; Grove and Esherick, 408–419; Bernhardt, chap. 1.

10. Bernhardt, chap. 1, esp. 35–42

11. Perkins, 140–151; Shehui jingji yanjiusuo, ed., preface and 1–2.

12. Liu Shiji, esp. 58–68, 120–127.

13. Ping-ti Ho 1962, 81.

14. Rankin 1986, esp. chaps. 2 and 3.

15. Ping-ti Ho 1962, 73–77; Chung-li Chang 1962, 150–151.

16. Rankin (1986, 17–21) provides an excellent discussion of the role of the *shendong*.

17. Ching-Chih Sun et al., 4, 98; Mantetsu 1940, 69–73; Kōain kachū renrakubu, 795–796.

18. On the Qing grain tribute system, see Hinton, 1–15. On Wuxi's role, see Shehui jingji yanjiusuo, preface and 1–2. For a general discussion of Wuxi's development as a major rice marketing center in Qing times, see Wuxi difangzhi bianji weiyuanhui, ed., 36–40.

19. On population growth in Jiangsu as a whole, see Perkins, 202–209. Population figures for Wuxi are derived from taxation records found in *Wuxi Jinkui xianzhi*, *juan* 8 and 9, and suggest a rise from 270,621 in 1726 to 1,075,323 by 1795. This is an improbably rapid rate of growth (approximately fourfold within a seventy-year period), reflecting underreporting before 1712 because potential taxpayers tried to keep their names off registers then used for taxes on both land and adult males. An imperial decree in 1712 resulted in the gradual merging of the head and land taxes, and by midcentury, we can assume that taxation records reflect real population more closely. A second problem is that the taxation rolls record only taxable males. I assume that taxable males made up about 53 percent of the population, a figure reported for Songjiang prefecture neighboring Wuxi. For the Songjiang figures, see Liang Fangzhong, 440–441.

20. *Xi-Jin shi xiaolu*, 6–7.

21. Dennerline 1988:76, 91–93.

22. Dennerline 1986, 171–181, 190–192; Dennerline 1979–80, 23, 27, 31–34; Dennerline 1988, 98–102.

23. Dennerline 1988, 102.

24. Ibid., 104–105.

25. Zhang Kai 1979, 54, states that Jiangyin, Wujin, Yixing, Liyang, and Changshou all became important new sericulture districts during this period. Also, a Mantetsu report discusses the growing importance of these counties as a new sericulture region in contrast to the older areas south of Lake Tai. Mantetsu 1940, 71–73; Kōain kachū renrakubu, 795–796.

26. Zhang Kai 1979, 54; Ching-chih Sun et al., 98; Mantetsu 1940, 69–73; Kōain kachū renrakubu, 795–796.

27. Bell 1985a, chap. 2; Bell 1985b; Bell, forthcoming. In these works, I use a Mantetsu survey study conducted in three Wuxi villages in 1940, to present a detailed analysis of small-peasant-family farming in Wuxi and the role of sericulture in that system. The data from this survey are found in Mantetsu 1941. Preliminary findings from a second survey study of 1,200 farming households in Wuxi conducted in 1929 by the Social Science Research Institute of the Academia Sinica also appear in Bell, forthcoming. These materials are cited in the bibliography as Guoli zhongyang yanjiuyuan shehui kexue yanjiusuo 1929. A more comprehensive analysis of this second set of materials will be found in Bell, draft ms.

28. Li Wenzhi 1981.

29. Rankin 1986, esp. chaps. 2 and 3.

30. Zhang Kai 1979, 53–54; *Wuxi Jinkui xianzhi*, 31:1.

31. Zhang Kai 1979, 53–54; Dongnan daxue nongke, ed., 2:26; *Gongshang banyuekan*, 2.15 (Aug. 1, 1930): investigation sec., 3.

32. Yan Jinqing, ed., 10:9; Gao Jingyue and Yan Xuexi, 4.

33. Zhang Kai 1979, 53.

34. *Wuxi Jinkui xianzhi*, 31:1.

35. Lu Guanying, 45; *Gongshang banyuekan*, 2.15 (Aug. 1, 1930): investigation sec., 3.

36. My analysis has benefited from Philip Huang's (1985) demonstration of a close relationship between population growth, labor intensification, and evolving class relationships in villages on the North China plain. Although the situation in Jiangnan was not identical, small-peasant-family farming in Wuxi reveals striking similarities in the correlation between demographic growth, parcelization of land-holdings, and an increasingly downward spiral of social differentiation among the peasantry.

37. Mantetsu 1941, 103–104.

38. On grain purchase by Wuxi peasant families, see Mantetsu 1941, 144–145. On the role of cash income in this process, see Mantetsu 1941, Table 15, 109.

39. Cadastral figures in gazetteers indicate 598,483 recorded taxpayers in 1830. In 1865, this number had dropped to 210,061. See *Wuxi Jinkui xianzhi*, 8:6–7; these figures are also cited in Li Wenzhi, ed., 1957, 1:151.

40. Accounts of poor migrants from northern Jiangsu coming to Wuxi and other counties south of the Yangzi abound in the periodical literature of the early twentieth century. E.g., Chen Yi, 34; Xue Muqiao, 58–60.

41. Mantetsu 1941, 88–89, 103–104. For descriptions of women working in sericulture, see Rong An, 113; and Mao Tun [Mao Dun], 1–26. For a fuller discussion of the female role in sericulture in Wuxi, see Bell 1985a, chap. 2.

42. Chen Huayin, 44–48.

43. Mantetsu 1941, 23.

44. Dwight Perkins (114–115, 300–301) has argued that the minimum subsistence requirements for grain consumption in China in the early twentieth century were approximately 400 *jin* per year. In the Mantetsu-surveyed villages, the average yearly rice consumption per adult villager was 312 *jin*. Wuxi peasants supplemented their

diets with broad beans and peas, which were both locally grown (see food purchase tables in Guoli zhongyang yanjiuyuan shehui kexue yanjiusuo). These calculations for Wuxi are made from data in Mantetsu 1940, 144–149, and Table 1. See also Bell (forthcoming) for a fuller discussion of minimum subsistence requirements.

45. *Jiangnan shangwu bao*, 9 (Apr. 21, 1900): commercial raw materials sec., 2; *Minguo ribao*, May 21, 1916, 3, 10; May 11, 1921, 3, 11; June 5, 1921, 2, 8; Sun Guoqiao, 985; Dongnan daxue nongke, 1:6, 2:49; Dier lishi dang'anguan, file no. 3504, subfile: 4.

46. Extensive data on debt are found in the Academia Sinica's 1929 survey of Wuxi (Guoli zhongyang yanjiuyuan shehui kexue yanjiusuo). Preliminary findings show that most peasant households in the villages surveyed had one or more loans at 20 percent yearly interest rates, and/or had mortgaged a portion of their land at average annual rental rates of 50 percent or more of its market value. Moreover, data in this survey also show a high rate of cocoon crop failure, an important factor contributing to accumulating debt.

47. The dispersion of cocoon firm facilities in many market town locations is documented in *Xi-Jin xiangtu dili* and also in Dier lishi dang'anguan, file no. 3242, subfile no. 32472.

48. *Xi-Jin xiangtu dili*, vol. 1, sec. 34; *Jiangsu sheng gongbao*, May 16, 1923, 2–3; Gao Jingyue interview; *Kaihua xiangzhi*, 1:52–53.

49. Wuxi difangzhi bianji weiyuanhui, 56–58; Qian Zhonghan 1961:123–125; *Xi-Jin xiangtu dili*, 2, sec. 3. Qian Zhonghan has also provided more specific details on Zhou Shunqing's cocoon firms and his role in new, locally based political organizations such as the Wuxi Chamber of Commerce and Agricultural Association during the New Policies period. See Qian Zhonghan 1983.

50. Qian Zhonghan 1961, 126; Wuxi difangzhi bianji weiyuanhui, 42.

51. Shanghai shehui kexueyuan jingji yanjiusuo, ed., 3–8.

52. *Gongsuo* was used since the latter Ming dynasty to refer to organizations that represented merchants in a given locale who participated in the same trade in contrast to *huiguan*, organizations of men from the same native place sojourning in the same city. For the early history of *gongsuo* and other forms of merchant organizations, see Fang Mingzhu 1963. For post-Opium War developments in *gongsuo* activity, see Peng Zeyi 1965.

53. Tōa dobunkai, 535.

54. Ibid.

55. Gao Jingyue, a former filature manager in Wuxi and member of the Wuxi People's Political Consultative Congress, makes the related point that when borrowing funds for silk filature operation, the "social standing" of the borrower was of crucial importance. See Gao 1983, 106.

56. For a detailed accounting of the types of contracts used and the responsibilities undertaken by comprador agents and cocoon firm owners, see Bell 1985a, 170–180. See also Lillian Li, 177–78.

57. I received a photographed copy of this contract from Zhang Kai, a Chinese scholar who has studied China's silk industry (interview, October 11, 1980).

58. Gao Jingyue interview; Zhang Kai interview. An interview with Xu Ruliang (May 24, 1980), a member of the Wuxi People's Political Consultative Congress

formerly involved in the Wuxi silk industry, confirmed this interpretation of the structure of the early cocoon firm system, claiming that "landlords" were the key link at the local level. Another Japanese source states that "wealthy rural folk" fulfilled this role. See Mantetsu 1940, 794–795.

59. Gao Jingyue 1980, 105.

60. A fuller accounting of cocoon merchant guild activities is found in Bell 1985a, 181–200.

61. For a discussion of "symbolic capital," see Bourdieu, chap. 4, esp. 171–183.

62. I am grateful to Yung-fa Chen for pointing out that gentry members often chose the name *wenshe* for organizations devoted to community service and local management activities.

63. *Kaihua xiangzhi*, 1:52–57. In the twentieth century, the adjective "foreign" continued to be used by the peasantry to describe individuals from the local elite involved in various aspects of silk industry development. When sericulture extension station workers, young female members of the local elite, went into the countryside in the 1920s and 1930s, peasants stood in their doorways gawking, calling these strangers who passed by "foreign teachers." Once again, we see that peasants used this term to indicate their growing awareness of the relationship between local elite management and the export-oriented silk industry. Fei Dasheng interview (May 18, 1981).

64. *Kaihua xiangzhi*, 1:52–57.

65. Gao Jingyue interview.

66. Ibid.

67. Ibid.

68. To petition for military protection from the naval police for boats carrying cocoons and cash was the first point in a list of guild functions Gao Jingyue provided in his interview. See Bell 1985a, 185. A sample of a provincial governor's response to a similar sort of petition by the joint guild organization of silk producers in Jiangsu, Zhejiang, and Anhui is found in *Jiangsu sheng gongbao*, May 11, 1923, 1–4. Newspaper and periodical accounts of cocoon marketing activity from the teens and twenties also discuss petitions from this joint guild and other merchant groups to the provincial governments in the region for military protection. See *Minguo ribao*, April 19, 1916, 2, 8; April 29, 1917, 3, 10, May 12, 1917, 3, 10; May 15, 1917, 2, 7, 3, 10; May 24, 1917, 3, 10. An extensive collection of original reports and petitions on cocoon marketing protection, including detailed discussions of why commerce should be protected, is in Dier lishi dang'anguan, file no. 3233. A newspaper account of May 1917 also reports that the Jiangsu provincial governor had instructed the Wuxi county magistrate to dispatch naval and land troops to protect areas in which there was cocoon marketing activity; see *Minguo ribao*, May 24, 1917, 2, 7. For the most part, the task of protection seems to have fallen to the naval police in each county where cocoon marketing took place. See *Jiangsu shiye yuezhi*, 67 (Oct. 1924):4–5.

69. Institute of Pacific Relations, ed., 1939b, 237–238. Translated from Qian Zhaoxiong, "Shangye ziben caozongxia de Wuxi cansang" (Wuxi sericulture under the control of commercial capital), *Zhongguo nongcun*, 1.4 (Jan. 1935):73–74.

70. *Minguo ribao*, May 25, 1917, 3, 10; June 4, 1917, 2, 7; June 5, 1917, 3, 10.

71. Ibid., June 5, 1917, 3, 10.

72. A vivid example of spontaneous peasant violence related to cocoon marketing is a 1929 incident where peasants became so angered over silkworm egg price manipulation that they began smashing equipment in the offices of a local sericulture cooperative. The assistance of the local ward head (*quzhang*) was sought in order to settle this dispute. See *Nongkuang gongbao*, 11 (May 1, 1929):73–75; 19 (Jan. 1, 1930):9–10; 21 (Mar. 1, 1930):28–29. Also see Bell 1985a, 240–245, for a detailed account of this incident and its political ramifications.

73. Although sources vary slightly, many cite approximately fifty filatures in Wuxi in the late 1920s. The reason for this variation is that filatures once built were rarely kept open continuously; they were rented only on a yearly basis according to market conditions for raw silk. Sources on Wuxi filatures include: Tōa kenkyujō, ed., 132–133, 142–146; *Wuxi shizheng*, 2 (Nov. 1, 1929):107–113; Wuxi shizheng choubei chu, 121–123; *Wuxi nianjian*: industry sec., 12–21; Mantetsu 1940, 79–80; Wuxi difangzhi bianji weiyuanhui, 42; Lu Guanying, 46–47; and Dier lishi dang'anguan, file no. 3242, subfile no. 32472. Similar problems exist for determining the exact number of cocoon firms in operation at any give time. From 1910 through the early 1930s, the reported number of licensed cocoon firms in Wuxi rose from 217 to 373. For numbers of cocoon firms in operation in Wuxi and other Jiangnan locales, see Tōa dobunkai, 528, 538–557; *Jiangsu shiye yuezhi*, 15 (June 1920):74–75; *Nongkuang gongbao*, 3 (Oct. 1, 1928): cocoon firm tables following 48; *Wuxi nianjian*: commerce sec. 28–37; and Dier lishi dang'anguan, file no. 3242, subfile no. 32472.

74. Although this statement is at odds with much prior research on the Nationalist government's role in promoting economic development, my research indicates that, at least in intent, its role was positive. See Bell 1985a, chaps. 3–5.

75. Wuxi difangzhi bianji weiyuanhui, 41–42, 57; Qian Zhonghan 1961, 123–126; Lü Huantai interview (May 24, 1980); Dier lishi dang'anguan, file No. 3242, subfile no. 32472.

76. For Xue's economic activities in Wuxi, see Wuxi difangzhi bianji weiyuanhui, 41–43; Qian Zhonghan 1961, 126–127; and Lü Huantai interview. For Xue's political roles, see *Gongshang banyuekan*, 3.2 (Jan. 15, 1931): commercial and industrial news sec., 7–9; *Jiangsu jianshe yuekan*, 2.3 (March 1935): report sec., 57–88; and Zhang Youyi, ed., 165.

77. Shanghai shehui kexueyuan jingji yanjiusuo, 8; Qian Zhonghan 1961, 127.

78. Lü Huantai interview; Qian Zhonghan 1961, 127; Wuxi difangzhi bianji weiyuanhui, 42.

79. On the "split ownership/management" system of filature operation, see *Gongshang banyuekan*, 2.1 (Jan. 1, 1930): investigation sec., 2–5; Zhuang Yaohe interview (May 27, 1980); Chūshi kensetsu shiryō seibi jimusho, ed., 42–43; Chen Tingfang, 113; *Nongshang gongbao*, 3.9 (April 15, 1917): special reports sec., 14–15; Wuxi difangzhi bianji weiyuanhui, 45–46; and Mantetsu 1940, 85–86. On problems for Chinese silk competing with its Japanese counterpart, see Lillian Li, 87; Yan Xuexi, 1; and Zhou Kuangming interview (Nov. 8 and 13, 1980).

80. Lü Huantai interview; Qian Zhonghan 1961, 127; Wuxi difangzhi bianji weiyuanhui, 42; *Shenbao*, May 6, 1934.

81. Qian Zhonghan 1961, 127; Wuxi difangzhi bianji weiyuanhui, 43; Shen Wenwei, 34; Lü Huantai interview; Wu Yaming interview (Nov. 7, 1980).

82. For the establishment of the Yongtai sericulture affairs office, see Hua Yin-chun, 17; Wu Yaming interview. On problems for filatures in maintaining an ade-quate cocoon supply, see Yin Liangying, 12; Wuxi difangzhi bianji weiyuanhui, 41; Mantetsu 1940, 94; *Yinhang zhoubao*, 3.34 (Sept. 3, 1929): weekly commerce sec., 2–3, and 3.37 (Sept. 24, 1929): weekly commerce sec., 4; *Gongshang banyuekan*, 2.17 (Sept. 1, 1930): legislation sec., 4–6; *Shenbao* (Jan. 19, 1937); 4, 14.

83. Kong Fanlin, 72–73; *Gongshang banyuekan*, 2.3 (Feb. 1, 1930): commercial news sec., 16, and 4.19 (Oct. 1, 1932): national economy sec., 1–2; He Bingxian, 18; Chūshi kensetsu shiryō seibi jimusho, 40.

84. Okumura Satoshi, 247.

85. *Gongshang banyuekan*, 3.2 (Jan. 15, 1931): commercial and industrial news sec., 7–9; He Bingxian, 20; Kong Fanlin, 72–73; *Gongshang banyuekan*, 3.10 (May 15, 1931): legislation sec., 8–9; *Nongye zhoubao*, 71 (Feb. 22, 1931):625–627; Okumura Satoshi, 246; and Dier lishi dang'anguan, file no. 1328. For a full discussion of the bond program, see Bell 1985a, 271–275.

86. *Gongshang banyuekan*, 3.2 (Jan. 15, 1931): commercial and industrial news sec., 7–9, and *Nongye zhoubao*, 71 (Feb. 22, 1931):625–627. Xue Shouxuan's designa-tion as "silk industry magnate" is found in Ku Nong 1937a, 103, and 1937b, 62–70. Excerpts from Ku Nong's second article appear in Zhang Youyi, 3:166–167.

87. Zhu Chuxin, 520. For a full accounting of the gradual process through which Xue acquired Wuxi filatures, including the formation of the Xingye Silk company, an umbrella organization that carried out much leasing activity, see Bell 1985a, 284–291.

88. Zhang Youyi, 3:163–164; Guan Yida, 1; *Jiangsu jianshe yuekan*, 2.3 (March 1935): report sec., 57.

89. *Shenbao*, May 17, 1934.

90. *Jiangsu jianshe yuekan*, 2.3 (March 1935): report sec., 57–88; Zhang Youyi, 3:163–165.

91. *Shenbao*, May 4, 1934.

92. *Shenbao*, June 2, 1934, 4, 13.

93. Dier lishi dang'anguan, file no. 3242, subfile no. 22061:42.

94. Guan Yida, 1.

95. Lü Huantai interview; Ku Nong 1937a, 67–70.

96. Bell 1985a, chap. 4.

97. Shen Wenwei, 34.

98. Ibid.

99. Ku Nong 1937b, 104.

100. On the constant fluctuation of cocoon prices, see the newspaper accounts in *Minguo ribao*, note 70 above. See also *Minguo ribao*, May 27, 1917, 3, 10; May 28, 1917, 3, 11; May 30, 1917, 3, 10.

101. Institute of Pacific Relations, ed., 1939a, 187. Translated from Ku Nong 1937b, 106.

102. *Shenbao*, June 2, 1936, 3, 11.

103. Raw silk prices are calculated from tables in Lillian Li, 74–77. Cocoon prices had risen to highs of seventy *yuan* per *dan* in the 1920s. See tables on sericulture and cocoon production in Guoli zhongyang yanjiuyuan shehui kexue yanjiusuo.

104. *Shenbao*, June 1, 1936, 4, 14.

NOTES TO CHAPTER FIVE

Abbreviations

MGS Maqi gaiba qiao ji
STYT Shaoxing Tianyue xiang Yinghu tang pu shibanlu zhengxin lu
SXZ Shaoxing xianzhi ziliao diyi ji
TZ Tianyue zhi

1. A general outline of this case is provided in Shiba 1984. The name of Tianyue came from a rock at the village of Fujiadun said to resemble a seven-stringed *guqin*, which, tradition said, was played by a Daoist immortal. See *Xiaoshan xian dimingzhi*, 184.

2. This description is based on *TZ*, 1b–2b.

3. *TZ*, 1a.

4. Professor Chen Qiaoyi (1981, 75) contends that the Qiyan excavation had occurred earlier and that the opening had been diked and reopened several times before the mid-fifteenth century.

5. *TZ*, 10b.

6. *Xiaoshan xianzhi gao* 3:23b.

7. The population density and the economic base in Middle Tianyue, which I denote as "peripheral," thus does not differ substantially from that of the surrounding core. In this sense, it may be, as Stevan Harrell has suggested, that the difference between Middle Tianyue and the surrounding core is a difference not in kind but in degree and scale. I would suggest, however, that although this "periphery" does not meet the standard definitional qualifications set forth by Skinner, it evidences key attributes of peripheries: poverty, domination by agents of the core, and a more uni-fied, less diverse elite social and political structure than core areas. This complex of sociopolitical attributes is suggested clearly by the term "periphery." Finally, I would argue that Tianyue's geographical and administrative position meant that the Middle Tianyue populace experienced problems common to those facing inhabitants of peripheries.

8. Gu Shijiang, 46.

9. *Xiaoshan xianzhi* 11:1.

10. Ibid., 1:37–38. In 1950 all of Linpu and Tianyue became part of Xiaoshan county.

11. Ibid., 8:11. For an important analysis of commerce and local markets, see Mann, esp. chaps. 4, 5, 9.

12. *Xiaoshan xianzhi* 23:27.

13. Ibid., 7:26.

14. See, e.g., *Minguo ribao*, Feb. 4, 1929, and *Dongnan ribao*, Jan. 22, 1948; June 21, 1948.

15. *Xiaoshan xianzhi* 16:22.

16. Ibid., *da shiji*, 20–22, 25; 16:22. For specifics on the May 1911 riot, see Cole 1986, 50.

17. *Shi bao*, Sept. 28, 1914; Sept. 30, 1914.

18. *Shen bao*, Aug. 3, 1927. This citation reports the establishment of surveillance units to prevent merchant price manipulation in earlier years.

19. *Xiaoshan xianzhi, da shiji*, 22.

20. *Xiaoshan xian dimingzhi* (184) indicates that the second son of a twelfth-century Xiaoshan magistrate first settled in Tianyue. *SXZ* (7:27b) contends that it was not until the ninth generation of this lineage (early Ming) that the first settlement in Tianyue occurred.

21. *SXZ*, 12:4a. All of Shouchong's river-dike and sluicegate repairs protected the land of his and other township lineages.

22. *STYT*. The remaining thirteen contributors came from a number of different lineages. See the characterization of the Tang family in Rankin 1986, 261–263.

23. *MGS*, preface: 2a.

24. *MGS*, 2:9a–b; *TZ*, 11a; and *SXZ*, 12:3a–b. Lu was also a founding member of the Ji Society.

25. *Shi bao*, May 20, 1914.

26. *Xiaoshan xianzhi gao*, 10:10a, and *TZ*, 22b–23a.

27. *TZ*, 20b.

28. *Shi bao*, May 20, 1914.

29. *SXZ*, 16:191b. This information is found in the biography of Tang's father, Pei'en. There is no extant biography of Shouchong.

30. *TZ*, 38a–b; *SXZ*, 16:192a–194a.

31. *Xiaoshan xianzhi gao*, 10:10a.

32. Rankin 1986, 261–263.

33. Shouqian's *jinshi* degree and widespread reputation enhanced the family's local position. He could not, however, provide the patronage and support for his native place and his kin that one might expect. Shouqian actually held office only briefly and spent much of his career in opposition to the government. I am indebted to Mary Rankin for this insight on Shouqian.

The extralocal involvement of the family continued on the provincial level in 1916 when Military Governor Lu Gongwang appointed the youngest brother Shouming an adviser. See *Shi bao*, Aug. 14, 1916.

34. It has been shown many times that local dominance in South China was often attained through developing effective lineage organizations. E.g., Rubie S. Watson 1982. Marriage ties were one method of increasing a lineage's local dominance.

35. Lineage control of the various villages was plotted using a composite map, taken from *Xiaoshan xian dimingzhi* (171, 180), and a village-by-village listing of contributors to the reconstruction of the lake dikes in Tianyue township in 1922. See *STYT* for the maiden names of widowed contributors to the lake dikes. Though the information is only suggestive, in the Tang lineage village, the wide variety of maiden names of Tang widows in contrast to the very limited variety in other villages is notable. Tracking interlineage marriage information through genealogies has proved impossible. Only two of six genealogies from Middle Tianyue at the Zhejiang Provincial Library date from after 1882, and neither provides relevant information.

36. See the biography of Tang Pei'en, *SXZ*, 16:191a–192a; *STYT*, and *SXZ, ce* 9. The Ges in that time period produced two *jinshi*, five *juren*, and two *gongsheng*.

37. The marriage patterns of Tianyue were strikingly local and suggest a tight unity among local elites. This situation suggests social patterns of a periphery,

perhaps a result of the constraints of poverty and geography. It is impossible to tell on the basis of available sources if some Tianyue families were able to marry their daughters "out" to other areas.

38. *TZ*. For his lineage, see *SXZ*, 7:32b.

39. *SXZ*, 7:1b.

40. *Shao-Xiao tangzha gongcheng yuekan*, 4 (January 1927): 29.

41. See Lu's account of reconstructing Linpu's Fire God Dike, *SXZ*, 12:3a–b.

42. *Shaoxing xian yihui minguo yuannian yijue an*, 12a–b; *MGS*, preface: 2a.

43. In certain areas such as the inner core, where elite structures were more diverse than in Middle Tianyue, self-government institutions themselves brought a new resource for local power to some among the wider variety of leaders. In peripheral situations, where local elite "oligarchies" had provided leadership for years, the establishment of self-government bodies headed by the same oligarchies did not bring an especially new import to their positions. See Schoppa 1982, esp. chaps. 8, 9.

44. Here "public" and "private" refer not to the nature of the deeds performed but to the status of the performer.

45. *Shaoxing xian yihui minguo yuannian yijue an*, 31b–32a.

46. By power, I mean "the capacity to produce intended and foreseen effects on others." See Wrong, 2.

47. By legitimacy, I mean the "type of support that derives not from force or its threat but from values held by the individuals formulating, influencing, and being affected by political ends." See Swartz, 10.

48. The phrase is Wrong's, 52.

49. Swartz, 14.

50. For a brief biography of Liu, see Hummel, 532–533.

51. *TZ*, 13a.

52. *Xiaoshan xianzhi gao*, 3:24b–25a.

53. Ibid., 3:25a.

54. *MGS*, 2:11a–b; 13a–15a.

55. *TZ*, 11a.

56. *MGS*, 4:1a–5b.

57. *SXZ*, 11:6a–8a.

58. The implication of immorality as a mask for attacking antagonistic power holders in Chinese society is discussed in Pye, 41. See also Schoppa 1989, esp. chaps. 2, 4.

59. See Cole 1986, chaps. 5, 6. There is no other evidence on which to judge the accuracy of this petition's claim about *muyou*.

60. Degree holders are listed in *SXZ*, 8, 9. Information on lineages and their elites are in *SXZ*, 7. The Kong, Tang, and Ge lineages were resident only in Middle Tianyue. Thus, though subdistrict residence is not included in the degree-listing, these three lineage totals can be quickly ascertained. Population data are in *TZ*, 5a–6a.

61. *TZ*, 16a. It is not possible to delineate the degree holders from Lower Tianyue (Suoqian) because residents in other areas of Shaoxing shared surnames with key lineages here (Zhao, Wang, Li, Jin, and Shen). I am therefore relying on qualitative evidence from the Tianyue petition and the circumstances of the case. It is also suggestive that Suoqian, containing 32 percent of the population of the original

Tianyue subdistrict, produced fourteen lineages illustrious enough to be included in the gazetteer lineage survey. Middle Tianyue, with 59 percent of the population, produced only nine. See *SXZ*, 7.

62. See the comments on the terms *daibiao* and the more traditional term *daili* ("agent" or "deputy") in Rankin 1986, 278.

63. See the description of patron-client relationships in S. N. Eisenstadt and L. Roniger 1984, 48–49. The authors note (205) the greater likelihood of patron-client relations in "peripheral units [which] possess few mechanisms through which they control corporate access to outside resources and loci of decisions which affect them."

64. Kuhn 1975, 274–277.

65. *MGS*, 4:6a–8b; *TZ*, 11a.

66. *MGS*, 4:12a–14b.

67. *MGS*, 3:10a.

68. *MGS*, 4:15a–16a. The map placed a large branch of the Puyang river in Middle Tianyue and put the dike of Lower Ying Lake along the Little West River (as if to indicate the acute danger of flooding).

69. E.g., the arguments in Schoppa (1989, chaps. 7, 8) regarding the reclamation of Xiang Lake in Xiaoshan county and those regarding the sale of some public river, lake, and pond land in the 1910s in *Xiaoshan hetang jinian lu*.

I use Richard Madsen's definition of "moral discourse": "an active social process of understanding, evaluating, and arguing about what is right and wrong in a given situation." See his statement in Madsen, 8. "Discourse" refers to more than simply verbal exchange as will shortly be evident.

For the importance of language as a social and political legitimator and the relationship between language and experience at times of crisis, see Bourdieu 1977, 170.

70. See Cohen, 5–9, 126–143.

71. *Shaoxing xian yihui minguo yuannian yijue an*, 66a–68b. Open meetings to discuss the danger were held in the subdistricts.

72. *MGS*, 1:14a–15a. On the potency of the threat of disharmony, see Pye's description (33) of the danger of "primitive power" as perceived in Chinese culture.

73. *MGS*, 3:11a. This threat brought a rebuke from Governor Qu.

74. *TZ*, 11a–b.

75. *MGS*, 3:3a–5a.

76. *MGS*, 3:11b.

77. *MGS*, preface: 2a.

78. *MGS*, 4:20a–b

79. Ibid.

80. *MGS*, preface: 2b; 3:3a–5a.

81. Bourdieu 1977, 183.

82. For He, see *Xiaoshan xianzhi gao*, 10:10a, 12a: *MGS*, 3:3a–5a. In the late 1920s he would become known as a "local bully, evil gentry" for his heading a rent collection organization called the "Property Protection Association." See *Shen bao*, Nov. 10, 1927.

83. Bourdieu 1977, 178–179. Madsen (18) uses the term "political capital." The crucial nature of "symbolic status" even in cultural play is underlined in Clifford Geertz 1973a, 412–453.

84. For the information on the Qiu lineage, see *Xiaoshan xingshi*, 45.

85. *STYT*. Among the remaining leaders, there were three Tang, four Ge, three Ye, one Hua, and one Tong.

86. *MGS*, 4:23a–b.

87. Ibid.

88. *MGS*, 3:32a, preface: 3a.

89. *TZ*, 12a.

90. An alternative interpretation of this episode might suggest that the resignations of Tang and his allies were a sham, that Tang knew what was going on or might even have actively encouraged the destruction behind the screen of "resignation." Although such a reading of the incident fits a political culture whose primary dynamic was the authority relationship between superior and subordinate, it does not explain why the Ji Society was formed *after* the completion of the episode (when it might earlier have served as an instrument to help solve the crisis) or why Qiu was notably missing from the list of the Ji Society founders. The sources (compiled by the Ji Society) give evidence of an obvious rupture between Tang and the villagers. See the text below.

91. See Schoppa 1982, 64, 222, n. 36. For discussion of the hostility, see *Shi bao*, May 2, 1914.

92. *Shi bao*, May 20, 1914. Shouchong had apparently been involved in some accident on his return to Datangwu from Linpu on May 16.

93. F. G. Bailey (*1969*, 82) argues that in fact the "main political capital of the leader of a moral group is his monopoly of the right to communicate with or symbolize whatever mystical value holds the group's devotion." Eisenstadt and Roniger (1984, 263–267) point to the instability of patron-client ties and frequent combinations of continuity and discontinuity.

94. *MGS*, 2:13a says summer; *TZ*, 20b indicates spring.

95. *MGS*, 2:13a–15a.

96. For a cogent presentation on the use and meaning of symbol, see Clifford Geertz 1973b, 91–94.

97. Madsen, 9.

98. The inscription is in *MGS*, 2:15a; Ge's record is in *TZ*, 39b–40a.

99. Cohen, 151–153.

100. *TZ*, 15a.

101. *SXZ*, 12:3b–4a.

102. For the Fire God Dike repairs, see *SXZ*, 12:3a–b, 11a–12b. Substantial discussion over the "private" or "public" nature of dams marked deliberations over this dike.

103. Shiba, 328.

104. *TZ*, 20b.

105. Bourdieu 1977, 191.

106. Bailey (1969, 84) denotes these resources "political capital." He calls those resources the client believes the patron holds "political credit."

107. On the import of synthetic social gradations, see Ossowski, 45–56.

108. On the tendency for elites with greater personal "credentials" to move to social and political levels of greater complexity and variety, see Teune and Mlinar, 142–150.

109. See the description of "practice theory" in Ortner, 153.

110. *TZ*, 12a.

NOTES TO CHAPTER SIX

1. Kuhn 1970.

2. One notable exception is Meskill 1979.

3. According to Skinner (1977c, 214–215, 241), the Yun-Gui macroregion consists of most of Yunnan, central and western Guizhou, and a portion of southern Sichuan. For a general description of the Yun-Gui macroregion, see Naquin and Rawski, 199–205.

4. "Topography of Kweichau," 530.

5. Neville and Bell, 105; *The Provinces of China*, 97–100; Xue Shaoming, 55.

6. *The Provinces of China*, 99–100; Neville and Bell, 105, 130; Bourne, 44–45; Tang Zaiyang, 13; Mo Jian and Lei Yongming, 40.

7. Bourne, 44–45.

8. Luo Raodian, 57.

9. Ai Bida, 191; *Xingyi fuzhi*, 35:2b.

10. Ai Bida, 185, 189.

11. Bourne, 44. Also see "Topography of Kweichau," 530.

12. Ai Bida, 191.

13. *Xingyi fuzhi* 47:26b–29a. Xingyi prefecture was composed of the counties of Xingyi, Pu'an, and Annan along with the department (*zhou*) of Zhenfeng and the subprefecture (*ting*) of Panzhou.

14. Wu Xuechou and Hu Gang, 195; Guizhou daxue lishixi, 186–187; Feng Zuyi 1984, 61.

15. Guizhou daxue lishixi, 187.

16. Ibid.

17. Wu Xuechou and Hu Gang, 195; He Jiwu, 267.

18. Yang Defang and Weng Jialie, 70–71.

19. Bourne, 44.

20. Bao Jianxing, 79–82; Wu Xuechou and Hu Gang, 187–188.

21. "Liu Guanli Xiawutun zhongyi ci ji," 4:29b; "Liu Tongzhi xiansheng nianpu," 4:31a–31b; Wu Xuechou and Hu Gang, 195.

22. Kuhn 1970, 67.

23. Schoppa 1973, 10, 16–17.

24. For a description of the local strongman as a social type, see Meskill, 88–91.

25. "Liu Guanli," 4:29b–30b; "Liu Tongzhi," 4:31b–34a.

26. "Liu Guanli," 4:30a–30b; "Liu Tongzhi," 4:31b, 34a; Wang Yanyu, 245; Guizhou daxue lishixi, 190.

27. "Liu Tongzhi," 4:32a–32b, 34a.

28. Kuhn 1970, 120–121.

29. Liu Guanli's troops had an unsavory reputation for their thorough plundering. In one place, their passing left a popular saying, "Liu's soldiers came to Longchang, and in one sweep left only dust and smoke." Long Shangxue, Chen Hanhui, and Fang Jian, 91–92.

30. Guizhou daxue lishixi, 189.

31. "Liu Tongzhi," 4:31b.

32. Wu Xuechou and Hu Gang, 197; Guizhou daxue lishixi, 190.

33. This feud began during the 1862–63 siege of Xiawutun when the Lius' surrender to besieging rebels allowed the rebels to turn and destroy a militia band that had been sent from the town of Bangzha to aid the Lius by three militia leaders, who originally had been Liu Guanzhen's close personal friends. One of these men was killed, and the other two swore to seek revenge against the Lius for what they saw as a betrayal. When Liu Guanzhen went on a militia inspection tour to Bangzha in 1865 these men took their revenge. Wu Xuechou and Hu Gang, 195–196.

34. Ibid., 196–197.

35. Zhou Suyuan 1963, 12.

36. Long Shangxue et al., 91.

37. Wu Xuechou and Hu Gang, 196.

38. E.g., Liu Yuezhao, 287–296.

39. Wu Xuechou and Hu Gang, 197; Guizhou daxue lishixi, 191; "Liu Tongzhi," 4:34a.

40. Zhou Suyuan 1963, 12; Feng Zuyi 1984, 62.

41. See McCord 1988.

42. Long Shangxue et al., 91.

43. Wu Xuechou and Hu Gang, 197.

44. Ling Ti'an, 4:28a–29b.

45. Zhou Suyuan 1963, 12.

46. Ibid.

47. Wu Xuezhou and Hu Gang, 197.

48. Bourne, 44.

49. Wu Xuechou and Hu Gang, 197.

50. Ibid.; Feng Zuyi 1984, 63.

51. Zhou Suyuan 1963, 12.

52. He Jiwu, 267; Li Defang, 71; Xiong Zongren 1987a, 151. Liu Xianshi's son, Liu Gangwu, also earned a *shengyuan* degree in the last years of the examination system. He Jiwu, 283.

53. Mo Jian and Le Yongming, 46–47.

54. Feng Zuyi 1982, 58–59.

55. He Jiwu, 267; Li Defang, 71.

56. "Liu Guanli," 4:30b; Wu Xuechou and Hu Gang, 198; Feng Zuyi 1984, 63; Feng Zuyi 1982, 59.

57. Zhou Suyuan 1963, 12; Feng Zuyi 1984, 63.

58. He Jiwu, 268.

59. Wu Xuechou and Hu Gang, 198; Zhou Suyuan 1963, 12.

60. He Jiwu, 268; Zhou Suyuan 1963, 3, 12.

61. Li Shi, 121.

62. Wu Xuechou and Hu Gang, 197–198.

63. Ibid.; He Jiwu, 268; Feng Zuyi 1984, 63–64.

64. Wu Xuechou and Hu Gang, 197; Feng Zuyi 1984, 63–64.

65. He Jiwu, 268, 287; Boorman and Howard, eds., 2:79.

66. Feng Zuyi 1984, 64; He Jiwu, 283.

67. Feng Zuyi 1984, 64; Li Defang, 71.

68. Wu Xuechou and Hu Gang, 198; Wu Xuechou 1979, 108.

69. Tang Eryong's grandfather, Tang Jiong, was a provincial degree holder who had held the post of provincial governor. Hummel, ed., 707–708.

70. Zhou Suyuan 1980, 6–7; Wu Xuechou and Hu Gang, 183; Li Shi, 121.

71. Feng Zuyi 1984, 64.

72. He Jiwu, 268.

73. Tang Eryong was eventually forced into retirement by an exposé of a Tang family scandal in a Self-Government Society newspaper. Zhou Suyuan 1980, 57–58.

74. Wu Xuezhou 1979, 72–87. The best discussion of the composition and character of Guizhou's two reformist factions is Li Shi 1982.

75. Wu Xuechou 1979, 92–93; Wu Xuechou and Hu Gang, 185–186; Zhou Suyuan 1963, 3.

76. Wu Xuechou 1979, 92; Zhou Suyuan 1963, 3–4.

77. Ping Gang 1981, 14.

78. He Jiwu, 270; Ping Gang 1959, 300; Yang Changming, 206.

79. Huang Jizhou, 164; Zhou Suyuan 1980, 63–64; Yang Changming, 206.

80. Zhou Suyuan 1980, 64; Wu Xuechou 1979, 98.

81. Wu Xuechou 1979, 103–107.

82. Zou Lu, 6:398; Sun Zhongyin, 239, 245–246, 253; Zhou Suyuan 1980, 67; Wu Xuechou 1979, 109.

83. One of Liu Xianzhi's Guizhou colleagues in the Yunnan government, Xiong Fanyu, was a metropolitan degree holder. For a time in the late Qing, Xiong had lectured in Xingyi schools. Together with Liu Xianzhi, Xiong had joined Liang Qichao's reformist circle in Japan and then obtained a post on the Yunnan governor-general's staff. Wu Xuechou and Zhang You, 108; Wu Xuechou and Hu Gang, 197; Sun Zhongyin, 245–246, 252.

84. Wu Xuechou 1979, 109–110, 114–115; Zhou Suyuan 1963, 7–8.

85. When the expeditionary force that had left the province during the Revolution tried to return to Guizhou later in 1912 they were blocked by Liu and Tang's armies, defeated and dispersed. Wu Xuechou 1979, 110–113; Zhou Suyuan 1963, 8–11.

86. Gui Baizhu, 102.

87. Xiong Zongren 1987a, 152–154.

88. Xiong Zongren 1987b, 70–73.

89. Boorman and Howard, eds., 2:79.

90. Gui Baizhu, 102–103; He Jiwu, 288.

91. He Jiwu, 283–284; Guizhou daxue lishixi, 198. Liu Gangwu's son, Liu Daren, later served as a foreign ministry spokesman and a diplomat for the Guomindang government in Taiwan. He Jiwu, 265, 284.

92. Boorman and Howard, eds., 2:80; He Jiwu, 288, 311.

93. Among other posts, Liu Xianqian served as brigade general of Anyi and Weining districts, west Guizhou circuit intendant and bandit commissioner, and as head of southwestern Guizhou salt administration. Zhang Youdong et al., 288; Xiong Zongren 1987a, 152–153.

94. He Jiwu, 282.

95. Guizhou daxue lishixi, 199–200.

96. Zhou Suyuan 1980, 93.

97. *Dagong bao* (Oct. 14, 1920).

98. The struggle between Liu Xianshi and Wang Wenhua emerged in late 1920 when Liu opposed the return of Wang's army from a three-year sojourn in Sichuan. Wang himself "retired" to Shanghai during the coup to avoid the opprobrium of direct involvement in his uncle's fall. Among the actual coup leaders, however, were He Yingqin, Wang's brother-in-law, and Sun Jianfeng, who was both Wang Wenhua's cousin on the Wang side and the brother of the wife of Liu Xianshi's eldest son, Liu Jianwu. Wang Wenhua gained little from the coup as he was assassinated in Shanghai soon after by another Guizhou military rival. Xiong Zongren 1987b, 74; Lin Zixian, 119.

99. Zhou Suyuan 1963, 16; Xiong Zongren 1987a, 155.

100. Guizhou daxue lishixi, 198–199.

NOTES TO CHAPTER SEVEN

1. Michael, xi–xliii.

2. This observation is made in Schoppa 1982, 3. For another statement of this position see Sheridan, 18–26.

3. E.g., Hanwell 1937a, 1937b; and Chen Han-seng.

4. Fei Hsiao-t'ung 1939; Alitto 1978–79.

5. On the chambers of commerce, see Bergère 1968, 241. On self-government organizations, see Fincher 1981 and Kuhn 1975. On Nationalist attempts to abolish *lijin* and impose a business tax, see Mann, 163–199. For a discussion of *dibao* and the establishment of subdistrict government offices, see Barkan 1983, 229–239.

6. Rankin 1986; Bastid 1989; Schoppa 1982.

7. Barkan 1983.

8. Geisert 1979.

9. Duara 1987, 132–161.

10. During their occupation of Rugao, the Japanese divided the county in two. During the early 1940s when Rugao was part of a Communist base area, and again after 1949, the Communists did likewise. Most of early twentieth-century Rugao has become the two counties of Rugao and Rudong. The northern part of the original Rugao is now part of Haian County.

11. *Jiangsu dangwu zhoukan* 27 (July 20, 1930):92; *Shi bao*, Mar. 14, 1929, 3. All population figures from this period are approximate.

12. For 1.5 million figure, see Chang Ch'un-ming, 243. For tenancy percentages, see Wang Haoran, 67. For plot sizes, see Jiangsu sheng nongmin yinhang zonghang, ed., 226. Statistics from this period are not accurate. *Gao Nong*, 1.8 (August 1931):11–13, breaks down tenancy and ownership rates by district within the county. Generally, the districts closest to Rugao City had the highest tenancy rates, and the districts along the coast and the county's southwestern boundary had the highest ownership rates. Districts along the southwestern boundary also had some of the county's poorest land. In these districts—i.e., those with the poorest land but with large numbers of owner-cultivators—the Rugao Communist movement started in the late 1920s.

13. Wang Haoran, 67; Jiangsu sheng nongmin yinhang zonghang, ed., 222; Yin Weihe, 126; *North China Herald*, Aug. 15, 1934, 240; June 5, 1935, 381; June 28, 1933, 490; July 4, 1934, 12.

14. Yin Weihe, 126–127. Cotton mills were established in Rugao from 1921–1924. None appears to have remained open longer than a year or two. *China Industrial Handbooks: Kiangsu*, 316.

15. *North China Herald*, Oct. 14, 1936, 54, and May 17, 1933, 254; Yin Weihe, 126.

16. Yin Weihe, 124.

17. Although Rugao sometimes was officially classified as a "first rank" county, it was always less important than Nantong, where prefects and other officials in charge of groups of counties including Nantong always resided. See Zhao Ruheng, 28, on how Jiangsu classified its counties for financial purposes, and 20–21, on classification for administrative purposes. See also *Jiangsu sheng zhengfu gongbao* 331 (Jan. 8, 1931):9.

18. For a more extended discussion of the elite, see Barkan 1983, 369–370.

19. At the beginning of the twentieth century the Shas, the Zhus, and the Mas were regarded as the three "big families" (*dahu*) upon which all officials had to call upon first reaching the county. In addition, with probably over 10,000 *mu* of acreage apiece, the Shas and the Zhus were regarded as the county's two biggest landholding families. It was said in Rugao that "the Shas are number one, and the Zhus are number two, but neither of them can surpass the Ding Hui Si [a Buddhist monastery]." "Rugao jiefang shinian shi," chap. 2:1; He Banghua 1981b, 43.

20. *Rugao xianzhi* (1808), 14:2b, 6b–7a, 9a–b, 10b, 11b, 14a, 16a–b, 21b, 23a, 32b, 39a; 16:24a–b, 34b–35a, 69a–b; 17:36a, 80b–81a, 97b–98a; 21:22b. *Rugao xian xuzhi* (1837), front, 1:11a, 2:1b–2a, 3:7a, 8:10a, 26a. *Rugao xian xuzhi* (1873), front, 1:19a; 6:17b, 18a; 8:23a–23b; 13:2a–3a.

21. E.g., Zheng Zhonghao 1980b, 66; Xu Laiqing, 22; Huang Qiwu 1961, 230; Yuan Caizhi 1980b, 2:36.

22. Sha Yan'gao, 66–67. Even after 1949, the loss of the Sha collection during the 1930s and 1940s Japanese occupation of the county was mourned by Rugao residents. Today, none of the volumes can be traced. Guan Weilin, 91.

23. Bastid, 46.

24. *Shi bao*, June 23, 1924, 2:4; Sha Yan'gao, 69.

25. Huang Qiwu 1980, 25–27; Yuan Caizhi 1981c, 113; *Rugao xianzhi* (1933), 1:2.

26. Mao Bijiang was a "gifted scholar," calligrapher, and Ming Dynasty loyalist. Zhang Zhengyu 1980a, 70; Ma Daolai, 13–14. The large Mao family compound, still in excellent repair, is being preserved as a museum. For references to other Mao family members, see *Rugao xian xuzhi* (1873), 6:17a, 18b, 20a, 22b, 24b, 25a, 25b, 26a, 29a, 29b, 30b.

27. On Mao, see Fu Dong, 132–136; Mao Xiao (?), 137–140.

28. On Zhang, see Xu Laiqing, 23; Yuan Caizhi 1981a, 105.

29. On Deng, see Yuan Caizhi 1981c, 113; Zhang Naicheng, 98; *Jiangsu sheng zhengzhi nianjian*, 352.

30. *Jiangsu sheng zhengzhi nianjian*, 352.

31. For a history of the legal profession in Rugao, see Zhang Naicheng, 99–100. For more details on Xu, see You Yanjia and Chen Baosheng, 87–90.

32. Yuan Caizhi (1980b), 2:36.

33. Hu Langru, 84; He Banghua 1981b, 43.

34. *Rugao xian xuzhi* (1873), 1:3b, 6b, 25a, 35a, 37a; 3:7a, 12a, 17b.

35. Zhou Deyin and You Yuangui, 28.

36. He Banghua 1981, 44.

37. Both Richard Bush, 47–53, and Schoppa, 72, note local leaders' increasingly specialized training. However, in Zhejiang Schoppa says that until the mid-1920s such individuals were "confined mainly to large centers." The Rugao case shows that in central Jiangsu trained professionals were common outside the inner core significantly earlier than Schoppa indicates.

38. It is a common mistake to look for the main impact of an event immediately after its occurrence. Even after 1927 older elites continued to be active in local affairs; many of those who compiled the 1933 Rugao gazetteer were Qing degree holders.

39. Chu, 11.

40. For descriptions of Jiang's activities, see Chu and Bastid.

41. Zhang Jian, 54. "Qingchao monian Rugao quanxian xuetang tongji biao," 7; Xu Laiqing, 23; Sha Yan'gao, 66. At various times, Sha also headed each of these institutions.

42. Fujii Masao, 28.

43. On Zhang's membership in the Society for Constitutional Government, see Zhejiang sheng xinhai geming shi yanjiu hui and Zhejiang sheng tushuguan, eds., 217; Bastid, 63. For a brief history of the society, see Wang Shuhuai, 143–151. For Zhang's assembly memberships, see *Jiangsu sheng zhengzhi nianjian*, 112; *Jiangsu sheng neiwu xingzheng baogao shu*, 2:60, 64; Xu Laiqing, 23.

44. Bastid, 33, 60, 63.

45. *Jiangsu sheng zhengzhi nianjian*, 427; *Shi bao*, July 16, 1924, 2:2, Mar. 21, 1927, 1:3; *Jiangsu sheng neiwu xingzheng baogao shu*, 1:83. *Gao ming bao*, June 29, 1913, 9.

46. When Huang told Sha that the arms of the antisalt-smuggling soldiers were insufficient to guard the county and that new weapons were needed, Sha wrote a letter of introduction to the cashier of the Da Sheng company's Shanghai office. The letter enabled Huang to borrow 30,000 yuan from the company to buy a large quantity of weapons and bullets from a Japanese merchant. Huang Qiwu 1961, 230.

47. Huang Qiwu 1961, 231; Xu Laiqing, 22. *Jiangsu sheng zhengzhi nianjian*, 39–40; *Jiangsu sheng neiwu xingzheng baogao shu*, 1(chart after page 10).

48. "Qingchao monian Rugao quan xian xuetang tongji biao," 6–15. Some members were traditional degree holders such as Zhang Fan, a *gongsheng* and member of the Qing cabinet; see Yuan Caizhi 1981b, 107. Others like Zhang Xiang, one of Rugao's first lawyers and member of the first Jiangsu Provincial Assembly, had modern educations; see *Jiangsu sheng zhengzhi nianjian*, 112; *Jiangsu sheng neiwu xingzheng baogao shu*, 2:64.

49. E.g., Chūzō Ichiko, 297.

50. See also Barkan 1983, 368–404. For details concerning Yuan's dissolution of the elected assemblies, see Young, 148–155. For local elite founding and running of local newspapers, see Cai Guanming, 77–78 ; Yu Men, 84–86.

51. Yuan Caizhi 1980a, 33; *Shi bao*, Mar. 2, 1927, 1:4. For Sha's negotiating and mediating, see *Shi bao*, May 13, 1924, 2:4, and Aug. 27, 1924, 2:4; Sha Yan'gao, 68–69.

52. Ma Tongke, 48–49; *Shi bao*, May 26, 1926, 1:2.

53. Yuan Caizhi 1980c, 40; Zhang Fengting 1980a, 1980b; *Shi bao*, May 16, 1924,

2:4, and Mar. 5, 1927, 1:4; *Tongtong ribao* Mar. 5, 1927, 3.

54. Yu Men, 1:84; Lin Xiao, 64; Sha Yan'gao, 68; *Shi bao*, Nov. 13, 1926, 1:4; Feb. 19, 1927, 1:4.

55. Sha Yan'gao, 67–68.

56. Yuan Caizhi 1980c, 38; Lin Xiao, 59.

57. Zhu Anjun, 109–111; Zheng Zhonghao, 65–67.

58. Zheng Zhonghao 1980b, 66; Ma Daolai, 14; Song Guihuang, 14–18. Zheng Zhonghao (1980a, 75) says the Pingmin she was founded in 1924. Because the first issue of the society's newspaper was dated January 1, 1922, Zheng cannot be correct. Display in Nantong Museum (Nantong bowuguan), seen November 11, 1983.

59. Liu Ruilong, 14; "Rugao xian diyige zhibu de jianli," 26–27. Display in Nantong Museum (Nantong bowuguan), seen Nov. 11, 1983; He Banghua 1981a, 25–26.

60. "Rugao xian diyige dang zhibu de jianli," 27; Song Guihuang, 19–20; Wang Yingchao, 45.

61. Interview with Liu Ruilong, Beijing, Oct. 1984; Song Guihuang, 19–20; "Rugao xian diyige zhibu de jianli," 26–27.

62. Song Guihuang, 20. For details on the Rugao Nationalist Party, see Barkan 1983, 80–179.

63. Zhu Anjun, 110–111; Xu Laiqing, 23.

64. Song Guihuang, 18.

65. Liu Ruilong, 17; Sha Yan'gao, 68–69; *Shi bao*, July 19, 1927, 1:4.

66. E.g., "Rugao dangwu gaikuang," 16; *Shi bao*, July 19, 1927, 2; Aug. 11, 1927, 5; Dec. 23, 1927, 3; Jan. 26, 1928, 8.

67. *Shi bao*, July 24, 1927, 3; Dec. 31, 1927, 2; July 8, 1928, 8; Aug. 1, 1928, 4; *Tongtong ribao*, July 26, 1927, 4; *Zhongyang ribao*, July 31, 1928, 3:2.

68. *Shi bao*, Dec. 22, 1928, 4; Aug. 19, 1928, 4.

69. *Zhongyang ribao*, Feb. 23, 1928, 3:3.

70. On Mao, see *Shi bao*, Aug. 10, 1928, 4; Sept. 6, 1928, 4. On Zhu, see *Shi bao*, Feb. 23, 1928, 3; July 18, 1928, 8. On Han, see Pan Yichen, 41–44; Interview in Nantong, Dec. 1984; Barkan 1986.

71. *Tongtong ribao*, July 8, 1927, 3. As of December 1927, the new Rugao city head was Ma Shaozhou; *Shi bao*, Dec. 21, 1927, 2.

72. *Tongtong ribao*, Aug. 13, 1927, 4.

73. See Barkan 1983, 80–179. For a more detailed analysis of the Nationalist government, 180–367.

74. Ibid., 132–133, 144.

75. For example, one morning when a gentry member from Zhenzhou and his father left for Rugao city, the two men were ambushed. The son was killed instantly; the father ran into a nearby river and escaped. *Shi bao*, Oct. 18, 1928, 4.

76. In 1928, the goal of the revolutionary troops was to burn and destroy a particular local landlord's dwelling; e.g., Liu Ruilong, 41. In later, larger battles, the emphasis remained the same. For example, when the Communists attacked Old Tiger Town, a main goal was to capture the fortified dwelling of the local gentry member who commanded the militia. Zhang Aiping, 942.

77. *Shi bao*, Dec. 11, 1927, 3.

78. Ibid., Nov. 14, 1928, 4; Nov. 26, 1928, 4; July 22, 1929, 4; July 29, 1929, 4; *Jiangsu jiaoyu gailan*, 1:88, 133.

79. *Shi bao*, Aug. 6, 1927, 5; Aug. 24, 1928, 8; June 20, 1929, 4; May 16, 1931, 4; "Jiangsu ge xian xinwen shiye diaocha," 64.

80. For lists of post-1927 Rugao district heads see *Shi bao*, Dec. 21, 1927, 2; Apr. 8, 1928, 7; Dec. 23, 1938, 4; May 8, 1929, 4; Aug. 13, 1929, 4.

81. Wang Haoran, 67–68; Wang Peitang, 265. For examples of the public property management office's involvement in county financial affairs, see *Shi bao*, Dec. 19, 1929, 3; *Zhongyang ribao*, Oct. 28, 1931, 2:3; Nov. 4, 1931, 2:3; May 10, 1933, 2:2.

82. *North China Herald*, Nov. 24, 1931, 269; Oct. 19, 1932, 92; July 12, 1933, 49; Oct. 18, 1933, 90; Mar. 14, 1934, 407; Dec. 26, 1934, 438.

83. *North China Herald*, Apr. 26, 1933, 134.

84. *Shi bao*, Apr. 9, 1928, 7; Dec. 29, 1928, 4.

85. Faced with threats from the Nationalists, then from Communists and sea bandits, subcounty leaders raised funds and formed sizable militias. County-level leaders, however, continued to depend on Nationalist government soldiers and police for protection. Between 1927 and 1937 outlying towns and villages were frequently attacked, but the county seat remained safe. In Rugao, gentry militarization only took place in response to a real threat. This example suggests that Chinese militarization was not a uniform linear process, but occurred irregularly in response to localized conditions. For details about the militia, see Barkan 1983, 503–508.

NOTES TO CHAPTER EIGHT

1. Li Hua 1980, 20.

2. *Yishibao*, Aug. 9, 1922, 7.

3. Ibid., Apr. 22, 1920, 7.

4. L. K. T'ao 1929, 258. The estimate is from 1925.

5. *North China Standard*, Apr. 18, 1926, 8; Gamble 1921, 101.

6. "Xi Ying," 127.

7. See Nathan (1976) for a profile and analysis of the early Republican political elite.

8. Yuan Shikai's bungled attempt to centralize state power through bureaucratic means suggests both continuity with late Qing reforms and the flaws inherent in a purely administrative strategy. See Young, 205–209.

9. In his study of the Nationalists in Shanghai, Joseph Fewsmith (1985) discusses splits between party-led mass constituencies and the civil and military officials loyal to Chiang Kai-shek. Parks Coble (1980) argues that the hostility characterizing relations between the Nationalist regime and Shanghai capitalists overrode any sense of shared interests.

10. Clapham, 39.

11. Migdal, 428.

12. Ibid., 427.

13. *Beijing Ruifuxiang*, 20–23.

14. Ibid., 6.

15. Zhang Yufa, 600.

16. *Yishibao*, Oct. 15, 1928, 7.

17. For a brief account of the store's history and current disposition, see *Renmin ribao*, Mar. 17, 1986, 3.

18. *Beijing Ruifuxiang*, 11.

19. Ibid.

20. Ibid., 6.

21. *Yishibao*, Jan. 10, 1922, 7.

22. *Beijing Ruifuxiang*, 7.

23. The silk and foreign goods guild participated in planning sessions to deal with war threats in autumn 1925 and contributed the entire monthly "luxury tax" demanded by Zhang Zuolin in spring 1928. *Shuntian shibao*, Nov. 19, 1925, 7; *Yishibao*, May 24, 1928, 3.

24. See a retrospective on Beijing economic life in *Yishibao*, Sept. 6, 1928, 7, and Sept. 14, 1928, 7; and Lou Xuexi, Chi Zehui, and Chen Wenxian, eds., 24–25, 53, 59.

25. *Yishibao*, Sept. 6, 1928, 7.

26. The controversy is described in Burgess, 6–10.

27. For example, during winter 1925–26 planning of food distribution began in November, but the soup kitchens failed to open until January. Meanwhile two hundred people a month died on the streets of the city. *North China Standard*, Jan. 5, 1926, 8.

28. Chesneaux, 192.

29. Zou Mingchu, 74.

30. Yue Tianyu, 35.

31. Liu Yifeng, 268.

32. Gamble 1921, 39; L. K. T'ao 1928, 39. Both discuss the class heterogeneity of city neighborhoods. T'ao notes the beginnings of slum formation at the end of the decade.

33. For the importance in the history of class relations of the moment when policing functions no longer are the direct, personal responsibility of the monied and propertied classes but instead are given to modern police forces, see Silver 1967.

34. *Yishibao*, Apr. 16, 1929, 11.

35. Tarrow, 113.

36. For example, the rural nobility in Europe long justified its privileges on the basis of "leadership over, responsibility for, and protection of" the peasantry until "the state had taken over these functions." Blum, 419.

37. Ibid. The term "deference society" is F. M. L. Thompson's (cited by Blum).

38. *Yishibao*, May 14, 1928, 7.

39. Tan Shih-hua, 282.

40. Tarrow, 111.

41. Philip Kuhn's concept of cadredom is discussed in Susan Mann Jones 1979, 79.

42. For a discussion of the rise of local elite activism in the nineteenth century see Rankin 1986.

43. Mann, 23.

44. Imahori Seiji 1947, 23.

45. Ibid., 59.

46. These "New Policies," as Rankin (1986, 28) notes, "can best be assessed in terms of their impact upon an already existing sphere of public activity."

47. Cooptation of local elites through liberal reforms of this kind is a common trait of centralizing, autocratic, and bureaucratic states. For this aspect of late Qing re-

form, see Fincher, 29. For comparable evidence from the Stolypin local governmental reforms in Russia, see Weissman, 140–142.

48. Johnson 1985.

49. Ibid., 47.

50. Rankin (1986, 16) describes this "intermediate arena where the state and society met" as a "dynamic and expanding sphere, which neither governmental nor societal leaders could fully claim as their own." Fewsmith (1985, 23) refers to developments like the formation of chambers of commerce as an "awakening of civil society." However, by describing chambers as "explicitly private associations" he misses their fundamentally public, as opposed to private or official, character. See Duara 1985, 117–118.

51. Qing reformers imagined that political life should consist only of "a bureaucracy and small surrounding public"; Nathan, 15. Yuan Shikai tried to drastically curtail the role of self-government; Young, 148–155.

52. "Civil society" connotes an organizational life separate from the "state." In European political and social thought, the term "society" came to refer to "an association of free men" as opposed to the "state" as "an organization of power, drawing on the senses of hierarchy and majesty." Williams 1976, 245. During this period of Chinese history, social organization, which once took its larger meaning from the sense of hierarchy associated with hegemonic Confucianism came to have a freer, more independent public profile. This shift in perception of the relationship between officialdom and public life did not constitute a clean break. Judging by the self-consciously independent stance taken by local elites and the corporate bodies they led, it was a break nonetheless.

53. Strand, 417–425.

54. *Yishibao*, Sept. 17, 1920, 3.

55. *Shuntian shibao*, Mar. 8, 1920, 7.

56. Gramsci, 229–239.

57. Tarrow, 128.

58. Lei Zhihui, 103. A portion of this increase was due to the increased jurisdiction covered by Beijing.

59. Mann, 1; see also chap. 8, "Tax-Farming and State-Building."

60. Imahori Seiji 1947.

61. *Shuntian shibao*, Feb. 12, 1922, 7.

62. *Yishibao*, Mar. 23, 1928, cited in *Gendai Shina no kiroku* (Records of Contemporary China), Hatano Ken'ichi, comp. (Mar. 1928).

63. Whereas, according to Rankin (1986, 19) the traditional "brokerage function was informal" and "based on personal ties" the local elite broker of the 1920s was a public figure in the modern sense who operated both backstage on a personal, informal level and on the open stage before public opinion and his constituents.

64. *North China Standard*, Nov. 17, 1927, 3.

65. Ibid., Mar. 29, 1928, 1; *Yishibao*, May 2, 1928, 2.

66. *Yishibao*, Mar. 2, 1928, cited in *Gendai Shina no kiroku* (March 1928).

67. Cohen, 220.

68. A classic statement of this kind of elite dilemma is found in Olson 1971.

69. E. P. Thompson 1978, 164.

70. Yoshikawa Kōjirō 1974.

71. This happened in the case of a particularly bitter conflict between rival groups in the nightsoil guild; *Yishibao,* July 17, 1924, 7.

72. Ibid., Feb. 24, 1925, 7; and June 9, 1924, 7, for cases where conflict between a policeman and a rickshaw man led to the puller's death and a fight between a work crew and shop personnel kept mediators at bay.

73. Boorman and Howard, eds., 2:108–110.

74. Guan Ruiwu, 155–166.

75. *Yishibao,* Feb. 18, 1929, 7.

76. Boorman and Howard, eds., 108–110.

77. *North China Standard,* Aug. 30, 1929, 1.

78. *Shuntian shibao,* Jan. 26, 1924, 7; Feb. 24, 1924, 7.

79. Ibid., Nov. 14, 1928, 7; *North China Standard,* Nov. 15, 1928, 12.

80. Bailey 1971, 2–3.

81. Ibid., 18.

82. Simmel, 46.

83. *Yishibao,* Jan. 19, 1923, 7.

84. Ibid., Mar. 1, 1925, 7; March 4, 1925, 7.

85. Conflict in the water trade among rival Shandong, Baoding, and Beijing factions accompanied attempts to reestablish a guild in the mid-1920s. *Yishibao,* Oct. 2, 1924, 7.

86. Yu Side, 125.

87. Deng Haoming, 91.

88. *Shuntian shibao,* Oct. 25, 1929, 7.

89. Lou Xuexi et al., 1.

90. Oswald Siren, 8.

91. *Beijing Ruifuxiang,* 20–25; *Chinese Economic Bulletin,* June 16, 1928, 300–330.

92. *Shuntian shibao,* Feb. 14, 1929, 7. Sources for the following account of the rise and fall of the clerks association include Wu Bannong, 54; *Shuntian shibao,* Feb. 15, 1929, 7; Feb. 16, 1929, 7; Feb. 18, 1929, 7; Feb. 19, 1929, 7; Feb. 22, 1929, 7; Mar. 8, 1929, 7; *North China Standard,* Feb. 15, 1929, 1; Feb. 20, 1929, 11.

93. *Shuntian shibao,* July 3, 1929, 7. The figure is from a post mortem statement on the movement by remnants of the association and may be exaggerated.

94. *Beijing Ruifuxiang,* 21.

95. *North China Standard,* Feb. 20, 1929, 11; Feb. 23, 1929, 11.

96. See Migdal, 402, for a discussion of the impact of an alliance between central state power and mass constituencies on the power of local elites.

NOTES TO CHAPTER NINE

1. See Chung-li Chang 1955; Yung-teh Chow 1966, 244; Ping-ti Ho 1962, 162–165; Kracke.

2. See Beattie 1979b, 8–9, 129; Dennerline 1986; Hartwell, 417–420; Hymes 1986a, 34–61; Twitchett 1959; Walton, 35–77; Odoric Wou 1979.

3. Ping-ti Ho 1962, 92–125; Kracke.

4. Hymes 1986a, 34–41; Hartwell, 418. See also Odoric Wou.

5. In addition to Hymes 1986a, see Beattie 1979b; Dennerline 1986; Walton.

6. Beattie 1979b.

7. Walton, 36.

8. On effects of partible inheritance in China generally, see Philip Huang, 78, 117; Myers 1970, 125, 160–162; Fei Hsiao-t'ung and Chang Chih-i, 19–20, 117.

9. See Le Roy Ladurie, 43–44; Netting; Stone and Stone.

10. Rubie Watson 1982, 1985.

11. Beattie 1979b.

12. Rubie Watson 1985, 137–168.

13. In this study *xiang* refers to a formal subdivision of the county. Until the 1950s this formal unit coincided with the area of Deng control.

14. On higher-order lineages, see James L. Watson 1982, 608–609.

15. Rubie Watson 1985, 128.

16. Rubie Watson 1981, 593–615.

17. For disscussion and examples of lineage land, see Ebrey 1986, 40–44; Twitchett 1959, 1960–61.

18. For a discussion of *tang*, see Kuhn 1970, 168–171; Sangren.

19. Twitchett 1959, 1960–61. For another example of *yizhuang*, see Dennerline 1979–80.

20. For a discussion of entail and "strict settlement," see Stone and Stone, 48–55.

21. Brim, 34.

22. Baker 1968, 171.

23. James L. Watson 1975, 36.

24. Potter, 96.

25. Chen Han-seng, 34–35.

26. In 1905 the Deng had a total of eighty-two ancestral estates in Ha Tsuen *xiang*.

27. Potter, 97.

28. See Grant, 56.

29. For a discussion of landownership and tenancy in Ha Tsuen, see Rubie Watson 1985, 61–72.

30. C. K. Yang, 47.

31. Dennerline 1979–80, 1986.

32. Dennerline 1986, 187.

33. On the difference between Dennerline's estates and Rubie Watson's estates in the New Territories, see ibid., 187.

34. Quoted in Freedman, 52.

35. Potter, 104.

36. On the importance of personal wealth, see also Beattie 1979b, 117.

37. See Chen Han-seng, 42. Hui-chen Wang Liu, 106.

38. See also Potter, 105.

39. Ibid., 107.

40. Rubie Watson 1985, 75–77.

41. For a detailed discussion of this case see Palmer, 40–52.

42. Ibid.

43. Rubie Watson 1985, 62.

44. The penetration of colonial legal procedures into the lives of New Territories residents may, however, have set this region off from its neighbors across the border. It is clear that previously disenfranchised satellite villagers used the new legal struc-

ture to their advantage as did the new urban elite. The extent to which the old rural elite of wealthy landowners used this structure in the early twentieth century is unclear at this point.

45. Kung-chuan Hsiao 1960; Kuhn 1970.

46. Rankin 1986, 166.

47. Cole 1986, 166; Mann 1987.

48. For a discussion of the Rural Committee system, see Miners 1979.

49. Rubie Watson 1985, 91–93. See also Baker, 52; Potter, 29.

50. See James L. Watson 1987.

51. Hayes, 38.

52. For a discussion of violence in the New Territories, see Rubie Watson 1985, 85–88.

53. See James L. Watson 1977, 169, 172; James L. Watson 1988.

54. James L. Watson 1988.

55. Elvin 1973, 258. See also Ping-ti Ho 1962, 257.

56. Philip Huang, 78. On this point, see also Myers 1970, 125. I have already noted (see above) that the effects of inheritance were not uniform, although in general inheritance did contribute to mobility patterns.

57. See Philip Huang, 29–30, 65–66, 223–224, 232, 234; Myers 1970, 125–126, 234; Buck 1937, map 3; Perkins, 90–91; Wilkinson, 6–13.

58. Myers 1970, 125.

59. Ibid., 126.

60. Gamble 1963, 33, 35, 54.

61. Ibid., 49–51.

62. See Rankin 1986.

63. See Myers 1970, 234–235. Elvin 1973, 254–255. Buck 1930, 145.

64. Esherick 1981, 401.

65. See Perkins, 87.

66. See Philip Huang, 82n.

67. See Perkins, 88–91.

68. Chen Han-seng, 3.

69. Ibid., viii.

70. C. K. Yang, 46.

71. Potter, 80.

72. It is important to note that although tenancy and landless rates tend to be higher in Guangdong than in the north, high rates of private and corporate landlordism are not found in all southeastern villages. Both Edgar Wickberg (1981, 31) and C. K. Yang (42) report a lower rate of corporate property than Ha Tsuen's 50 percent or Ping Shan's 93 percent: Wickberg gives a corporate rate of 35 percent for Pat Hueng (an area near Ha Tsuen), and Yang provides a rate of 6.2 percent for Nanching. A comparison between those Pearl River delta villages that have high rates of corporate property and those that do not would be illuminating, especially with regard to elite dominance and leadership. Perkins (90) has argued that the level of commerce is a major factor in explaining the differing rates of landlessness and tenancy.

73. The comparison between Tongcheng and Wuxi on the one hand and Ha Tsuen on the other cannot produce definitive answers to the questions discussed here.

The works of Beattie and Dennerline have been used because, among the historical work on Lower Yangzi lineages, they deal most explicitly with questions of corporate property, landownership, and elite leadership.

74. Beattie 1979b, 135.

75. Dennerline 1979–80, 54; on the period from 1745–1878, see Dennerline 1986, 188.

76. Dennerline 1979–80; 64n. See also Chen Han-seng, 31.

77. See Potter, 96.

78. See Dennerline 1986, 187.

79. See Dennerline 1979–80.

80. Perkins, 88–91.

81. Ibid., 91.

82. Buck 1937, 58. For more figures on Wuxi land distribution, see *China Industrial Handbooks: Kiangsu*, 31.

83. Mazumdar, 221. On this general point, see also Esherick 1981, 405; Grove and Esherick.

NOTES TO CHAPTER TEN

Abbreviation

CN   *Chūgoku nōson kankō chōsa* (Investigation of Chinese village customs) 6 vols. Tokyo, 1981.

1. See Philip Huang, 177–179; the other authoritative study of the rural economy of North China is Myers 1970.

2. The principal source for this study is the six-volume Japanese survey of villages in the North China plain, known as *Chūgoku nōson kankō chōsa* (*CN*). I draw particularly from the contracts and interviews in these volumes to gain an understanding of customary law. These investigations were conducted in the early 1940s, but the contracts and other written records date from the turn of the century and even earlier. A fuller picture of the villages themselves can be found in Duara 1988, Myers 1970, and Philip Huang 1985.

3. Philip Huang, 65.

4. Ibid., 78.

5. See Duara 1988.

6. Weber 1978, 1:215.

7. See Bourdieu 1984, esp. 125–168.

8. Baker 1968.

9. See also Rubie Watson 1985, 169.

10. Ibid., 89.

11. Duara 1983, 249–250.

12. Traditional community activities in the village and the effects of state penetration upon them are analyzed in detail in Duara 1988.

13. Myers and Chen, 1–32.

14. *CN* 2:56; *CN* 5:438.

15. *CN* 5:206. See also Duara 1988, 188.

16. See for instance *CN* 4:221; *CN* 3:275; *CN* 5:206, 578.

17. *CN*: 3 278–279. See also Duara 1988, 188.
18. Martin Yang, 167, 171.
19. *CN* 5:preface, 5.
20. *CN* 5:204.
21. *CN* 5:268.
22. *CN* 5:258, 260.
23. *CN* 5:37–38.
24. *CN* 5:39.
25. *CN* 5:5, 39, 37, 41, 50, 58, 131, 258.
26. *CN* 5:5, 11, 14, 41, 42–43, 152, 258.
27. *CN* 5:43, 56–58, 100.
28. *CN* 5:18.
29. *CN* 5:100.
30. *CN* 5:17, 24, 32, 39, 58, 95, 206, 258.
31. *CN* 1:76.
32. *CN* 2:40, 194, 195.
33. *CN* 2:40, 195.
34. *CN* 2:488; *CN* 1:187, 189, 190.
35. *CN* 1:124, 138, 139; *CN* 2:238–239.
36. *CN* 1:124; *CN* 2:32, 41, 44, 77, 107, 108, 260, 311.
37. *CN* 2:107, 195.
38. *CN* 2:40, 44, 46.
39. *CN* 2:20, 143, 169, 211, 229–230.
40. *CN* 3:preface, 5. *Luancheng xianzhi*, 2:23.
41. Philip Huang, 129.
42. *CN* 3:preface, 5–7.
43. *CN* 3:preface, 5–6.
44. *CN* 3:preface, 5–6.
45. *CN* 3:preface, 6–7.
46. *CN* 3:163–164, 173–174, 193, 215, 226.
47. *CN* 3:preface, 6, 41, 50.
48. *CN* 3:50, 51, 53, 56, 63, 170.
49. *CN* 3:53, 250, 275, 278–279, 348.
50. *CN* 3:164, 170, 171–172.
51. *CN* 3:179, 206.
52. *CN* 3:263, 269, 277, 281, 282, 300, 304, 353.
53. *CN* 3:275.
54. *CN* 5:525.
55. *CN* 5:preface, 6; *Liangxiang xianzhi*, 3:6.
56. *CN* 5:preface, 6. The average family owned less than ten *mu* of land.
57. *CN* 5:preface, 6, 7.
58. *CN* 5:420, 426, 430. For the wars, see Sheridan, 60–64.
59. *CN* 3:13–14; *CN* 5:435, 579–580.
60. Hosokawa Kazutoshi, 164.
61. Eisenstadt and Roniger 1980. See also Gellner and Waterbury, eds., 1977, and Schmidt, Guasti, Lande, and Scott, eds. 1977.
62. Gouldner, 28–43.

NOTES TO CHAPTER ELEVEN

1. Yan Xiuyu and Xie Yingju, 1:213–222; Mao Zedong 1982, 41–181. The text of Mao's "Xunwu Investigation" was first published in this 1982 collection, using an original copy from the Central Party Archives. *Reports from Xunwu,* an annotated translation by Roger Thompson, is scheduled for publication by Stanford University Press in 1990.

2. Mao Zedong 1982, 44–55. For the concept of macroregion, see Skinner 1977a. Originally Skinner included Jiangxi within the Middle Yangzi macroregion as it appears on Map 1.1., but he has since come to consider it a macroregion in its own right.

3. *Ganzhou fuzhi* 2:41a, 42a; *Ruijin xianzhi gao,* 54; Jiang Yuchang, *Gongdu cungao* 1:60a; Yang Chaolin, 1:28b–29a.

4. This general description of the southern Jiangxi hill country is derived mainly from my earlier work. See Averill 1983, 1987, esp. 280–281. For a vivid series of reports on social unrest and antigovernmental activity in early twentieth-century southern Jiangxi, including Xunwu (then known as Changning), see Jiang Yuchang.

5. Mao Zedong 1982, 56–61, 79–81, 87–88, 99.

6. I accept Robert Hymes's definition of local elites as those "whose access to wealth, power, or prestige was, in the local scheme of things, especially privileged: whose control of material resources, hold over men's actions and decisions, or special place in the regard of their contemporaries, set them apart from . . . society as a whole and made them people to be reckoned with." Hymes 1986a, 7.

7. In the "Xunwu Investigation," Mao Zedong (1982) also distinguishes among local elites, dividing them into categories such as "merchants" and "landlords," then ranking them on the basis of economic criteria such as amount of capital or quantity of grain produced on land owned. The present account draws heavily on the information Mao provides but seeks to set it in an analytical framework that more systematically includes noneconomic factors and other elite categories.

8. The term *shi* (picul) as Mao uses it appears to be equivalent to a *dan* (also translated picul), which is usually considered to contain 100 *jin* (catties), each of which is approximately one-half kilogram. Chinese measures varied considerably by region, however, and Mao notes that in Xunwu the *shi* contained 180 *jin* (i.e., 90 kg.). I have therefore used this figure in the text when converting *shi* into metric figures. To put these figures into some context, Mao reported that two *shi* of grain per year was enough to support a person. See Mao Zedong 1982, 170.

9. Mao Zedong 1982, 113–115.

10. Ibid., 113–114; Pan Shanfu, 25.

11. For a description of the central place hierarchy, see Skinner 1977a.

12. Mao Zedong 1982, 67, 100, 102.

13. Ibid., 162–163; Zeng Biyi, 88.

14. Mao Zedong 1982, 118–119.

15. Ibid., 126–130.

16. Ibid. See also Jiang Yuchang (c. 1908) for descriptions of local elite irregularities and antigovernment attitudes.

17. Mao Zedong 1982, 119.

18. Zeng Biyi, 88.

19. Mao Zedong 1982, 105. Mao estimated that landlords constituted 3.45 percent of the total Xunwu population, a figure supported by extrapolations from information provided elsewhere in his text. If allowance is made for nonlandowning merchants, teachers, and other elites not included in Mao's estimate, a figure of 3.5 to 4.0 percent seems reasonable.

20. Mao Zedong 1982, 115, 359n.

21. Hsien-chin Hu 1948; Hui-chen Wang Liu 1959b; Mao Zedong 1982, 106–108.

22. Hsien-chih Hu, 20–30; Mao Zedong 1949a, 22; Jiang Yuchang, 64b; Xiao Hua, 227.

23. Mao Zedong 1982, 129–131, 145–149; Mao Zedong 1949a, 22–24.

24. Mao Zedong 1949a, 22; Polachek, 812–813.

25. See essays by William Rowe and Timothy Brook in this volume, and Beattie 1979b.

26. Xunwu, and doubtless many other peripheral Jiangxi counties, had relatively few gentry during the Qing period. By the late nineteenth century the county elite could claim only 4 civil and 1 military *jinshi* (metropolitan graduate), 10 civil, 4 "imperial favor," and 52 military *juren* (provincial graduate), and 186 *gongsheng* (senior licentiate) degree winners. The Pans (present in the county from Song times onward and whose patriarch, Pan Mingzheng, was the dominant elite figure in the county in the early twentieth century) had won no major degrees whatsoever during the Qing and had only a handful of the honorific *gongsheng* degrees presented to elderly men who had repeatedly taken but failed the regular examinations. Even acknowledging the likely presence in the county at any one time of several hundred *shengyuan* (whose names are not listed in the local gazetteers) there must have been many local elites who were not degree holders and whose elite status was based on other attributes. *Changning xianzhi, juan* 2.

27. Deng Zihui, 60.

28. Qiu Zhou, 64–65.

29. Interview, Xiao Zhengqing et al., Xingguo county, May 26, 1984.

30. These comments on county magistrates are derived from such Republican period Jiangxi gazetteers and other sources as *Ninggang xianzhi, houzhi*: 3–14; *Fenyi xianzhi*, 10; *Jiangxi minzheng gongbao*, 8 (Apr. 16, 1928). For Qing conditions, see Watt 1972.

31. Zhonggong Ruijin xianwei, 6a.

32. For other examples, see ibid., 5a–b; Jiang Yuchang, 1:60a.

33. E.g., Tse-tsung Chow 1960. This and most other relevant works concentrate upon the political impact of urban institutions of higher education. As this essay hopes to show, the politics of the May Fourth era and after were also shaped by events in lower-level, more rural schools.

34. This section on education follows Averill (1987, 282–285) and the sources cited therein.

35. For examples of provincial government inspection of schools, see *Jiangxi jiaoyu gongbao*, 2.14 (Jan. 1, 1929):25–28; 3.2 (May 11, 1929):37–45.

36. For examples of such networks, see Yang Yuanming, 35, and Jiang Bozhang.

37. It is unclear just when this involvement in factional politics began, but certainly the late Qing reformist and revolutionary movements set in motion various changes—the formation of study associations (*xuehui*), the New Policies (including

the establishment of the new schools themselves), and the founding of organized political parties—that encouraged its growth.

38. Comments on county-level schools are based on republican period gazetteers; comments on old-style village schools are based on similar biographical materials published in the Taiwan journal, *Jiangxi wenxian,* and a variety of PRC sources. For an example from Huichang county, on Xunwu's northern border, see Liu Lucheng, 116–119. Information on Xunwu is from Mao Zedong 1982, 160–163. Altogether in 1930 the county had 30 university graduates (6 of whom had also studied abroad), 500 middle-school graduates, and 800 upper elementary-school graduates. It also had 400 living Qing *shengyuan* and one *juren.*

39. Mao Zedong 1982, 125–126, 161–162.

40. Ibid., 126–131, 161–162. Mao's impressionistic comments on educational attitudes should be read with caution. But his conclusions are plausible, consistent with other available evidence, and well informed. He drew his information from local CCP cadres, such as Gu Bo, who had past personal involvement in Xunwu's educational circles and considerable recent opportunity to reflect upon the county's class structure.

41. Hobsbawm, chaps. 2, 6; Liu Xiaonong 1980; Zou Fuguang 1984.

42. Ibid.; Jiang Yuchang, 1:58a–60a. Many themes mentioned in this discussion of hill-country banditry have been discussed at greater length in Billingsley 1988, which appeared after this article was completed. For an account of banditry elsewhere that also emphasizes connections between bandits and local elites, see Lewin 1979.

43. Hobsbawm, 35.

44. Liu Xiaonong, 106–107; Zou Fuguang, 94.

45. The following account of the revolutionary movement in Xunwu is based primarily on Zeng Biyi, 91–98; Bousfield, 109–124; Zhonggong Jiangxi shengwei dangshi yanjiushi, 183–185; Mao Zedong 1982, 67, 100, 127–129.

46. Averill 1987, 284–290.

47. Ibid., 283–284; Zhonggong Ruijin xianwei, 6b; Li Jishan, 26:123; Yifeng xian difang zhi bianzuan wei, 8–9.

48. For sources discussing these various issues, see Chen Qihan, 408–410; Huang Muxian 1981; Qiu Zhou, 77–79; Mao Zedong 1949a, 90; Guo Qi and Dong Xia 1982.

49. Deng Zihui, 57; Xiao Hua, 239; Chen Qihan, 409; Qiu Zhou, 75.

50. Huang Muxian 1981; He Changgong 1959; Chen Qihan, 408–410; Liu Xiaonong, 116–119.

51. The general point that Communist cadres used their family status and lineage ties to further the movement is well established. E.g., Chen Qihan, 410; Fang Zhichun, 145–146. Although much more indirect, evidence of the use of small lineages against large ones is considerable. E.g., Mao Zedong 1949a, 90; Yan Yaxian 1959; Hu Yueyi, 90; Shao Shiping, 62.

52. Mao Zedong 1982, 127–130.

53. In Mao's listing of over 125 landlords from around the county, he explicitly identified seventeen people belonging to or "colluding with" the New Xunwu clique: two from upper-elite, fourteen from middle-elite, and one from lower-elite families. As of 1930, eight of the seventeen were also active members of the GMD. Mao also mentions names of eleven people who were members of or "linked with" (*jiehe*) the

Cooperative Society and four who were linked with the Zhongshan clique or the Zhongshan School: twelve of these fifteen men were from lower-elite and two from middle-elite family backgrounds. Mao also specified that nine of the eleven people explicitly connected with the Cooperative Society were from declining households, a fact that he found characteristic of all people in the society. The vast majority of these fifteen individuals ultimately became CCP members and/or active participants in the revolution, though a few later abandoned the movement. Mao Zedong 1982, 67, 115–124, 128–129.

54. Data gathered on thirty-one pre-1927 Jiangxi CCP members whose biographies contain usable family-background information show that two-thirds of this group (all themselves well-educated individuals) were from families of local school teachers, small merchants, peasants, or artisans. The biographies indicate that some of these families (particularly the school teachers) represented declining branches of formerly more prosperous elites. Other Communists, especially those from peasant or artisan background, were only able to obtain the schooling that made them elites because of money borrowed from elite patrons, lineages, or distant relations. These figures are derived from research still in progress: the main sources are collections of biographies such as Zhonggong Jiangxi shengwei; Jiangxi sheng minzheng ting 1960, Jiangxi sheng minzheng ting 1980.

55. See Averill 1987, 294–295.

56. Somewhat exceptional in this regard are Yung-fa Chen 1986 and Galbiatti 1985. Neither, however, makes local elites a central part of his discussion.

57. See, among other studies, Moore 1966, Skocpol 1979, and Goldstone, ed. 1986.

NOTES TO CONCLUDING REMARKS

1. Blum, 11–12, 21–22, chap. 4.

2. See Goody, Thirsk, and Thompson, eds.

3. Stone and Stone, 69–104.

4. Wakeman (1975b, 19–28) points to the significance of elite life-styles. Articles by Rowe and Brook in this volume provide detailed treatment.

5. On merchants as spreaders of elite life-styles, see Naquin and Rawski, 59–60. On frontier gentrification, see Meskill, chaps. 12, 13; McCord and Zelin in this volume.

6. Robert Forster raised the issue of continuity of elite institutions versus continuity of personnel at the Banff conference.

7. Ping-ti Ho 1962 (esp. 258) is the best representative of this argument.

8. See especially Hymes 1986a; Wou, 69–88; and the local studies cited in note 9.

9. Beattie 1979b, 129; Meskill.

10. Esherick 1981, 401.

11. Mingay, 59; see also F. M. L. Thompson, 32, 112–117. For calculations on Chinese landholding, see Esherick 1981, 401. The English figures derive from the New Doomsday Survey of 1873. Because the social categories are different it is hard to make exact comparisons between even late-nineteenth-century England and early-

twentieth-century China. However, clearly the English aristocratic and gentry land-owners were not only far fewer than the approximately one million Chinese degree holders (c. 1.3 percent of the population, Chang Chung-li 1955, 111) of the early nineteenth century but also constituted a small percentage of the population compared with the 3 to 4 percent who appear as landlords in the twentieth-century Chinese surveys. The English 1871 census figure was 21,299,683 (see Wrigley, 588). Taking the simplest figures from the New Doomsday Survey—that 7,000 persons owned 80 percent of the land in 1873 (F. M. L. Thompson, 27)—and assuming that these people and their families totaled 35,000 people, they only constituted .0016 percent of the population of 21,300,000 and perhaps 30 percent of these were not members of the peerage, gentry or baronetcy.

12. Blum, 19–20.

13. Ossowski, 66; Forster 1987.

14. E. P. Thompson 1978, 133–165.

15. Ye Xian'en 1983; Wiens, 12–20.

16. For a powerful statement of this view, see Kuhn 1984, 17, 27.

17. For a summary of stratification in the Lower Yangzi, see Bell in this volume; on Hunan, see Perdue 1987, 150–163, 179–180; on North China, see Philip Huang; on Taiwan, see Harrell 1987.

18. Johnson, 36.

19. Min Tu-ki, chap. 2, esp. 22, 49.

20. Dennerline 1981, chap. 2; 1986, 170–209.

21. See Cao Xueqin, 1:111, for a reference to a published "Magistrate's Life Preserver" identifying the rich and powerful of a county.

22. Ping-ti Ho 1962, 227–229.

23. Esherick 1987, 30; Rankin 1986, 313–315.

24. Meskill, chap. 10.

25. Schoppa 1989.

26. See also Von Glahn, 181–202; Perdue 1987; Harrell 1987.

27. Lamley, 1–39.

28. Meskill, chaps. 11–12; Harrell 1987.

29. Kuhn 1970, chap. 3; McCord, 156–197.

30. Perdue 1987, 205–218; Faure, 42–43, 173.

31. Skinner 1964, 1965, 1977a, 1977c. For examples of progressive marketing integration in the Lower Yangzi, see Yoshinobu Shiba 1977 and Elvin 1977.

32. Rozman, 278–284.

33. Elman, 112–129.

34. Skinner 1976.

35. Cole 1980.

36. Robert Forster, comments at the Conference on Chinese Local Elites and Patterns of Dominance, Banff, 1987.

37. On this cultural tempering of conflict, see Harrell 1986, 135–136.

38. For a survey of the literature, see James Watson 1982, 589–622. Articles in Ebrey and Watson contain much historical information on lineages. On the history of lineages in Anhui, see Beattie 1979; Ye Xian'en 1983; and Zurndorfer. On the New Territories lineage history, see Faure. On Zhejiang, see Ueda Makoto.

39. Beattie 1979b, 88.

40. Dennerline 1979–80, 41.

41. This observation was made by Keith Schoppa.

42. Faure (56–60), also uses the term "trust" to refer to these lineage corporations. On corporate aspects of Chinese social organization, see Sangren.

43. Ebrey 1983.

44. Dennerline (1979–80, 42) also treats charitable estates as corporate and managerial entities, but he stresses their community educational and welfare functions as a way to maintain group unity and expand combined resources.

45. Naquin 1986; Rawski 1986; Duara 1988.

46. Barnes, 39–58.

47. Wang Dahua, 82–89.

48. Kuhn 1970, 84; Folsom.

49. He Bingdi 1966.

50. Eisenstadt and Roniger 1980, 66, 73. China partly fits Eisenstadt's model, though in such respects as lack of community cohesion and weak kin structures, North China fits better than the Yangzi valley and South China.

51. See Skinner 1976 (334, 342, 357) for a general statement about the better political access of cores with many degree holders. The account, in Meskill (chap. 10) of the Lin family's long struggle to get a hearing at court is a wonderful example of the difficulties faced by poorly connected elites on the periphery when they needed the protection of high officials.

52. For a useful general discussion of patronage and its functions in China, see Eisenstadt and Roniger 1984, esp. 48–50, 139–145, 203–219.

53. See Bourdieu (1977, 190–197) for a discussion of "symbolic violence."

54. This concept originated in Gramsci, 12; see also Williams 1977, 108–109; E. P. Thompson 1978, 163; and Lears.

55. See Johnson, Nathan, and Rawski, eds., esp. the articles by Evelyn Rawski, James Hayes, and Victor Mair.

56. Johnson 1985, 47–48.

57. Ortner, 153; Weller.

58. We thank Keith Schoppa for this observation.

59. Cao Xueqin, 1:chap. 18; 2:196–197; 3:248.

60. Meskill, chaps. 11–12.

61. Weller, 55.

62. E. P. Thompson 1974, 389.

63. Bourdieu 1977, 171–183. Bourdieu creates his definition around the ostensibly reciprocal gift giving in North Africa, but the principle can be applied to a variety of social situations.

64. Bailey 1971, 2.

65. E. P. Thompson 1978, 151, 154.

66. This idea comes from E. P. Thompson 1978 (163) who hypothesizes that the poor imposed some of their own terms as a price for the hegemony of the nobility. E. P. Thompson 1974, 403, explores this same issue.

67. Cf. Rowe 1989, chap. 5.

68. Esherick 1987, 235–240.

69. The remark by a Haifeng landlord that the main order of business was to teach troublesome peasants a "lesson in the law" (Marks, 184) can be interpreted in this sense. For the escalation of violence in Haifeng in the mid-1920s, see Galbiatti.

70. This view is shared by Ping-ti Ho (1962, 55, 230–231) and Beattie (1979b, 268–269).

71. Elvin 1973, 164–178. For a general summary of the issues, see Myers 1974, 265–278.

72. On Shanxi merchants, see Wei Qingyuan and Wu Qiyan, 127–144; Li Hua 1983. On the Huizhou salt merchants, see Ping-ti Ho 1954.

73. Huang Qichen and Deng Kaisong; Yu Siwei; Luo Yixing.

74. Peterson, 67–80.

75. Angela Hsi, 135–136, 138–142, 171–178.

76. The Huizhou salt merchants provide some of the best examples of this process. In addition to Ping-ti Ho 1954, see Ye Xian'en 1983.

77. Luo Yixing 1985.

78. See also Yen-p'ing Hao.

79. Chung-li Chang 1955, 114–141. This process led Ho Ping-ti (1962, 256) to conclude that "money, after 1850 at the latest, had overshadowed higher academic degrees as a determinant of higher status."

80. See Stone and Stone, on the English case. The Stones argue against the notion of an open English elite but present much evidence that seems, in comparative terms, to support it. They summarize (3–6) some effects attributed to England's "open" elite and note the literature arguing for them.

81. Cited in Stone and Stone, 23.

82. Wang Shizhen (mid-sixteenth century) cited in Elvin 1973, 223.

83. See Grove (forthcoming, chap. 2) for a full discussion; also Elvin 1973, 172–175.

84. Stone and Stone, 420.

85. On the wide geographic range of the Shanxi merchants see Li Hua. The investment of Shaanxi merchants in the Ziliugong salt wells is an example of such scattering of investment; see Zelin's article in this volume.

86. Ye Xian'en 1983 (123–143) provides compelling examples of this "feudalization" of merchant profits through "contributions" to the state and the purchase of land.

87. Bastid-Bruguière, 539–540.

88. McCord, 156–197.

89. Edmund Fung, 62–113.

90. See Alitto, 220–221; also Perry for a general view of how militarized groups fitted into nineteenth- and twentieth-century North China society.

91. Elman, 87–138.

92. Dennerline 1981, 118–119; on the English case, see Miles, 196–210.

93. On private secretaries, see Cole 1980; on pettifoggers, Macauley.

94. Liang Qizi, 309–310, 313, 317, 322; cf. Joanna H. Smith, 309–338; and more generally, Naquin and Rawski, 44–46, 58.

95. Perdue 1987, 164–233.

96. Zelin 1984, 264–302.

97. Perdue 1987, 75; Mann 1987; Rowe 1989, chap. 4.

98. Kuhn 1970; Mann 1987; Rowe 1989; Rankin 1986.

99. Ping-ti Ho 1964, 236.

100. Rankin 1986, 8, 62, 176, 217, 258; Schoppa 1982, 67, 95–109, 121–124, 136, 140–141, 152, 186–190.

101. Esherick 1976, 66–69, 99–105, 243–252; Kuhn 1970, 224. Note that Rankin rejects this notion of a split between urban and rural elites in economically developed cores; see Rankin 1986, 232–233, 243; and 1977, 67–104.

102. On the twentieth-century use of this term, *tuhao lieshen*, see Kuhn 1975, 287–295.

103. Perdue 1987; Will 1980a; Naquin and Rawski. See also Wong, Will, Lee, Perdue, and Oi.

104. Kuhn 1970.

105. One of the best textbooks on twentieth-century China is *China in Disintegration* by James E. Sheridan. For an application of this idea to local elites, see Alitto.

106. In addition to his article in this volume, see Duara 1987, 156.

107. Kuhn 1986, 344–352.

108. This conceptualization is employed in Fewsmith, 163–164, 189–191.

109. Bailey 1969, 77.

110. Ibid., 171.

111. Kuhn 1975, 287–295.

GLOSSARY

The large number of names and phrases in the text makes it necessary to restrict this list. Characters are given for most terms, but only for the most essential personal and geographical names. Characters for most authors and places in the bibliography are not repeated here. For names of nationally prominent individuals during the Qing dynasty, a standard reference is Arthur W. Hummel, ed., *Eminent Chinese of the Ch'ing Period*. For the Republican period, consult Howard L. Boorman and Richard C. Howard, eds., *Biographical Dictionary of Republican China*.

An Disheng	安迪生
ban dizhu xing de funong	半地主性的富農
banggui	帮櫃
baolan	包攬
bendi	本地
bian'an	邊岸
biao	標
Boquan	柏泉
bu gong dao	不公道
Caidian	蔡店
cehui ju	測繪局
Chahu Zhang	茶湖張
Changcun	昌村
changlu	長路
chanye	產業
Chen Zhaoshen	陳兆申
Cheng Bingruo	程炳若
Chengxi Fan	城西范
Chongde (Shrine)	崇德祠

Chongyi	崇義
Chuankou	沌口
Cong Peigong	叢佩功
da citang	大祠堂
Da tongmeng	大同盟
daguan guiren	達官貴人
dahu	大戶
daibiao	代表
Dangkou	蕩口
dao	道
Datangwu	大湯塢
Datong shangdian	大同商店
Dayan shan	大巖山
Deng Yu'an	鄧宇安
dianyuan gonghui	店員公會
dibao	地保
difang shenshi	地方紳士
Dingyuan Wan	定遠萬
dongfang	冬防
Dongze	東澤
douzhong	斗種
Duqing tang	都慶堂
Fan Zhongyan	范仲淹
fatuan	法團
Fengyang	鳳陽
fenzheng	分正
Fu Ju	傅菊
Fushi Zhou	浮石周
Gan	贛
gaodeng xiaoxue	高等小學
Ge Bilun	葛陛綸
gengdu	耕讀
gonghui	公會
Gongkuan gongchan guanli chu	公款公產管理處
Gongping	公平
gongsheng	貢生
gongsuo	公所
gongtang	公堂
Gouyue *zu*	鉤月祖
Gu Bo	古柏
Gu Dengzhi	顧澄之
Gu Guangming	古光明
Gu Lesan	古樂三
guandai	管帶

guanliao liumang	官僚流氓
Guanqiao	官橋
guanzhang	管賬
guifang	櫃房
gunpi	棍痞
Guomindang	國民黨
Ha Tsuen	厦村
Hakka	客家
Han-Huang-Chu	漢黃楚
Hanbang	漢帮
hang	行
Hankou	漢口
Hanyang	漢陽
He Bingzao	何丙藻
He Yingqin	何應欽
He Zizhen	何子貞
Hongshanmiao	洪山廟
Hou Dasheng	候大生
Houjiaying	候家營
houxue	後學
Hu Yuanhai	胡元海
Hu Yuanhe	胡元和
Hua Guanyi	華綸翼
Hua Zhisan	華芝三
Huaishang *shi*	懷上市
Huang Qiwu	黃七五
Huang Zhiqing	黃植青
Huangcaoba	黃草壩
Huanglingji	黃陵磯
Huangpi	黃陂
Huaxin *sichang*	華新絲廠
Huguang	湖廣
huiguan	會館
Huizhou	徽州
huowu gu	貨物股
ji-Chu	濟楚
Ji she	蕺社
jia	家
ji'an	計岸
Ji'an	吉安
Jiangbei Tu	江北屠
Jiangbei yunhe gongcheng ju	江北運河工程局
Jiangjing hui	講經會
Jiangnan	江南
Jiangshan Chen	姜山陳

Jiangxia	江夏
jiaoji gu	交際股
jiaoxiao	教孝
Jiaoyu xingzheng weiyuanhui	教育行政委員會
jiashu	家塾
Jiaxing	嘉興
Jiayu	嘉魚
jie	界
jiehe	結合
jikou shouyan	計口授鹽
jin	斤
Jingbian ying	靖邊營
Jingchuan Yang	鏡川楊
jingjie tang	精洁堂
Jingshan	京山
Jingshe	精舍
Jingshi xuetang	經世學堂
Jinkou	金口
Jinkui	金匱
jinshi	進士
Jinxi zhiyan hui	禁吸紙煙會
jitian	祭田
jiu pai	舊派
Jiuji yuan	救濟院
jiyin	積引
ju	局
junji	軍籍
juntian	軍田
junzi	君子
juren	舉人
Jurong	句容
jushen	巨紳
Kaihua *xiang*	開化鄉
kemin	客民
Kong Zhaomian	孔昭晃
Kong Ziming	孔子明
Lan Dashun	藍大順
laojiao	老教
laorenjia	老人家
laoshen	老紳
Li Bichun	李筆春
Li Shao	李韶
Li Siyou	李四友
Li Weiji	李維基
Li Yonghe	李永和

Li Yuanqing	李元慶
lian	臉
Lian xiang zizhi huiyi	聯鄉自治會議
Liang-Huai	兩淮
Lianghu Wu	兩湖吳
Lianhuati	蓮花堤
lieshen	劣紳
lijin	釐金
Linchuan	臨川
Linpu	臨浦
Linshi junzheng zong silingbu	臨時軍政總司令部
Lishui	溧水
Liu Gangwu	劉剛吾
Liu Gongliang	劉公亮
Liu Guande	劉官德
Liu Guanli	劉官禮
Liu Xianqian	劉顯潛
Liu Xianshi	劉顯世
Liu Yanshan	劉燕山
Liu Yue xueyou hui	留粵學友會
Liu Zixing	劉子馨
Liu Zongzhou	劉宗周
Longgu Chen	龍谷陳
Lou	樓
Lou Kehui	婁克輝
Lu Luosheng	魯雒生
Luoshe *zhen*	洛社鎮
Ma Jinfan	馬錦繁
Ma Jizhi	馬繼之
Ma Laichi	馬來迟
Macheng	麻城
Mao Guangsheng	冒廣生
Maodong Zhu	茅東朱
Maoshan zha	茅山閘
Maqi ba	麻溪壩
Meixian	梅縣
Meng Jinhou	孟覲侯
Meng Luochuan	孟洛川
menqiang	門墻
Mianyang	沔陽
mianzi	面子
minsheng	民生
mintian	民田
miye gonghui	米業公會
mu	畝
muyou	幕友

Nanhu Shen	南湖瀋
Nankang	南康
Nanling	南嶺
Nitang	泥迖
Nong xuebao	農學報
nonghui	農會
nongzhuang gu	農莊股
pai	派
Pan Mingzheng	潘明征
Pan Shusheng	潘樹聲
Pingmin she	平民社
poluo hu	破落戶
puhui	譜諱
Qian Fenggao	錢鳳高
qiandian	錢店
Qiantang	錢塘
qianzhuang	錢莊
Qijie Li	砌街李
Qinghua shan	清化山
Qingnian geming tongzhi hui	青年革命同志會
qingzhang ju	清丈局
Qiu Shaoyao	裘韶堯
Qixu She	棄繻社
qu	區
Qu Yingguang	屈映光
quanxuesuo	勸學所
quzhang	區長
ren	仁
Ren Kecheng	任可澄
Ren Sanzhai	任三宅
Ren Yuanbing	任元炳
Renchang *jianhang*	仁昌繭行
renshi	人士
rexin gongyi	熱心公益
Rong Desheng	榮德生
Rong Zongjing	榮宗敬
Rongxian	榮縣
Rongxiang *zhen*	榮鄉鎮
Rongyang	榮陽
Ruifuxiang	瑞蚨祥
Sandian hui	三點會
saosichang	繰絲廠
Sha Yuanbing	沙元炳

Sha Yuanqu	沙元渠
Shajing	沙井
shan laoshu	山老鼠
Shantoubu	山頭埠
Shaoyaozhi Qian	芍藥沚錢
shehui	社會
Shen Yuqing	瀋瑜慶
shencha	審查
shendong	紳董
Shengchang *tiehao*	昇昌鐵号
shengyuan	生員
Shenyi	愼怡
shi (picul)	石
Shi (surname)	史
shi (sub-district)	市
shi/ying ye	實營業
shifan xuexiao	師範學校
Shijinshan *miao*	十金山廟
shimin (scholars and people)	士民
shimin (townspeople)	市民
shiye	師爺
shizu	始祖
shuihui	水會
Shuili hui	水利會
shuixun	水巡
shumi yuan	樞密院
shuyuan	書院
Sibeichai	寺北柴
sichang	絲廠
sili	私利
sili	司理
sishu	私塾
Sun Chuanfang	孫傳芳
Sun Xueshi	孫學仕
Sun Xunchu	孫詢芻
Suoqian *xiang*	所前鄉
taidou	泰斗
tang	堂
Tang Eryong	唐爾鏞
Tang Pei'en	湯沛恩
Tang Shouchong	湯壽崇
Tang Shouqian	湯壽潛
Tangbei	塘背
tangzhang	塘長
Tianyi ge	天一閣
Tianyue xiang	天樂鄉

tongling	統領
Tongmeng hui	同盟會
tongnian	同年
tongxing zhiyi	同姓支異
tongzhi	同知
tongzu	同族
tuanfang zongju	團防總局
tuanlian	團練
tuanti	團體
tuanti zidong	團體自動
tuhao lieshen	土豪劣紳
tulie	土劣
tuntian	屯田
tuntou	屯頭
Wan Bangfu	萬邦孚
wan hu	萬戶
Wan Sinian	萬斯年
Wan'an	萬安
Wang Boqun	王伯群
Wang Langyun	王朗雲
Wang Sanwei	王三畏
Wang Wenhua	王文華
Wanzhu Gao	萬竹高
wei	衛
wenshe	文社
Wuchang	武昌
wudang	吾黨
Wudian	吳店
Wujin	武進
Wuxian	吳縣
Wuxiangqi Fu	五鄉砌傅
Xiakou	夏口
xian	縣
xian dangbu	縣黨部
xiang	鄉
Xiang-Han	襄漢
xiangdang	鄉黨
xiangdong	鄉董
xiangshen	鄉紳
xiangzhen	鄉鎮
xiangzu	鄉族
xianjin gu	現金股
Xiantao	仙桃
Xianzheng yubeihui	憲政預備會
Xiao Huisheng	蕭惠生

Xiaogan	孝感
Xiaoshan	蕭山
xiaoyi	孝義
Xiashao tang	下邵塘
Xiawutun	下五屯
Xicheng Dong	西城董
xiechou	挾仇
Xihu Chen	西湖陳
Xihu Lu	西湖陸
xin pai	新派
Xincheng	新城
Xincheng *yinhang*	信誠銀行
xinfa hu	新發戶
Xingguo	興國
Xinjian	新建
Xintan	新攤
Xinxun	新尋
Xiong Xiling	熊希齡
Xu Guozhen	許國楨
Xu Jiajin	徐家瑾
Xue Fucheng	薛福成
Xue Nanming	薛南溟
Xue Shouxuan	薛壽宣
xuehui	學會
xuemao	學貿
xunding	巡丁
xunfang ying	巡防營
Xunwu pingmin hezuo she	尋烏平民合作社
yahang	牙行
Yan Guixing	顏桂馨
Yan Guoxing	嚴國興
Yan Shenyu	嚴慎予
Yan Xiu	嚴修
Yan Yongxing	顏永興
Yang Jincheng	楊芐城
Yang Yuan	楊源
Yangmei	楊眉
yangshang	洋商
yanhao	鹽號
yanjing	鹽警
yanyan jing	鹽岩井
Yaojiazui	姚家嘴
Ye Mingchen	葉名琛
yijing banjing	以井辦井
yin	引
Yingshan	應山

yinshi shishen	殷實士紳
yitian	義田
Yixing *xian*	宜興縣
yizhang	議長
Yizhong shangye xuexiao	乙种商業學校
yizhuang	義莊
Yong River	甬河
Yongtai *sichang*	永泰絲廠
youfu wugui	有富無貴
youji	游擊
yuan	元
Yuantai qianzhuang	沅泰钱莊
Yubei lixian gonghui	預備立憲公會
Yudu	于都
Yugan	餘干
Yushui	于水
yuyin	餘引
zhai	寨
Zhaimen	寨門
Zhang Bailin	張百麟
Zhang Jian	張謇
Zhang Jing	張京
Zhang Rui	張瑞
Zhang Shiche	張時徹
Zhang Shizhao	章士釗
Zhang Xiang	張相
Zhang Yinqing	張寅卿
Zhang Yueqing	張樂卿
zhangfang guanshi	賬房管事
zhanggui	賬櫃
Zhao Laoyou	趙老有
Zhao Xi	趙熙
zhen	鎮
Zhenshuai she	眞率社
zhi	支
zhifu	知府
zhishi	知事
zhongbaoren	中保人
zhongren	中人
Zhongshan	中山
zhongyi ci	忠義祠
Zhongyi gonghui	中醫公會
Zhou Shunqing	周舜卿
Zhou Xiangqian	周祥千
Zhou Yingzhi	周應治
Zhouhanzhen Zhou	周漢鎮周

Zhouxin *zhen*	周新鎮
Zhuang Hao	莊濠
Zigong linshi yishihui	自貢臨時議事會
Ziliujing	自流井
zipai	字派
Zizhi xueshe	自治學社
zong	宗
zong guifang	總櫃房
zong zhanggui	總賬櫃
zu	族
zupu	族譜
zusong	族訟
zuzhang	族長

BIBLIOGRAPHY

Ai Bida 愛必達. [1847?] 1968. *Qiannan shilue* 黔南識畧 (A record of south Guizhou). Reprint, Taibei.

Ai Nanying 艾南英. [1836] 1980. *Tian yongzi ji* 天庸子集 (The collected writings of heaven's hired hand). Reprint, Taibei.

Alitto, Guy S. 1978–79. "Rural Elites in Transition: China's Cultural Crisis and the Problem of Legitimacy." In *Select Papers from the Center for Chinese Studies*, University of Chicago, no. 3, 218–276. Chicago.

Averill, Stephen C. 1987. "Party, Society and Local Elite in the Jiangxi Communist Movement." *Journal of Asian Studies* 46, no. 2 (May): 279–303.

———. 1983. "The Shed People and the Opening of the Yangzi Highlands." *Modern China* 9, no. 1: 84–126.

Bailey, F. G. 1971. "Gifts of Poison." In *Gifts and Poison: The Politics of Reputation*, edited by F. G. Bailey, 1–25. Oxford.

———. 1969. *Stratagems and Spoils: A Social Anthropology of Politics*. New York.

Baker, Hugh H. D. 1977. "Extended Kinship in the Traditional City." In Skinner, ed., 499–518. Stanford.

———. 1968. *A Chinese Lineage Village: Sheung Shui*. Stanford.

Balazs, Etiènne. 1964. *Chinese Civilization and Bureaucracy: Variations on a Theme*. Translated by H. M. Wright. New Haven.

Bao Jianxing 保健行. 1981. "Xian-Tong nianjian Guizhou Huimin de fan-Qing douzheng" 咸同年間貴州回民的反清鬥爭 (Anti-Qing struggles of Guizhou's Muslims in the Xianfeng-Tongzhi period). *Guizhou wenshi congkan* 貴州文史叢刊 (Collected articles on Guizhou's culture and history), 1:78–86.

Barkan, Lenore, 1986. "Retrenchment through Progress: Sub-county Government in a Nationalist Setting." Paper presented at the 38th meeting of the Association for Asian Studies, March 21–23.

———. 1983. "Nationalists, Communists and Local Leaders: Political Dynamics in a Chinese County, 1927–1937." Ph.D. diss., University of Washington.

Barnes, J. A. 1954. "Class and Committees in a Norwegian Island Parish." *Human Relations* 7:39–58.

Bastid, Marianne. 1989. *Educational Reform in Early Twentieth-Century China*. Translated by Paul J. Bailey. Ann Arbor.

Bastid-Bruguière, Marianne. 1980. "Currents of Social Change." In *The Cambridge History of China*, edited by John K. Fairbank and Kwang-ching Liu. Vol. 11, *The Late Ch'ing, 1800–1911, Part 2*, 535–602. Cambridge.

Beattie, Hilary. 1979a. "The Alternative to Resistance: The Case of T'ung-ch'eng, Anhui." In *From Ming to Ch'ing: Conquest, Region and Continuity in Seventeenth-Century China*, edited by Jonathan D. Spence and John E. Wills, Jr., 239–276. New Haven.

———. 1979b. *Land and Lineage in China: A Study of T'ung-ch'eng County, Anhwei, in the Ming and Ch'ing Dynasties*. Cambridge.

Beijing Ruifuxiang 北京瑞蚨祥 (Ruifuxiang of Beijing). 1959. Edited by Ziben zhuyi jingji gaizao yanjiushi, Zhongguo kexueyuan jingji yanjiusuo 資本主義經濟改造研究室, 中國科學院經濟研究所 (Research Office for the Transformation of the Capitalist Economy, Chinese Academy of Sciences Economic Research Institute). Beijing.

Bell, Lynda S. Draft manuscript. "The Dynamics of Chinese Development: Agriculture, Commercialization, and Industry in Wuxi County."

———. Forthcoming. "Farming, Sericulture and Peasant Rationality in Wuxi County in the Early Twentieth Century." In *Chinese History in Economic Perspective*, edited by Thomas Rawski and Lilian Li. Berkeley.

———. 1985a. "Merchants, Peasants, and the State: The Organization and Politics of Chinese Silk Production, Wuxi County, 1870–1937." Ph.D. diss. University of California, Los Angeles.

———. 1985b. "Explaining China's Rural Crisis: Observations from Wuxi County in the Early Twentieth Century," *Republican China* 11, no. 1 (Nov.): 15–31.

Bergère, Marie-Claire. 1983. "The Chinese Bourgeoisie, 1911–37." In *The Cambridge History of China*, edited by John K. Fairbank. Vol. 12, *Republican China, 1912–1949*, Part 1, 722–827. Cambridge.

———. 1968. "The Role of the Bourgeoisie." In *China in Revolution*, edited by Mary Clabaugh Wright, 229–295. New Haven.

Bernhardt, Kathryn, Draft manuscript. "Peasants, Elites, and the State in the Lower Yangzi Valley, 1800–1937."

Billingsley, Phil. 1988. *Bandits in Republican China*. Stanford.

Blum, Jerome. 1978. *The End of the Old Order in Rural Europe*. Princeton.

Boorman, Howard L., and Richard C. Howard, eds. 1968. *Biographical Dictionary of Republican China*. New York.

Bourdieu, Pierre. 1984. *Distinction: A Social Critique of the Judgement of Taste*. Translated by Richard Nice. Cambridge, Mass.

———. 1977. *An Outline of a Theory of Practice*. Translated by Richard Nice. Cambridge.

Bourne, Frederick. 1898. *Report of the Mission to China of the Blackburn Chamber of Commerce, 1896–1897: F. S. A. Bourne's Section*. Blackburn.

Bousfield, Lillian. 1932. *Sun-wu Stories*. Shanghai.

Brim, John, 1970. "Local Systems and Modernizing Change in the New Territories." Ph.D. diss., Stanford University.

Brook, Timothy. Forthcoming. *Patronage and Power: Buddhist Monasteries and the Chinese Gentry, 1522–1722*.

———. 1988. "Must Lineages Own Land?" *Bulletin of Concerned Asian Scholars* 20, no. 4 (Dec.): 72–79.

Buck, John Lossing. 1937. *Land Utilization in China.* Nanking.

———. 1930. *Chinese Farm Economy: A Study of 2,866 Farms in Seventeen Localities and Seven Provinces in China.* Chicago.

Burgess, John. 1925. *The Significance of Social Work in China.* Vol. 10. Beijing.

Bush, Richard C. 1982. *The Politics of Cotton Textiles in Kuomintang China, 1927–1937.* New York.

Cai Guanming 蔡觀明. 1980. "*Gao ming bao* de huiyi"《皋鳴報的回憶》(Reminiscences of the Rugao crier). *Rugao wenshi zhiliao* 1:77–78.

Cannadine, David. 1980. *Lords and Landlords: The Aristocracy and the Towns, 1774–1967.* Leicester.

Cao Xueqin. 1973, 1977. *The Story of the Stone.* Vol. 1: *The Golden Days*; Vol. 2: *The Crab-Flower Club*; Vol. 3: *The Warning Voice.* Translated by David Hawkes. Baltimore.

Chai Degeng 柴德賡. 1982. *Shixue congkao* 史學叢考 (A collection of historical studies). Beijing.

Chang, Ch'un-ming. 1936. "A New Government for Rural China: The Political Aspect of Rural Reconstruction." *Nankai Social and Economic Quarterly* 9, no. 2 (July): 239–295.

Chang, Chung-li. 1962. *The Income of the Chinese Gentry.* Seattle.

———. 1955. *The Chinese Gentry: Studies on Their Role in Nineteenth-Century Chinese Society.* Seattle.

Changning xianzhi 長寧縣志. 1877. (Gazetteer of Changning [Xunwu] county).

Chen, Han-seng. 1936. *Landlord and Peasant in China: A Study of the Agrarian Crisis in South China.* New York.

———. 1933. *The Present Agrarian Problem in China.* Shanghai.

Chen Huayin 陳華寅. 1929. "Jiangsu sheng renkou yu yiken tianmu zhi xilian" 江蘇省人口與已墾田畝之系聯. (Correlation between population and cultivated land in Jiangsu), *Tongji yuebao* 統計月報 1, no. 3 (May): 44–48.

Chen Qiaoyi 陳橋驛. 1981. "Lun lishi shiqi Puyangjiang xiayou de hedao bianqian" 論歷史時期浦陽江下游的河道變迁 (On the changes in the course of the Puyang river throughout history). *Lishi dili* 歷史地理 1:65–79.

Chen Qihan 陳奇涵. 1959. "Xingguo de chuqi geming douzheng" 興國的初期革命鬥爭 (The first period of revolutionary struggle in Xingguo). *Xinghuo liaoyuan* 星火燎原 1:407–417.

Chen Tingfang 陳廷芳. 1943. "Jindai Zhongguo zhi saosiye" 近代中國之繅絲业 (Modern China's silk-reeling industry). *Qiye zhoukan* 企業週刊 1 (Nov.–Dec.): 46–47; reprinted as "Juyou fengjian de maiban xingzhi de Zhongguo saosiye" (China's feudalistic, comprador-nature silk-reeling industry), in Chen Zhen 4:111–113.

Chen Yi 陳一. 1935. "Wuxi nongcun zhi xianzhuang" 無錫農村之現狀 (Current conditions in the Wuxi countryside). *Nonghang yuekan* 農行月刊 2, no. 4 (April): 31–34.

Chen, Yung-fa. 1986. *Making Revolution: The Communist Movement in Eastern and Central China, 1937–1945.* Berkeley.

Chen Zhen 陳眞 et al., eds. 1957–1961. *Zhongguo jindai gongye shi ziliao* 中國近代工業史資料 (Materials on the industrial history of modern China), 4 vols. Beijing.

Chesneaux, Jean. 1968. *The Chinese Labor Movement, 1919–1927.* Stanford.

China Industrial Handbooks: Kiangsu. 1933. Ministry of Industry, Bureau of Foreign Trade, comp. Shanghai.

Chinese Economic Bulletin. 1921–27. Beijing.

Chow, Tse-tsung, 1960. *The May Fourth Movement: Intellectual Revolution in Modern China*. Cambridge, Mass.

Chow, Yung-teh. 1966. *Social Mobility in China: Status Careers Among the Gentry in a Chinese Community*. New York.

Chu, Samuel C. 1965. *Reformer in Modern China*. New York.

Ch'ü, T'ung-tsu. 1962. *Local Government in China Under the Ch'ing*. Stanford.

Chūgoku nōson kankō chōsa 中國農村慣行調查. 1981. (Investigation of Chinese village customs). 6 vols. Tokyo.

Chūshi kensetsu shiryō seibi jimusho, ed. 1941. 中支建設資料整備事務所. *Mushaku kōgyō jijō* 無錫工業事情 (Wuxi industry). Shanghai.

Clapham, Christopher. 1985. *Third World Politics: An Introduction*. Madison.

Coble, Parks. 1980. *The Shanghai Capitalists and the Nationalist Government, 1927–1937*. Cambridge, Mass.

Cohen, Abner. 1981. *The Politics of Elite Culture: Explorations in the Dramaturgy of Power in a Modern African Society*. Berkeley.

Cole, James. 1986. *Shaohsing: Competition and Cooperation in Nineteenth Century China*. Tucson, Ariz.

———. 1980. "The Shaoxing Connection: A Vertical Administrative Clique in Late Qing China." *Modern China* 6, no. 3 (July): 317–326.

Curtin, Philip. 1975. *Economic Change in Precolonial Africa*. Madison.

Dagong bao 大公報 (L'Impartial). Changsha.

Davis, Richard. 1986. *Court and Family in Sung China, 960–1279: Bureaucratic Success and Kinship Fortunes for the Shih of Ming-chou*. Durham, N. C.

Deng Haoming 鄧昊明. 1981. "'Benshe' shimo" "本社"始末 (The whole story of the "Foundation Society"). *Wenshi ziliao xuanbian* 文史資料选編, Beijing, vol. 9.

Deng Zihui 鄧子恢. 1982. "Huiyi Chongyi 'wuyi' baodong" 回憶崇義"五一"暴動 (Remembering the May First Uprising in Chongyi). *Jiangxi wenshi ziliao* 江西文史資料 8:54–61.

Dennerline, Jerry. 1988. *Qian Mu and the World of Seven Mansions*. New Haven.

———. 1986. "Marriage, Adoption, and Charity in the Development of Lineages in Wu-hsi from Sung to Ch'ing." In Ebrey and Watson, eds., 170–209. Berkeley.

———. 1981. *The Chia-ting Loyalists: Confucian Leadership and Social Change in Seventeenth-Century China*. New Haven.

———. 1979–80. "The New Hua Charitable Estate and Local Level Leadership in Wuxi County at the End of the Qing." In *Papers from the Center for Far Eastern Studies*, University of Chicago 4:19–70.

Dier lishi dang'anguan 第二歷史檔案館 (Number Two National History Archive, Nanjing). *File no. 1328* (Materials from the Ministry of Industry, dated Sept. 24, 1932), "Zhengli Jiang-Zhe chenchangsi chenjian weiyuanhui zhuyue huiyi an" 整理江浙陳廠絲陳茧委員會逐月會議案 (Monthly meeting reports of the committee to arrange for dealing with old stocks of filature silk and cocoons).

———. *File no. 3233* (Materials of the Ministry of Industry and Commerce) Jiang-Zhe-Wan sijianye tuanti guanyu baohu jianshi, xianzhi jianhang jianzao jianyi 江浙皖絲茧業團體關于保護茧市，限制茧行茧灶建議 (Proposals from silk industry groups in Jiangsu, Zhejiang, and Anhui for protection of cocoon marketing and control of cocoon firms and cocoon-drying rooms), 1927–31.

————. *File no. 3242* (Materials from the Ministry of Industry)—*Subfile no. 22061* "Jiangsu sheng gexian jianhang yilan" 江蘇省各縣茧行一覽 (An overview by county of Jiangsu cocoon firms), 1930.

————. *File no. 3242—Subfile no. 32472* "Ershier nianfen jiansi chanliang deng diaocha biao xudao gexian yilanbiao" 二十二年份茧絲產量等調查表續到各縣一覽表 (Supplementary tables by county on the investigation of cocoon and silk production in 1933).

————. *File no. 3504 Jiang-Zhe-Wan-Hu qudi canzhong qingxing* 江浙皖滬取締蚕种情形 (The regulation of silkworm eggs in Jiangsu, Zhejiang, Anhui, and Shanghai)— *Subfile*: "Liangnian lai bensheng (Zhejiang) canzhong zhizao ji qudi jingguo gaikuang, Minguo ershinian—Minguo ershiernian" 兩年來本省(浙江)蚕种制造及取締經过概況,民國二十年－民國二十二年 (The manufacture and regulation of silkworm eggs in Zhejiang for the past two years—1931–33).

Dinghai xianzhi 定海縣志. 1563. (Gazetteer of Dinghai County).

Dongnan daxue nongke 東南大學農科, ed. 1923–24. *Jiangsu sheng nongye diaochalu* 江蘇省農業調查录 (Records of an investigation into agriculture in Jiangsu province). 3 vols. Changzhou.

Dongnan ribao 東南日報. 1948. Hangzhou ed. January–December.

Duara, Prasenjit. 1988. *Culture, Power, and the State: Rural North China, 1900–1942.* Stanford.

————. 1987. "State Involution: A Study of Local Finances in North China, 1911–1935." *Comparative Studies in Society and History* 29 (January): 132–161.

————. 1985. "Review of Joseph Fewsmith, *Party, State and Local Elites in Republican China.*" *Journal of Asian Studies* 45, no. 1 (November): 117–118.

————. 1983. "Power in Rural Society: North China Villages, 1900–1940." Ph.D. diss., Harvard University.

Eberhard, Wolfram, 1971. *A History of China.* Berkeley.

————. 1970. *Conquerors and Rulers: Social Forces in Medieval China.* Leiden.

Ebrey, Patricia Buckley. 1986. "The Early Stages in the Development of Descent Group Organization." In Ebrey and Watson, eds., 16–61. Berkeley.

————. 1983. "Types of Lineages in Ch'ing China: A Reexamination of the Chang Lineage of T'ung-ch'eng." *Ch'ing-shih wen-t'i* 4, no. 9 (June): 1–20.

Ebrey, Patricia, and James L. Watson. 1986a. "Introduction." In Ebrey and Watson, eds., 1–15. Berkeley.

————. eds. 1986b. *Kinship Organization in Late Imperial China, 1000–1940.* Berkeley.

Eisenstadt, S. N., and L. Roniger. 1984. *Patrons, Clients, and Friends: Interpersonal Relations and the Structure of Trust in Society.* Cambridge, England.

————. 1980. "Patron-Client Relations as a Model of Structuring Social Exchange." *Comparative Studies in Society and History* 22, no. 1 (Jan.): 42–77.

Elman, Benjamin. 1984. *From Philosophy to Philology: Intellectual and Social Aspects of Change in Late Imperial China.* Cambridge, Mass.

Elvin, Mark. 1977. "Market Towns and Waterways: The County of Shang-hai from 1480–1910." In Skinner, ed., 441–473.

————. 1973. *The Pattern of the Chinese Past.* Stanford.

Entenmann, Robert E. 1982. "Migration and Settlement in Sichuan, 1644–1796."

Ph.D. diss. Harvard University.

Esherick, Joseph N. 1987. *The Origins of the Boxer Uprising*. Berkeley.

———. 1981. "Number Games: A Note on Land Distribution in Prerevolutionary China," *Modern China* 7:387–411.

———. 1976. *Reform and Revolution in China: The 1911 Revolution in Hunan and Hubei*. Berkeley.

Everitt, Alan. 1966. "Social Mobility in Early Modern England." *Past and Present* 33 (April): 56–73.

Fan Zhiqing 范植清. 1985. "Mingmo nongmin daqiyi yu Hankouzhen de fazhan" 明末農民大起義與漢口鎮的發展 (The great late Ming peasant rebellions and the development of Hankou). *Zhongguo nongmin zhanzheng shi yanjiu jikan* 中國農民戰爭史研究季刊 4:156–163.

Fang Mingzhu 方銘竹. 1963. "Qingdai yapian zhanzheng qian tongye shangren de hangbang zuzhi" 清代鴉片戰爭前同業商人的行帮組織 (Organization among merchants of the same trade in the Qing period prior to the Opium War), *Shangye yanjiu* 商業研究 3 (Dec. 20): 59–61.

Fang Zhichun 方志純. 1983. *Huainian ji* 懷念集 (A collection of cherished memories). Beijing.

Faure, David. 1986. *The Structure of Chinese Rural Society: Lineage and Village in the Eastern New Territories, Hong Kong*. Oxford.

Fei Dasheng 費達生. 1981. Interview, May 18, at the Suzhou Silk Industry Institute in Suzhou, an affiliate of the Suzhou School for Sericulture in Hushuguan.

Fei, Hsiao-t'ung (Fei Xiaotong). 1953. *China's Gentry: Essays on Rural-Urban Relations*. Edited by Margaret Park Redfield. Chicago.

———. 1939. *Peasant Life in China: A Study of County Life in the Yangtze Valley*. London.

Fei, Hsiao-t'ung, and Chang Chih-i. 1948. *Earthbound China: A Study of Rural Economy in Yunnan*. London.

Fei Xiaotong (Fei Hsiao-t'ung) 費孝通 et al. 1984. *Xiao chengzhen da wenti* 小城鎮大問題 (Major questions regarding small cities and towns). Nanjing.

Feng Hefa 馮和法. 1935. *Zhongguo nongcun jingji ziliao xubian* 中國農村經濟資料續編 (Supplementary materials on China's rural economy). Shanghai.

Feng shi zongpu 馮氏宗譜. 1946. (Genealogy of the Feng lineage).

Feng Zuyi 馮祖貽. 1984. "Xingyi Liushi jiazu yu jindai Guizhou zhengzhi" 興義劉氏家族與近代貴州政治 (The Liu family of Xingyi and modern Guizhou's politics). *Guizhou wenshi congkan* 貴州文史叢刊 (Collected articles on Guizhou's culture and history) 4:61–70.

———. 1982. "1902–1905 nian Guangxi huidang qiyi jun zai Guizhou, Yunnan de huodong" 1902–1905 年廣西會黨起義軍在貴州、雲南的活動 (The activities of Guangxi secret society uprising armies in Guizhou and Yunnan from 1902 to 1905). *Guizhou shehui kexue* 貴州社會科學 3:58–63.

Fenyi xianzhi 分宜縣志. 1940 (Gazetteer of Fenyi county).

Fewsmith, Joseph. 1985. *Party, State and Local Elites in Republican China: Merchant Organizations and Politics in Shanghai, 1870–1930*. Honolulu.

Fincher, John. 1981. *Chinese Democracy: The Self-Government Movement in Local Provincial and National Politics, 1905–1914*. London.

Folsom, Kenneth E. 1968. *Friends, Guests and Colleagues: The "Mu-fu" System in the Late Ch'ing Period*. Berkeley.

Forster, Robert. 1987. "Comments: Some Perspectives of a European Historian." Paper written for the Conference on Chinese Local Elites and Patterns of Dominance. Banff.

———. 1980. *Merchants, Landlords, Magistrates: The Depont Family in Eighteenth-Century France*. Baltimore.

Freedman, Maurice. 1966. *Chinese Lineage and Society: Fukien and Kwangtung*. London.

———. 1958. *Lineage Organization in Southeast China*. London.

Fried, Morton. 1966. "Some Political Aspects of Clanship in a Modern Chinese City." In *Political Anthropology*, edited by Marc J. Swartz, Victor W. Turner, and Arthur Tuden, 285–300. Chicago.

Fu Dong 傅冬. 1981. "Bawu laoren yi xi hua" 八五老人一席話 (A talk with an eighty-five-year-old man). *Rugao wenshi ziliao* 3:132–136.

Fu Yiling 傅衣凌. 1982. "Lun xiangzu shili duiyu Zhongguo fengjian jingji de ganshe" 論鄉族勢力對于中國封建經濟的干涉 (The negative influence of *xiang*-level lineages on China's feudal economy). In Fu Yiling, *Ming-Qing shehui jingji shi lunwenji* 明清社會經濟史論文集 (Collected essays on Ming and Qing socioeconomic history). 78–102. Beijing.

Fujii Masao 藤井正夫. 1955. "Shimmatsu Kō-Setsu ni okeru tetsuro mondai to burujoa seiryoku no ichi sokumen" 清末江浙における鉄路問題とブルジョア勢力の一側面 (The late Qing railway question in Jiangsu and Zhejiang, and one aspect of the power of the bourgeoisie). *Rekishingaku kenkyū* 歷史學研究 5:22–30.

Fung, Edmund S. K. 1980. *The Military Dimension of the Chinese Revolution: The New Army and Its Role in the Revolution of 1911*. Canberra.

Fushun xianzhi 富順縣志. 1932. (Gazetteer of Fushun county).

Fushun Ziliujing Zhenzhushan Wangshi Baoshan ci sixiu jiapu. n.d. 富順自流井珍珠山王氏宝善祠四修家譜 (The fourth edition of the genealogy of the Wang family of the Baoshan ancestral hall, Zhenzhushan, Ziliujing, Fushun).

Galbiatti, Fernando. 1985. *P'eng P'ai and the Hai-Lu-Feng Soviet*. Stanford.

Gamble, Sidney. 1963. *North China Villages*. Berkeley.

———. 1921. *Peking: A Social Survey*. New York.

Ganzhou fuzhi 贛州府志. 1778. (Gazetteer of Ganzhou prefecture).

Gao Jingyue 高景岳. 1983. "Wuxi saosi gongye de fazhan he qiye guanli de yanbian, 1904–1956" 無錫繅絲工業的發展和企業管理的演變 (Development of the Wuxi filature industry and the evolution of industrial management, 1904–1956), *Zhongguo shehui jingji shi yanjiu* 中國社會經濟史研究 1:102–110.

———. 1980. Interview, May 24, at the headquarters of the Wuxi People's Political Consultative Congress, Wuxi.

Gao Jingyue, and Yan Xuexi 嚴學熙. 1980. "Wuxi zuizao de sangyuan" 無錫最早的桑园 (Wuxi's first mulberry tract), *Wuxi xianbao* 無錫縣報, Aug. 20: 4.

Gao ming bao 皋鳴報 1913. (The Rugao crier). Rugao.

Gao nong 皋農. 1931. (Rugao agriculture). Rugao.

Gates, Hill. 1981. "Social Class and Ethnicity." In *The Anthropology of Taiwanese Society*, edited by Emily Ahern and Hill Gates. Stanford.

Geertz, Clifford. 1973a. "Deep Play: Notes on the Balinese Cockfight." In *The Interpretation of Cultures*, edited by Clifford Geertz, 412–453. New York.

———. 1973b. "Religion as a Cultural System." In *The Interpretation of Cultures*, edited by Clifford Geertz, 87–125. New York.

Geisert, Bradley Kent. 1979. "Power and Society: The Kuomintang and Local Elites in Kiangsu Province, China, 1924–1937." Ph.D. diss., University of Virginia.

Gellner, Ernest, and J. Waterbury, eds. 1977. *Patrons and Clients in Mediterranean Societies*. London.

Gendai Shina no kiroku 近代支那の記錄. 1928. (Records of contemporary China). Compiled by Hatano Ken'ichi 波多野乾. Tokyo.

Genealogical Society of Utah, ed. 1983. *Chinese Genealogies at the Genealogical Society of Utah: An Annotated Bibliography*. Taipei.

Goldstone, Jack, ed. 1986. *Revolutions: Theoretical, Comparative and Historical Studies*. New York.

Gongshang banyuekan 工商半月刊. 1930–31. Shanghai.

Goody, Jack, Joan Thirsk, and E. P. Thompson, eds. 1976. *Family and Inheritance: Rural Society in Western Europe, 1200–1800*. Cambridge.

Gouldner, Alvin. 1977. "The Norm of Reciprocity: A Preliminary Statement." In *Friends, Followers and Factions*, edited by S. W. Schmidt, L. Guasti, C. H. Lande, and J. C. Scott, 28–43. Berkeley.

Gramsci, Antonio. 1971. *Selections from the Prison Notebooks*. Edited and translated by Quintin Hoare and Geoffrey N. Smith. New York.

Grant, Charles. 1964. "The Extension of the Arable Area in Hong Kong." In *Land Use Problems in Hong Kong*, edited by S. G. Davis. Hong Kong.

Grove, Linda. Forthcoming. *Rural Manufacture in China's Modernization: The Gaoyang Textile Industry from 1900 to the 1980s.*

Grove, Linda, and Christian Daniels, eds. 1984. *State and Society in China: Japanese Perspectives on Ming-Qing Social and Economic History*. Tokyo.

Grove, Linda, and Joseph W. Esherick. 1980. "From Feudalism to Capitalism: Japanese Scholarship on the Transformation of Chinese Rural Society." *Modern China* 6, no. 4 (Oct.): 397–438.

Gu Shijiang 顧士江. 1933. *Xiaoshan xiangtu zhi* 蕭山鄉土志 (A gazetteer of Xiaoshan county). Hangzhou.

Gu Yanwu 顧炎武. 1959. "Shengyuan lun" 生員論 (On *shengyuan*). In *Gu Tinglin shiwenji* 顧亭林詩文集 (Poetry and essays of Gu Yanwu), 22–26. Beijing.

Guan Ruiwu 關瑞梧. 1980. "Jiefang qian de Beijing Xiangshan ciyou yuan" 解放前的北京香山慈幼院 (Beijing's Xiangshan orphanage prior to liberation). *Wenshi ziliao xuanji* 文史資料選輯 31 (November): 155–166.

Guan Weilin 管維霖. 1980. "Yu Zhiwen fenmo zayi" 于志文粉墨雜憶 (Recollections of Yu Zhiwen in politics). *Rugao wenshi ziliao* 2:88–92.

Guan Yida 管義達. 1935. "Jiangsusheng ershisannian canye tongzhi baogao" 江蘇省二十三年蠶業統制報告 (Report on Jiangsu's sericulture control for 1934). *Jiangsu jianshe yuekan* 江蘇建設月刊 2, no. 3 (March): report sec., 1–6.

Guangxu Hubei yudi ji 光緒湖北輿地記. 1894. (Geography of Hubei). Wuchang.

Gui Baizhu 桂百鑄. 1963. "Liu Xianshi jituan neibu douzheng sanji" 劉顯世集團內部鬥爭散記 (Notes on the internal struggles in Liu Xianshi's clique). *Guizhou wenshi ziliao xuanji* 1:98–114.

Gui shi zongpu 桂氏宗譜. 1935. (Genealogy of the Gui lineage).

Guizhou daxue lishixi 貴州大學歷史系. 1979. "Guizhou junfa Liu Xianshi fajia shi" 貴州軍閥劉顯世發家史 (The family history of the Guizhou warlord Liu Xianshi).

Guizhou wenshi ziliao xuanji 3:186–200.

Guizhou wenshi ziliao xuanji 貴州文史資料選輯 (Selected Guizhou cultural and historical materials), edited by Zhongguo renmin zhengzhi xieshang huiyi, Guizhou sheng weiyanhui, wenshi ziliao weiyuanhui.

Guo Qi 國琦 and Dong Xia 東霞 . 1982. "Jiangxi suqu chuqi de sufan yu Futian shibian" 江西蘇區初期的肅反與富田事變 (The Futian Incident and the suppression of counterrevolutionaries in the early period of the Jiangxi soviet areas). *Dangshi yanjiu ziliao* 黨史研究資料 5:7–25.

Guoli zhongyang yanjiusuo shehui kexue yanjiusuo 國立中央研究院社會科學研究所. 1929. *Jiangsu Wuxi nongmin-dizhu jingji diaocha* 江蘇無錫農民地主經濟調查 (A survey of the peasant-landlord economy in Wuxi county, Jiangsu province). Wuxi.

Han shi zongpu 韓氏宗譜. 1946. (Genealogy of the Han lineage).

Hanwell, Norman, 1937a. "The Dragnet of Local Government in China." *Pacific Affairs* 10, no. 1 (March): 43–63.

———. 1937b. "Rotten Gentry of China." *Asia* 37, no. 4 (April): 297–300.

Hanyang xian xiangtu 漢陽縣詳圖. 1933. (Detailed map of Hanyang county).

Hanyang xian yutu 漢陽縣輿圖. 1901. (Map of Hanyang county).

Hanyang xianshi 漢陽縣識. 1884. (Unofficial gazetteer of Hanyang county).

Hanyang xianzhi 漢陽縣志. 1867. (Gazetteer of Hanyang county).

Hanyang xianzhi. 1818. (Gazetteer of Hanyang county).

Hanyang Yao shi fangpu 漢陽姚氏方譜. 1923. (Genealogy of the Hanyang branch of the Yao lineage).

Hanyang Zhang shi zongpu 漢陽張氏宗譜. 1921. (Genealogy of the Zhang lineage of Hanyang).

Hao, Yen-p'ing. 1970. *The Comprador in Nineteenth-Century China: Bridge between East and West*. Cambridge, Mass.

Harrell, Stevan. 1987. "The Decline of Ethnicity and the Transformation of the North Taiwan Local Elite." Paper presented at the Conference on Chinese Local Elites and Patterns of Dominance. Banff.

———. 1986. *Ploughshare Village: Culture and Context in Taiwan*. Seattle.

Hartwell, Robert. 1982. "Demographic, Political, and Social Transformations of China, 750–1550." *Harvard Journal of Asiatic Studies* 42, no. 2 (Dec.): 365–442.

Hayes, James. 1977. *The Hong Kong Region 1850–1911*. Hamden, Conn.

He Banghua 何邦華. 1981a. "Lunxian yu Rikou qian hou de Rugao" 淪陷于日寇前后的如皋 (Rugao before and after the Japanese bandit occupation). *Rugao wenshi ziliao* 4:43–47.

———. 1981b. "Wo suo zhidao de Xu Jiajin lieshi" 我所知道的徐家瑾烈士 (The martyr Xu Jiajin whom I knew). *Rugao wenshi ziliao* 3:25–26.

He Bingdi 何炳棣 (Ping-ti Ho). 1966. *Zhongguo huiguan shilun.* 中國會館史論 Historical Survey of Landsmannshaften in China). Taibei.

He Bingxian 何炳賢. 1933. "Minguo ershiyi nian Zhongguo gongshangye de huigu" 民國二十一年中國工商業的回顧 (A review of Chinese commerce and industry in 1932). *Gongshang banyuekan* 工商半月刊 5, no. 1 (Jan. 1): articles sec., 1–39.

He Changgong 何長工. 1959. "Gaizao Wang Zuo budui" 改造王佐部隊 (Reforming Wang Zuo's detachment). *Xinghuo liaoyuan* 星火燎原 (Beijing) 1:270–277.

He Jiwu 何輯五. 1982. *Guizhou zhengtan yiwang* 貴州政壇憶往 (A remembrance of

Guizhou's political arena). Taibei.

Hinton, Harold C. 1956. *The Grain Tribute System of China (1845–1911)*. Cambridge, Mass.

Ho, Ping-ti (He Bingdi). 1962. *The Ladder of Success in Imperial China: Aspects of Social Mobility, 1368–1911*. New York.

———. 1954. "The Salt Merchants of Yangzhou." *Harvard Journal of Asiatic Studies* 17:130–168.

Hobsbawm, Eric. 1981. *Bandits*. New York.

Holmes, Clive. 1974. *The Eastern Association in the English Civil War*. Cambridge.

Hongshanmiao Luo shi zongpu 洪山廟羅氏宗譜 1918. (Genealogy of the Luo lineage of Hongshanmiao).

Hoshi, Ayao. 1969. *The Ming Tribute Grain System*. Abstracted and translated by Mark Elvin. Ann Arbor.

Hosie, Alexander. 1922. *Szechuan, its Products, Industries and Resources*. Shanghai.

Hosokawa Kazutoshi. 細川一敏. 1984. "'Chūjin' yori mita Chūgoku gōson no tochi shoyū ishiki to ningen kankei" "中人"より観た中國郷村の土地所有意識と人間関係 (Human relations and the consciousness of landownership in Chinese villages, as seen through the "middleman"). *Hiromae Daigaku Jimbun Gakubu "Bunkei Ronsō"* 弘前大学人文学部「文経論叢」 (Collected essays of the Humanities Division of Hiromae University) 19, no. 3 (March): 143–195.

Hsi, Angela Ning-Jy Sun. 1972. "Social and Economic Status of the Merchant Class of the Ming Dynasty, 1368–1644." Ph.D diss., University of Illinois at Urbana-Champaign.

Hsiao, Kung-chuan. 1960. *Rural China: Imperial Control in the Nineteenth Century*. Seattle.

Hsieh, Winston. 1974. "Peasant Insurrection and the Marketing Hierarchy in the Canton Delta, 1911–1912." In *The Chinese City Between Two Worlds*, edited by Mark Elvin and G. William Skinner, 119–141. Stanford.

Hu, Hsien-chin. 1948. *The Common Descent Group in China and Its Functions*. New York.

Hu Langru 胡烺如. 1981. "Rugao xian shatian qingkuang de diaocha" 如皋縣沙田情況的調查 (An investigation of the conditions on Rugao's sandbars). *Rugao wenshi ziliao* 3:79–95.

Hu Shanquan and Luo Xiaoyuan. 胡善權、羅筱元. 1984. "Qingji Zigong difang wu shuyuan" 清季自貢地方五書院 (The five academies in Zigong during the Qing period). *Zigong wenshi ziliao xuanji* 14:189–190.

Hu Shaoquan. 胡少權. 1981. "Gongjing Hu Yuanhe de xingqi yu shuailuo" 貢井胡元和的興起与衰落 (The rise and fall of Hu Yuanhe of Gongjing). *Zigong wenshi ziliao xuanji* 12:49–79.

Hu Yueyi 胡越一. 1982. "Da geming chuqi Jiujiang, Xiushui jiandang pianduan" 大革命初期九江、修水建黨片斷 (Fragments concerning the establishment of the Jiujiang and Xiushui party during the early period of the Great Revolution). *Jiangxi wenshi ziliao xuanji* 8:83–90.

Hua Yinchun 華印椿. 1931. *Wuxi nongcun pinkun zhi yuanyin ji jiuzhi zhi fangfa* 無錫農村貧困之原因及救治之方法 (The reasons for rural impoverishment in Wuxi and methods for recovery). Wuxi.

Huang Jizhou 黃濟舟. 1959. "Xinhai Guizhou geming jilue" 辛亥貴州革命紀畧 (Record of Guizhou's 1911 Revolution). *Yunnan Guizhou xinhai geming ziliao*, 147–173.

Huang Muxian 黃慕憲. 1981. "Jiangxi gongnong hongjun di qi, di jiu zongdui de chuangjian" 江西工農紅軍第七、第九纵隊的創建 (The founding of the Jiangxi Worker-Peasant Red Army's Seventh and Ninth columns). *Jiangxi shehui kexue* 江西社會科學 1:59–62.

Huang, Philip C. C. 1985. *The Peasant Economy and Social Change in North China*. Stanford.

Huang Qichen 黃启臣. 1983. "Shilun Ming-Qing shiqi shangye ziben liuxiang tudi de wenti" 試論明清时期商业資本流向土地的问題(A discussion of the question of merchant capital invested in land in the Ming-Qing period). *Zhongshan daxue xuebao* 中山大學學報 1:66–84.

Huang Qichen and Deng Kaisong 鄧開頌. 1984. "Ming Jiajing zhi Chongzhen nian-jian Aomen duiwai maoyi de fazhan" 明嘉靖至崇禎年間澳门对外貿易的發展 (The development of Macao's foreign trade between the Ming Jiajing and Chong-zhen periods). *Zhongshan daxue xuebao* 中山大學學報 3:88–97.

Huang Qiwu 黃七五. 1980. "Chongti jiushi hua dangnian" 重提舊事話當年 (Re-collecting the past by speaking of one's youth). *Xinhua ribao* 新華日報 (Nov. 16, 1956); reprinted in *Rugao wenshi ziliao* 1:25–29.

———. 1961. "Rugao guangfu zhi huiyi" 如皋光复之回憶 (Recollections of the 1911 Revolution in Rugao). In *Xinhai geming Jiangsu diqu shiliao* 辛亥革命江蘇地區史料 (Historical materials on the 1911 Revolution in Jiangsu), edited by Yangzhou shi-fan xueyuan lishixi 揚州師範學院歷史系, 230–231. Nanjing.

Huang, Ray. 1974. *Taxation and Government Finance in Sixteenth-Century Ming China*. Cambridge, Mass.

Huang Zhiqing and Nie Wufang. 黃植青, 聶無放. 1982. "Zigong yanchang fazhan pianduan" 自貢塩場發展片斷 (Passages on the development of the Zigong salt yard). *Zigong wenshi ziliao xuanji*, 6–10:251–57.

Hummel, Arthur W., ed. 1943. *Eminent Chinese of the Ch'ing Period (1644–1912)*. Washington, D.C.

Hymes, Robert. 1986a. *Statesmen and Gentlemen: The Elite of Fu-chou, Chiang-hsi, in Northern and Southern Sung*. Cambridge.

———. 1986b. "Marriage, Descent Groups, and the Localist Strategy in Sung and Yuan Fu-chou." In Ebrey and Watson, eds., 95–136.

Ichiko, Chūzō. 1968. "The Role of the Gentry: An Hypothesis." In *China in Revolution: The First Phase, 1900–1913*, edited by Mary Clabaugh Wright, 297–317. New Haven.

Imahori Seiji 今堀誠二. 1956. "Shindai ni okeru nōson kikō no kindaika ni tsuite— Kantōsho Kōsanken dōkai chihō ni okeru 'kyōdōtai' suiden katei" 清代における農村機構の近代について―廣東省香山縣東海地方における「共同體」推轉過程 *Rekishigaku kenkyū* 歷史學研究 191 (Jan.) 3–17; 192 (Feb.): 14–29.

———. 1953. *Chūgoku no shakai kōzō* 中國の社會構造 (Chinese social structure). Tokyo.

———. 1947. *Pekin shimin no jichi-kōsei*. 北平市民の自治構成 (The self-governing organizations of the citizens of Peking). Tokyo.

Institute of Pacific Relations, ed. 1939a. "Silk Filature and Silkworm Cooperatives in Wusih." In *Agrarian China. Selected Source Materials from Chinese Authors*, 184–188. London.

———. 1939b. "Trade Capital and Silk Farming in Wushi." In *Agrarian China*.

Selected Source Materials from Chinese Authors, 235–239. London.

Jenkins, Philip. 1983. *The Making of a Ruling Class: The Glamorgan Gentry, 1640–1790*. Cambridge.

Ji Runqing. 吉潤卿. 1964. "Gongjing yan chang fazhan yipie" 貢井盐場發展一瞥 (A glance at the development of the Gongjing salt yard). *Sichuan wenshi ziliao xuanji* 四川文史資料選輯 11:187–203.

Jiang Bozhang 姜伯彰. 1972. "Zhishi sanshi nian" 芝師三十年 (Thirty years of the Zhiyang normal school). In *Jiang Bozhang xiansheng shiwen ji* 姜伯彰先生詩文集 (The collected poetry and prose of Mr. Jiang Bozhang), edited by Lu Tangping 魯蕩平 et al., 34–51. Taibei.

Jiang Xiangcheng and Luo Xiaoyuan et al. 姜相成、羅筱元. 1982. "Zigong yanchang de niu" 自貢盐場的牛 (Buffalo at the Zigong salt yard). *Zigong wenshi ziliao xuanji* 12:108–127.

Jiang Yuchang (?) 江毓昌. c. 1908. *Gongdu cungao* 公牘存稿 (A draft collection of public correspondence). N.p.

Jiangnan shangwu bao 江南商務報 (Jiangnan commerce). 1900–01. Shanghai.

Jiangsu dangwu zhoukan 江蘇黨務周刊. 1930. (Jiangsu party affairs weekly). Zhenjiang (?).

"Jiangsu ge xian xinwen shiye diaocha" 江蘇各縣新聞事業調查. 1936. (An investigation of Jiangsu's county newspapers). *Suheng banyuekan* 蘇衡半月刊 17–18 (Aug.): 60–66.

Jiangsu jianshe yuekan 江蘇建設月刊. 1935. (Jiangsu Reconstruction monthly). Zhenjiang.

Jiangsu jiaoyu gailan 江蘇教育概覽. [1933] 1971. (An overview of Jiangsu education). Reprint, Taibei.

Jiangsu sheng gongbao 江蘇省公報. 1923. (Bulletin of the Jiangsu provincial government). Zhenjiang.

Jiangsu sheng neiwu xingzheng baogao shu 江蘇省內務行政報告書. 1914 (?). (Report on Jiangsu's internal administration). Shanghai.

Jiangsu sheng nongmin yinhang zonghang 江蘇省農民銀行總行, ed. 1930–32. *Disan nian zhi Jiangsu sheng nongmin yinhang* 第三年之江蘇省農民銀行 (The third year of the Jiangsu Farmers' Bank). Zhenjiang.

Jiangsu sheng zhengfu gongbao 江蘇省政府公報. 1930–31. (Jiangsu provincial gazette). Zhenjiang.

Jiangsu sheng zhengzhi nianjian 江蘇省政治年鑑. 1924. (Jiangsu political yearbook).

Jiangsu shiye yuezhi 江蘇事業月誌. 1920–24. (Jiangsu industrial monthly). Nanjing.

Jiangxi jiaoyu gongbao 江西教育公報. 1928–30. (Jiangxi educational gazette). Compiled by Jiangxi sheng zhengfu jiaoyu ting 江西省政府教育廳. Nanchang.

Jiangxi minzheng gongbao 江西民政公報. 1928–30. (Jiangxi civil affairs gazette). Compiled by Jiangxi sheng zhengfu minzheng ting 江西省政府民政廳. Nanchang.

Jiangxi nianjian 江西年鑑. 1936. (Jiangxi yearbook). Compiled by Jiangxi sheng zhengfu tongji shi. 江西省政府統計室. Nanchang.

Jiangxi sheng minzheng ting 江西省民政廳. 1960. *Buxiu de geming zhanshi* 不朽的革命戰士 (Immortal revolutionary comrades). Nanchang.

———. 1980. *Bixue danxin* 碧血丹心 (Loyalty until death). Nanchang.

Jiangxi wenshi ziliao xuanji 江西文史資料选輯. 1980–. (Selected materials on the culture and history of Jiangxi). Compiled by Zhongguo renmin zhengzhi xie-shang huiyi Jiangxi sheng weiyuan hui wenshi ziliao yanjiu weiyuan hui 中國人民政治协商會議江西省委員會文史資料研究委員會. Nanchang.

Jiangxi wenxian 江西文獻. 1966–. (Documents of Jiangxi). Taibei.

Jing Su and Luo Lun. 1978. *Landlord and Labor in Late Imperial China: Case Studies from Shandong.* Translated by Endymion Wilkinson. Cambridge, Mass.

Johnson, David. 1985. "Communication, Class, and Consciousness in Late Imperial China." In Johnson, Nathan, and Rawski, eds., 34–72. Berkeley.

Johnson, David, Andrew Nathan, Evelyn Rawski, eds. 1985. *Popular Culture in Late Imperial China.* Berkeley.

Jones, Susan Mann [Susan Mann]. 1979. "The Organization of Trade at the County Level: Brokerage and Tax Farming in the Republican Period." In *Select Papers from the Center for Far Eastern Studies* (University of Chicago) 3:70–79. Chicago.

———. 1974. "The Ningbo Pang and Financial Power at Shanghai." In *The Chinese City between Two Worlds,* edited by Mark Elvin and G. William Skinner, 73–96. Stanford.

Kaihua xiangzhi 開化鄉志. 1916. (A gazetteer of Kaihua subdistrict). Wuxi.

Kōain kachū renrakubu 興亞院華中連絡部. 1941. *Chū-Shina jūyō kokubō shigen kiito chōsa hōkoku* 中支那重要國防資源生絲調查報告 (A report on an investigation of raw silk in Central China, a raw material for national defense). Shanghai.

Kobayashi, Kazumi. 1984. "The Other Side of Rent and Tax Resistance Struggles, Ideology and the Road to Rebellion." In Grove and Daniels, eds., 215–243. Tokyo.

Kong Fanlin 孔繁霖. 1935. "Zhongguo nongcun wenti zhi jiantao." 中國農村問題之檢討 (A self-criticism of China's rural problems). *Nongcun jingji* 農村經濟 2, no. 12 (Oct. 1): 63–82.

Kracke. E. A. 1947. "Family vs. Merit in the Examination System." *Harvard Journal of Asiatic Studies* 10:103–123.

Ku Nong 苦農. 1937a. "Yangcan hezuo yundong zai Wuxi" 养蚕合作運動在無錫 (The sericulture cooperative movement in Wuxi). *Zhongguo nongcun* 中國農村 3, no. 6 (June 1): 103–106.

———. 1937b. "Sijian tongzhixia de Wuxi cansang" 絲茧統制下的無錫蚕桑 (Wuxi sericulture under [government policies] of cocoon control). In *Zhongguo nongcun dongtai* 中國農村動态 (Trends in rural China), edited by Zhongguo nongcun jingji yanjiuhui 中國農村經濟研究會. Shanghai.

Kuhn, Philip A. 1986. "The Development of Local Government." In *The Cambridge History of China,* edited by John K. Fairbank and Albert Feuerwerker. Vol. 13, *Republican China, 1912–1949, Part 2.* 329–360. Cambridge.

———. 1984. "Chinese Views of Social Classification." In *Class and Social Classification in Post-Revolutionary China,* edited by James Watson, 16–28. Cambridge, Mass.

———. 1975. "Local Self-Government under the Republic: Problems of Control, Autonomy, and Mobilization." In *Conflict and Control in Late Imperial China,* edited by Frederic Wakeman, Jr., and Carolyn Grant, 257–298. Berkeley.

———. 1970. *Rebellion and Its Enemies in Late Imperial China: Militarization and Social Structure, 1769–1864.* Cambridge, Mass.

Kuhn, Philip A., and Susan Mann Jones. 1978–79. "Introduction." In *Select Papers from the Center for Far Eastern Studies* (University of Chicago) 3:ii–xix. Chicago.

Lai Mingqin, et al. 賴明欽. 1982. "Yanyanjing fazhan gaikuang" 盐岩井發展概况 (A general survey of the development of the rock salt wells). *Zigong wenshi ziliao xuanji* 6–10:3–52.

Lamley, Harry J. 1977. "Hsieh-tou: The Pathology of Violence in Southeastern China." *Ch'ing-shih wen-t'i* 3, no. 7 (Nov.): 1–39.

Lao shi zupu 勞氏族譜. 1755. (Genealogy of the Lao lineage).

Lapidus, Ira M. 1975. "Hierarchies and Networks: A Comparison of Chinese and Islamic Societies." In *Conflict and Control in Late Imperial China*, edited by Frederic Wakeman, Jr., and Carolyn Grant, 26–42. Berkeley.

Le Roy Ladurie, Emmanuel. 1976. "Family Structures and Inheritance Customs in Sixteenth-Century France." In *Family and Inheritance: Rural Society in Western Europe, 1200–1800*, edited by Jack Goody, Joan Thrisk, and E. P. Thompson, 37–70. Cambridge.

Lears, T. J. Jackson. 1985. "The Concept of Cultural Hegemony: Problems and Possibilities." *American Historical Review* 90, no. 3 (June): 567–593.

Lei Jihui 雷輯輝. 1933. *Beiping shuizhuan kaolue* 北平稅捐考略 (A brief examination of taxes in Beiping). Beiping.

Lewin, Linda. 1979. "The case of the 'good thief' Antonio Silvino." *Past and Present* 82 (Feb.): 116–146.

Li Defang 李德芳. 1980. "Liu Xianshi" 劉顯世. *Guizhou shehui kexue* 貴州社會科學 2:71–74.

Li Hua 李華, ed. 1983. "Shilun Qingdai qianqi de Shanxi bang shangren." 試論清代前期的山西帮商人. *Lishi yanjiu* 歷史研究 3:304–32.

———. 1980. *Ming-Qing yilai Beijing gongshang huiguan beike xuanbian* 明清以來北京工商會館碑刻選編 (Selected stele of industrial and commercial guilds in Ming-Qing Beijing). Beijing.

Li Jishan 李継善. 1985. "Zou Nu." 鄒努 In *Zhonggong dangshi renwu zhuan* 中共黨史人物傳 (Biographies of personages in the history of the CCP). Compiled by Zhonggong dangshi renwu yanjiu hui 中共黨史人物研究會 26:122–136. Xi'an.

Li, Lillian M. 1981. *China's Silk Trade: Traditional Industry in the Modern World*. Cambridge, Mass.

Li, Rong. 李榕. 1948. "An Account of the Salt Industry at Tzu-liu-ching" (*Ziliujing ji*). Translated by Lien-che Tu Fang. *ISIS* 39, no. 4 (Nov.): 228–234.

Li Shi 李實. 1982. "Lun xinhai geming shiqi Guizhou lixian pai de fenhua" 論辛亥革命时期貴州立憲派的分化 (Divisions in the constitutionalist party in the period of the 1911 Revolution). *Guizhou wenshi ziliao xuanji* 10, supplement: 120–143.

Li Wenzhi 李文治. 1981. "Lun Qingdai houqi Jiang-Zhe-Wan sansheng yuan Taiping Tianguo zhanlingqu tudi guanxi de bianhua" 論清代后期江浙皖三省原太平天國占領區土地關係的變化 (On changes in land tenure in late Qing in areas of Jiangsu, Zhejiang, and Anhui formerly occupied by the Taipings). *Lishi yanjiu* 歷史研究 12:81–96.

———, ed. 1957. *Zhongguo jindai nongye shi ziliao* 中國近代農業史資料 (Materials on the agricultural history of modern China). Vol. 1 (1840–1911). Beijing.

Li Yesi 李業嗣. n.d. *Gaotang shichao* 杲堂詩鈔 (The unedited poetry of Li Yesi). *Siming congshu* ed.

Li Zilin et al. 李子琳. 1962 and 1963. "Ziliujing Li Siyou tang you faren dao shuaiwang" 自流井李四友堂由發軔到衰亡 (The Li Siyou tang of Ziliujing from its development to its decline). *Sichuan wenshi ziliao xuanji* 四川文史資料選輯 4:145–171, 5:199–211.

Liang Fangzhong 梁方仲. 1980. *Zhongguo lidai hukou, tiandi, tianfu tongji* 中國歷代戶口、田地、田賦統計 (China's dynastic statistics on household population, land, and land taxes). Shanghai.

Liang Qizi 梁其姿 (Angela Leung). 1986. "Mingmo Qingchu minjian cishan huodong de xingqi—yi Jiang-Zhe diqu weili" 明末清初民間慈善活動的興起—以浙江地區為例 (The rise of private philanthropy in the late Ming and early Qing—examples from Jiangsu and Zhejiang). *Shihuo yuekan* 食貨月刊 15, nos. 7–8: 304–331.

Liangxiang xianzhi 艮鄉縣志. 1924. (Liangxiang county gazetteer).

Lin Xiangrui 林祥瑞. 1985. "Qingdai qianqi Fujian dizhu jingji de ruogan tedian" 清代前期福建地主經濟的若干特點. *Lishi yanjiu* 歷史研究 1:61–72.

Lin Xiao 林嘯. 1981. "Yi shi shiling" 醫史拾零 (Tidbits of medical history). *Rugao wenshi ziliao* 4:59–65.

Lin Zhenhan 林振翰. 1919. *Chuanyan jiyao* 川盐紀要 (Fundamental facts about Sichuan Salt). n.p.

Lin Zixian 林子贤. 1963. "Guizhou 'Minjiu shibian' qinliji" 貴州民九事變親歷記 (A personal record of Guizhou's 1920 incident). *Guizhou wenshi ziliao xuanji* 1:115–121.

Ling shi zongpu 凌氏宗譜. 1883. (Genealogy of the Ling lineage).

Ling Ti'an 凌惕安, ed. 1932. *Xian-Tong Guizhou junshi shi* 咸同貴州軍事史 (A military history of Guizhou in the Xianfeng-Tongzhi period). Guizhou.

Ling Yaolun 凌耀倫. 1982. "Qingdai Zigong jingyanye zibenzhuyi mengya fazhan daolu chutan" 清代自貢井盐業資本主義萌芽的發展道路初談 (A preliminary investigation of the sprouts of capitalism in the Zigong salt industry). *Sichuan daxue xuebao congkan* 四川大學學報叢刊 14:76–108.

Lishi jiapu 李氏家譜. n.d. (Genealogy of the Li family). Ancestral hall ed.

Lishi zupu 李氏族譜 (Genealogy of the Li lineage). Qianlong rev. ed.

Liu Chunyuan, et al. 劉春源. 1977. "Wo guo Songdai jingyan gongyi de zhongyao gexin—Sichuan 'zhuotong jing'" 我國宋代井盐工艺的重要革新—四川卓筒井 (An important reform of our country's salt-well industry during the Song—The Sichuan "lofty-pipe" well). *Wenwu* 文物 12:66–72.

Liu Guangjing 劉廣京 (K. C. Liu). 1978. "Wan Qing difang guan zishu zhi shiliao jiazhi: Dao-Xian zhi ji guan-shen guan-min guanxi chutan" 晚清地方官自述之史料價值：道咸之際官紳官民關係初探(The value of documents written by local officials in the late Qing: A preliminary investigation of official-gentry and official-commoner relations in the Daoguang and Xianfeng eras). In *Zhongyang yanjiuyuan chengli wushi zhounian jinian lunwen ji* 中央研究院成立五十周年紀念論文集 (Essays in commemoration of the fiftieth anniversary of the founding of the Academia Sinica). Taibei.

"Liu Guanli Xiawutun zhongyi ci ji" 劉官禮下五屯忠義祠記. 1932. (Record of the Xiawutun loyalty temple of Liu Guanli). In *Xian-Tong Guizhou junshi shi* (A military history of Guizhou in the Xianfeng-Tongzhi period), edited by Ling Ti'an, 4:29b–30a.

Liu, Hui-chen Wang. 1959a. "An Analysis of Chinese Clan Rules: Confucian

Theories in Action." In *Confucianism in Action*, edited by David Nivison and Arthur Wright, 63–96. Stanford.

———. 1959b'. *The Traditional Chinese Clan Rules*. Locust Valley, N.Y.

Liu Lucheng 劉祿成. 1984–85. "Shaonian qiuxue suoyi" 少年求學瑣憶 (Sundry reminiscences of attending school as a youth). *Jiangxi wenxian* 116 (Apr.): 63–67; 117 (July): 54–56; 118 (Oct.): 59–61; 119 (Jan.): 29, 59–61.

Liu Ruilong 劉瑞龍. 1981. *Huiyi hong shisi jun* 回憶紅十四軍 (Remembrances of the Fourteenth Red Army). Nanjing?.

Liu shi zongpu 劉氏宗譜. 1924. (Genealogy of the Liu lineage).

Liu shi zongpu 劉氏宗譜. 1932. (Genealogy of the Liu lineage).

Liu Shiji 劉石吉. 1987. *Ming-Qing shidai Jiangnan shizhen yanjiu* 明清時代江南市鎮研究 (Research on Jiangnan market towns in the Ming and Qing periods). Beijing.

"Liu Tongzhi xiansheng nianpu" 劉統之先生年譜. 1932. (Biography of Mr. Liu Tongzhi). In *Xian-Tong Guizhou junshi shi* (A military history of Guizhou in the Xianfeng-Tongzhi period), edited by Ling Ti'an, 4:31a–34b.

Liu Xiaonong 劉曉農. 1980. "Yuan Wencai, Wang Zuo ji qi budui shimo" 袁文才、王佐及其部隊始末(Yuan Wenzai, Wang Zuo and the complete story of their detachment). *Jiangxi wenshi ziliao xuanji* 3:101–120.

Liu Yifeng 劉一峯. 1980. "Beijing dianche gongsi jianwen huiyi" 北京電車公司見聞回憶 (An eyewitness account of the Beijing Streetcar Company). *Wenshi ziliao xuanji* 文史資料選輯 31 (Nov.): 261–290.

Liu Yuezhao 劉岳昭. [1888] 1970. Dian Qian zouyi 滇黔奏議 (Yunnan and Guizhou memorials). Reprint, Taibei.

Long Shangxue 龍尙學, Chen Hanhui 陳翰輝, and Fang Jian 房健. 1982. "Yuan Zuming jiazu bainian shi" 袁祖銘家族百年史 (A hundred year history of the family of Yuan Zuming). *Guizhou wenshi congkan* 貴州文史叢刊 1:90–101.

Lou Xuexi 婁學熙, Chi Zehui 池澤匯, and Chen Wenxian 陳問咸, eds. 1932. *Beiping shi gongshangye gaikuang* 北平市工商業概況 (A survey of industry and commerce in the city of Beiping). Beiping.

Lu Guanying 盧冠英. 1921. "Jiangsu Wuxi xian ershi nian lai zhi siye guan" 江蘇無錫縣二十年來之絲業观 (An overview of the Wuxi silk industry during the last twenty years). *Nongshang gongbao* 8, no. 1 (Aug. 15): articles and translations sec., 45–47.

Lu, Hsün. 1974. *The Selected Stories of Lu Hsün*. Translated by Yang Hsien-yi and Gladys Yang. Peking.

Lu Zijian. 魯子健. 1984. "Chuanyan ji-Chu yu Sichuan yanye fazhan" 川盐濟楚與四川盐業發展 (Sichuan salt in aid to Huguang and the development of the Sichuan salt industry). *Shehui kexue yanjiu* 社會科學研究 2:75–82.

Lü Huantai 呂渙泰. 1980. Interview, May 24, at the headquarters of the Wuxi People's Political Consultative Congress, Wuxi.

Luancheng xianzhi 欒城縣志. 1971. (Luancheng county gazetteer).

Luo Raodian 羅绕典. [1847] 1974. *Qiannan zhifang jilue* 黔南职方紀畧 (A record of south Guizhou). Reprint, Taibei.

Luo Xiaoyuan 羅筱元. 1984. "Furong guanyun ju de bihai" 富荣官運局的弊害 (Malpractices in the Furong Official Salt Distribution Bureau). *Zigong wenshi ziliao xuanji* 14:58–75.

————. 1981. "Zhang Xiaopo dui Zigong yanchang de yingxiang" 張筱坡對自貢盐場的影响 (The influence of Zhang Xiaopo on the Zigong salt yard). *Zigong wenshi ziliao xuanji* 12:178–192.

————. 1963. "Ziliujing Wang Sanwei tang xingwang jiyao" 自流井王三畏堂興亡紀要 (A summary of the rise and fall of the Wang Sanwei tang of Ziliujing). *Sichuan wenshi ziliao xuanji* 四川文史資料選輯 7:164–177; 8:185–198.

Luo Xiaoyuan and Jiang Xiangcheng 姜相成. 1983. "Zigong yanchang de jian-shang" 自貢盐場的筧商 (Pipe merchants at the Zigong salt yard). *Zigong wenshi ziliao xuanji* 13:135–145.

Luo Xiaoyuan, et al. 1981. "Zigong difang de gelao hui" 自貢地方的哥老會 (The Elder Brother Society in Zigong). *Zigong wenshi ziliao xuanji* 12:89–107.

Luo Yixing 羅一星. 1985. "Ming-Qing shiqi de Foshan shangren" 明清时期的佛山商人 (Foshan merchants of the Ming and Qing). *Xueshu yanjiu* 學術研究 6:81–90.

Ma Daolai 馬道來. 1980. "Rugao shi hua" 如皋史話 (A few words on Rugao's history). *Rugao wenshi zhiliao* 2:5–22.

Ma Fangbo. 馬仿波. 1982. "Zigong yanchang de mucai shangye" 自貢盐場的木材商業 (The lumber business at the Zigong salt yard). *Zigong wenshi ziliao xuanji* 6–10:271–286.

Ma Tongke 馬同科. 1980. "Yao Ru dianqi gongsi chuangban qianhou dagai" 耀如電氣公司創辦前后大概 (A general description of the Rugao Illumination Company's founding). *Rugao wenshi ziliao* 2:48–52.

Macauley, Melissa. 1987. "Pondering the 'Pernicious' Pettifoggers of Late Imperial China." University of California, Berkeley, seminar paper.

Madsen, Richard. 1984. *Morality and Power in a Chinese Village.* Berkeley.

Mann, Susan [Susan Mann Jones]. 1987. *Local Merchants and the Chinese Bureaucracy, 1750–1950.* Stanford.

Manyin [pseud.] 曼因. 1944. *Ziliujing* 自流井. Chengdu.

Mao Tun (Mao Dun) 矛盾. 1979. "Spring Silkworms" (Chuncan 春蚕). Translated and reprinted in his *Spring Silkworms and Other Stories,* 1–26. Beijing.

Mao Xiao (?) 冒效. 1981. "Ji wode fuqin Mao Heting" 記我的父親冒鶴亭 (I remember my father, Mao Heting). *Rugao wenshi ziliao* 3:136–140.

Mao Zedong 毛澤東. 1982. "Xunwu diaocha" 尋烏調查 (Xunwu investigation). In *Mao Zedong nongcun diaocha wenji* 毛澤東農村調查文集 (A collection of Mao Zedong's rural investigations), compiled by *Zhonggong zhongyang wenxian yanjiu shi* 中共中央文獻研究室, 41–181. Beijing.

————. 1949a. "Ganxi tudi fenpei qingxing" 贛西土地分配情形 (The general condition of land distribution in West Jiangxi). In *Nongcun diaocha* 農村調查, 88–95. Shanghai.

————. 1949b. "Xingguo diaocha" 興國調查 (Investigation of Xingguo). In *Nongcun diaocha* 農村調查, 1–73. Shanghai.

Maqi gaiba wei qiao shimo ji 麻溪改壩爲橋始末記. 1916. (A record of the circumstances of changing the Maqi embankment to a bridge).

Marks, Robert B. 1984. *Rural Revolution in South China: Peasants and the Making of History in Haifeng County, 1570–1930.* Madison, Wis.

Marsh, Robert. 1961. *The Mandarins: The Circulation of Elites in China, 1600–1900.* New York.

Mazumdar, Sucheta. 1984. "A History of the Sugar Industry in China: The Political

Economy of a Cash Crop in Guangdong, 1644–1834." Ph.D. diss., University of California at Los Angeles.

McCord, Edward A. 1988. "Militia and Local Militarization in Late Qing and Early Republican China: The Case of Hunan." *Modern China* 14, no. 2 (Apr.): 156–197.

Mencius. 1963. *Mencius*. Translated by W. A. C. H. Dobson. Toronto.

Meskill, Johanna Menzel. 1979. *A Chinese Family: The Lins of Wu-feng, Taiwan, 1729–1895*. Princeton.

Michael, Franz, 1964. "Regionalism in Nineteenth-Century China". Introduction to *Li Hung-chang and the Huai Army*, by Stanley Spector. xxi–xliii. Seattle.

Migdal, Joel. 1987. "Strong States, Weak States: Power and Accommodation." In *Understanding Political Development*, edited by Myron Weiner and Samuel P. Huntington. 391–434. Boston.

Miles, Michael. 1986. "'A haven for the privileged': recruitment into the profession of attorney in England, 1709–1792." *Social History* 11, no. 2 (May): 197–210.

Min Tu-ki. 1989. *National Polity and Local Power: The Transformation of Late Imperial China*. Edited by Philip Kuhn and Timothy Brook. Cambridge, Mass.

Minami Manshū tetsudō kabushiki kaisha, Shanhai jimusho chōsashitsu 南滿洲鐵道株式會社,上海事務所調查室 1941. (Shanghai Research Office of the South Manchurian Railway Company). *Kōsoshō Mushakuken nōson jittai chōsa hōkokusho* 江蘇省無錫縣農村實態調查報告書 (A report on an investigation of rural conditions in Wuxi county, Jiangsu province). Shanghai.

———. 1940. *Mushaku kōgyō jittai chōsa hōkokusho* 無錫工業實態調查報告書 (A report on an investigation of industry in Wuxi). Shanghai.

Miners, Norman. 1979. *The Government and Politics of Hong Kong*. Hong Kong.

Mingay, G. E. 1976. *The Gentry: The Rise and Fall of a Ruling Class*. London.

Minguo ribao 民國日報. 1916–1930. (Republican daily news). Shanghai.

Mo Jian and Lei Yongming 莫健, 雷永明 1982. "Xinhai geming qiande Guizhou shehui" 辛亥革命前的貴州社會 (Guizhou society before the 1911 Revolution). *Guizhou wenshi ziliao xuanji* 10, supplement: 37–59.

Moore, Barrington. 1966. *Social Origins of Dictatorship and Democracy*. Boston.

Mori Masao 森正夫. 1985. "Kyōzoku o megutte" 鄉族をめぐつて (On xiang-level lineages). *Tōyōshi kenkyū* 東洋史研究 44, no. 1:137–153.

———. 1980. "The Gentry in the Ming Period—An Outline of the Relations between the Shih-ta-fu and Local Society." *Acta Asiatica* 38:31–53.

———. 1975–76. "Nihon no Min-Shin jidai shi kenkyū no okeru kyōshinron ni tsuite" 日本の明清近代史研究における鄉紳論について (Theories of local gentry in Japanese studies of the Ming-Qing period). *Rekishi Hyōron* 歷史評論. 308 (Dec.); 312 (Apr.); and 314 (July).

Mote. F. W. 1977. "The Transformation of Nanking, 1350–1400." In Skinner, ed., 101–154. Stanford.

Mousnier, Roland E. 1979 and 1984. *The Institutions of France under the Absolute Monarchy, 1598–1789*. Vol. 1: *Society and State*. Translated by Brian Pearce. Vol. 2: *The Organs of State and Society*. Translated by Arthur Goldhammer. Chicago.

Muramatsu Yūji 村松祐次. 1970. *Kindai Kōnan no sokan* 近代江南の租棧 (Rent bursaries in modern Jiangnan). Tokyo.

Myers, Ramon. 1974. "Transformation and Continuity in Chinese Social and Economic History." *Journal of Asian Studies* 33, no. 2 (Feb.): 265–278.

———. 1970. *The Chinese Peasant Economy: Agricultural Development in Hopei and Shantung, 1890–1949.* Cambridge, Mass.

Myers, Ramon, and Fu-mei Chang Chen. 1976. "Customary Law and Economic Growth in China During the Ch'ing Period." *Ch'ing-shih wen-t'i* 3, no. 5 (Nov.): 1–32.

Nanjing daxue lishixi 南京大學歷史系, ed. 1983. *Zhongguo zibenzhuyi mengya wenti lunwenji* 中國資本主義萌芽問題論文集 (Collected studies on capitalist sprouts in China). Nanjing.

———. 1981. *Ming-Qing zibenzhuyi mengya yanjiu lunwenji* 明清資本主義萌芽研究論文集 (Collected studies on capitalist sprouts in the Ming and Qing). Shanghai.

Naquin, Susan. 1986. "Two Descent Groups in North China: The Wangs of Yungp'ing Prefecture, 1500–1800." In Ebrey and Watson, eds., 210–244.

———. 1981. *Shantung Rebellion: The Wang Lun Uprising of 1774.* New Haven.

Naquin, Susan, and Evelyn S. Rawski. 1987. *Chinese Society in the Eighteenth Century.* New Haven.

Nathan, Andrew. 1976. *Peking Politics, 1918–1923: Factionalism and the Failure of Constitutionalism.* Berkeley.

Netting, Robert McC. 1981. *Balancing on an Alp: Ecological Change and Continuity in a Swiss Mountain Community.* Cambridge.

Neville, Henry, and Henry Bell. 1898. *Report of the Mission to China of the Blackburn Chamber of Commerce, 1896–1897: H. Neville and H. Bell's Section.* Blackburn.

Niida Noboru et al., eds. 仁井田陞. 1981. *Chūgoku nōson kanko chōsa* 中國農村慣行調查 (A survey of village customs in China). Tokyo.

Ningbo fuzhi 寧波府志. 1846. (Gazetteer of Ningbo prefecture). Prefaces dated 1733, 1741.

Ninggang xianzhi 寧岡縣志. 1937. (Gazetteer of Ninggang county).

Nongkuang gongbao 農礦公報. 1928–30. (Bulletin of Jiangsu Department of Agriculture and Mines). Zhenjiang.

Nongshang gongbao 農商公報. 1917 (Bulletin of the Ministry of Agriculture and Commerce). Beijing.

Nongye zhoubao 農業週報. 1931. (Agricultural weekly). Nanjing.

North China Herald. 1933–36. Shanghai.

North China Standard. 1926–29. Beijing.

Okumura Satoshi 奧村哲 1978. "Kyōkōka Kō-Setsu sanshigyo no saihen" 恐慌下江浙蠶絲業の再編 (The reorganization of sericulture in Jiangsu and Zhejiang due to the depression). *Tōyōshi kenkyū* 東洋史研究 37, no. 2 (Sept.): 242–278.

Olson, Mancur. 1971. *The Logic of Collective Action: Public Goods and the Theory of Groups.* New York.

Ortner, Sherry B. 1984. "Theory in Anthropology since the Sixties." *Comparative Studies in Society and History* 26, no. 1 (Jan.): 124–166.

Ossowski, Stanislaw. 1963. *Class Structure in the Social Consciousness.* New York.

Ouyang Yuemou et al. 歐陽樾牟. 1983. "Zigong difang de diandangye". 自貢地方的典當業 (The pawnshop business in Zigong). *Zigong wenshi ziliao xuanji* 13:146–155.

Oyama Masaaki. 1984. "Large Landownership in the Jiangnan Delta Region during the Late Ming-Early Qing Period." In Grove and Daniels, eds., 101–163. Tokyo.

Palmer, Michael. 1987. "The Surface-Subsoil Form of Divided Ownership in Late Imperial China: Some Examples from the New Territories of Hong Kong." *Modern Asian Studies* 21:1–119.

Pan Guangdan 潘光旦. 1947. *Ming-Qing liangdai Jiaxing de wangzu* 明清兩代嘉興的望族 (The prominent lineages of Jiaxing in the Ming and Qing dynasties). Shanghai.

Pan Shanfu 潘善福. 1983. "Xunwu xian jianjie" 尋烏縣簡介 (A brief introduction to Xunwu county). *Jiangxi wenxian* 111 (Jan.): 21–25.

Pan Yichen 潘逸尘. 1980. "Han Zishi guo Rugao beikou ji" 韓紫石過如皋被扣記 (An account of the arrest of Han Zishi as he crossed Rugao). *Rugao wenshi ziliao* 1:41–44.

Pasternak, Burton. 1968. "The Role of the Frontier in Chinese Lineage Development." *Journal of Asian Studies* 28, no. 3 (May): 551–561.

Peng Zeyi 彭澤益. 1965. "Shijiu shiji houqi Zhongguo chengshi shougongye shangye hanghui de chongjian he zuoyong" 十九世紀後期中國城市手工業商業行會的重建和作用 (The reestablishment and functions of Chinese urban handicraft and commercial guilds at the end of the nineteenth century), *Lishi yanjiu* 歷史研究, issue no. 1 (Jan.): 71–102.

Perdue, Peter C. 1987. *Exhausting the Earth: State and Peasant in Hunan, 1500–1850.* Cambridge, Mass.

———. 1986. "Insiders and Outsiders: The Xiangtan Riot of 1819 and Collective Action in Hunan." *Modern China* 12, no. 2 (April): 166–201.

Perkins, Dwight. 1969. *Agricultural Development in China 1368–1968.* Chicago.

Perry, Elizabeth J. 1980. *Rebels and Revolutionaries in North China, 1845–1945.* Stanford.

Peterson, Willard. 1979. *Bitter Gourd: Fang I-chih and the Impetus for Intellectual Change.* New Haven.

Ping Gang 平剛. 1981. "Guizhou guangfu shishi" 貴州光复史實 (Facts on the history of Guizhou's 1911 Revolution). In *Guiyang wenshi ziliao xuanji* 貴陽文史資料選輯 (Selected Guiyang cultural and historical materials), edited by Zhongguo renmin zhengzhi xieshang huiyi, Guizhou sheng Guiyang shi weiyanhui, wenshi ziliao yanjiu weiyuanhui 中國人民政治协商會議, 貴州省貴陽市委員會, 文史資料研究委員會 2:10–14. Guiyang.

———. 1959. "Guizhou geming xianlie shilue" 貴州革命先烈事略 (Brief biographies of Guizhou revolutionary martyrs). *Yunnan Guizhou xinhai geming ziliao,* 273–310.

Polachek, James. 1983. "The Moral Economy of the Kiangsi Soviet (1928–1934)." *Journal of Asian Studies* 42, no. 4 (Aug.): 805–829.

Potter, Jack. 1968. *Capitalism and the Chinese Peasant.* Berkeley.

The Provinces of China together with a History of the First Year of H.I.M. Hsuan Tung and an Account of the Government of China. 1910. Shanghai.

Pye, Lucien. 1985. *Asian Power and Politics, The Cultural Dimensions of Authority.* Cambridge, Mass.

Qian Zhaoxiong 錢兆熊. 1935. "Shangye ziben caozongxia de Wuxi cansang" 商業資本操纵下的無錫蚕桑 (Wuxi sericulture under the control of commerical capital). *Zhongguo nongcun* 中國農村 1, no. 4 (Jan.): 71–74.

Qian Zhonghan 錢鍾漢. 1983. "Zhou Shunqing" 周舜卿. In *Gongshang jingji shiliao congkan* 工商經濟史料叢刊 (Collections of historical materials on commerce and industry), edited by Zhongguo renmin zhengzhi xieshang huiyi quanguo yanjiu weiyuanhui, wenshi ziliao yanjiu weiyuanhui 中國人民政治协商會議全國研究委員會, 文史資料研究委員會. 4:105–110.

———. 1961. "Wuxi wuge zhuyao chanye ziben xitong de xingcheng yu fazhan" 無錫五個主要產業資本系統的形成與發展 (The formation and development of five important industrial capital networks in Wuxi). *Wenshi ziliao xuanji* 文史資料選輯 (Selected historical reminiscences) 24 (Dec.): 98–154. Beijing.

Qiao Fu 樵斧. 1916. *Ziliujing diyiji* 自流井第一集 (Ziliujing, vol. 1). n.p.

"Qingchao monian Rugao quanxian xuetang tongji biao" 清朝末年如皋全縣學堂統計表. 1980. (Statistical table on all Rugao schools in the last years of the Qing dynasty). *Rugao wenshi ziliao* 1:6–15.

Qingchao xuwenxian tongkao 清朝續文獻通考 [1747] 1958. (Further compendium of historical records of the Qing dynasty). Reprint, Taibei.

Qiu Zhou 丘偈. 1982. "Huiyi Yudu baodong" 回憶余都暴動 (Remembering the Yudu Uprising). *Jiangxi wenshi ziliao xuanji* 8:62–82.

Quan Zuwang. 全祖望. 1814. *Yongshang zuwang biao* 甬上族望表 (Table of prominent members of Yin county lineages).

———. 1803. *Jieqi ting ji* 鮚埼亭集 (Collected writings from Jieqi Pavilion). *Sibu congkan* edition.

Ran Guangrong and Zhang Xuejun 冉光榮, 張學君. 1984. *Ming-Qing Sichuan jingyan shigao* 明清四川井盐史稿 (A draft history of the well-salt industry in Sichuan during the Ming and Qing periods). Chengdu.

———. 1981. "Sichuan jingyan ye zibenzhuyi mengya wenti yanjiu" 四川井盐業資本主義萌芽問題研究 (A study of the problem of the sprouts of capitalism in the Sichuan well-salt industry). In *Ming-Qing zibenzhuyi mengya yanjiu lunwenji* 明清資本主義萌芽研究論文集 (Collected essays in the study of the sprouts of capitalism during the Ming-Qing period), edited by Nanjing daxue lishixi and Ming-Qing yanjiushi. Shanghai.

———. 1980. "Sichuan jingyanye zibenzhuyi mengya de tantao—guanyu Qingdai Fu-Rong yanchang jingying qiyue de chubu fenxi" 四川井盐業資本主義萌芽的探討—关于清代富榮盐場經營契約的初步分析 (An exploration of the sprouts of capitalism in the Sichuan well-salt industry—a preliminary analysis of Qing period Furong salt yard management contracts). *Sichuan daxue xuebao congkan* 四川大學學報叢刊 5:30–42.

Rankin, Mary Backus. 1986. *Elite Activism and Political Transformation in China, Zhejiang Province, 1865–1911.* Stanford.

———. 1977. "Rural-Urban Continuities: Leading Families of Two Chekiang Market Towns." *Ch'ing-shih wen-t'i* 3, no. 2 (Nov.): 67–104.

Rawski, Evelyn S. 1986. "The Ma Landlords of Yang-chia-kou in Late Ch'ing and Republican China." In Ebrey and Watson, eds., 245–273. Berkeley.

Renmin ribao 人民日報 (People's Daily). Beijing.

Rong An 容鑫. 1927. "Gedi nongmin zhuangkuang diaocha: Wuxi" 各地農民狀況調查：無錫 (Investigation of peasant circumstances in various locales: Wuxi). *Dongfang zazhi* 東方雜誌 24, no. 16 (Aug. 25): 109–113.

Rong xianzhi 容縣志. 1929. (Gazetteer of Rong county).

Rowe, William T. Forthcoming. "Economic Change in the Middle Yangtze Macroregion, 1736–1938." In *Markets and Regions in Chinese Economic History*, edited by Robert M. Hartwell, Albert Feuerwerker, and Robert F. Dernberger.

———. 1989. *Hankow: Conflict and Community in a Chinese City, 1796–1895*. Stanford.

———. 1985. "Approaches to Chinese Social History." In *Reliving the Past: The Worlds of Social History*, edited by Oliver Zunz. 236–296. Chapel Hill.

———. 1984. *Hankow: Commerce and Society in a Chinese City, 1796–1889*. Stanford.

Rozman, Gilbert. 1973. *Urban Networks in Ch'ing China and Tokugawa Japan*. Princeton.

"Rugao dangwu gaikuang" 如皋黨務概況. 1928. (Conditions of party affairs in Rugao). *Jiangsu dang sheng* 江蘇黨聲 (Jiangsu party voice), 16 (Nov. 11): 14–18.

"Rugao jiefang shinian shi" 如皋解放十年史. 1959. (Liberated Rugao's ten-year history). Manuscript.

Rugao wenshi ziliao 如皋文史資料. 1980–81. (Materials on the history and culture of Rugao).

"Rugao xian diyige dang zhibu de jianli" 如皋縣第一个黨支部的建立. 1981. (The establishment of the first Rugao party branch). *Rugao wenshi ziliao* 3:26–27.

Rugao xian xuzhi 如皋縣續志. 1837. (Supplementary gazetteer of Rugao county).

Rugao xian xuzhi. 1873. (Supplementary gazetteer of Rugao county).

Rugao xianzhi 如皋縣志. 1933. (Gazetteer of Rugao county).

Rugao xianzhi. 1808. (Gazetteer of Rugao county).

Ruijin xianzhi gao 瑞金縣志稿. 1941. (Draft gazetteer of Ruijin county).

Sahlins, Marshall. 1985. *Islands of History*. Chicago.

———. 1981. *Historical Metaphors and Mythical Realities: Structure in the Early History of the Sandwich Islands Kingdom*. Ann Arbor.

Sangren, P. Steven. 1984. "Traditional Chinese Corporations: Beyond Kinship." *Journal of Asian Studies* 3, no. 3 (May): 391–415.

Santai xianzhi 三台縣志. 1937. (Gazetteer of Santai county).

Sasaki Masaya 佐佐木正哉. 1963. "Kanpō ninen Gin-ken no kōryō bōdō" 咸豐二年鄞縣の抗糧暴動 (An anti-tax uprising in Yin county in 1852). *Tōyo bunka kenkyūjo kiyo* 東洋文化研究所紀要 5:185–299.

Schmidt, S. W., L. Guasti, C. H. Lande, and J. C. Scott, eds. 1977. *Friends, Followers and Factions*. Berkeley.

Schoppa, R. Keith. 1989. *Xiang Lake—Nine Centuries of Chinese Life*. New Haven.

———. 1982. *Chinese Elites and Political Change: Zhejiang Province in the Early Twentieth Century*. Cambridge, Mass.

———. 1973. "The Composition and Functions of the Local Elite in Szechwan, 1851–1874." *Ch'ing-shi wen-t'i* 2, no. 10 (Nov.): 7–23.

Sha Yan'gao 沙彥高. 1981. "Dui wo fuqin Sha Yuanbing de jidian huiyi 對我父親沙元炳的几点回憶 (A few recollections of my father, Sha Yuanbing). *Rugao wenshi ziliao* 4:66–69.

Shan xianzhi 單县志. 1759. (Gazetteer of Shan county).

Shanghai qianzhuang shiliao 上海錢莊史料. 1961. (Historical materials on Shanghai old-style banks). Edited by Zhongguo renmin yinhang, Shanghai shi fenhang 中國人民銀行, 上海市分行. Shanghai.

Shanghai shehui kexueyuan jingji yanjiusuo, ed. 上海社會科學院經濟研究所. 1962. *Rongjia chiye shiliao* 容家企業史料 (Historical materials concerning the Rong family enterprises). Vol. 1, *1896–1937*. Shanghai.

Shao Shiping 邵式平. 1959. "Zhongguo gongnong hongjun di shi juntuan de dan-sheng" 中國工農紅軍第十軍團的誕生 (The birth of the Chinese Worker-Peasant Red Tenth Army Group). *Hongqi piao piao* 紅旗飄飄 12:55–64.

Shao-Xiao tangzha gongcheng yuekan 紹蕭塘閘工程月刊. 1926–27. (The Shaoxing-Xiaoshan Dike and Sluicegate Engineering Monthly). October–July.

Shaoxing Tianyue xiang Yinghu tang pu shibanlu zhengxin lu. 1922 紹興天樂鄉溢湖塘鋪石板路徵信錄 (The financial report of laying the stone slab dike of Ying Lake in Tianyue subdistrict).

Shaoxing xian yihui minguo yuannian yijue an 紹興縣議會民國元年議決案. 1912. (Decisions of the Shaoxing county assembly in 1912).

Shaoxing xianzhi ziliao diyi ji 紹興縣志資料第一輯. 1937. (First compilation of materials for a gazetteer of Shaoxing county).

Shehui jingji yanjiusuo 社會經濟研究所, ed. 1935. *Wuxi mishi diaocha* 無錫米市調查 (An investigation of the Wuxi rice market). Shanghai.

Shen bao. 申報. 1923–36. (The Shanghai news). Shanghai.

Shen Wenwei 潘文緯. 1934. "Fuxing Jiang-Zhe cansi shiye" 復興江浙蠶絲事業 (Revival of the silk industry in Jiangsu and Zhejiang). *Nongcun jingji* 農村經濟 1, no. 6 (Apr. 1): 32–35.

Sheridan, James E. 1975. *China in Disintegration: The Republican Era in Chinese History.* New York.

Shi bao 時報. 1909–31. (The Eastern Times). Shanghai.

Shiba Yoshinobu. 斯波義信. 1984. "*Maqi gaiba wei qiao shimoji* ni tsuite" 麻溪改壩爲橋始末記について. In *Nishijima Sadao hakushi kan reki kinen: To Ajia shi ni okeru kokka to nōmin* 西嶋定生博士還暦記念：東アジア史における国家と農民 (Essays in honor of the sixtieth birthday of Dr. Nishijima Sadao: State and peasant in East Asian history), 327–348. Tokyo.

———. 1977. "Ningpo and its Hinterland." In Skinner, ed., 391–439.

Shigeta, Atsushi. 1984. "The Origins and Structure of Gentry Rule." In Grove and Daniels, eds., 335–385.

Shu Wencheng et al. 舒文成. 1981. "Ziliujing shaoyan gongren de hanghui zuzhi—Yandigong" 自流井燒盐工人的行會組織—炎帝宮 (The guild organization of the Ziliujing salt evaporators—the Yandigong). *Zigong wenshi ziliao xuanji* 12:35–48.

Shuntian shibao 順天時報. 1920–29. (Beijing Times).

Sibu congkan 四部叢刊. 1920–21. (The great compendium of the four treasuries).

Sichuan yanfazhi 四川盐法志. 1883. (Gazetteer of the Sichuan Salt Administration).

Sichuan yanzheng shi 四川盐政史. 1932. (The History of the Sichuan Salt Administration).

Silver, Alan. 1967. "The Demand for Order in Civil Society: A Review of Some Themes in the History of Urban Crime, Police and Riot." In *The Police: Six Sociological Essays*, edited by David Bordura. New York.

Siming congshu 四明叢書. [1915] 1966. (Collectanea on Ningbo). Edited by Zhang Shouyong 張壽鏞. Reprint, Taibei.

Simmel, Georg. 1955. *Conflict and the Web of Group-Affiliations.* New York.

Siren, Oswald. 1924. *The Walls and Gates of Peking.* London.

Skinner, G. William. 1987. "Sichuan's Population in the Nineteenth Century: Lessons from Disaggregated Data." *Late Imperial China* 8, no. 1 (June): 1–79.

———. 1985. "The Structure of Chinese History." *Journal of Asian Studies* 44, no. 2 (Feb.): 271–292.

Skinner, G. William. 1977a. "Cities and the Hierarchy of Local Systems." In Skinner, ed., 275–351.

———. 1977b. "Introduction: Urban and Rural in Chinese Society." In Skinner, ed., 219–260.

———. 1977c. "Regional Urbanization in Nineteenth-Century China." In Skinner, ed., 211–249.

———. 1976. "Mobility Strategies in Late Imperial China." In *Regional Analysis*. Vol. 1: *Economic Systems*, edited by Carol A. Smith. New York.

———. 1964–65. "Marketing and Social Structure in Rural China." Parts 1, 2. *Journal of Asian Studies* 24, no. 1 (Nov.): 3–43; 24, no. 2 (Feb.): 195–228.

———, ed. 1977. *The City in Late Imperial China*. Stanford.

Skocpol, Theda. 1979. *States and Social Revolutions: A Comparative Analysis of France, Russia, and China*. Cambridge.

Smith, Joanna F. Handlin. 1987. "Benevolent Societies: The Reshaping of Charity During the Late Ming and Early Ch'ing." *Journal of Asian Studies* 46, no. 2 (May): 309–338.

Smith, Paul, 1984. "Commerce, Agriculture, and Core Formation in the Upper Yangtze, 2 A.D. to 1948." Paper prepared for the Conference on Spatial and Temporal Trends and Cycles in Chinese Economic History, 980–1980. Bellagio, Italy, August 17–23.

Song Guihuang 宋桂煌 1981. "Rugao diqu qingnian yundong de huigu" 如皋地區青年運動的回顧 (Reminiscences of Rugao's youth movement). *Rugao wenshi ziliao* 3:13–25.

Song Lanxi. 宋艮曦. 1984. "Shilun Qingdai Sichuan yanshang de faren" 試論清代四川盐商的發軔 (A preliminary discussion of the beginnings of the Sichuan salt merchants). *Jingyan shi tongxun* 井盐史通訊 1:30–38.

Spring, David, ed. 1977. *European Landed Elites in the Nineteenth Century*. Baltimore.

———. 1971. "English Landowners and Nineteenth-Century Industrialization." In *Land and Industry: The Landed Estate and the Industrial Revolution*, edited by J. T. Ward and R. G. Wilson, 16–62. Newton Abbot, England.

Spring, David, and Eileen Spring, 1986. "Social Mobility and the English Landed Elite." *Canadian Journal of History* 21, no. 3 (Dec.): 333–351.

Stone, Lawrence, and Jeanne Fawtier Stone. 1986. *An Open Elite? England 1540–1880*. Oxford.

Strand, David, 1985. "Feuds, Fights and Factions: Group Politics in 1920s Beijing." *Modern China* 11, no. 4 (Oct.): 411–435.

Struve, Lynn. 1987. "The Early Qing Legacy of Huang Tsung-hsi: A Reexamination." *Asia Major*, 3d ser. 1, no. 1 (Nov.): 83–122.

Sun, Ching-chih, et al. 1961. *Economic Geography of the East China Region (Shanghai, Kiangsu, Anhwei, Chekiang)*. Translated from *Huadong diqu jingji dili* 華東地區經濟地理 (Beijing, Nov. 1959). Published by Joint Publications Research Service, no. 11,438. Washington, D.C.

Sun Guoqiao 孫國乔. 1931. "Wuxi zhidao yu yangcan shiye zhi yaodian" 無錫植稻與养蚕事業之要點 (The essentials of rice cultivation and sericulture in Wuxi). *Nongye zhoubao* 農業週報 1, no. 25 (Oct. 16): 982–985.

Sun Zhongyin 孫種因. 1957. "Chongjiu zhanji" 重九戰記 (A record of the double-nine war). In *Xinhai geming* 辛亥革命 (The 1911 Revolution), edited by Chai Degeng 柴德賡 et al., 6:239–254. Shanghai.

Suzuki Tomoo 鈴木智夫. 1977. *Kindai Chūgoku no jinushi sei* 近代中國の地主制 (The landlord system of modern China). Tokyo.

Swartz, Marc J. 1968. "Introduction." In *Local-Level Politics: Social and Cultural Perspectives*, edited by Marc J. Swartz, 1–46. Chicago.

Swartz, Marc J., Victor W. Turner, and Arthur Tuden, eds. 1966. *Political Anthropology*. Chicago.

Taga Akigōrō 多賀秋五郎. 1960. *Sōfu no kenkyū* 宗譜の研究 (A study of Chinese lineages). Tokyo.

Tan, Shih-hua. 1934. *A Chinese Testament*. New York.

Tanaka, Issei. 1985. "The Social and Historical Context of Ming-Ch'ing Local Drama." In Johnson, Nathan, and Rawski, eds., 163–168.

Tang Zaiyang 唐載陽. 1987. "Qingdai Guizhou de gongshangye" 清代貴州的工商業 (The industry and commerce of Guizhou in the Qing dynasty). *Guizhou wenshi congkan* 貴州文史叢刊 (Collected articles on Guizhou's culture and history) 1:8–14.

T'ao, L. K. 1929. "Unemployment among Intellectual Workers in China." *Chinese Social and Political Science Review* 13, no. 3 (July): 251–261.

———. 1928. *Livelihood in Beijing: An Analysis of the Budgets of Sixty Families*. Beijing.

Tarrow, Sidney. 1977. *Between Center and Periphery: Grassroots Politicians in Italy and France*. New Haven.

Tawney, R. H. 1941. "The Rise of the Gentry, 1558–1640." *Economic History Review* 11:1–38.

Taylor, Romeyn. 1969. "Yuan Origins of the Wei-so System." In *Chinese Government in Ming Times: Seven Studies*, edited by Charles O. Hucker, 23–40. New York.

Teune, Henry, and Zdravko Mlinar. 1974. "Development and Participation." In *Local Politics, Development and Participation*, edited by F. C. Bruhns, Franco Cazzola, and Jerzy Wiatr. Pittsburgh.

Thompson, E. P. 1978. "Eighteenth-Century English Society: Class Struggle without Class?" *Past and Present* 3, no. 2 (May): 133–165.

———. 1974. "Patrician Society, Plebian Culture." *Journal of Social History* 7, no. 4 (Summer): 382–405.

Thompson, F. M. L. 1963. *English Landed Society in the Nineteenth Century*. London.

Tian Maode 田茂德. 1984. "Piaohao zai Sichuan de yixie huodong" 票号在四川的一些活動 (Some activities of remittance shops in Sichuan). *Sichuan wenshi ziliao xuanji* 32:56–72.

Tianyue zhi 天樂志. 1937. (A gazetteer of Tianyue subdistrict). In *Shaoxing xianzhi ziliao diyi ji*.

Tōa dobunkai 東亞同文會. 1920. *Shina shōbetsu zenshi* 支那省別全誌 (A provincial gazetteer of China). Vol. 15, *Jiangsu* 江蘇. Tokyo.

Tōa kenkyūjo 東亞研究所, ed. 1943. *Shina sanshigyō kenkyū* 支那蠶絲業研究 (Research on China's silk industry). Tokyo.

Tongtong ribao 通通日報 (Tongtong daily). 1927. Nantong.

"Topography of Kweichau; its extent, subdivisions, surface, inhabitants, production, rivers, and mountains." 1849. *Chinese Repository* 18 (Oct.): 525–532.

Tu Long 屠隆. 1977. *Baiyu ji* 白榆集 (The collected writings of Tu Long). Reprint, Taibei.

Tsur, Nyok-ching. 1983. "Forms of Business in the City of Ningbo in China." *Chinese Sociology and Anthropology* 15, no. 4: 3–131.

Twitchett, Dennis. 1960–61. "Documents of Clan Administration I, The Rules of Administration of the Charitable Estate of the Fan Clan." *Asia Major* 8:1–35.

———. 1959. "The Fan Clan's Charitable Estate, 1050–1760." In *Confucianism in Action*, edited by David Nivison and Arthur Wright. Stanford.

Ueda Makoto 上田信. 1984. "Chiiki to sōzoku—Sekkō shō sankanbu" 地域と宗族— 浙江省山間部 (Locality and lineage—the hill country of Zhejiang). *Tōyō bunka kenkyūjo kiyō* 東洋文化研究所紀要 94:115–160.

Vincent, Joan. 1986. "System and Process, 1974–1985." *Annual Review of Anthropology* 15:99–119.

———. 1978. "Political Anthropology: Manipulative Strategies." *Annual Review of Anthropology* 7 (1978): 175–194.

Von Glahn, Richard. 1987. *The Country of Streams and Grottoes: Expansion, Settlement and Civilization of the Sichuan Frontier in Song Times.* Cambridge, Mass.

Wakeman, Frederic, Jr. 1985. *The Great Enterprise: The Manchu Reconstruction of Imperial Order in Seventeenth-Century China.* Berkeley.

———. 1975a. "Introduction: The Evolution of Local Control in Late Imperial China." In *Conflict and Control in Late Imperial China*, edited by Frederic Wakeman, Jr. and Carolyn Grant. Berkeley.

———. 1975b. *The Fall of Imperial China.* New York.

Walton, Linda. 1984. "Kinship, Marriage, and Status in Song China: A Study of the Lou Lineage of Ningbo, c. 1050–1250." *Journal of Asian History* 18, no. 1: 35–77.

Wan Yan 萬言. n.d. *Guancun wenchao* 管邨文鈔 (The unedited writings of Wan Yan). *Siming congshu* edition.

Wang Baoxin 王葆心. 1932. *Ji Hankou zongtan* 繼漢口叢談 (Continuation of the Hankou compendium).

Wang Dahua 王大華. 1984. "Guangdong shexue yu shangren" 廣東社學與商人 (Guangdong community schools and merchants). *Shaanxi shifan daxue xuebao* 陝西师范大學學報 1:82–89.

Wang Haoran 王浩然. 1928. "Rugao xian xianzheng gaikuang" 如皋縣縣政概況 (Conditions of Rugao county government). *Jiangsu xunkan* 江蘇旬刊 5 (Oct. 11): 63–72.

Wang Peitang 王培棠. 1938. *Jiangsu sheng xiangtu zhi* 江蘇省鄉土誌 (The geography and local history of Jiangsu province). Changsha.

Wang Roude 王柔德. 1983. "Jiefang qian Zigong yanshang de Fengjianxing" 解放前自貢盐商的封建性 (The feudal nature of the Zigong salt merchants before liberation). *Jingyan shi tongxun* 經盐史通訊 1:21–27.

Wang Roude and Zhong Langhua 钟朗華, comps. 1985. "Luo Xiaoyuan sishinian de Yanye jingying ji qi wannian shilue" 羅筱元四十年的盐業經營及其晚年事略 (Luo Xiaoyuan's forty years in the salt industry and a short biographical account of his later years). *Zigong wenshi ziliao xuanji* 15:70–113.

Wang Shouji 王守基. 1903. *Yanfa yilue* 盐法議略 (A brief account of the imperial salt administration). Shanghai.

Wang Shuhuai 王樹槐. 1985. *Zhongguo xiandaihua de quyu yanjiu: Jiangsu sheng, 1860–1916* 中國現代化的區域研究:江蘇省 1860–1916 (Modernization in China, 1860–1916: A regional study of social, political and economic change in Jiangsu province). Taibei.

Wang Yanyu 王燕玉. 1980. *Guizhou shi zhuanti kao* 貴州史專題考察 (An examination of special topics in Guizhou history). Guiyang.

Wang Yingchao 王盈朝. 1980. "Huiyi Subei Rugao 'wuyi' nongmin shouci qiyi" 回憶蘇北如皋"五一"農民首次起義 (Recollections of the North Jiangsu Rugao's May First first peasant uprising). *Rugao wenshi ziliao* 1:45–69.

Wang, Yu-chuan. 1940. "The Organization of a Typical Guerrilla Area in South Shantung." In *The Chinese Army: Its Organization and Military Efficiency*, edited by Evans Fordyce Carlson. New York.

Watson, James L. 1988. "Self Defense Corps, Violence, and the Bachelor Sub-Culture in South China: Two Case Studies." In *Proceedings of the Second International Conference on Sinology*, edited by Liu Pin-hsiung. Vol. 4. Taipei.

———. 1987. "From the Common Pot: Feasting with Equals in Chinese Society." *Anthropos* 82:389–401.

———. 1982. "Chinese Kinship Reconsidered: Anthropological Perspectives on Historical Research." *The China Quarterly* 92:589–622.

———. 1975. *Emigration and the Chinese Lineage*. Berkeley.

Watson, Rubie S. 1985. *Inequality Among Brothers: Class and Kinship in South China*. Cambridge.

———. 1982. "The Creation of a Chinese Lineage: The Teng of Ha Tsuen, 1669–1751." *Modern Asian Studies* 16, no. 1: 69–100.

———. 1981. "Class Differences and Affinal Relations in South China." *Man* 16:593–615.

Watt, John. 1972. *The District Magistrate in Late Imperial China*. New York.

Weber, Max. 1978. *Economy and Society*. Edited by Guenther Roth and Claus Wittich. 2 vols. Berkeley.

———. 1958. "Class, Status, Party." In *From Max Weber: Essays in Sociology*, edited by H. H. Gerth and C. Wright Mills, 180–195. New York.

———. 1951. *The Religion of China: Confucianism and Taoism*. Translated by H. M. Wright. New Haven.

Wei Qingyuan 韋慶遠 and Wu Qiyan 吳奇衍. 1981. "Qingdai zhuming huangshang Fan-shi de xingshuai" 清代著名皇商范氏的興衰 (The rise and decline of the famous Qing-period imperial merchants, the Fans). *Lishi yanjiu* 歷史研究 3:127–144.

Weiner, Myron, and Samuel P. Huntington, eds. 1987. *Understanding Political Development*. Boston.

Weissman, Neil B. 1981. *Reform in Tsarist Russia: The State Bureaucracy and Local Government, 1900–1914*. New Brunswick, N.J.

Weller, Robert. 1987. *Unities and Diversities in Chinese Religion*. Seattle.

Wickberg, Edgar. 1981. "Another Look at Land and Lineage in the New Territories, ca. 1900." *Journal of the Hong Kong Branch of the Royal Asiatic Society* 21:25–42.

Wiens, Mi Chu. 1980. "Lord and Peasant: The Sixteenth to the Eighteenth Century." *Modern China* 6, no. 1: 3–40.

Wilkinson, Endymion. 1978. "Introduction." In *Landlord and Labor in Late Imperial China: Case Studies from Shandong*, by Jing Su and Luo Lun, 1–38. Translated by Endymion Wilkinson. Cambridge.

Will, Pierre-Etienne. 1980a. *Bureaucratie et Famine en Chine au 18e Siècle*. Paris.

————. 1980b. "Un Cycle Hydraulique en Chine: La Province du Hubei du XVIe au XIXe Siècles." *Bulletin de l'Ecole Francais d'Extreme Orient* 68:261–287.

Williams, Raymond. 1977. *Marxism and Literature*. Oxford.

————. 1976. *Keywords: A Vocabulary of Culture and Society*. New York.

Wilson, R. G. 1971. "The Denisons and Milneses: Eighteenth-Century Merchant Landowners." In *Land and Industry: The Landed Estate and the Industrial Revolution*, edited by J. T. Ward and R. G. Wilson, 145–172. Newton Abbot, England.

Wittfogel, Karl. 1953. *Oriental Despotism*. New Haven.

Wong, R. Bin, Pierre-Etienne Will, James Lee, Peter C. Perdue, and Jean Oi. 1990. *Nourishing the People: The State Civilian Granary System in China, 1650–1850*. Ann Arbor.

Wou, Odoric Y. K. 1979. "The Political Kin Unit and the Family Origin of Ch'ing Local Officials." In *Perspectives on a Changing China: Essays in Honor of Prof. C. Martin Wilbur*, edited by Joshua A. Fogel and William T. Rowe, 69–88. Boulder, Colo.

Wrigley, E. A., and R. S. Schofield. 1981. *The Population History of England, 1541–1871*. Cambridge, Mass.

Wrong, Dennis. 1979. *Power: Its Forms, Bases, and Uses*. New York.

Wu Bannong 吳半農. 1929. "Hebei sheng ji Ping-Jin liangshi laozi zhengyi de fenxi" 河北省及平津兩市勞資爭議底分析 (An analysis of labor disputes in Hebei province and the cities of Beiping and Tianjin). *Shehui kexue jikan* 社會科學季刊 (Social Sciences Quarterly) 4.3–4 (July–December): 1–71.

Wu Duo 吳鐸. 1971. "Chuanyan guanyun zhi shimo" 川盐官運之始末 (The whole story of official transport of Sichuan salt). *Zhongguo jindai shehui jingji shi lunji* 中國近代社會經濟史論集. Hong Kong.

Wu Xuechou 吳雪儔. 1979. "Guizhou xinhai geming shimo" 貴州辛亥革命始末 (The beginning and end of Guizhou's 1911 Revolution). *Guizhou wenshi ziliao xuanji* 3:70–117.

Wu Xuechou and Hu Gang 胡剛. 1959. "Guizhou xinhai geming sanji" 貴州辛亥革命散記 (A sketch of Guizhou's 1911 Revolution). In *Yunnan Guizhou xinhai geming ziliao*, 174–198.

Wu Xuechou and Zhang You 張油. 1981. "Guizhou xinhai geming xianxingzhe Zhang Min shilue" 貴州辛亥革命先行者張忞事畧 (Biography of Zhang Min, a precursor of Guizhou's 1911 Revolution). *Guizhou wenshi ziliao xuanji* 10:146–158.

Wu Yaming 武亞明. 1980. Interview, Nov. 7, at the Sericulture Research Institute of the Jiangsu Academy of Agricultural Science, Zhenjiang.

Wuhan Municipal Commercial Industrial Alliance. 1965. "Yekaitai lishi ziliao" 葉開泰歷史資料 (Materials on the Yekaitai Store). Manuscript.

————. n.d. "Wuhan Yekaitai yaodian jianshi" 武漢葉開泰藥店簡史 (A short history of the Wuhan Yekaitai Medicine Store). Manuscript.

Wuxi difangzhi bianji weiyuanhui 無錫地方志編輯委員會. 1959. *Wuxi gushi xuan* 無錫故事選 (Selected stories from Wuxi). Wuxi.

Wuxi Jinkui xianzhi 無錫金匱縣志. 1881. (A gazetteer of Wuxi and Jinkui counties).

Wuxi mishi diaocha 無錫米市調查. 1935. (An investigation of the Wuxi rice market). Shanghai.

Wuxi nianjian 無錫年鑒. 1930. (Wuxi yearbook). Wuxi.

Wuxi shizheng 無錫市政. 1929–30. (Wuxi city government). Wuxi.

Wuxi shizheng choubei chu 無錫市政籌備處, ed. 1929. "Wuxi saosichang yilanbiao" 無錫繰絲廠一覽表 (A table of Wuxi's silk filatures). *Wuxi shizheng choubei shilu* 無錫市政籌備史录 (Records of planning work of the Wuxi city government), 3 (Dec. 1): 121–123.

Xi-Jin shi xiaolu 錫金識小录. 1752. (A brief record of what is known about Wuxi and Jinkui counties). Wuxi.

Xi-Jin xiangtu dili 錫金乡土地理. 1909. (The rural geography of Wuxi and Jinkui counties). Wuxi.

"Xi Ying" 西瀅 [pseud.] 1928. *Xi Ying xianhua* 西瀅閒話 (Idle gossip from Xi Ying). Shanghai.

Xiao Hua 肖華. 1983. "Mofan de Xingguo, yingxiong de renmin" 模范的興國, 英雄的人民 (Model Xingguo, heroic people). *Zhonggong dangshi ziliao* 中共黨史資料 7:226–263.

Xiaoshan hetang jinian lu 蕭山河塘紀念錄. 1920. (A commemorative record of the river and pond case in Xiaoshan).

Xiaoshan xian dimingzhi 蕭山縣地名志. 1980. (Gazetteer of Xiaoshan place names).

Xiaoshan xianzhi 蕭山縣志. 1985. (Gazetteer of Xiaoshan county).

Xiaoshan xianzhi gao 蕭山縣志稿. 1935. (Draft gazetteer of Xiaoshan county).

Xiaoshan xingshi 蕭山姓氏. 1984. (Xiaoshan family names).

Xingyi fuzhi 興義府志. 1851. (Gazetteer of Xingyi prefecture).

Xiong Zongren 熊宗仁. 1987a. "Liu Xianqian" 劉顯潛. In *Minguo renwu zhuan* 民國人物傳 (Biographies of Republican personalities), edited by Zong Zhiwen 宗志文 and Yan Ruping 嚴如平, 6:151–155. Beijing.

———. 1987b. "Wang Wenhua" 王文华. In *Minguo renwu zhuan* (Biographies of Republican personalities), edited by Zong Zhiwen and Yan Ruping, 6:69–75. Beijing.

Xu Dixin 許滌新 and Wu Chengming 吳承明, eds. 1985. *Zhongguo zibenzhuyi fazhan shi* 中國資本主義發展史 (A history of the development of capitalism in China). Beijing.

Xu Laiqing 許來青. 1980. "Xinhai geming hou Rugao qingkuang diandi" 辛亥革命后如皋情況点滴 (A tidbit about conditions in Rugao after the 1911 Revolution). *Rugao wenshi ziliao* 2:22–24.

Xu Ruliang 許汝艮. 1980. Interview, May 24, at the headquarters of the Wuxi People's Political Consultative Congress, Wuxi.

Xue Muqiao 薛暮橋. 1936. "Nongcun fuye he nongmin li cun" 農村副業和農民离村 (Rural subsidiary industry and peasant migration). *Zhongguo nongcun* 中國農村 2, no. 9: 53–62.

Xue Shaoming 薛紹銘. 1937. *Qian-Dian-Chuan luxing ji* 黔滇川旅行記 (A travel diary of Guizhou, Yunnan, and Sichuan). Hong Kong.

Yamane Yukio 山根幸夫. 1985. "Shindai Santō no shishū to shinshiso" 清代山東の市集と紳士層 (Markets and the gentry stratum in Shandong in the Qing). *Tōyō gakuhō* 東洋学報 66:539–560.

Yan Jinqing 嚴金清, ed. 1923. *Yan Lianfang (Yan Ziqing) yigao* 嚴廉訪[嚴紫卿]遺稿 (The posthumous manuscripts of Yan Lianfang [Yan Ziqing]). Wuxi.

Yan Ruyi 嚴如煜. 1822. *Sansheng bianfang beilan* 三省邊防備覽 (A reference on the defense of the three-province border region).

Yan Xiuyu 嚴修余 and Xie Yingju 謝應舉. 1978. "Xunwu diaocha" 尋烏調查 (Xunwu investigation). In *Guanshan zhenzhen cang—zhongyang geming genjudi de douzheng* 關山陣陣蒼—中央革命根据地的鬪爭 (The pass and the lines of hills are blue—the struggle for the central revolutionary base area), compiled by Jiangxi renmin chuban she 江西人民出版社, 1:213–222. Nanchang.

Yan Xuexi 嚴學熙. n.d. "Chuncan daosi sibujin: Ji jiechu de cansi jiaoyujia he gexinjia Zheng Qunjiang xiansheng" 春蠶到死絲不盡：記傑出的蠶絲教育家和革新家郑群疆先生 (A lifelong commitment to sericulture: A record of the prominent sericulture educator and innovator, Mr. Zheng Qunjiang). Manuscript.

Yan Yaxian. 晏亞仙. 1959. "San da Caojia" 三打曹家 (Three times attacking the Cao family). In Hongse fengbao 紅色風暴, compiled by Jiangxi renmin chuban she, 7:130–150. Nanchang.

Yang, C. K. 1959. A Chinese Village in Early Communist Transition. Cambridge, Mass.

Yang Changming 楊昌銘. 1959. "Guizhou guangfu jishi" 貴州光复紀實 (Record of Guizhou's revolution). In Yunnan Guizhou xinhai geming ziliao, 199–209.

Yang Chaolin 楊朝麟. 1716. Xijiang zhenglue 西江政畧 (A brief account of governing Jiangxi).

Yang Defang 楊德芳 and Weng Jialie 翁家烈. 1981. "Guanyu Taiping tianguo geming shiqi Guizhou gezu renmin qiyi de jige wenti" 関于太平天國革命時期貴州各族人民起義的几个問題 (A few questions concerning the uprisings of Guizhou's nationalities during the period of the Taiping revolution). Guizhou wenshi congkan 貴州文史丛刊 (Collected articles on Guizhou's culture and history) 1:70–77.

Yang Duxing et al. 楊篤行. 1982. "Zigong yanchang zhengqi jiche jilu gaishu" 自貢盐場蒸氣機車汲卤概述 (A general discussion of steam pumping at the Zigong salt yard). Zigong wenshi ziliao xuanji, nos. 1–5:137–153.

Yang, Martin. 1965. A Chinese Village. New York.

Yang Yuanming 楊遠鳴. 1976. "Xianshi Yang Shaogeng xiansheng zhuanlue" 先師楊紹耕先生傳略 (A brief biography of Mr. Yang Shaogeng). Jiangxi wenxian 85 (July): 35.

Yao shi zongpu 姚氏宗譜. 1930. (Genealogy of the Yao lineage).

Ye shi zongpu 葉氏宗譜. 1873. (Genealogy of the Ye lineage).

Ye Xian'en 葉顯恩. 1987. "Huishang lirun de fengjianhua yu zibenzhuyi mengya" 徽商利润的封建化與資本主義萌芽 (The feudalization of Huizhou merchants' profits and the sprouts of capitalism). Zhongshan daxue xuebao 中山大學學報 1:50–63.

———. 1983. Ming-Qing Huizhou nongcun shehui yu dianpuzhi 明清徽州農村社會與佃僕制 (The system of servile tenancy in the rural society of Huizhou). Anhui.

Yifeng xian difang zhi bianzuan wei 宜豐縣地方志編纂委. 1985. Yifeng renmin geming shi 宜豐人民革命史 (Revolutionary history of the people of Yifeng). n.p.

Yin Liangyin 尹良瑩. 1931. Zhongguo canye shi 中國蠶業史 (A history of Chinese sericulture). Nanjing.

Yin Weihe 殷惟龢. 1936. Jiangsu liushiyi xianzhi 江蘇六十一縣志 (Annals of Jiangsu's sixty-one counties). Shanghai.

Yinhang zhoubao 銀行週報. 1929. (Bankers' weekly). Beijing.

Yinxian tongzhi 鄞縣通志. 1937. (Comprehensive gazetteer of Yin county).

Yinxian zhi 鄞縣志. 1788. (Gazetteer of Yin county).

Yinxian zhi 鄞縣志. 1877. (Gazetteer of Yin county).

Yishibao 益世報. 1920–29. (Social Welfare). Beijing.

Yongkang xianzhi 永康縣志. 1822. (Gazetteer of Yongkang county).

Yongshang Leigongqiao Wu shi jiapu 甬上雷公橋吳氏家譜. 1927. (The family genealogy of the Leigongqiao Wus of Yin county).

Yongshang Lu shi Jingmu Tang zongpu 甬上盧氏敬睦堂宗譜. 1903. (The Jingmu Shrine genealogy of the Lus of Yin county).

Yoshikawa Kōjirō 吉川幸次郎. 1974. "Chūgoku no keisatsu" 中國の警察 (The police of China). In *Yoshikawa Kōjirō zenshū* 吉川幸次郎全集 (Complete works of Yoshikawa Kojiro). Vol. 16. Tokyo.

You Yanjia 尤延甲 and Chen Baosheng 陳宝生. 1980. "Gao Yu feiliao gongsi de gaikuang" 皋腴肥料公司的概況 (General narrative of the Gao Yu Fertilizer Company). *Rugao wenshi ziliao* 1:87–90.

Young, Ernest P. 1977. *The Presidency of Yuan Shi-k'ai: Liberalism and Dictatorship in Early Republican China*. Ann Arbor.

Yu Men, 禹門. 1980. "Rugao *Yixue bao* de huiyi" 如皋醫學報的回憶 (Reminiscences of *Rugao Medicine*). *Rugao wenshi ziliao* 1:84–86.

Yu Side 于思德. 1930. "Beiping gonghui diaocha" 北平工會調查 (An investigation of Beiping unions). *Shehuixue jie* 社會學界 (Sociological World), 4.

Yu Siwei 余思偉. 1983. "Qingdai qianqi Guangzhou yu Dongnanya de maoyi guanxi" 清代前期廣州與東南亞的貿易關係 (Trade between Canton and Southeast Asia in the early Qing). *Zhongshan daxue xuebao* 中山大學學報 2:73–83.

Yuan Caizhi 袁采之. 1980a. "Rugao xian shuilihui ji fushe cehuiju zhi huiyi" 如皋縣水利及附設測绘局之回憶 (Remembrances of the Rugao County Water Conservancy Committee and its subordinate surveying office). *Rugao wenshi ziliao* 2:32–34.

———. 1980b. "Tantan Tong-Yu gonglu Rugao duan de luxian" 談談通榆公路如皋段的路綫 (Talks about the Rugao section of the Tong-Yu road). *Rugao wenshi ziliao* 2:36–37.

———. 1980c. "Rugao xian qingzhangju zhi qingkuang" 如皋縣清丈局之情況 (Conditions in the Rugao surveyor's office). *Rugao wenshi ziliao* 2:38–41.

———. 1981a. "Rugao quangban xuetang de qingkuang" 如皋創辦學堂的情況 (Conditions surrounding the establishment of Rugao's schools.) *Rugao wenshi ziliao* 3:105–107.

———. 1981b. "Ku lin" 哭臨 (Grieving for the emperor). *Rugao wenshi ziliao* 3:107–108.

———. 1981c. "Wo suo zhidao de yijiuyier nian yihou de Rugao xian shufa renwu 我所知道的一九一二年以后的如皋縣書法人物 (Post-1912 Rugao calligraphers that I knew). *Rugao wenshi ziliao* 3:113–114.

Yue Tianyu 樂天宇. 1981. "Wo suo zhidao de Zhonggong Beijing diwei zaoqi de geming huodong" 我所知道的中共北京地委早期的革命活動 (What I know about the revolutionary activity of the Beijing Committee of the Chinese Communist Party). *Wenshi ziliao xuanbian* 文史資料選編 (A compilation of historical materials) 11 (Sept.): 1–44.

Yunnan Guizhou xinhai geming ziliao 雲南貴州辛亥革命資料. 1959. (Materials on the 1911 Revolution in Yunnan and Guizhou). Edited by Zhongguo kexueyuan lishi yanjiusuo 中国科學院歷史研究所. Beijing.

Zelin, Madeleine. 1988. "Capital Accumulation and Investment Strategies in Early Modern China: The Case of the Furong Salt Yard." *Late Imperial China* 9, no. 1 (June): 79–122.

———. 1986. "The Rights of Tenants in Mid-Qing Sichuan: A Study of Land-related Lawsuits in the Baxian Archives." *Journal of Asian Studies* 45, no. 3 (May): 499–526.

——— 1984. *The Magistrate's Tael: Rationalizing Fiscal Reform in Eighteenth-Century Ch'ing China*. Berkeley.

Zeng Biyi 曾碧漪. 1980. "Yi Gu Bo tongzhi" 憶古柏同志 (Remembering comrade Gu Bo). *Hongqi piao piao* 紅旗飄飄 19:88–105.

Zhang Aiping 張愛萍. 1958–60. "Weigong laohu zhuang" 圍攻老虎庄 (Seige of Old Tiger Town). *Xinghuo liaoyuan* 星火燎原 (Sparks that started a prairie fire) 2:941–947.

Zhang Duanfu. 張端甫. 1979–80. "Jianle diqu shouqu yizhi de danchangshang—Wu Jingrang tang" 犍樂地區首屈一指的大場商—吳景讓堂 (A Jianle area salt-yard merchant lineage second to none—the Wu Jingrang tang). Parts 1, 2 *Jingyan shi tongxun* 井盐史通訊 6:49–56; 7:51–56.

Zhang Fengting 張風亭. 1980a. "Rugao cehuiju zhangliang dixing shimo" 如皋測繪局丈量地形始末 (The beginning and end of the surveying done by the Rugao surveying office). *Rugao wenshi ziliao* 2:42.

———. 1980b. "Rugao she qingzhangju zhangliang tianmu de shimo 如皋設清丈局丈量田亩的始末 (The beginning and end of Rugao's establishing a surveying office to survey land). *Rugao wenshi ziliao* 2:43.

Zhang Jian 張謇. 1925. *Seweng ziding nianpu* 嗇翁自訂年譜 (Chronological autobiography of Zhang Jian). Nantong.

Zhang Kai 章楷. 1980. Interview, Oct. 11, at the Jiangsu Academy of Agricultural Science, Nanjing.

———. 1979. "Mantan lishishang Jiangsu de canye" 漫談歷史上江蘇的蚕業 (An informal history of Jiangsu sericulture). Parts 1, 2. *Canye keji* 蚕業技術 2 (July): 54–56; 3 (Oct.): 53–56.

Zhang Naicheng 張乃成. 1981. "Huiyi jiefang qian Rugao de sifa qingkuang" 回憶解放前如皋的司法情況 (Remembrances of Rugao's prerevolutionary judicial system). *Rugao wenshi ziliao* 3:95–100.

Zhang shi sanxiu jiapu 張氏三修家譜. 1876. (Genealogy of the Zhang lineage, 3rd rev. ed.).

Zhang shi zongpu 張氏宗譜. 1948. (Genealogy of the Zhang lineage).

Zhang Xiaomei 張肖梅, ed. 1939. *Sichuan jingji cankao ziliao* 四川經濟參考資料 (Reference materials on the economy of Sichuan). Shanghai.

Zhang Xingzhou 張行周. 1973. *Ningbo xiguan congtan* 寧波習慣叢談 (Notes on the customs of Ningbo). Taibei.

Zhang Xuecheng 張學誠. 1922. *Zhang shi yishu* 張氏遺書 (Surviving works of Zhang Xuecheng).

Zhang Youdong et al. 張友棟. 1959. "Wei Liu Xianshi deng cansha Qianren shang canyi yuan shu" 為劉顯世等慘杀黔人上參議院書 (Report to the national assembly on the massacre of Guizhou people by Liu Xianshi et al.). *Yunnan Guizhou xinhai geming wenxian*, 226–230.

Zhang Youyi 章有義, ed. 1957. *Zhongguo jindai nongye shi ziliao* 中國近代農業史資料 (Materials on the agricultural history of modern China). Vol. 3: *1927–37*. Beijing.

Zhang Yufa 張玉法. 1982. *Zhongguo xiandaihua de quyu yanjiu: Shandong sheng, 1860–1916* 中國現代化的區域研究：山東省 (Regional studies on Chinese modernization: Shandong, 1860–1916). Taibei.

Zhang Zhengyu 張正峓. 1980a. "Wo tigong yi dian xiansuo" 我提供一点綫索 (I offer a few clues). *Rugao wenshi ziliao* 1:69–74.

Zhao Ruheng 趙如珩, comp. 1935. *Jiangsu shengjian* 江蘇省鑑 (Handbook on Jiangsu Province). Shanghai.

Zhejiang sheng xinhai geming shi yanjiu hui 浙江省辛亥革命史研究會 and Zhejiang sheng tushuguan 浙江省圖书馆, eds. 1981. *Xinhai geming Zhejiang shiliao xuanji* 辛亥革命浙江史料选集 (Collected materials on the 1911 Revolution in Zhejiang). Hangzhou.

Zhenhai xian xinzhi beigao 鎮海縣新志備高 (A prepared draft for a new gazetteer of Zhenhai). 1922.

Zheng Zhonghao 鄭仲豪. 1980a. "Guanyu Rugao pingmin she de ersan shi" 關于如皋平民社的二三事 (Several events of the Rugao Common People's Association). *Rugao wenshi ziliao* 1:75–76.

———. 1980b. "Xian xuelian de huodong yu shoucuo" 縣學联的活動與受挫 (The activities and defeat of the county student association). *Rugao wenshi ziliao* 2:65–67.

Zhonggong Jiangxi shengwei dangshi yanjiu shi 中共江西省委黨史研究室. 1984. *Jiangxi yinglie* 江西英烈 (Heroic martyrs of Jiangxi). Nanchang.

Zhonggong Ruijin xianwei dangshi bianzuan weiyuan hui 中共瑞金縣委黨史編纂委員會. 1959. *Ruijin renmin geming douzheng shi (chu gao)* 瑞金人民革命鬪爭史（初稿）(Draft history of the revolutionary struggle of the people of Ruijin county). Ruijin (?).

Zhongyang ribao 中央日報. 1928–33. (The central daily news). Shanghai.

Zhou Daozun 周道遵. 1848. *Yongshang shuili zhi* 甬上水利志 (Gazetteer of the water resources of Yin county). *Siming congshu* ed.

Zhou Deyin 周德銀 and You Yuangui 尤元桂. 1981. "Sanshi nian qian de Rugao huangbaoche gongren bagong" 三十年前的如皋黃包車工人罷工 (The Rugao rickshaw pullers strike of thirty years ago). *Rugao wenshi ziliao* 3:28–32.

Zhou Kuangming 周匡明. 1980. Interviews, Nov. 8 and 13, at the Sericulture Research Institute of the Jiangsu Academy of Agricultural Science, Zhenjiang.

Zhou Suyuan 周素園. 1980. "Guizhou mindang tongshi" 貴州民黨痛史 (The painful history of Guizhou's people's parties). *Guizhou wenshi ziliao xuanji* 4:1–112.

———. 1963. "Guizhou lujun shi shuyao" 貴州陸軍史迹要 (A summary history of the Guizhou army). *Guizhou wenshi ziliao xuanji* 1:1–43.

Zhou Xun 周詢. [1948] 1966. *Shuhai congtan* 蜀海叢談 (Collected comments on Sichuan). Reprinted in *Jindai Zhongguo shiliao congkan* 近代中國史料叢刊 1, no. 7. Taipei.

Zhu Anjun 朱安俊. 1981. "Ru cheng xuesheng dizhi Ri huo" 如城學生抵制日貨 (Rugao city students boycott Japanese goods). *Rugao wenshi ziliao* 3:109–111.

Zhu Chuxin 朱楚辛. 1936. "Zhongguo de sijianye" 中國的絲蠶業 (China's raw silk and cocoon industries). *Shenbao zhoukan* 申報週刊 1, no. 22 (June 7): 519–520.

Zhuang Yaohe 庄幺鶴. 1980. Interview, May 27, at the No. 1 Silk Factory in Wuxi, formerly the Dingchang silk filature, founded in 1928 by Zhou Shunqing.

Zigongshi dang'anguan, Beijing jingji xueyuan, Sichuan daxue, ed. 自貢市档案館, 北京經濟學院, 四川大學. 1985. *Zigong yanye qiyue dang'an xuanji* 自貢盐業契約档案選輯 (Selected Zigong salt industry contracts and documents). Beijing.

Zigong wenshi ziliao xuanji 自貢文史資料選輯 1981–85. (Selected materials on the history and culture of Zigong).

Zou Fuguang 鄒馥光. 1984. "Wang Zuo yu Yin Daoyi you jiaowang dao polie" 王佐與尹道一由交往到破裂 (Wang Zuo and Yin Daoyi from contact to rupture). *Jiangxi wenshi ziliao xuanji* 15:92–95.

Zou Lu 鄒魯. 1957. "Guizhou guangfu" 貴州光复 (Guizhou's revolution). In *Xinhai geming* 辛亥革命 (The 1911 Revolution), edited by Chai Degeng 柴德賡 et al., 6:396–399. Shanghai.

Zou Mingchu 鄒明初. 1981. "Huiyi Sun Zhongshan xiansheng beishang ji *Beijing minguo ribao* bei chafeng de jingguo" 回憶孫中山先生北上及北京民國日報被查封的經過 (Remembering Mr. Sun Yat-sen's trip north and the closure of the *Beijing Republican Daily*). *Wenshi ziliao xuanbian* 文史資料選編 9 (Feb.): 70–78.

Zurndorfer, Harriet. 1981. "The Hsin-an ta-tsu chih and the Development of Chinese Gentry Society, 800–1600." *T'oung-fao* 67:154–215.

INDEX

Names of individuals mentioned in only one section of an article and of localities treated in only one study have not been included in this index.

Compositor: Asco Trade Typesetting Ltd.
Text: 10/12 Baskerville
Display: Baskerville
Printer: Edwards Brothers, Inc.
Binder: Edwards Brothers, Inc.